Pearson New International Edition

Fundamentals of Futures
and Options Markets
John C. Hull
Eighth Edition

PEARSON®

Pearson Education Limited
Edinburgh Gate
Harlow
Essex CM20 2JE
England and Associated Companies throughout the world

Visit us on the World Wide Web at: www.pearsoned.co.uk

PEARSON®

ISBN 10: 1-292-04190-0
ISBN 13: 978-1-292-04190-2

British Library Cataloguing-in-Publication Data
A catalogue record for this book is available from the British Library

Printed in the United States of America

Table of Contents

CHAPTER 1

Introduction

Derivatives markets have become increasingly important in the world of finance and investments. It is now essential for all finance professionals to understand how these markets work, how they can be used, and what determines prices in them. This book addresses these issues.

Derivatives are traded on exchanges and in what are termed "over-the-counter" (OTC) markets. The two main products trading on exchanges are futures and options. In the over-the counter markets forwards, swaps, options, and a wide range of other derivatives transactions are agreed to. Prior to the crisis which started in 2007, the OTC derivatives market was relatively free from regulation. This has now changed. As we will explain, OTC market participants are now subject to rules specifying how trading must be done, how trades must be reported, and the collateral that must be provided.

This opening chapter starts by providing an introduction to futures markets and futures exchanges. It then compares exchange-traded derivatives markets with OTC derivatives markets and discusses forward contracts, which are the OTC counterpart of futures contracts. After that, it introduces options and outlines the activities of hedgers, speculators, and arbitrageurs in derivatives markets.

1.1 FUTURES CONTRACTS

A *futures contract* is an agreement to buy or sell an asset at a certain time in the future for a certain price. There are many exchanges throughout the world trading futures contracts. The Chicago Board of Trade, the Chicago Mercantile Exchange, and the New York Mercantile Exchange have merged to form the CME Group (www.cmegroup.com). Other large exchanges include NYSE Euronext (www.euronext.com), Eurex (www.eurexchange.com), BM&FBOVESPA (www.bmfbovespa.com.br), and the Tokyo Financial Exchange (www.tfx.co.jp). A table at the end of this book gives a more complete list.

Futures exchanges allow people who want to buy or sell assets in the future to trade with each other. In June a trader in New York might contact a broker with instructions to buy 5,000 bushels of corn for September delivery. The broker would immediately communicate the client's instructions to the CME Group. At about the same time,

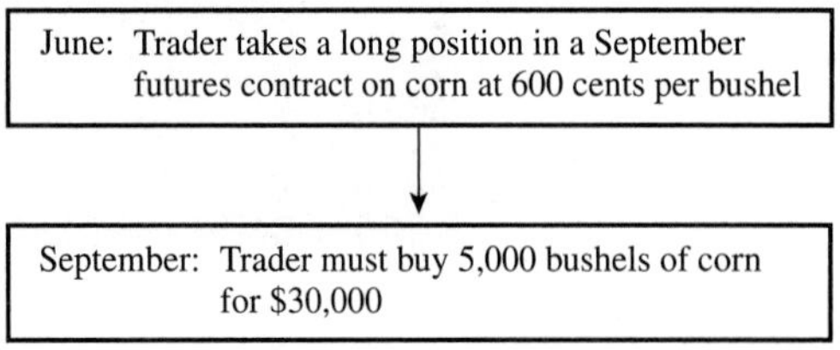

Figure 1.1 A futures contract (assuming it is held to maturity)

another trader in Kansas might instruct a broker to sell 5,000 bushels of corn for September delivery. These instructions would also be passed on to the CME Group. A price would be determined and the deal would be done.

The trader in New York who agreed to buy has what is termed a *long futures position*; the trader in Kansas who agreed to sell has what is termed a *short futures position*. The price is known as the *futures price*. We will suppose the price is 600 cents per bushel. This price, like any other price, is determined by the laws of supply and demand. If at a particular time more people wish to sell September corn than to buy September corn, the price goes down. New buyers will then enter the market so that a balance between buyers and sellers is maintained. If more people wish to buy September corn than to sell September corn, the price goes up—for similar reasons.

Issues such as margin requirements, daily settlement procedures, trading practices, commissions, bid–offer spreads, and the role of the exchange clearing house will be discussed in Chapter 2. For the time being, we can assume that the end result of the events just described is that the trader in New York has agreed to buy 5,000 bushels of corn for 600 cents per bushel in September and the trader in Kansas has agreed to sell 5,000 bushels of corn for 600 cents per bushel in September. Both sides have entered into a binding contract. The contract is illustrated in Figure 1.1.

A futures price can be contrasted with the *spot price*. The spot price is for immediate, or almost immediate, delivery. The futures price is the price for delivery at some time in the future. The two are not usually equal. As we will see in later chapters, the futures price may be greater than or less than the spot price.

1.2 HISTORY OF FUTURES MARKETS

Futures markets can be traced back to the Middle Ages. They were originally developed to meet the needs of farmers and merchants. Consider the position of a farmer in June of a certain year who will harvest a known amount of corn in September. There is uncertainty about the price the farmer will receive for the corn. In years of scarcity it might be possible to obtain relatively high prices, particularly if the farmer is not in a hurry to sell. On the other hand, in years of oversupply the corn might have to be disposed of at fire-sale prices. The farmer and the farmer's family are clearly exposed to a great deal of risk.

Consider next a company that has an ongoing requirement for corn. The company is also exposed to price risk. In some years an oversupply situation may create favorable prices; in other years scarcity may cause the prices to be exorbitant. It can make sense for the farmer and the company to get together in June (or even earlier) and agree on a price for the farmer's production of corn in September. This involves them negotiating a type of futures contract. The contract provides a way for each side to eliminate the risk it faces because of the uncertain future price of corn.

We might ask what happens to the company's requirements for corn during the rest of the year. Once the harvest season is over, the corn must be stored until the next season. In undertaking this storage, the company does not bear any price risk, but does incur the costs of storage. If the farmer or some other person stores the corn, the company and the storer both face risks associated with the future corn price, and again there is a clear role for futures contracts.

The Chicago Board of Trade

The Chicago Board of Trade (CBOT) was established in 1848 to bring farmers and merchants together. Initially, its main task was to standardize the quantities and qualities of the grains that were traded. Within a few years, the first futures-type contract was developed. It was known as a *to-arrive contract*. Speculators soon became interested in the contract and found trading the contract to be an attractive alternative to trading the grain itself. The CBOT developed futures contracts on many different underlying assets, including corn, oats, soybeans, soybean meal, soybean oil, wheat, Treasury bonds, and Treasury notes. It is now part of the CME Group.

The Chicago Mercantile Exchange

In 1874 the Chicago Produce Exchange was established, providing a market for butter, eggs, poultry, and other perishable agricultural products. In 1898 the butter and egg dealers withdrew from the exchange to form the Chicago Butter and Egg Board. In 1919, this was renamed the Chicago Mercantile Exchange (CME) and was reorganized for futures trading. Since then, the exchange has provided a futures market for many commodities, including pork bellies (1961), live cattle (1964), live hogs (1966), and feeder cattle (1971). In 1982 it introduced a futures contract on the Standard & Poor's (S&P) 500 Stock Index.

The Chicago Mercantile Exchange started futures trading in foreign currencies in 1972. The currency futures traded now include the euro, British pound, Canadian dollar, Japanese yen, Swiss franc, Australian dollar, Mexican peso, Brazilian real, South African rand, New Zealand dollar, Russian rouble, Chinese renminbi, Swedish krona, Czech koruna, Hungarian forint, Israeli shekel, Korean won, Polish złoty, and Turkish lira. The Chicago Mercantile Exchange developed the very popular Eurodollar futures contract. (As later chapters will explain, this is a contract on the future value of a short-term interest rate.) It has also introduced futures contracts on weather and real estate.

Electronic Trading

Traditionally futures have been traded using what is known as the *open-outcry system*. This involves traders physically meeting on the floor of the exchange, known as the "trading pit," and using a complicated set of hand signals to indicate the trades they would like to carry out. In the example we considered earlier, one floor trader would represent the investor in New York who wanted to buy September corn and another floor trader would represent the investor in Kansas who wanted to sell September corn.

Business Snapshot 1.1 The Lehman Bankruptcy

On September 15, 2008, Lehman Brothers filed for bankruptcy. This was the largest bankruptcy filing in US history and its ramifications were felt throughout derivatives markets. Almost until the end, it seemed as though there was a good chance that Lehman would survive. A number of companies (e.g., the Korean Development Bank, Barclays Bank in the UK, and Bank of America) expressed interest in buying it, but none of these was able to close a deal. Many people thought that Lehman was "too big to fail" and that the US government would have to bail it out if no purchaser could be found. This proved not to be the case.

How did this happen? It was a combination of high leverage, risky investments, and liquidity problems. Commercial banks that take deposits are subject to regulations on the amount of capital they must keep. Lehman was an investment bank and not subject to these regulations. By 2007, its leverage ratio had increased to 31:1, which means that a 3–4% decline in the value of its assets would wipe out its capital. Dick Fuld, Lehman's Chairman and Chief Executive, encouraged an aggressive deal-making, risk-taking culture. He is reported to have told his executives: "Every day is a battle. You have to kill the enemy." The Chief Risk Officer at Lehman was competent, but did not have much influence and was even removed from the executive committee in 2007. The risks taken by Lehman included large positions in the instruments created from subprime mortgages, which will be described in Chapter 8. Lehman funded much of its operations with short-term debt. When there was a loss of confidence in the company, lenders refused to roll over this funding, forcing it into bankruptcy.

Lehman was very active in the over-the-counter derivatives markets. It had hundreds of thousands of transactions outstanding with about 8,000 different counterparties. Lehman's counterparties were often required to post collateral and this collateral had in many cases been used by Lehman for various purposes. It is easy to see that sorting out who owes what to whom in this type of situation is a nightmare!

Exchanges have largely replaced the open outcry system by *electronic trading*. This involves traders entering their required trades at a keyboard and a computer being used to match buyers and sellers. Most futures exchanges throughout the world are entirely electronic. Electronic trading has led to a growth in algorithmic trading, also known as black-box, automated, high-frequency, or robo trading. This involves the use of computer programs to initiate trades, often without human intervention.

1.3 THE OVER-THE-COUNTER MARKET

Futures contracts are very popular exchange-traded contracts. Options, which are introduced later in this chapter, also trade very actively on exchanges. But not all trading of derivatives is on exchanges. Many trades take place in the *over-the-counter* (OTC) market. Banks, other large financial institutions, fund managers, and corporations are the main participants in OTC derivatives markets. The number of derivatives transactions per year in OTC markets is smaller than in exchange-traded markets, but the average size of the transactions is much greater.

Traditionally, participants in the OTC derivatives markets have contacted each other

Business Snapshot 1.2 Systemic risk

Systemic risk is the risk that a default by one financial institution will create a "ripple effect" that leads to defaults by other financial institutions and threatens the stability of the financial system. There are huge numbers of over-the-counter transactions between banks. If Bank A fails, Bank B may take a huge loss on the transactions it has with Bank A. This in turn could lead to Bank B failing. Bank C that has many outstanding transactions with both Bank A and Bank B might then take a large loss and experience severe financial difficulties; and so on.

The financial system has survived defaults such as Drexel in 1990 and Lehman Brothers in 2008, but regulators continue to be concerned. During the market turmoil of 2007 and 2008, many large financial institutions were bailed out, rather than being allowed to fail, because governments were concerned about systemic risk.

directly or have found counterparties for their trades using an interdealer broker. Banks often act as market makers for the more commonly traded instruments. This means that they are always prepared to quote a bid price (at which they are prepared to take one side of a derivatives transaction) and an offer price (at which they are prepared to take the other side). When they start trading with each other, two market participants often sign an agreement covering all transactions they might enter into in the future. The issues covered in the agreement include the circumstances under which outstanding transactions can be terminated, how settlement amounts are calculated in the event of a termination, and how the collateral (if any) that must be posted by each side is calculated.

Prior to the credit crisis, which started in 2007 and is discussed in some detail in Chapter 8, OTC derivatives markets were largely unregulated. Following the credit crisis and the failure of Lehman Brothers (see Business Snapshot 1.1), we have seen the development many new regulations affecting the operation of OTC markets. The purpose of the regulations is to improve the transparency of OTC markets, improve market efficiency, and reduce systemic risk (see Business Snapshot 1.2 for a discussion of systemic risk). The over-the-counter market in some respects is being forced to become more like the exchange-traded market. Three important changes are:

1. Standardized OTC derivatives in the United States must whenever possible be traded on what are referred to as *swap execution facilities* (SEFs). These are platforms where market participants can post bid and offer quotes and where they can choose to trade by accepting the quotes of other market participants.
2. There is a requirement in most parts of the world that a central clearing party (CCP) be used for most standardized derivatives transactions. The CCP's role is to stand between the two sides in an over-the-counter derivatives transaction in much the same way that an exchange does in the exchange-traded derivatives market. CCPs are discussed in more detail in Chapter 2.
3. All trades must be reported to a central registry.

Market Size

Both the over-the-counter and the exchange-traded market for derivatives are huge. Although the statistics that are collected for the two markets are not exactly comparable,

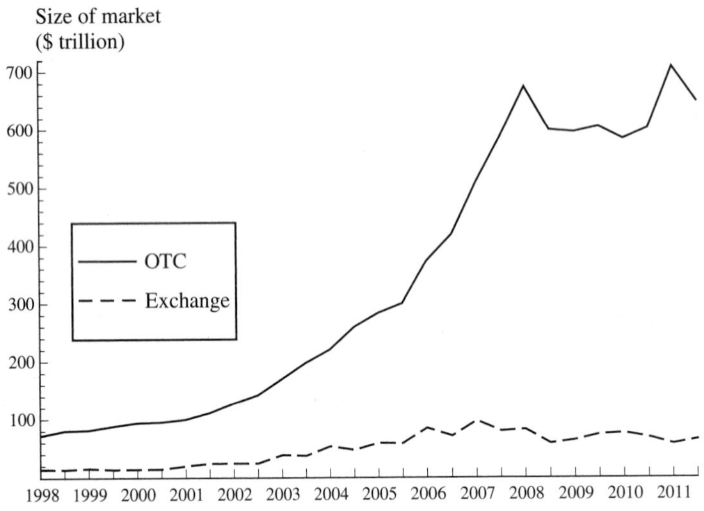

Figure 1.2 Size of over-the-counter and exchange-traded derivatives markets

it is clear that the over-the-counter market is much larger than the exchange-traded market. The Bank for International Settlements (www.bis.org) started collecting statistics on the markets in 1998. Figure 1.2 compares (a) the estimated total principal amounts underlying transactions that were outstanding in the over-the-counter markets between 1998 and 2011 and (b) the estimated total value of the assets underlying exchange-traded contracts during the same period. Using these measures, the size of the over-the-counter market was \$648 trillion in December 2011 and that of the exchange-traded market was \$64 trillion at this time.

In interpreting these numbers we should bear in mind that the principal underlying an over-the-counter transaction is not the same as its value. An example of an over-the-counter transaction is an agreement to buy 100 million U.S. dollars with British pounds at a predetermined exchange rate in one year. The total principal amount underlying this transaction is \$100 million. However, the value of the transaction at a particular point in time might be only \$1 million. The Bank for International Settlements estimates the gross market value of all OTC contracts outstanding in December 2011 to be about \$27 trillion.[1]

1.4 FORWARD CONTRACTS

A forward contract is similar to a futures contracts in that it is an agreement to buy or sell an asset at a certain time in the future for a certain price. But, whereas futures contracts are traded on exchanges, forward contracts trade in the over-the-counter market.

Forward contracts on foreign exchange are very popular. Most large banks employ both spot and forward foreign exchange traders. Spot traders are trading a foreign currency for almost immediate delivery. Forward traders are trading for delivery at a

[1] A contract that is worth \$1 million to one side and −\$1 million to the other side would be counted as having a gross market value of \$1 million.

Table 1.1 Spot and forward quotes for the USD/GBP exchange rate, June 22, 2012 (GBP = British pound; USD = U.S. dollar; quote is number of USD per GBP)

	Bid	*Offer*
Spot	1.5585	1.5589
1-month forward	1.5582	1.5587
3-month forward	1.5579	1.5585
6-month forward	1.5573	1.5580

future time. Table 1.1 provides the quotes for the exchange rate between the British pound (GBP) and the U.S. dollar (USD) that might be made by a large international bank on June 22, 2012. The quote is for the number of USD per GBP. The first row indicates that the bank is prepared to buy GBP (also known as sterling) in the spot market (i.e., for virtually immediate delivery) at the rate of $1.5585 per GBP and sell sterling in the spot market at $1.5589 per GBP. The second row indicates that the bank is prepared to buy sterling in one month at $1.5582 per GBP and sell sterling in one month at $1.5587 per GBP; the third row indicates that it is prepared to buy sterling in three months at $1.5579 per GBP and sell sterling in three months at $1.5585 per GBP; and so on.

The quotes are for very large transactions. (As anyone who has traveled abroad knows, retail customers face much larger spreads between bid and offer quotes than those in Table 1.1.) After examining the quotes in Table 1.1, a large corporation might agree to sell £100 million in six months for $155.73 million to the bank as part of its hedging program.

There is a relationship between the forward price of a foreign currency, the spot price of the foreign currency, domestic interest rates, and foreign interest rates. This is explained in Chapter 5.

1.5 OPTIONS

Options are traded both on exchanges and in the over-the-counter markets. There are two types of option: calls and puts. A *call option* gives the holder the right to buy an asset by a certain date for a certain price. A *put option* gives the holder the right to sell an asset by a certain date for a certain price. The price in the contract is known as the *exercise price* or the *strike price*; the date in the contract is known as the *expiration date* or the *maturity date*. A *European option* can be exercised only on the maturity date; an *American option* can be exercised at any time during its life.

It should be emphasized that an option gives the holder the right to do something. The holder does not have to exercise this right. This fact distinguishes options from futures (or forward) contracts. The holder of a long futures contract is committed to buying an asset at a certain price at a certain time in the future. By contrast, the holder of a call option has a choice as to whether to buy the asset at a certain price at a certain time in the future. It costs nothing (except for margin requirements, which will be discussed in Chapter 2) to enter into a futures contract. By contrast, an

Table 1.2. Prices of call options on Google, June 25, 2012; stock price: bid \$561.32; offer \$561.51

Strike price	*July 2012*		*Sept. 2012*		*Dec. 2012*	
(\$)	*Bid*	*Offer*	*Bid*	*Offer*	*Bid*	*Offer*
520	46.50	47.20	55.40	56.80	67.70	70.00
540	31.70	32.30	41.60	42.50	55.30	56.20
560	20.00	20.40	30.20	30.70	44.20	45.00
580	11.30	11.60	20.70	21.20	34.50	35.30
600	5.60	5.90	13.50	13.90	26.30	27.10

investor must pay an up-front price, known as the *option premium*, for an option contract.

The largest exchange in the world for trading stock options is the Chicago Board Options Exchange (CBOE; www.cboe.com). Table 1.2 gives the bid and offer quotes for some of the call options trading on Google (ticker symbol: GOOG) on June 25, 2012. Table 1.3 does the same for put options trading on Google on that date. The tables have been constructed from data on the CBOE web site. The Google stock price at the time of the quotes was bid 561.32, offer 561.51. The bid–offer spread on an option, as a percentage of its price, is greater than that on the underlying stock and depends on the volume of trading. The option strike prices in the tables are \$520, \$540, \$560, \$580, and \$600. The maturities are July 2012, September 2012, and December 2012. The July options have a maturity date of July 21, 2012, the September options have a maturity date of September 22, 2012, and the December options have a maturity date of December 22, 2012.

The tables illustrate a number of properties of options. The price of a call option decreases as the strike price increases; the price of a put option increases as the strike price increases. Both types of options tend to become more valuable as their time to maturity increases. These properties of options will be discussed further in Chapter 10.

Suppose an investor instructs a broker to buy one December call option contract on Google with a strike price of \$580. The broker will relay these instructions to a trader at the CBOE and the deal will be done. The (offer) price is \$35.30, as indicated in Table 1.2. This is the price for an option to buy one share. In the United States, an

Table 1.3 Prices of put options on Google, June 25, 2012; stock price: bid \$561.32; offer \$561.51

Strike price	*July 2012*		*Sept. 2012*		*Dec. 2012*	
(\$)	*Bid*	*Offer*	*Bid*	*Offer*	*Bid*	*Offer*
520	5.00	5.30	13.60	14.00	25.30	26.10
540	10.20	10.50	19.80	20.30	32.80	33.50
560	18.30	18.70	28.10	28.60	41.50	42.30
580	29.60	30.00	38.40	39.10	51.80	52.60
600	43.80	44.40	51.10	52.10	63.50	64.90

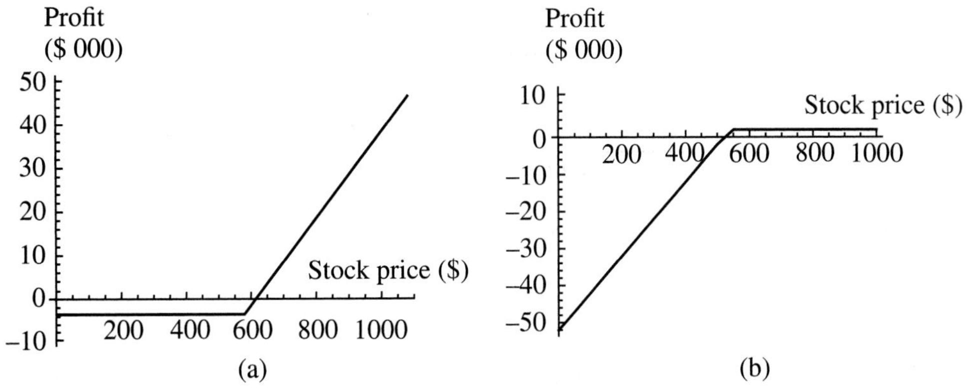

Figure 1.3 Net profit from (a) purchasing a contract consisting of 100 Google December call options with a strike price of \$580 and (b) selling a contract consisting of 100 Google September put options with a strike price of \$540

option contract is an agreement to buy or sell 100 shares. Therefore, the investor must arrange for \$3,530 to be remitted to the exchange through the broker. The exchange will then arrange for this amount to be passed on to the party on the other side of the transaction.

In our example, the investor has obtained at a cost of \$3,530 the right to buy 100 Google shares for \$580 each. If the price of Google does not not rise above \$580.00 by December 22, 2012, the option is not exercised and the investor loses \$3,530.[2] But if Google does well and the option is exercised when the bid price for the stock is \$650, the investor is able to buy 100 shares at \$580 and immediately sell them for \$650 for a profit of \$7,000—or \$3,470 when the initial cost of the options is taken into account.[3]

An alternative trade would be to sell one September put option contract with a strike price of \$540 at the bid price of \$19.80. This would lead to an immediate cash inflow of $\$100 \times 19.80 = \$1{,}980$. If the Google stock price stays above \$540, this option is not exercised and the investor makes a \$1,980 profit. However, if stock price falls and the option is exercised when the stock price is \$500 there is a loss. The investor must buy 100 shares at \$540 when they are worth only \$500. This leads to a loss of \$4,000, or \$2,020 when the initial amount received for the option contract is taken into account.

The stock options trading on the CBOE are American (i.e., they can be exercised at any time). If we assume for simplicity that they are European, so that they can be exercised only at maturity, the investor's profit as a function of the final stock price for the two trades we have considered is shown in Figure 1.3.

Further details about the operation of options markets and how prices such as those in Tables 1.2 and 1.3 are determined by traders are given in later chapters. At this stage we note that there are four types of participants in options markets:

1. Buyers of calls
2. Sellers of calls

[2] The calculations here ignore commissions paid by the investor.

[3] The calculations here ignore the effect of discounting. Theoretically, the \$7,000 should be discounted from the time of exercise to June 25, 2012 when calculating the payoff.

3. Buyers of puts
4. Sellers of puts

Buyers are referred to as having *long positions*; sellers are referred to as having *short positions*. Selling an option is also known as *writing the option*.

1.6 HISTORY OF OPTIONS MARKETS

The first trading in put and call options began in Europe and in the United States as early as the eighteenth century. In the early years the market got a bad name because of certain corrupt practices. One of these involved brokers being given options on a certain stock as an inducement for them to recommend the stock to their clients.

Put and Call Brokers and Dealers Association

In the early 1900s a group of firms set up the Put and Call Brokers and Dealers Association. The aim of this association was to provide a mechanism for bringing buyers and sellers together. Investors who wanted to buy an option would contact one of the member firms. This firm would attempt to find a seller or writer of the option from either its own clients or those of other member firms. If no seller could be found, the firm would undertake to write the option itself in return for what was deemed to be an appropriate price.

The options market of the Put and Call Brokers and Dealers Association suffered from two deficiencies. First, there was no secondary market. The buyer of an option did not have the right to sell it to another party prior to expiration. Second, there was no mechanism to guarantee that the writer of the option would honor the contract. If the writer did not live up to the agreement when the option was exercised, the buyer had to resort to costly lawsuits.

The Formation of Options Exchanges

In April 1973 the Chicago Board of Trade set up a new exchange, the Chicago Board Options Exchange, specifically for the purpose of trading stock options. Since then options markets have become increasingly popular with investors. By the early 1980s the volume of trading had grown so rapidly that the number of shares underlying the stock option contracts traded each day in United States exceeded the daily volume of shares traded on the New York Stock Exchange.

The exchanges trading options in the United States now include the Chicago Board Options Exchange (www.cboe.com), NASDAQ OMX (www.nasdaqtrader.com), NYSE Euronext (www.euronext.com), the International Securities Exchange (www.iseoptions.com), and the Boston Options Exchange (www.bostonoptions.com). Options trade on several thousand different stocks as well as stock indices, foreign currencies, and other assets.

Most exchanges offering futures contracts also offer options on these contracts. Thus, the CME Group offers options on corn futures, live cattle futures, and so on. Options exchanges exist all over the world (see the table at the end of this book).

The Over-the-Counter Market for Options

The over-the-counter market for options has grown very rapidly since the early 1980s and is now bigger than the exchange-traded market. One advantage of options traded in the over-the-counter market is that they can be tailored to meet the particular needs of a corporate treasurer or fund manager. For example, a corporate treasurer who wants a European call option to buy 1.6 million British pounds at an exchange rate of 1.5580 may not find exactly the right product trading on an exchange. However, it is likely that many derivatives dealers would be pleased to provide a quote for an over-the-counter contract that meets the treasurer's precise needs.

1.7 TYPES OF TRADER

Futures, forward, and options markets have been outstandingly successful. The main reason is that they have attracted many different types of trader and have a great deal of liquidity. When an investor wants to take one side of a contract, there is usually no problem in finding someone who is prepared to take the other side.

Three broad categories of trader can be identified: hedgers, speculators, and arbitrageurs. Hedgers use futures, forwards, and options to reduce the risk that they face from potential future movements in a market variable. Speculators use them to bet on the future direction of a market variable. Arbitrageurs take offsetting positions in two or more instruments to lock in a profit. As described in Business Snapshot 1.3, hedge funds have become big users of derivatives for all three purposes.

In the next few sections, we consider the activities of each type of trader in more detail.

1.8 HEDGERS

In this section we illustrate how hedgers can reduce their risks with forward contracts and options.

Hedging Using Forward Contracts

Suppose that it is June 22, 2012, and ImportCo, a company based in the United States, knows that it will have to pay £10 million on September 22, 2012, for goods it has purchased from a British supplier. The USD/GBP exchange rate quotes made by a financial institution are shown in Table 1.1. ImportCo could hedge its foreign exchange risk by buying pounds (GBP) from the financial institution in the three-month forward market at 1.5585. This would have the effect of fixing the price to be paid to the British exporter at $15,585,000.

Consider next another U.S. company, which we will refer to as ExportCo, that is exporting goods to the United Kingdom and on June 22, 2012, knows that it will receive £30 million three months later. ExportCo can hedge its foreign exchange risk by selling £30 million in the three-month forward market at an exchange rate of 1.5579. This would have the effect of locking in the U.S. dollars to be realized for the pounds at $46,737,000.

Business Snapshot 1.3 Hedge funds

Hedge funds have become major users of derivatives for hedging, speculation, and arbitrage. They are similar to mutual funds in that they invest funds on behalf of clients. However, they accept funds only from financially sophisticated individuals and do not publicly offer their securities. Mutual funds are subject to regulations requiring that the shares be redeemable at any time, that investment policies be disclosed, that the use of leverage be limited, and so on. Hedge funds are relatively free of these regulations. This gives them a great deal of freedom to develop sophisticated, unconventional, and proprietary investment strategies. The fees charged by hedge fund managers are dependent on the fund's performance and are relatively high—typically 2 plus 20%, i.e., 2% of the amount invested plus 20% of the profits. Hedge funds have grown in popularity, with about $2 trillion being invested in them throughout the world. "Funds of funds" have been set up to invest in a portfolio of hedge funds.

The investment strategy followed by a hedge fund manager often involves using derivatives to set up a speculative or arbitrage position. Once the strategy has been defined, the hedge fund manager must:

1. Evaluate the risks to which the fund is exposed
2. Decide which risks are acceptable and which will be hedged
3. Devise strategies (usually involving derivatives) to hedge the unacceptable risks.

Here are some examples of the labels used for hedge funds together with the trading strategies followed:

Long/Short Equities: Purchase securities considered to be undervalued and short those considered to be overvalued in such a way that the exposure to the overall direction of the market is small.

Convertible Arbitrage: Take a long position in a thought-to-be-undervalued convertible bond combined with an actively managed short position in the underlying equity.

Distressed Securities: Buy securities issued by companies in, or close to, bankruptcy.

Emerging Markets: Invest in debt and equity of companies in developing or emerging countries and in the debt of the countries themselves.

Global Macro: Carry out trades that reflect anticipated global macroeconomic trends.

Merger Arbitrage: Trade after a possible merger or acquisition is announced so that a profit is made if the announced deal takes place.

Example 1.1 summarizes the hedging strategies open to ImportCo and ExportCo. Note that a company might do better if it chooses not to hedge than if it chooses to hedge. Alternatively, it might do worse. Consider ImportCo. If the exchange rate is 1.5000 on September 22 and the company has not hedged, the £10 million that it has to pay will cost $15,000,000, which is less than $15,585,000. On the other hand, if the exchange rate is 1.6000, the £10 million will cost $16,000,000—and the company will wish it had hedged! The position of ExportCo if it does not hedge is the reverse. If the exchange rate in September proves to be less than 1.5579, the company will wish it had hedged; if the rate is greater than 1.5579, it will be pleased it has not done so.

Example 1.1 Hedging with forward contracts

It is June 22, 2012. ImportCo must pay £10 million on September 22, 2012, for goods purchased from Britain. Using the quotes in Table 1.1, it buys £10 million in the three-month forward market to lock in an exchange rate of 1.5585 for the pounds it will pay.

ExportCo will receive £30 million on September 22, 2012, from a customer in Britain. Using quotes in Table 1.1, it sells £30 million in the three-month forward market to lock in an exchange rate of 1.5579 for the pounds it will receive.

This example illustrates a key aspect of hedging. Hedging reduces the risk, but it is not necessarily the case that the outcome with hedging will be better than the outcome without hedging.

Hedging Using Options

Options can also be used for hedging. Example 1.2 considers an investor who in May of a particular year owns 1,000 shares of a company. The share price is \$28 per share. The investor is concerned about a possible share price decline in the next two months and wants protection. The investor could buy 10 July put option contracts on the company's stock on the Chicago Board Options Exchange with a strike price of \$27.50. This would give the investor the right to sell a total of 1,000 shares for a price of \$27.50. If the quoted option price is \$1, each option contract would cost $100 \times \$1 = \$100$ and the total cost of the hedging strategy would be $10 \times \$100 = \$1{,}000$.

The strategy costs \$1,000 but guarantees that the shares can be sold for at least \$27.50 per share during the life of the option. If the market price of the stock falls below \$27.50, the options will be exercised so that \$27,500 is realized for the entire holding. When the cost of the options is taken into account, the amount realized is \$26,500. If the market price stays above \$27.50, the options are not exercised and expire worthless. However, in this case the value of the holding is always above \$27,500 (or above \$26,500 when the cost of the options is taken into account). Figure 1.4 shows the net value of the portfolio (after taking the cost of the options into account) as a function of the stock price in two months. The dotted line shows the value of the portfolio assuming no hedging.

Example 1.2 Hedging with options

It is May. An investor who owns 1,000 shares of a company and wants protection against a possible decline in the share price over the next two months. Market quotes are as follows:

Current share price: \$28
July 27.50 put price: \$1

The investor buys 10 put option contracts for a total cost of \$1,000. This gives the investor the right to sell 1,000 shares for \$27.50 per share during the next two months.

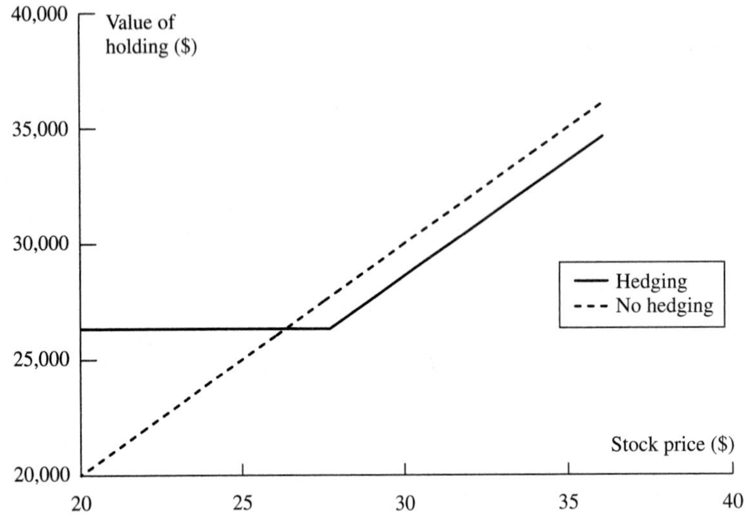

Figure 1.4 Value in Example 1.2 of the investor's holding in two months

A Comparison

There is a fundamental difference between the use of forward contracts and options for hedging. Forward contracts are designed to neutralize risk by fixing the price that the hedger will pay or receive for the underlying asset. Option contracts, by contrast, provide insurance. They offer a way for investors to protect themselves against adverse price movements in the future while still allowing them to benefit from favorable price movements. Unlike forwards, options involve the payment of an up-front fee.

1.9 SPECULATORS

We now move on to consider how futures and options markets can be used by speculators. Whereas hedgers want to avoid an exposure to adverse movements in the price of an asset, speculators wish to take a position in the market. Either they are betting that the price of the asset will go up or they are betting that it will go down.

Speculation Using Futures

Consider a U.S. speculator who in February thinks that the British pound will strengthen relative to the U.S. dollar over the next two months and is prepared to back that hunch to the tune of £250,000. One thing the speculator can do is purchase £250,000 in the spot market in the hope that the sterling can be sold later at higher price. (The sterling once purchased would be kept in an interest-bearing account.) Another possibility is to take a long position in four CME April futures contracts on sterling. (Each futures contract is for the purchase of £62,500.) Table 1.4 summarizes the two alternatives on the assumption that the current exchange rate is 1.5470 dollars

Table 1.4 Speculation using spot and futures contracts. One futures contract is on £62,500. Initial margin for four futures contracts = \$20,000

	Possible Trade	
	Buy £250,000 *Spot price = 1.5470*	*Buy 4 futures contracts* *Futures price = 1.5410*
Investment	\$386,750	\$20,000
Profit if April spot = 1.6000	\$13,250	\$14,750
Profit if April spot = 1.5000	−\$11,750	−\$10,250

per pound and the April futures price is 1.5410 dollars per pound. If the exchange rate turns out to be 1.6000 dollars per pound in April, the futures contract alternative enables the speculator to realize a profit of $(1.6000 - 1.5410) \times 250{,}000 = \$14{,}750$. The spot market alternative leads to 250,000 units of an asset being purchased for \$1.5470 in February and sold for \$1.6000 in April, so that a profit of $(1.6000 - 1.5470) \times 250{,}000 = \$13{,}250$ is made. If the exchange rate falls to 1.5000 dollars per pound, the futures contract gives rise to a $(1.5410 - 1.5000) \times 250{,}000 = \$10{,}250$ loss, whereas the spot market alternative gives rise to a loss of $(1.5470 - 1.5000) \times 250{,}000 = \$11{,}750$. The alternatives appear to give rise to slightly different profits and losses, but these calculations do not reflect the interest that is earned or paid.

What then is the difference between the two alternatives? The first alternative of buying sterling requires an up-front investment of \$386,750 ($= 250{,}000 \times 1.5470$). By contrast, the second alternative requires only a small amount of cash—perhaps \$20,000—to be deposited by the speculator in what is termed a margin account (this is explained in Chapter 2). The futures market allows the speculator to obtain leverage. With a relatively small initial outlay, the investor is able to take a large speculative position.

Speculation Using Options

Options can also be used for speculation. Suppose that it is October and a speculator considers that a stock is likely to increase in value over the next two months. The stock price is currently \$20, and a two-month call option with a \$22.50 strike price is currently selling for \$1. Table 1.5 illustrates two possible alternatives assuming that the speculator is willing to invest \$2,000. One alternative is to purchase 100 shares.

Table 1.5 Comparison of profits from two alternative strategies for using \$2,000 to speculate on a stock worth \$20 in October

Investor's strategy	*December stock price*	
	\$15	*\$27*
Buy 100 shares	−\$500	\$700
Buy 2,000 call options	−\$2,000	\$7,000

Another involves the purchase of 2,000 call options (i.e., 20 call option contracts). Suppose that the speculator's hunch is correct and the price of the stock rises to \$27 by December. The first alternative of buying the stock yields a profit of

$$100 \times (\$27 - \$20) = \$700$$

However, the second alternative is far more profitable. A call option on the stock with a strike price of \$22.50 gives a payoff of \$4.50, because it enables something worth \$27 to be bought for \$22.50. The total payoff from the 2,000 options that are purchased under the second alternative is

$$2{,}000 \times \$4.50 = \$9{,}000$$

Subtracting the original cost of the options yields a net profit of

$$\$9{,}000 - \$2{,}000 = \$7{,}000$$

The options strategy is, therefore, ten times more profitable than the strategy of buying the stock.

Options also give rise to a greater potential loss. Suppose the stock price falls to \$15 by December. The first alternative of buying stock yields a loss of

$$100 \times (\$20 - \$15) = \$500$$

Because the call options expire without being exercised, the options strategy would lead to a loss of \$2,000—the original amount paid for the options. Figure 1.5 shows the profit or loss from the two strategies as a function of the price of the stock in two months.

Options like futures provide a form of leverage. For a given investment, the use of options magnifies the financial consequences. Good outcomes become very good, while bad outcomes result in the whole initial investment being lost.

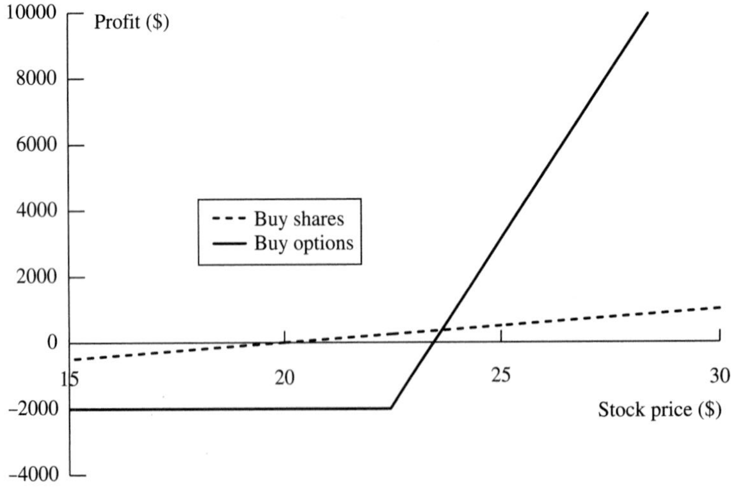

Figure 1.5 Profit or loss from two alternative strategies for speculating on a stock currently worth \$20

A Comparison

Futures and options are similar instruments for speculators in that they both provide a way in which a type of leverage can be obtained. However, there is an important difference between the two. When a speculator uses futures the potential loss as well as the potential gain is very large. When options are used, no matter how bad things get, the speculator's loss is limited to the amount paid for the options.

1.10 ARBITRAGEURS

Arbitrageurs are a third important group of participants in futures, forward, and options markets. Arbitrage involves locking in a riskless profit by simultaneously entering into transactions in two or more markets. In later chapters we will see how arbitrage is sometimes possible when the futures price of an asset gets out of line with its spot price. We will also examine how arbitrage can be used in options markets. This section illustrates the concept of arbitrage with a very simple example.

Example 1.3 considers a stock that is traded in both New York and London. Suppose that the stock price is \$152 in New York and £100 in London at a time when the exchange rate is \$1.5500 per pound. An arbitrageur could simultaneously buy 100 shares of the stock in New York and sell them in London to obtain a risk-free profit of

$$100 \times [(\$1.55 \times 100) - \$152]$$

or \$300 in the absence of transactions costs. Transactions costs would probably eliminate the profit for a small investor. However, a large investment bank faces very low transactions costs in both the stock market and the foreign exchange market. It would find the arbitrage opportunity very attractive and would try to take as much advantage of it as possible.

Arbitrage opportunities such as the one in Example 1.3 cannot last for long. As arbitrageurs buy the stock in New York, the forces of supply and demand will cause the

Example 1.3 An arbitrage opportunity

A stock is traded in both New York and London. The following quotes have been obtained:

New York: \$152 per share
London: £100 per share
Value of £1: \$1.5500

A trader does the following:

1. Buys 100 shares in New York
2. Sells the shares in London
3. Converts the sale proceeds from pounds to dollars.

This leads to a profit of

$$100 \times [(\$1.55 \times 100) - \$152] = \$300$$

dollar price to rise. Similarly, as they sell the stock in London, the sterling price will be driven down. Very quickly the two prices will become equivalent at the current exchange rate. Indeed, the existence of profit-hungry arbitrageurs makes it unlikely that a major disparity between the sterling price and the dollar price could ever exist in the first place. Generalizing from this example, we can say that the very existence of arbitrageurs means that in practice only very small arbitrage opportunities are observed in the prices that are quoted in most financial markets. In this book most of the arguments concerning futures prices, forward prices, and the values of option contracts will be based on the assumption that there are no arbitrage opportunities.

1.11 DANGERS

Derivatives are very versatile instruments. As we have seen they can be used for hedging, for speculation, and for arbitrage. It is this very versatility that can cause problems. Sometimes traders who have a mandate to hedge risks or follow an arbitrage strategy become (consciously or unconsciously) speculators. The results can be disastrous. One example of this is provided by the activities of Jérôme Kerviel at Société Général (see Business Snapshot 1.4).

To avoid the type of problems Société Général encountered it is very important for both financial and nonfinancial corporations to set up controls to ensure that derivatives are being used for their intended purpose. Risk limits should be set and the activities of traders should be monitored daily to ensure that the risk limits are adhered to.

Unfortunately, even when traders follow the risk limits that have been specified, big mistakes can happen. Some of the activities of traders in the derivatives market during the period leading up to the start of the credit crisis in July 2007 proved to be much riskier than they were thought to be by the financial institutions they worked for. As will be discussed in Chapter 8, house prices in the United States had been rising fast. Most people thought that the increases would continue—or, at worst, that house prices would simply level off. Very few were prepared for the steep decline that actually happened. Furthermore, very few were prepared for the high correlation between mortgage default rates in different parts of the country. Some risk managers did express reservations about the exposures of the companies for which they worked to the US real estate market. But, when times are good (or appear to be good), there is an unfortunate tendency to ignore risk managers and this is what happened at many financial institutions during the 2006–2007 period. The key lesson from the credit crisis is that financial institutions should always be dispassionately asking "What can go wrong?", and they should follow that up with the question "If it does go wrong, how much will we lose?"

SUMMARY

In this chapter we have taken a first look at futures, forward, and options markets. Futures and forward contracts are agreements to buy or sell an asset at a certain time in the future for a certain price. Futures contracts are traded on an exchange, whereas forward contracts are traded in the over-the-counter market. There are two types of

Business Snapshot 1.4 SocGen's big loss in 2008

Derivatives are very versatile instruments. They can be used for hedging, speculation, and arbitrage. One of the risks faced by a company that trades derivatives is that an employee who has a mandate to hedge or to look for arbitrage opportunities may become a speculator.

Jérôme Kerviel joined Société Général (SocGen) in 2000 to work in the compliance area. In 2005, he was promoted and became a junior trader in the bank's Delta One products team. He traded equity indices such as the German DAX index, the French CAC 40, and the Euro Stoxx 50. His job was to look for arbitrage opportunities. These might arise if a futures contract on an equity index was trading for a different price on two different exchanges. They might also arise if equity index futures prices were not consistent with the prices of the shares constituting the index. (This type of arbitrage is discussed in Chapter 5.)

Kerviel used his knowledge of the bank's procedures to speculate while giving the appearance of arbitraging. He took big positions in equity indices and created fictitious trades to make it appear that he was hedged. In reality, he had large bets on the direction in which the indices would move. The size of his unhedged position grew over time to tens of billions of euros.

In January 2008, his unauthorized trading was uncovered by SocGen. Over a three-day period, the bank unwound his position for a loss of 4.9 billion euros. This was at the time the biggest loss created by fraudulent activity in the history of finance. (Later in the year, a much bigger loss from Bernard Madoff's Ponzi scheme came to light.)

Rogue trader losses were not unknown at banks prior to 2008. For example, in the 1990s, Nick Leeson, who worked at Barings Bank, had a mandate similar to that of Jérôme Kerviel. His job was to arbitrage between Nikkei 225 futures quotes in Singapore and Osaka. Instead he found a way to make big bets on the direction of the Nikkei 225 using futures and options, losing $1 billion and destroying the 200-year old bank in the process. In 2002, it was found that John Rusnak at Allied Irish Bank had lost $700 million from unauthorized foreign exchange trading. The lessons from these losses are that it is important to define unambiguous risk limits for traders and then to monitor what they do very carefully to make sure that the limits are adhered to.

options: calls and puts. A call option gives the holder the right to buy an asset by a certain date for a certain price. A put option gives the holder the right to sell an asset by a certain date for a certain price. Options trade both on exchanges and in the over-the-counter market.

Futures, forwards, and options have been very successful innovations. Three main types of participants in the markets can be identified: hedgers, speculators, and arbitrageurs. Hedgers are in the position of facing risk associated with the price of an asset. They use futures, forward, or option contracts to reduce or eliminate this risk. Speculators wish to bet on future movements in the price of an asset. Futures, forward, and option contracts can give them extra leverage; that is, the contracts can increase both the potential gains and potential losses in a speculative investment. Arbitrageurs are in business to take advantage of a discrepancy between prices in two different markets. If, for example, they see the futures price of an asset getting out of line with the spot price, they will take offsetting positions in the two markets to lock in a profit.

FURTHER READING

Chancellor, E. *Devil Take the Hindmost—A History of Financial Speculation*. New York: Farra Straus Giroux, 2000.

Merton, R. C. "Finance Theory and Future Trends: The Shift to Integration," *Risk*, 12, 7 (July 1999): 48–51.

Miller, M. H. "Financial Innovation: Achievements and Prospects," *Journal of Applied Corporate Finance*, 4 (Winter 1992): 4–11.

Zingales, L. "Causes and Effects of the Lehman Bankruptcy," Testimony before Committee on Oversight and Government Reform, United States House of Representatives, October 6, 2008.

Quiz (Answers at End of Book)

1.1. What is the difference between a long futures position and a short futures position?

1.2. Explain carefully the difference between (a) hedging, (b) speculation, and (c) arbitrage.

1.3. What is the difference between (a) entering into a long futures contract when the futures price is $50 and (b) taking a long position in a call option with a strike price of $50?

1.4. An investor enters into a short forward contract to sell 100,000 British pounds for U.S. dollars at an exchange rate of 1.4000 U.S. dollars per pound. How much does the investor gain or lose if the exchange rate at the end of the contract is (a) 1.3900 and (b) 1.4200?

1.5. Suppose that you write a put contract with a strike price of $40 and an expiration date in three months. The current stock price is $41 and one put option contract is on 100 shares. What have you committed yourself to? How much could you gain or lose?

1.6. You would like to speculate on a rise in the price of a certain stock. The current stock price is $29 and a three-month call with a strike price of $30 costs $2.90. You have $5,800 to invest. Identify two alternative strategies. Briefly outline the advantages and disadvantages of each.

1.7. What is the difference between the over-the-counter and the exchange-traded market? What are the bid and offer quotes of a market maker in the over-the-counter market?

Practice Questions (Answers in Solutions Manual/Study Guide)

1.8. Suppose you own 5,000 shares that are worth $25 each. How can put options be used to provide you with insurance against a decline in the value of your holding over the next four months?

1.9. A stock when it is first issued provides funds for a company. Is the same true of an exchange-traded stock option? Discuss.

1.10. Explain why a futures contract can be used for either speculation or hedging.

1.11. A cattle farmer expects to have 120,000 pounds of live cattle to sell in three months. The live-cattle futures contract on the Chicago Mercantile Exchange is for the delivery of 40,000 pounds of cattle. How can the farmer use the contract for hedging? From the farmer's viewpoint, what are the pros and cons of hedging?

1.12. It is July 2013. A mining company has just discovered a small deposit of gold. It will take six months to construct the mine. The gold will then be extracted on a more or less continuous basis for one year. Futures contracts on gold are available on the New York Mercantile Exchange. There are delivery months every two months from August 2013 to December 2014. Each contract is for the delivery of 100 ounces. Discuss how the mining company might use futures markets for hedging.

1.13. Suppose that a March call option on a stock with a strike price of \$50 costs \$2.50 and is held until March. Under what circumstances will the holder of the option make a gain? Under what circumstances will the option be exercised? Draw a diagram showing how the profit on a long position in the option depends on the stock price at the maturity of the option.

1.14. Suppose that a June put option on a stock with a strike price of \$60 costs \$4 and is held until June. Under what circumstances will the holder of the option make a gain? Under what circumstances will the option be exercised? Draw a diagram showing how the profit on a short position in the option depends on the stock price at the maturity of the option.

1.15. It is May and a trader writes a September call option with a strike price of \$20. The stock price is \$18 and the option price is \$2. Describe the investor's cash flows if the option is held until September and the stock price is \$25 at this time.

1.16. An investor writes a December put option with a strike price of \$30. The price of the option is \$4. Under what circumstances does the investor make a gain?

1.17. The CME Group offers a futures contract on long-term Treasury bonds. Characterize the investors likely to use this contract.

1.18. An airline executive has argued: "There is no point in our using oil futures. There is just as much chance that the price of oil in the future will be less than the futures price as there is that it will be greater than this price." Discuss the executive's viewpoint.

1.19. "Options and futures are zero-sum games." What do you think is meant by this statement?

1.20. A trader enters into a short forward contract on 100 million yen. The forward exchange rate is \$0.0080 per yen. How much does the trader gain or lose if the exchange rate at the end of the contract is (a) \$0.0074 per yen; (b) \$0.0091 per yen?

1.21. A trader enters into a short cotton futures contract when the futures price is 50 cents per pound. The contract is for the delivery of 50,000 pounds. How much does the trader gain or lose if the cotton price at the end of the contract is (a) 48.20 cents per pound; (b) 51.30 cents per pound?

1.22. A company knows that it is due to receive a certain amount of a foreign currency in four months. What type of option contract is appropriate for hedging?

1.23. A United States company expects to have to pay 1 million Canadian dollars in six months. Explain how the exchange rate risk can be hedged using (a) a forward contract; (b) an option.

1.24. A trader buys a call option with a strike price of \$30 for \$3. Does the trader ever exercise the option and lose money on the trade. Explain.

1.25. A trader sells a put option with a strike price of \$40 for \$5. What is the trader's maximum gain and maximum loss? How does your answer change if it is a call option?

1.26. "Buying a stock and a put option on the stock is a form of insurance." Explain this statement.

Further Questions

1.27. Trader A enters into a forward contract to buy an asset for \$1,000 in one year. Trader B buys a call option to buy the asset for \$1,000 in one year. The cost of the option is \$100. What is the difference between the positions of the traders? Show the profit as a function of the price of the asset in one year for the two traders.

1.28. On June 25, 2012, as indicated in Table 1.2, the spot offer price of Google stock is \$561.51 and the offer price of a call option with a strike price of \$560 and a maturity date of September is \$30.70. A trader is considering two alternatives: buy 100 shares of the stock and buy 100 September call options. For each alternative, what is (a) the upfront cost, (b) the total gain if the stock price in September is \$620, and (c) the total loss if the stock price in September is \$500. Assume that the option is not exercised before September and if stock is purchased it is sold in September.

1.29. What is arbitrage? Explain the arbitrage opportunity when the price of a dually listed mining company stock is \$50 (USD) on the New York Stock Exchange and \$52 (CAD) on the Toronto Stock Exchange. Assume that the exchange rate is such that 1 USD equals 1.01 CAD. Explain what is likely to happen to prices as traders take advantage of this opportunity.

1.30. In March, a U.S. investor instructs a broker to sell one July put option contract on a stock. The stock price is \$42 and the strike price is \$40. The option price is \$3. Explain what the investor has agreed to. Under what circumstances will the trade prove to be profitable? What are the risks?

1.31. A U.S. company knows it will have to pay 3 million euros in three months. The current exchange rate is 1.4500 dollars per euro. Discuss how forward and options contracts can be used by the company to hedge its exposure.

1.32. A stock price is \$29. An investor buys one call option contract on the stock with a strike price of \$30 and sells a call option contract on the stock with a strike price of \$32.50. The market prices of the options are \$2.75 and \$1.50, respectively. The options have the same maturity date. Describe the investor's position.

1.33. The price of gold is currently \$1,800 per ounce. Forward contracts are available to buy or sell gold at \$2,000 per ounce for delivery in one year. An arbitrageur can borrow money at 5% per annum. What should the arbitrageur do? Assume that the cost of storing gold is zero and that gold provides no income.

1.34. Discuss how foreign currency options can be used for hedging in the situation described in Example 1.1 so that (a) ImportCo is guaranteed that its exchange rate will be less than 1.5800, and (b) ExportCo is guaranteed that its exchange rate will be at least 1.5400.

1.35. The current price of a stock is \$94, and three-month European call options with a strike price of \$95 currently sell for \$4.70. An investor who feels that the price of the stock will increase is trying to decide between buying 100 shares and buying 2,000 call options (20 contracts). Both strategies involve an investment of \$9,400. What advice would you give? How high does the stock price have to rise for the option strategy to be more profitable?

1.36. On June 25, 2012, an investor owns 100 Google shares. As indicated in Table 1.3, the bid share price is \$561.32 and a December put option with a strike price of \$520 costs \$26.10. The investor is comparing two alternatives to limit downside risk. The first involves buying one December put option contract with a strike price of \$520. The second involves instructing a broker to sell the 100 shares as soon as Google's price reaches \$520. Discuss the advantages and disadvantages of the two strategies.

1.37. A trader buys a European call option and sells a European put option. The options have the same underlying asset, strike price, and maturity. Describe the trader's position. Under what circumstances does the price of the call equal the price of the put?

CHAPTER 2 Mechanics of Futures Markets

In Chapter 1 we explained that both futures and forward contracts are agreements to buy or sell an asset at a future time for a certain price. Futures contracts are traded on an exchange and the contract terms are standardized by that exchange. Forward contracts are traded in the over-the-counter market.

This chapter covers the details of how futures markets work. We examine issues such as the specification of contracts, the operation of margin accounts, the organization of exchanges, the regulation of markets, the way in which quotes are made, and the treatment of futures transactions for accounting and tax purposes. We explain how some of the ideas pioneered by futures exchanges are now being adopted by over-the-counter markets.

2.1 OPENING AND CLOSING FUTURES POSITIONS

A futures contract is an agreement to buy or sell an asset for a certain price at a certain time in the future. A contract is usually referred to by its delivery month. Thus an investor could instruct a broker to buy one October oil futures contract. There is a period of time during the delivery month (often the whole month) when delivery can be made. Trading in the contract usually ceases some time during the delivery period. The party with the short position chooses when delivery is made.

The reader may be surprised to learn that the vast majority of the futures contracts that are initiated do not lead to delivery. The reason is that most investors choose to close out their positions prior to the delivery period specified in the contract. Making or taking delivery under the terms of a futures contract is often inconvenient and in some instances quite expensive. This is true even for a hedger who wants to buy or sell the asset underlying the futures contract. Such a hedger usually prefers to close out the futures position and then buy or sell the asset in the usual way.

Closing a position involves entering into an opposite trade to the original one that opened the position. For example, an investor who buys five July corn futures contracts on May 6 can close out the position on June 20 by selling (i.e., shorting) five July corn futures contracts. An investor who sells (i.e., shorts) five July contracts on May 6 can close out the position on June 20 by buying five July contracts. In each case, the

From Chapter 2 of *Fundamentals of Futures and Options Markets*, Eighth Edition. John C. Hull.

investor's total gain or loss is determined by the change in the futures price between May 6 and June 20.

Delivery is so unusual that traders sometimes forget how the delivery process works (see Business Snapshot 2.1). Nevertheless we will spend part of this chapter reviewing the delivery arrangements in futures contracts. This is because it is the possibility of final delivery that ties the futures price to the spot price.[1]

2.2 SPECIFICATION OF A FUTURES CONTRACT

When developing a new contract, the exchange must specify in some detail the exact nature of the agreement between the two parties. In particular, it must specify the asset, the contract size (exactly how much of the asset will be delivered under one contract), where delivery will be made, and when delivery will be made.

Sometimes alternatives are specified for the grade of the asset that will be delivered or for the delivery locations. As a general rule, it is the party with the short position (the party that has agreed to sell the asset) that chooses what will happen when alternatives are specified by the exchange.[2] When the party with the short position is ready to deliver, it files a *notice of intention to deliver* with the exchange. This notice indicates selections it has made with respect to the grade of asset that will be delivered and the delivery location.

The Asset

When the asset is a commodity, there may be quite a variation in the quality of what is available in the marketplace. When the asset is specified, it is therefore important that the exchange stipulate the grade or grades of the commodity that are acceptable. The IntercontinentalExchange (ICE) has specified the asset in its orange juice futures contract as frozen concentrates that are U.S. Grade A, with Brix value of not less than 62.5 degrees.

For some commodities a range of grades can be delivered, but the price received depends on the grade chosen. For example, in the CME Group corn futures contract, the standard grade is "No. 2 Yellow," but substitutions are allowed with the price being adjusted in a way established by the exchange. No. 1 Yellow is deliverable for 1.5 cents per bushel more than No. 2 Yellow. No. 3 Yellow is deliverable for 1.5 cents per bushel less than No. 2 Yellow.

The financial assets in futures contracts are generally well defined and unambiguous. For example, there is no need to specify the grade of a Japanese yen. However, there are some interesting features of the Treasury bond and Treasury note futures contracts traded by the CME Group. The underlying asset in the Treasury bond contract is any U.S. Treasury bond that has a maturity between 15 and 25 years on the first day of the delivery month. In the 10-year Treasury note futures contract, the underlying asset is any Treasury note with a maturity between 6.5 and 10 years on the first day of the

[1] As mentioned in Chapter 1, the spot price is the price for almost immediate delivery.

[2] There are exceptions. As pointed out by J. E. Newsome, G. H. K. Wang, M. E. Boyd, and M. J. Fuller in "Contract Modifications and the Basis Behavior of Live Cattle Futures," *Journal of Futures Markets*, 24, 6 (2004), 557–90, the CME gave the buyer some options on how delivery could be made in live cattle futures in 1995.

Business Snapshot 2.1 The unanticipated delivery of a futures contract

This story (which may well be apocryphal) was told to the author of this book a long time ago by a senior executive of a financial institution. It concerns a new employee of the financial institution who had not previously worked in the financial sector. One of the clients of the financial institution regularly entered into a long futures contract on live cattle for hedging purposes and issued instructions to close out the position on the last day of trading. (Live cattle futures contracts are traded by the CME Group and each contract is on 40,000 pounds of cattle.) The new employee was given responsibility for handling the account.

When the time came to close out a contract, the employee noted that the client was long one contract and instructed a trader at the exchange to buy (not sell) one contract. The result of this mistake was that the financial institution ended up with a long position in two live cattle futures contracts. By the time the mistake was spotted, trading in the contract had ceased.

The financial institution (not the client) was responsible for the mistake. As a result it started to look into the details of the delivery arrangements for live cattle futures contracts—something it had never done before. Under the terms of the contract, cattle could be delivered by the party with the short position to a number of different locations in the United States during the delivery month. Because it was long, the financial institution could do nothing but wait for a party with a short position to issue a *notice of intention to deliver* to the exchange and for the exchange to assign that notice to the financial institution.

It eventually received a notice from the exchange and found that it would receive live cattle at a location 2,000 miles away the following Tuesday. The new employee was sent to the location to handle things. It turned out that the location had a cattle auction every Tuesday. The party with the short position that was making delivery bought cattle at the auction and then immediately delivered them. Unfortunately the cattle could not be resold until the next cattle auction the following Tuesday. The employee was therefore faced with the problem of making arrangements for the cattle to be housed and fed for a week. This was a great start to a first job in the financial sector!

delivery month.. In both cases, the exchange has a formula for adjusting the price received according to the coupon and maturity date of the bond delivered. This is discussed in Chapter 6.

The Contract Size

The contract size specifies the amount of the asset that has to be delivered under one contract. This is an important decision for the exchange. If the contract size is too large, many investors who wish to hedge relatively small exposures or who wish to take relatively small speculative positions will be unable to use the exchange. On the other hand, if the contract size is too small, trading may be expensive as there is a cost associated with each contract traded.

The correct size for a contract clearly depends on the likely user. Whereas the value of what is delivered under a futures contract on an agricultural product might be $10,000 to $20,000, it is much higher for some financial futures. For example, under the

Treasury bond futures contract traded by the CME Group, instruments with a face value of $100,000 are delivered.

In some cases exchanges have introduced "mini" contracts to attract smaller investors. For example, the CME Group's Mini Nasdaq 100 contract is on 20 times the Nasdaq 100 index whereas the regular contract is on 100 times the index. (We will cover futures on indices more fully in Chapter 3.)

Delivery Arrangements

The place where delivery will be made must be specified by the exchange. This is particularly important for commodities that involve significant transportation costs. In the case of the ICE frozen concentrate orange juice contract, delivery is to exchange-licensed warehouses in Florida, New Jersey, or Delaware.

When alternative delivery locations are specified, the price received by the party with the short position is sometimes adjusted according to the location chosen by that party. The price tends to be higher for delivery locations that are relatively far from the main sources of the commodity.

Delivery Months

A futures contract is referred to by its delivery month. The exchange must specify the precise period during the month when delivery can be made. For many futures contracts, the delivery period is the whole month.

The delivery months vary from contract to contract and are chosen by the exchange to meet the needs of market participants. For example, corn futures traded by the CME Group have delivery months of March, May, July, September, and December. At any given time, contracts trade for the closest delivery month and a number of subsequent delivery months. The exchange specifies when trading in a particular month's contract will begin. The exchange also specifies the last day on which trading can take place for a given contract. Trading generally ceases a few days before the last day on which delivery can be made.

Price Quotes

The exchange defines how prices will be quoted. For example, in the U.S., crude oil futures prices are quoted in dollars and cents, but Treasury bond and Treasury note futures prices are quoted in dollars and thirty-seconds of a dollar.

Price Limits and Position Limits

For most contracts, daily price movement limits are specified by the exchange. If in a day the price moves down from the previous day's close by an amount equal to the daily price limit, the contract is said to be *limit down*. If it moves up by the limit, it is said to be *limit up*. A *limit move* is a move in either direction equal to the daily price limit. Normally, trading ceases for the day once the contract is limit up or limit down. However, in some instances the exchange has the authority to step in and change the limits.

The purpose of daily price limits is to prevent large price movements from occurring because of speculative excesses. However, limits can become an artificial barrier to trading when the price of the underlying commodity is advancing or declining rapidly. Whether price limits are, on balance, good for futures markets is controversial.

Position limits are the maximum number of contracts that a speculator may hold. The purpose of these limits is to prevent speculators from exercising undue influence on the market.

2.3 CONVERGENCE OF FUTURES PRICE TO SPOT PRICE

As the delivery period for a futures contract is approached, the futures price converges to the spot price of the underlying asset. When the delivery period is reached, the futures price equals, or is very close to the spot price.

To see why this is so, we first suppose that the futures price is above the spot price during the delivery period. Traders then have a clear arbitrage opportunity:

1. Sell (i.e., short) a futures contract
2. Buy the asset
3. Make delivery

These steps are certain to lead to a profit equal to the amount by which the futures price exceeds the spot price. As traders exploit this arbitrage opportunity, the futures price will fall. Suppose next that the futures price is below the spot price during the delivery period. Companies interested in acquiring the asset will find it attractive to buy a futures contract and then wait for delivery to be made. As they do so, the futures price will tend to rise.

The result is that the futures price is very close to the spot price during the delivery period. Figure 2.1 illustrates the convergence of the futures price to the spot price. In Figure 2.1a the futures price is above the spot price prior to the delivery period, and in Figure 2.1b the futures price is below the spot price prior to the delivery period. The circumstances under which these two patterns are observed are discussed in Chapter 5.

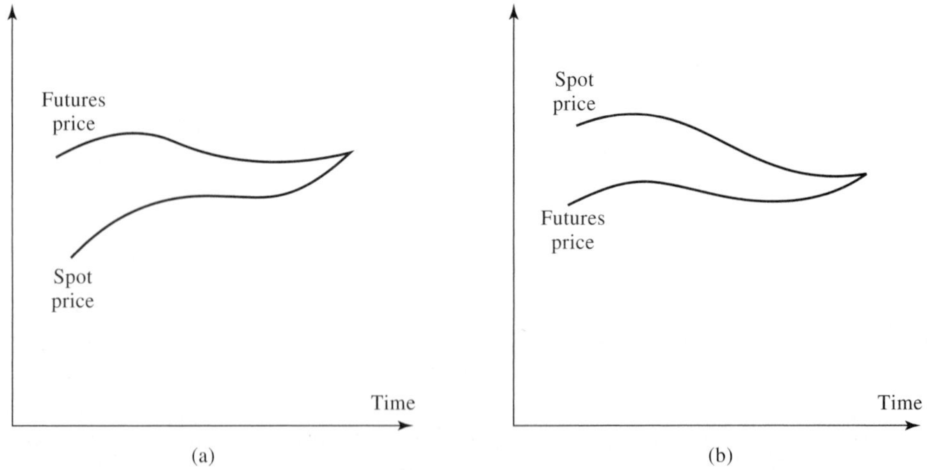

Figure 2.1 Relationship between futures price and spot price as the delivery month is approached: (a) futures price above spot price; (b) futures price below spot price

2.4 THE OPERATION OF MARGIN ACCOUNTS

If two investors get in touch with each other directly and agree to trade an asset in the future for a certain price, there are obvious risks. One of the investors may regret the deal and try to back out. Alternatively, the investor simply may not have the financial resources to honor the agreement. One of the key roles of the exchange is to organize trading so that contract defaults are avoided. This is where margin accounts come in.

Daily Settlement

To illustrate how margin accounts work, we consider an investor who contacts his or her broker on June 5 to buy two December gold futures contracts. We suppose that the current futures price is \$1,650 per ounce. Because the contract size is 100 ounces, the investor has contracted to buy a total of 200 ounces at this price. The broker will require the investor to deposit funds in a *margin account*. The amount that must be deposited at the time the contract is entered into is known as the *initial margin*. We suppose this is \$6,000 per contract, or \$12,000 in total. At the end of each trading day, the margin account is adjusted to reflect the investor's gain or loss. This practice is referred to as *daily settlement* or *marking to market*.

Suppose, for example, that by the end of June 5 the futures price has dropped from \$1,650 to \$1,641. The investor has a loss of \$1,800 (= 200 × \$9), because the 200 ounces of December gold, which the investor contracted to buy at \$1,650, can now be sold for only \$1,641. The balance in the margin account would therefore be reduced by \$1,800 to \$10,200. Similarly, if the price of December gold rose to \$1,659 by the end of June 5, the balance in the margin account would be increased by \$1,800 to \$13,800. A trade is first settled at the close of the day on which it takes place. It is then settled at the close of trading on each subsequent day.

Note that daily settlement is not merely an arrangement between broker and client. When there is a decrease in the futures price so that the margin account of an investor with a long position is reduced by \$1,800, the investor's broker has to pay the exchange clearing house \$1,800 and this money is passed on to the broker of an investor with a short position. Similarly, when there is an increase in the futures price, brokers for parties with short positions pay money to the exchange clearing house and brokers for parties with long positions receive money from the exchange clearing house. Later we will examine in more detail the mechanism by which this happens.

The investor is entitled to withdraw any balance in the margin account in excess of the initial margin. To ensure that the balance in the margin account never becomes negative, a *maintenance margin*, which is somewhat lower than the initial margin, is set. If the balance in the margin account falls below the maintenance margin, the investor receives a margin call and is expected to top up the margin account to the initial margin level the next day. The extra funds deposited are known as a *variation margin*. If the investor does not provide the variation margin, the broker closes out the position. In the case considered above, closing out the position would involve neutralizing the existing contract by selling 200 ounces of gold for delivery in December.

Table 2.1 illustrates the operation of the margin account for one possible sequence of futures prices in the case of the investor considered earlier. The maintenance margin is assumed for the purpose of the illustration to be \$4,500 per contract, or \$9,000 in total. On Day 7 the balance in the margin account falls \$1,020 below the maintenance margin

Table 2.1 Operation of margin account for a long position in two gold futures contracts. The initial margin is \$6,000 per contract, or \$12,000 in total; the maintenance margin is \$4,500 per contract, or \$9,000 in total. The contract is entered into on Day 1 at \$1,650 and closed out on Day 16 at \$1,626.90

Day	*Trade price (\$)*	*Settlement price (\$)*	*Daily gain (\$)*	*Cumulative gain (\$)*	*Margin account balance (\$)*	*Margin call (\$)*
1	1,650.00				12,000	
1		1,641.00	−1,800	−1,800	10,200	
2		1,638.30	−540	−2,340	9,660	
3		1,644.60	1,260	−1,080	10,920	
4		1,641.30	−660	−1,740	10,260	
5		1,640.10	−240	−1,980	10,020	
6		1,636.20	−780	−2,760	9,240	
7		1,629.90	−1,260	−4,020	7,980	4,020
8		1,630.80	180	−3,840	12,180	
9		1,625.40	−1,080	−4,920	11,100	
10		1,628.10	540	−4,380	11,640	
11		1,611.00	−3,420	−7,800	8,220	3,780
12		1,611.00	0	−7,800	12,000	
13		1,614.30	660	−7,140	12,660	
14		1,616.10	360	−6,780	13,020	
15		1,623.00	1,380	−5,400	14,400	
16	1,626.90		780	−4,620	15,180	

level. This drop triggers a margin call from the broker for additional \$4,020 to bring the margin account balance up to \$12,000. Table 2.1 assumes that the investor does in fact provide this margin by the close of trading on Day 8. On Day 11 the balance in the margin account again falls below the maintenance margin level, and a margin call for \$3,780 is sent out. The investor provides this margin by the close of trading on Day 12. On Day 16 the investor decides to close out the position by selling two contracts. The futures price on that day is \$1,626.90, and the investor has a cumulative loss of \$4,620. Note that the investor has excess margin on Days 8, 13, 14, and 15. Table 2.1 assumes that the excess is not withdrawn.

Further Details

Most brokers pay investors interest on the balance in a margin account. The balance in the account does not, therefore, represent a true cost, providing the interest rate is competitive with what could be earned elsewhere. To satisfy the initial margin requirements (but not subsequent margin calls), an investor can usually deposit securities with the broker. Treasury bills are usually accepted in lieu of cash at about 90% of their face value. Shares are also sometimes accepted in lieu of cash—but at about 50% of their market value.

Whereas a forward contract is settled at the end of its life, a futures contract is settled daily. At the end of each day, the investor's gain (loss) is added to (subtracted from) the margin account, bringing the value of the contract back to zero. A futures contract is in effect closed out and rewritten at a new price each day.

Minimum levels for the initial and maintenance margin are set by the exchange clearing house. Individual brokers may require more margin from their clients than the minimum level specified by the exchange clearing house. Minimum margin levels are determined by the variability of the price of the underlying asset and are revised when necessary. The higher the variability, the higher the margin levels. The maintenance margin is usually about 75% of the initial margin.

Margin requirements may depend on the objectives of the trader. A bona fide hedger, such as a company that produces the commodity on which the futures contract is written, is often subject to lower margin requirements than a speculator. The reason is that there is deemed to be less risk of default. Day trades and spread transactions often give rise to lower margin requirements than do hedge transactions. In a *day trade* the trader announces to the broker an intent to close out the position in the same day. In a *spread transaction* the trader simultaneously buys (i.e., takes a long position in) a contract on an asset for one maturity month and sells (i.e., takes a short position in) a contract on the same asset for another maturity month.

Note that margin requirements are the same on short futures positions as they are on long futures positions. It is just as easy to take a short futures position as it is to take a long one. The spot market does not have this symmetry. Taking a long position in the spot market involves buying the asset for immediate delivery and presents no problems. Taking a short position involves selling an asset that you do not own. This is a more complex transaction that may or may not be possible in a particular market. It is discussed further in Chapter 5.

The Clearing House and Clearing Margin

A *clearing house* acts as an intermediary in futures transactions. It guarantees the performance of the parties to each transaction. The clearing house has a number of members, who must contribute to a default fund. Brokers who are not members themselves must channel their business through a member. The main task of the clearing house is to keep track of all the transactions that take place during a day so that it can calculate the net position of each of its members.

Just as an investor is required to maintain a margin account with a broker, the broker is required to maintain margin with a clearing house member and the clearing house member is required to maintain a margin account with the clearing house. The latter is known as a *clearing margin*. The margin accounts for clearing house members are adjusted for gains and losses at the end of each trading day in the same way as are the margin accounts of investors. However, in the case of the clearing house member, there is an original margin, but no maintenance margin. Every day the account balance for each contract must be maintained at an amount equal to the original margin times the number of contracts outstanding. Thus, depending on transactions during the day and price movements, the clearing house member may have to add funds to its margin account at the end of the day, or it may find it can remove funds from the account at this time. Brokers who are not clearing house members must maintain a margin account with a clearing house member.

In determining a clearing margin, the exchange clearing house calculates the number of contracts outstanding on either a gross or a net basis. When the gross basis is used, the number of contracts equals the sum of long and short positions; when the net basis is used, these are offset against each other. Suppose a clearing house member has two clients: one with a long position in 20 contracts, the other with a short position in 15 contracts. Gross margining would calculate the clearing margin on the basis of 35 contracts; net margining would calculate the clearing margin on the basis of 5 contracts. Most exchanges currently use net margining.

Credit Risk

The whole purpose of the margining system is to ensure that funds are available to pay traders when they make a profit. Overall the system has been very successful. Traders entering into contracts at major exchanges have always had their contracts honored. Futures markets were tested on October 19, 1987, when the S&P 500 index declined by over 20% and traders with long positions in S&P 500 futures found they had negative margin balances. Traders who did not meet margin calls were closed out but still owed their brokers money. Some did not pay, and as a result some brokers went bankrupt because, without their clients' money, they were unable to meet margin calls on contracts they had entered into on behalf of their clients. However, the clearing house had sufficient funds to ensure that everyone who had a short futures position on the S&P 500 got paid.

2.5 OTC MARKETS

Over-the-counter (OTC) markets, introduced in Chapter 1, are markets where companies agree to derivatives transactions without involving an exchange. Credit risk has traditionally been a feature of OTC derivatives markets. Consider two companies, A and B, that have entered into a number of derivatives transactions. If A defaults when the net value of the outstanding transactions to B is positive, a loss is liable to be taken by B. Similarly, if B defaults when the net value of outstanding transactions to A is positive, a loss is likely to be taken by A.

In an attempt to reduce credit risk, the OTC market has used some of the procedures of exchange-traded markets. The agreement between company A and company B may require A or B, or both, to post margin. (In this case of OTC markets, margin is referred to as collateral.) Also, as mentioned in Section 1.3, A and B may use a central clearing party, which is similar to an exchange clearing house, for its transactions. We will now explain these developments.

Collateral

Consider again two companies, A and B, that have entered into a number of OTC derivatives transactions. A collateral agreement between the companies is likely to involve the transactions being valued each day. The agreement may be one-way, where only one side is liable to have to post collateral, or two-way, where both sides are liable to have to post collateral. Many different types of collateral arrangements can be negotiated. A simple two-way agreement might work as follows. If from one day to the next the transactions increase in value to A by $\$X$ (and decrease in value to B by $\$X$), company B is required to provide $\$X$ of collateral to A. If the reverse happens and the transactions increase in value to B by $\$X$ (and decrease in value to A by $\$X$),

Business Snapshot 2.2 Long-Term Capital Management's big loss

Long-Term Capital Management (LTCM), a hedge fund formed in the mid-1990s, always collateralized its transactions. The hedge fund's investment strategy was known as convergence arbitrage. A very simple example of what it might do is the following. It would find two bonds, X and Y, issued by the same company that promised the same payoffs, with X being less liquid (i.e., less actively traded) than Y. The market places a value on liquidity. As a result the price of X would be less than the price of Y. LTCM would buy X, short Y, and wait, expecting the prices of the two bonds to converge at some future time.

When interest rates increased, the company expected both bonds to move down in price by about the same amount so that the collateral it paid on bond X would be about the same as the collateral it received on bond Y. Similarly, when interest rates decreased LTCM expected both bonds to move up in price by about the same amount so that the collateral it received on bond X would be about the same as the collateral it paid on bond Y. It therefore expected that there would be no significant outflow of funds as a result of its collateralization agreements.

In August 1998, Russia defaulted on its debt and this led to what is termed a "flight to quality" in capital markets. One result was that investors valued liquid instruments more highly than usual and the spreads between the prices of the liquid and illiquid instruments in LTCM's portfolio increased dramatically. The prices of the bonds LTCM had bought went down and the prices of those it had shorted increased. It was required to post collateral on both. The company experienced difficulties because it was highly leveraged. Positions had to be closed out and LTCM lost about \$4 billion. If the company had been less highly leveraged, it would probably have been able to survive the flight to quality and could have waited for the prices of the liquid and illiquid bonds to move back closer to each other.

company A is required to provide $\$X$ to B. To use the terminology of exchange-traded markets, in this arrangement the companies would be required to post variation margin, but no initial margin.

The collateral can be in the form of cash or acceptable marketable securities. Interest is usually paid on cash collateral. The market value of securities is usually reduced by a certain percentage amount to determine their value for collateral purposes. This reduction is known as a *haircut*.

Collateralization significantly reduces the credit risk in over-the-counter contracts. Collateralization agreements were used by a hedge fund, Long-Term Capital Management (LTCM) in the 1990s. They allowed LTCM to be highly levered. The contracts did provide credit risk protection, but as described in Business Snapshot 2.2 the high leverage left the hedge fund vulnerable to other risks.

The Use of Clearing Houses in OTC Markets

Prior to the credit crisis that started in 2007, most OTC trades were handled by bilateral agreements between market participants.[3] As just described, the agreements often

[3] The most common such agreement was an International Swaps and Derivatives Association (ISDA) Master Agreement.

involved collateral being posted, but the amount of collateral required was not usually as great as the amount of margin that would be required for similar transactions in the exchange-traded market. As a result, whereas exchange-traded markets were almost completely free of credit risk, OTC markets were not.

Following the credit crisis that started in 2007, regulators have become more concerned about systemic risk (see Business Snapshot 1.2). This has led them to look for ways reducing credit risk by making the OTC markets more like exchange-traded markets. The result has been legislation requiring that standard OTC transactions (with a few exceptions) be handled by what are known as *central clearing parties* (CCPs).

CCPs are similar to exchange clearing houses. Once it has been agreed between two parties A and B, a standard OTC derivative transaction is presented to a CCP. Assuming the CCP accepts the transaction, it becomes the counterparty to both A and B. (This is similar to the way the clearing house for a futures exchange becomes the counterparty to the two sides of a futures trade). For example, if the transaction is a forward contract where A has agreed to buy an asset from B in one year for a certain price, the clearing house agrees to

1. Buy the asset from B in one year for the agreed price, and
2. Sell the asset to A in one year for the agreed price.

It takes on the credit risk of both A and B. It manages this risk by requiring an initial margin and a daily variation margin from each of them.

Figure 2.2 illustrates the way bilateral and central clearing work. (It makes the simplifying assumption that there are only eight market participants and one CCP.) Under bilateral clearing there are many different agreements between market participants as indicated in Figure 2.2a. If all OTC contracts were cleared through a single CCP we would move to the situation shown in Figure 2.2b. In practice, because not all OTC transaction are routed through CCPs and there is more than one CCP, the market has elements of both Figure 2.2a and 2.2b.

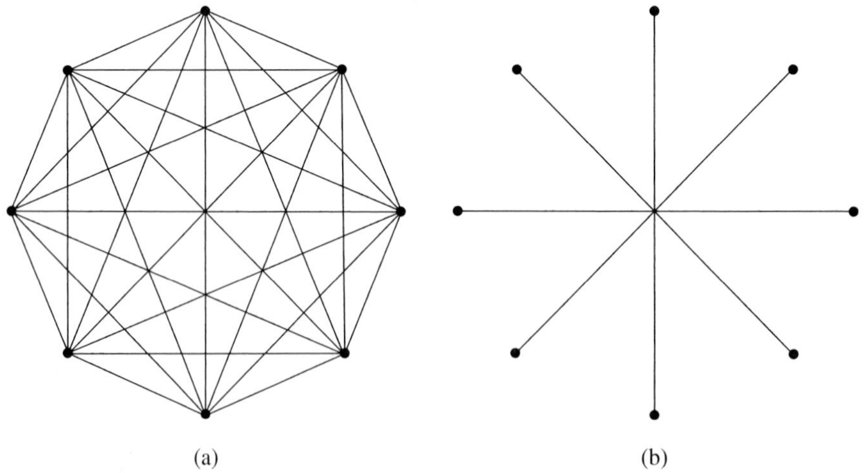

Figure 2.2 (a) The traditional way in which OTC markets have operated: a series of bilateral agreements between market participants; (b) how OTC markets would operate with a single central clearing house.

Table 2.2 Futures quotes for a selection of CME Group contracts on commodities on July 13, 2012

	Open	*High*	*Low*	*Prior settlement*	*Last trade*	*Change*	*Volume*
Gold, 100 oz, $ per oz							
Aug. 2012	1571.2	1596.5	1565.6	1565.3	1589.7	+24.4	115,296
Sept. 2012	1570.4	1597.5	1567.1	1566.4	1590.2	+23.8	303
Oct. 2012	1574.0	1598.3	1570.0	1567.6	1593.6	+26.0	726
Dec. 2012	1576.5	1601.0	1570.7	1570.0	1596.0	+26.0	11,283
June 2013	1598.0	1604.6	1598.0	1576.1	1604.6	+28.5	250
Crude Oil, 1,000 barrels, $ per barrel							
Aug. 2012	85.86	87.61	85.58	86.08	87.28	+1.20	223,698
Sept. 2012	86.33	88.00	85.95	86.46	87.68	+1.22	87,931
Dec. 2012	87.45	89.21	87.39	87.73	88.94	+1.21	31,701
Dec. 2013	88.85	90.15	88.78	88.92	89.95	+1.03	11,128
Dec. 2014	87.20	87.74	87.20	86.98	87.74	+0.76	2,388
Corn, 5,000 bushels, cents per bushel							
Sept. 2012	730.00	748.00	726.50	731.25	742.25	+11.00	78,317
Dec. 2012	731.25	749.00	727.25	732.25	742.25	+10.00	179,010
Mar. 2013	733.00	748.25	729.00	734.50	743.50	+9.00	22,588
May 2013	731.00	744.25	726.75	732.75	739.75	+7.00	4,548
July 2013	728.00	739.00	721.00	728.75	733.50	+4.75	7,874
Dec. 2013	618.75	626.50	613.75	618.25	626.00	+7.75	4,260
Soybeans, 5,000 bushels, cents per bushel							
Aug. 2012	1572.00	1600.00	1571.50	1572.50	1596.00	+23.50	19,194
Sept. 2012	1544.50	1574.00	1544.50	1545.50	1570.00	+24.50	7,024
Nov. 2012	1528.00	1561.50	1526.50	1529.00	1552.75	+23.75	98,526
Jan. 2013	1527.75	1557.25	1523.75	1526.00	1548.00	+22.00	11,621
Mar. 2013	1486.25	1508.00	1482.25	1481.25	1500.25	+19.00	6,226
May 2013	1432.25	1453.25	1428.00	1430.25	1449.00	+18.75	5,234
Wheat, 5,000 bushels, cents per bushel							
Sept. 2012	845.75	865.75	842.00	846.75	846.25	−0.50	41,301
Dec. 2012	859.00	877.75	856.00	859.75	861.50	+1.75	29,450
Mar. 2013	868.00	885.75	865.00	869.00	870.00	+2.00	6,972
May 2013	865.00	881.00	863.00	864.50	867.00	+2.50	2,339
July 2013	824.50	840.00	824.25	826.75	832.50	+5.75	4,118
Live Cattle, 40,000 lbs, cents per lb							
Aug. 2012	116.900	117.600	116.300	117.025	117.225	+0.200	23,117
Oct. 2012	121.450	121.650	120.525	121.650	121.600	−0.050	18,427
Dec. 2012	124.900	125.000	124.050	124.975	124.950	−0.025	6,561
Feb. 2013	128.500	128.500	127.525	128.550	128.500	−0.050	2,450
Apr. 2013	131.225	131.400	130.300	131.375	131.250	−0.125	1,615

2.6 MARKET QUOTES

Futures quotes are available from exchanges and several online sources. Table 2.2 is constructed from quotes provided by the CME Group for a number of different commodities at a particular time on July 13, 2012. Quotes for index, currency, and interest rate futures are given in Chapters 3, 5, and 6, respectively.

The asset underlying the futures contract, the contract size, and the way the price is quoted are shown at the top of each section of Table 2.2. The first asset is gold. The contract size is 100 ounces and the price is quoted as dollars per ounce. The maturity month of the contract is indicated in the first column of the table.

Prices

The first three numbers in each row of Table 2.2 show the opening price, the highest price in trading so far during the day, and the lowest price in trading so far during the day. The opening price is representative of the prices at which contracts were trading immediately after the start of trading on July 13, 2012. For the August 2012 gold contract, the opening price on July 13, 2012 was $1,571.2 per ounce. The highest price during the day was $1,596.5 per ounce and the lowest price during the day was $1,565.6 per ounce.

Settlement Price

The *settlement price* is the price used for calculating daily gains and losses and margin requirements. It is usually calculated as the price at which the contract traded immediately before the end of a day's trading session. The fourth number in Table 2.2 shows the settlement price the previous day (i.e., July 12, 2012). The fifth number shows the most recent trading price, and the sixth number shows the price change from the previous day's settlement price. In the case of the August 2012 gold contract, the previous day's settlement price was $1,565.3. The most recent trade was at $1,589.7, $24.4 higher than the previous day's settlement price. If $1,589.7 proved to be the settlement price on July 13, 2012, the margin account of a trader with a long position in one contract would gain $2,440 on July 13 and the margin account of a trader with a short position would lose this amount on July 13.

Trading Volume and Open Interest

The final column of Table 2.2 shows the *trading volume*. The trading volume is the number of contracts traded in a day. It can be contrasted with the *open interest*, which is the number of contracts outstanding, that is, the number of long positions or, equivalently, the number of short positions.

If there is a large amount of trading by day traders (i.e., traders who enter into a position and close it out on the same day) the volume of trading in a day can be greater than either the beginning-of-day or end-of-day open interest.

Patterns of Futures

Futures prices can show a number of different patterns. In Table 2.2, gold futures prices and live cattle futures prices are an increasing function of maturity. This is known as a *normal market*. Soybean futures prices are a decreasing function of maturity. This is known as an *inverted market*. Other commodities such as crude oil, corn, and wheat showed patterns that were partly normal and partly inverted on July 13, 2012.

2.7 DELIVERY

As mentioned earlier in this chapter, very few of the futures contracts that are entered into lead to delivery of the underlying asset. Most are closed out early. Nevertheless, it is the possibility of eventual delivery that determines the futures price. An understanding of delivery procedures is therefore important.

The period during which delivery can be made is defined by the exchange and varies from contract to contract. The decision on when to deliver is made by the party with the short position, whom we shall refer to as investor A. When investor A decides to deliver, investor A's broker issues a notice of intention to deliver to the exchange clearing house. This notice states how many contracts will be delivered and, in the case of commodities, also specifies where delivery will be made and what grade will be delivered. The exchange then chooses a party with a long position to accept delivery.

Suppose that investor B was the party on the other side of investor A's futures contract when it was entered into. It is important to realize that there is no reason to expect that it will be investor B who takes delivery. Investor B may well have closed out his or her position by trading with investor C, investor C may have closed out his or her position by trading with investor D, and so on. The usual rule chosen by the exchange is to pass the notice of intention to deliver on to the party with the oldest outstanding long position. Parties with long positions must accept delivery notices. However, if the notices are transferable, long investors have a short period of time, usually half an hour, to find another party with a long position that is prepared to accept the notice from them.

In the case of a commodity, taking delivery usually means accepting a warehouse receipt in return for immediate payment. The party taking delivery is then responsible for all warehousing costs. In the case of livestock futures, there may be costs associated with feeding and looking after the animals (see Business Snapshot 2.1). In the case of financial futures, delivery is usually made by wire transfer. For all contracts, the price paid is usually the most recent settlement price. If specified by the exchange, this price is adjusted for grade, location of delivery, and so on. The whole delivery procedure from the issuance of the notice of intention to deliver to the delivery itself generally takes two to three days.

There are three critical days for a contract. These are the first notice day, the last notice day, and the last trading day. The *first notice day* is the first day on which a notice of intention to make delivery can be submitted to the exchange. The *last notice day* is the last such day. The *last trading day* is generally a few days before the last notice day. To avoid the risk of having to take delivery, an investor with a long position should close out his or her contracts prior to the first notice day.

Cash Settlement

Some financial futures, such as those on stock indices discussed in Chapter 3, are settled in cash because it is inconvenient or impossible to deliver the underlying asset. In the case of the futures contract on the S&P 500, for example, delivering the underlying asset would involve delivering a portfolio of 500 stocks. When a contract is settled in cash, all outstanding contracts are declared closed on a predetermined day. The final settlement price is set equal to the spot price of the underlying asset at either the open or close of trading on that day. For example, in the S&P 500 futures contract traded by the CME Group, the predetermined day is the third Friday of the delivery month and final settlement is at the opening price.

2.8 TYPES OF TRADER AND TYPES OF ORDER

There are two main types of trader executing trades: *futures commission merchants* (FCMs) and *locals*. FCMs are following the instructions of their clients and charge a commission for doing so; locals are trading on their own account.

Individuals taking positions, whether locals or the clients of FCMs, can be categorized as hedgers, speculators, or arbitrageurs, as discussed in Chapter 1. Speculators can be classified as scalpers, day traders, or position traders. *Scalpers* are watching for very short term trends and attempt to profit from small changes in the contract price. They usually hold their positions for only a few minutes. *Day traders* hold their positions for less than one trading day. They are unwilling to take the risk that adverse news will occur overnight. *Position traders* hold their positions for much longer periods of time. They hope to make significant profits from major movements in the markets.

Orders

The simplest type of order placed with a broker is a *market order*. It is a request that a trade be carried out immediately at the best price available in the market. However, there are many other types of orders. We will consider those that are more commonly used.

A *limit order* specifies a particular price. The order can be executed only at this price or at one more favorable to the investor. Thus, if the limit price is $30 for an investor wanting to buy, the order will be executed only at a price of $30 or less. There is, of course, no guarantee that the order will be executed at all, because the limit price may never be reached.

A *stop order* or *stop-loss order* also specifies a particular price. The order is executed at the best available price once a bid or offer is made at that particular price or a less-favorable price. Suppose a stop order to sell at $30 is issued when the market price is $35. It becomes an order to sell when and if the price falls to $30. In effect, a stop order becomes a market order as soon as the specified price has been hit. The purpose of a stop order is usually to close out a position if unfavorable price movements take place. It limits the loss that can be incurred.

A *stop–limit order* is a combination of a stop order and a limit order. The order becomes a limit order as soon as a bid or offer is made at a price equal to or less favorable than the stop price. Two prices must be specified in a stop–limit order: the stop price and the limit price. Suppose that, at the time the market price is $35, a stop–limit order to buy is issued with a stop price of $40 and a limit price of $41. As soon as there is a bid or offer at $40, the stop–limit becomes a limit order at $41. If the stop price and the limit price are the same, the order is sometimes called a *stop-and-limit order*.

A *market-if-touched order* (MIT) is executed at the best available price after a trade occurs at a specified price or at a price more favorable than the specified price. In effect, an MIT becomes a market order once the specified price has been hit. An MIT is also known as a *board order*. Consider an investor who has a long position in a futures contract and is issuing instructions that would lead to closing out the contract. A stop order is designed to place a limit on the loss that can occur in the event of unfavorable price movements. By contrast, a market-if-touched order is designed to ensure that profits are taken if sufficiently favorable price movements occur.

A *discretionary order* or *market-not-held order* is traded as a market order except that execution may be delayed at the broker's discretion in an attempt to get a better price.

Some orders specify time conditions. Unless otherwise stated, an order is a day order and expires at the end of the trading day. A *time-of-day order* specifies a particular period of time during the day when the order can be executed. An *open order* or a *good-till-canceled order* is in effect until executed or until the end of trading in the particular contract. A *fill-or-kill order*, as its name implies, must be executed immediately on receipt or not at all.

2.9 REGULATION

Futures markets in the United States are currently regulated federally by the Commodity Futures Trading Commission (CFTC; www.cftc.gov), which was established in 1974.

The CFTC looks after the public interest. It is responsible for ensuring that prices are communicated to the public and that futures traders report their outstanding positions if they are above certain levels. The CFTC also licenses all individuals who offer their services to the public in futures trading. The backgrounds of these individuals are investigated, and there are minimum capital requirements. The CFTC deals with complaints brought by the public and ensures that disciplinary action is taken against individuals when appropriate. It has the authority to force exchanges to take disciplinary action against members who are in violation of exchange rules.

With the formation of the National Futures Association (NFA; www.nfa.futures.org) in 1982, some of responsibilities of the CFTC were shifted to the futures industry itself. The NFA is an organization of individuals who participate in the futures industry. Its objective is to prevent fraud and to ensure that the market operates in the best interests of the general public. It is authorized to monitor trading and take disciplinary action when appropriate. The agency has set up an efficient system for arbitrating disputes between individuals and its members.

From time to time other bodies such as the Securities and Exchange Commission (SEC; www.sec.gov), the Federal Reserve Board (www.federalreserve.gov), and the U.S. Treasury Department (www.treas.gov) have claimed jurisdictional rights over some aspects of futures trading. These bodies are concerned with the effects of futures trading on the spot markets for securities such as stocks, Treasury bills, and Treasury bonds.

Trading Irregularities

Most of the time futures markets operate efficiently and in the public interest. However, from time to time trading irregularities do come to light. One type of trading irregularity occurs when an investor group tries to "corner the market."[4] The investor group takes a huge long futures position and also tries to exercise some control over the supply of the underlying commodity. As the maturity of the futures contracts is approached, the investor group does not close out its position, so that the number of outstanding futures contracts may exceed the amount of the commodity available for delivery. The holders of short positions realize that they will find it difficult to deliver and become desperate to close out their positions. The result is a large rise in both futures and spot prices. Regulators usually deal with this type of abuse of the market by increasing margin requirements or imposing stricter position limits or prohibiting trades that increase a speculator's open position or requiring market participants to close out their positions.

Other types of trading irregularities can involve the traders on the floor of the exchange. These received some publicity early in 1989 when it was announced that the FBI had carried out a two-year investigation, using undercover agents, of trading on the Chicago Board of Trade and the Chicago Mercantile Exchange. The investigation was initiated because of complaints filed by a large agricultural concern. The alleged offenses included overcharging customers, not paying customers the full proceeds of sales, and traders using their knowledge of customer orders to trade first for themselves. (The latter is known as *front running*.)

2.10 ACCOUNTING AND TAX

The full details of the accounting and tax treatment of futures contracts are beyond the scope of this book. A trader who wants detailed information on this should obtain professional advice. This section provides some general background information.

Accounting

Accounting standards require changes in the market value of a futures contract to be recognized when they occur unless the contract qualifies as a hedge. If the contract does qualify as a hedge, then gains or losses are generally recognized for accounting purposes in the same period in which the gains or losses from the item being hedged are recognized. The latter treatment is referred to as *hedge accounting*.

Example 2.1 considers a company with a December year end. In September 2013 it buys a March 2014 corn futures contract and closes out the position at the end of February 2014. Suppose that the futures prices are 750 cents per bushel when the contract is entered into, 770 cents per bushel at the end of 2013, and 780 cents per bushel when the contract is closed out. The contract is for the delivery of 5,000 bushels. If the contract does not qualify as a hedge, the gains for accounting purposes are

$$5{,}000 \times (7.70 - 7.50) = \$1{,}000$$

in 2013 and

$$5{,}000 \times (7.80 - 7.70) = \$500$$

in 2014. If the company is hedging the purchase of 5,000 bushels of corn in February

[4] Possibly the best known example of this involves the activities of the Hunt brothers in the silver market in 1979–80. Between the middle of 1979 and the beginning of 1980, their activities led to a price rise from \$6 per ounce to \$50 per ounce.

Example 2.1 Accounting treatment of a futures transaction

A company buys 5,000 bushels of March 2014 corn in September 2013 for 750 cents per bushel and closes out the position in February 2014 for 780 cents per bushel. The price of March 2014 corn on December 31, 2013, the company's year end, is 770 cents per bushel.

If contract is not a hedge, the treatment of these transactions leads to:
Accounting profit in 2013 = 5,000 × 20 cents = \$1,000.
Accounting profit in 2014 = 5,000 × 10 cents = \$500.

If contract is hedging a purchase of corn in 2014, the result is:
Accounting profit in 2013 = \$0.
Accounting profit in 2014 = 5,000 × 30 cents = \$1,500.

2014 so that the contract qualifies for hedge accounting, the entire gain of \$1,500 is realized in 2014 for accounting purposes.

The treatment of hedging gains and losses is sensible. If the company is hedging the purchase of 5,000 bushels of corn in February 2014, the effect of the futures contract is to ensure that the price paid is close to 750 cents per bushel. The accounting treatment reflects that this price is paid in 2014.

In June 1998, the Financial Accounting Standards Board issued Statement No. 133 (FAS 133), Accounting for Derivative Instruments and Hedging Activities. FAS 133 applies to all types of derivatives (including futures, forwards, swaps, and options). It requires all derivatives to be included on the balance sheet at fair market value.[5] It increases disclosure requirements. It also gives companies far less latitude than previously in using hedge accounting. For hedge accounting to be used, the hedging instrument must be highly effective in offsetting exposures and an assessment of this effectiveness is required every three months. A similar standard IAS 39 has been issued by the International Accounting Standards Board.

Tax

Under the U.S. tax rules, two key issues are the nature of a taxable gain or loss and the timing of the recognition of the gain or loss. Gains or losses are either classified as capital gains/losses or as part of ordinary income.

For a corporate taxpayer, capital gains are taxed at the same rate as ordinary income, and the ability to deduct losses is restricted. Capital losses are deductible only to the extent of capital gains. A corporation may carry back a capital loss for three years and carry it forward for up to five years. For a noncorporate taxpayer, short-term capital gains are taxed at the same rate as ordinary income, but long-term capital gains are taxed at a lower rate than ordinary income. (Long-term capital gains are gains from the sale of a capital asset held for longer than one year; short term capital gains are the gains from the sale of a capital asset held one year or less.) The Taxpayer Relief Act of 1997 widened the rate differential between ordinary income and long-term capital gains. For a noncorporate taxpayer, capital losses are deductible to the extent of capital gains plus ordinary income up to \$3,000 and can be carried forward indefinitely.

[5] Previously the attraction of derivatives in some situations was that they were "off-balance-sheet" items.

Generally, positions in futures contracts are treated as if they are closed out on the last day of the tax year. For the noncorporate taxpayer this gives rise to capital gains and losses. These are treated as if they are 60% long term and 40% short term without regard to the holding period. This is referred to as the "60/40" rule. A noncorporate taxpayer may elect to carry back for three years any net losses from the 60/40 rule to offset any gains recognized under the rule in the previous three years.

Hedging transactions are exempt from this rule. The definition of a hedge transaction for tax purposes is different from that for accounting purposes. The tax regulations define a hedging transaction as a transaction entered into in the normal course of business primarily for one of the following reasons:

1. To reduce the risk of price changes or currency fluctuations with respect to property that is held or to be held by the taxpayer for the purposes of producing ordinary income
2. To reduce the risk of price or interest rate changes or currency fluctuations with respect to borrowings made by the taxpayer.

A hedging transaction must be clearly identified in a timely manner in the company's records as a hedge. Gains or losses from hedging transactions are treated as ordinary income. The timing of the recognition of gains or losses from hedging transactions generally matches the timing of the recognition of income or expense associated with the transaction being hedged.

2.11 FORWARD vs. FUTURES CONTRACTS

As explained in Chapter 1, forward contracts are similar to futures contracts in that they are agreements to buy or sell an asset at a certain time in the future for a certain price. Whereas futures contracts are traded on an exchange, forward contracts are traded in the over-the-counter market. They are typically entered into by two financial institutions or by a financial institution and one of its clients.

One of the parties to a forward contract assumes a *long position* and agrees to buy the asset on a certain specified date for a certain price. The other party assumes a *short position* and agrees to sell the asset on the same date for the same price. Forward contracts do not have to conform to the standards of a particular exchange. The contract delivery date can be any date mutually convenient to the two parties. Usually, in forward contracts a single delivery date is specified, whereas in futures contracts there is a range of possible delivery dates.

Unlike futures contracts, forward contracts are not settled daily. The two parties contract to settle up on the specified delivery date. Whereas most futures contracts are closed out prior to delivery, most forward contracts do lead to delivery of the physical asset or to final settlement in cash. Table 2.3 summarizes the main differences between forward and futures contracts.

Profits from Forward and Futures Contracts

Suppose that the sterling exchange rate for a 90-day forward contract is 1.6000 dollars per pound and that this rate is also the futures price for a contract that will be delivered in exactly 90 days. Under the forward contract, the whole gain or loss is realized at the

Table 2.3 Comparison of forward and futures contracts

Forward	*Futures*
Private contract between two parties	Traded on an exchange
Not standardized	Standardized contract
Usually one specified delivery date	Range of delivery dates
Settled at end of contract	Settled daily
Delivery or final cash settlement usually takes place	Contract is usually closed out prior to maturity
Some credit risk	Virtually no credit risk

end of the life of the contract. Under the futures contract, the gain or loss is realized day by day because of the daily settlement procedures. Figure 2.3 shows the net profit as a function of the exchange rate for 90-day long and short forward or futures positions on £1 million.

Example 2.2 considers the situation where investor A is long £1 million in a 90-day forward contract, and investor B is long £1 million in 90-day futures contracts. (Each futures contract is for the purchase or sale of £62,500, so investor B has purchased a total of 16 contracts.) Assume that the spot exchange rate in 90 days proves to be 1.7000 dollars per pound. Investor A makes a gain of $100,000 on the 90th day. Investor B makes the same gain—but spread out over the 90-day period. On some days investor B may realize a loss, whereas on other days he or she makes a gain. However, in total, when losses are netted against gains, there is a gain of $100,000 over the 90-day period.

Foreign Exchange Quotes

Both forward and futures contracts trade actively on foreign currencies. However, there is sometimes a difference in the way exchange rates are quoted in the two markets. Futures prices are always quoted as the number of U.S. dollars per unit of the foreign

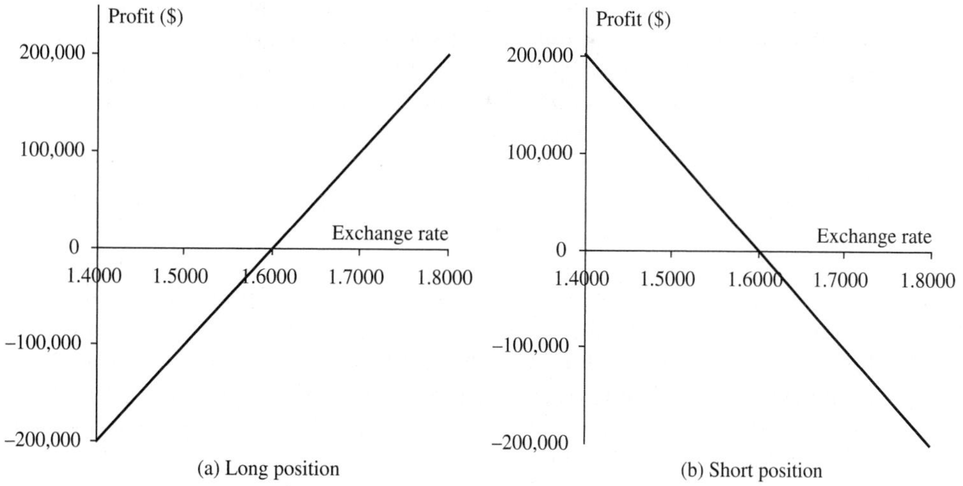

Figure 2.3 Profit from (a) long and (b) short forward or futures position on £1 million

Example 2.2 Futures vs. forwards

Investor A takes a long position in a 90-day forward contract on £1 million. The forward price is 1.6000 dollars per pound. Investor B takes a long position in 90-day futures contracts on £1 million. The futures price is also 1.6000 dollars per pound. At the end of the 90 days, the exchange rate proves to be 1.7000.

The result of this is that investors A and B each make a total gain equal to

$$(1.7000 - 1.6000) \times 1{,}000{,}000 = \$100{,}000$$

Investor A's gain is made entirely on the 90th day. Investor B's gain is realized day by day over the 90-day period. On some days investor B may realize a loss, whereas on other days he or she will realize a gain.

currency or as the number of U.S. cents per unit of the foreign currency. Forward prices are always quoted in the same way as spot prices. This means that for the British pound, the euro, the Australian dollar, and the New Zealand dollar, the forward quotes show the number of U.S. dollars per unit of the foreign currency and are directly comparable with futures quotes. For other major currencies, forward quotes show the number of units of the foreign currency per U.S. dollar (USD). Consider the Canadian dollar (CAD). A futures price quote of 0.9500 USD per CAD corresponds to a forward price quote of 1.0526 CAD per USD (1.0526 = 1/0.9500).

SUMMARY

A very high proportion of the futures contracts that are traded do not lead to the delivery of the underlying asset. This is because traders usually enter into offsetting contracts to close out their positions before the delivery period is reached. However, it is the possibility of final delivery that drives the determination of the futures price. For each futures contract, there is a range of days during which delivery can be made and a well-defined delivery procedure. Some contracts, such as those on stock indices, are settled in cash rather than by delivery of the underlying asset.

The specification of contracts is an important activity for a futures exchange. The two sides to any contract must know what can be delivered, where delivery can take place, and when delivery can take place. They also need to know details on the trading hours, how prices will be quoted, maximum daily price movements, and so on. New contracts must be approved by the Commodity Futures Trading Commission before trading starts.

Margin requirements are an important aspect of futures markets. An investor keeps a margin account with his or her broker. The account is adjusted daily to reflect gains or losses, and from time to time the broker may require the account to be topped up if adverse price movements have taken place. The broker either must be a clearing house member or must maintain a margin account with a clearing house member. Each clearing house member maintains a margin account with the exchange clearing house. The balance in the account is adjusted daily to reflect gains and losses on the business for which the clearing house member is responsible.

In over-the-counter derivatives markets, transactions are cleared either bilaterally or centrally. When bilateral clearing is used, collateral frequently has to be posted by one or both parties to reduce credit risk. When central clearing is used, a central clearing party (CCP) stands between the two sides and performs much the same function as an exchange clearing house.

Forward contracts differ from futures contracts in a number of ways. Forward contracts are private arrangements between two parties, whereas futures contracts are traded on exchanges. There is generally a single delivery date in a forward contract, whereas futures contracts frequently involve a range of such dates. Because they are not traded on exchanges, forward contracts do not need to be standardized. A forward contract is not usually settled until the end of its life, and most contracts do in fact lead to delivery of the underlying asset or a cash settlement at this time.

In the next few chapters we will examine in more detail the ways in which forward and futures contracts can be used for hedging. We will also look at how forward and futures prices are determined.

FURTHER READING

Duffie, D., and H. Zhu. "Does a Central Clearing Counterparty Reduce Counterparty Risk?" *Review of Asset Pricing Studies*, 1 (2011), 74–95.

Gastineau, G. L., D. J. Smith, and R. Todd. *Risk Management, Derivatives, and Financial Analysis under SFAS No. 133*. The Research Foundation of AIMR and Blackwell Series in Finance, 2001.

Hull, J. "CCPs, Their Risks, and How They Can Be Reduced," *Journal of Derivatives*, 20, 1 (Fall 2012): 26–29.

Jones, F. J., and R. J. Teweles. *The Futures Game* (B. Warwick, ed.), 3rd edn. New York: McGraw-Hill, 1998.

Jorion, P. "Risk Management Lessons from Long-Term Capital Management," *European Financial Management*, 6, 3 (September 2000): 277–300.

Kawaller, I. G., and P. D. Koch. "Meeting the Highly Effective Expectation Criterion for Hedge Accounting," *Journal of Derivatives*, 7, 4 (Summer 2000): 79–87.

Lowenstein, R. *When Genius Failed: The Rise and Fall of Long-Term Capital Management*. New York: Random House, 2000.

Quiz (Answers at End of Book)

2.1. Distinguish between the terms *open interest* and *trading volume*.

2.2. What is the difference between a *local* and a *futures commission merchant*?

2.3. Suppose that you enter into a short futures contract to sell July silver for $27.20 per ounce. The size of the contract is 5,000 ounces. The initial margin is $4,000, and the maintenance margin is $3,000. What change in the futures price will lead to a margin call? What happens if you do not meet the margin call?

2.4. Suppose that in September 2013 a company takes a long position in a contract on May 2014 crude oil futures. It closes out its position in March 2014. The futures price (per barrel) is $88.30 when it enters into the contract, $90.50 when it closes out the position, and $89.10 at the end of December 2013. One contract is for the delivery of

1,000 barrels. What is the company's profit? When is it realized? How is it taxed if it is (a) a hedger and (b) a speculator? Assume that the company has a December 31 year end.

2.5. What does a stop order to sell at \$2 mean? When might it be used? What does a limit order to sell at \$2 mean? When might it be used?

2.6. What is the difference between the operation of the margin accounts administered by a clearing house and those administered by a broker?

2.7. What differences exist in the way prices are quoted in the foreign exchange futures market, the foreign exchange spot market, and the foreign exchange forward market?

Practice Questions (Answers in Solutions Manual/Study Guide)

2.8. The party with a short position in a futures contract sometimes has options as to the precise asset that will be delivered, where delivery will take place, when delivery will take place, and so on. Do these options increase or decrease the futures price? Explain your reasoning.

2.9. What are the most important aspects of the design of a new futures contract?

2.10. Explain how margin accounts protect investors against the possibility of default.

2.11. A trader buys two July futures contracts on orange juice. Each contract is for the delivery of 15,000 pounds. The current futures price is 160 cents per pound, the initial margin is \$6,000 per contract, and the maintenance margin is \$4,500 per contract. What price change would lead to a margin call? Under what circumstances could \$2,000 be withdrawn from the margin account?

2.12. Show that, if the futures price of a commodity is greater than the spot price during the delivery period, then there is an arbitrage opportunity. Does an arbitrage opportunity exist if the futures price is less than the spot price? Explain your answer.

2.13. Explain the difference between a market-if-touched order and a stop order.

2.14. Explain what a stop-limit order to sell at 20.30 with a limit of 20.10 means.

2.15. At the end of one day a clearing house member is long 100 contracts, and the settlement price is \$50,000 per contract. The original margin is \$2,000 per contract. On the following day the member becomes responsible for clearing an additional 20 long contracts, entered into at a price of \$51,000 per contract. The settlement price at the end of this day is \$50,200. How much does the member have to add to its margin account with the exchange clearing house?

2.16. On July 1, 2013, a Japanese company enters into a forward contract to buy \$1 million with yen on January 1, 2014. On September 1, 2013, it enters into a forward contract to sell \$1 million on January 1, 2014. Describe the profit or loss the company will make in dollars as a function of the forward exchange rates on July 1, 2013, and September 1, 2013.

2.17. The forward price of the Swiss franc for delivery in 45 days is quoted as 1.1000. The futures price for a contract that will be delivered in 45 days is 0.9000. Explain these two quotes. Which is more favorable for an investor wanting to sell Swiss francs?

2.18. Suppose you call your broker and issue instructions to sell one July hogs contract. Describe what happens.

2.19. "Speculation in futures markets is pure gambling. It is not in the public interest to allow speculators to trade on a futures exchange." Discuss this viewpoint.

2.20. Explain the difference between bilateral and central clearing for OTC derivatives.

2.21. What do you think would happen if an exchange started trading a contract in which the quality of the underlying asset was incompletely specified?

2.22. "When a futures contract is traded on the floor of the exchange, it may be the case that the open interest increases by one, stays the same, or decreases by one." Explain this statement.

2.23. Suppose that on October 24, 2013, a company sells one April 2014 live-cattle futures contract. It closes out its position on January 21, 2014. The futures price (per pound) is 91.20 cents when it enters into the contract, 88.30 cents when it closes out the position, and 88.80 cents at the end of December 2013. One contract is for the delivery of 40,000 pounds of cattle. What is the profit? How is it taxed if the company is (a) a hedger and (b) a speculator? Assume that the company has a December 31 year end.

2.24. Explain how CCPs work. What are the advantages to the financial system of requiring all standardized derivatives transactions to be cleared through CCPs?

Further Questions

2.25. Trader A enters into futures contracts to buy 1 million euros for 1.4 million dollars in three months. Trader B enters in a forward contract to do the same thing. The exchange rate (dollars per euro) declines sharply during the first two months and then increases for the third month to close at 1.4300. Ignoring daily settlement, what is the total profit of each trader? When the impact of daily settlement is taken into account, which trader has done better?

2.26. Explain what is meant by open interest. Why does the open interest usually decline during the month preceding the delivery month? On a particular day, there were 2,000 trades in a particular futures contract. This means that there were 2,000 buyers (going long) and 2,000 sellers (going short). Of the 2,000 buyers, 1,400 were closing out positions and 600 were entering into new positions. Of the 2,000 sellers, 1,200 were closing out positions and 800 were entering into new positions. What is the impact of the day's trading on open interest?

2.27. One orange juice futures contract is on 15,000 pounds of frozen concentrate. Suppose that in September 2013 a company sells a March 2015 orange juice futures contract for 120 cents per pound. In December 2013, the futures price is 140 cents; in December 2014, it is 110 cents; and in February 2015, it is closed out at 125 cents. The company has a December year end. What is the company's profit or loss on the contract? How is it realized? What is the accounting and tax treatment of the transaction if the company is classified as (a) a hedger and (b) a speculator?

2.28. A company enters into a short futures contract to sell 5,000 bushels of wheat for 450 cents per bushel. The initial margin is \$3,000 and the maintenance margin is \$2,000. What price change would lead to a margin call? Under what circumstances could \$1,500 be withdrawn from the margin account?

2.29. Suppose that there are no storage costs for crude oil and the interest rate for borrowing or lending is 5% per annum. How could you make money if the June and December futures contracts for a particular year trade at \$80 and \$86, respectively.

2.30. What position is equivalent to a long forward contract to buy an asset at K on a certain date and a put option to sell it for K on that date.

2.31. A company has derivatives transactions with Banks A, B, and C that are worth +\$20 million, −\$15 million, and −\$25 million, respectively, to the company. How much margin or collateral does the company have to provide in each of the following two situations?

(a) The transactions are cleared bilaterally and are subject to one-way collateral agreements where the company posts variation margin but no initial margin. The banks do not have to post collateral.

(b) The transactions are cleared centrally through the same CCP and the CCP requires a total initial margin of \$10 million.

2.32. A bank's derivatives transactions with a counterparty are worth +\$10 million to the bank and are cleared bilaterally. The counterparty has posted \$10 million of cash collateral. What credit exposure does the bank have?

2.33. The author's website (`www.rotman.utoronto.ca/~hull/data`) contains daily closing prices for the crude oil futures contract and the gold futures contract. Download the data and answer the following:

(a) How high do the maintenance margin levels for oil and gold have to be set so that there is a 1% chance that an investor with a balance slightly above the maintenence margin level on a particular day has a negative balance two days later. How high do they have to be for a 0.1% chance? Assume daily price changes are normally distributed with mean zero. Explain why the exchange might be interested in this calculation.

(b) Imagine an investor who starts with a long position in the oil contract at the beginning of the period covered by the data and keeps the contract for the whole of the period of time covered by the data. Margin balances in excess of the initial margin are withdrawn. Use the maintenance margin you calculated in part (a) for a 1% risk level and assume that the maintenance margin is 75% of the initial margin. Calculate the number of margin calls and the number of times the investor has a negative margin balance. Assume that all margin calls are met in your calculations. Repeat the calculations for an investor who starts with a short position in the gold contract.

CHAPTER 3 Hedging Strategies Using Futures

Many of the participants in futures markets are hedgers. Their aim is to use futures markets to reduce a particular risk they face. This risk might relate to fluctuations in the price of oil, a foreign exchange rate, the level of the stock market, or some other variable. A *perfect hedge* is one that completely eliminates the risk. Perfect hedges are rare. For the most part, therefore, a study of hedging using futures contracts is a study of the ways in which hedges can be constructed so that they perform as close to perfect as possible.

In this chapter we consider a number of general issues associated with the way hedges are set up. When is a short futures position appropriate? When is a long futures position appropriate? Which futures contract should be used? What is the optimal size of the futures position for reducing risk? At this stage, we restrict our attention to what might be termed *hedge-and-forget* strategies. We assume that no attempt is made to adjust the hedge once it has been put in place. The hedger simply takes a futures position at the beginning of the life of the hedge and closes out the position at the end of the life of the hedge. In Chapter 17, we will examine dynamic hedging strategies in which the hedge is monitored closely and frequent adjustments are made.

The chapter initially treats futures contracts as forward contracts (i.e., it ignores daily settlement). Later it explains an adjustment known as "tailing" that takes account of the difference between futures and forwards.

3.1 BASIC PRINCIPLES

When an individual or company chooses to use futures markets to hedge a risk, the objective is usually to take a position that neutralizes the risk as far as possible. Consider a company that knows it will gain \$10,000 for each 1 cent increase in the price of a commodity over the next three months and lose \$10,000 for each 1 cent decrease in the price during the same period. To hedge, the company's treasurer should take a short futures position that is designed to offset this risk. The futures position should lead to a loss of \$10,000 for each 1 cent increase in the price of the commodity over the three months and a gain of \$10,000 for each 1 cent decrease in the price during this period. If the price of the commodity goes down, the gain on the futures position offsets the loss

From Chapter 3 of *Fundamentals of Futures and Options Markets*, Eighth Edition. John C. Hull.

on the rest of the company's business. If the price of the commodity goes up, the loss on the futures position is offset by the gain on the rest of the company's business.

Short Hedges

A *short hedge* is a hedge, such as the one just described, that involves a short position in futures contracts. A short hedge is appropriate when the hedger already owns an asset and expects to sell it at some time in the future. For example, a short hedge could be used by a farmer who owns some hogs and knows that they will be ready for sale at the local market in two months. A short hedge can also be used when an asset is not owned right now but will be owned at some time in the future. Consider, for example, a U.S. exporter who knows that he or she will receive euros in three months. The exporter will realize a gain if the euro increases in value relative to the U.S. dollar and will sustain a loss if the euro decreases in value relative to the U.S. dollar. A short futures position leads to a loss if the euro increases in value and a gain if it decreases in value. It has the effect of offsetting the exporter's risk.

We will use Example 3.1 to provide a more detailed illustration of the operation of a short hedge. It is May 15 today and an oil producer has just negotiated a contract to sell 1 million barrels of crude oil. It has been agreed that the price that will apply in the contract is the market price on August 15. The oil producer is therefore in the position where it will gain \$10,000 for each 1 cent increase in the price of oil over the next three months and lose \$10,000 for each 1 cent decrease in the price during this period. The spot price on May 15 is \$80 per barrel and the crude oil futures price for August delivery for the CME Group contract is \$79 per barrel. Because each futures contract traded by the CME Group is for the delivery of 1,000 barrels, the company can hedge its exposure by shorting 1,000 futures contracts. If the oil producer closes out its position on August 15, the effect of the strategy should be to lock in a price close to \$79 per barrel.

To illustrate what might happen, suppose that the spot price on August 15 proves to be \$75 per barrel. The company realizes \$75 million for the oil under its sales contract. Because August is the delivery month for the futures contract, the futures price on August 15 should be very close to the spot price of \$75 on that date. The company therefore gains approximately

$$\$79 - \$75 = \$4$$

Example 3.1 A short hedge

It is May 15. An oil producer has negotiated a contract to sell 1 million barrels of crude oil. The price in the sales contract is the spot price on August 15. Quotes:

Spot price of crude oil: \$80 per barrel
August oil futures price: \$79 per barrel

The oil producer can hedge with the following transactions:

May 15: Short 1,000 August futures contracts on crude oil
August 15: Close out futures position

After gains or losses on the futures are taken into account, the price received by the company is close to \$79 per barrel.

per barrel, or \$4 million in total from the short futures position. The total amount realized from both the futures position and the sales contract is therefore approximately \$79 per barrel, or \$79 million in total.

For an alternative outcome, suppose that the price of oil on August 15 proves to be \$85 per barrel. The company realizes \$85 for the oil and loses approximately

$$\$85 - \$79 = \$6$$

per barrel on the short futures position. Again, the total amount realized is approximately \$79 million. It is easy to see that in all cases the company ends up with approximately \$79 million.

Long Hedges

Hedges that involve taking a long position in a futures contract are known as *long hedges*. A long hedge is appropriate when a company knows it will have to purchase a certain asset in the future and wants to lock in a price now.

This is illustrated in Example 3.2, where a copper fabricator knows it will need 100,000 pounds of copper on May 15. The futures price for May delivery is 320 cents per pound. The fabricator can hedge its position by taking a long position in four futures contracts traded by the CME Group and closing its position on May 15. Each contract is for the delivery of 25,000 pounds of copper. The strategy has the effect of locking in the price of the required quantity of copper at close to 320 cents per pound.

Suppose that the spot price of copper on May 15 proves to be 325 cents per pound. Because May is the delivery month for the futures contract, this should be very close to the futures price. The fabricator therefore gains approximately

$$100{,}000 \times (\$3.25 - \$3.20) = \$5{,}000$$

on the futures contracts. It pays $100{,}000 \times \$3.25 = \$325{,}000$ for the copper, making the net cost approximately $\$325{,}000 - \$5{,}000 = \$320{,}000$. For an alternative outcome, suppose that the spot price is 305 cents per pound on May 15. The fabricator then loses approximately

$$100{,}000 \times (\$3.20 - \$3.05) = \$15{,}000$$

on the futures contract and pays $100{,}000 \times \$3.05 = \$305{,}000$ for the copper. Again, the net cost is approximately \$320,000, or 320 cents per pound.

Example 3.2 A long hedge

It is January 15. A copper fabricator knows it will require 100,000 pounds of copper on May 15 to meet a certain contract. The spot price of copper is 340 cents per pound and the May futures price is 320 cents per pound.

The copper fabricator can hedge with the following transactions:

January 15: Take a long position in four May futures contracts on copper
May 15: Close out the position

After gains or losses on the futures are taken into account, the price paid by the company is close to 320 cents per pound.

Note that in this case it is better for the company to use futures contracts than to buy the copper on January 15 in the spot market. If it does the latter, it will pay 340 cents per pound instead of 320 cents per pound and will incur both interest costs and storage costs. For a company using copper on a regular basis, this disadvantage would be offset by the convenience of having the copper on hand.[1] However, for a company that knows it will not require the copper until May 15, the futures contract alternative is likely to be preferred.

In Examples 3.1 and 3.2, we assume that the futures position is closed out in the delivery month. The hedge has the same basic effect if delivery is allowed to happen. However, making or taking delivery can be costly and inconvenient. For this reason, delivery is not usually made even when the hedger keeps the futures contract until the delivery month. As will be discussed later, hedgers with long positions usually avoid any possibility of having to take delivery by closing out their positions before the delivery period.

We have also assumed in the two examples that a futures contract is the same as a forward contract. In practice, daily settlement does have a small effect on the performance of a hedge. As explained in Chapter 2, it means that the payoff from the futures contract is realized day by day throughout the life of the hedge rather than all at the end.

3.2 ARGUMENTS FOR AND AGAINST HEDGING

The arguments in favor of hedging are so obvious that they hardly need to be stated. Most companies are in the business of manufacturing, or retailing or wholesaling, or providing a service. They have no particular skills or expertise in predicting variables such as interest rates, exchange rates, and commodity prices. It makes sense for them to hedge the risks associated with these variables as they become aware of them. The companies can then focus on their main activities—for which presumably they do have particular skills and expertise. By hedging, they avoid unpleasant surprises, such as sharp rises in the price of a commodity that is being purchased.

In practice, many risks are left unhedged. In the rest of this section, we will explore some of the reasons for this.

Hedging and Shareholders

One argument sometimes put forward is that the shareholders can, if they wish, do the hedging themselves. They do not need the company to do it for them. This argument is, however, open to question. It assumes that shareholders have as much information as the company's management about the risks faced by the company. In most instances, this is not the case. The argument also ignores commissions and other transactions costs. These are less expensive per dollar of hedging for large transactions than for small transactions. Hedging is therefore likely to be less expensive when carried out by the company than when it is carried out by individual shareholders. Indeed, the size of futures contracts makes hedging by individual shareholders impossible in many situations.

---

[1] See Chapter 5 for a discussion of convenience yields.

One thing that shareholders can do far more easily than a corporation is diversify risk. A shareholder with a well-diversified portfolio may be immune to many of the risks faced by a corporation. For example, in addition to holding shares in a company that uses copper, a well-diversified shareholder may hold shares in a copper producer, so that there is very little overall exposure to the price of copper. If companies are acting in the best interests of well-diversified shareholders, it can be argued that hedging is unnecessary in many situations. However, the extent to which managers are in practice influenced by this type of argument is open to question.

Hedging and Competitors

If hedging is not the norm in a certain industry, it may not make sense for one particular company to choose to be different from all others. Competitive pressures from within the industry may be such that the prices of the goods and services produced by the industry fluctuate to reflect raw material costs, interest rates, exchange rates, and so on. A company that does not hedge can expect its profit margin to be roughly constant. However, a company that does hedge can expect its profit margin to fluctuate!

To illustrate this point, consider two manufacturers of gold jewelry, SafeandSure Company and TakeaChance Company. We assume that most companies in the industry do not hedge against movements in the price of gold and that TakeaChance Company is no exception. However, SafeandSure Company has decided to be different from its competitors and to use futures contracts to hedge its purchase of gold over the next 18 months. If the price of gold goes up, economic pressures will tend to lead to a corresponding increase in the wholesale price of jewelry, so that TakeaChance Company's gross profit margin is unaffected. In contrast, SafeandSure Company's profit margin will increase after the effects of the hedge have been taken into account. If the price of gold goes down, economic pressures will tend to lead to a corresponding decrease in the wholesale price of jewelry. Again, TakeaChance Company's profit margin is unaffected. However, SafeandSure Company's profit margin goes down. In extreme conditions, SafeandSure Company's profit margin could become negative as a result of the "hedging" carried out! The situation is summarized in Table 3.1.

This example emphasizes the importance of looking at the big picture when hedging. All the implications of price changes on a company's profitability should be taken into account in the design of a hedging strategy to protect against the price changes.

Table 3.1 Danger in hedging when competitors do not hedge

Change in gold price	*Effect on Price of gold jewelry*	*Effect on Profits of TakeaChance Co.*	*Effect on Profits of SafeandSure Co.*
Increase	Increase	None	Increase
Decrease	Decrease	None	Decrease

Hedging Can Lead to a Worse Outcome

It is important to realize that a hedge using futures contracts can result in a decrease or an increase in a company's profits relative to its position with no hedging. In Example 3.1, if the price of oil goes down, the company loses money on its sale of 1 million barrels of oil, and the futures position leads to an offsetting gain. The treasurer can be congratulated for having had the foresight to put the hedge in place. Clearly, the company is better off than it would be with no hedging. Other executives in the organization, it is hoped, will appreciate the contribution made by the treasurer. If the price of oil goes up, the company gains from its sale of the oil, and the futures position leads to an offsetting loss. The company is in a worse position than it would have been in with no hedging. Although the hedging decision was perfectly logical, the treasurer may in practice have a difficult time justifying it. Suppose that the price of oil is $89 on August 15 in Example 3.1, so that the company loses $10 per barrel on the futures contract. We can imagine a conversation such as the following between the treasurer and the president:

President: This is terrible. We've lost $10 million in the futures market in the space of three months. How could it happen? I want a full explanation.

Treasurer: The purpose of the futures contracts was to hedge our exposure to the price of oil—not to make a profit. Don't forget that we made about $10 million from the favorable effect of the oil price increases on our business.

President: What's that got to do with it? That's like saying that we do not need to worry when our sales are down in California because they are up in New York.

Treasurer: If the price of oil had gone down...

President: I don't care what would have happened if the price of oil had gone down. The fact is that it went up. I really do not know what you were doing playing the futures markets like this. Our shareholders will expect us to have done particularly well this quarter. I'm going to have to explain to them that your actions reduced profits by $10 million. I'm afraid this is going to mean no bonus for you this year.

Treasurer: That's unfair. I was only...

President: Unfair! You are lucky not to be fired. You lost $10 million.

Treasurer: It all depends how you look at it...

It is easy to see why many treasurers are reluctant to hedge! Hedging reduces risk for the company. However, it may increase risks for the treasurer if others do not fully understand what is being done. The only real solution to this problem involves ensuring that all senior executives within the organization fully understand the nature of hedging before a hedging program is put in place. Ideally, hedging strategies are set by a company's board of directors and are clearly communicated to both the company's management and the shareholders. (See Business Snapshot 3.1 for a discussion of hedging by gold mining companies.)

Business Snapshot 3.1 Hedging by gold mining companies

It is natural for a gold mining company to consider hedging against changes in the price of gold. Typically it takes several years to extract all the gold from a mine. Once a gold mining company decides to go ahead with production at a particular mine, it has a big exposure to the price of gold. Indeed a mine that looks profitable at the outset could become unprofitable if the price of gold plunges.

Gold mining companies are careful to explain their hedging strategies to potential shareholders. Some gold mining companies do not hedge. They tend to attract shareholders who buy gold stocks because they want to benefit when the price of gold increases and are prepared to accept the risk of a loss from a decrease in the price of gold. Other companies choose to hedge. They estimate the number of ounces of gold they will produce each month for the next few years and enter into short futures or forward contracts to lock in the price for all or part of this.

Suppose you are Goldman Sachs and are approached by a gold mining company that wants to sell you a large amount of gold in one year at a fixed price. How do you set the price and then hedge your risk? The answer is that you can hedge by borrowing the gold from a central bank and immediately selling it in the spot market, investing the proceeds at the risk-free rate. At the end of the year, you buy the gold from the gold mining company and use it to repay the central bank. The fixed forward price you set for the gold reflects the risk-free rate you can earn and the lease rate you pay the central bank for borrowing the gold.

3.3 BASIS RISK

The hedges in the examples considered so far have been almost too good to be true. The hedger was able to identify the precise date in the future when an asset would be bought or sold. The hedger was then able to use futures contracts to remove almost all the risk arising from the price of the asset on that date. In practice, hedging is often not quite as straightforward. Some of the reasons are as follows:

1. The asset whose price is to be hedged may not be exactly the same as the asset underlying the futures contract.
2. The hedger may not be certain of the exact date the asset will be bought or sold.
3. The hedge may require the futures contract to be closed out before its delivery month.

These problems give rise to what is termed *basis risk*. This concept will now be explained.

The Basis

The *basis* in a hedging situation is as follows:[2]

$$\text{Basis} = \text{Spot price of asset to be hedged} - \text{Futures price of contract used}$$

[2] This is the usual definition. However, an alternative definition, Basis = Futures price − Spot price, is sometimes used, particularly when the futures contract is on a financial asset.

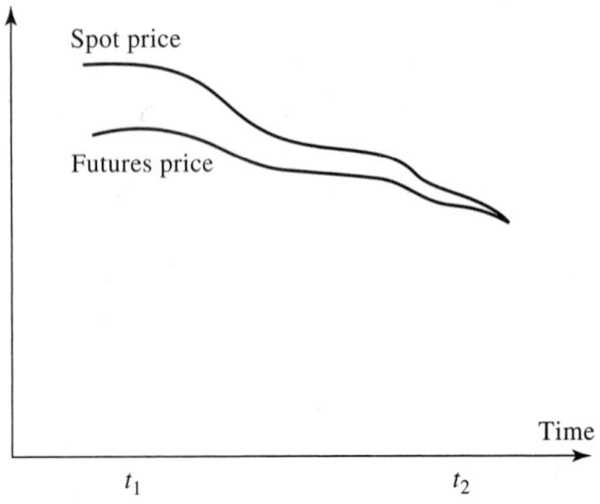

Figure 3.1 Variation of basis over time

If the asset to be hedged and the asset underlying the futures contract are the same, the basis should be zero at the expiration of the futures contract. Prior to expiration, the basis may be positive or negative.

As time passes, the spot price and a particular month's futures price do not necessarily change by the same amount and, as a result, the basis changes. An increase in the basis is referred to as a *strengthening of the basis* and a decrease in the basis is referred to as a *weakening of the basis*. Figure 3.1 illustrates how a basis might change over time in a situation where the basis is positive prior to expiration of the futures contract.

To examine the nature of basis risk, we will use the following notation:

S_1: Spot price at time t_1
S_2: Spot price at time t_2
F_1: Futures price at time t_1
F_2: Futures price at time t_2
b_1: Basis at time t_1
b_2: Basis at time t_2

We will assume that a hedge is put in place at time t_1 and closed out at time t_2. As an example, we will consider the case where the spot and futures prices at the time the hedge is initiated are \$2.50 and \$2.20, respectively, and that at the time the hedge is closed out they are \$2.00 and \$1.90, respectively. This means that $S_1 = 2.50$, $F_1 = 2.20$, $S_2 = 2.00$, and $F_2 = 1.90$. From the definition of the basis,

$$b_1 = S_1 - F_1 \quad \text{and} \quad b_2 = S_2 - F_2$$

so that, in our example, $b_1 = 0.30$ and $b_2 = 0.10$.

Consider first the situation of a hedger who knows that the asset will be sold at time t_2 and takes a short futures position at time t_1. The price realized for the asset is S_2 and the profit on the futures position is $F_1 - F_2$. The effective price obtained for the asset with hedging is therefore

$$S_2 + F_1 - F_2 = F_1 + b_2$$

In our example, this is \$2.30. The value of F_1 is known at time t_1. If b_2 were also known at this time, a perfect hedge would result. The hedging risk is the uncertainty associated with b_2 and is known as *basis risk*. Consider next a situation where a company knows it will buy the asset at time t_2 and initiates a long hedge at time t_1. The price paid for the asset is S_2 and the loss on the hedge is $F_1 - F_2$. The effective price paid with hedging is therefore

$$S_2 + F_1 - F_2 = F_1 + b_2$$

This is the same expression as before and is \$2.30 in the example. The value of F_1 is known at time t_1, and the term b_2 represents basis risk.

Note that basis risk can lead to an improvement or a worsening of a hedger's position. Consider a company that uses a short hedge because it plans to sell the asset. If the basis strengthens (i.e., increases) unexpectedly, the company's position improves because it will get a higher price for the asset after futures gains or losses are considered; if the basis weakens (i.e., decreases) unexpectedly, the company's position worsens. For a company using a long hedge because it plans to buy the asset, the reverse holds. If the basis strengthens unexpectedly, the company's position worsens because it will pay a higher price for the asset after futures gains and losses are considered; if the basis weakens unexpectedly, the company's position improves.

The asset that gives rise to the company's exposure is sometimes different from the asset underlying the futures contract that is used for hedging. This is known as *cross hedging* and is discussed in the next section. It leads to an increase in basis risk. Define S_2^* as the price of the asset underlying the futures contract at time t_2. As before, S_2 is the price of the asset being hedged at time t_2. By hedging, a company ensures that the price that will be paid (or received) for the asset is

$$S_2 + F_1 - F_2$$

This can be written as

$$F_1 + (S_2^* - F_2) + (S_2 - S_2^*)$$

The terms $S_2^* - F_2$ and $S_2 - S_2^*$ represent the two components of the basis. The $S_2^* - F_2$ term is the basis that would exist if the asset being hedged were the same as the asset underlying the futures contract. The $S_2 - S_2^*$ term is the basis arising from the difference between the two assets.

Choice of Contract

One key factor affecting basis risk is the choice of the futures contract to be used for hedging. This choice has two components:

1. The choice of the asset underlying the futures contract
2. The choice of the delivery month

If the asset being hedged exactly matches an asset underlying a futures contract, the first choice is generally fairly easy. In other circumstances, it is necessary to carry out a careful analysis to determine which of the available futures contracts has futures prices that are most closely correlated with the price of the asset being hedged.

The choice of delivery month can be influenced by several factors. In the examples earlier in this chapter, we assumed that when the expiration of the hedge corresponds to a delivery month, the contract with that delivery month is chosen. In fact, a contract with a later delivery month is usually chosen in these circumstances. The reason is that futures prices can be quite erratic during the delivery month. Also, a long hedger runs the risk of having to take delivery of the physical asset if the contract is held during the delivery month. Taking delivery can be expensive and inconvenient. (Long hedgers normally prefer to close out the futures contract and buy the asset from their usual suppliers.)

In general, basis risk increases as the time difference between the hedge expiration and the delivery month increases. A good rule of thumb is therefore to choose a delivery month that is as close as possible to, but later than, the expiration of the hedge. Suppose delivery months are March, June, September, and December for futures on a particular asset. For hedge expirations in December, January, and February, the March contract will be chosen; for hedge expirations in March, April, and May, the June contract will be chosen; and so on. This rule of thumb assumes that there is sufficient liquidity in all contracts to meet the hedger's requirements. In practice, liquidity tends to be greatest in short maturity futures contracts. The hedger may therefore, in some situations, be inclined to use short maturity contracts and roll them forward. This strategy is discussed later in the chapter.

Illustrations

Example 3.3 illustrates some of the points made so far in this section. It is March 1. A U.S. company expects to receive 50 million Japanese yen at the end of July. Yen futures contracts offered by the CME Group have delivery months of March, June, September, and December. One contract is for the delivery of 12.5 million yen. The criteria mentioned earlier for the choice of a contract suggest that the September contract be chosen for hedging purposes.

The company shorts four September yen futures contracts on March 1. When the yen are received at the end of July, the company closes out its position. The basis risk arises from uncertainty about the difference between the futures price and the spot price at this time. We suppose that the futures price on March 1 in cents per yen is 1.2800 and that the spot and futures prices when the contract is closed out are 1.2200 and 1.2250 cents per yen, respectively. The basis is −0.0050, and the gain from the futures

Example 3.3 Basis risk in a short hedge

It is March 1. A U.S. company expects to receive 50 million Japanese yen at the end of July. The September futures price for the yen is currently 1.2800 cents per yen. Its hedging strategy is as follows:

1. Short four September yen futures contracts on March 1 at a futures price of 1.2800
2. Close out the contract when the yen arrive at the end of July

One possible outcome is:

Spot price at end of July = 1.2200
September futures price at end of July = 1.2250
Basis at end of July = −0.0050

There are two alternative ways of calculating the net exchange rate after hedging:

Spot price in July + Gain on futures = 1.2200 + 0.0550 = 1.2750
Futures price in March + Basis in July = 1.2800 − 0.0050 = 1.2750

Example 3.4 Basis risk in a long hedge

It is June 8. A company knows that it will need to purchase 20,000 barrels of crude oil some time in October or November. The current December oil futures price is \$88.00 per barrel. Its hedging strategy is as follows:

1. Take a long position in 20 December oil futures contracts on June 8 at a futures price of \$88
2. Close out the contract when ready to purchase the oil

One possible outcome is:

Company is ready to purchase oil on November 10
Spot price on November 10 = \$92
December futures price on November 10 = \$92
Basis on November 10 = \$3

There are two alternative ways of calculating the net cost of oil after hedging:

Spot price on Nov. 10 − Gain on Futures = \$95 − \$4 = \$91
Futures price on June 8 + Basis on November 10 = \$88 + \$3 = \$91

contracts is 0.0550. The effective price obtained in cents per yen is the spot price plus the gain on the futures:

$$1.2200 + 0.0550 = 1.2750$$

This can also be written as the initial futures price plus the basis:

$$1.2800 + (-0.0050) = 1.2750$$

The company receives a total of 50×0.01275 million dollars, or \$637,500.

Example 3.4 considers a long hedge. It is June 8, and a company knows that it will need to purchase 20,000 barrels of crude oil at some time in October or November. Oil futures contracts are traded for delivery every month, and the contract size is 1,000 barrels. Following the criteria indicated, the company decides to use the December contract for hedging. On June 8 it takes a long position in 20 December contracts. At that time, the futures price is \$88.00 per barrel. The company finds that it is ready to purchase the crude oil on November 10. It therefore closes out its futures contract on that date. The basis risk arises from uncertainty as to what the basis will be on the day the contract is closed out. We suppose that the spot price and futures price on November 10 are \$95 per barrel and \$92 per barrel, respectively. The basis is therefore \$3, and the effective price paid is \$91 per barrel, or \$1,820,000 in total.

3.4 CROSS HEDGING

In Examples 3.1 to 3.4, the asset underlying the futures contract is the same as the asset whose price is being hedged. *Cross hedging* occurs when the two assets are different. Consider, for example, an airline that is concerned about the future price of jet fuel. Since jet fuel futures are not actively traded, it might choose to use heating oil futures contracts to hedge its exposure.

The *hedge ratio* is the ratio of the size of the position taken in futures contracts to the size of the exposure. When the asset underlying the futures contract is the same as the asset being hedged it is natural to use a hedge ratio of 1.0. This is the hedge ratio we have used in the examples considered so far. In Example 3.4, for instance, the hedger's exposure was on 20,000 barrels of oil, and futures contracts were entered into for the delivery of exactly this amount of oil.

When cross hedging is used, setting the hedge ratio equal to 1.0 is not always optimal. The hedger should choose a value for the hedge ratio that minimizes the variance of the value of the hedged position. We now consider how the hedger can do this.

Calculating the Minimum Variance Hedge Ratio

The minimum variance hedge ratio depends on the relationship between changes in the spot price and changes in the futures price. Define:

ΔS: Change in spot price, S, during a period of time equal to the life of the hedge

ΔF: Change in futures price, F, during a period of time equal to the life of the hedge

We will denote the minimum variance hedge ratio by h^*. It can be shown that h^* is the slope of the best-fit line from a linear regression of ΔS against ΔF (see Figure 3.2). This result is intuitively reasonable. We would expect h^* to be the ratio of the average change in S for a particular change in F.

The appendix to this chapter provides a review of key statistical concepts: standard deviation, coefficient of correlation, and linear regression. The formula for calculating the best-fit slope in equation (3A.4) gives:

$$h^* = \rho \frac{\sigma_S}{\sigma_F} \tag{3.1}$$

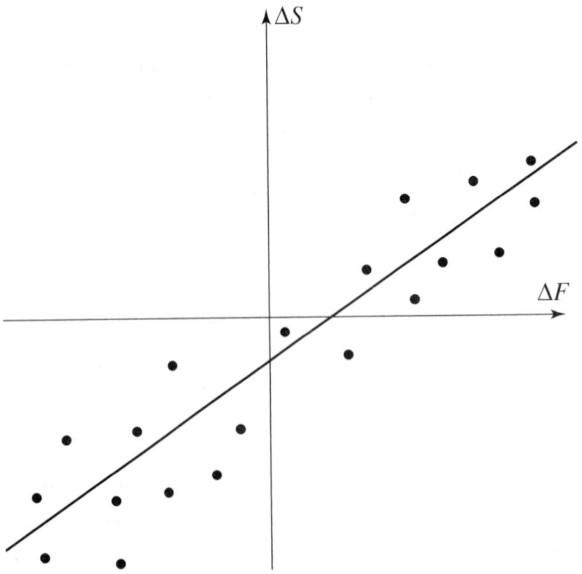

Figure 3.2 Regression of change in spot price against change in futures price

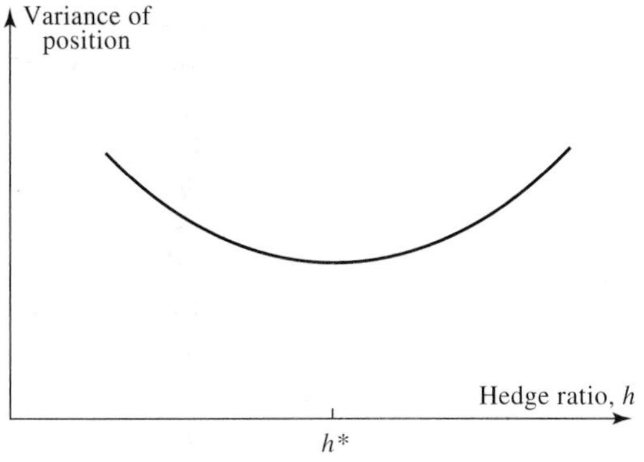

Figure 3.3 Dependence of variance of hedger's position on hedge ratio

where σ_S is the standard deviation of ΔS, σ_F is the standard deviation of ΔF, and ρ is the coefficient of correlation between the two.

Equation (3.1) shows that the optimal hedge ratio is the product of the coefficient of correlation between ΔS and ΔF and the ratio of the standard deviation of ΔS to the standard deviation of ΔF. Figure 3.3 shows how the variance of the value of the hedger's position depends on the hedge ratio chosen.

If $\rho = 1$ and $\sigma_F = \sigma_S$, the hedge ratio, h^*, is 1.0. This result is to be expected, because in this case the futures price mirrors the spot price perfectly. If $\rho = 1$ and $\sigma_F = 2\sigma_S$, the hedge ratio h^* is 0.5. This result is also as expected, because in this case the futures price always changes by twice as much as the spot price. The *hedge effectiveness* can be defined as the proportion of the variance that is eliminated by hedging. This is the R^2 from the regression of ΔS against ΔF and equals ρ^2.

The parameters ρ, σ_F, and σ_S in equation (3.1) are usually estimated from historical data on ΔS and ΔF. (The implicit assumption is that the future will in some sense be like the past.) A number of equal nonoverlapping time intervals are chosen, and the values of ΔS and ΔF for each of the intervals are observed. Ideally, the length of each time interval is the same as the length of the time interval for which the hedge is in effect. In practice, this sometimes severely limits the number of observations that are available, and a shorter time interval is used.

Example 3.5 shows how the results in this section can be used by an airline using heating oil futures to hedge the purchase of jet fuel.[3]

Optimal Number of Contracts

To calculate the number of contracts that should be used in hedging, define:

Q_A: Size of position being hedged (units)

Q_F: Size of one futures contract (units)

N^*: Optimal number of futures contracts for hedging

From equation (3.1), the futures contracts should be on $h^* Q_A$ units of the asset. The

[3] Heating oil futures are more actively traded than jet fuel futures contracts. For an account of how Delta Airlines used heating oil futures to hedge its future purchases of jet fuel, see A. Ness, "Delta Wins on Fuel," *Risk*, June 2001: 8.

Example 3.5 Calculation of the minimimum variance hedge ratio

An airline expects to purchase two million gallons of jet fuel in one month and decides to use heating oil futures for hedging. We suppose that Table 3.2 gives, for 15 successive months, data on the change, ΔS, in the jet fuel price per gallon and the corresponding change, ΔF, in the futures price for the contract on heating oil that would be used for hedging price changes during the month.

To evaluate the minimum variance hedge ratio, we can use the STDEV and CORREL functions in Excel to obtain $\sigma_F = 0.0313$, $\sigma_S = 0.0263$, and $\rho = 0.928$. Equation (3.1) then gives

$$h^* = 0.928 \times \frac{0.0263}{0.0313} = 0.7777$$

Alternatively we can use the SLOPE function in Excel to get this answer directly. (See worksheet on author's website for the calculations.)

This result means that the airline should hedge by taking a position in heating oil futures corresponding to 77.77% of its exposure. The hedge effectiveness is $0.928^2 = 0.862$.

number of futures contracts required is therefore given by

$$N^* = \frac{h^* Q_A}{Q_F} \tag{3.2}$$

In Example 3.5, the optimal hedge ratio, h^*, is 0.7777. Each heating oil contract traded by the CME Group is on 42,000 gallons of heating oil and the airline has an exposure to the price of 2 million gallons of jet fuel. From equation (3.2), the optimal number of contracts is

$$\frac{0.7777 \times 2{,}000{,}000}{42{,}000} = 37.03$$

or, rounding to the nearest whole number, 37.

Tailing the Hedge

When futures are used for hedging, a small adjustment, known as *tailing the hedge*, can be made to allow for the impact of daily settlement. In practice this means that equation (3.2) becomes

$$N^* = \frac{h^* V_A}{V_F} \tag{3.3}$$

where V_A is the dollar value of the position being hedged and V_F is the dollar value of one futures contract (the futures price times Q_F). Suppose that in Example 3.5 the futures price and the spot price are 1.99 and 1.94 dollars per gallon, respectively. Then $V_A = 2{,}000{,}000 \times 1.94 = 3{,}880{,}0000$, while $V_F = 42{,}000 \times 1.99 = 83{,}580$, so that the optimal number of contracts is

$$\frac{0.7777 \times 3{,}880{,}000}{83{,}580} = 36.10$$

Table 3.2 Data to calculate minimum variance hedge ratio when heating oil futures contract is used to hedge purchase of jet fuel

Month i	*Change in heating oil futures price per gallon* (ΔF)	*Change in jet fuel price per gallon* (ΔS)
1	0.021	0.029
2	0.035	0.020
3	−0.046	−0.044
4	0.001	0.008
5	0.044	0.026
6	−0.029	−0.019
7	−0.026	−0.010
8	−0.029	−0.007
9	0.048	0.043
10	−0.006	0.011
11	−0.036	−0.036
12	−0.011	−0.018
13	0.019	0.009
14	−0.027	−0.032
15	0.029	0.023

If we round this to the nearest whole number, the optimal number of contracts is now 36 rather than 37. The effect of tailing the hedge is to multiply the hedge ratio in equation (3.2) by the ratio of the spot price to the futures price. Theoretically, the futures position used for hedging should then be adjusted as V_A and V_F change, but in practice this usually makes very little difference.

If forward contracts rather than futures are used, there is no daily settlement and equation (3.2) should be used.

3.5 STOCK INDEX FUTURES

We now move on to consider stock index futures and how they are used to hedge or manage exposures to equity prices.

A *stock index* tracks changes in the value of a hypothetical portfolio of stocks. The weight of a stock in the portfolio at a particular time equals the proportion of the hypothetical portfolio invested in the stock at that time. The percentage increase in the stock index over a small interval of time is set equal to the percentage increase in the value of the hypothetical portfolio. Dividends are usually not included in the calculation, so that the index tracks the capital gain/loss from investing in the portfolio.[4]

[4] An exception to this is a *total return index*. This is calculated by assuming that dividends on the hypothetical portfolio are reinvested in the portfolio.

If the hypothetical portfolio of stocks remains fixed, the weights assigned to individual stocks in the portfolio do not remain fixed. When the price of one particular stock in the portfolio rises more sharply than others, more weight is automatically given to that stock. Sometimes indices are constructed from a hypothetical portfolio consisting of one of each of a number of stocks. The weights assigned to the stocks are then proportional to their market prices, with adjustments being made when there are stock splits. Other indices are constructed so that weights are proportional to market capitalization (stock price × number of shares outstanding). The underlying portfolio is then automatically adjusted to reflect stock splits, stock dividends, and new equity issues.

Stock Indices

Table 3.3 gives futures prices for contracts on three different stock indices on July 13, 2012.

The *Dow Jones Industrial Average* is based on a portfolio consisting of 30 blue-chip stocks in the United States. The weights given to the stocks are proportional to their prices. The CME Group trades two futures contracts on the index. One is on $10 times the index. The other (the Mini DJ Industrial Average) is on $5 times the index. The Mini contract trades most actively.

The *Standard & Poor's 500* (S&P 500) *Index* is based on a portfolio of 500 different stocks: 400 industrials, 40 utilities, 20 transportation companies, and 40 financial institutions. The weights of the stocks in the portfolio at any given time are proportional to their market capitalizations. The stocks are those of large publicly held companies that trade on NYSE Euronext or NASDAQ OMX. The CME Group trades two futures contracts on the S&P 500. One is on $250 times the index; the other (the Mini S&P 500 contract) is on $50 times the index. The Mini contract trades most actively.

The *NASDAQ-100* is based on 100 stocks using the National Association of Securities Dealers Automatic Quotations Service. The CME Group trades two contracts. One is on $100 times the index; the other (the Mini NASDAQ-100 contract) is on $20 times the index. The Mini contract trades most actively.

Table 3.3 Futures quotes for a selection of CME Group contracts on stock indices on July 13, 2012

	Open	*High*	*Low*	*Prior settlement*	*Last trade*	*Change*	*Volume*
Mini Dow Jones Industrial Average, $5 times index							
Sept. 2012	12,500	12,714	12,500	12,502	12,713	+211	100,898
Dec. 2012	12,501	12,625	12,501	12,424	12,625	+201	9
Mini S&P 500, $50 times index							
Sept. 2012	1329.25	1353.25	1328.75	1329.25	1351.50	+22.25	1,437,896
Dec. 2012	1323.00	1346.00	1322.00	1322.00	1344.75	+22.75	1,907
Mini NASDAQ-100, $20 times index							
Sept. 2012	2537.50	2584.75	2537.50	2537.75	2584.00	+46.25	156,547
Dec. 2012	2538.75	2575.00	2538.75	2531.00	2575.00	+44.00	2

As mentioned in Chapter 2, futures contracts on stock indices are settled in cash, not by delivery of the underlying asset. All contracts are marked to market to either the opening price or the closing price of the index on the last trading day, and the positions are then deemed to be closed. For example, contracts on the S&P 500 are closed out at the opening price of the S&P 500 index on the third Friday of the delivery month.

Hedging an Equity Portfolio

Stock index futures can be used to hedge a well-diversified equity portfolio. Define:

V_A: Current value of the portfolio

V_F: Current value of one futures contract (the futures price times the contract size)

If the portfolio mirrors the index, a hedge ratio very close to 1.0 is clearly appropriate, and equation (3.3) shows that the number of futures contracts that should be shorted is

$$N^* = \frac{V_A}{V_F} \tag{3.4}$$

Suppose, for example, that a portfolio worth \$5.05 million mirrors the S&P 500. The index futures price is 1,010 and each futures contract is on \$250 times the index. In this case, $V_A = 5{,}050{,}000$ and $V_F = 1{,}010 \times 250 = 252{,}500$, so that $5{,}050{,}000/252{,}500 = 20$ contracts should be shorted to hedge the portfolio.

When the portfolio does not exactly mirror the index, we can use the parameter beta (β) from the capital asset pricing model to determine the appropriate number of contracts to short. As explained in the appendix to this chapter, the beta of an asset is the slope of the best-fit line when the return on the asset is regressed against the return of a well-diversified stock index. When the beta of a portfolio equals 1.0, the return on the portfolio tends to mirror the return on the index; when $\beta = 2.0$, the changes in the return on the portfolio tend to be twice as great as the corresponding changes in the return from the index; when $\beta = 0.5$, they tend to be half as great; and so on.

A portfolio with a β of 2.0 is twice as sensitive to index movements as a portfolio with a beta of 1.0. It is therefore necessary to use twice as many contracts to hedge the portfolio. Similarly, a portfolio with a beta of 0.5 is half as sensitive to the index as a portfolio with a beta of 1.0 and we should use half as many contracts to hedge it. In general, we adjust equation (3.4) for a portfolio with a beta different from 1.0 as follows:

$$N^* = \beta\frac{V_A}{V_F} \tag{3.5}$$

This formula assumes that the maturity of the futures contract is close to the maturity of the hedge.

Comparing equation (3.5) with equation (3.3), we see that they imply $h^* = \beta$. This is not surprising. The hedge ratio h^* is the slope of the best-fit line when changes in the portfolio are regressed against changes in the futures price of the index. Beta (β) is the slope of the best-fit line when the return from the portfolio is regressed against the return from the the index. The two slopes are very similar.

We will show that equation (3.5) gives good results by extending our earlier example. Suppose that a futures contract with four months to maturity is used to hedge the value of a portfolio over the next three months in the following situation:

S&P 500 index = 1,000

S&P 500 futures price = 1,010

Value of portfolio = \$5,050,000

Risk-free interest rate = 4% per annum

Dividend yield on index = 1% per annum

Beta of portfolio = 1.5

One futures contract is for delivery of \$250 times the index. As before, $V_F = 250 \times 1{,}010 = 252{,}500$. From equation (3.5), the number of futures contracts that should be shorted to hedge the portfolio is

$$1.5 \times \frac{5{,}050{,}000}{252{,}500} = 30$$

Suppose the index turns out to be 900 in three months and the futures price is 902. The gain from the short futures position is then

$$30 \times (1{,}010 - 902) \times 250 = \$810{,}000$$

The loss on the index is 10%. The index pays a dividend of 1% per annum, or 0.25% per three months. When dividends are taken into account, an investor in the index would therefore earn −9.75% over the three-month period. As shown in the appendix to this chapter, the capital asset pricing model gives

$$\begin{aligned}\text{Expected return on portfolio} = {} & \text{Risk-free interest rate} \\ & + 1.5 \times (\text{Return on index} - \text{Risk-free interest rate})\end{aligned}$$

The risk-free interest rate is approximately 1% per three months. It follows that the expected return (%) on the portfolio during the three months is

$$1.0 + [1.5 \times (-9.75 - 1.0)] = -15.125$$

The expected value of the portfolio (inclusive of dividends) at the end of the three months is therefore

$$\$5{,}050{,}000 \times (1 - 0.15125) = \$4{,}286{,}187$$

It follows that the expected value of the hedger's position, including the gain on the hedge, is

$$\$4{,}286{,}187 + \$810{,}000 = \$5{,}096{,}187$$

Table 3.4 summarizes these calculations together with similar calculations for other values of the index at maturity. It can be seen that the total value of the hedger's position in three months is almost independent of the value of the index.

One thing we have not covered in this example is the relationship between futures prices and spot prices. We will see in Chapter 5 that the 1,010 assumed for the futures

Table 3.4 Performance of stock index hedge

Value of index in three months:	900	950	1,000	1,050	1,100
Futures price of index today:	1,010	1,010	1,010	1,010	1,010
Futures price of index in three months:	902	952	1,003	1,053	1,103
Gain on futures position ($):	810,000	435,000	52,500	−322,500	−697,500
Return on market:	−9.750%	−4.750%	0.250%	5.250%	10.250%
Expected return on portfolio:	−15.125%	−7.625%	−0.125%	7.375%	14.875%
Expected portfolio value in three months including dividends ($):	4,286,187	4,664,937	5,043,687	5,422,437	5,801,187
Total value of position in three months ($):	5,096,187	5,099,937	5,096,187	5,099,937	5,103,687

price today is roughly what we would expect given the interest rate and dividend we are assuming. The same is true of the futures prices in three months shown in Table 3.4.[5]

Reasons for Hedging an Equity Portfolio

Table 3.4 shows that the hedging procedure results in a value for the hedger's position at the end of the three months being about 1% higher than at the beginning of the three months. There is no surprise here. The risk-free rate is 4% per annum or 1% per three months. The hedge results in the investor's position growing at the risk-free rate.

It is natural to ask why the hedger should go to the trouble of using futures contracts. To earn the risk-free interest rate, the hedger can simply sell the portfolio and invest the proceeds in risk-free instruments such as Treasury bills.

One answer to this question is that hedging can be justified if the hedger feels that the stocks in the portfolio have been chosen well. In these circumstances, the hedger might be very uncertain about the performance of the market as a whole, but confident that the stocks in the portfolio will outperform the market (after appropriate adjustments have been made for the beta of the portfolio). A hedge using index futures removes the risk arising from market moves and leaves the hedger exposed only to the performance of the portfolio relative to the market. (This will be discussed shortly.) Another reason for hedging may be that the hedger is planning to hold a portfolio for a long period of time and requires short-term protection in an uncertain market situation. The alternative strategy of selling the portfolio and buying it back later might involve unacceptably high transaction costs.

Changing the Beta of a Portfolio

In the example in Table 3.4, the beta of the hedger's portfolio is reduced to zero so that the expected return is independent of the performance of the index. Sometimes futures

[5] The calculations in Table 3.4 assume that the dividend yield on the index is predictable, the risk-free interest rate remains constant, and the return on the index over the three-month period is perfectly correlated with the return on the portfolio. In practice, these assumptions do not hold perfectly, and the hedge works rather less well than is indicated by Table 3.4.

contracts are used to change the beta of a portfolio to some value other than zero. Continuing with our earlier example:

S&P 500 index = 1,000

S&P 500 futures price = 1,010

Value of portfolio = $5,050,000

Beta of portfolio = 1.5

As before, $V_F = 250 \times 1{,}010 = 252{,}500$ and a complete hedge requires

$$1.5 \times \frac{5{,}050{,}000}{252{,}500} = 30$$

contracts to be shorted. To reduce the beta of the portfolio from 1.5 to 0.75, the number of contracts shorted should be 15 rather than 30; to increase the beta of the portfolio to 2.0, a long position in 10 contracts should be taken; and so on. In general, to change the beta of the portfolio from β to β^*, where $\beta > \beta^*$, a short position in

$$(\beta - \beta^*)\frac{V_A}{V_F}$$

contracts is required. When $\beta < \beta^*$, a long position in

$$(\beta^* - \beta)\frac{V_A}{V_F}$$

contracts is required.

Locking in the Benefits of Stock Picking

Suppose you consider yourself to be good at picking stocks that will outperform the market. You own a single stock or a small portfolio of stocks. You do not know how well the market will perform over the next few months, but you are confident that your portfolio will do better than the market. What should you do?

You should short $\beta V_A/V_F$ index futures contracts, where β is the beta of your portfolio, V_A is the total value of the portfolio, and V_F is the current value of one index futures contract. If your portfolio performs better than a well-diversified portfolio with the same beta, you will then make money.

Consider an investor who in April holds 20,000 shares of a company, each worth $100. The investor feels that the market will be very volatile over the next three months but that the company has a good chance of outperforming the market. The investor decides to use the August futures contract on the S&P 500 to hedge the market's return during the three-month period. The β of the company is estimated at 1.1. Suppose that the current futures price for the August contract on the S&P 500 is 900. Each contract is for delivery of $250 times the index. In this case, $V_A = 20{,}000 \times 100 = 2{,}000{,}000$ and $V_F = 900 \times 250 = 225{,}000$. The number of contracts that should be shorted is therefore

$$1.1 \times \frac{2{,}000{,}000}{225{,}000} = 9.78$$

Rounding to the nearest integer, the investor shorts 10 contracts, closing out the position in July. Suppose that the company's stock falls to \$90 and the futures price of the S&P 500 falls to 750. The investor loses 20,000 × (\$100 − \$90) = \$200,000 on the stock, while gaining 10 × 250 × (900 − 750) = \$375,000 on the futures contracts.

The overall gain to the investor in this case is \$175,000 because the company's stock did not go down by as much as a well-diversified portfolio with a β of 1.1. If the market had gone up and the company's stock went up by more than a portfolio with a β of 1.1 (as expected by the investor), then a profit would be made in this case as well.

3.6 STACK AND ROLL

Sometimes the expiration date of the hedge is later than the delivery dates of all the futures contracts that can be used. The hedger must then roll the hedge forward by closing out one futures contract and taking the same position in a futures contract with a later delivery date. Hedges can be rolled forward many times. Consider a company that wishes to use a short hedge to reduce the risk associated with the price to be received for an asset at time T. If there are futures contracts 1, 2, 3, ..., n (not all necessarily in existence at the present time) with progressively later delivery dates, the company can use the following strategy:

Time t_1: Short futures contract 1

Time t_2: Close out futures contract 1
Short futures contract 2

Time t_3: Close out futures contract 2
Short futures contract 3

⋮

Time t_n: Close out futures contract $n-1$
Short futures contract n

Time T: Close out futures contract n

Suppose that in April 2013 a company realizes that it will have 1 million barrels of oil to sell in June 2014 and decides to hedge its risk with a hedge ratio of 1.0. (In this example, we do not make the "tailing" adjustment described in Section 3.4.) The current spot price is \$89. Although futures contracts are traded with maturities stretching several years into the future, we suppose that only the first six delivery months have sufficient liquidity to meet the company's needs. The company therefore shorts 1,000 October 2013 contracts. In September 2013, it rolls the hedge forward into the March 2014 contract. In February 2014, it rolls the hedge forward again into the July 2014 contract.

One possible outcome is shown in Table 3.5. The October 2013 contract is shorted at \$88.20 per barrel and closed out at \$87.40 per barrel for a profit of \$0.80 per barrel; the March 2014 contract is shorted at \$87.00 per barrel and closed out at \$86.50 per barrel for a profit of \$0.50 per barrel. The July 2014 contract is shorted at \$86.30 per barrel and closed out at \$85.90 per barrel for a profit of \$0.40 per barrel. The final spot price is \$86.

The dollar gain per barrel of oil from the short futures contracts is

$$(88.20 - 87.40) + (87.00 - 86.50) + (86.30 - 85.90) = 1.70$$

Table 3.5 Data for the example on rolling oil hedge forward

Date	*Apr. 2013*	*Sept. 2013*	*Feb. 2014*	*June 2014*
Oct. 2013 futures price	88.20	87.40		
Mar. 2014 futures price		87.00	86.50	
July 2014 futures price			86.30	85.90
Spot price	89.00			86.00

The oil price declined from \$89 to \$86. Receiving only \$1.70 per barrel compensation for a price decline of \$3.00 may appear unsatisfactory. However, we cannot expect total compensation for a price decline when futures prices are below spot prices. The best we can hope for is to lock in the futures price that would be applicable to a contract maturing in June 2014.

In practice, a company usually has an exposure every month to the underlying asset and uses a one-month futures contract for hedging because it is the most liquid. Initially it enters into ("stacks") sufficient contracts to cover its exposure to the end of its hedging horizon. One month later, it closes out all the contracts and "rolls" them into new one-month contracts to cover its new exposure, and so on.

As described in Business Snapshot 3.2, a German company, Metallgesellschaft, followed this strategy in the early 1990s to hedge contracts it had entered into to supply commodities at a fixed price. It ran into difficulties because the prices of the commodities declined so that there were immediate cash outflows on the futures and the expectation of eventual gains on the contracts. This mismatch between the timing of the cash flows on hedge and the timing of the cash flows from the position being hedged led to liquidity problems that could not be handled. The moral of the story is that potential liquidity problems should always be considered when a hedging strategy is being planned.

SUMMARY

This chapter has discussed various ways in which a company can take a position in futures contracts to offset an exposure to the price of an asset. If the exposure is such that the company gains when the price of the asset increases and loses when the price of the asset decreases, a short hedge is appropriate. If the exposure is the other way round (i.e., the company gains when the price of the asset decreases and loses when the price of the asset increases), a long hedge is appropriate.

Hedging is a way of reducing risk. As such, it should be welcomed by most executives. In reality, there are a number of theoretical and practical reasons why companies do not hedge. On a theoretical level, we can argue that shareholders, by holding well-diversified portfolios, can eliminate many of the risks faced by a company. They do not require the company to hedge these risks. On a practical level, a company may find that it is increasing rather than decreasing risk by hedging if none of its competitors does so. Also, a treasurer may fear criticism from other executives if the company makes a gain from movements in the price of the underlying asset and a loss on the hedge.

Business Snapshot 3.2 Metallgesellschaft: Hedging gone awry

Sometimes rolling hedges forward can lead to cash flow pressures. This problem was illustrated dramatically by the activities of a German company, Metallgesellschaft (MG), in the early 1990s.

MG sold a huge volume of 5- to 10-year heating oil and gasoline fixed-price supply contracts to its customers at 6 to 8 cents above market prices. It hedged its exposure with long positions in short-dated futures contracts that were rolled forward. As it turned out, the price of oil fell and there were margin calls on the futures positions. Considerable short-term cash flow pressures were placed on MG. The members of MG who devised the hedging strategy argued that these short-term cash outflows were offset by positive cash flows that would ultimately be realized on the long-term fixed-price contracts. However, the company's senior management and its bankers became concerned about the huge cash drain. As a result, the company closed out all the hedge positions and agreed with its customers that the fixed-price contracts would be abandoned. The outcome was a loss to MG of \$1.33 billion.

An important concept in hedging is basis risk. The basis is the difference between the spot price of an asset and its futures price. Basis risk arises from a hedger's uncertainty as to what the basis will be at maturity of the hedge.

The hedge ratio is the ratio of the size of the position taken in futures contracts to the size of the exposure. It is not always optimal to use a hedge ratio of 1.0. If the hedger wishes to minimize the variance of a position, a hedge ratio different from 1.0 may be appropriate. The optimal hedge ratio is the slope of the best-fit line obtained when changes in the spot price are regressed against changes in the futures price.

Stock index futures can be used to hedge the systematic risk in an equity portfolio. The number of futures contracts required is the beta of the portfolio multiplied by the ratio of the value of the portfolio to the value of one futures contract. Stock index futures can also be used to change the beta of a portfolio without changing the stocks comprising the portfolio.

When there is no liquid futures contract that matures later than the expiration of the hedge, a strategy known as stack and roll may be appropriate. This involves entering into a sequence of futures contracts. When the first futures contract is near expiration, it is closed out and the hedger enters into a second contract with a later delivery month. When the second contract is close to expiration, it is closed out and the hedger enters into a third contract with a later delivery month; and so on. The result of all this is the creation of a long-dated futures contract by trading a series of short-dated contracts.

FURTHER READING

Allayannis, G., and J. Weston. "The Use of Foreign Currency Derivatives and Firm Market Value," *Review of Financial Studies*, 14, 1 (Spring 2001): 243–76.

Bodnar, G.M., G.S. Hayt, and R.C. Marston. "1998 Wharton Survey of Financial Risk Management by U.S. Non-Financial Firms," *Financial Management* 2, 4 (1998): 70–91.

Brown, G. W. "Managing Foreign Exchange Risk with Derivatives," *Journal of Financial Economics*, 60 (2001): 401–48.

Campbell, J. Y., K. Serfaty-de Medeiros, and L. M. Viceira, "Global Currency Hedging," *Journal of Finance*, 65, 1 (February 2010): 87–121.

Cotter, J., and J. Hanly, "Hedging: Scaling and the Investor Horizon," *Journal of Risk*, 12, 2 (Winter 2009/10): 49–77.

Culp, C., and M. Miller. "Metallgesellschaft and the Economics of Synthetic Storage," *Journal of Applied Corporate Finance* 7, 4 (Winter 1995): 62–76.

Ederington, L. H. "The Hedging Performance of the New Futures Market," *Journal of Finance* 34 (March 1979): 157–70.

Edwards, F. R., and M. S. Canter. "The Collapse of Metallgesellschaft: Unhedgeable Risks, Poor Hedging Strategy, or Just Bad Luck?" *Journal of Applied Corporate Finance*, 8, 1 (Spring 1995): 86–105.

Geczy, C., B. A. Minton, and C. Schrand. "Why Firms Use Currency Derivatives," *Journal of Finance*, 52, 4 (1997): 1323–54.

Graham, J. R., and C. W. Smith Jr. "Tax Incentives to Hedge," *Journal of Finance*, 54, 6 (1999): 2241–62.

Haushalter, G. D. "Financing Policy, Basis Risk, and Corporate Hedging: Evidence from Oil and Gas Producers," *Journal of Finance*, 55, 1 (2000): 107–52.

Mello, A. S., and J. E. Parsons. "Hedging and Liquidity," *Review of Financial Studies*, 13 (Spring 2000): 127–53.

Neuberger, A. J. "Hedging Long-Term Exposures with Multiple Short-Term Futures Contracts," *Review of Financial Studies*, 12 (1999): 429–59.

Petersen, M. A., and S. R. Thiagarajan, "Risk Management and Hedging: With and Without Derivatives," *Financial Management*, 29, 4 (Winter 2000): 5–30.

Rendleman, R. "A Reconciliation of Potentially Conflicting Approaches to Hedging with Futures," *Advances in Futures and Options*, 6 (1993): 81–92.

Stulz, R. M. "Optimal Hedging Policies," *Journal of Financial and Quantitative Analysis*, 19 (June 1984): 127–40.

Tufano, P. "Who Manages Risk? An Empirical Examination of Risk Management Practices in the Gold Mining Industry," *Journal of Finance*, 51, 4 (1996): 1097–1138.

Tufano, P. "The Determinants of Stock Price Exposure: Financial Engineering and the Gold Mining Industry," *Journal of Finance*, 53, 3 (1998): 1015–52.

Quiz (Answers at End of Book)

3.1. Under what circumstances are (a) a short hedge and (b) a long hedge appropriate?

3.2. Explain what is meant by *basis risk* when futures contracts are used for hedging.

3.3. Explain what is meant by a *perfect hedge*. Does a perfect hedge always lead to a better outcome than an imperfect hedge? Explain your answer.

3.4. Under what circumstances does a minimum variance hedge portfolio lead to no hedging at all?

3.5. Give three reasons why the treasurer of a company might not hedge the company's exposure to a particular risk.

3.6. Suppose that the standard deviation of quarterly changes in the prices of a commodity is \$0.65, the standard deviation of quarterly changes in a futures price on the commodity is \$0.81, and the coefficient of correlation between the two changes is 0.8. What is the optimal hedge ratio for a three-month contract? What does it mean?

3.7. A company has a \$20 million portfolio with a beta of 1.2. It would like to use futures contracts on the S&P 500 to hedge its risk. The index futures price is currently 1080, and each contract is for delivery of \$250 times the index. What is the hedge that minimizes risk? What should the company do if it wants to reduce the beta of the portfolio to 0.6?

Practice Questions (Answers in Solutions Manual/Study Guide)

3.8. In the Chicago Board of Trade's corn futures contract, the following delivery months are available: March, May, July, September, and December. State the contract that should be used for hedging when the expiration of the hedge is in (a) June, (b) July, and (c) January.

3.9. Does a perfect hedge always succeed in locking in the current spot price of an asset for a future transaction? Explain your answer.

3.10. Explain why a short hedger's position improves when the basis strengthens unexpectedly and worsens when the basis weakens unexpectedly.

3.11. Imagine you are the treasurer of a Japanese company exporting electronic equipment to the United States. Discuss how you would design a foreign exchange hedging strategy and the arguments you would use to sell the strategy to your fellow executives.

3.12. Suppose that in Example 3.4 the company decides to use a hedge ratio of 0.8. How does the decision affect the way in which the hedge is implemented and the result?

3.13. "If the minimum variance hedge ratio is calculated as 1.0, the hedge must be perfect." Is this statement true? Explain your answer.

3.14. "If there is no basis risk, the minimum variance hedge ratio is always 1.0." Is this statement true? Explain your answer.

3.15. "For an asset where futures prices are usually less than spot prices, long hedges are likely to be particularly attractive." Explain this statement.

3.16. The standard deviation of monthly changes in the spot price of live cattle is (in cents per pound) 1.2. The standard deviation of monthly changes in the futures price of live cattle for the closest contract is 1.4. The correlation between the futures price changes and the spot price changes is 0.7. It is now October 15. A beef producer is committed to purchasing 200,000 pounds of live cattle on November 15. The producer wants to use the December live-cattle futures contracts to hedge its risk. Each contract is for the delivery of 40,000 pounds of cattle. What strategy should the beef producer follow?

3.17. A corn farmer argues: "I do not use futures contracts for hedging. My real risk is not the price of corn. It is that my whole crop gets wiped out by the weather." Discuss this viewpoint. Should the farmer estimate his or her expected production of corn and hedge to try to lock in a price for expected production?

3.18. On July 1, an investor holds 50,000 shares of a certain stock. The market price is \$30 per share. The investor is interested in hedging against movements in the market over the next month and decides to use the September Mini S&P 500 futures contract. The index futures price is 1,500 and one contract is for delivery of \$50 times the index. The beta of the stock is 1.3. What strategy should the investor follow? Under what circumstances will it be profitable?

3.19. Suppose that in Table 3.5 the company decides to use a hedge ratio of 1.5. How does the decision affect the way the hedge is implemented and the result?

3.20. A futures contract is used for hedging. Explain why the daily settlement of the contract can give rise to cash-flow problems.

3.21. The expected return on the S&P 500 is 12% and the risk-free rate is 5%. What is the expected return on an investment with a beta of (a) 0.2, (b) 0.5, and (c) 1.4?

Further Questions

3.22. It is now June. A company knows that it will sell 5,000 barrels of crude oil in September. It uses the October CME Group futures contract to hedge the price it will receive. Each contract is on 1,000 barrels of "light sweet crude." What position should it take? What price risks is it still exposed to after taking the position?

3.23. Sixty futures contracts are used to hedge an exposure to the price of silver. Each futures contract is on 5,000 ounces of silver. At the time the hedge is closed out, the basis is \$0.20 per ounce. What is the effect of the basis on the hedger's financial position if (a) the trader is hedging the purchase of silver and (b) the trader is hedging the sale of silver?

3.24. A trader owns 55,000 units of a particular asset and decides to hedge the value of her position with futures contracts on another related asset. Each futures contract is on 5,000 units. The spot price of the asset that is owned is \$28 and the standard deviation of the change in this price over the life of the hedge is estimated to be \$0.43. The futures price of the related asset is \$27 and the standard deviation of the change in this over the life of the hedge is \$0.40. The coefficient of correlation between the spot price change and futures price change is 0.95.
(a) What is the minimum variance hedge ratio?
(b) Should the hedger take a long or short futures position?
(c) What is the optimal number of futures contracts with no tailing of the hedge?
(d) What is the optimal number of futures contracts with tailing of the hedge?

3.25. A company wishes to hedge its exposure to a new fuel whose price changes have a 0.6 correlation with gasoline futures price changes. The company will lose \$1 million for each 1 cent increase in the price per gallon of the new fuel over the next three months. The new fuel's price changes have a standard deviation that is 50% greater than price changes in gasoline futures prices. If gasoline futures are used to hedge the exposure, what should the hedge ratio be? What is the company's exposure measured in gallons of the new fuel? What position, measured in gallons, should the company take in gasoline futures? How many gasoline futures contracts should be traded? Each futures contract is on 42,000 gallons.

3.26. A portfolio manager has maintained an actively managed portfolio with a beta of 0.2. During the last year, the risk-free rate was 5% and equities performed very badly providing a return of −30%. The portfolio manager produced a return of −10% and claims that in the circumstances it was a good performance. Discuss this claim.

3.27. It is July 16. A company has a portfolio of stocks worth \$100 million. The beta of the portfolio is 1.2. The company would like to use the CME December futures contract on

the S&P 500 to change the beta of the portfolio to 0.5 during the period July 16 to November 16. The index futures price is 1,000, and each contract is on $250 times the index.
(a) What position should the company take?
(b) Suppose that the company changes its mind and decides to increase the beta of the portfolio from 1.2 to 1.5. What position in futures contracts should it take?

3.28. The following table gives data on monthly changes in the spot price of a commodity and the futures price of a contract used to hedge it. Use the data to calculate a minimum variance hedge ratio.

Spot price change	+0.50	+0.61	−0.22	−0.35	+0.79
Futures price change	+0.56	+0.63	−0.12	−0.44	+0.60
Spot price change	+0.04	+0.15	+0.70	−0.51	−0.41
Futures price change	−0.06	+0.01	+0.80	−0.56	−0.46

3.29. It is now October 2013. A company anticipates that it will purchase 1 million pounds of copper in each of February 2014, August 2014, February 2015, and August 2015. The company has decided to use the futures contracts traded by the CME Group to hedge its risk. One contract is for the delivery of 25,000 pounds of copper. The initial margin is $2,000 per contract and the maintenance margin is $1,500 per contract. The company's policy is to hedge 80% of its exposure. Contracts with maturities up to 13 months into the future are considered to have sufficient liquidity to meet the company's needs. Devise a hedging strategy for the company. (Do not make the "tailing" adjustment described in Section 3.4.)

Assume the market prices (in cents per pound) today and at future dates are as in the following table. What is the impact of the strategy you propose on the price the company pays for copper? What is the initial margin requirement in October 2010? Is the company subject to any margin calls?

Date	*Oct. 2013*	*Feb. 2014*	*Aug. 2014*	*Feb. 2015*	*Aug. 2015*
Spot price	372.00	369.00	365.00	377.00	388.00
Mar. 2014 futures price	372.30	369.10			
Sept. 2014 futures price	372.80	370.20	364.80		
Mar. 2015 futures price		370.70	364.30	376.70	
Sept. 2015 futures price			364.20	376.50	388.20

3.30. A fund manager has a portfolio worth $50 million with a beta of 0.87. The manager is concerned about the performance of the market over the next two months and plans to use three-month futures contracts on the S&P 500 to hedge the risk. The current index level is 1,250, one contract is on 250 times the index, the risk-free rate is 6% per annum, and the dividend yield on the index is 3% per annum. The current three-month futures price is 1,259.
(a) What position should the fund manager take to hedge exposure to the market over the next two months?
(b) Calculate the effect of your strategy on the fund manager's returns if the index in two months is 1,000, 1,100, 1,200, 1,300, and 1,400. Assume that the one-month futures price is 0.25% higher than the index level at this time.

APPENDIX

Review of Key Concepts in Statistics and the CAPM

The material in Chapter 3 requires a knowledge of standard deviation, correlation, linear regression, and the capital asset pricing model. This appendix provides a review of these topics. An Excel worksheet to illustrate the calculations can be found on the author's website.

Standard Deviation

Standard deviation is a measure of the extent to which observations on a particular variable are different form each other. It is usually denoted by the Greek letter σ (sigma). If the observations on the variable are all the same, their standard deviation is zero. As they become more different, their standard deviation increases.

As an example, suppose that you own six finance textbooks. The weights of the books (in pounds) are 5, 7, 5, 4, 9, and 6. The mean (i.e., average) weight is $\frac{1}{6}(5+7+5+4+9+6) = 6$ pounds. To calculate the standard deviation, we first take the difference between each observation and the mean and square the result. For our example, these squared differences are as follows:

$$(5-6)^2 = 1$$
$$(7-6)^2 = 1$$
$$(5-6)^2 = 1$$
$$(4-6)^2 = 4$$
$$(9-6)^2 = 9$$
$$(6-6)^2 = 0$$

The standard deviation is the square root of the mean of the squared differences (sometimes referred to as the *root mean square* of the differences):

$$\sigma = \sqrt{\frac{1+1+1+4+9+0}{6}} = 1.633$$

The *variance* of a set of observations is the square of the standard deviation. In our example, it is 2.667.

Often the calculation of standard deviation or variance distinguishes between situations where the data is for the whole population and where it is for a sample from the population. The calculation we have just given is correct for the situation where the data is for the whole population. When it is for a sample from the population, σ is estimated by dividing the sum of squared differences by one less than the number of observations—not by the number of observations—and taking the square root of the result.

In our example, if you were concerned with calculating the standard deviation of the weights of finance textbooks that you own, then the calculation we have given would be correct because the data you have is for the whole population. If you are interested in calculating the standard deviation of all finance textbooks (and regard the ones you own as a random sample), then the standard deviation would be estimated as

$$\sigma = \sqrt{\frac{1+1+1+4+9+0}{5}} = 1.789$$

and the variance would be 3.2.

In finance we are usually interested in estimating standard deviations from sample data, so that the second approach, where the number of observations is reduced by one in the calculation of the root mean square, is used. The formula for standard deviation when there are n observations $x_1, x_2, \dots, x_n$ is therefore

$$\sigma = \sqrt{\frac{\sum_{i=1}^{n}(x_i - \bar{x})^2}{n-1}} \quad \textbf{(3A.1)}$$

where $\bar{x}$ is the mean of the observations.

In Excel, the function STDEV can be used to calculate a standard deviation from sample data. If the data on the weights of books are put in cells B2 to B7 of an Excel worksheet, the instruction

=STDEV(B2:B7)

in another cell gives the standard deviation as 1.789.

Correlation

Correlation is a measure of the extent to which there is a linear relationship between two variables. It is usually measured by the *coefficient of correlation*, which is a number between −1 and +1. A correlation of 0 would indicate no linear relationship; a correlation of +1 would indicate a perfect positive relationship between the variables; a correlation of −1 would indicate a perfect negative relationship between the variables. As explained in Section 3.4, in hedging we are looking for situations where there is a high correlation between (a) the gain or loss on a company's exposure and (b) the gain or loss on a instrument used for hedging. The coefficient of correlation is usually denoted by the Greek letter ρ (rho).

Suppose that the observations on the first variable x are $x_1, x_2, \dots, x_n$ and that the corresponding observations on the second variable y, are $y_1, y_2, \dots, y_n$. Denote $\bar{x}$ as the mean of the observations on variable x and $\bar{y}$ as the mean of the observations on variable y. The formula for calculating the coefficient of correlation is

$$\rho = \frac{\sum_{i=1}^{n}(x_i - \bar{x})(y_i - \bar{y})}{\sqrt{\sum_{i=1}^{n}(x_i - \bar{x})^2 \sum_{i=1}^{n}(y_i - \bar{y})^2}} \quad \textbf{(3A.2)}$$

Let us continue our example involving finance textbooks. Suppose that the variable x is the weight of a finance textbook and the observations are those given above: 5, 7, 5, 4, 9, and 6 pounds. Suppose that the variable y is the number of pages in a finance textbook and the observations on variable y corresponding to the six observations on variable x are 420, 630, 330, 380, 800, and 500, respectively (see Table 3A.1). In this case,

Table 3A.1 Weights of finance textbooks and number of pages. S.D. = standard deviation

Observation	*Weights (pounds)*	*Number of pages*
1	5	420
2	7	630
3	5	330
4	4	380
5	9	800
6	6	500
Mean	6.000	510.000
S.D.	1.789	176.635

$\bar{y} = \frac{1}{6}(420 + 630 + 330 + 380 + 800 + 500) = 510$. Also, $\bar{x} = 6$, as calculated earlier, so equation (3A.1) gives

$$\rho = 0.962$$

Not surprisingly, the correlation between the weights of finance texts and the number of pages in them is close to 1.

The Excel function CORREL can be used to calculate a coefficient of correlation. If the weights are in cells B2 to B7 and the page counts are in cells C2 to C7, then

= CORREL(B2:B7, C2:C7)

gives 0.962.

Linear Regression

Linear regression is used to estimate a best-fit linear relationship of the form

$$y = a + bx \tag{3A.3}$$

between two variables y and x. The parameter b is the slope and the parameter a is the intercept.

The slope b is estimated from observations on y and x as

$$b = \rho\frac{\sigma_y}{\sigma_x} \tag{3A.4}$$

where ρ is the coefficient of correlation between the observations on y and x, σ_y is the standard deviation of the observations on y, and σ_x is the standard deviation of the observations on x. The intercept a is then estimated as $\bar{y} - b\bar{x}$ where $\bar{x}$ and $\bar{y}$ are the means of the observations on x and y, respectively.

Suppose we are interested in predicting the number of pages in a finance textbook from its weight using the data in Table 3A.1. We have already calculated $\rho = 0.962$. In this case, $\sigma_x = 1.789$ and $\sigma_y = 176.635$, so that

$$b = 0.962 \times \frac{176.635}{1.789} = 95$$

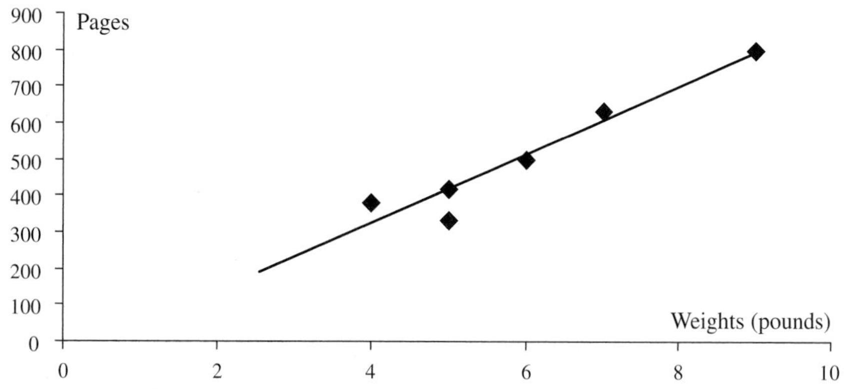

Figure 3A.1 Best-fit relationship for data in Table 3A.1

Setting $\bar{x} = 6$ and $\bar{y} = 510$, we obtain

$$a = 510 - 95 \times 6 = -60$$

The best-fit regression relationship is therefore

$$y = -60 + 95x$$

This is shown in Figure 3A.1.

Using Excel, the intercept and and slope can be calculated using the INTERCEPT and SLOPE functions. When the x values are in cells B2 to B7 and the y values are in cells C2 to C7, the instructions are:

=INTERCEPT(C2:C7, B2:B7)

and

=SLOPE(C2:C7, B2:B7)

The R^2 of a linear regression of y on x is the proportion of the variance of y that is accounted for by x. It is the square of the coefficient of correlation (0.926 in our example).

Capital Asset Pricing Model

The capital asset pricing model is a model that can be used to calculate the expected rate of return from an asset from a measure of that part of its risk that cannot be diversified away. The formula is[6]

$$\text{Expected return on asset} = R_F + \beta(R_M - R_F) \qquad \textbf{(3A.5)}$$

where R_M is the return on the portfolio of all available investments, R_F is the return on a risk-free investment, and β (the Greek letter beta) is the value of the slope obtained from the linear regression in equation (3A.3) when variable y is the return on the asset and variable x is R_M. The return from the portfolio of all available investments, R_M, is referred to as the *return on the market* and is usually approximated as the return on a well-diversified stock index such as the S&P 500.

[6] If the return on the market is not known, R_M is replaced by the expected value of R_M in this formula.

Beta (β) measures the sensitivity of returns from the asset to returns from the market. When $\beta = 0$, there is no sensitivity; when $\beta = 0.5$, the excess return on the asset over the risk-free rate is on average half of the excess return of the market over the risk-free rate; when $\beta = 1$, the excess return on the asset over the risk-free rate is equal to the excess return of the market over the risk-free rate; and so on.

According to the capital asset pricing model, the risk in the returns from an asset can be divided into two parts. *Systematic risk* is risk related to returns from the market and cannot be diversified away. *Nonsystematic risk* is risk that is unique to the asset and can be diversified away by choosing a large portfolio of different assets. The parameter β is a measure of systematic risk. Equation (3A.5) shows that, when an asset has no systematic risk ($\beta = 0$), its expected return is the risk-free rate. As β increases, the expected return increases. When $\beta = 1$, so that it has the same systematic risk as the market, the expected return is the return of the market.

When the asset is an individual stock, the expected return given by equation (3A.5) is an unbiased—but not particularly good—predictor of the actual return. But, when the asset is a well-diversified portfolio of stocks, it is a much better predictor. As a result, the equation

$$\text{Return on diversified portfolio} = R_F + \beta(R_M - R_F)$$

can be used as a basis for hedging a diversified portfolio. The β in the equation is the beta of the portfolio and can be calculated as the weighted average of the betas of the stocks in the portfolio.

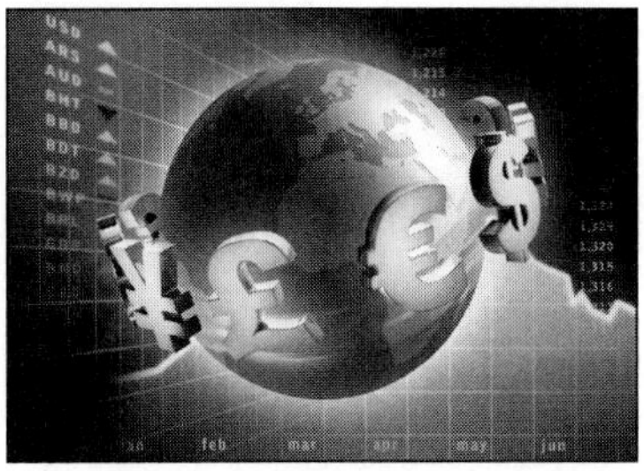

CHAPTER 4 Interest Rates

Interest rates are a factor in the valuation of virtually all derivatives and will feature prominently in much of the material presented in the rest of this book. This chapter deals with some fundamental issues concerned with the way interest rates are measured and analyzed. It explains the compounding frequency used to define an interest rate and the meaning of continuously compounded interest rates, which are used extensively in the analysis of derivatives. It covers zero rates, par yields, and yield curves, discusses bond pricing, and outlines a "bootstrap" procedure commonly used by a derivatives trading desk to calculate zero-coupon interest rates. It also covers forward rates and forward rate agreements, and reviews different theories of the term structure of interest rates.

Chapter 6 will cover interest rate futures and duration. For ease of exposition, we ignore day count conventions in this chapter. The nature of these conventions and their impact on calculations will be discussed in Chapters 6 and 7.

4.1 TYPES OF RATES

An interest rate in a particular situation defines the amount of money a borrower promises to pay the lender. For any given currency, many different types of interest rates are regularly quoted. These include mortgage rates, deposit rates, prime borrowing rates, and so on. The interest rate applicable in a situation depends on the credit risk. This is the risk that there will be a default by the borrower of funds, so that the interest and principal are not paid to the lender as promised. The higher the credit risk, the higher the interest rate that is promised by the borrower.

Treasury Rates

Treasury rates are the rates an investor earns on Treasury bills and Treasury bonds. These are the instruments used by a government to borrow in its own currency. Japanese Treasury rates are the rates at which the Japanese government borrows in yen; U.S. Treasury rates are the rates at which the U.S. government borrows in U.S. dollars; and so on. It is usually assumed that there is no chance that a government will default on an obligation denominated in its own currency. Treasury rates are therefore

From Chapter 4 of *Fundamentals of Futures and Options Markets*, Eighth Edition. John C. Hull.

totally risk-free rates in the sense that an investor who buys a Treasury bill or Treasury bond is certain that interest and principal payments will be made as promised.

LIBOR

LIBOR is short for *London Interbank Offered Rate*. It is a reference interest rate, produced once a day, designed to reflect the rate of interest at which banks can obtain unsecured loans from other banks. Traditionally, LIBOR has been determined by submissions from large banks to the British Bankers Association at 11 a.m. each business day. LIBOR is quoted in all major currencies for maturities up to 12 months: 1-month LIBOR is the rate of interest on 1-month loans, 3-month LIBOR is the rate of interest on 3-month loans, and so on.

A bank must satisfy certain creditworthiness criteria in order to be able to borrow at LIBOR from another bank. A rule of thumb is that borrowing at LIBOR is only possible for a bank with a AA credit rating or better.[1]

A rate closely related to LIBOR is LIBID. This is the *London Interbank Bid Rate* and is the rate at which banks are prepared to borrow from (i.e., accept deposits from) other banks. At any specified time, there is a small spread between LIBID and LIBOR rates (with LIBOR higher than LIBID). If more banks want to borrow U.S. dollars for 3 months than lend U.S. dollars for 3 months, the 3-month U.S. LIBID and LIBOR rates will increase. Similarly, if more banks want to lend 3-month funds than borrow these funds, the 3-month LIBID and LIBOR rates will decrease. LIBOR borrowing and lending is part of what is known as the *Eurocurrency market*, which is an international market outside the control of any one government.

Repo Rates

Sometimes trading activities are funded with a *repurchase agreement*, *repo*. This is a contract where an investment dealer who owns securities agrees to sell them to another company now and buy them back later at a slightly higher price. The other company is providing a loan to the investment dealer. The difference between the price at which the securities are sold and the price at which they are repurchased is the interest it earns. The interest rate is referred to as the *repo rate*. If structured carefully, the loan involves very little credit risk. If the borrower does not honor the agreement, the lending company simply keeps the securities. If the lending company does not keep to its side of the agreement, the original owner of the securities keeps the cash. The most common type of repo is an *overnight repo*, in which the agreement is renegotiated each day. However, longer-term arrangements, known as *term repos*, are sometimes used.

The Risk-Free Rate

The "risk-free rate" is used extensively in the evaluation of derivatives. It might be thought that derivatives traders would use the interest rates implied by Treasury bills and bonds as risk-free rates. In fact, they do not do this. As indicated in Business Snapshot 4.1, there are a number of tax and regulatory issues that cause Treasury rates to be artificially low.

[1] The best credit rating given to a company by rating agencies S&P and Fitch is AAA. The second best is AA. The corresponding ratings from Moody's are Aaa and Aa, respectively.

Business Snapshot 4.1 What Is the Risk-Free Rate?

Derivatives dealers argue that the interest rates implied by Treasury bills and Treasury bonds are artificially low because:

1. Treasury bills and Treasury bonds must be purchased by financial institutions to fulfill a variety of regulatory requirements. This increases demand for these Treasury instruments driving the price up and the yield down.
2. The amount of capital a bank is required to hold to support an investment in Treasury bills and bonds is substantially smaller than the capital required to support a similar investment in other instruments with very low risk.
3. In the United States, Treasury instruments are given a favorable tax treatment compared with most other fixed-income investments because they are not taxed at the state level.

Traditionally derivatives dealers have assumed that LIBOR rates are risk-free, but this is an approximation. LIBOR rates are not totally risk-free. A LIBOR loan has the risk that the bank borrowing funds will default during the life of the loan. Following the credit crisis that started in 2007, many dealers switched to using overnight indexed swap rates as risk-free rates. These rates are discussed in Section 7.6.

Financial institutions have traditionally used LIBOR rates as risk-free rates. For a AA-rated financial institution LIBOR is the short-term opportunity cost of capital. The financial institution can borrow short-term funds at the LIBOR quotes of other financial institutions and can lend funds to other financial institutions at its own LIBOR quotes. LIBOR rates are not totally free of credit risk. For example, when funds are lent at 3-month LIBOR to a AA-rated financial institution, there is a small chance that it will default during the 3 months. However, they are close to risk-free in normal market conditions. LIBOR rates have maturities up to 1 year. As we will explain later, traders have traditionally used Eurodollar futures and interest rate swaps to extend the risk-free LIBOR yield curve beyond 1 year.

The credit crisis that started in 2007 caused many derivatives dealers to critically review the practice of using LIBOR as the risk-free rate. This is because banks became very reluctant to lend to each other during the crisis and LIBOR rates soared. As will be explained in Chapter 7, many dealers use what is known as the overnight indexed swap (OIS) rate as the risk-free rate—particularly when collateralized transactions are valued.

4.2 MEASURING INTEREST RATES

A statement by a bank that the interest rate on one-year deposits is 10% per annum sounds straightforward and unambiguous. In fact, its precise meaning depends on the way the interest rate is measured.

If the interest rate is measured with annual compounding, the bank's statement that the interest rate is 10% means that \$100 grows to

$$\$100 \times 1.1 = \$110$$

at the end of one year. When the interest rate is measured with semiannual compounding, it means that 5% is earned every six months, with the interest being reinvested. In this case, \$100 grows to

$$\$100 \times 1.05 \times 1.05 = \$110.25$$

at the end of one year. When the interest rate is measured with quarterly compounding, the bank's statement means that 2.5% is earned every three months, with the interest being reinvested. The \$100 then grows to

$$\$100 \times 1.025^4 = \$110.38$$

at the end of one year. Table 4.1 shows the effect of increasing the compounding frequency further.

The compounding frequency defines the units in which an interest rate is measured. A rate expressed with one compounding frequency can be converted into an equivalent rate with a different compounding frequency. For example, from Table 4.1 we see that 10.25% with annual compounding is equivalent to 10% with semiannual compounding. We can think of the difference between one compounding frequency and another to be analogous to the difference between kilometers and miles. They are two different units of measurement.

To generalize our results, suppose that an amount A is invested for n years at an interest rate of R per annum. If the rate is compounded once per annum, the terminal value of the investment is

$$A(1+R)^n$$

If the rate is compounded m times per annum, the terminal value of the investment is

$$A\left(1+\frac{R}{m}\right)^{mn} \tag{4.1}$$

When $m = 1$ the rate is sometimes referred to as the *equivalent annual interest rate*.

Continuous Compounding

The limit as the compounding frequency, m, tends to infinity is known as *continuous compounding*. With continuous compounding, it can be shown (see the appendix to this

Table 4.1 Effect of the compounding frequency on the value of \$100 at the end of one year when the interest rate is 10% per annum

Compounding frequency	*Value of \$100 at end of year (\$)*
Annually ($m = 1$)	110.00
Semiannually ($m = 2$)	110.25
Quarterly ($m = 4$)	110.38
Monthly ($m = 12$)	110.47
Weekly ($m = 52$)	110.51
Daily ($m = 365$)	110.52

chapter) that an amount A invested for n years at rate R grows to

$$Ae^{Rn} \tag{4.2}$$

where e is approximately 2.71828. The function e^x is the exponential function and is built into most calculators, so the computation of the expression in equation (4.2) presents no problems. In the example in Table 4.1, $A = 100$, $n = 1$, and $R = 0.1$, so that the value to which A grows with continuous compounding is

$$100e^{0.1} = \$110.52$$

This is (to two decimal places) the same as the value with daily compounding. For most practical purposes, continuous compounding can be thought of as being equivalent to daily compounding. Compounding a sum of money at a continuously compounded rate R for n years involves multiplying it by e^{Rn}. Discounting it at a continuously compounded rate R for n years involves multiplying by e^{-Rn}.

In this book interest rates will be measured with continuous compounding except where otherwise stated. Readers used to working with interest rates that are measured with annual, semiannual, or some other compounding frequency may find this a little strange at first. However, continuously compounded interest rates are used to such a great extent in pricing derivatives that it makes sense to get used to working with them now.

Suppose that R_c is a rate of interest with continuous compounding and R_m is the equivalent rate with compounding m times per annum. From the results in equations (4.1) and (4.2), we must have

$$Ae^{R_c n} = A\left(1 + \frac{R_m}{m}\right)^{mn}$$

or

$$e^{R_c} = \left(1 + \frac{R_m}{m}\right)^{m}$$

This means that

$$R_c = m \ln\left(1 + \frac{R_m}{m}\right) \tag{4.3}$$

and

$$R_m = m(e^{R_c/m} - 1) \tag{4.4}$$

These equations can be used to convert a rate with a compounding frequency of m times per annum to a continuously compounded rate and vice versa (see Example 4.1). The function $\ln x$ is the natural logarithm function and is built into most calculators. It is defined so that, if $y = \ln x$, then $x = e^y$ (see the Appendix to this chapter).

4.3 ZERO RATES

The n-year zero-coupon interest rate is the rate of interest earned on an investment that starts today and lasts for n years. All the interest and principal is realized at the end of n years. There are no intermediate payments. The n-year zero-coupon interest rate is sometimes also referred to as the n-year *spot rate*, the n-year *zero rate*, or just the n-year *zero*. Suppose a five-year zero rate with continuous compounding is quoted as 5% per

Example 4.1 Changing the compounding frequency

1. Consider an interest rate that is quoted as 10% per annum with semiannual compounding. From equation (4.3), with $m = 2$ and $R_m = 0.1$, the equivalent rate with continuous compounding is

$$2\ln\left(1+\frac{0.1}{2}\right) = 0.09758$$

or 9.758% per annum.

2. Suppose that a lender quotes the interest rate on loans as 8% per annum with continuous compounding, and that interest is actually paid quarterly. From equation (4.4), with $m = 4$ and $R_c = 0.08$, the equivalent rate with quarterly compounding is

$$4 \times (e^{0.08/4} - 1) = 0.0808$$

or 8.08% per annum. This means that on a $1,000 loan, interest payments of $20.20 would be required each quarter.

annum. This means that $100, if invested for five years, grows to

$$100 \times e^{0.05\times 5} = 128.40$$

Most of the interest rates we observe directly in the market are not pure zero rates. Consider a five-year government bond that provides a 6% coupon. The price of this bond does not by itself determine the five-year Treasury zero rate because some of the return on the bond is realized in the form of coupons prior to the end of year five. Later in this chapter we will discuss how we can determine Treasury zero rates from the prices of coupon-bearing bonds.

4.4 BOND PRICING

Most bonds pay coupons to the holder periodically. The bond's principal (which is also known as its par value or face value) is paid at the end of its life. The theoretical price of a bond can be calculated as the present value of all the cash flows that will be received by the owner of the bond. Sometimes bond traders use the same discount rate for all the cash flows underlying a bond, but a more accurate approach is to use the appropriate zero rate for each cash flow.

To illustrate this, consider the situation where Treasury zero rates, measured with continuous compounding, are as in Table 4.2. (We explain later how these can be calculated.) Suppose that a two-year Treasury bond with a principal of $100 provides coupons at the rate of 6% per annum semiannually. To calculate the present value of the first coupon of $3, we discount it at 5.0% for six months; to calculate the present value of the second coupon of $3, we discount it at 5.8% for one year; and so on. The theoretical price of the bond is therefore

$$3e^{-0.05\times 0.5} + 3e^{-0.058\times 1.0} + 3e^{-0.064\times 1.5} + 103e^{-0.068\times 2.0} = 98.39$$

or $98.39.

Table 4.2 Treasury zero rates

Maturity (years)	*Zero rate (%) (cont. comp.)*
0.5	5.0
1.0	5.8
1.5	6.4
2.0	6.8

Bond Yield

A bond's yield is the single discount rate that, when applied to all cash flows, gives the bond's value equal to its market price. Suppose that the theoretical price of the bond we have been considering, \$98.39, is also its market value (that is, the market's price of the bond is in exact agreement with the data in Table 4.2). If y is the yield on the bond expressed with continuous compounding, it must be true that

$$3e^{-y\times 0.5} + 3e^{-y\times 1.0} + 3e^{-y\times 1.5} + 103e^{-y\times 2.0} = 98.39$$

This equation can be solved using an iterative ("trial and error") procedure to give $y = 6.76\%$.

Par Yield

The *par yield* for a certain bond maturity is the coupon rate that causes the bond price to equal its par value. (The par value is the same as the principal value). Usually the bond is assumed to provide semiannual coupons. Suppose that the coupon on a two-year bond in our example is c per annum (or $c/2$ per six months). Using the zero rates in Table 4.2, the value of the bond is equal to its par value of 100 when

$$\frac{c}{2}e^{-0.05\times 0.5} + \frac{c}{2}e^{-0.058\times 1.0} + \frac{c}{2}e^{-0.064\times 1.5} + \left(100 + \frac{c}{2}\right)e^{-0.068\times 2.0} = 100$$

This equation can be solved in a straightforward way to give $c = 6.87$. The two-year par yield is therefore 6.87% per annum.

More generally, if d is the present value of \$1 received at the maturity of the bond, A the value of an annuity that pays one dollar on each coupon payment date, and m the number of coupon payments per year, then the par yield c must satisfy

$$100 = A\frac{c}{m} + 100d$$

so that

$$c = \frac{(100 - 100d)m}{A}$$

In our example, $m = 2$, $d = e^{-0.068\times 2} = 0.87284$, and

$$A = e^{-0.05\times 0.5} + e^{-0.058\times 1.0} + e^{-0.064\times 1.5} + e^{-0.068\times 2.0} = 3.70027$$

The formula confirms that the par yield is 6.87% per annum. This is the rate expressed with semiannual compounding; with continuous compounding it would be 6.75%.

4.5 DETERMINING TREASURY ZERO RATES

One way of determining Treasury zero rates such as those in Table 4.2 is to observe yields on "strips." These are zero-coupon bonds that are synthetically created by traders when they sell coupons on a Treasury bond separately from the principal.

Another way to determine Treasury zero rates is from Treasury bills and coupon-bearing bonds. The most popular approach is known as the *bootstrap method.* To illustrate the nature of the method, consider the data in Table 4.3 on the prices of five bonds. Because the first three bonds pay no coupons, the zero rates corresponding to the maturities of these bonds can be easily calculated. The three-month bond has the effect of turning an investment of 97.5 into 100 three months later. The continuously compounded three-month rate R is therefore given by solving

$$100 = 97.5e^{R\times 0.25}$$

It is 10.127% per annum. The six-month rate is similarly given by solving

$$100 = 94.9e^{R\times 0.5}$$

It is 10.469% per annum with continuous compounding. Similarly, the one-year rate with continuous compounding is given by solving

$$100 = 90e^{R\times 1.0}$$

It is 10.536% per annum.

The fourth bond lasts 1.5 years. The payments are as follows:

6 months: \$4
1 year: \$4
1.5 years: \$104

From our earlier calculations, we know that the discount rate for the payment at the end of six months is 10.469% and that the discount rate for the payment at the end of one year is 10.536%. We also know that the bond's price, \$96, must equal the present value of all the payments received by the bondholder. Suppose the 1.5-year zero rate is denoted by R. It follows that

$$4e^{-0.10469\times 0.5} + 4e^{-0.10536\times 1.0} + 104e^{-R\times 1.5} = 96$$

Table 4.3 Data for bootstrap method

Bond principal (\$)	*Time to maturity (years)*	*Annual coupon* (\$)*	*Bond price (\$)*
100	0.25	0	97.5
100	0.50	0	94.9
100	1.00	0	90.0
100	1.50	8	96.0
100	2.00	12	101.6

* Half the stated coupon is assumed to be paid every six months.

Table 4.4 Continuously compounded zero rates determined from data in Table 4.3

Maturity (years)	*Zero rate (%) (cont. comp.)*
0.25	10.127
0.50	10.469
1.00	10.536
1.50	10.681
2.00	10.808

This reduces to

$$e^{-1.5R} = 0.85196$$

or

$$R = -\frac{\ln(0.85196)}{1.5} = 0.10681$$

The 1.5-year zero rate is therefore 10.681%. This is the only zero rate that is consistent with the six-month rate, one-year rate, and the data in Table 4.3.

The two-year zero rate can be calculated similarly to the six-month, one-year, and 1.5-year zero rates, together with the information on the last bond in Table 4.3. If R is the two-year zero rate, then

$$6e^{-0.10469\times 0.5} + 6e^{-0.10536\times 1.0} + 6e^{-0.10681\times 1.5} + 106e^{-R\times 2.0} = 101.6$$

This gives $R = 0.10808$, or 10.808%.

The rates we have calculated are summarized in Table 4.4. A chart showing the zero rate as a function of maturity is known as the *zero curve*. A common assumption is that the zero curve is linear between the points determined using the bootstrap method. (This means that the 1.25-year zero rate is $0.5 \times 10.536 + 0.5 \times 10.681 = 10.6085\%$ in our example.) It is also usually assumed that the zero curve is horizontal prior to the first point and horizontal beyond the last point. Figure 4.1 shows the zero curve for our data using these assumptions. By using longer maturity bonds, the zero curve would be more accurately determined beyond two years.

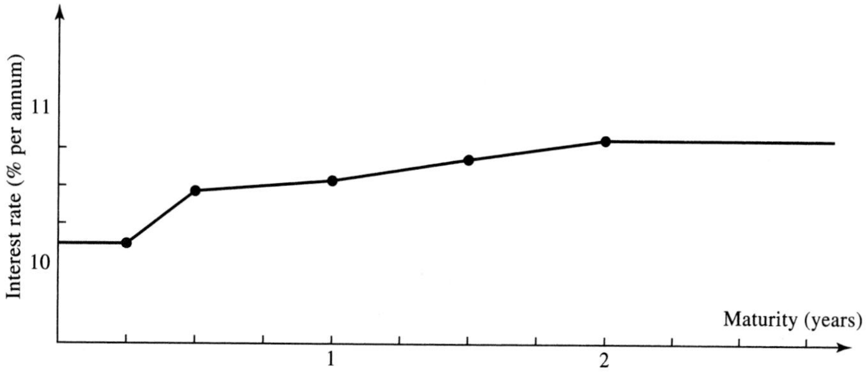

Figure 4.1 Zero rates given by the bootstrap method

In practice, we do not usually have bonds with maturities equal to exactly 1.5 years, 2 years, 2.5 years, and so on. The approach often used by analysts is to interpolate between the bond price data before it is used to calculate the zero curve. For example, if they know that a 2.3-year bond with a coupon of 6% sells for 98 and a 2.7-year bond with a coupon of 6.5% sells for 99, they might assume that a 2.5-year bond with a coupon of 6.25% would sell for 98.5.

4.6 FORWARD RATES

Forward interest rates are the rates of interest implied by current zero rates for periods of time in the future. To illustrate how they are calculated, we suppose that risk-free zero rates are as shown in the second column of Table 4.5. The rates are assumed to be continuously compounded. Thus, the 3% per annum rate for one year means that, in return for an investment of \$100 today, an amount $100e^{0.03\times 1} = \$103.05$ is received in one year; the 4% per annum rate for two years means that, in return for an investment of \$100 today, an amount $100e^{0.04\times 2} = \$108.33$ is received in two years; and so on.

The forward interest rate in Table 4.5 for year 2 is 5% per annum. This is the rate of interest that is implied by the zero rates for the period of time between the end of the first year and the end of the second year. It can be calculated from the one-year zero interest rate of 3% per annum and the two-year zero interest rate of 4% per annum. It is the rate of interest for year 2 that, when combined with 3% per annum for year 1, gives 4% overall for the two years. To show that the correct answer is 5% per annum, suppose that \$100 is invested. A rate of 3% for the first year and 5% for the second year gives

$$100e^{0.03\times 1}e^{0.05\times 1} = \$108.33$$

at the end of the second year. A rate of 4% per annum for two years gives

$$100e^{0.04\times 2}$$

which is also \$108.33. This example illustrates the general result that when interest rates are continuously compounded and rates in successive time periods are combined, the overall equivalent rate is simply the average rate during the whole period. (This is explained in the appendix to this chapter.) In our example, 3% for the first year and 5% for the second year average to 4% for the two years. The result is only approximately true when the rates are not continuously compounded.

Table 4.5 Calculation of forward rates

Year (n)	*Zero rate for an n-year investment (% per annum)*	*Forward rate for nth year (% per annum)*
1	3.0	
2	4.0	5.0
3	4.6	5.8
4	5.0	6.2
5	5.3	6.5

Business Snapshot 4.2 Orange County's yield curve plays

Suppose a large investor can borrow or lend at the rates in Table 4.5 and thinks that one-year interest rates will not change much over the next five years. The investor can borrow one-year funds and invest for five years. The one-year borrowings can be rolled over for further one-year periods at the end of the first, second, third, and fourth years. If interest rates do stay about the same, this strategy will yield a profit of about 2.3% per year because interest will be received at 5.3% and paid at 3%. This type of trading strategy is known as a *yield curve play*. The investor is speculating that rates in the future will be quite different from the forward rates observed in the market today. (In our example forward rates observed in the market today for future one-year periods are 5%, 5.8%, 6.2%, and 6.5%.)

Robert Citron, the Treasurer at Orange County, used yield curve plays similar to the one we have just described very successfully in 1992 and 1993. The profit from Mr. Citron's trades became an important contributor to Orange County's budget and he was re-elected. (No one listened to his opponent in the election, who said his trading strategy was too risky.)

In 1994 Mr. Citron expanded his yield curve plays. He invested heavily in *inverse floaters*. These pay a rate of interest equal to a fixed rate of interest minus a floating rate. He also leveraged his position by borrowing in the repo market. If short-term interest rates had remained the same or declined he would have continued to do well. As it happened, interest rates rose sharply during 1994. On December 1, 1994, Orange County announced that its investment portfolio had lost $1.5 billion and several days later it filed for bankruptcy protection.

The forward rate for year 3 is the rate of interest that is implied by a 4% per annum two-year zero rate and a 4.6% per annum three-year zero rate. It is 5.8% per annum. The reason is that an investment for two years at 4% per annum combined with an investment for one year at 5.8% per annum gives an overall average return for the three years of 4.6% per annum. The other forward rates can be calculated similarly and are shown in the third column of the table. In general, if R_1 and R_2 are the zero rates for maturities T_1 and T_2, respectively, and R_F is the forward interest rate for the period of time between T_1 and T_2:

$$R_F = \frac{R_2 T_2 - R_1 T_1}{T_2 - T_1} \qquad \textbf{(4.5)}$$

To illustrate this formula, consider the calculation of the year 4 forward rate from the data in Table 4.5: $T_1 = 3$, $T_2 = 4$, $R_1 = 0.046$, and $R_2 = 0.05$, and the formula gives $R_F = 0.062$.

Equation (4.5) can be written

$$R_F = R_2 + (R_2 - R_1)\frac{T_1}{T_2 - T_1} \qquad \textbf{(4.6)}$$

This shows that if the zero curve is upward sloping between T_1 and T_2, so that $R_2 > R_1$, then $R_F > R_2$ (i.e., the forward rate for a period of time ending at T_2 is greater than the T_2 zero rate). Similarly, if the zero curve is downward sloping, with $R_2 < R_1$, then $R_F < R_2$ (i.e., the forward rate for a period of time ending at T_2 is less than the T_2 zero rate).

By borrowing and lending at zero rates, a large financial institution can lock in forward rates. Suppose zero rates are as in Table 4.5. It can borrow \$100 at 3% for one year and invest the money at 4% for two years, the result is a cash outflow of $100e^{0.03\times 1} = \$103.05$ at the end of year 1 and an inflow of $100e^{0.04\times 2} = \$108.33$ at the end of year 2. Because $108.33 = 103.05e^{0.05}$, a return equal to the forward rate (5%) is earned on \$103.05 during the second year. Alternatively it can borrow \$100 for four years at 5% and invest it for three years at 4.6%. The result is a cash inflow of $100e^{0.046\times 3} = \$114.80$ at the end of the third year and a cash outflow of $100e^{0.05\times 4} = \$122.14$ at the end of the fourth year. Because $122.14 = 114.80e^{0.062}$, money is being borrowed for the fourth year at the forward rate of 6.2%.

If a large investor thinks that rates in the future will be different from today's forward rates there are many trading strategies that the investor will find attractive (see Business Snapshot 4.2). One of these involves entering into a contract known as a *forward rate agreement*. We will now discuss how this contract works and how it is valued.

4.7 FORWARD RATE AGREEMENTS

A forward rate agreement (FRA) is an over-the-counter agreement designed to ensure that a certain interest rate will apply to either borrowing or lending a certain principal during a specified future period of time. The usual assumption underlying the contract is that the borrowing or lending would normally be done at LIBOR. For the purposes of the analysis in this section, we assume that LIBOR is the proxy used for the risk-free rate. (In Chapter 7 we explain what happens when another proxy is used.)

Consider a forward rate agreement where company X is agreeing to lend money at LIBOR to company Y for the period of time between T_1 and T_2. Define:

R_K: The rate of interest agreed to in the FRA

R_F: The forward LIBOR interest rate for the period between times T_1 and T_2, calculated today[2]

R_M: The actual LIBOR interest rate observed in the market at time T_1 for the period between times T_1 and T_2

L: The principal underlying the contract.

We will depart from our usual assumption of continuous compounding and assume that the rates R_K, R_F, and R_M are all measured with a compounding frequency reflecting the length of the period they apply to. This means that, if $T_2 - T_1 = 0.5$, they are expressed with semiannual compounding; if $T_2 - T_1 = 0.25$, they are expressed with quarterly compounding; and so on. (This assumption corresponds to the usual market practices for FRAs.)

Normally company X would earn R_M from the LIBOR loan. The FRA means that it will earn R_K. The extra interest rate (which may be negative) that it earns as a result of entering into the FRA is $R_K - R_M$. The interest rate is set at time T_1 and paid at time T_2. The extra interest rate therefore leads to a cash flow to company X at time T_2 of

$$L(R_K - R_M)(T_2 - T_1) \tag{4.7}$$

[2] LIBOR forward rates are calculated as described in Section 4.6 from the LIBOR/swap zero curve. The latter is determined in the way described in Section 7.8.

Example 4.2 Cash flows from an FRA

Suppose that a company enters into an FRA that is designed to ensure it will receive a fixed rate of 4% on a principal of $100 million for a three-month period starting in three years. If three-month LIBOR proves to be 4.5% for the three-month period the cash flow to the lender will be

$$100{,}000{,}000 \times (0.040 - 0.045) \times 0.25 = -\$125{,}000$$

at the 3.25-year point. This is equivalent to a cash flow of

$$-\frac{125{,}000}{1 + 0.045 \times 0.25} = -\$123{,}609$$

at the three-year point. The cash flow to the party on the opposite side of the transaction will be +$125,000 at the 3.25 point or +$123,609 at the three-year point. (All interest rates in this example are expressed with quarterly compounding.)

Similarly there is a cash flow to company Y at time T_2 of

$$L(R_M - R_K)(T_2 - T_1) \tag{4.8}$$

From equations (4.7) and (4.8) we see that there is another interpretation of the FRA. It is an agreement where company X will receive interest on the principal between T_1 and T_2 at the fixed rate of R_K and pay interest at the realized LIBOR rate of R_M. Company Y will pay interest on the principal between T_1 and T_2 at the fixed rate of R_K and receive interest at R_M. This interpretation will be important when we come to consider swaps in Chapter 7.

Usually FRAs are settled at time T_1 rather than T_2. The payoff must then be discounted from time T_2 to T_1. For company X the payoff at time T_1 is

$$\frac{L(R_K - R_M)(T_2 - T_1)}{1 + R_M(T_2 - T_1)}$$

and for company Y the payoff at time T_1 is

$$\frac{L(R_M - R_K)(T_2 - T_1)}{1 + R_M(T_2 - T_1)}$$

Example 4.2 illustrates the calculation of cash flows from an FRA. In this case, LIBOR is paid and 4% is received for a three-month period.

Valuation

To value an FRA, we first note that it is always worth zero when $R_K = R_F$.[3] This is because, as noted in Section 4.6, a large financial institution can at no cost lock in the forward rate for a future time period. For example, it can ensure that it earns the forward rate for the time period between years 2 and 3 by borrowing a certain amount of money for two years and investing it for three years. Similarly, it can ensure that it

[3] It is usually the case that R_K is set equal to R_F when the FRA is first initiated.

Example 4.3 Valuation of an FRA

Suppose that zero and forward rates are as in Table 4.5. Consider an FRA where a company will receive a rate of 6%, measured with annual compounding, on a principal of \$100 million between the end of year 1 and the end of year 2. In this case, the forward rate is 5% with continuous compounding or 5.127% with annual compounding. From equation (4.9), it follows that the value of the FRA is

$$100{,}000{,}000 \times (0.06 - 0.05127)e^{-0.04\times 2} = \$805{,}800$$

pays the forward rate for the time period between years 2 and 3 by borrowing a certain amount of money three years and investing it for two years.

Compare two FRAs. The first promises that the LIBOR forward rate R_F will be received on a principal of L between times T_1 and T_2; the second promises that R_K will be received on the same principal between the same two dates. The two contracts are the same except for the interest payments received at time T_2. The excess of the value of the second contract over the first is, therefore, the present value of the difference between these interest payment, or

$$L(R_K - R_F)(T_2 - T_1)e^{-R_2T_2}$$

where R_2 is the continuously compounded riskless zero rate for a maturity T_2.[4] Because the value of the first FRA (where R_F is received) is zero, the value of the second FRA (where R_K is received) is

$$V_{\text{FRA}} = L(R_K - R_F)(T_2 - T_1)e^{-R_2T_2} \tag{4.9}$$

Similarly, the value of an FRA which promises that an interest rate of R_K will be paid on borrowings of L between T_1 and T_2 is

$$V_{\text{FRA}} = L(R_F - R_K)(T_2 - T_1)e^{-R_2T_2} \tag{4.10}$$

By comparing equations (4.7) and (4.9) (or equations (4.8) and (4.10)), we see that an FRA can be valued if we:

1. Calculate the payoff on the assumption that forward rates are realized (that is, on the assumption that $R_M = R_F$)
2. Discount this payoff at the risk-free rate

We will use this result when we come to value swaps (which are porfolios of FRAs) in Chapter 7. Example 4.3 illustrates the valuation of FRAs.

4.8 THEORIES OF THE TERM STRUCTURE OF INTEREST RATES

It is natural to ask what determines the shape of the zero curve. Why is it sometimes downward sloping, sometimes upward sloping, and sometimes partly upward sloping

[4] Note that R_K, R_M, and R_F are expressed with a compounding frequency corresponding to $T_2 - T_1$, whereas R_2 is expressed with continuous compounding.

and partly downward sloping? A number of different theories have been proposed. The simplest is *expectations theory*, which conjectures that long-term interest rates should reflect expected future short-term interest rates. More precisely, it argues that a forward interest rate corresponding to a certain future period is equal to the expected future zero interest rate for that period. Another idea, *market segmentation theory*, conjectures that there need be no relationship between short-, medium-, and long-term interest rates. Under the theory, a major investor such as a large pension fund invests in bonds of a certain maturity and does not readily switch from one maturity to another. The short-term interest rate is determined by supply and demand in the short-term bond market; the medium-term interest rate is determined by supply and demand in the medium-term bond market; and so on.

The theory that is most appealing is *liquidity preference theory*. The basic assumption underlying the theory is that investors prefer to preserve their liquidity and invest funds for short periods of time. Borrowers, on the other hand, usually prefer to borrow at fixed rates for long periods of time. This leads to a situation in which forward rates are greater than expected future zero rates. The theory is also consistent with the empirical result that yield curves tend to be upward sloping more often than they are downward sloping.

The Management of Net Interest Income

To understand liquidity preference theory, it is useful to consider the interest rate risk faced by banks when they take deposits and make loans. The *net interest income* of the bank is the excess of the interest received over the interest paid and needs to be carefully managed.

Consider a simple situation where a bank offers consumers a one-year and a five-year deposit rate as well as a one-year and five-year mortgage rate. The rates are shown in Table 4.6. We make the simplifying assumption that the expected one-year interest rate for future time periods to equal the one-year rates prevailing in the market today. Loosely speaking this means that the market considers interest rate increases to be just as likely as interest rate decreases. As a result, the rates in Table 4.6 are "fair" in that they reflect the market's expectations (i.e., they correspond to expectations theory). Investing money for one year and reinvesting for four further one-year periods give the same expected overall return as a single five-year investment. Similarly, borrowing money for one year and refinancing each year for the next four years leads to the same expected financing costs as a single five-year loan.

Suppose you have money to deposit and agree with the prevailing view that interest rate increases are just as likely as interest rate decreases. Would you choose to deposit your money for one year at 3% per annum or for five years at 3% per annum? The chances are that you would choose one year because this gives you more financial flexibility. It ties up your funds for a shorter period of time.

Table 4.6 Example of rates offered by a bank to its customers

Maturity (years)	*Deposit rate*	*Mortgage rate*
1	3%	6%
5	3%	6%

Table 4.7 Five-year rates are increased in an attempt to match maturities of assets and liabilities

Maturity (years)	*Deposit rate*	*Mortgage rate*
1	3%	6%
5	4%	7%

Now suppose that you want a mortgage. Again you agree with the prevailing view that interest rate increases are just as likely as interest rate decreases. Would you choose a one-year mortgage at 6% or a five-year mortgage at 6%? The chances are that you would choose a five-year mortgage because it fixes your borrowing rate for the next five years and subjects you to less refinancing risk.

When the bank posts the rates shown in Table 4.6, it is likely to find that the majority of its customers opt for one-year deposits and five-year mortgages. This creates an asset/liability mismatch for the bank and subjects it to risks. There is no problem if interest rates fall. The bank will find itself financing the five-year 6% loans with deposits that cost less than 3% in the future and net interest income will increase. However, if rates rise, the deposits that are financing these 6% loans will cost more than 3% in the future and net interest income will decline. A 3% rise in interest rates would reduce the net interest income to zero.

It is the job of the asset/liability management group to ensure that the maturities of the assets on which interest is earned and the maturities of the liabilities on which interest is paid are matched. One way it can do this is by increasing the five-year rate on both deposits and mortgages. For example, it could move to the situation in Table 4.7 where the five-year deposit rate is 4% and the five-year mortgage rate 7%. This would make five-year deposits relatively more attractive and one-year mortgages relatively more attractive. Some customers who chose one-year deposits when the rates were as in Table 4.6 will switch to five-year deposits in the Table 4.7 situation. Some customers who chose five-year mortgages when the rates were as in Table 4.6 will choose one-year mortgages. This may lead to the maturities of assets and liabilities being matched. If there is still an imbalance with depositors tending to choose a one-year maturity and borrowers a five-year maturity, five-year deposit and mortgage rates could be increased even further. Eventually the imbalance will disappear.

The net result of all banks behaving in the way we have just described is liquidity preference theory. Long-term rates tend to be higher than those that would be predicted by expected future short-term rates. The yield curve is upward sloping most of the time. It is downward sloping only when the market expects a really steep decline in short-term rates.

Many banks now have sophisticated systems for monitoring the decisions being made by customers so that, when they detect small differences between the maturities of the assets and liabilities being chosen by customers they can fine tune the rates they offer. Sometimes derivatives such as interest rate swaps (which will be discussed in Chapter 7) are also used to manage their exposure. The result of all this is that net interest income is usually very stable. This has not always been the case. In the United States, the failure of Savings and Loan companies in the 1980s and the failure of Continental Illinois in 1984 were to a large extent a result of the fact that they did not match the maturities of assets and liabilities. Both failures proved very expensive for U.S. taxpayers.

Business Snapshot 4.3 Liquidity and the 2007–2009 Financial Crisis

During the credit crisis that started in July 2007 there was a "flight to quality," where financial institutions and investors looked for safe investments and were less inclined than before to take credit risks. Financial institutions that relied on short-term funding experienced liquidity problems. One example is Northern Rock in the United Kingdom, which chose to finance much of its mortgage portfolio with wholesale deposits, some lasting only three months. Starting in September 2007, the depositors became nervous and refused to roll over the funding they were providing to Northern Rock, i.e., at the end of a three-month period they would refuse to deposit their funds for a further three-month period. As a result, Northern Rock was unable to finance its assets. It was taken over by the UK government in early 2008. In the U.S., financial institutions such as Bear Stearns and Lehman Brothers experienced similar liquidity problems because they had chosen to fund part of their operations with short-term funds.

Liquidity

In addition to creating problems in the way that has been described, a portfolio where maturities are mismatched can lead to liquidity problems. Consider a financial institution that funds five-year fixed rate loans with wholesale deposits that last only three months. It might recognize its exposure to rising interest rates and hedge its interest rate risk. (One way of doing this is by using interest rate swaps, as mentioned earlier.) However, it still has a liquidity risk. Wholesale depositors may, for some reason, lose confidence in the financial institution and refuse to continue to provide the financial institution with short-term funding. The financial institution, even if it has adequate equity capital, will then experience a severe liquidity problem that could lead to its downfall. As described in Business Snapshot 4.3, these types of liquidity problems were the root cause of some of the failures of financial institutions during the crisis that started in 2007.

SUMMARY

Two important interest rates for derivatives traders are Treasury rates and LIBOR rates. Treasury rates are the rates paid by a government on borrowings in its own currency. LIBOR rates are short-term lending rates offered by banks in the interbank market.

The compounding frequency used for an interest rate defines the units in which it is measured. The difference between an annually compounded rate and a quarterly compounded rate is analogous to the difference between a distance measured in miles and a distance measured in kilometers. Traders frequently use continuous compounding when analyzing the value of options and more complex derivatives.

Many different types of interest rate are quoted in financial markets and calculated by analysts. The n-year zero rate or n-year spot rate is the rate applicable to an investment lasting for n years when all of the return is realized at the end. The par yield on a bond of a certain maturity is the coupon rate that causes the bond to sell for its par value. Forward rates are the rates applicable to future periods of time implied by today's zero rates.

The method most commonly used to calculate zero rates is known as the bootstrap method. It involves starting with short-term instruments and moving progressively to longer-term instruments, making sure that the zero rates calculated at each stage are consistent with the prices of the instruments. It is used daily by trading desks to calculate a Treasury zero-rate curve.

A forward rate agreement (FRA) is an over-the-counter agreement that an interest rate (usually LIBOR) will be exchanged for a specified interest rate during a specified future period of time. An FRA can be valued by assuming that forward rates are realized and discounting the resulting payoff.

Liquidity preference theory can be used to explain the interest rate term structures that are observed in practice. The theory argues that most individuals and most companies like to borrow long and lend short. To match the maturities of borrowers and lenders, it is necessary for financial intermediaries to raise long-term rates so that forward interest rates are higher than expected future spot interest rates.

FURTHER READING

Allen, S. L., and A. D. Kleinstein. *Valuing Fixed-Income Investments and Derivative Securities: Cash Flow Analysis and Calculation.* New York: New York Institute of Finance, 1991.

Fabozzi, F. J. *Fixed-Income Mathematics: Analytical and Statistical Techniques*, 4th edn. New York: McGraw-Hill, 2006.

Grinblatt, M., and F. A. Longstaff. "Financial Innovation and the Role of Derivatives Securities: An Empirical Analysis of the Treasury Strips Program," *Journal of Finance*, 55, 3 (2000): 1415–36.

Jorion, P. *Big Bets Gone Bad: Derivatives and Bankruptcy in Orange County.* New York: Academic Press, 1995.

Stigum, M., and F. L. Robinson. *Money Markets and Bond Calculations.* Chicago: Irwin, 1996.

Quiz (Answers at End of Book)

4.1. A bank quotes an interest rate of 14% per annum with quarterly compounding. What is the equivalent rate with (a) continuous compounding and (b) annual compounding?

4.2. What is meant by LIBOR and LIBID. Which is higher?

4.3. The six-month and one-year zero rates are both 10% per annum. For a bond that has a life of 18 months and pays a coupon of 8% per annum semiannually (with a coupon payment having just been made), the yield is 10.4% per annum. What is the bond's price? What is the 18-month zero rate? All rates are quoted with semiannual compounding.

4.4. An investor receives $1,100 in one year in return for an investment of $1,000 now. Calculate the percentage return per annum with (a) annual compounding, (b) semiannual compounding, (c) monthly compounding, and (d) continuous compounding.

4.5. Suppose that zero interest rates with continuous compounding are as follows:

Maturity (months)	*Rate (% per annum)*
3	8.0
6	8.2
9	8.4
12	8.5
15	8.6
18	8.7

Calculate forward interest rates for the second, third, fourth, fifth, and sixth quarters.

4.6. Assuming that zero rates are as in Problem 4.5, what is the value of an FRA that enables the holder to earn 9.5% for a three-month period starting in one year on a principal of $1,000,000? The interest rate is expressed with quarterly compounding.

4.7. The term structure of interest rates is upward sloping. Put the following in order of magnitude:
a. The five-year zero rate
b. The yield on a five-year coupon-bearing bond
c. The forward rate corresponding to the period between 4.75 and 5 years in the future

What is the answer to this question when the term structure of interest rates is downward sloping?

Practice Questions (Answers in Solutions Manual/Study Guide)

4.8. The cash prices of six-month and one-year Treasury bills are 94.0 and 89.0. A 1.5-year bond that will pay coupons of $4 every six months currently sells for $94.84. A two-year bond that will pay coupons of $5 every six months currently sells for $97.12. Calculate the six-month, one-year, 1.5-year, and two-year zero rates.

4.9. What rate of interest with continuous compounding is equivalent to 15% per annum with monthly compounding?

4.10. A deposit account pays 12% per annum with continuous compounding, but interest is actually paid quarterly. How much interest will be paid each quarter on a $10,000 deposit?

4.11. Suppose that 6-month, 12-month, 18-month, 24-month, and 30-month zero rates continuously compounded are 4%, 4.2%, 4.4%, 4.6%, and 4.8% per annum, respectively. Estimate the cash price of a bond with a face value of 100 that will mature in 30 months pays a coupon of 4% per annum semiannually.

4.12. A three-year bond provides a coupon of 8% semiannually and has a cash price of 104. What is the bond's yield?

4.13. Suppose that the 6-month, 12-month, 18-month, and 24-month zero rates are 5%, 6%, 6.5%, and 7%, respectively. What is the two-year par yield?

4.14. Suppose that zero interest rates with continuous compounding are as follows:

Maturity (years)	*Rate (% per annum)*
1	2.0
2	3.0
3	3.7
4	4.2
5	4.5

Calculate forward interest rates for the second, third, fourth, and fifth years.

4.15. Use the rates in Problem 4.14 to value an FRA where you will pay 5% (compounded annually) for the third year on $1 million.

4.16. A 10-year 8% coupon bond currently sells for $90. A 10-year 4% coupon bond currently sells for $80. What is the 10-year zero rate? (Hint: Consider taking a long position in two of the 4% coupon bonds and a short position in one of the 8% coupon bonds.)

4.17. Explain carefully why liquidity preference theory is consistent with the observation that the term structure of interest rates tends to be upward sloping more often than it is downward sloping.

4.18. "When the zero curve is upward sloping, the zero rate for a particular maturity is greater than the par yield for that maturity. When the zero curve is downward sloping, the reverse is true." Explain why this is so.

4.19. Why are U.S. Treasury rates significantly lower than other rates that are close to risk-free?

4.20. Why does a loan in the repo market involve very little credit risk?

4.21. Explain why an FRA is equivalent to the exchange of a floating rate of interest for a fixed rate of interest.

4.22. Explain how a repo agreement works and why it involves very little risk for the lender.

Further Questions

4.23. When compounded annually an interest rate is 11%. What is the rate when expressed with (a) semiannual compounding, (b) quarterly compounding, (c) monthly compounding, (d) weekly compounding, and (e) daily compounding.

4.24. The following table gives Treasury zero rates and cash flows on a Treasury bond:

Maturity (years)	*Zero rate*	*Coupon payment*	*Principal*
0.5	2.0%	$20	
1.0	2.3%	$20	
1.5	2.7%	$20	
2.0	3.2%	$20	$1000

Zero rates are continuously compounded.

(a) What is the bond's theoretical price?

(b) What is the bond's yield?

4.25. A five-year bond provides a coupon of 5% per annum payable semiannually. Its price is 104. What is the bond's yield? You may find Excel's Solver useful.

4.26. Suppose that LIBOR rates for maturities of one, two, three, four, five, and six months are 2.6%, 2.9%, 3.1%, 3.2%, 3.25%, and 3.3% with continuous compounding. What are the forward rates for future one-month periods?

4.27. A bank can borrow or lend at LIBOR. The two-month LIBOR rate is 0.28% per annum with continuous compounding. Assuming that interest rates cannot be negative, what is the arbitrage opportunity if the three-month LIBOR rate is 0.1% per year with continuous compounding. How low can the three-month LIBOR rate become without an arbitrage opportunity being created?

4.28. A bank can borrow or lend at LIBOR. Suppose that the six-month rate is 5% and the nine-month rate is 6%. The rate that can be locked in for the period between six months and nine months using an FRA is 7%. What arbitrage opportunities are open to the bank? All rates are continuously compounded.

4.29. An interest rate is quoted as 5% per annum with semiannual compounding. What is the equivalent rate with (a) annual compounding, (b) monthly compounding, and (c) continuous compounding.

4.30. The 6-month, 12-month. 18-month, and 24-month zero rates are 4%, 4.5%, 4.75%, and 5% with semiannual compounding.

(a) What are the rates with continuous compounding?

(b) What is the forward rate for the six-month period beginning in 18 months?

(c) What is the value of an FRA that promises to pay you 6% (compounded semiannually) on a principal of $1 million for the six-month period starting in 18 months?

4.31. What is the two-year par yield when the zero rates are as in Problem 4.30? What is the yield on a two-year bond that pays a coupon equal to the par yield?

4.32. The following table gives the prices of bonds:

Bond principal ($)	*Time to maturity (years)*	*Annual coupon* ($)*	*Bond price ($)*
100	0.50	0.0	98
100	1.00	0.0	95
100	1.50	6.2	101
100	2.00	8.0	104

* Half the stated coupon is assumed to be paid every six months.

(a) Calculate zero rates for maturities of 6 months, 12 months, 18 months, and 24 months.

(b) What are the forward rates for the periods: 6 months to 12 months, 12 months to 18 months, 18 months to 24 months?

(c) What are the 6-month, 12-month, 18-month, and 24-month par yields for bonds that provide semiannual coupon payments?

(d) Estimate the price and yield of a two-year bond providing a semiannual coupon of 7% per annum.

APPENDIX

Exponential and Logarithmic Functions

The exponential function and the natural logarithm function are widely used in mathematics and in formulas that are encountered in the derivatives business. Here we give a quick review of their properties. The exponential function is closely related to the mathematical constant e. This constant can be defined as an infinite series:

$$e = 1 + \frac{1}{1!} + \frac{1}{2!} + \frac{1}{3!} + \frac{1}{4!} + \cdots$$

where $n! = n \times (n-1) \times (n-2) \times \cdots \times 3 \times 2 \times 1$. It can be calculated to any desired accuracy by evaluating enough terms in the series. Using the first four terms, we get

$$e = 1 + 1 + \frac{1}{2} + \frac{1}{6} = 2.66667$$

Using the first six terms, we get

$$e = 1 + 1 + \frac{1}{2} + \frac{1}{6} + \frac{1}{24} + \frac{1}{120} = 2.71667$$

Using the first ten terms, we get $e = 2.71828$, which is accurate to five decimal places.

The exponential function is e^x. It is sometimes also written as $\exp(x)$. It is calculated as is 2.71828^x. For example, $e^3 = 2.71828^3 = 20.0855$. The exponential function has many interesting properties. One of these is that

$$e^R = \lim_{m \longrightarrow \infty} \left(1 + \frac{R}{m}\right)^m$$

In other words, as the value of m is increased in the expression on the right-hand side, we get closer and closer to e^R. This property of e leads directly to

$$Ae^{Rn} = \lim_{m \longrightarrow \infty} A\left(1 + \frac{R}{m}\right)^{mn}$$

and shows why equation (4.1) becomes equation (4.2) as m becomes very large.

An important property of the exponential function is

$$e^x e^y = e^{x+y}$$

(This property arises because exponents add when expressions are multiplied.) Suppose that an investor invests \$100 for four years. The rate of interest is 5% for the first two years and 7% for the last two years, with the rates expressed using continuous compounding. From equation (4.2), by the end of two years the \$100 has grown to $100e^{0.05\times 2} = \$110.52$. During the next two years, this 110.52 grows to $110.52e^{0.07\times 2} = \$127.13$. The value at the end of four years can be written as

$$100e^{0.05\times 2}e^{0.07\times 2} = 100e^{(0.05\times 2)+(0.07\times 2)} = 100e^{0.06\times 4}$$

This shows that continuously compounded rates of 5% for two years and 7% for two years average to 6% for four years. Rates measured with some other compounding frequency do not have this simplifying property.

The natural logarithm function, $\ln(x)$, is the inverse of the exponential function. If $y = e^x$, then $x = \ln(y)$. In our earlier example, we found that $e^3 = 20.0855$. It follows that $\ln 20.0855 = 3$. Important properties of this function are:

$$\ln(XY) = \ln(X) + \ln(Y) \quad \text{and} \quad \ln(X/Y) = \ln(X) - \ln(Y).$$

For example, $\ln(2) = 0.69$, $\ln(3) = 1.10$, and $\ln(6) = 0.69 + 1.10 = 1.79$.

CHAPTER 5

Determination of Forward and Futures Prices

In this chapter we examine how forward prices and futures prices are related to the spot price of the underlying asset. Forward contracts are easier to analyze than futures contracts because there is no daily settlement—only a single payment at maturity. We therefore start this chapter by considering the relationship between forward prices and spot prices. Luckily it can be shown that the forward price and futures price of an asset are usually very close when the maturities of the two contracts are the same. This is convenient because it means that results obtained for forwards are usually also true for futures.

In the first part of the chapter we derive some important general results on the relationship between forward prices and spot prices. We then use the results to examine the relationship between forward or futures prices and spot prices for contracts on stock indices, foreign exchange, and commodities. We will consider interest rate futures contracts in the next chapter.

5.1 INVESTMENT ASSETS vs. CONSUMPTION ASSETS

When considering forward and futures contracts, it is important to distinguish between investment assets and consumption assets. An *investment asset* is an asset that is held for investment purposes by significant numbers of investors. Stocks and bonds are clearly investment assets. Gold and silver are also examples of investment assets. Note that investment assets do not have to be held exclusively for investment. (Silver, for example, has a number of industrial uses.) However, they do have to satisfy the requirement that they are held by significant numbers of investors solely for investment. A *consumption asset* is an asset that is held primarily for consumption and not usually for investment purposes. Examples of consumption assets are commodities such as copper, oil, and pork bellies.

As we will see later in this chapter, we can use arbitrage arguments to determine the forward and futures prices of an investment asset from its spot price and other observable market variables. We cannot do this for consumption assets.

5.2 SHORT SELLING

Some of the arbitrage strategies presented in this chapter involve *short selling*. This trade, usually simply referred to as "shorting," involves selling an asset that is not owned. It is something that is possible for some, but not all, investment assets. We will illustrate how it works by considering a short sale of shares of a stock.

Suppose an investor instructs a broker to short 500 shares of company X. The broker will carry out the instructions by borrowing the shares from someone who owns them and selling them in the market in the usual way. At some later stage, the investor will close out the position by purchasing 500 shares of company X in the market. These shares are then used to replace the shares that were borrowed, so that the short position is closed out. The investor takes a profit if the stock price has declined and a loss if it has risen. If at any time while the contract is open the broker has to return the borrowed shares and there are no other shares that can be borrowed, the investor is forced to close out the position, even if not ready to do so. Sometimes a fee is charged for lending shares or other securities to the party doing the shorting.

An investor with a short position must pay to the broker any income, such as dividends or interest, that would normally be received on the securities that have been shorted. The broker will transfer this to the account of the client from whom the securities have been borrowed. Consider the position of an investor who shorts 500 shares in April when the price per share is \$120 and closes out the position by buying them back in July when the price per share is \$100. Suppose that a dividend of \$1 per share is paid in May. The investor receives $500 \times \$120 = \$60{,}000$ in April when the short position is initiated. The dividend leads to a payment by the investor of $500 \times \$1 = \$500$ in May. The investor also pays $500 \times \$100 = \$50{,}000$ for shares when the position is closed out in July. The net gain is, therefore,

$$\$60{,}000 - \$500 - \$50{,}000 = \$9{,}500$$

assuming no fee for borrowing the shares. Table 5.1 illustrates this example and shows that the cash flows from the short sale are the mirror image of the cash flows from purchasing the shares in April and selling them in July (again assuming no borrowing fee).

Table 5.1 Cash flows from short sale and purchase of shares

Purchase of shares	
April: Purchase 500 shares for \$120	−\$60,000
May: Receive dividend	+\$500
July: Sell 500 shares for \$100 per share	+\$50,000
	Net profit = −\$9,500
Short sale of shares	
April: Borrow 500 shares and sell them for \$120	+\$60,000
May: Pay dividend	−\$500
July: Buy 500 shares for \$100 per share	−\$50,000
Replace borrowed shares to close short position	
	Net profit = +\$9,500

The investor is required to maintain a *margin account* with the broker. The margin account consists of cash or marketable securities deposited by the investor with the broker to guarantee that the investor will not walk away from the short position if the share price increases. It is similar to the margin account discussed in Chapter 2 for futures contracts. An initial margin is required and if there are adverse movements (i.e., increases) in the price of the asset that is being shorted, additional margin may be required. If the additional margin is not provided, the short position is closed out. The margin account should not represent a cost to the investor. This is because interest is usually paid on the balance in margin accounts and, if the interest rate offered is unacceptable, marketable securities such as Treasury bills can be used to meet margin requirements. The proceeds of the sale of the asset belong to the investor and normally form part of the initial margin.

From time to time regulations are changed on short selling. In 1938 the uptick rule was introduced. This allowed shares to be shorted on an "uptick"—that is when the most recent movement in the share price was an increase. The SEC abolished the uptick rule in July 2007, but introduced an "alternative uptick" rule in February 2010. Under this rule, when the price of a stock has decreased by more than 10% in one day, there are restrictions on short selling for that day and the next day. These restrictions are that the stock can be shorted only at a price that is higher than the best current bid price. Occasionally there are temporary bans on short selling. This happened in a number of countries in 2008 because it was considered that short selling contributed to the high market volatility that was being experienced.

5.3 ASSUMPTIONS AND NOTATION

In this chapter we will assume that the following are all true for some market participants:

1. They are subject to no transactions costs when they trade.
2. They are subject to the same tax rate on all net trading profits.
3. They can borrow money at the same risk-free rate of interest as they can lend money.
4. They take advantage of arbitrage opportunities as they occur.

Note that we do not require these assumptions to be true for all market participants. All that we require is that they be true—or at least approximately true—for a few key market participants such as large derivatives dealers. It is the trading activities of these key market participants and their eagerness to take advantage of arbitrage opportunities as they occur that determine the relationship between forward and spot prices.

The following notation will be used throughout this chapter:

T: Time until delivery date in a forward or futures contract (in years)

S_0: Price of the asset underlying the forward or futures contract today

F_0: Forward or futures price today

r: Zero-coupon risk-free rate of interest per annum, expressed with continuous compounding, for an investment maturing at the delivery date (i.e., in T years)

The risk-free rate, r, is the rate at which money is borrowed or lent when there is no credit risk so that the money is certain to be repaid. As discussed in Chapter 4, financial institutions and other participants in derivatives markets have traditionally used LIBOR as a proxy for the risk-free rate, but events during the credit crisis starting in 2007 have caused them to look for other alternatives.

5.4 FORWARD PRICE FOR AN INVESTMENT ASSET

The easiest forward contract to value is one written on an investment asset that provides the holder with no income. Non-dividend-paying stocks and zero-coupon bonds are examples of such investment assets.

Consider a long forward contract to purchase a non-dividend-paying stock in three months.[1] Assume the current stock price is \$40 and the three-month risk-free interest rate is 5% per annum.

Suppose first that the forward price is relatively high at \$43. An arbitrageur can borrow \$40 at the risk-free interest rate of 5% per annum, buy one share, and short a forward contract to sell one share in three months. At the end of the three months, the arbitrageur delivers the share and receives \$43. The sum of money required to pay off the loan is

$$40e^{0.05\times 3/12} = \$40.50$$

By following this strategy, the arbitrageur locks in a profit of \$43.00 − \$40.50 = \$2.50 at the end of the three-month period.

Suppose next that the forward price is relatively low at \$39. An arbitrageur can short one share, invest the proceeds of the short sale at 5% per annum for three months, and take a long position in a three-month forward contract. The proceeds of the short sale grow to $40e^{0.05\times 3/12}$, or \$40.50, in three months. At the end of the three months, the

Table 5.2 Arbitrage opportunities when forward price is out of line with spot price for asset providing no income (asset price = \$40; interest rate = 5%; maturity of forward contract = 3 months)

Forward Price = \$43	***Forward Price = \$39***
Action now:	*Action now*:
Borrow \$40 at 5% for 3 months	Short 1 unit of asset to realize \$40
Buy one unit of asset	Invest \$40 at 5% for 3 months
Enter into forward contract to sell asset in 3 months for \$43	Enter into a forward contract to buy asset in 3 months for \$39
Action in 3 months:	*Action in 3 months*:
Sell asset for \$43	Buy asset for \$39
Use \$40.50 to repay loan with interest	Close short position
	Receive \$40.50 from investment
Profit realized = \$2.50	Profit realized = \$1.50

[1] Forward contracts on individual stocks do not often arise in practice. However, they form useful examples for developing our ideas. Futures on individual stocks started trading in the United States in November 2002.

arbitrageur pays \$39, takes delivery of the share under the terms of the forward contract, and uses it to close out the short position. A net gain of

$$\$40.50 - \$39.00 = \$1.50$$

is therefore made at the end of the three months. The two trading strategies we have considered are summarized in Table 5.2.

Under what circumstances do arbitrage opportunities such as those in Table 5.2 not exist? The first arbitrage works when the forward price is greater than \$40.50. The second arbitrage works when the forward price is less than \$40.50. We deduce that, for there to be no arbitrage, the forward price must be exactly \$40.50.

A Generalization

To generalize this example, we consider a forward contract on an investment asset with price S_0 that provides no income. Using our notation, T is the time to maturity, r is the risk-free rate, and F_0 is the forward price. The relationship between F_0 and S_0 is

$$F_0 = S_0 e^{rT} \qquad \textbf{(5.1)}$$

If $F_0 > S_0 e^{rT}$, arbitrageurs can buy the asset and short forward contracts on the asset. If $F_0 < S_0 e^{rT}$, they can short the asset and enter into long forward contracts on it.[2] In our example, $S_0 = 40$, $r = 0.05$, and $T = 0.25$, so that equation (5.1) gives

$$F_0 = 40e^{0.05\times 0.25} = \$40.50$$

which is in agreement with our earlier calculations. Example 5.1 provides another application of equation (5.1).

A long forward contract and a spot purchase both lead to the asset being owned at time T. The forward price is higher than the spot price because of the cost of financing the spot purchase of the asset during the life of the forward contract. This cost was overlooked by Kidder Peabody in 1994 (see Business Snapshot 5.1).

Example 5.1 Forward price of an asset providing no income

Consider a four-month forward contract to buy a zero-coupon bond that will mature one year from today. (This means that the bond will have eight months to go when the forward contract matures.) The current price of the bond is \$930. We assume that the four-month risk-free rate of interest (continuously compounded) is 6% per annum. Because zero-coupon bonds provide no income, we can use equation (5.1), with $T = 4/12$, $r = 0.06$, and $S_0 = 930$. The forward price, F_0, is given by

$$F_0 = 930e^{0.06\times 4/12} = \$948.79$$

This would be the delivery price in a contract negotiated today.

[2] For another way of seeing that equation (5.1) is correct, consider the following strategy: buy one unit of the asset and enter into a short forward contract to sell it for F_0 at time T. This costs S_0 and is certain to lead to a cash inflow of F_0 at time T. So S_0 must equal the present value of F_0; that is, $S_0 = F_0 e^{-rT}$, or equivalently $F_0 = S_0 e^{rT}$.

Business Snapshot 5.1 Kidder Peabody's embarrassing mistake

Investment banks have developed a way of creating a zero-coupon bond, called a *strip*, from a coupon-bearing Treasury bond by selling each of the cash flows underlying the coupon-bearing bond as a separate security. Joseph Jett, a trader working for Kidder Peabody, had a relatively simple trading strategy. He would buy strips and sell them in the forward market. As equation (5.1) shows, the forward price of a security providing no income is always higher than the spot price. Suppose, for example, that the three-month interest rate is 4% per annum and the spot price of a strip is \$70. The three-month forward price of the strip is $70e^{0.04\times 3/12} = \$70.70$.

Kidder Peabody's computer system reported a profit on each of Jett's trades equal to the excess of the forward price over the spot price (\$0.70 in our example). In fact this profit was nothing more than the cost of financing the purchase of the strip. But, by rolling his contracts forward, Jett was able to prevent this cost from accruing to him.

The result was that the system reported a profit of \$100 million on Jett's trading (and Jett received a big bonus) when in fact there was a loss in the region of \$350 million. This shows that even large financial institutions can get relatively simple things wrong!

What If Short Sales Are Not Possible?

Short sales are not possible for all investment assets. As it happens, this does not matter. To derive equation (5.1), we do not need to be able to short the asset. All that we require is that there be a significant number of people who hold the asset purely for investment (and by definition this is always true of an investment asset). If the forward price is too low, they will find it attractive to sell the asset and take a long position in a forward contract.

Suppose the underlying investment asset gives rise to no storage costs or income. If $F_0 > S_0e^{rT}$, an investor can adopt the following strategy:

1. Borrow S_0 dollars at an interest rate r for T years.
2. Buy one unit of the asset.
3. Short a forward contract on one unit of the asset.

At time T, the asset is sold for F_0. An amount S_0e^{rT} is required to repay the loan at this time and the investor makes a profit of $F_0 - S_0e^{rT}$.

Suppose next that $F_0 < S_0e^{rT}$. Then an investor who owns the asset can:

1. Sell the asset for S_0.
2. Invest the proceeds at interest rate r for time T.
3. Take a long position in a forward contract on the asset.

At time T, the cash invested has grown to S_0e^{rT}. The asset is repurchased for F_0 and the investor makes a profit of $S_0e^{rT} - F_0$ relative to the position the investor would have been in if the asset had been kept.

As in the non-dividend-paying stock example considered earlier, we can expect the forward price to adjust so that neither of the two arbitrage opportunities we have considered exists. This means that the relationship in equation (5.1) must hold.

5.5 KNOWN INCOME

In this section we consider a forward contract on an investment asset that will provide a perfectly predictable cash income to the holder. Examples are stocks paying known dividends and coupon-bearing bonds. We adopt the same approach as in the previous section. We first look at a numerical example and then review the formal arguments.

Consider a long forward contract to purchase a coupon-bearing bond whose current price is \$900. We will suppose that the forward contract matures in nine months. We will also suppose that a coupon payment of \$40 is expected after four months. We assume the four-month and nine-month risk-free interest rates continuously compounded are 3% and 4% per annum, respectively.

Suppose first that the forward price is relatively high at \$910. An arbitrageur can borrow \$900 to buy the bond and short a forward contract. The coupon payment has a present value of $40e^{-0.03\times 4/12} = \$39.60$. Of the \$900, 39.60 is therefore borrowed at 3% per annum for four months so that it can be repaid with the coupon payment. The remaining \$860.40 is borrowed at 4% per annum for nine months. The amount owing at the end of nine months is $860.40e^{0.04\times 0.75} = \$886.60$. A sum of \$910 is received for the bond under the terms of the forward contract. The arbitrageur therefore makes a net profit of

$$910.00 - 886.60 = \$23.40$$

Suppose next that the forward price is relatively low at \$870. An investor can short the bond and enter into a long forward contract. Of the \$900 realized from shorting the bond, \$39.60 is invested for four months at 3% per annum, so that it grows into an amount sufficient to pay the coupon on the bond. The remaining \$860.40 is invested for nine months at 4% per annum and grows to \$886.60. A sum of \$870 is paid under the

Table 5.3 Arbitrage opportunities when 9-month forward price is out of line with spot price for asset providing known cash income (asset price = \$900; income of \$40 occurs at 4 months; 4-month and 9-month rates are 3% and 4% per annum)

Forward price = \$910	***Forward price = \$870***
Action now:	*Action now*:
Borrow \$900: \$39.60 for 4 months and \$860.40 for 9 months	Short 1 unit of asset to realize \$900
Buy one unit of asset	Invest \$39.60 for 4 months and \$860.40 for 9 months
Enter into forward contract to sell asset in 9 months for \$910	Enter into a forward contract to buy asset in 9 months for \$870
Action in 4 months:	*Action in 4 months*:
Receive \$40 of income on asset	Receive \$40 from 4-month investment
Use \$40 to repay first loan with interest	Pay income of \$40 on asset
Action in 9 months:	*Action in 9 months*:
Sell asset for \$910	Receive \$886.60 from 9-month investment
Use \$886.60 to repay second loan with interest	Buy asset for \$870
	Close short position
Profit realized = \$23.40	Profit realized = \$16.60

terms of the forward contract to buy the bond and the short position is closed out. The investor therefore gains

$$886.60 - 870 = \$16.60$$

The two strategies we have considered are summarized in Table 5.3.[3]

The first strategy in Table 5.3 produces a profit when the forward price is greater than \$886.60, whereas the second strategy produces a profit when the forward price is less than \$886.60. It follows that, if there are no arbitrage opportunities, the forward price must be \$886.60.

A Generalization

We can generalize from this example to argue that, when an investment asset provides income with a present value of I during the life of a forward contract, we have

$$F_0 = (S_0 - I)e^{rT} \tag{5.2}$$

In our example, $S_0 = 900.00$, $I = 40e^{-0.03\times 4/12} = 39.60$, $r = 0.04$, and $T = 0.75$, so that

$$F_0 = (900.00 - 39.60)e^{0.04\times 0.75} = \$886.60$$

This is in agreement with our earlier calculation. Equation (5.2) applies to any investment asset that provides a known cash income. Example 5.2 provides another application of equation (5.2).

If $F_0 > (S_0 - I)e^{rT}$, an arbitrageur can lock in a profit by buying the asset and shorting a forward contract on the asset. If $F_0 < (S_0 - I)e^{rT}$ an arbitrageur can lock in a profit by shorting the asset and taking a long position in a forward contract. If

Example 5.2 Forward price of an asset providing a known income

Consider a 10-month forward contract on a stock when the stock price is \$50. We assume that the risk-free rate of interest continuously compounded is 8% per annum for all maturities. We also assume that dividends of \$0.75 per share are expected after three months, six months, and nine months. The present value of the dividends, I, is given by

$$I = 0.75e^{-0.08\times 3/12} + 0.75e^{-0.08\times 6/12} + 0.75e^{-0.08\times 9/12} = 2.162$$

The variable T is 10 months, so that the forward price, F_0, from equation (5.2), is given by

$$F_0 = (50 - 2.162)e^{0.08\times 10/12} = \$51.14$$

If the forward price were less than this, an arbitrageur would short the stock spot and buy forward contracts. If the forward price were greater than this, an arbitrageur would short forward contracts and buy the stock in the spot market.

[3] If shorting the bond is not possible, investors who already own the bond will sell it and buy a forward contract on the bond, thereby increasing the value of their position by \$16.60. This is similar to the strategy we described for the asset in the previous section.

Example 5.3 Forward price of an asset providing a known yield

Consider a six-month forward contract on an asset that is expected to provide income equal to 2% of the asset price once during a six-month period. The risk-free rate of interest with continuous compounding is 10% per annum. The asset price is \$25. In this case $S_0 = 25$, $r = 0.10$, and $T = 0.5$. The yield is 4% per annum with semiannual compounding. From equation (4.3), this is 3.96% per annum with continuous compounding. It follows that $q = 0.0396$, so that from equation (5.3) the forward price F_0 is given by

$$F_0 = 25e^{(0.10-0.0396)\times 0.5} = \$25.77$$

short sales are not possible, investors who own the asset will find it profitable to sell the asset and enter into long forward contracts.[4]

5.6 KNOWN YIELD

We now consider the situation where the asset underlying a forward contract provides a known yield rather than a known cash income. This means that the income is known when expressed as a percent of the asset's price at the time the income is paid. Suppose that an asset is expected to provide a yield of 5% per annum. This could mean that income is paid once a year and is equal to 5% of the asset price at the time it is paid. (The yield would then be 5% with annual compounding.) It could mean that income is paid twice a year and is equal to 2.5% of the asset price at the time it is paid. (The yield would then be 5% per annum with semiannual compounding.) In Section 4.2 we explained that we will normally measure interest rates with continuous compounding. Similarly we will normally measure yields with continuous compounding. Formulas for translating a yield measured with one compounding frequency to a yield measured with another compounding frequency are the same as those given for interest rates in Section 4.2.

Define q as the average yield per annum on an asset during the life of a forward contract with continuous compounding. It can be shown (see Problem 5.20) that

$$F_0 = S_0 e^{(r-q)T} \tag{5.3}$$

Example 5.3 provides an application of this formula.

5.7 VALUING FORWARD CONTRACTS

The value of a forward contract at the time it is first entered into is zero. At a later stage it may prove to have a positive or negative value. Banks are required to value all the

[4] For another way of seeing that equation (5.2) is correct, consider the following strategy: buy one unit of the asset and enter into a short forward contract to sell it for F_0 at time T. This costs S_0 and is certain to lead to a cash inflow of F_0 at time T and income with a present value of I. The initial outflow is S_0. The present value of the inflows is $I + F_0e^{-rT}$. Hence $S_0 = I + F_0e^{-rT}$, or equivalently $F_0 = (S_0 - I)e^{rT}$.

contracts in their trading books each day. We now consider how they can do this for forward contracts.

Using the notation introduced earlier, we suppose F_0 is the current forward price for a contract that was negotiated some time ago, the delivery date is T years from today, and r is the T-year risk-free interest rate. We also define:

K: Delivery price in the contract

f: Value of forward contract today

A general result, applicable to all long forward contracts (on both investment assets and consumption assets), is

$$f = (F_0 - K)e^{-rT} \tag{5.4}$$

It is important to understand the difference between F_0, the forward price today and f, the value of the forward contract today. At the beginning of the life of the forward contract, the delivery price is set equal to the forward price and $f = 0$. As time passes, both the forward price and the value of the forward contract, f, change.

To see why equation (5.4) is correct, we use an argument analogous to the one we used for forward rate agreements in Section 4.7. We compare a long forward contract that has a delivery price of F_0 with an otherwise identical long forward contract that has a delivery price of K. The difference between the two is only in the amount that will be paid for the underlying asset at time T. Under the first contract this amount is F_0; under the second contract it is K. A cash outflow difference of $F_0 - K$ at time T translates to a difference of $(F_0 - K)e^{-rT}$ today. The contract with a delivery price F_0 is therefore less valuable than the contract with delivery price K by an amount $(F_0 - K)e^{-rT}$. The value of the long forward contract that has a delivery price of F_0 is by definition zero. It follows that the value of the contract with a delivery price of K is $(F_0 - K)e^{-rT}$. This proves equation (5.4). Similarly, the value of a short forward contract with delivery price K is

$$(K - F_0)e^{-rT}$$

Example 5.4 provides an application of equation (5.4).

Equation (5.4) shows that we can value a long forward contract on an asset by making the assumption that the price of the asset at the maturity of the forward contract equals the forward price F_0. To see this, note that when we make that

Example 5.4 Valuing a forward contract

A long forward contract on a non-dividend-paying stock was entered into some time ago. It currently has six months to maturity. The risk-free rate of interest (with continuous compounding) is 10% per annum, the stock price is \$25, and the delivery price is \$24. In this case $S_0 = 25$, $r = 0.10$, $T = 0.5$, and $K = 24$. From equation (5.1) the six-month forward price, F_0, is given by

$$F_0 = 25e^{0.1\times 0.5} = \$26.28$$

From equation (5.4), the value of the forward contract is

$$f = (26.28 - 24)e^{-0.1\times 0.5} = \$2.17$$

Business Snapshot 5.2 A systems error?

A foreign exchange trader working for a bank enters into a long forward contract to buy 1 million pounds sterling at an exchange rate of 1.6000 in three months. At the same time, another trader on the next desk takes a long position in 16 three-month futures contracts on sterling. The futures price is 1.6000 and each contract is on 62,500 pounds. The positions taken by the forward and futures traders are therefore the same. Within minutes of the positions being taken the forward and the futures prices both increase to 1.6040. The bank's systems show that the futures trader has made a profit of \$4,000 while the forward trader has made a profit of only \$3,900. The forward trader immediately calls the bank's systems department to complain. Does the forward trader have a valid complaint?

The answer is no! The daily settlement of futures contracts ensures that the futures trader realizes an almost immediate profit corresponding to the increase in the futures price. If the forward trader closed out the position by entering into a short contract at 1.6040, the forward trader would have contracted to buy 1 million pounds at 1.6000 in three months and sell 1 million pounds at 1.6040 in three months. This would lead to a \$4,000 profit—but in three months' time. The forward trader's profit is the present value of \$4,000. This is consistent with equation (5.4).

The forward trader can gain some consolation from the fact that gains and losses are treated symmetrically. If the forward/futures prices dropped to 1.5960 instead of rising to 1.6040 the futures trader would take a loss of \$4,000, while the forward trader would take a loss of only \$3,900.

assumption a long forward contract provides a payoff at time T of $F_0 - K$. This has a present value of $(F_0 - K)e^{-rT}$, which is the value of f in equation (5.4). Similarly, we can value a short forward contract on the asset by assuming that the current forward price of the asset is realized. These results are analogous to the result in Section 4.7 that we can value a forward rate agreement on the assumption that forward rates are realized.

Using equation (5.4) in conjunction with (5.1) gives the following expression for the value of a forward contract on an investment asset that provides no income:

$$f = S_0 - Ke^{-rT} \tag{5.5}$$

Similarly, using equation (5.4) in conjunction with (5.2) gives the following expression for the value of a long forward contract on an investment asset that provides a known income with present value I:

$$f = S_0 - I - Ke^{-rT} \tag{5.6}$$

Finally, using equation (5.4) in conjunction with (5.3) gives the following expression for the value of a long forward contract on an investment asset that provides a known yield at rate q:

$$f = S_0e^{-qT} - Ke^{-rT} \tag{5.7}$$

When a futures price changes, the gain or loss on a futures contract is calculated as the change in the futures price multiplied by the size of the position. This gain is realized almost immediately because of the way futures contracts are settled daily.

Equation (5.4) shows that, when a forward price changes, the gain or loss is the present value of the change in the forward price multiplied by the size of the position. The difference between the gain/loss on forward and futures contracts can cause confusion on foreign exchange trading desks (see Business Snapshot 5.2).

5.8 ARE FORWARD PRICES AND FUTURES PRICES EQUAL?

It can be shown that, when there is no uncertainty about future interest rates, the forward price for a contract with a certain delivery date is in theory the same as the futures price for a contract with that delivery date. When interest rates vary unpredictably (as they do in the real world), forward and futures prices are in theory no longer the same.

We can get a sense of the nature of the relationship by considering the situation where the price S of the underlying asset is strongly positively correlated with interest rates. When S increases, an investor who holds a long futures position makes an immediate gain because of the daily settlement procedure. The positive correlation indicates that it is likely that interest rates have also increased. The gain will therefore tend to be invested at a higher than average rate of interest. Similarly, when S decreases, the investor will incur an immediate loss. This loss will tend to be financed at a lower than average rate of interest. An investor holding a forward contract rather than a futures contract is not affected in this way by interest rate movements. It follows that a long futures contract will be slightly more attractive than a similar long forward contract. Hence, when S is strongly positively correlated with interest rates, futures prices will tend to be slightly higher than forward prices. When S is strongly negatively correlated with interest rates, a similar argument shows that forward prices will tend to be slightly higher than futures prices.

The theoretical differences between forward and futures prices for contracts that last only a few months are in most circumstances sufficiently small to be ignored. In practice, there are a number of factors not reflected in theoretical models that may cause forward and futures prices to be different. These include taxes, transactions costs, and the use of margin accounts. The risk that the counterparty will default may be less in the case of a futures contract because of the role of the exchange clearinghouse. Also, in some instances, futures contracts are more liquid and easier to trade than forward contracts. Despite all these points, for most purposes it is reasonable to assume that forward and futures prices are the same. This is the assumption we will usually make in this book. We will use the symbol F_0 to represent both the futures price and the forward price of an asset today.

One exception to the rule that futures and forward contracts can be assumed to be the same concerns Eurodollar futures. This will be discussed in Section 6.3.

5.9 FUTURES PRICES OF STOCK INDICES

We introduced futures on stock indices in Section 3.5 and showed how a stock index futures contract is a useful tool in managing equity portfolios. We are now in a position to consider how index futures prices are determined.

Business Snapshot 5.3 The CME Nikkei 225 futures contract

The arguments in this chapter on how index futures prices are determined require that the index be the value of investment asset. This means that it must be the value of a portfolio of assets that can be traded. The asset underlying the Chicago Mercantile Exchange's futures contract on the Nikkei 225 Index does not qualify. The reason is quite subtle. Suppose that S is the value of the Nikkei 225 Index. This is the value of a portfolio of 225 Japanese stocks measured in yen. The variable underlying the CME futures contract on the Nikkei 225 has a *dollar value* of $5S$. In other words, the futures contract takes a variable that is measured in yen and treats it as though it is dollars.

We cannot invest in a portfolio whose value will always be $5S$ dollars. The best we can do is to invest in one that is always worth $5S$ yen or in one that is always worth $5QS$ dollars, where Q is the dollar value of one yen. The variable $5S$ dollars is not therefore the price of an investment asset and equation (5.8) does not apply.

CME's Nikkei 225 futures contract is an example of a *quanto*. A quanto is a derivative where the underlying asset is measured in one currency and the payoff is in another currency.

A stock index can usually be regarded as the price of an investment asset that pays dividends.[5] The investment asset is the portfolio of stocks underlying the index, and the dividends paid by the investment asset are the dividends that would be received by the holder of this portfolio. It is usually assumed that the dividends provide a known yield rather than a known cash income. If q is the dividend yield rate, equation (5.3) gives the futures price, F_0, as

$$F_0 = S_0 e^{(r-q)T} \tag{5.8}$$

Example 5.5 provides an application of this formula.

In practice, the dividend yield on the portfolio underlying an index varies throughout the year. For example, a large proportion of the dividends on the NYSE stocks are paid in the first week of February, May, August, and November each year. The value of q should represent the average annualized dividend yield during the life of the contract. The dividends used for estimating q should be those for which the ex-dividend date is during the life of the futures contract. In Table 3.3 of Chapter 3, the December settlement price for the S&P 500 is about 0.5% below the September settlement price. Using equation (5.8), this suggests that the S&P 500 dividend yield exceeds the U.S. short-term risk-free rate by about 0.5% per quarter, or 2% per year.

Example 5.5 Calculation of index futures price

Consider a three-month futures contract on the S&P 500. Suppose that the stocks underlying the index provide a dividend yield of 1% per annum, that the current value of the index is 1,300, and that the continuously compounded risk-free interest rate is 5% per annum. In this case, $r = 0.05$, $S_0 = 1{,}300$, $T = 0.25$, and $q = 0.01$. Hence, the futures price, F_0, is given by $F_0 = 1{,}300e^{(0.05-0.01)\times 0.25} = \$1{,}313.07$.

[5] Occasionally this is not the case: see Business Snapshot 5.3.

Business Snapshot 5.4 Index arbitrage in October 1987

To do index arbitrage, a trader must be able to trade both the index futures contract and the portfolio of stocks underlying the index very quickly at the prices quoted in the market. In normal market conditions, this is possible using program trading, and the relationship in equation (5.8) holds well. Examples of days when the market was anything but normal are October 19 and 20 of 1987. On what is termed "Black Monday," October 19, 1987, the market fell by more than 20%, and the 604 million shares traded on the New York Stock Exchange easily exceeded all previous records. The exchange's systems were overloaded, and if you placed an order to buy or sell shares on that day, there could be a delay of up to two hours before your order was executed.

For most of October 19, 1987, futures prices were at a significant discount to the underlying index. For example, at the close of trading the S&P 500 Index was at 225.06 (down 57.88 on the day), whereas the futures price for December delivery on the S&P 500 was 201.50 (down 80.75 on the day). This was largely because the delays in processing orders made index arbitrage impossible. On the next day, Tuesday, October 20, 1987, the New York Stock Exchange placed temporary restrictions on the way in which program trading could be done. This also made index arbitrage very difficult and the breakdown of the traditional linkage between stock indices and stock index futures continued. At one point the futures price for the December contract was 18% less than the S&P 500 Index. However, after a few days the market returned to normal, and the activities of arbitrageurs ensured that equation (5.8) governed the relationship between futures and spot prices of indices.

Index Arbitrage

If $F_0 > S_0e^{(r-q)T}$, profits can be made by buying spot (i.e., for immediate delivery) the stocks underlying the index and shorting futures contracts. If $F_0 < S_0e^{(r-q)T}$, profits can be made by doing the reverse—that is, shorting or selling the stocks underlying the index and taking a long position in futures contracts. These strategies are known as *index arbitrage*. When $F_0 < S_0e^{(r-q)T}$, index arbitrage might be done by a pension fund that owns an indexed portfolio of stocks. When $F_0 > S_0e^{(r-q)T}$, it might be done by a corporation holding short-term money market investments. For indices involving many stocks, index arbitrage is sometimes accomplished by trading a relatively small representative sample of stocks whose movements closely mirror those of the index. Usually index arbitrage is implemented through *program trading*, whereby a computer system is used to generate the trades.

Most of the time the activities of arbitrageurs ensure that equation (5.8) holds, but occasionally arbitrage is impossible and the futures price does get out of line with the spot price (see Business Snapshot 5.4).

5.10 FORWARD AND FUTURES CONTRACTS ON CURRENCIES

We now move on to consider forward and futures foreign currency contracts. We take the perspective of a U.S. investor. The underlying asset is one unit of the foreign currency. We will therefore define the variable S_0 as the current spot price in U.S. dollars of one unit of the foreign currency and F_0 as the forward or futures price in U.S. dollars of one unit of the foreign currency. This is consistent with the way we have defined S_0 and F_0 for other assets underlying forward and futures contracts. (However, as mentioned in Section 2.11, it does not necessarily correspond to the way spot and forward exchange rates are quoted. For major exchange rates other than the British pound, euro, Australian dollar, and New Zealand dollar, a spot or forward exchange rate is normally quoted on a "foreign currency per dollar" basis.)

A foreign currency has the property that the holder of the currency can earn interest at the risk-free interest rate prevailing in the foreign country. For example, the holder can invest the currency in a foreign-denominated bond. We define r_f as the value of the foreign risk-free interest rate when money is invested for time T. The variable r is the U.S. dollar risk-free rate when money is invested for this period of time.

The relationship between F_0 and S_0 is

$$F_0 = S_0 e^{(r-r_f)T} \tag{5.9}$$

This is the well-known interest rate parity relationship from international finance. The reason it is true is illustrated in Figure 5.1. Suppose that an individual starts with 1,000 units of the foreign currency. There are two ways it can be converted to dollars at time T. One is by investing it for T years at r_f and entering into a forward contract to sell the proceeds for dollars at time T. This generates $1{,}000e^{r_f T} F_0$ dollars. The other is by exchanging the foreign currency for dollars in the spot market and investing the proceeds for T years at rate r. This generates $1{,}000S_0e^{rT}$ dollars. In the absence of

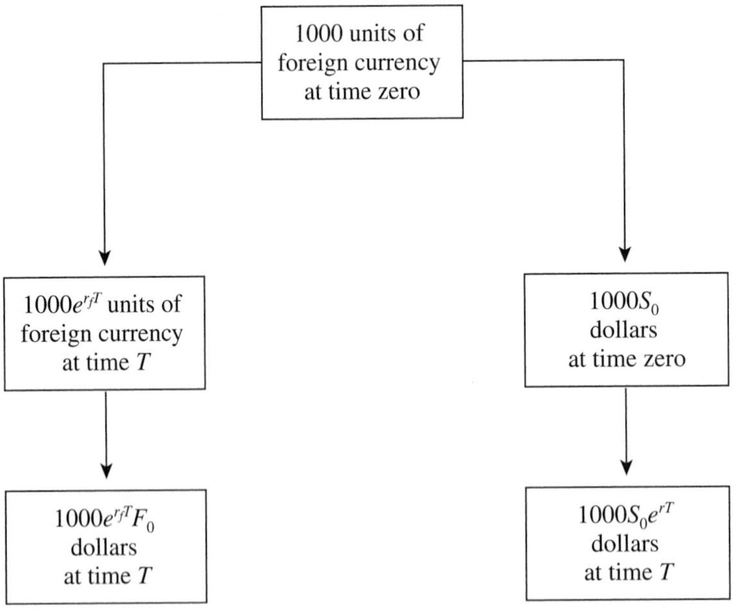

Figure 5.1 Two ways of converting 1,000 units of a foreign currency to dollars at time T. S_0 is spot exchange rate; F_0 is forward exchange rate; r and r_f are dollar and foreign risk-free rates

arbitrage opportunites, the two strategies must give the same result. Hence

$$1{,}000e^{r_f T}F_0 = 1{,}000S_0e^{rT}$$

so that

$$F_0 = S_0e^{(r-r_f)T}$$

Example 5.6 shows how an arbitrageur could make a profit if this relationship does not hold for the exchange rate between the U.S. and Australian dollars.

Table 5.4 shows currency futures quotes on July 13, 2012. The quotes indicate the value of the foreign currency in U.S. dollars. This is the usual quotation convention for futures contracts. Equation (5.9) applies with r equal to the U.S. risk-free rate and r_f equal to the foreign risk-free rate.

Example 5.6 Arbitrage in forward and spot foreign exchange markets

Suppose that the two-year interest rates in Australia and the United States are 5% and 7%, respectively, and the spot exchange rate is 0.6200 USD per AUD. (As indicated by Table 5.4, this is quite a bit different from the exchange rate in 2012!) From equation (5.9), the two-year forward exchange rate should be

$$0.62e^{(0.07-0.05)\times 2} = 0.6453$$

Suppose first the two-year forward exchange rate is less than this, say 0.6300. An arbitrageur can

1. Borrow 1,000 AUD at 5% per annum for two years, convert to 620 USD and invest the USD at 7%. (Both rates are continuously compounded.)
2. Enter into a forward contract to buy 1,105.17 AUD for $1{,}105.17 \times 0.63 = 696.26$ USD.

The 620 USD that are invested at 7% grow to $620e^{0.07\times 2} = 713.17$ USD in two years. Of this, 696.26 USD are used to purchase 1,105.17 AUD under the terms of the forward contract. This is exactly enough to repay principal and interest on the 1,000 AUD that are borrowed ($1{,}000e^{0.05\times 2} = 1{,}105.17$). The strategy therefore gives rise to a riskless profit of $713.17 - 696.26 = 16.91$ USD. (If this does not sound very exciting, consider following a similar strategy where you borrow 100 million AUD!)

Suppose next that the two-year forward rate is 0.6600 (greater than the 0.6453 value given by equation (5.9)). An arbitrageur can:

1. Borrow 1,000 USD at 7% per annum for two years, convert to $1{,}000/0.6200 = 1{,}612.90$ AUD, and invest the AUD at 5%.
2. Enter into a forward contract to sell 1,782.53 AUD for $1{,}782.53 \times 0.66 = 1{,}176.47$ USD.

The 1,612.90 AUD that are invested at 5% grow to $1{,}612.90e^{0.05\times 2} = 1{,}782.53$ AUD in two years. The forward contract has the effect of converting this to 1,176.47 USD. The amount needed to payoff the USD borrowings is $1{,}000e^{0.07\times 2} = 1{,}150.27$ USD. The strategy therefore gives rise to a riskless profit of $1{,}176.47 - 1{,}150.27 = 26.20$ USD.

Table 5.4 Futures quotes for a selection of CME Group contracts on foreign currencies on July 13, 2012

	Open	*High*	*Low*	*Prior settlement*	*Last trade*	*Change*	*Volume*
Australian Dollar, USD per AUD							
Sept. 2012	1.0076	1.0170	1.0063	1.0075	1.0167	+0.0092	130,216
Dec. 2012	1.0000	1.0093	0.9990	1.0000	1.0085	+0.0085	58
British Pound, USD per GBP							
Sept. 2012	1.5428	1.5578	1.5411	1.5427	1.5578	+0.0151	103,578
Dec. 2012	1.5430	1.5575	1.5430	1.5424	1.5575	+0.0151	37
Canadian Dollar, USD per CAD							
Sept. 2012	0.9797	0.9858	0.9787	0.9804	0.9851	+0.0047	91,472
Dec. 2012	0.9780	0.9838	0.9769	0.9785	0.9832	+0.0047	527
Euro, USD per EUR							
Sept. 2012	1.2211	1.2267	1.2171	1.2206	1.2257	+0.0051	218,890
Dec. 2012	1.2230	1.2282	1.2193	1.2222	1.2273	+0.0051	169
Japanese Yen, USD per 100 yen							
Sept. 2012	1.2620	1.2665	1.2604	1.2619	1.2623	+0.0004	46,503
Dec. 2012	1.2622	1.2677	1.2622	1.2635	1.2640	+0.0005	92
Swiss Franc, USD per CHF							
Sept. 2012	1.0173	1.0219	1.0142	1.0170	1.0209	+0.0039	39,278
Dec 2012	1.0237	1.0246	1.0237	1.0198	1.0238	+0.0040	5

On July 13, 2012, short-term interest rates on the euro, Japanese yen, and Swiss franc were lower than the interest rate on the U.S. dollar. This corresponds to the $r > r_f$ situation and explains why the December settlement futures price for these currencies is higher than the September settlement price in Table 5.4. For the Australian dollar, British pound, and Canadian dollar, interest rates were higher than in the United States. This corresponds to the $r_f > r$ situation and explains why the December settlement futures price of these currencies is lower than the September settlement price in Table 5.4.

Example 5.7 estimates the interest rate difference between Australia and the United States from Table 5.4.

Example 5.7 Estimating interest rate differentials

In Table 5.4, the December settlement price for the Australian dollar is 0.744% lower than the September settlement price. This indicates that short-term futures prices are decreasing at a rate of about 2.976% per year. From equation (5.9), this is an estimate of the amount by which short-term Australian interest rates exceeded short-term U.S. interest rates.

A Foreign Currency as an Asset Providing a Known Yield

Note that equation (5.9) is identical to equation (5.3) with q replaced by r_f. This is not a coincidence. A foreign currency can be regarded as an investment asset paying a known yield. The yield is the risk-free rate of interest in the foreign currency.

To understand this, note that the value of interest paid in a foreign currency depends on the value of the foreign currency. Suppose that the interest rate on British pounds is 5% per annum. To a U.S. investor the British pound provides an income equal to 5% of the value of the British pound per annum. In other words it is an asset that provides a yield of 5% per annum.

5.11 FUTURES ON COMMODITIES

We now move on to consider futures contracts on commodities. First we look at the futures prices of commodities that are investment assets such as gold and silver.[6] We then move on to examine the futures prices of consumption assets.

Income and Storage Costs

As explained in Business Snapshot 3.1, the hedging strategies of gold producers leads to a requirement on the part of investment banks to borrow gold. Gold owners such as central banks charge interest in the form of what is known as the *gold lease rate* when they lend gold. The same is true of silver. Gold and silver can therefore provide income to the holder. For the purposes of our examples, we ignore this income. However, we will take account of storage costs.

Equation (5.1) shows that in the absence of storage costs and income the forward price of a commodity that is an investment asset is given by

$$F_0 = S_0 e^{rT} \tag{5.10}$$

Storage costs can be treated as negative income. If U is the present value of all the storage costs during the life of a forward contract, it follows from equation (5.2) that

$$F_0 = (S_0 + U)e^{rT} \tag{5.11}$$

Example 5.8 provides an application of this formula.

If the storage costs (net of income) incurred at any time are proportional to the price of the commodity, they can be treated as negative yield. In this case, from equation (5.3), we have

$$F_0 = S_0 e^{(r+u)T} \tag{5.12}$$

where u denotes the storage costs per annum as a proportion of the spot price net of any yield earned on the asset.

---

[6] Recall that, for an asset to be an investment asset, it need not be held solely for investment purposes. What is required is that some individuals hold it for investment purposes and that these individuals be prepared to sell their holdings and go long forward contracts, if the latter look more attractive. This explains why silver, although it has significant industrial uses, is an investment asset.

Consumption Commodities

Commodities that are consumption assets rather than investment assets usually provide no income, but can be subject to significant storage costs. We now review carefully the arbitrage strategies used to determine futures prices from spot prices.[7] Suppose that, instead of equation (5.11), we have

$$F_0 > (S_0 + U)e^{rT} \tag{5.13}$$

To take advantage of this opportunity, an arbitrageur can implement the following strategy:

1. Borrow an amount $S_0 + U$ at the risk-free rate and use it to purchase one unit of the commodity and to pay storage costs.
2. Short a futures contract on one unit of the commodity.

If we regard the futures contract as a forward contract, so that there is no daily settlement, this strategy leads to a profit of $F_0 - (S_0 + U)e^{rT}$ at time T. Example 5.8 illustrates the strategy for gold. There is no problem in implementing the strategy for any commodity. However, as arbitrageurs do so, there will be a tendency for S_0 to increase and F_0 to decrease until equation (5.13) is no longer true. We conclude that equation (5.13) cannot hold for any significant length of time.

Suppose next that

$$F_0 < (S_0 + U)e^{rT} \tag{5.14}$$

In the case of investment assets such as gold and silver, we can argue that many investors hold the commodity solely for investment. When they observe the inequality in equation (5.14), they will find it profitable to:

1. Sell the commodity, save the storage costs, and invest the proceeds at the risk-free interest rate.
2. Take a long position in a futures contract.

This strategy is illustrated for gold in Example 5.8. The result is a riskless profit at maturity of $(S_0 + U)e^{rT} - F_0$ relative to the position the investors would have been in if they had held the commodity. It follows that equation (5.14) cannot hold for long. Because neither equation (5.13) nor (5.14) can hold for long, we must have $F_0 = (S_0 + U)e^{rT}$.

This argument cannot be used for commodities that are not, to any significant extent, held for investment. Individuals and companies who keep such a commodity in inventory do so because of its consumption value, not because of its value as an investment. They are reluctant to sell the commodity in the spot market and buy futures or forward contracts, because futures and forward contracts cannot be used in a manufacturing process or consumed in some other way. There is therefore nothing to stop equation (5.14) from holding. All we can assert for a consumption commodity is therefore

$$F_0 \leqslant (S_0 + U)e^{rT} \tag{5.15}$$

[7] For some commodities the spot price depends on the delivery location. We assume that the delivery location for spot and futures are the same.

Example 5.8 Gold futures price

Consider a one-year futures contract on gold. We assume no income and that it costs \$2 per ounce per year to store gold, with the payment being made at the end of the year. The spot price is \$1,600 and the risk-free rate is 5% per annum for all maturities. This corresponds to $r = 0.05$, $S_0 = 1{,}600$, $T = 1$, and

$$U = 2e^{-0.05\times 1} = 1.90$$

From equation (5.11) the theoretical futures price, F_0, is given by

$$F_0 = (1{,}600 + 1.90)e^{0.05\times 1} = \$1{,}684.03$$

Futures Price Too High

Suppose the actual gold futures price is greater than \$1,684.03, say \$1,700. An arbitrageur can:

1. Borrow \$160,000 at the risk-free interest rate of 5% to buy 100 ounces of gold.
2. Short one gold futures contract for delivery in one year.

The futures contract ensures that the purchased gold can be sold for \$170,000. An amount \$168,203 is used to pay interest and principal on the loan and \$200 is used to pay storage, so that the net gain is

$$\$170{,}000 - \$168{,}203 - \$200 = \$1{,}587$$

Futures Price Too Low

Suppose next the futures price is less than \$1,684.03, say \$1,650. An investor who already holds 100 ounces of gold for investment purposes can:

1. Sell the gold for \$160,000.
2. Enter into one long gold futures contract for delivery in one year.

The \$160,000 is invested at the risk-free interest rate of 5% for one year and grows to \$168,203. The futures contract ensures that the gold can be repurchased for \$165,000. The investor saves \$200 in storage costs. The futures contract therefore improves the investor's position by

$$168{,}203 - 165{,}000 + 200 = \$3{,}403$$

If storage costs are expressed as a proportion u of the spot price, the equivalent result is

$$F_0 \leqslant S_0e^{(r+u)T} \tag{5.16}$$

Convenience Yields

We do not necessarily have equality in equations (5.15) and (5.16) because users of a consumption commodity may feel that ownership of the physical commodity provides benefits that are not obtained by holders of futures contracts. For example, an oil refiner is unlikely to regard a futures contract on crude oil in the same way as crude oil held in inventory. The crude oil in inventory can be an input to the refining process whereas a futures contract cannot be used for this purpose. In general, ownership of the physical asset enables a manufacturer to keep a production process running and perhaps profit from temporary local shortages. A futures contract does not do the same. The benefits from holding the physical asset are sometimes referred to as the *convenience yield* provided by the commodity. If the dollar amount of storage costs is known and has a present value, U, the convenience yield, y, is defined so that

$$F_0 e^{yT} = (S_0 + U)e^{rT}$$

If the storage costs per unit are a constant proportion, u, of the spot price, then y is defined so that

$$F_0 e^{yT} = S_0 e^{(r+u)T}$$

or

$$F_0 = S_0 e^{(r+u-y)T} \qquad \textbf{(5.17)}$$

The convenience yield simply measures the extent to which the left-hand side is less than the right-hand side in equation (5.15) or (5.16). For investment assets the convenience yield must be zero; otherwise, there are arbitrage opportunities such as those in Example 5.8. Table 2.2 of Chapter 2 shows that the futures price of soybeans tended to decrease as the time to maturity of the contract increased on July 13, 2012. This suggests that the convenience yield, y, is greater than $r + u$ for soybeans on this date.

The convenience yield reflects the market's expectations concerning the future availability of the commodity. The greater the possibility of shortages, the higher the convenience yield. If users of the commodity have high inventories, there is very little chance of shortages in the near future and the convenience yield tends to be low. If inventories are low, then shortages are more likely and the convenience yield is usually higher.

5.12 THE COST OF CARRY

The relationship between futures prices and spot prices can be summarized in terms of the *cost of carry*. This measures the storage cost plus the interest that is paid to finance the asset less the income earned on the asset. For a non-dividend-paying stock, the cost of carry is r, because there are no storage costs and no income is earned; for a stock index, it is $r - q$, because income is earned at rate q on the asset. For a currency, it is $r - r_f$; for a commodity that provides income at rate q and requires storage costs at rate u, it is $r - q + u$; and so on.

Define the cost of carry as c. For an investment asset, the futures price is

$$F_0 = S_0 e^{cT} \qquad \textbf{(5.18)}$$

For a consumption asset, it is

$$F_0 = S_0 e^{(c-y)T} \qquad \textbf{(5.19)}$$

where y is the convenience yield.

5.13 DELIVERY OPTIONS

Whereas a forward contract normally specifies that delivery is to take place on a particular day, a futures contract often allows the party with the short position to choose to deliver at any time during a certain period. (Typically the party has to give a few days' notice of its intention to deliver.) The choice introduces a complication into the determination of futures prices. Should the maturity of the futures contract be assumed to be the beginning, middle, or end of the delivery period? Even though most futures contracts are closed out prior to maturity, it is important to know when delivery would have taken place in order to calculate the theoretical futures price.

If the futures price is an increasing function of the time to maturity, it can be seen from equation (5.19) that $c > y$, so that the benefits from holding the asset (including convenience yield and net of storage costs) are less than the risk-free rate. It is usually optimal in such a case for the party with the short position to deliver as early as possible, because the interest earned on the cash received outweighs the benefits of holding the asset. As a rule, futures prices in these circumstances should be calculated on the basis that delivery will take place at the beginning of the delivery period. If futures prices are decreasing as time to maturity increases ($c < y$), the reverse is true. It is then usually optimal for the party with the short position to deliver as late as possible, and futures prices should, as a rule, be calculated on this assumption.

5.14 FUTURES PRICES AND EXPECTED SPOT PRICES

We refer to the market's average opinion about what the spot price of an asset will be at a certain future time as the *expected spot price* of the asset at that time. Suppose that it is now June and the September futures price of corn is 350 cents. It is interesting to ask what the expected spot price of corn in September is. Is it less that 350 cents, greater than 350 cents, or exactly equal to 350 cents? As illustrated in Figure 2.1, the futures price converges to the spot price at maturity. If the expected spot price is less than 350 cents, the market must be expecting the September futures price to decline so that traders with short positions gain and traders with long positions lose. If the expected spot price is greater than 350 cents the reverse must be true. The market must be expecting the September futures price to increase so that traders with long positions gain while those with short positions lose.

Keynes and Hicks

Economists John Maynard Keynes and John Hicks argued that if hedgers tend to hold short positions and speculators tend to hold long positions, the futures price of an asset will be below the expected spot price.[8] This is because speculators require compensation for the risks they are bearing. They will trade only if they can expect to make money on average. Hedgers will lose money on average, but they are likely to be prepared to accept this because the futures contract reduces their risks. If hedgers tend to hold long positions while speculators hold short positions, Keynes and Hicks argued that the futures price will be above the expected spot price for a similar reason.

Risk and Return

The modern approach to explaining the relationship between futures prices and expected spot prices is based on the relationship between risk and expected return in

[8] See J. M. Keynes, *A Treatise on Money*. London: Macmillan, 1930; and J. R. Hicks, *Value and Capital*. Oxford: Clarendon Press, 1939.

the economy. In general, the higher the risk of an investment, the higher the expected return demanded by an investor. The capital asset pricing model, which is explained in the appendix to Chapter 3, shows that there are two types of risk in the economy: systematic and nonsystematic. Nonsystematic risk should not be important to an investor. It can be almost completely eliminated by holding a well-diversified portfolio. An investor should not therefore require a higher expected return for bearing nonsystematic risk. Systematic risk, by contrast, cannot be diversified away. It arises from a correlation between returns from the investment and returns from the whole stock market. An investor generally requires a higher expected return than the risk-free interest rate for bearing positive amounts of systematic risk. Also, an investor is prepared to accept a lower expected return than the risk-free interest rate when the systematic risk in an investment is negative.

The Risk in a Futures Position

Let us consider a speculator who takes a long position in a futures contract that lasts for T years in the hope that the spot price of the asset will be above the futures price at the end of the life of the futures contract. We ignore daily settlement and assume that the futures contract can be treated as a forward contract. We suppose that the speculator puts the present value of the futures price into a risk-free investment while simultaneously taking a long futures position. The proceeds of the risk-free investment are used to buy the asset on the delivery date. The asset is then immediately sold for its market price. The cash flows to the speculator are:

Today: $-F_0e^{-rT}$

End of Futures Contract: $+S_T$

where F_0 is the futures price today, S_T is the price of the asset at time T at the end of the futures contract, and r is the risk-free return on funds invested for time T.

How do we value this investment? The discount rate we should use for the expected cash flow at time T equals an investor's required return on the investment. Suppose that k is an investor's required return for this investment. The present value of this investment is

$$-F_0e^{-rT} + E(S_T)e^{-kT}$$

where E denotes expected value. We can assume that all investments in securities markets are priced so that they have zero net present value. This means that

$$-F_0e^{-rT} + E(S_T)e^{-kT} = 0$$

or

$$F_0 = E(S_T)e^{(r-k)T} \tag{5.20}$$

As we have just discussed, the returns investors require on an investment depend on its systematic risk. The investment we have been considering is in essence an investment in the asset underlying the futures contract. If the returns from this asset are uncorrelated with the stock market, the correct discount rate to use is the risk-free rate r, so we should set $k = r$. Equation (5.20) then gives

$$F_0 = E(S_T)$$

Table 5.5 Relationship between futures price and expected future spot price

Underlying asset	*Relationship of expected return k from asset to risk-free rate r*	*Relationship of futures price F to expected future spot price $E(S_T)$*
No systematic risk	$k = r$	$F_0 = E(S_T)$
Positive systematic risk	$k > r$	$F_0 < E(S_T)$
Negative systematic risk	$k < r$	$F_0 > E(S_T)$

This shows that the futures price is an unbiased estimate of the expected future spot price when the return from the underlying asset is uncorrelated with the stock market.

If the return from the asset is positively correlated with the stock market, $k > r$ and equation (5.20) leads to $F_0 < E(S_T)$. This shows that, when the asset underlying the futures contract has positive systematic risk, we should expect the futures price to understate the expected future spot price. An example of an asset that has positive systematic risk is a stock index. The expected return of investors on the stocks underlying an index is generally more than the risk-free rate, r. The dividends provide a return of q. The expected increase in the index must therefore be more than $r - q$. Equation (5.8) is therefore consistent with the prediction that the futures price understates the expected future stock price for a stock index.

If the return from the asset is negatively correlated with the stock market, $k < r$ and equation (5.20) shows that $F_0 > E(S_T)$. This shows that when the asset underlying the futures contract has negative systematic risk we should expect the futures price to overstate the expected future spot price.

These results are summarized in Table 5.5.

Normal Backwardation and Contango

When the futures price is below the expected future spot price, the situation is known as *normal backwardation*; when the futures price is above the expected future spot price, the situation is known as *contango*. However, it should be noted that sometimes these terms are used to refer to whether the futures price is below or above the current spot price, rather than whether it is below or above the expected future spot price.

SUMMARY

For most purposes, the futures price of a contract with a certain delivery date can be considered to be the same as the forward price for a contract with the same delivery date. It can be shown that in theory the two should be exactly the same when interest rates are perfectly predictable.

For the purposes of understanding futures (or forward) prices, it is convenient to divide futures contracts into two categories: those in which the underlying asset is held for investment by a significant number of investors, and those in which the underlying asset is held primarily for consumption purposes.

Table 5.6 Summary of results for a contract with time to maturity T on an investment asset with price S_0 when the risk-free interest rate for a T-year period is r

Asset	*Forward/futures price*	*Value of long forward contract with delivery price K*
Provides no income	$S_0 e^{rT}$	$S_0 - Ke^{-rT}$
Provides known income with present value I	$(S_0 - I)e^{rT}$	$S_0 - I - Ke^{-rT}$
Provides known yield, q	$S_0 e^{(r-q)T}$	$S_0 e^{-qT} - Ke^{-rT}$

In the case of investment assets, we have considered three different situations:

1. The asset provides no income.
2. The asset provides a known dollar income.
3. The asset provides a known yield.

The results are summarized in Table 5.6. They enable futures prices to be obtained for contracts on stock indices, currencies, gold, and silver. Storage costs can be treated as negative income.

In the case of consumption assets, it is not possible to obtain the futures price as a function of the spot price and other observable variables. Here the parameter known as the asset's convenience yield becomes important. It measures the extent to which users of the commodity feel that ownership of the physical asset provides benefits that are not obtained by the holders of the futures contract. These benefits may include the ability to profit from temporary local shortages or the ability to keep a production process running. We can obtain an upper bound for the futures price of consumption assets using arbitrage arguments, but we cannot nail down an equality relationship between futures and spot prices.

The concept of cost of carry is sometimes useful. The cost of carry is the storage cost of the underlying asset plus the cost of financing it minus the income received from it. In the case of investment assets, the futures price is greater than the spot price by an amount reflecting the cost of carry. In the case of consumption assets, the futures price is greater than the spot price by an amount reflecting the cost of carry net of the convenience yield.

If we assume the capital asset pricing model is true, the relationship between the futures price and the expected future spot price depends on whether the return on the asset is positively or negatively correlated with the return on the stock market. Positive correlation will tend to lead to a futures price lower than the expected future spot price. Negative correlation will tend to lead to a futures price higher than the expected future spot price. Only when the correlation is zero will the theoretical futures price be equal to the expected future spot price.

FURTHER READING

Cox, J. C., J. E. Ingersoll, and S. A. Ross. "The Relation between Forward Prices and Futures Prices," *Journal of Financial Economics*, 9 (December 1981): 321–46.

Ghon, R. S. and R. P. Chang. "Intra-day Arbitrage in Foreign Exchange and Eurocurrency Markets," *Journal of Finance*, 47, 1 (1992): 363–80.

Jarrow, R. A., and G. S. Oldfield. "Forward Contracts and Futures Contracts," *Journal of Financial Economics*, 9 (December 1981): 373–82.

Kane, E. J. "Market Incompleteness and Divergences between Forward and Futures Interest Rates," *Journal of Finance*, 35 (May 1980): 221–34.

Pindyck R. S. "Inventories and the Short-Run Dynamics of Commodity Prices," *Rand Journal of Economics*, 25, 1 (1994): 141–59.

Richard, S., and S. Sundaresan. "A Continuous-Time Model of Forward and Futures Prices in a Multigood Economy," *Journal of Financial Economics*, 9 (December 1981): 347–72.

Routledge, B. R., D. J. Seppi, and C. S. Spatt. "Equilibrium Forward Curves for Commodities," *Journal of Finance*, 55, 3 (2000): 1297–1338.

Quiz (Answers at End of Book)

5.1. Explain what happens when an investor shorts a certain share.

5.2. What is the difference between the forward price and the value of a forward contract?

5.3. Suppose that you enter into a six-month forward contract on a non-dividend-paying stock when the stock price is \$30 and the risk-free interest rate (with continuous compounding) is 12% per annum. What is the forward price?

5.4. A stock index currently stands at 350. The risk-free interest rate is 8% per annum (with continuous compounding) and the dividend yield on the index is 4% per annum. What should the futures price for a four-month contract be?

5.5. Explain carefully why the futures price of gold can be calculated from its spot price and other observable variables whereas the futures price of copper cannot.

5.6. Explain carefully the meaning of the terms *convenience yield* and *cost of carry*. What is the relationship between futures price, spot price, convenience yield, and cost of carry?

5.7. Explain why a foreign currency can be treated as an asset providing a known yield.

Practice Questions (Answers in Solutions Manual/Study Guide)

5.8. Is the futures price of a stock index greater than or less than the expected future value of the index? Explain your answer.

5.9. A one-year long forward contract on a non-dividend-paying stock is entered into when the stock price is \$40 and the risk-free rate of interest is 10% per annum with continuous compounding. (a) What are the forward price and the initial value of the forward contract? (b) Six months later, the price of the stock is \$45 and the risk-free interest rate is still 10%. What are the forward price and the value of the forward contract?

5.10. The risk-free rate of interest is 7% per annum with continuous compounding, and the dividend yield on a stock index is 3.2% per annum. The current value of the index is 150. What is the six-month futures price?

5.11. Assume that the risk-free interest rate is 9% per annum with continuous compounding and that the dividend yield on a stock index varies throughout the year. In February, May, August, and November, dividends are paid at a rate of 5% per annum. In other months, dividends are paid at a rate of 2% per annum. Suppose that the value of the index on July 31 is 1,300. What is the futures price for a contract deliverable on December 31 of the same year?

5.12. Suppose that the risk-free interest rate is 10% per annum with continuous compounding and that the dividend yield on a stock index is 4% per annum. The index is standing at 400, and the futures price for a contract deliverable in four months is 405. What arbitrage opportunities does this create?

5.13. Estimate the difference between short-term interest rates in Japan and the United States on July 13, 2012, from the information in Table 5.4.

5.14. The two-month interest rates in Switzerland and the United States are 2% and 5% per annum, respectively, with continuous compounding. The spot price of the Swiss franc is \$0.8000. The futures price for a contract deliverable in two months is \$0.8100. What arbitrage opportunities does this create?

5.15. The current price of silver is \$30 per ounce. The storage costs are \$0.48 per ounce per year payable quarterly in advance. Assuming that interest rates are 10% per annum for all maturities, calculate the futures price of silver for delivery in nine months.

5.16. Suppose that F_1 and F_2 are two futures contracts on the same commodity with times to maturity, t_1 and t_2, where $t_2 > t_1$. Prove that

$$F_2 \leqslant F_1 e^{r(t_2-t_1)}$$

where r is the interest rate (assumed constant) and there are no storage costs. For the purposes of this problem, assume that a futures contract is the same as a forward contract.

5.17. When a known future cash outflow in a foreign currency is hedged by a company using a forward contract, there is no foreign exchange risk. When it is hedged using futures contracts, the daily settlement process does leave the company exposed to some risk. Explain the nature of this risk. In particular, consider whether the company is better off using a futures contract or a forward contract when:
(a) The value of the foreign currency falls rapidly during the life of the contract.
(b) The value of the foreign currency rises rapidly during the life of the contract.
(c) The value of the foreign currency first rises and then falls back to its initial value.
(d) The value of the foreign currency first falls and then rises back to its initial value.
Assume that the forward price equals the futures price.

5.18. It is sometimes argued that a forward exchange rate is an unbiased predictor of future exchange rates. Under what circumstances is this so?

5.19. Show that the growth rate in an index futures price equals the excess return on the portfolio underlying the index over the risk-free rate. Assume that the risk-free interest rate and the dividend yield are constant.

5.20. Show that equation (5.3) is true by considering an investment in the asset combined with a short position in a futures contract. Assume that all income from the asset is reinvested in the asset. Use an argument similar to that in footnotes 2 and 4 of this chapter to explain in detail what an arbitrageur would do if equation (5.3) did not hold.

5.21. Explain carefully what is meant by the expected price of a commodity on a particular future date. Suppose that the future price for crude oil declines with the maturity of the contract at the rate of 2% per year. Assume that speculators tend to be short crude oil futures and hedgers tend to be long crude oil futures. What does the Keynes and Hicks argument imply about the expected future price of oil?

5.22. The Value Line index is designed to reflect changes in the value of a portfolio of over 1,600 equally weighted stocks. Prior to March 9, 1988, the change in the index from one day to the next was calculated as the *geometric* average of the changes in the prices of the stocks underlying the index. In these circumstances, does equation (5.8) correctly relate the futures price of the index to its cash price? If not, does the equation overstate or understate the futures price?

5.23. What is meant by (a) an investment asset and (b) a consumption asset. Why is the distinction between investment and consumption assets important in the determination of forward and futures prices?

5.24. What is the cost of carry for (a) a non-dividend-paying stock, (b) a stock index, (c) a commodity with storage costs, and (d) a foreign currency?

Further Questions

5.25. In early 2012, the spot exchange rate between the Swiss Franc and U.S. dollar was 1.0404 ($ per franc). Interest rates in the U.S. and Switzerland were 0.25% and 0% per annum, respectively, with continuous compounding. The three-month forward exchange rate was 1.0300 ($ per franc). What arbitrage strategy was possible? How does your answer change if the exchange rate is 1.0500 ($ per franc).

5.26. An index is 1,200. The three-month risk-free rate is 3% per annum and the dividend yield over the next three months is 1.2% per annum. The six-month risk-free rate is 3.5% per annum and the dividend yield over the next six months is 1% per annum. Estimate the futures price of the index for three-month and six-month contracts. All interest rates and dividend yields are continuously compounded.

5.27. The current USD/euro exchange rate is 1.4000 dollar per euro. The six-month forward exchange rate is 1.3950. The six-month USD interest rate is 1% per annum continuously compounded. Estimate the six-month euro interest rate.

5.28. The spot price of oil is $80 per barrel and the cost of storing a barrel of oil for one year is $3, payable at the end of the year. The risk-free interest rate is 5% per annum continuously compounded. What is an upper bound for the one-year futures price of oil?

5.29. A stock is expected to pay a dividend of $1 per share in two months and in five months. The stock price is $50, and the risk-free rate of interest is 8% per annum with continuous compounding for all maturities. An investor has just taken a short position in a six-month forward contract on the stock.

(a) What are the forward price and the initial value of the forward contract?

(b) Three months later, the price of the stock is $48 and the risk-free rate of interest is still 8% per annum. What are the forward price and the value of the short position in the forward contract?

5.30. A bank offers a corporate client a choice between borrowing cash at 11% per annum and borrowing gold at 2% per annum. (If gold is borrowed, interest must be repaid in gold. Thus, 100 ounces borrowed today would require 102 ounces to be repaid in one year.) The risk-free interest rate is 9.25% per annum, and storage costs are 0.5% per annum. Discuss whether the rate of interest on the gold loan is too high or too low in relation to the rate of interest on the cash loan. The interest rates on the two loans are expressed with annual compounding. The risk-free interest rate and storage costs are expressed with continuous compounding.

5.31. A company that is uncertain about the exact date when it will pay or receive a foreign currency may try to negotiate with its bank a forward contract that specifies a period during which delivery can be made. The company wants to reserve the right to choose the exact delivery date to fit in with its own cash flows. Put yourself in the position of the bank. How would you price the product that the company wants?

5.32. A trader owns a commodity as part of a long-term investment portfolio. The trader can buy the commodity for \$950 per ounce and sell it for \$949 per ounce. The trader can borrow funds at 6% per year and invest funds at 5.5% per year. (Both interest rates are expressed with annual compounding.) For what range of one-year forward prices does the trader have no arbitrage opportunities? Assume there is no bid–offer spread for forward prices.

5.33. A company enters into a forward contract with a bank to sell a foreign currency for K_1 at time T_1. The exchange rate at time T_1 proves to be S_1 ($> K_1$). The company asks the bank if it can roll the contract forward until time T_2 ($> T_1$) rather than settle at time T_1. The bank agrees to a new delivery price, K_2. Explain how K_2 should be calculated.

CHAPTER 6

Interest Rate Futures

So far we have covered futures contracts on commodities, stock indices, and foreign currencies. We have seen how they work, how they are used for hedging, and how futures prices are determined. We now move on to consider interest rate futures.

The first half of this chapter explains the popular Treasury bond futures contracts and Eurodollar futures contracts that trade in the United States. Many of the other interest rate futures contracts throughout the world have been modeled on these contracts. The second half discusses the duration measure and shows how it can be used to measure the sensitivity of a portfolio to interest rates. It describes how interest rate futures contracts, when used in conjunction with the duration measure, can be used to hedge a company's exposure to interest rate movements.

6.1 DAY COUNT AND QUOTATION CONVENTIONS

As a preliminary to the material in this chapter, we consider the day count and quotation conventions that apply to bonds and other interest-rate-dependent securities.

Day Counts

The day count defines the way in which interest accrues over time. Generally, we know the interest earned over some reference period (e.g., the time between coupon payments on a bond), and we are interested in calculating the interest earned over some other period.

The day count convention is usually expressed as X/Y. When we are calculating the interest earned between two dates, X defines the way in which the number of days between the two dates is calculated, and Y defines the way in which the total number of days in the reference period is measured. The interest earned between the two dates is

$$\frac{\text{Number of days between dates}}{\text{Number of days in reference period}} \times \text{Interest earned in reference period}$$

Three day count conventions that are commonly used in the United States are:

1. Actual/actual (in period)
2. 30/360
3. Actual/360

From Chapter 6 of *Fundamentals of Futures and Options Markets*, Eighth Edition. John C. Hull.

Business Snapshot 6.1 Day counts can be deceptive

Between February 28, 2014, and March 1, 2014, you have a choice between owning a U.S. government bond paying a 10% coupon and a U.S. corporate bond paying a 10% coupon, with all else equal. Which would you prefer?

It sounds as though there should not be much difference. In fact, you should have a marked preference for the corporate bond. Under the 30/360 day count convention used for corporate bonds there are three days between February 28, 2014, and March 1, 2014. Under the actual/actual (in period) day count convention used for government bonds, there is only one day. You would earn approximately three times as much interest by holding the corporate bond!

Actual/actual (in period) is used for U.S. Treasury bonds, 30/360 is used for U.S. corporate and municipal bonds, and actual/360 is used for U.S. Treasury bills and other money market instruments.

The use of actual/actual (in period) for Treasury bonds indicates that the interest earned between two dates is based on the ratio of the actual days elapsed to the actual number of days in the period between coupon payments. Assume that the bond principal is \$100, coupon payment dates are March 1 and September 1, and the coupon rate is 8% per annum. This means that \$4 of interest is paid on each of March 1 and September 1. Suppose that we wish to calculate the interest earned between March 1 and July 3. The reference period is from March 1 to September 1. There are 184 (actual) days in the reference period, and interest of \$4 is earned during the period. There are 124 (actual) days between March 1 and July 3. The interest earned between March 1 and July 3 is therefore

$$\frac{124}{184} \times 4 = 2.6957$$

The use of 30/360 for corporate and municipal bonds indicates that we assume 30 days per month and 360 days per year when carrying out calculations. With 30/360, the total number of days between March 1 and September 1 is 180. The total number of days between March 1 and July 3 is $(4 \times 30) + 2 = 122$. In a corporate bond with the same terms as the Treasury bond just considered, the interest earned between March 1 and July 3 would therefore be

$$\frac{122}{180} \times 4 = 2.7111$$

As shown in Business Snapshot 6.1, sometimes the 30/360 day count convention has surprising consequences.

The use of actual/360 for a money market instrument indicates that the reference period is 360 days. The interest earned during part of a year is calculated by dividing the actual number of elapsed days by 360 and multiplying by the rate. The interest earned in 90 days is therefore exactly one-fourth of the quoted rate. Note that the interest earned in a whole year of 365 days is 365/360 times the quoted rate.

Conventions vary from country to country and instrument to instrument. For example, money market instruments are quoted on an actual/365 basis in Australia, Canada, and New Zealand. LIBOR is quoted on an actual/360 basis for all currencies except sterling, for which it is quoted on an actual/365 basis. Euro-denominated and sterling bonds are usually calculated on an actual/actual basis.

Price Quotations of U.S. Treasury Bills

The prices of money market instruments are sometimes quoted using a *discount rate*. This is the interest earned as a percent of the final face value rather than as a percent of the initial price paid for the instrument. An example is Treasury bills in the United States. If the price of a 91-day Treasury bill is quoted as 8, this means that the rate of interest earned is 8% of the face value per 360 days. Suppose that the face value is \$100. Interest of \$2.0222 (= \$100 × 0.08 × 91/360) is earned over the 91-day life. This corresponds to a true rate of interest of 2.0222/(100 − 2.0222) = 2.064% for the 91-day period. In general, the relationship between the cash price and quoted price of a Treasury bill in the United States is

$$P = \frac{360}{n}(100 - Y)$$

where P is the quoted price, Y is the cash price, and n is the remaining life of the Treasury bill measured in calendar days.

Price Quotations of U.S. Treasury Bonds

Treasury bond prices in the United States are quoted in dollars and thirty-seconds of a dollar. The quoted price is for a bond with a face value of \$100. Thus, a quote of 90-05 indicates that the quoted price for a bond with a face value of \$100,000 is \$90,156.25.

The quoted price, which traders refer to as the *clean price*, is not the same as the cash price that has to be paid by the purchaser of the bond, which is referred to as the *dirty price* by traders. In general, we have

$$\text{Cash price} = \text{Quoted price} + \text{Accrued interest since last coupon date}$$

To illustrate this formula, suppose that it is March 5, 2013, and the bond under consideration is an 11% coupon bond maturing on July 10, 2028, with a quoted price of 95-16 or \$95.50. Because coupons are paid semiannually on government bonds (and the final coupon is at maturity), the most recent coupon date is January 10, 2013, and the next coupon date is July 10, 2013. The number of days between January 10, 2013, and March 5, 2013, is 54, whereas the number of days between January 10, 2013, and July 10, 2013, is 181. On a bond with \$100 face value, the coupon payment is \$5.50 on January 10 and July 10. The accrued interest on March 5, 2013, is the share of the July 10 coupon accruing to the bondholder on March 5, 2013. Because actual/actual in period is used for Treasury bonds in the United States, this is

$$\frac{54}{181} \times \$5.50 = \$1.64$$

The cash price per \$100 face value for the bond is therefore

$$\$95.50 + \$1.64 = \$97.14$$

Thus, the cash price of a \$100,000 bond is \$97,140.

6.2 TREASURY BOND FUTURES

Table 6.1 shows interest rate futures quotes on July 13, 2012. One of the most popular long-term interest rate futures contracts is the Treasury bond futures contract traded by the CME Group. In this contract, any government bond that has between 15 and 25 years to maturity on the first day of the delivery month can be delivered. In 2010, the CME Group started trading the Ultra T-Bond contract, where any bond with maturity over 25 years can be delivered. As will be explained later in this section, the exchange has developed a procedure for adjusting the price received by the party with the short position according to the particular bond it chooses to deliver.

Other contracts are the 10-year, 5-year, and 2-year Treasury note futures. In the 10-year Treasury note futures contract, any government note (i.e., bond) with a maturity between $6\frac{1}{2}$ and 10 years can be delivered; in the 5-year and 2-year contracts, the note delivered has a remaining life of about 5 and 2 years, respectively. (The original life must be less than 5.25 years.)

The remaining discussion in this section focuses on CME Group Treasury bond futures. The Treasury note futures traded in the United States and many other futures contracts in the rest of the world are designed in a similar way to CME Group Treasury bond futures so that many of the points we will make are applicable to these contracts as well.

Quotes

Treasury bond futures contracts are quoted in dollars and thirty-seconds of a dollar per \$100 face value. This is similar to the way the bonds are quoted in the spot market. In Table 6.1, the settlement price of the September 2012 Treasury bond futures contract is specified as 151-20. This means $151\frac{20}{32}$, or 151.625. The settlement price of the September 2012 10-year Treasury note futures contract is quoted to the nearest half of a thirty-second. Thus the open of 134-215 should be interpreted as $134\frac{21.5}{32}$, or 134.671875. The 5-year and 2-year Treasury note contracts are quoted even more precisely, to the nearest quarter of a thirty-second. Thus the settlement price of 124-152 for the 5-year Treasury note contract should be interpreted as $124\frac{15.25}{32}$, or 124.4765625. Similarly, a quote of 124-157 would be interpreted as $124\frac{15.75}{32}$.

Conversion Factors

As mentioned, the Treasury bond futures contract allows the party with the short position to choose to deliver any bond that has a maturity of more than 15 years but less than 25 years. When a particular bond is delivered, a parameter known as its *conversion factor* defines the price received for the bond. The applicable quoted price for the bond delivered is the product of the conversion factor and the most recent settlement price for the futures contract. Taking accrued interest into account, as described in Section 6.1, the cash received for each \$100 face value of bond delivered is

$$(\text{Most recent settlement price} \times \text{Conversion factor}) + \text{Accrued interest}$$

Each contract is for the delivery of \$100,000 face value of bonds. Suppose the most recent settlement price is 90-00, the conversion factor for the bond delivered is 1.3800, and the accrued interest on this bond at the time of delivery is \$3 per \$100 face value.

Table 6.1 Futures quotes for a selection of CME Group contracts on interest rates on July 13, 2012

	Open	*High*	*Low*	*Prior settlement*	*Last trade*	*Change*	*Volume*
Treasury Bonds, $100,000							
Sept. 2012	151-21	151-28	150-27	151-20	151-05	−0-15	251,347
Dec. 2012	152-22	152-30	151-30	152-24	152-09	−0-15	332
10-Year Treasury Notes, $100,000							
Sept. 2012	134-215	134-245	134-115	134-210	134-170	−0-040	548,058
5-Year Treasury Notes, $100,000							
Sept. 2012	124-155	124-170	124-120	124-152	124-150	−0-002	228,972
2-Year Treasury Notes, $200,000							
Sept. 2012	110-072	110-080	110-070	110-072	110-080	+0-007	151,875
30-Day Fed Funds Rate, $5,000,000							
July 2012	99.8350	99.8350	99.8325	99.8350	99.8350	0.0000	4,925
Nov. 2012	99.8450	99.8500	99.8400	99.8400	99.8450	+0.0050	2,701
Eurodollar, $1,000,000							
Sept. 2012	99.595	99.595	99.575	99.595	99.590	−0.005	146,635
Dec. 2012	99.575	99.580	99.550	99.575	99.570	−0.005	195,863
Dec. 2013	99.485	99.490	99.465	99.485	99.480	−0.005	91,097
Dec. 2014	99.305	99.305	99.270	99.305	99.275	−0.030	45,543
Dec. 2016	98.410	98.410	98.345	98.405	98.370	−0.035	8,284

The cash received by the party with the short position (and paid by the party with the long position) is then

$$(1.3800 \times 90.00) + 3.00 = \$127.20$$

per $100 face value. A party with the short position in one contract would deliver bonds with face value of $100,000 and receive $127,200.

The conversion factor for a bond is set equal to the quoted price the bond would have per dollar of principal on the first day of the delivery month on the assumption that the interest rate for all maturities equals 6% per annum (with semiannual compounding). The bond maturity and the times to the coupon payment dates are rounded down to the nearest three months for the purposes of the calculation. The practice enables the exchange to produce comprehensive tables. If, after rounding, the bond lasts for an exact number of six month periods, the first coupon is assumed to be paid in six months. If, after rounding, the bond does not last for an exact number of six-month periods (i.e., there is an extra three months), the first coupon is assumed to be paid after three months and accrued interest is subtracted.

As a first example of these rules, consider a 10% coupon bond with 20 years and two months to maturity. For the purposes of calculating the conversion factor, the bond is assumed to have exactly 20 years to maturity. The first coupon payment is assumed to be made after six months. Coupon payments are then assumed to be made at six-month intervals until the end of the 20 years when the principal payment is made. Assume that the face value is \$100. When the discount rate is 6% per annum with semiannual compounding (or 3% per six months), the value of the bond is

$$\sum_{i=1}^{40} \frac{5}{1.03^i} + \frac{100}{1.03^{40}} = \$146.23$$

Dividing by the face value gives a conversion factor of 1.4623.

As a second example of the rules, consider an 8% coupon bond with 18 years and 4 months to maturity. For the purposes of calculating the conversion factor, the bond is assumed to have exactly 18 years and 3 months to maturity. Discounting all the payments back to a point in time three months from today at 6% per annum (compounded semiannually) gives a value of

$$4 + \sum_{i=1}^{36} \frac{4}{1.03^i} + \frac{100}{1.03^{36}} = \$125.83$$

The interest rate for a three-month period is $\sqrt{1.03} - 1$ or 1.4889%. Hence, discounting back to the present gives the bond's value as $125.83/1.014889 = \$123.99$. Subtracting the accrued interest of 2.0, this becomes \$121.99. The conversion factor is therefore 1.2199.

Cheapest-to-Deliver Bond

At any given time during the delivery month, there are many bonds that can be delivered in the Treasury bond futures contract, with a wide variety of coupon payments and maturity dates. The party with the short position can choose which of the available bonds is "cheapest" to deliver. Since the party with the short position receives

(Most recent settlement price × Conversion factor) + Accrued interest

Example 6.1 Choosing the cheapest-to-deliver bond

The party with the short position has decided to deliver and is trying to choose between the following three bonds. Assume that the most recent settlement price is 93-08, or 93.25.

Bond	*Quoted bond price (\$)*	*Conversion factor*
1	99.50	1.0382
2	143.50	1.5188
3	119.75	1.2615

The cost of delivering each of the bonds is as follows:

Bond 1: $99.50 - (93.25 \times 1.0382) = \$2.69$

Bond 2: $143.50 - (93.25 \times 1.5188) = \$1.87$

Bond 3: $119.75 - (93.25 \times 1.2615) = \$2.12$

The cheapest-to-deliver bond is bond 2.

Business Snapshot 6.2 The wild card play

The settlement price in the CME Group's Treasury bond futures contract is the price at 2:00 p.m. Chicago time. However, Treasury bonds continue trading in the spot market beyond this time and a trader with a short position can issue to the clearing house a notice of intention to deliver later in the day. If the notice is issued, the invoice price is calculated on the basis of the settlement price that day, that is, the price at 2:00 p.m.

This practice gives rise to an option known as the *wild card play*. If bond prices decline after 2:00 p.m. on the first day of the delivery month, the party with the short position can issue a notice of intention to deliver at, say, 3:45 p.m. and proceed to buy bonds in the spot market for delivery at a price calculated from the 2:00 p.m. futures price. If the bond price does not decline, the party with the short position keeps the position open and waits until the next day when the same strategy can be used.

As with the other options open to the party with the short position, the wild card play is not free. Its value is reflected in the futures price, which is lower than it would be without the option.

and the cost of purchasing a bond is

$$\text{Quoted bond price} + \text{Accrued interest}$$

the cheapest-to-deliver bond is the one for which

$$\text{Quoted bond price} - (\text{Most recent settlement price} \times \text{Conversion factor})$$

is least. Once the party with the short position has decided to deliver, it can determine the cheapest-to-deliver bond by examining each of the deliverable bonds in turn. The calculations are illustrated in Example 6.1.

A number of factors determine the cheapest-to-deliver bond. When bond yields are in excess of 6%, the conversion factor system tends to favor the delivery of low-coupon long-maturity bonds. When yields are less than 6%, the system tends to favor the delivery of high-coupon short-maturity bonds. Also, when the yield curve is upward sloping, there is a tendency for bonds with a long time to maturity to be favored, whereas when it is downward sloping, there is a tendency for bonds with a short time to maturity to be delivered.

In addition to the cheapest-to-deliver bond option, the party with a short position has an option known as the wild card play. See Business Snapshot 6.2 for a description of this option.

Determining the Futures Price

An exact theoretical futures price for the Treasury bond contract is difficult to determine because the short party's options concerned with the timing of delivery and choice of the bond that is delivered cannot easily be valued. However, if we assume that both the cheapest-to-deliver bond and the delivery date are known, the Treasury bond futures contract is a futures contract on a traded security (the bond)

Example 6.2 Calculation of Treasury bond futures price

Suppose that, in a Treasury bond futures contract, it is known that the cheapest-to-deliver bond will be a 12% coupon bond with a conversion factor of 1.6000. Suppose also that it is known that delivery will take place in 270 days. Coupons are payable semiannually on the bond. As illustrated in the time chart below, the last coupon date was 60 days ago, the next coupon date is in 122 days, and the coupon date thereafter is in 305 days. The term structure is flat, and the rate of interest (with continuous compounding) is 10% per annum.

Assume that the current quoted bond price is \$115. The cash price of the bond is obtained by adding to this quoted price the proportion of the next coupon payment that accrues to the holder. The cash price is therefore

$$115 + \frac{60}{60+122} \times 6 = 116.978$$

A coupon of \$6 will be received after 122 days (= 0.3342 year). The present value of this is

$$6e^{-0.1\times 0.3342} = 5.803$$

The futures contract lasts for 270 days (0.7397 year). The cash futures price if the contract were written on the 12% bond would therefore be

$$(116.978 - 5.803)e^{0.1\times 0.7397} = 119.711$$

At delivery there are 148 days of accrued interest. The quoted futures price if the contract were written on the 12% bond is calculated by subtracting the accrued interest

$$119.711 - 6 \times \frac{148}{148+35} = 114.859$$

From the definition of the conversion factor, 1.6000 standard bonds are considered equivalent to each 12% bond. The quoted futures price should therefore be

$$\frac{114.859}{1.6000} = 71.79$$

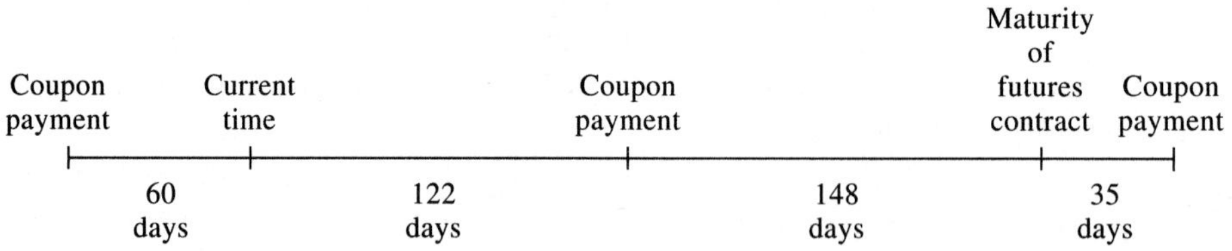

that provides the holder with known income.[1] Equation (5.2) then shows that the futures price, F_0, is related to the spot price, S_0, by

$$F_0 = (S_0 - I)e^{rT} \tag{6.1}$$

[1] In practice, for the purposes of estimating the cheapest-to-deliver bond, analysts usually assume that zero rates at the maturity of the futures contract will equal today's forward rates.

where I is the present value of the coupons during the life of the futures contract, T is the time until the futures contract matures, and r is the risk-free interest rate applicable to a time period of length T. Example 6.2 provides an application of equation (6.1).

6.3 EURODOLLAR FUTURES

The most popular interest rate futures contract in the United States is the three-month Eurodollar futures contract traded by the CME Group. A Eurodollar is a dollar deposited in a U.S. or foreign bank outside the United States. The Eurodollar interest rate is the rate of interest earned on Eurodollars deposited by one bank with another bank. It is essentially the same as the London Interbank Offered Rate (LIBOR) introduced in Chapter 4.

A three-month Eurodollar futures contract is a futures contract on the interest that will be paid (by someone who borrows at the Eurodollar interest rate) on \$1 million for a future three-month period. It allows a trader to speculate on a future three-month interest rate or to hedge an exposure to a future three-month interest rate. Eurodollar futures contracts have maturities in March, June, September, and December for up to 10 years into the future. This means that in 2013 a trader can use Eurodollar futures to take a position on what interest rates will be as far into the future as 2023. Short-maturity contracts trade for months other than March, June, September, and December.

To understand how Eurodollar futures contracts work, consider the December 2012 contract in Table 6.1. The contract traded at 99.570 on July 13, 2012. Contracts end on the third Wednesday of the delivery month. In the case of this contract, the third Wednesday of the delivery month is December 19, 2012. The contract is settled daily in the usual way until that date. On December 19, 2012, the settlement price is set equal to $100 - R$, where R is the actual three-month Eurodollar interest rate on that day, expressed with quarterly compounding and an actual/360 day count convention. Thus, if the three-month Eurodollar interest rate on December 19, 2012, turned out to be 0.5% (actual/360 with quarterly compounding), the final settlement price would be 99.500. Once a final settlement has taken place, all contracts are declared closed.

The contract is designed so that a one-basis-point (= 0.01) move in the futures quote corresponds to a gain or loss of \$25 per contract. When a Eurodollar futures quote increases by one basis point, a trader who is long one contract gains \$25 and a trader who is short one contract loses \$25. Similarly, when the quote decreases by one basis point a trader who is long one contract loses \$25 and a trader who is short one contract gains \$25. Suppose, for example, a settlement price changes from 99.120 to 99.230. Traders with long positions gain $11 \times 25 = \$275$ per contract; traders with short positions lose \$275 per contract. A one-basis-point change in the futures quote corresponds to a 0.01% change in the futures interest rate. This in turn leads to a

$$1{,}000{,}000 \times 0.0001 \times 0.25 = 25$$

or \$25 change in the interest that will be earned on \$1 million in three months. The \$25 per basis point rule is therefore consistent with the point made earlier that the contract locks in an interest rate on \$1 million for three months.

Table 6.2 Possible sequence of prices for December 2012 Eurodollar futures contract

Date	*Futures price*	*Change*	*Gain per contract ($)*
July 13, 2012	99.570		
July 16, 2012	99.530	−0.040	−100
July 17, 2012	99.580	+0.050	+125
⋮	⋮	⋮	⋮
Dec. 19, 2012	99.500	−0.060	+150
Total		−0.070	−175

The futures quote is 100 minus the futures interest rate. An investor who is long gains when interest rates fall and one who is short gains when interest rates rise. Table 6.2 shows a possible set of outcomes for the December 2012 contract in Table 6.1.

The CME defines the contract price as

$$10{,}000 \times [100 - 0.25 \times (100 - Q)] \tag{6.2}$$

where Q is the quote. Thus, the price of 99.570 for the December 2012 contract in Table 6.1 corresponds to a contract price of

$$10{,}000 \times [100 - 0.25 \times (100 - 99.570)] = \$998{,}925$$

In Table 6.2 the final contract price is

$$10{,}000 \times [100 - 0.25 \times (100 - 99.500)] = \$998{,}750$$

and the difference between the initial and final contract price is $175, This is consistent with the loss calculated in Table 6.2 using the "$25 per one-basis-point move" rule.

Table 6.1 shows that the interest rate term structure in the U.S. was upward sloping in July 2012. The settlement futures rate for a three-month period beginning September 19, 2012, was 0.405%; for a three-month period beginning December 19, 2012, it was 0.425%; and for a three-month period beginning December 18, 2013, it was 0.515%.

Example 6.3 shows how Eurodollar futures contracts can be used by an investor who wants to hedge the interest that will be earned during a future three-month period starting on September 16, 2015. Note that the timing of the cash flows from the hedge does not line up exactly with the timing of the interest cash flows. This is because the futures contract is settled daily. Also, the final settlement is on September 16, 2015, whereas interest payments on the investment are received three months after this date. As indicated in the example, a small adjustment can be made to the hedge position in an attempt to allow for this second point.

Other contracts similar to the CME Eurodollar futures contracts trade on interest rates in other countries. The CME trades Euroyen contracts. The London International Financial Futures and Options Exchange (part of Euronext) trades three-month Euribor contracts (i.e., contracts on the three-month LIBOR rate for the euro) and three-month Euroswiss futures.

Example 6.3 Use of Eurodollar futures for hedging

An investor wants to lock in the interest rate for a three-month period beginning September 16, 2015, on a principal of \$100 million. We suppose that the September 2015 Eurodollar futures quote is 96.500, indicating that the investor can lock in an interest rate of 100 – 96.5 or 3.5% per annum. The investor hedges by buying 100 contracts. Suppose that on September 16, 2015, the three-month Eurodollar rate turns out to be 2.6%. The final settlement in the contract is then at a price of 97.400. The investor gains

$$100 \times 25 \times (9{,}740 - 9{,}650) = 225{,}000$$

or \$225,000 on the Eurodollar futures contracts. The interest earned on the three-month investment is

$$100{,}000{,}000 \times 0.25 \times 0.026 = 650{,}000$$

or \$650,000. The gain on the Eurodollar futures brings this up to \$875,000, which is what the interest would be at 3.5% ($100{,}000{,}000 \times 0.25 \times 0.035 = 875{,}000$).

It appears that the futures trade has the effect of exactly locking an interest rate of 3.5% in all circumstances. In fact, the hedge is less than perfect because (a) futures contracts are settled daily (not all at the end) and (b) the final settlement in the futures contract happens on September 16, 2015, whereas the interest payment on the investment is three months later. One way of adjusting for the second point is to reduce the size of the hedge to reflect the difference between funds received on September 16, 2015, and funds received three months later. In this case, we would assume an interest rate of 3.5% for the three-month period and multiply the number of contracts by $1/(1 + 0.035 \times 0.25) = 0.9913$. This would lead to 99 rather than 100 contracts being purchased.

Forward vs. Futures Interest Rates

The Eurodollar futures contract is similar to a forward rate agreement in that it locks in an interest rate for a future period. (See Section 4.7 for a discussion of forward rate agreements.) For short maturities (up to one year or so), the two contracts can be assumed to be the same and the Eurodollar futures interest rate can be assumed to be the same as the corresponding forward interest rate. For longer-dated contracts differences between the contracts mentioned earlier become important. Compare a Eurodollar futures contract on an interest rate for the period between times T_1 and T_2 with a forward rate agreement for the same period. The Eurodollar futures contract is settled daily. The final settlement is at time T_1 and reflects the realized interest rate for the period between times T_1 and T_2. By contrast the forward rate agreement is not settled daily and the final settlement reflecting the realized interest rate between times T_1 and T_2 is made at time T_2.[2]

There are therefore two differences between a Eurodollar futures contract and a forward rate agreement. These are:

1. The difference between a Eurodollar futures contract and a similar contract where there is no daily settlement. The latter is a hypothetical forward contract where a

[2] As mentioned in Section 4.7, settlement may occur at time T_1, but it is then equal to the present value of what the forward contract payoff would be at time T_2.

Example 6.4 Calculation of convexity adjustment

Consider the situation where $\sigma = 0.012$ and we wish to calculate the forward rate when the eight-year Eurodollar futures price quote is 94. In this case, $T_1 = 8$, $T_2 = 8.25$, and the convexity adjustment is

$$\tfrac{1}{2} \times 0.012^2 \times 8 \times 8.25 = 0.00475$$

or 0.475% (47.5 basis points). The futures rate is 6% per annum on an actual/360 basis with quarterly compounding. This is $6 \times 365/360 = 6.083\%$ per annum on an actual/365 basis with quarterly compounding or 6.038% with continuous compounding. The forward rate is therefore $6.038 - 0.475 = 5.563\%$ per annum with continuous compounding. Table 6.3 shows how the size of the adjustment increases with the time to maturity. It is approximately proportional to the square of the time to maturity.

payoff equal to the difference between the forward interest rate and the realized interest rate is paid at time T_1.

2. The difference between the hypothetical forward contract where there is settlement at time T_1 and a true forward contract where there is settlement equal to the difference between the forward interest rate and realized interest rate at time T_2.

Both decrease the forward rate relative to the futures rate.

Convexity Adjustment

Analysts make what is known as a *convexity adjustment* to account for the differences between the two rates. One popular adjustment is

$$\text{Forward rate} = \text{Futures rate} - \tfrac{1}{2}\sigma^2 T_1 T_2 \qquad \textbf{(6.3)}$$

where, as above, T_1 is the time to maturity of the futures contract and T_2 is the time to the maturity of the rate underlying the futures contract. The variable σ is the standard deviation of the change in the short-term interest rate in one year. Both rates are expressed with continuous compounding.[3] The adjustment is illustrated in Example 6.4.

The forward rate is less than the futures rate. As can be seen from equation (6.3), the size of the adjustment is roughly proportional to the square of the time to maturity of the futures contract. Thus, the convexity adjustment for the eight-year contract is approximately 16 times that for a two-year contract.

6.4 DURATION

The *duration* of a bond, as its name implies, is a measure of how long on average the holder of the bond has to wait before receiving cash payments. A zero-coupon bond that matures in n years has a duration of n years. However, a coupon-bearing bond

[3] This formula is based on the Ho–Lee interest rate model. See T. S. Y. Ho and S.-B. Lee, "Term Structure Movements and Pricing Interest Rate Contingent Claims," *Journal of Finance*, 41 (December 1986), 1011–29.

Table 6.3 Convexity adjustment for the futures rate in Example 6.4

Maturity of futures (years)	*Convexity adjustments (basis points)*
2	3.2
4	12.2
6	27.0
8	47.5
10	73.8

maturing in n years has a duration of less than n years, because the holder receives some of the cash payments prior to year n.

Suppose that a bond provides the holder with cash flows c_i at time t_i $(1 \leqslant i \leqslant n)$. The bond price B and bond yield y (continuously compounded) are related by

$$B = \sum_{i=1}^{n} c_i e^{-yt_i} \tag{6.4}$$

The duration, D, of the bond is defined as

$$D = \frac{\sum_{i=1}^{n} t_i c_i e^{-yt_i}}{B} \tag{6.5}$$

This can be written as

$$D = \sum_{i=1}^{n} t_i \left[\frac{c_i e^{-yt_i}}{B} \right]$$

The term in square brackets is the ratio of the present value of the cash flow at time t_i to the bond price. The bond price is the present value of all payments. The duration is therefore a weighted average of the times when payments are made, with the weight applied to time t_i being equal to the proportion of the bond's total present value provided by the cash flow at time t_i. The sum of the weights is 1.0. (Note that, for the purposes of the definition of duration, all discounting is done at the bond yield rate of interest y. We do not use the a different zero rate for each cash flow in the way described in Section 4.4.)

From equation (6.4), it is approximately true that

$$\Delta B = -\Delta y \sum_{i=1}^{n} c_i t_i e^{-yt_i} \tag{6.6}$$

where Δy is a small change in y and ΔB is the corresponding small change in B. (Note that there is a negative relationship between B and y. When bond yields increase, bond prices decrease; and when bond yields decrease, bond prices increase.) From equations (6.5) and (6.6), we can derive the key duration relationship

$$\Delta B = -BD\,\Delta y \tag{6.7}$$

Table 6.4 Calculation of duration

Time (years)	*Cash flow ($)*	*Present value*	*Weight*	*Time × Weight*
0.5	5	4.709	0.050	0.025
1.0	5	4.435	0.047	0.047
1.5	5	4.176	0.044	0.066
2.0	5	3.933	0.042	0.083
2.5	5	3.704	0.039	0.098
3.0	105	73.256	0.778	2.333
Total	130	94.213	1.000	2.653

This can be written

$$\frac{\Delta B}{B} = -D\,\Delta y \tag{6.8}$$

Equation (6.8) is an approximate relationship between percentage changes in a bond price and changes in its yield. It is easy to use and is the reason why duration, which was suggested by Macaulay in 1938, has become such a popular measure.

Consider a three-year 10% coupon bond with a face value of \$100. Suppose that the yield on the bond is 12% per annum with continuous compounding. This means that $y = 0.12$. Coupon payments of \$5 are made every six months. Table 6.4 shows the calculations necessary to determine the bond's duration. The present values of the bond's cash flows, using the yield as the discount rate, are shown in column 3. (For example, the present value of the first cash flow is $5e^{-0.12\times 0.5} = 4.709$.) The sum of the numbers in column 3 gives the bond's price as 94.213. The weights are calculated by dividing the numbers in column 3 by 94.213. The sum of the numbers in column 5 gives the duration as 2.653 years. Example 6.5 tests the accuracy of the duration relationship in equation (6.7).

Example 6.5 Testing the duration relationship

For the bond in Table 6.4, the bond price B is 94.213 and the duration D is 2.653, so that equation (6.7) gives

$$\Delta B = -94.213 \times 2.653 \times \Delta y = -249.95 \times \Delta y$$

When the yield on the bond increases by 10 basis points (= 0.1%), $\Delta y = +0.001$. The duration relationship predicts that $\Delta B = -249.95 \times 0.001 = -0.250$, so that the bond price goes down to $94.213 - 0.250 = 93.963$. How accurate is this? When the bond yield increases by 10 basis points to 12.1%, the bond price is

$$5e^{-0.121\times 0.5} + 5e^{-0.121\times 1.0} + 5e^{-0.121\times 1.5} + 5e^{-0.121\times 2.0} + 5e^{-0.121\times 2.5} + 105e^{-0.121\times 3.0} = 93.963$$

which is (to three decimal places) the same as that predicted by the duration relationship.

Small changes in interest rates are often measured in *basis points*. As mentioned earlier, a basis point is 0.01% per annum.

Modified Duration

The preceding analysis is based on the assumption that y is expressed with continuous compounding. If y is expressed with annual compounding, it can be shown that the approximate relationship in equation (6.7) becomes

$$\Delta B = -\frac{BD\,\Delta y}{1+y}$$

More generally, if y is expressed with a compounding frequency of m times per year, then

$$\Delta B = -\frac{BD\,\Delta y}{1+y/m}$$

A variable D^* defined by

$$D^* = \frac{D}{1+y/m}$$

is sometimes referred to as the bond's *modified duration*. It allows the duration relationship to be simplified to

$$\Delta B = -BD^*\Delta y \tag{6.9}$$

when y is expressed with a compounding frequency of m times per year. Example 6.6 investigates the accuracy of the modified duration relationship.

Another term that is sometimes used is *dollar duration*. This is the product of modified duration and bond price, so that $\Delta B = -D^{**}\Delta y$, where D^{**} is dollar duration.

Example 6.6 Testing the modified duration relationship

The bond in Table 6.4 has a price of 94.213 and a duration of 2.653. The yield, expressed with semiannual compounding, is 12.3673%. The modified duration, D^*, is given by

$$D^* = \frac{2.653}{1+0.123673/2} = 2.499$$

From equation (6.9), we have

$$\Delta B = -94.213 \times 2.4985 \times \Delta y = -235.39 \times \Delta y$$

When the yield (semiannually compounded) increases by 10 basis points ($= 0.1\%$), $\Delta y = +0.001$. The duration relationship predicts that we expect ΔB to be $-235.39 \times 0.001 = -0.235$, so that the bond price to goes down to $94.213 - 0.235 = 93.978$. How accurate is this? When the bond yield (semiannually compounded) increases by 10 basis points to 12.4673% (or to 12.0941% with continuous compounding), an exact calculation similar to that in the previous example shows that the bond price becomes 93.978. This shows that the modified duration calculation gives good accuracy for small yield changes.

Bond Portfolios

The duration, D, of a bond portfolio can be defined as a weighted average of the durations of the individual bonds in the portfolio, with the weights being proportional to the bond prices. Equations (6.7) to (6.9) then apply with B being defined as the value of the bond portfolio. They estimate the change in the value of the bond portfolio for a particular change Δy in the yields of all the bonds.

It is important to realize that, when duration is used for bond portfolios, there is an implicit assumption that the yields of all bonds will change by approximately the same amount. When the bonds have widely differing maturities, this happens only when there is a parallel shift in the yield curve. We should therefore interpret equations (6.7) to (6.9) as providing estimates of the impact on the price of a bond portfolio of a parallel shift, Δy, in the yield curve.

The duration relationship applies only to small changes in yields. This is illustrated in Figure 6.1, which shows the relationship between the percentage change in value and change in yield for two bond portfolios having the same duration. The gradients of the two curves are the same at the origin. This means that both bond portfolios change in value by the same percentage for small yield changes and is consistent with equation (6.8). For large yield changes, the portfolios behave differently. Portfolio X has more curvature in its relationship with yields than portfolio Y. A factor known as *convexity* measures this curvature and can be used to improve the relationship in equation (6.8).

Hedging Portfolios of Assets and Liabilities

Financial institutions sometimes attempt to hedge themselves against interest rate risk by ensuring that the average duration of their assets equals the average duration of their liabilities. (The liabilities can be regarded as short positions in bonds.) This strategy is

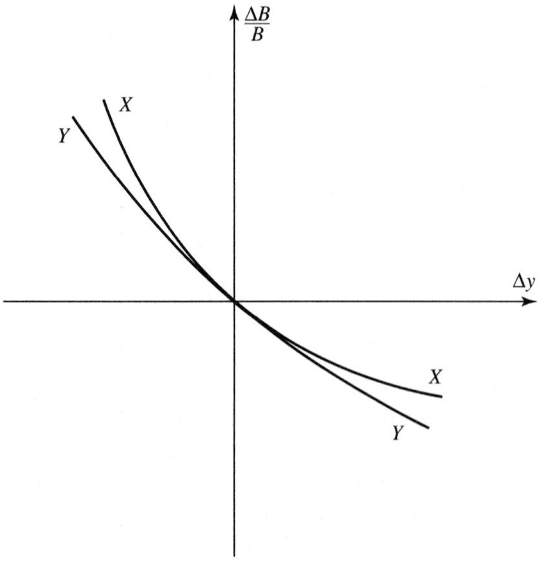

Figure 6.1 Two bond portfolios with the same duration

Business Snapshot 6.3 Asset–liability management by banks

The asset–liability management (ALM) committees of banks now monitor their exposure to interest rates very carefully. Matching the durations of assets and liabilities is sometimes a first step, but this does not protect a bank against non-parallel shifts in the yield curve. A popular approach is known as *GAP management*. This involves dividing the zero-coupon yield curve into segments, known as *buckets*. The first bucket might be 0 to 1 month, the second 1 to 3 months, and so on. The ALM committee then investigates the effect on the values of both assets and liabilities of the zero rates corresponding to one bucket changing while those corresponding to all other buckets stay the same.

If there is a mismatch, then corrective action is usually taken. This can involve changing deposit and lending rates in the way described in Section 4.8. Alternatively, tools such as swaps, FRAs, bond futures, Eurodollar futures, and other interest rate derivatives can be used.

known as *duration matching* or *portfolio immunization*. When implemented it ensures that a small parallel shift in interest rates will have little effect on the value of the portfolio of assets and liabilities. The gain (loss) on the assets should offset the loss (gain) on the liabilities.

Duration matching does not immunize a portfolio against nonparallel shifts in the zero curve. This is a weakness of the approach. In practice, short-term rates are usually more volatile than and are not perfectly correlated with long-term rates. Sometimes it even happens that short- and long-term rates move in opposite directions to each other. Duration matching is therefore only a first step and financial institutions have developed other tools to help them manage their interest rate exposure (see Business Snapshot 6.3).

6.5 DURATION-BASED HEDGING STRATEGIES USING FUTURES

Consider the situation where a position in an interest rate dependent asset such as a bond portfolio or a money market security is being hedged using an interest rate futures contract.

Define:

V_F: Contract price for one interest rate futures contract

D_F: Duration of the asset underlying the futures contract at the maturity of the futures contract

P: Forward value of the portfolio being hedged at the maturity of the hedge. In practice this is usually assumed to be the same as the portfolio value today.

D_P: Duration of the portfolio at the maturity of the hedge.

If we assume that the change in the yield, Δy, is the same for all maturities, which means that only parallel shifts in the yield curve can occur, it is approximately true that

$$\Delta P = -PD_P\,\Delta y$$

It is also approximately true that

$$\Delta V_F = -V_F D_F\,\Delta y$$

The number of contracts required to hedge against an uncertain Δy is therefore given by

$$N^* = \frac{PD_P}{V_F D_F} \quad \textbf{(6.10)}$$

This is the *duration-based hedge ratio*. It is sometimes also called the *price sensitivity hedge ratio*.[4] Using it has the effect of making the duration of the entire position zero.

When the hedging instrument is a Treasury bond futures contract, the hedger must base D_F on an assumption that one particular bond will be delivered. This means that the hedger must estimate which of the available bonds is likely to be cheapest to deliver at the time the hedge is put in place. If, subsequently, the interest rate environment changes so that it looks as though a different bond will be cheapest to deliver, the hedge has to be adjusted, and as a result its performance may be worse than anticipated.

When hedges are constructed using interest rate futures, it is important to bear in mind that interest rates and futures prices move in opposite directions. When interest rates go up, an interest rate futures price goes down. When interest rates go down, the reverse happens, and the interest rate futures price goes up. Thus, a company in a position to lose money if interest rates drop should hedge by taking a long futures position. Similarly, a company in a position to lose money if interest rates rise should hedge by taking a short futures position.

The hedger tries to choose the futures contract so that the duration of the underlying asset is as close as possible to the duration of the asset being hedged. Eurodollar futures tend to be used for exposures to short-term interest rates, whereas Treasury bond and Treasury note futures contracts are used for exposures to longer-term rates.

Hedging a Bond Portfolio

Consider the situation of a fund manager who has \$10 million invested in government bonds on August 2 and is concerned that interest rates are expected to be highly volatile over the next three months. The fund manager decides to use the December Treasury bond futures contract to hedge the value of the portfolio. The current futures price is 93-02 or 93.0625. Because each contract is for the delivery of \$100,000 face value of bonds, the futures contract price is \$93,062.50.

The duration of the bond portfolio in three months is 6.8 years. The cheapest-to-deliver bond in the Treasury bond contract is expected to be a 20-year 12% per annum coupon bond. The yield on this bond is currently 8.8% per annum, and the duration will be 9.2 years at maturity of the futures contract.

The fund manager requires a short position in Treasury bond futures to hedge the bond portfolio. If interest rates go up, a gain will be made on the short futures position, and a loss will be made on the bond portfolio. If interest rates decrease, a loss will be

[4] For a more detailed discussion of equation (6.10), see R. Rendleman, "Duration-Based Hedging with Treasury Bond Futures," *Journal of Fixed Income*, 9, 1 (June 1999): 84–91.

Example 6.7 Hedging a bond portfolio

It is August 2. A fund manager responsible for a \$10 million bond portfolio is concerned that interest rates are expected to be highly volatile over the next three months. The fund manager decides to use Treasury bond futures to hedge the value of the bond portfolio. The quoted price for the December Treasury bond futures contract is 93-02. This means that the contract price is \$93,062.50. The strategy followed is:

1. Short 79 December Treasury bond futures contracts on August 2.
2. Close out the position on November 2.

Suppose that during the period August 2 to November 2, interest rates decline rapidly and the value of the bond portfolio increases from \$10 million to \$10,450,000. On November 2, the Treasury bond futures price is 98-16. (This corresponds to a contract price of \$98,500.00.) A loss of

$$79 \times (\$98{,}500.00 - \$93{,}062.50) = \$429{,}562.50$$

is therefore made on the Treasury bond futures contracts. The value of the portfolio manager's position changes by only

$$\$450{,}000.00 - \$429{,}562.50 = \$20{,}437.50.$$

made on the short position, but there will be a gain on the bond portfolio. The number of bond futures contracts that should be shorted can be calculated from equation (6.10) as

$$\frac{10{,}000{,}000 \times 6.80}{93{,}062.50 \times 9.20} = 79.42$$

Rounding to the nearest whole number, the portfolio manager should short 79 contracts.

Example 6.7 illustrates how the hedge might work out. Suppose that during the period from August 2 to November 2, interest rates decline rapidly and the value of the bond portfolio increases from \$10 million to \$10,450,000. Suppose further that on November 2, the Treasury bond futures price is 98-16. This corresponds to a contract price of \$98,500. The total loss on the Treasury bond futures contracts is

$$79 \times (\$98{,}500.00 - \$93{,}062.50) = \$429{,}562.50$$

The net change in the value of the portfolio manager's position is therefore only

$$\$450{,}000.00 - \$429{,}562.50 = \$20{,}437.50$$

Since the fund incurs a loss on the futures position, the manager may regret implementing the hedge. On average, we can expect half of our hedges to lead to this sort of regret. This is in the nature of hedging.

Hedging a Floating-Rate Loan

Interest rate futures can be used to hedge the rate of interest paid by a large corporation on a floating-rate loan. Eurodollar futures are ideal for this because the

Eurodollar interest rate is closely related to the rate of interest at which large corporations borrow.

Consider a company that in April borrows \$15 million for three months. The interest rate for each of the three one-month periods will be the one-month LIBOR rate plus 1%. At the time the loan is negotiated, the one-month LIBOR rate is 8% per annum, so the company must pay 9% per annum for the first month. Because the one-month LIBOR rate is quoted with monthly compounding, the interest for the first month is 0.75% of \$15 million, or \$112,500. This is known for certain at the time the loan is negotiated and does not have to be hedged.

The interest paid at the end of the second month is determined by the one-month LIBOR rate at the beginning of the second month. It can be hedged by taking a position in the June Eurodollar futures contract. Suppose that the quoted price for this contract is 91.88. From Section 6.3, the contract price is

$$10{,}000 \times [100 - 0.25 \times (100 - 91.88)] = \$979{,}700$$

The company will lose money if interest rates rise and gain if interest rates fall. It therefore requires a short position in the futures contracts. The duration of the asset underlying the futures contract at maturity of the contract is three months, or 0.25 years. The duration of the liability being hedged is one month, or 0.08333 years. From equation (6.10), the number of contracts that should be used to hedge the interest payment in the second month is

$$\frac{15{,}000{,}000 \times 0.08333}{979{,}700 \times 0.25} = 5.10$$

Rounding to the nearest whole number, five contracts are required.

For the third month, the September Eurodollar futures contract can be used. Suppose the quoted price for this contract is 91.44, which corresponds to a futures price of \$978,600. The number of futures contracts that should be shorted can be calculated as before:

$$\frac{15{,}000{,}000 \times 0.08333}{978{,}600 \times 0.25} = 5.11$$

Again, we find that, to the nearest whole number, five contracts are required. Thus, five of the June contracts should be shorted to hedge the LIBOR rate applicable to the second month, and five of the September contracts should be shorted to hedge the LIBOR rate applicable to the third month. The June contracts are closed out on May 29, and the September contracts are closed out on June 29.

Example 6.8 illustrates how the hedge might work. Suppose that on May 29 the one-month LIBOR rate is 8.8% and the June futures price is 91.12. The latter corresponds to a contract price of \$977,800, so that the company makes a profit of

$$5 \times (\$979{,}700 - \$977{,}800) = \$9{,}500$$

on the June contracts. This provided compensation for the extra \$10,000 interest (one-twelfth of 0.8% of \$15 million) that had to be paid at the end of the second month as a result of the LIBOR increase from 8% to 8.8%.

Suppose further that on June 29 the one-month LIBOR rate is 9.4% and the September futures price is 90.16. A similar calculation to that just given shows that

Example 6.8 Hedging a floating-rate loan

It is April 29. A company has just borrowed \$15 million for three months at an interest rate equal to one-month LIBOR plus 1% and would like to hedge its risk. The following quotes have been obtained:

1. The one-month LIBOR rate is 8%.
2. The June Eurodollar futures price is 91.88.
3. The September Eurodollar futures price is 91.44.

The company decides to take the following actions:

1. Short five June contracts and five September contracts.
2. Close out the June contracts on May 29.
3. Close out the September contracts on June 29.

On May 29, the one-month LIBOR rate proves to be 8.8%, and the June futures price proves to be 91.12. The company gains 5 × (\$979,700 − \$977,800) = \$9,500 on the five June contracts. This provides compensation for the \$10,000 extra interest payment necessary in the second month because of the increase in LIBOR from 8% to 8.8%.

On June 29, the one-month LIBOR rate proves to be 9.4% and the September futures price proves to be 90.16. The company gains \$16,000 on the five September contracts. This provides compensation for extra interest costs of \$17,500.

the company gains \$16,000 on the short futures position, but incurs extra interest costs of \$17,500 as a result of the increase in one-month LIBOR from 8% per annum to 9.4% per annum.

As discussed in Example 6.3, the timing of hedge cash flows does not exactly line up with that of the interest cash flows.

SUMMARY

Two very popular interest rate contracts are the Treasury bond and Eurodollar futures contracts that trade in the United States. In the Treasury bond futures contracts, the party with the short position has a number of interesting delivery options:

1. Delivery can be made on any day during the delivery month.
2. There are a number of alternative bonds that can be delivered.
3. On any day during the delivery month, the notice of intention to deliver at the 2:00 p.m. settlement price can be made later in the day.

These options all tend to reduce the futures price.

The Eurodollar futures contract is a contract on the three-month rate starting on the third Wednesday of the delivery month. Eurodollar futures are frequently used to estimate LIBOR forward rates for the purpose of constructing a LIBOR zero curve. When long-dated contracts are used in this way, it is important to make what is termed a convexity adjustment to allow for the difference between a futures and a forward contract.

The concept of duration is important in hedging interest rate risk. Duration measures how long on average an investor has to wait before receiving payments. It is a weighted average of the times until payments are received, with the weight for a particular payment time being proportional to the present value of the payment.

A key result underlying the duration-based hedging procedure described in this chapter is

$$\Delta B = -BD\,\Delta y$$

where B is a bond price, D is its duration, Δy is a small change in its yield (continuously compounded), and ΔB is the resultant small change in B. The equation enables a hedger to assess the sensitivity of a bond price to small changes in its yield. It also enables the hedger to assess the sensitivity of an interest rate futures price to small changes in the yield of the underlying instrument. If the hedger is prepared to assume that Δy is the same for all bonds, the result enables the hedger to calculate the number of futures contracts necessary to protect a bond or bond portfolio against small changes in interest rates.

The key assumption underlying duration-based hedging is that all interest rates change by the same amount. This means that only parallel shifts in the term structure are allowed for. In practice, short-term interest rates are generally more volatile than long-term interest rates, and hedge performance is liable to be poor if the duration of the bond underlying the futures contract differs markedly from the duration of the asset being hedged.

FURTHER READING

Burghardt, G., and W. Hoskins. "The Convexity Bias in Eurodollar Futures," *Risk*, 8, 3 (1995): 63–70.

Duffie, D. "Debt Management and Interest Rate Risk" in W. Beaver and G. Parker (eds.), *Risk Management: Challenges and Solutions*. New York: McGraw-Hill, 1994.

Fabozzi, F. J. *Duration, Convexity, and Other Bond Risk Measures*, Frank J. Fabozzi Assoc., 1999.

Grinblatt, M., and N. Jegadeesh. "The Relative Price of Eurodollar Futures and Forward Contracts," *Journal of Finance*, 51, 4 (September 1996): 1499–1522.

Quiz (Answers at End of Book)

6.1. A U.S. Treasury bond pays a 7% coupon on January 7 and July 7. How much interest accrues per $100 of principal to the bond holder between July 7, 2013, and August 9, 2013? How would your answer be different if it were a corporate bond?

6.2. It is January 9, 2013. The price of a Treasury bond with a 12% coupon that matures on October 12, 2020, is quoted as 102-07. What is the cash price?

6.3. How is the conversion factor of a bond calculated by the CME Group? How is it used?

6.4. A Eurodollar futures price changes from 96.76 to 96.82. What is the gain or loss to an investor who is long two contracts?

6.5. What is the purpose of the convexity adjustment made to Eurodollar futures rates? Why is the convexity adjustment necessary?

6.6. What does duration tell you about the sensitivity of a bond portfolio to interest rates. What are the limitations of the duration measure?

6.7. It is January 30. You are managing a bond portfolio worth $6 million. The duration of the portfolio in six months will be 8.2 years. The September Treasury bond futures price is currently 108-15, and the cheapest-to-deliver bond will have a duration of 7.6 years in September. How should you hedge against changes in interest rates over the next six months?

Practice Questions (Answers in Solutions Manual/Study Guide)

6.8. The price of a 90-day Treasury bill is quoted as 10.00. What continuously compounded return (on an actual/365 basis) does an investor earn on the Treasury bill for the 90-day period?

6.9. It is May 5, 2013. The quoted price of a U.S. government bond with a 12% coupon that matures on July 27, 2024, is 110-17. What is the cash price?

6.10. Suppose that the Treasury bond futures price is 101-12. Which of the following four bonds is cheapest to deliver?

Bond	*Price*	*Conversion factor*
1	125-05	1.2131
2	142-15	1.3792
3	115-31	1.1149
4	144-02	1.4026

6.11. It is July 30, 2015. The cheapest-to-deliver bond in a September 2015 Treasury bond futures contract is a 13% coupon bond, and delivery is expected to be made on September 30, 2015. Coupon payments on the bond are made on February 4 and August 4 each year. The term structure is flat, and the rate of interest with semiannual compounding is 12% per annum. The conversion factor for the bond is 1.5. The current quoted bond price is $110. Calculate the quoted futures price for the contract.

6.12. An investor is looking for arbitrage opportunities in the Treasury bond futures market. What complications are created by the fact that the party with a short position can choose to deliver any bond with a maturity of over 15 years?

6.13. Suppose that the nine-month LIBOR interest rate is 8% per annum and the six-month LIBOR interest rate is 7.5% per annum (both with actual/365 and continuous compounding). Estimate the three-month Eurodollar futures price quote for a contract maturing in six months.

6.14. A five-year bond with a yield of 11% (continuously compounded) pays an 8% coupon at the end of each year.

(a) What is the bond's price?
(b) What is the bond's duration?
(c) Use the duration to calculate the effect on the bond's price of a 0.2% decrease in its yield.

(d) Recalculate the bond's price on the basis of a 10.8% per annum yield and verify that the result is in agreement with your answer to (c).

6.15. Suppose that a bond portfolio with a duration of 12 years is hedged using a futures contract in which the underlying asset has a duration of four years. What is likely to be the impact on the hedge of the fact that the 12-year rate is less volatile than the four-year rate?

6.16. Suppose that it is February 20 and a treasurer realizes that on July 17 the company will have to issue $5 million of commercial paper with a maturity of 180 days. If the paper were issued today, the company would realize $4,820,000. (In other words, the company would receive $4,820,000 for its paper and have to redeem it at $5,000,000 in 180 days' time.) The September Eurodollar futures price is quoted as 92.00. How should the treasurer hedge the company's exposure?

6.17. On August 1, a portfolio manager has a bond portfolio worth $10 million. The duration of the portfolio in October will be 7.1 years. The December Treasury bond futures price is currently 91-12 and the cheapest-to-deliver bond will have a duration of 8.8 years at maturity. How should the portfolio manager immunize the portfolio against changes in interest rates over the next two months?

6.18. How can the portfolio manager change the duration of the portfolio to 3.0 years in Problem 6.17?

6.19. Between October 30, 2015, and November 1, 2015, you have a choice between owning a U.S. government bond paying a 12% coupon and a U.S. corporate bond paying a 12% coupon. Consider carefully the day count conventions discussed in this chapter and decide, all else being equal, which of the two bonds you would prefer to own.

6.20. Suppose that a Eurodollar futures quote is 88 for a contract maturing in 60 days. What is the LIBOR forward rate for the 60- to 150-day period? Ignore the difference between futures and forwards for the purposes of this question.

6.21. The three-month Eurodollar futures price for a contract maturing in six years is quoted as 95.20. The standard deviation of the change in the short-term interest rate in one year is 1.1%. Estimate the forward LIBOR interest rate for the period between 6.00 and 6.25 years in the future.

6.22. Explain why the forward interest rate is less than the corresponding futures interest rate calculated from a Eurodollar futures contract.

Further Questions

6.23. It is April 7, 2014. The quoted price of a U.S. government bond with a 6% per annum coupon (paid semiannually) is 120-00. The bond matures on July 27, 2023. What is the cash price? How does your answer change if it is a corporate bond?

6.24. A Treasury bond futures price is 103-12. The prices of three deliverable bonds are 115-06, 135-12, and 155-28. Their conversion factors are 1.0679, 1.2264, and 1.4169, respectively. Which bond is cheapest to deliver?

6.25. The December Eurodollar futures contract is quoted as 98.40 and a company plans to borrow $8 million for three months starting in December at LIBOR plus 0.5%.

(a) What rate can the company lock in by using the Eurodollar futures contract?
(b) What position should the company take in the contracts?

(c) If the actual three-month rate turns out to be 1.3%, what is the final settlement price on the futures contracts.

Explain why timing mismatches reduce the effectiveness of the hedge.

6.26. A Eurodollar futures quote for the period between 5.1 and 5.35 years in the future is 97.1. The standard deviation of the change in the short-term interest rate in one year is 1.4%. Estimate the forward interest rate in an FRA.

6.27. It is March 10, 2014. The cheapest-to-deliver bond in a December 2014 Treasury bond futures contract is an 8% coupon bond, and delivery is expected to be made on December 31, 2014. Coupon payments on the bond are made on March 1 and September 1 each year. The rate of interest with continuous compounding is 5% per annum for all maturities. The conversion factor for the bond is 1.2191. The current quoted bond price is $137. Calculate the quoted futures price for the contract.

6.28. Assume that a bank can borrow or lend money at the same interest rate in the LIBOR market. The 90-day rate is 10% per annum, and the 180-day rate is 10.2% per annum, both expressed with continuous compounding and an actual/actual day count. The Eurodollar futures price for a contract maturing in 90 days is quoted as 89.5. What arbitrage opportunities are open to the bank?

6.29. Portfolio A consists of a 1-year zero-coupon bond with a face value of $2,000 and a 10-year zero-coupon bond with a face value of $6,000. Portfolio B consists of a 5.95-year zero-coupon bond with a face value of $5,000. The current yield on all bonds is 10% per annum.
(a) Show that both portfolios have the same duration.
(b) Show that the percentage changes in the values of the two portfolios for a 0.1% per annum increase in yields are the same.
(c) What are the percentage changes in the values of the two portfolios for a 5% per annum increase in yields?

6.30. It is June 25, 2013. The futures price for the June 2013 bond futures contract is 118-23.
(a) Calculate the conversion factor for a bond maturing on January 1, 2026, paying a coupon of 10%.
(b) Calculate the conversion factor for a bond maturing on October 1, 2031, paying a coupon of 7%.
(c) Suppose that the quoted prices of the bonds in (a) and (b) are 169.00 and 136.00, respectively. Which bond is cheaper to deliver?
(d) Assuming that the cheapest-to-deliver bond is actually delivered on June 25, 2013, what is the cash price received for the bond?

6.31. A portfolio manager plans to use a Treasury bond futures contract to hedge a bond portfolio over the next three months. The portfolio is worth $100 million and will have a duration of 4.0 years in three months. The futures price is 122, and each futures contract is on $100,000 of bonds. The bond that is expected to be cheapest to deliver will have a duration of 9.0 years at the maturity of the futures contract. What position in futures contracts is required?
(a) What adjustments to the hedge are necessary if after one month the bond that is expected to be cheapest to deliver changes to one with a duration of seven years?
(b) Suppose that all rates increase over the three months, but long-term rates increase less than short-term and medium-term rates. What is the effect of this on the performance of the hedge?

CHAPTER 7

Swaps

The first swap contracts were negotiated in the early 1980s. Since then the market has seen phenomenal growth. Swaps now occupy a position of central importance in derivatives markets.

A swap is an over-the-counter derivatives agreement between two companies to exchange cash flows in the future. The agreement defines the dates when the cash flows are to be paid and the way in which they are to be calculated. Usually the calculation of the cash flows involves the future value of an interest rate, an exchange rate, or other market variable.

A forward contract can be viewed as a simple example of a swap. Suppose it is March 1, 2014, and a company enters into a forward contract to buy 100 ounces of gold for \$1,800 per ounce in one year. The company can sell the gold in one year as soon as it is received. The forward contract is therefore equivalent to a swap where the company agrees that on March 1, 2015, it will pay \$180,000 and receive $100 \times S$, where S is the market price of one ounce of gold on that date.

Whereas a forward contract is equivalent to the exchange of cash flows on just one future date, swaps typically lead to cash-flow exchanges taking place on several future dates. In this chapter we examine how swaps are designed, how they are used, and how they can be valued. Our discussion centers on interest rate swaps and currency swaps. Other types of swaps are briefly reviewed at the end of the chapter and discussed in more detail in Chapter 22.

7.1 MECHANICS OF INTEREST RATE SWAPS

The most common type of swap is a "plain vanilla" interest rate swap. In this a company agrees to pay cash flows equal to interest at a predetermined fixed rate on a notional principal for a predetermined number of years. In return, it receives interest at a floating rate on the same notional principal for the same period of time.

LIBOR

The floating rate in most interest rate swap agreements is the London Interbank Offered Rate (LIBOR), which we introduced in Chapter 4. It is the rate of interest at which a

From Chapter 7 of *Fundamentals of Futures and Options Markets*, Eighth Edition. John C. Hull.

bank is prepared to lend money to other banks that have a AA credit rating. As explained in Chapter 4, LIBOR rates are published each day for a number of different currencies. Several different borrowing periods, ranging from overnight to one year, are considered.

Just as prime is often the reference rate of interest for floating-rate loans in the domestic financial market, LIBOR is a reference rate of interest for loans in international financial markets. To understand how it is used, consider a five-year bond with a rate of interest specified as six-month LIBOR plus 0.5% per annum. The life of the bond is divided into 10 periods each six months in length. For each period, the rate of interest is set at 0.5% per annum above the six-month LIBOR rate (i.e., LIBOR for a borrowing period of six months) at the beginning of the period. Interest is paid at the end of the period.

Illustration

Consider a hypothetical three-year swap initiated on March 5, 2013, between Microsoft and Intel. We suppose Microsoft agrees to pay Intel an interest rate of 5% per annum on a principal of \$100 million, and in return Intel agrees to pay Microsoft the six-month LIBOR rate on the same principal. We assume the agreement specifies that payments are to be exchanged every six months, and the 5% interest rate is quoted with semiannual compounding. This swap is represented diagrammatically in Figure 7.1.

The first exchange of payments would take place on September 5, 2013, six months after the initiation of the agreement. Microsoft would pay Intel \$2.5 million. This is the interest on the \$100 million principal for six months at 5%. Intel would pay Microsoft interest on the \$100 million principal at the six-month LIBOR rate prevailing six months prior to September 5, 2013—that is, on March 5, 2013. Suppose that the six-month LIBOR rate on March 5, 2013, is 4.2%. Intel pays Microsoft $0.5 \times 0.042 \times \$100 = \$2.1$ million.[1] Note that there is no uncertainty about this first exchange of payments because it is determined by the LIBOR rate at the time the transaction is agreed to.

The second exchange of payments would take place on March 5, 2014, one year after the initiation of the agreement. Microsoft would pay \$2.5 million to Intel, and Intel would pay interest on the \$100 million principal to Microsoft at the six-month LIBOR rate prevailing six months prior to March 5, 2014—that is, on September 5, 2013. Suppose that the six-month LIBOR rate on September 5, 2013, proves to be 4.8%. Intel pays $0.5 \times 0.048 \times \$100 = \$2.4$ million to Microsoft.

In total, there are six exchanges of payment on the swap. The fixed payments are always \$2.5 million. The floating-rate payments on a payment date are calculated using the six-month LIBOR rate prevailing six months before the payment date. An interest rate swap is generally structured so that one side remits the difference between

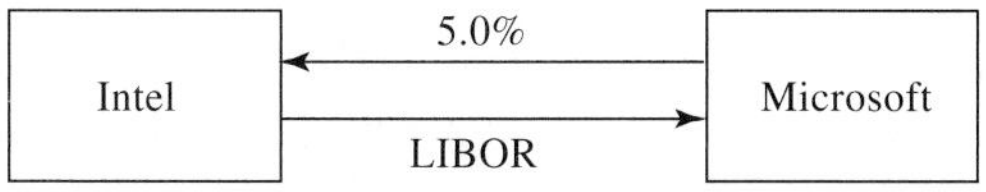

Figure 7.1 Interest rate swap between Microsoft and Intel

[1] The calculations here are simplified in that they ignore day count conventions. This point is discussed in more detail later in the chapter.

Table 7.1 Cash flows (millions of dollars) to Microsoft in a \$100 million three-year interest rate swap when a fixed rate of 5% is paid and LIBOR is received

Date	*Six-month LIBOR rate (%)*	*Floating cash flow received*	*Fixed cash flow paid*	*Net cash flow*
Mar. 5, 2013	4.20			
Sept. 5, 2013	4.80	+2.10	−2.50	−0.40
Mar. 5, 2014	5.30	+2.40	−2.50	−0.10
Sept. 5, 2014	5.50	+2.65	−2.50	+0.15
Mar. 5, 2015	5.60	+2.75	−2.50	+0.25
Sept. 5, 2015	5.90	+2.80	−2.50	+0.30
Mar. 5, 2016		+2.95	−2.50	+0.45

the two payments to the other side. In our example, Microsoft would pay Intel \$0.4 million (= \$2.5 million − \$2.1 million) on September 5, 2013, and \$0.1 million (= \$2.5 million − \$2.4 million) on March 5, 2014.

Table 7.1 provides a complete example of the payments made under the swap for one particular set of six-month LIBOR rates. The table shows the swap cash flows from the perspective of Microsoft. Note that the \$100 million principal is used only for the calculation of interest payments. The principal itself is not exchanged. For this reason, it is usually termed the *notional principal*, or just the *notional*.

If the notional principal were exchanged at the end of the life of the swap, the nature of the deal would not be changed in any way. The notional principal is the same for both the fixed and floating payments. Exchanging \$100 million for \$100 million at the end of the life of the swap is a transaction that would have no financial value to either Microsoft or Intel. Table 7.2 shows the cash flows in Table 7.1 with a final exchange of principal added in. This provides an interesting way of viewing the swap. The cash flows in the third column of this table are the cash flows from a long position in a floating-rate bond. The cash flows in the fourth column of the table are the cash flows from a short position in a fixed-rate bond. The table shows that the swap can be regarded as the exchange of a fixed-rate bond for a floating-rate bond. Microsoft, whose position is described by Table 7.2, is long a floating-rate bond and short a fixed-rate bond. Intel is long a fixed-rate bond and short a floating-rate bond.

Table 7.2 Cash flows (millions of dollars) from Table 7.1 when there is a final exchange of principal

Date	*Six-month LIBOR rate (%)*	*Floating cash flow received*	*Fixed cash flow paid*	*Net cash flow*
Mar. 5, 2013	4.20			
Sept. 5, 2013	4.80	+2.10	−2.50	−0.40
Mar. 5, 2014	5.30	+2.40	−2.50	−0.10
Sept. 5, 2014	5.50	+2.65	−2.50	+0.15
Mar. 5, 2015	5.60	+2.75	−2.50	+0.25
Sept. 5, 2015	5.90	+2.80	−2.50	+0.30
Mar. 5, 2016		+102.95	−102.50	+0.45

Example 7.1 The versatility of swaps

Swaps have been so successful because they can be used in so many different ways. The swap in Figure 7.1 can be used to transform the nature of liabilities or assets.

Transforming Liabilities
Figure 7.2 shows that the swap can be used by Microsoft to switch its borrowings from floating to fixed and by Intel to do the reverse:

	Microsoft	*Intel*
Loan payment	LIBOR + 0.1%	5.2%
Add: Paid under swap	5.0%	LIBOR
Less: Received under swap	−LIBOR	−5.0%
Net payment	5.1%	LIBOR + 0.2%

Transforming Assets
Using the same swap, Figure 7.3 shows Microsoft can switch its assets from fixed to floating and Intel can do the reverse:

	Microsoft	*Intel*
Investment income	4.7%	LIBOR − 0.2%
Less: Paid under swap	−5.0%	−LIBOR
Add: Received under swap	LIBOR	5.0%
Net income	LIBOR − 0.3%	4.8%

This characterization of the cash flows in the swap helps to explain why the floating rate in the swap is set six months before it is paid. On a floating-rate bond, interest is generally set at the beginning of the period to which it will apply and is paid at the end of the period. The calculation of the floating-rate payments in a "plain vanilla" interest rate swap such as the one in Table 7.2 reflects this.

Swaps are versatile financial instruments. This is what has made them so popular. Example 7.1 uses Figures 7.2 and 7.3 to summarize some of the reasons Microsoft and Intel might have for entering into the transactions in Figure 7.1.

Using the Swap to Transform a Liability

For Microsoft, the swap could be used to transform a floating-rate loan into a fixed-rate loan. Suppose that Microsoft has arranged to borrow \$100 million at LIBOR plus 10 basis points. (One basis point is one-hundredth of 1%, so the rate is LIBOR plus 0.1%.) After

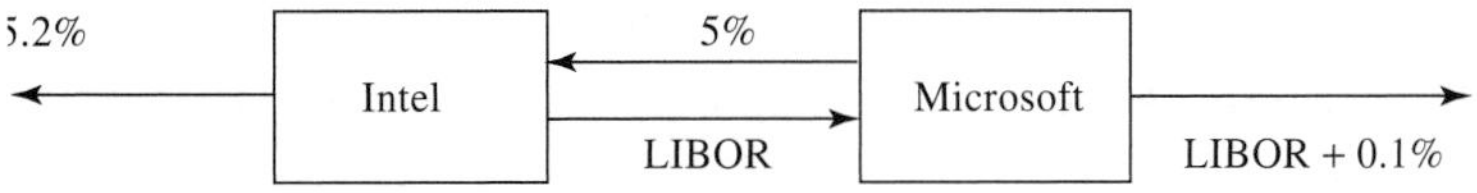

Figure 7.2 Microsoft and Intel use the swap to transform a liability

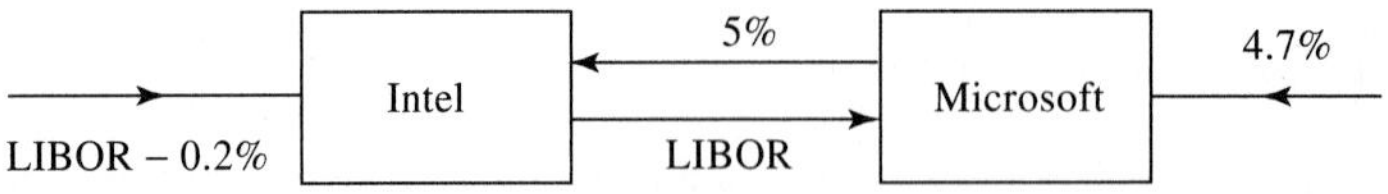

Figure 7.3 Microsoft and Intel use the swap to transform an asset

Microsoft has entered into the swap, it has three sets of cash flows:

1. It pays LIBOR plus 0.1% to its outside lenders.
2. It receives LIBOR under the terms of the swap.
3. It pays 5% under the terms of the swap.

These three sets of cash flows net out to an interest rate payment of 5.1%. Thus, for Microsoft the swap could have the effect of transforming borrowings at a floating rate of LIBOR plus 10 basis points into borrowings at a fixed rate of 5.1%.

For Intel the swap could have the effect of transforming a fixed-rate loan into a floating-rate loan. Suppose that Intel has a three-year $100 million loan outstanding on which it pays 5.2%. After it has entered into the swap, it has three sets of cash flows:

1. It pays 5.2% to its outside lenders.
2. It pays LIBOR under the terms of the swap.
3. It receives 5% under the terms of the swap.

These three sets of cash flows net out to an interest rate payment of LIBOR plus 0.2% (or LIBOR plus 20 basis points). Thus, for Intel the swap could have the effect of transforming borrowings at a fixed rate of 5.2% into borrowings at a floating rate of LIBOR plus 20 basis points.

Using the Swap to Transform an Asset

Swaps can also be used to transform the nature of an asset. Consider Microsoft in our example. The swap could have the effect of transforming an asset earning a fixed rate of interest into an asset earning a floating rate of interest. Suppose that Microsoft owns $100 million in bonds that will provide interest at 4.7% per annum over the next three years. After Microsoft has entered into the swap, it has three sets of cash flows:

1. It receives 4.7% on the bonds.
2. It receives LIBOR under the terms of the swap.
3. It pays 5% under the terms of the swap.

These three sets of cash flows net out to an interest rate inflow of LIBOR minus 30 basis points. Thus, one possible use of the swap for Microsoft is to transform an asset earning 4.7% into an asset earning LIBOR minus 30 basis points.

Next, consider Intel. The swap could have the effect of transforming an asset earning a floating rate of interest into an asset earning a fixed rate of interest. Suppose that Intel has an investment of $100 million that yields LIBOR minus 20 basis points. After it has entered into the swap, it has three sets of cash flows:

1. It receives LIBOR minus 20 basis points on its investment.
2. It pays LIBOR under the terms of the swap.
3. It receives 5% under the terms of the swap.

Figure 7.4 Interest rate swap from Figure 7.2 when financial institution is involved

These three sets of cash flows net out to an interest rate inflow of 4.8%. Thus, one possible use of the swap for Intel is to transform an asset earning LIBOR minus 20 basis points into an asset earning 4.8%.

Role of Financial Intermediary

Usually two nonfinancial companies such as Intel and Microsoft do not get in touch directly to arrange a swap in the way indicated in Figures 7.2 and 7.3. They each deal with a bank or other financial institution. "Plain vanilla" fixed-for-floating swaps on U.S. interest rates are usually structured so that the financial institution earns about 3 or 4 basis points (0.03% or 0.04%) on a pair of offsetting transactions.

Figure 7.4 shows what the role of the financial institution might be in the situation in Figure 7.2. The financial institution enters into two offsetting swap transactions with Intel and Microsoft. Assuming that both companies honor their obligations, the financial institution is certain to make a profit of 0.03% (3 basis points) per year multiplied by the notional principal of $100 million. (This amounts to $30,000 per year for the three-year period.) Microsoft ends up borrowing at 5.115% (instead of 5.1%, as in Figure 7.2). Intel ends up borrowing at LIBOR plus 21.5 basis points (instead of at LIBOR plus 20 basis points, as in Figure 7.2).

Figure 7.5 illustrates the role of the financial institution in the situation in Figure 7.3. The swap is the same as before and the financial institution is certain to make a profit of 3 basis points if neither company defaults. Microsoft ends up earning LIBOR minus 31.5 basis points (instead of LIBOR minus 30 basis points, as in Figure 7.3). Intel ends up earning 4.785% (instead of 4.8%, as in Figure 7.3).

Note that in each case the financial institution has entered into two separate transactions: one with Intel and the other with Microsoft. In most instances, Intel will not even know that the financial institution has entered into an offsetting swap with Microsoft, and vice versa. If one of the companies defaults, the financial institution still has to honor its agreement with the other company. The 3-basis-point spread earned by the financial institution is partly to compensate it for the risk that one of the two companies will default on the swap payments.

Market Makers

In practice, it is unlikely that two companies will contact a financial institution at the same time and want to take opposite positions in exactly the same swap. For this reason, many large financial institutions act as market makers for swaps. This means that they

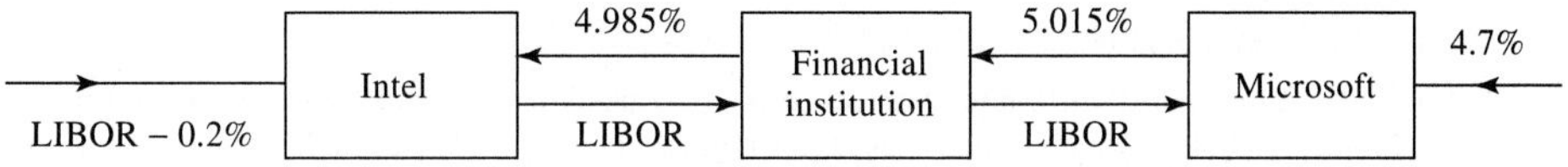

Figure 7.5 Interest rate swap from Figure 7.3 when financial institution is involved

Table 7.3 Bid and offer fixed rates in the swap market and swap rates (percent per annum); payments exchanged semiannually

Maturity (years)	*Bid*	*Offer*	*Swap rate*
2	6.03	6.06	6.045
3	6.21	6.24	6.225
4	6.35	6.39	6.370
5	6.47	6.51	6.490
7	6.65	6.68	6.665
10	6.83	6.87	6.850

are prepared to enter into a swap without having an offsetting swap with another counterparty.[2] Market makers must carefully quantify and hedge the risks they are taking. Bonds, forward rate agreements, and interest rate futures are examples of the instruments that can be used for hedging by swap market makers. Table 7.3 shows quotes for plain vanilla U.S. dollar swaps that might be posted by a market maker.[3] Typically, the bid–offer spread is 3 to 4 basis points. The average of the bid and offer fixed rates is known as the *swap rate*. This is shown in the final column of Table 7.3.

Consider a new swap where the fixed rate equals the current swap rate. It is reasonable to assume that the value of this swap is zero. (Why else would a market maker choose bid–offer quotes centered on the swap rate?) In Table 7.2, we saw that a swap can be characterized as the difference between a fixed-rate and a floating-rate bond. Define:

B_{fix}: Value of fixed-rate bond underlying the swap we are considering

B_{fl}: Value of floating-rate bond underlying the swap we are considering

Because the swap is worth zero, it follows that

$$B_{\text{fix}} = B_{\text{fl}} \tag{7.1}$$

We will use this result later in the chapter when discussing how the LIBOR/swap zero curve is determined.

7.2 DAY COUNT ISSUES

We discussed day count conventions in Section 6.1. The day count conventions affect payments on a swap, and some of the numbers calculated in the examples we have given do not exactly reflect these day count conventions. Consider, for example, the six-month LIBOR payments in Table 7.1. Because it is a U.S. money market rate, six-month LIBOR is quoted on an actual/360 basis. The first floating payment in Table 7.1, based

[2] This is sometimes referred to as *warehousing* swaps.

[3] The standard swap in the United States is one where fixed payments made every six months are exchanged for floating LIBOR payments made every three months. In Table 7.1, we assumed that both fixed and floating payments are exchanged every six months. The fixed rate should in theory be the same regardless of whether floating payments are made every three months or every six months.

on the LIBOR rate of 4.2%, is shown as \$2.10 million. Because there are 184 days between March 5, 2013, and September 5, 2013, it should be

$$100 \times 0.042 \times \frac{184}{360} = \$2.1467 \text{ million}$$

In general, a LIBOR-based floating-rate cash flow on a swap payment date is calculated as $LRn/360$, where L is the principal, R is the relevant LIBOR rate, and n is the number of days since the last payment date.

The fixed rate that is paid in a swap transaction is similarly quoted with a particular day count basis being specified. As a result, the fixed payments may not be exactly equal on each payment date. The fixed rate is usually quoted as actual/365 or 30/360. It is not therefore directly comparable with LIBOR because it applies to a full year. To make the rates approximately comparable, either the six-month LIBOR rate must be multiplied by 365/360 or the fixed rate must be multiplied by 360/365. For clarity of exposition, we will ignore day count issues in the calculations in the rest of this chapter.

7.3 CONFIRMATIONS

A *confirmation* is the legal agreement underlying a swap and is signed by representatives of the two parties. The drafting of confirmations has been facilitated by the work of the International Swaps and Derivatives Association (ISDA; www.isda.org) in New York. This organization has produced a number of Master Agreements that consist of clauses defining in some detail the terminology used in swap agreements, what happens in the event of default by either side, and so on. Master Agreements usually cover all outstanding transactions between two parties. In Business Snapshot 7.1, we show a possible extract from the confirmation for the swap between Microsoft and the financial institution (assumed to be Goldman Sachs) in Figure 7.4. Almost certainly, the full confirmation would state that the provisions of an ISDA Master Agreement apply to the contract.

The confirmation specifies that the following business day convention is to be used and that the U.S. calendar determines which days are business days and which days are holidays. This means that, if a payment date falls on a weekend or a U.S. holiday, the payment is made on the next business day.[4] March 5, 2016, is a Saturday. The last exchange of payments in the swap between Microsoft and Goldman Sachs is therefore on Monday, March 7, 2016.

7.4 THE COMPARATIVE-ADVANTAGE ARGUMENT

An explanation commonly put forward to explain the popularity of swaps concerns comparative advantages. Consider the use of an interest rate swap to transform a liability. Some companies, it is argued, have a comparative advantage when borrowing in fixed-rate markets, whereas others have a comparative advantage in floating-rate

[4] Another business day convention that is sometimes specified is the *modified following* business day convention, which is the same as the following business day convention except that, when the next business day falls in a different month from the specified day, the payment is made on the immediately preceding business day. *Preceding* and *modified preceding* business day conventions are defined analogously.

Business Snapshot 7.1 Extract from hypothetical swap confirmation

Trade date:	27-February-2013
Effective date:	5-March-2013
Business day convention (all dates):	Following business day
Holiday calendar:	U.S.
Termination date:	5-March-2013
Fixed amounts	
Fixed-rate payer:	Microsoft
Fixed-rate notional principal:	USD 100 million
Fixed rate:	5.015% per annum
Fixed-rate day count convention:	Actual/365
Fixed-rate payment dates:	Each 5-March and 5-September commencing 5-September, 2013, up to and including 5-March, 2016
Floating amounts	
Floating-rate payer:	Goldman Sachs
Floating-rate notional principal:	USD 100 million
Floating rate:	USD six-month LIBOR
Floating-rate day count convention:	Actual/360
Floating-rate payment dates:	Each 5-March and 5-September commencing 5-September, 2013, up to and including 5-March, 2016

markets. To obtain a new loan, it makes sense for a company to go to the market where it has a comparative advantage. As a result, the company may borrow fixed when it wants floating, or borrow floating when it wants fixed. The swap is used to transform a fixed-rate loan into a floating-rate loan, and vice versa.

Suppose that two companies, AAACorp and BBBCorp, both wish to borrow $10 million for five years and have been offered the rates shown in Table 7.4. AAACorp has a AAA credit rating; BBBCorp has a BBB credit rating.[5] We assume that BBBCorp wants to borrow at a fixed rate of interest, whereas AAACorp wants to borrow at a floating rate linked to six-month LIBOR. Since it has a worse credit rating than AAACorp, BBBCorp pays a higher rate of interest than AAACorp in both the fixed and floating markets.

A key feature of the rates offered to AAACorp and BBBCorp is that the difference between the two fixed rates is greater than the difference between the two floating rates.

Table 7.4 Borrowing rates that provide a basis for the comparative-advantage argument

	Fixed	*Floating*
AAACorp	4.0%	Six-month LIBOR − 0.1%
BBBCorp	5.2%	Six-month LIBOR + 0.6%

[5] The credit ratings assigned to companies by S&P and Fitch (in order of decreasing creditworthiness) are AAA, AA, A, BBB, BB, B, CCC, CC, and C. The corresponding ratings assigned by Moody's are Aaa, Aa, A, Baa, Ba, B, Caa, Ca, and C, respectively.

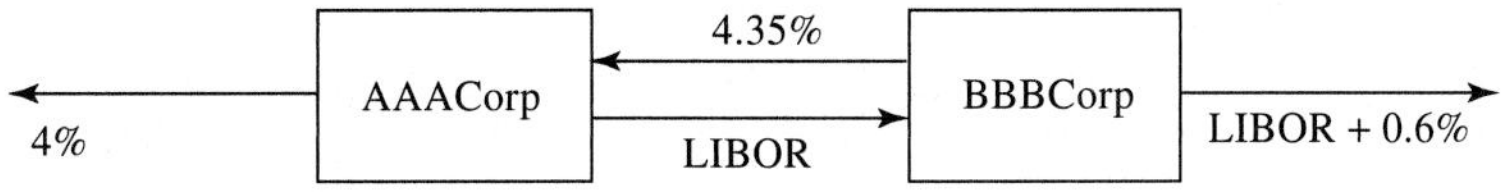

Figure 7.6 Swap agreement between AAACorp and BBBCorp when the rates in Table 7.4 apply

BBBCorp pays 1.2% more than AAACorp in fixed-rate markets and only 0.7% more than AAACorp in floating-rate markets. BBBCorp appears to have a comparative advantage in floating-rate markets, whereas AAACorp appears to have a comparative advantage in fixed-rate markets.[6] It is this apparent anomaly that can lead to a swap being negotiated. AAACorp borrows fixed-rate funds at 4% per annum. BBBCorp borrows floating-rate funds at LIBOR plus 0.6% per annum. They then enter into a swap agreement to ensure that AAACorp ends up with floating-rate funds and BBBCorp ends up with fixed-rate funds.

To understand how the swap might work, we first assume that AAACorp and BBBCorp get in touch with each other directly. The sort of swap they might negotiate is shown in Figure 7.6. This is very similar to our example in Figure 7.2. AAACorp agrees to pay BBBCorp interest at six-month LIBOR on $10 million. In return, BBBCorp agrees to pay AAACorp interest at a fixed rate of 4.35% per annum on $10 million.

AAACorp has three sets of interest rate cash flows:

1. It pays 4% per annum to outside lenders.
2. It receives 4.35% per annum from BBBCorp.
3. It pays LIBOR to BBBCorp.

The net effect of the three cash flows is that AAACorp pays LIBOR minus 0.35% per annum. This is 0.25% per annum less than it would pay if it went directly to floating-rate markets. BBBCorp also has three sets of interest rate cash flows:

1. It pays LIBOR + 0.6% per annum to outside lenders.
2. It receives LIBOR from AAACorp.
3. It pays 4.35% per annum to AAACorp.

The net effect of the three cash flows is that BBBCorp pays 4.95% per annum. This is 0.25% per annum less than it would pay if it went directly to fixed-rate markets.

The swap arrangement appears to improve the position of both AAACorp and BBBCorp by 0.25% per annum. The total gain is therefore 0.5% per annum. It can be shown that the total apparent gain from this type of interest rate swap arrangement is always $a - b$, where a is the difference between the interest rates facing the two companies in fixed-rate markets, and b is the difference between the interest rates facing the two companies in floating-rate markets. In this case, $a = 1.2\%$ and $b = 0.7\%$.

If AAACorp and BBBCorp did not deal directly with each other and used a financial institution, an arrangement such as that shown in Figure 7.7 might result. (This is

[6] Note that BBBCorp's comparative advantage in floating-rate markets does not imply that BBBCorp pays less than AAACorp in this market. It means that the extra amount that BBBCorp pays over the amount paid by AAACorp is less in this market. One of my students summarized the situation as follows: "AAACorp pays more less in fixed-rate markets; BBBCorp pays less more in floating-rate markets."

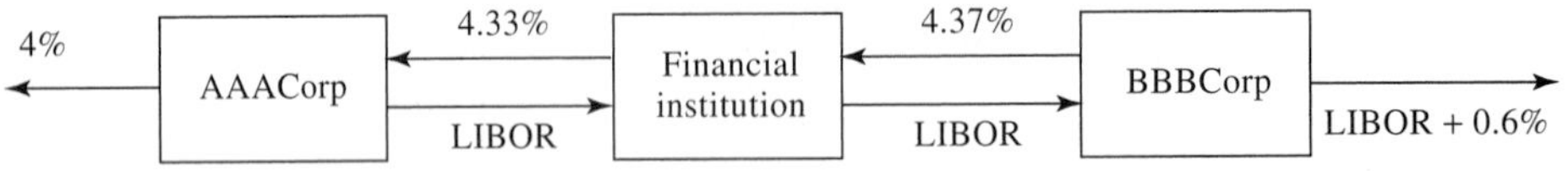

Figure 7.7 Swap agreement between AAACorp and BBBCorp when rates in Table 7.4 apply and a financial intermediary is involved

similar to the example in Figure 7.4.) In this case, AAACorp ends up borrowing at LIBOR minus 0.33%, BBBCorp ends up borrowing at 4.97%, and the financial institution earns a spread of 4 basis points per year. The gain to AAACorp is 0.23%; the gain to BBBCorp is 0.23%; and the gain to the financial institution is 0.04%. The total gain to all three parties is 0.50% as before.

Criticism of the Argument

The comparative-advantage argument we have just outlined for explaining the attractiveness of interest rate swaps is open to question. Why, in Table 7.4, should the spreads between the rates offered to AAACorp and BBBCorp be different in fixed and floating markets? Now that the interest rate swap market has been in existence for a long time, we might reasonably expect these types of differences to have been arbitraged away.

The reason that spread differentials appear to exist is due to the nature of the contracts available to companies in fixed and floating markets. The 4.0% and 5.2% rates available to AAACorp and BBBCorp in fixed-rate markets are five-year rates (e.g., the rates at which the companies can issue five-year fixed-rate bonds). The LIBOR − 0.1% and LIBOR + 0.6% rates available to AAACorp and BBBCorp in floating-rate markets are six-month rates. In the floating-rate market, the lender usually has the opportunity to review the floating rates every six months. If the creditworthiness of AAACorp or BBBCorp has declined, the lender has the option of increasing the spread over LIBOR that is charged. In extreme circumstances, the lender can refuse to roll over the loan at all. The providers of fixed-rate financing do not have the option to change the terms of the loan in this way.[7]

The spreads between the rates offered to AAACorp and BBBCorp are a reflection of the extent to which BBBCorp is more likely to default than AAACorp. During the next six months, there is very little chance that either AAACorp or BBBCorp will default. As we look further ahead, the probability of a default by a company with a relatively low credit rating (such as BBBCorp) is liable to increase faster than the probability of a default by a company with a relatively high credit rating (such as AAACorp). This is why the spread between the five-year rates is greater than the spread between the six-month rates.

After negotiating a floating-rate loan at LIBOR + 0.6% and entering into the swap shown in Figure 7.7, BBBCorp appears to obtain a fixed-rate loan at 4.97%. The arguments just presented show that this is not really the case. In practice, the rate paid is 4.97% only if BBBCorp can continue to borrow floating-rate funds at a spread of 0.6% over LIBOR. If, for example, the credit rating of BBBCorp declines so that the floating-rate loan is rolled over at LIBOR + 1.6%, the rate paid by BBBCorp increases to 5.97%. The market expects that BBBCorp's spread over six-month LIBOR will on

[7] If the floating rate loans are structured so that the spread over LIBOR is guaranteed in advance regardless of changes in credit rating, then the spread differentials, and therefore the comparative advantage, disappear.

average rise during the swap's life. BBBCorp's expected average borrowing rate when it enters into the swap is therefore greater than 4.97%.

The swap in Figure 7.7 locks in LIBOR − 0.33% for AAACorp for all of the next five years, not just for the next six months. This appears to be a good deal for AAACorp. The downside is that it is bearing the risk of a default by the financial institution. If it borrowed floating-rate funds in the usual way, it would not be bearing this risk.

7.5 THE NATURE OF SWAP RATES

It is now appropriate to examine the nature of swap rates and the relationship between swap and LIBOR markets. LIBOR is the rate of interest at which a AA-rated bank can borrow for a short period of time from other banks. It is not totally risk-free because there is a small chance that a bank currently rated AA will default during the life of the LIBOR loan.

A financial institution can earn the five-year swap rate on a certain principal by:

1. Lending the principal for the first six months to a AA borrower and then relending it for successive six-month periods to other AA borrowers, and
2. Entering into a swap to exchange the LIBOR income for the five-year swap rate.

This shows that the five-year swap rate is an interest rate with a credit risk corresponding to the situation where 10 consecutive six-month LIBOR loans to AA companies are made. Similarly the seven-year swap rate is an interest rate with a credit risk corresponding to the situation where 14 consecutive six-month LIBOR loans to AA companies are made. Swap rates of other maturities can be interpreted analogously.

Note that five-year swap rates are less than five-year AA borrowing rates. It is much more attractive to lend money for successive six-month periods to borrowers who are always AA at the beginning of the periods than to lend it to one borrower for the whole five years when all we can be sure of is that the borrower is AA at the beginning of the five years.

In discussing the above points, Collin-Dufresne and Solnik refer to swap rates as "continually refreshed" LIBOR rates.[8]

Financial institutions frequently calculate a zero curve from LIBOR rates and swap rates, as we will describe shortly. Pre-crisis this was used as the risk-free zero curve for discounting the payoffs from swaps and other derivatives. Since the crisis, rates calculated from overnight indexed swaps have been regarded as better estimates of risk-free rates.

7.6 OVERNIGHT INDEXED SWAPS

Since their introduction, overnight-indexed swaps have become popular in all major currencies. They are related to the unsecured overnight borrowing and lending that banks do at the end of each day to satisfy their liquidity needs. (Banks with excess funds lend; banks short of funds borrow.) The interest rate on these overnight loans is monitored by

[8] See P. Collin-Dufresne and B. Solnik, "On the Term Structure of Default Premia in the Swap and Libor Market," *Journal of Finance*, 56, 3 (June 2001).

the central bank which may intervene with its own transactions in an attempt to raise or lower the rate. In the U.S., the rate is referred to as the federal funds rate.

An overnight indexed swap (OIS) is a swap where where a fixed rate for a period (e.g., one month or three months) is exchanged for the geometric average of the overnight rates during the period.[9] If, during a certain period, a bank borrows funds at the overnight rate (rolling the interest and principal forward each day), the interest rate it pays for the period is the geometric average of the overnight interest rates. Similarly, if it lends money at the overnight interest rate every day (rolling the interest and principal forward each day), the interest it earns for the period is the geometric average of the overnight interest rates. An OIS therefore allows overnight borrowing or lending to be swapped for borrowing or lending at a fixed rate. The fixed rate in an OIS is referred to as the OIS rate. If the fixed rate is greater than the geometric average of daily rates, there is a payment from the fixed-rate payer to the floating-rate payer; otherwise there is a payment from the floating-rate payer to the fixed-rate payer.

OIS swaps tend to have relatively short lives (often three months or less). However, transactions that last as long as five to ten years are becoming more common. Longer-term OIS swaps are typically divided into three-month sub-periods and at the end of each sub-period the geometric average of the overnight rates during the sub-period is exchanged for the OIS fixed rate. In the previous section, we explained that the interest rate swap rate is a continually refreshed LIBOR rate: the rate that can be earned on a series of short-term loans to AA-rated financial institutions. Similarly, the OIS rate is a continually refreshed overnight rate: it is the rate that can be earned by a financial institution from a series of overnight loans to other financial institutions.

A bank (Bank A) can engage in the following transactions:

1. Borrow $100 million in the the overnight market for three months, rolling the interest and principal on the loan forward each night.
2. Lend the $100 million for three months at LIBOR to another bank (Bank B).
3. Use an OIS to exchange the overnight borrowings for borrowings at the three-month OIS rate.

This will lead to Bank A receiving the three-month LIBOR rate and (assuming its creditworthiness remains acceptable to the overnight market) paying the three-month overnight indexed swap rate. We might therefore expect the three-month overnight indexed swap rate to equal the three-month LIBOR rate. However, it is generally lower. This is because Bank A requires some compensation for the risk it is taking that Bank B will default on the three-month LIBOR loan. The lenders to Bank A bear much less risk than Bank A because they have the option of ceasing to lend if A's credit quality declines.

The excess of the three-month LIBOR rate over the three-month overnight indexed swap rate is known as the LIBOR–OIS spread. It is used as a measure of stress in financial markets. In normal market conditions it is about 10 basis points. However, it rose sharply during the 2007–2009 credit crisis because banks became less willing to lend to each other for three-month periods. In October 2008, the spread spiked to an all time high of 364 basis points. By a year later it had returned to more normal levels. It rose again when there were stresses in financial markets. For example, it rose to about

[9] In the U.S., the relevant overnight rate is the "effective federal funds rate", which is the average of the rates reported by brokers.

50 basis points at the end of December 2011 as a result of concerns about European countries such as Greece.

7.7 VALUATION OF INTEREST RATE SWAPS

We now move on to discuss the valuation of interest rate swaps. An interest rate swap is worth close to zero when it is first initiated. After it has been in existence for some time, its value may be positive or negative.

Each exchange of payments in an interest rate swap is a forward rate agreement (FRA) where interest at a predetermined fixed rate is exchanged for interest at the LIBOR floating rate. Consider, for example, the swap between Microsoft and Intel in Figure 7.1. The swap is a three-year deal entered into on March 5, 2013, with semiannual payments. The first exchange of payments is known at the time the swap is negotiated. The other five exchanges can be regarded as FRAs. The exchange on March 5, 2014, is an FRA where interest at 5% is exchanged for interest at at the six-month LIBOR rate observed in the market on September 5, 2013; the exchange on September 5, 2014, is an FRA where interest at 5% is exchanged for interest at at the six-month LIBOR rate observed in the market on March 5, 2014; and so on.

As shown at the end of Section 4.7, an FRA can be valued by assuming that forward rates are realized. Because it is nothing more than a portfolio of FRAs, an interest rate swap can also be valued by assuming that forward rates are realized. The procedure is as follows:

1. Calculate forward rates for each of the LIBOR rates that will determine swap cash flows.
2. Calculate the swap cash flows on the assumption that LIBOR rates will equal forward rates.
3. Discount the swap cash flows at the risk-free rate.

Example 7.2 provides an illustration. The procedure requires us (a) to estimate a risk-free zero curve for discounting and (b) to estimate forward LIBOR rates for each of the payments underlying the swap. The next two sections deal with some technical issues concerned with the estimates and the difference between using LIBOR and OIS rates for discounting. These issues are of great concern to derivatives practitioners, but some readers, once they have understood Example 7.2, may wish to jump to Example 7.6 and Section 7.11.

7.8 ESTIMATING THE ZERO CURVE FOR DISCOUNTING

Derivatives practitioners have traditionally used LIBOR and swap rates to define a risk-free zero curve and have used this curve to calculate discount rates when valuing derivatives. However, the credit crisis has caused this practice to be questioned. As explained in Sections 7.5 and 7.6, LIBOR rates incorporate a risk premium to allow for the possibility of a bank counterparty experiencing financial difficulties and defaulting on an interbank loan. Many derivatives dealers choose to use OIS rates when determining the discount rate for collateralized transactions and LIBOR/swap

Example 7.2 Valuing an interest rate swap using FRAs

Suppose that some time ago a financial institution entered into a swap where it agreed to make semiannual payments at a rate of 3% per annum and receive LIBOR on a notional principal of \$100 million. The swap now has a remaining life of 1.25 years. Payments will therefore be made 0.25, 0.75, and 1.25 years from today. The risk-free rates with continuous compounding for maturities of 3 months, 9 months and 15 months are 2.8%, 3.2%, and 3.4%. We suppose that the forward LIBOR rates for the 3-month to 9-month and the 9-month to 15-month periods are 3.4% and 3.7%, respectively, with continuous compounding. Using equation (4.4), the 3-month to 9-month forward rate becomes $2 \times (e^{0.034 \times 0.5} - 1)$, or 3.429%, with semiannual compounding. Similarly, the 9-month to 15-month forward rate becomes 3.734% with semiannual compounding. The LIBOR rate applicable to the exchange in 0.25 years was determined 0.25 years ago. We suppose that it is 2.9% with semiannual compounding.

The calculation of swap cash flows on the assumption that LIBOR rates will equal forward rates and the discounting of the cash flows are shown in the following table. (All cash flows are in millions of dollars.)

Time (years)	*Fixed cash flow*	*Floating cash flow*	*Net cash flow*	*Discount factor*	*Present value of net cash flow*
0.25	−1.5000	+1.4500	−0.0500	0.9930	−0.0497
0.75	−1.5000	+1.7145	+0.2145	0.9763	+0.2094
1.25	−1.5000	+1.8672	+0.3672	0.9584	+0.3519
Total					0.5117

Consider, for example, the 0.75 year row. The fixed cash flow is $-0.5 \times 0.03 \times 100$, or −\$1.5000 million. The floating cash flow, assuming forward rates are realized, is $0.5 \times 0.03429 \times 100$, or \$1.7145 million. The net cash flow is therefore \$0.2145 million. The discount factor is $e^{-0.032 \times 0.75} = 0.9763$, so that the present value is $0.2145 \times 0.9763 = 0.2094$.

The value of the swap is obtained by summing the present values. It is \$0.5177 million. (Note that these calculations do not take account of holiday calendars and day count conventions.)

rates when determining the discount rate for noncollateralized transactions.[10] (See Section 2.5 for a discussion of the use of collateral in OTC markets.) In this section and the next, we explain how valuation is accomplished using both assumptions. We start by considering the construction of the risk-free zero curve.

Determining Zero Rates for LIBOR Discounting

When LIBOR rates and swap rates are used to define discount rates, the value of a newly issued floating-rate bond that pays LIBOR is always equal to its principal value

[10] In J. Hull and A. White, "LIBOR vs. OIS: The Derivatives Discounting Dilemma, Working Paper, University of Toronto, 2012, it is argued that OIS rates should be used for discounting both collateralized and noncollateralized transactions.

Example 7.3 Determining zero rates from swaps

Suppose that the 6-month, 12-month, and 18-month LIBOR/swap zero rates have been determined as 4%, 4.5%, and 4.8% with continuous compounding and that the 2-year swap rate (for a swap where payments are made semiannually) is 5%. This 5% swap rate means that a bond with a principal of \$100 and a semiannual coupon of 5% per annum sells for par. It follows that, if R is the 2-year zero rate, then

$$2.5e^{-0.04\times 0.5} + 2.5e^{-0.045\times 1.0} + 2.5e^{-0.048\times 1.5} + 102.5e^{-2R} = 100$$

Solving this, we obtain $R = 4.953\%$. (Note that this calculation is simplified in that it does not take the swap's day count conventions and holiday calendars into account. See Section 7.2.)

(or par value). The reason is that the bond provides a rate of interest of LIBOR and LIBOR is the discount rate so that the interest on the bond exactly matches the discount rate. As a result, the bond is fairly priced at par.

As shown in Table 7.2, a swap can be regarded as the exchange of a fixed-rate bond for a floating-rate bond. In equation (7.1) we showed that, for a newly issued swap, the value of the fixed-rate bond equals the value of the floating-rate bond. We have just argued that the value of the floating-rate bond equals the notional principal. It follows that the value of the fixed-rate bond also equals the swap's notional principal. Swap rates therefore define a set of par yield bonds. For example, from the swap rates in Table 7.3 we can deduce that the two-year LIBOR/swap par yield is 6.045%, the three-year LIBOR/swap par yield is 6.225%, and so on.[11]

Section 4.5 shows how the bootstrap method can be used to determine the Treasury zero curve from Treasury bill and Treasury bond quotes. It can be used in a similar way to obtain the LIBOR/swap zero curve from the par yield bonds that are defined by swap rates. Example 7.3 illustrates this. Forward rates calculated from Eurodollar futures are sometimes used to help bootstrap the LIBOR/swap zero curve. A forward rate for time T_1 to time T_2 can be used to calculate the T_2 zero rate from the T_1 zero rate.

Determining Zero Rates for OIS Discounting

When OIS rates are used to define risk-free rates for discounting, the procedure for constructing the OIS zero curve is the similar to that just given for LIBOR/swap rates. The one-month OIS rate defines the one-month zero rate, the three-month OIS rate defines the three-month zero rate, and so on. When there are periodic settlements in the OIS contract, the OIS rate defines a par yield bond. Suppose, for example, that the five-year OIS rate is 3.5% with quarterly settlement. (This means that, at the end of each quarter, 3.5% is exchanged for the geometric average of the overnight rates during the quarter.) A bond paying a quarterly coupon at a rate of 3.5% per annum would be assumed to sell for par.

LIBOR interest rate swaps are traded for longer maturities than OIS swaps. If the OIS zero curve is required for long maturities, a natural approach is to assume that

[11] Analysts frequently interpolate between swap rates before calculating the zero curve. For example, for the data in Table 7.3, the 2.5-year swap rate could be assumed to be 6.135%, the 7.5-year swap rate could be assumed to be 6.696%, and so on.

the spread between the OIS rates and LIBOR swap rates is the same at the long end as it is for the longest OIS maturity for which there is reliable data. Suppose, for example, that there is no reliable data on OIS swaps for maturities longer than five years. If at the five-year point the LIBOR–OIS spread is 20 basis points, this could be assumed to continue at the same level beyond five years. LIBOR–OIS basis swaps (see Section 7.16), which have longer maturities than OIS swaps, can also sometimes be used.

7.9 FORWARD RATES

The calculation of forward LIBOR rates depends on the rates used for discounting. This means that again we must consider two cases.

Forward Rates When LIBOR Discounting Is Used

When LIBOR/swap rates are used to determine risk-free discount rates, forward LIBOR rates can be calculated using equation (4.5). (Note that the data given in Example 7.2 is consistent with the assumption of LIBOR discounting. For example, the three-month and nine-month rates with continuous compounding were 2.8% and 3.2% and the forward rate given for the three to nine month period was given as 3.4% with continuous compounding. Because

$$\frac{0.032 \times 0.75 - 0.028 \times 0.25}{0.5} = 0.034$$

this is what equation (4.5) would give.)

An alternative approach to calculating the forward rates, which can be used in more general situations, is to use ensure that swaps of all maturities are worth zero. This approach is illustrated in Example 7.4. The example shows that the forward rate calculated for the 18 to 24 month period using the approach agrees with the forward rate given by equation (4.5).

Forward Rates When OIS Discounting Is Used

When OIS rates are assumed to determine risk-free discount rates, it is necessary to follow an approach similar to that in Example 7.4 and bootstrap forward rates in such a way that swaps of different maturity have a value of zero. This is illustrated in Example 7.5. The OIS zero rates for 6, 12, 18, and 24 months, with continuous compounding, are assumed to be 3.8%, 4.3%, 4.6%, and 4.75% (about 20 basis points less than the corresponding LIBOR/swap zero rates in Example 7.4). The 6-month LIBOR rate, 6 to 12 month LIBOR forward rate, and the 12 to 18 month LIBOR forward rate are assumed to have been already calculated and to be the same as in Example 7.4. The calculations in Example 7.5 show that the 18 to 24 month forward rate is 5.483%, about 0.2 basis points less than when LIBOR is assumed to be risk-free. In the highly competitive interest rate swap market, the impact of this small difference when combined with the impact of lower discount rates has an effect of swap valuations which market participants cannot ignore.

Example 7.4 Bootstrapping LIBOR forward rates with LIBOR discounting

Consider again the data in Example 7.3. The 6-, 12-, 18-month, and (calculated) 24-month rates are, with continuous compounding, 4%, 4.5%, 4.8%, and 4.953%, respectively. The 6-month rate is 4.040% with semiannual compounding. From equation (4.5), the forward rate for the period between 6 and 12 months is 5% with continuous compounding or 5.063% with semiannual compounding. Similarly, the forward rate for the period between 12 and 18 months is 5.4% with continuous compounding or 5.474% with semiannual compounding. We suppose that we do not know the forward rate for the 18 to 24 month period.

The two-year swap rate is 5%. This means that a swap where LIBOR is exchanged for 5% is worth zero. It follows that the sum of the values of (a) the known exchange at 6 months and (b) the forward contracts corresponding to the exchanges at 12, 18, and 24 months must be zero. This can be used to determine the forward rate for the 18 to 24 month period.

The value of the first payment, assuming fixed is paid and floating is received on a principal of 100, is

$$0.5 \times (0.4040 - 0.5000) \times 100 \times e^{-0.04 \times 0.5} = -0.4704$$

The value of the second payment is

$$0.5 \times (0.05063 - 5.000) \times 100 \times e^{-0.045 \times 1} = 0.0301$$

The value of the third payment is

$$0.5 \times (0.05474 - 5.000) \times 100 \times e^{-0.048 \times 1.5} = 0.2203$$

The total value of the first three payments is $-0.4704 + 0.0301 + 0.2203 = -0.2199$. Suppose that the (assumed unknown) forward rate for the final payment is F with semiannual compounding. For the swap to be worth zero, we must have

$$0.5 \times (F - 0.05) \times 100 \times e^{-0.04953 \times 2} = 0.2199$$

This gives $F = 0.05486$, or 5.486%. This is 5.412% with continuous compounding. It is consistent with using equation (4.5) in conjunction with the 18-month zero rate of 4.8% and the 24-month zero rate of 4.953% because

$$(2.0 \times 0.04953 - 1.5 \times 0.048)/0.5 = 0.05412$$

7.10 VALUATION IN TERMS OF BONDS

Principal payments are not exchanged in an interest rate swap. However, as illustrated in Table 7.2, we can assume that principal payments are both received and paid at the end of the swap without changing its value. By doing this, we find that a swap where fixed cash flows are received and floating cash flows are paid can be regarded as a long position in a fixed-rate bond and a short position in a floating-rate bond, so that

$$V_{\text{swap}} = B_{\text{fix}} - B_{\text{fl}}$$

where V_{swap} is the value of the swap, B_{fl} is the value of the floating rate bond underlying

Example 7.5 Bootstrapping LIBOR forward rates with OIS discounting

Suppose that the 6-month, 12-month, 18-month, and 24-month OIS zero rates, with continuous compounding, are 3.8%, 4.3%, 4.6%, and 4.75%, respectively. Suppose further that the LIBOR and LIBOR forward rates out to 18 months have been calculated and are as in Example 7.4. The 6-month LIBOR rate is 4.040% with semiannual compounding. The forward rate for the period between 6 and 12 months is 5.063% with semiannual compounding. The forward rate for the period between 12 and 18 months is 5.474% with semiannual compounding. We show how the forward rate for the 18- to 24-month period can be calculated.

The two-year swap rate is 5%. The value of a two-year swap where LIBOR is paid and 5% is received is therefore zero. We know that the swap can be valued by assuming that forward rates are realized. The value of the first payment in the swap, assuming a principal of 100 is

$$0.5 \times (0.4040 - 0.5000) \times 100 \times e^{-0.038\times 0.5} = -0.4708$$

The value of the second payment is

$$0.5 \times (0.05063 - 5.000) \times 100 \times e^{-0.043\times 1} = 0.0302$$

The value of the third payments is

$$0.5 \times (0.05474 - 5.000) \times 100 \times e^{-0.046\times 1.5} = 0.2210$$

The total value of the first three payments is $-0.4708 + 0.0302 + 0.2210 = -0.2197$. Suppose that the (assumed unknown) forward rate for the final payment is F. For the swap to be worth zero, we must have $0.5 \times (F - 0.05) \times 100 \times e^{-0.0475\times 2} = 0.2197$. This gives $F = 0.05483$, or 5.483%.

the swap and B_{fix} is the value of the fixed rate payments underlying the swap. Similarly, a swap where floating cash flows are received and fixed cash flows are paid is a long position in a floating-rate bond and a short position in a fixed-rate bond, so that the value of the swap is

$$V_{\text{swap}} = B_{\text{fl}} - B_{\text{fix}}$$

The value of the fixed rate bond, B_{fix} can be determined as described in Section 4.4. To calculate the value of the floating-rate bond when the LIBOR/swap zero curve is used for discounting, we note the bond is worth the par value, L, immediately after an interest payment. This is because at this time the bond is a "fair deal" where the borrower pays LIBOR for each subsequent accrual period.

Suppose that the next exchange of payments is at time t^* and the floating payment that will be made at time t^* (which was determined at the last payment date) is k^*. Immediately after the payment $B_{\text{fl}} = L$, where L is the notional principal, for the reason just explained. It follows that immediately before the payment $B_{\text{fl}} = L + k^*$. The floating-rate bond can therefore be regarded as an instrument providing a single cash flow of $L + k^*$ at time t^*. Discounting this, the value of the floating-rate bond today is $(L + k^*)e^{-r^*t^*}$, where r^* is the LIBOR/swap zero rate for a maturity of t^*. The argument is illustrated in Figure 7.8 and Example 7.6.

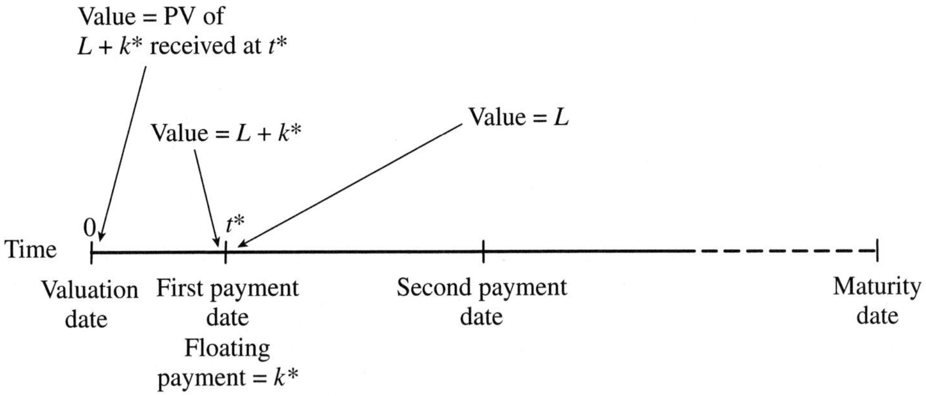

Figure 7.8 Valuation of floating-rate bond when bond principal is L and next payment is k^* at t^*

Example 7.6 Valuation in terms of bonds for LIBOR discounting

Consider again the situation in Example 7.2. The financial institution is paying 3% semiannually and receiving LIBOR on a notional principal of \$100 million. The next exchange is in 0.25 years when the floating cash flow will be 1.45 million. Hence $t^* = 0.25$, $L = 100$ million and $k^* = 1.45$ million. Subsequent exchanges will take place in 0.75 and 1.25 years. The (LIBOR/swap) risk-free rates for maturities of 0.25, 0.75, and 1.25 years are 2.8%, 3.2%, and 3.4%, respectively, with continuous compounding. The floating-rate bond has the same value as a cash flow of 101.45 in 0.25 years. The valuation of the fixed- and floating-rate bonds are shown in the following table (where all cash flows are in millions of dollars):

Time (years)	B_{fix} *cash flow*	B_{fl} *cash flow*	*Discount factor*	*Present value* B_{fix} *cash flow*	*Present value* B_{fl} *cash flow*
0.25	1.5000	+101.4500	0.9930	1.4895	100.7423
0.75	1.5000		0.9763	1.4644	
1.25	101.5000		0.9584	97.2766	
Total				100.2306	100.7423

The value of the fixed-rate bond is 100.2306. The value of the floating-rate bond is 100.7423. In this case, the financial institution is long the floating-rate bond and short the fixed-rate bond because it is receiving floating and paying fixed. The value of the swap is therefore

$$100.7423 - 100.2306 = 0.5117$$

This is in agreement with the value obtained in Example 7.2. (This is as expected because the forward rates in Example 7.2 are consistent with LIBOR being used as the discount rate.)

Unfortunately when OIS rates are used for discounting there is no short cut for determining B_{fl}. Each floating rate cash flow must be calculated on the assumption that forward rates are realized and the results discounted at OIS rates.

7.11 TERM STRUCTURE EFFECTS

The fixed rate in an interest rate swap is chosen so that the swap is worth zero (or close to zero) initially. This means that at the outset of a swap the sum of the values of the FRAs underlying the swap is zero. It does not mean that the value of each individual FRA is zero. In general, some FRAs will have positive values whereas others will have negative values.

Consider the FRAs underlying the swap between the Microsoft and Intel in Figure 7.1:

Value of FRA to Microsoft $>$ 0 when forward interest rate $>$ 5.0%

Value of FRA to Microsoft $=$ 0 when forward interest rate $=$ 5.0%

Value of FRA to Microsoft $<$ 0 when forward interest rate $<$ 5.0%

Suppose that the term structure of interest rates is upward sloping at the time the swap is negotiated. This means that the forward interest rates increase as the maturity of the FRA increases. Because the sum of the values of the FRAs is zero, the forward interest rate must be less than 5.0% for the early payment dates and greater than 5.0% for the later payment dates. The value to Microsoft of the FRAs corresponding to early payment dates is therefore negative, whereas the value of the FRAs corresponding to later payment dates is positive. If the term structure of interest rates is downward sloping at the time the swap is negotiated, the reverse is true. The impact of the shape of the term structure of interest rates on the values of the forward contracts underlying a swap is illustrated in Figure 7.9.

7.12 FIXED-FOR-FIXED CURRENCY SWAPS

Another popular type of swap is a *fixed-for-fixed currency swap*. This involves exchanging principal and payments at a fixed rate of interest in one currency for principal and payments at a fixed rate of interest in another currency.

A currency swap agreement requires the principal to be specified in each of the two currencies. The principal amounts are usually exchanged at the beginning and at the end of the life of the swap. Usually the principal amounts are chosen to be approximately equivalent using the exchange rate at the swap's initiation.

Illustration

Consider a hypothetical five-year currency swap agreement between IBM and British Petroleum entered into on February 1, 2013. We suppose that IBM pays a fixed rate of interest of 5% in sterling and receives a fixed rate of interest of 6% in dollars from British Petroleum. Interest rate payments are made once a year and the principal amounts are $15 million and £10 million. This is termed a fixed-for-fixed currency swap because the interest rate in each currency is at a fixed rate. The swap is shown in

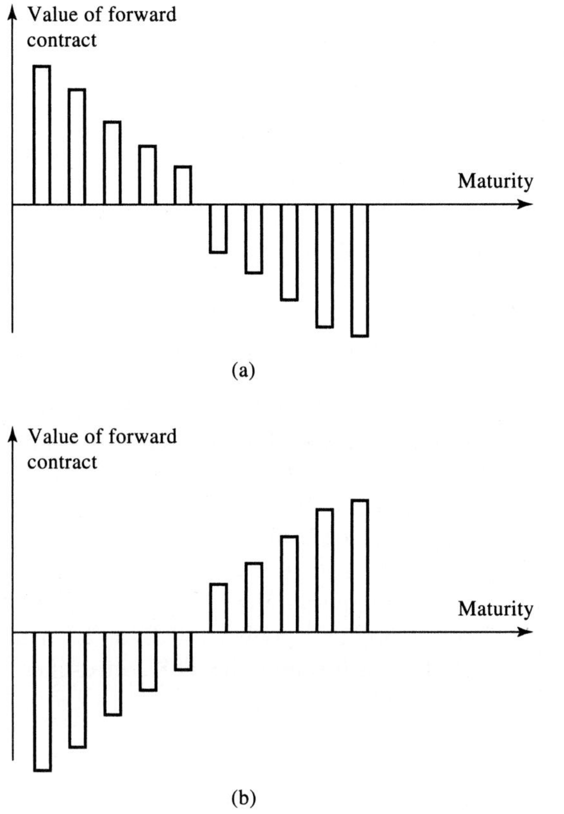

Figure 7.9 Value of forward rate agreements underlying a swap as a function of maturity. In (a) the term structure of interest rates is upward sloping and we receive fixed, or it is downward sloping and we receive floating; in (b) the term structure of interest rates is upward sloping and we receive floating, or it is downward sloping and we receive fixed.

Figure 7.10. Initially, the principal amounts flow in the opposite direction to the arrows in Figure 7.10. The interest payments during the life of the swap and the final principal payment flow in the same direction as the arrows. Thus, at the outset of the swap, IBM pays \$15 million and receives £10 million. Each year during the life of the swap contract, IBM receives \$0.90 million (= 6% of \$15 million) and pays £0.50 million (= 5% of £10 million). At the end of the life of the swap, it pays a principal of £10 million and receives a principal of \$15 million. These cash flows are shown in Table 7.5.

Use of a Currency Swap to Transform Liabilities and Assets

A swap such as the one just considered can be used to transform borrowings in one currency to borrowings in another currency. Suppose that IBM can issue \$18 million of

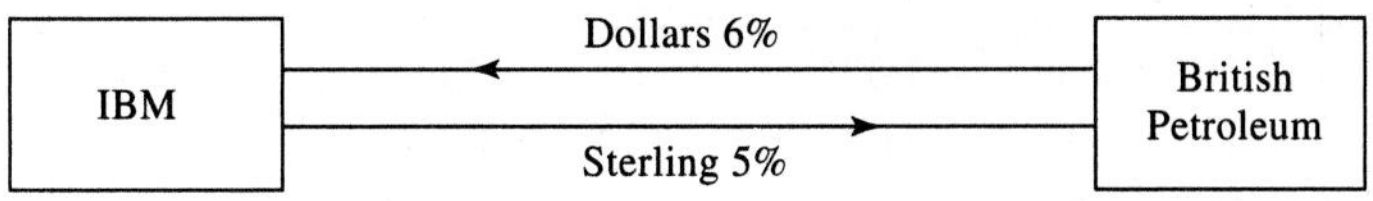

Figure 7.10 A currency swap

Table 7.5 Cash flows to IBM in currency swap

Date	*Dollar cash flow (millions)*	*Sterling cash flow (millions)*
February 1, 2013	−15.00	+10.0
February 1, 2014	+0.90	−0.5
February 1, 2015	+0.90	−0.5
February 1, 2016	+0.90	−0.5
February 1, 2017	+0.90	−0.5
February 1, 2018	+15.90	−10.5

U.S.-dollar-denominated bonds at 6% interest. The swap has the effect of transforming this transaction into one where IBM has borrowed £10 million at 5% interest. The initial exchange of principal converts the proceeds of the bond issue from U.S. dollars to sterling. The subsequent exchanges in the swap have the effect of swapping the interest and principal payments from dollars to sterling.

The swap can also be used to transform the nature of assets. Suppose that IBM can invest £10 million in the U.K. to yield 5% per annum for the next five years, but feels that the U.S. dollar will strengthen against sterling and prefers a U.S.-dollar-denominated investment. The swap has the effect of transforming the U.K. investment into an $15 million investment in the U.S. yielding 6%.

Comparative Advantage

Currency swaps can be motivated by comparative advantage. To illustrate this, we consider another hypothetical example. Suppose the five-year fixed-rate borrowing costs to General Electric and Qantas Airways in U.S. dollars (USD) and Australian dollars (AUD) are as shown in Table 7.6. The data in the table suggest that Australian rates are higher than USD interest rates, and also that General Electric is more creditworthy than Qantas Airways because it is offered a more favorable rate of interest in both currencies. From the viewpoint of a swap trader, the interesting aspect of Table 7.6 is that the spreads between the rates paid by General Electric and Qantas Airways in the two markets are not the same. Qantas Airways pays 2% more than General Electric in the U.S. dollar market and only 0.4% more than General Electric in the AUD market.

This situation is analogous to that in Table 7.4. General Electric has a comparative advantage in the USD market, whereas Qantas Airways has a comparative advantage in the AUD market. In Table 7.4, where a plain vanilla interest rate swap was considered, we argued that comparative advantages are largely illusory. Here we are

Table 7.6 Borrowing rates providing basis for currency swap

	*USD**	*AUD**
General Electric	5.0%	7.6%
Qantas Airways	7.0%	8.0%

* Quoted rates have been adjusted to reflect the differential impact of taxes.

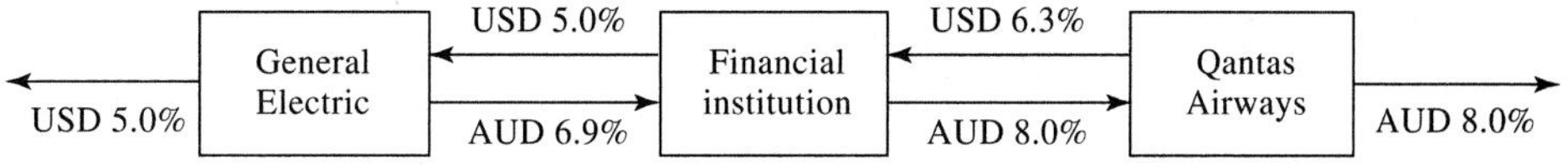

Figure 7.11 A currency swap motivated by comparative advantage

comparing the rates offered in two different currencies, and it is more likely that the comparative advantages are genuine. One possible source of comparative advantage is tax. General Electric's position might be such that USD borrowings lead to lower taxes on its worldwide income than AUD borrowings. Qantas Airways' position might be the reverse. (Note that we assume that the interest rates shown in Table 7.6 have been adjusted to reflect these types of tax advantages.)

We suppose that General Electric wants to borrow 20 million AUD and Qantas Airways wants to borrow 15 million USD and that the current exchange rate (USD per AUD) is 0.7500. This creates a perfect situation for a currency swap. General Electric and Qantas Airways each borrow in the market where they have a comparative advantage; that is, General Electric borrows USD and Qantas Airways borrows AUD. They then use a currency swap to transform General Electric's loan into a AUD loan and Qantas Airways' loan into a USD loan.

As already mentioned, the difference between the dollar interest rates is 2%, whereas the difference between the AUD interest rates is 0.4%. By analogy with the interest rate swap case, we expect the total gain to all parties to be $2.0 - 0.4 = 1.6\%$ per annum.

There are several ways in which the swap can be arranged. Figure 7.11 shows one way swaps might be entered into with a financial institution. General Electric borrows USD and Qantas Airways borrows AUD. The effect of the swap is to transform the USD interest rate of 5% per annum to an AUD interest rate of 6.9% per annum for General Electric. As a result, General Electric is 0.7% per annum better off than it would be if it went directly to AUD markets. Similarly, Qantas exchanges an AUD loan at 8% per annum for a USD loan at 6.3% per annum and ends up 0.7% per annum better off than it would be if it went directly to USD markets. The financial institution gains 1.3% per annum on its USD cash flows and loses 1.1% per annum on its AUD flows. If we ignore the difference between the two currencies, the financial institution makes a net gain of 0.2% per annum. As predicted, the total gain to all parties is 1.6% per annum.

Each year the financial institution makes a gain of USD 195,000 (= 1.3% of 15 million) and incurs a loss of AUD 220,000 (= 1.1% of 20 million). The financial institution can avoid any foreign exchange risk by buying AUD 220,000 per annum in the forward market for each year of the life of the swap, thus locking in a net gain in USD.

It is possible to redesign the swap so that the financial institution makes a 0.2% spread in USD. Figures 7.12 and 7.13 present two alternatives. These alternatives are unlikely to be used in practice because they do not lead to General Electric and Qantas

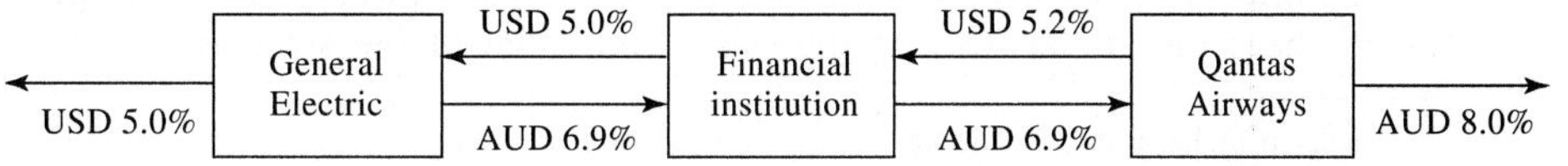

Figure 7.12 Alternative arrangement for currency swap: Qantas Airways bears some foreign exchange risk

Figure 7.13 Alternative arrangement for currency swap: General Electric bears some foreign exchange risk

being free of foreign exchange risk.[12] In Figure 7.12, Qantas bears some foreign exchange risk because it pays 1.1% per annum in AUD and 5.2% per annum in USD. In Figure 7.13, General Electric bears some foreign exchange risk because it receives 1.1% per annum in USD and pays 8% per annum in AUD.

7.13 VALUATION OF FIXED-FOR-FIXED CURRENCY SWAPS

Like interest rate swaps, fixed-for-fixed currency swaps can be decomposed into either the difference between two bonds or a portfolio of forward contracts.

Valuation in Terms of Bond Prices

If we define V_{swap} as the value in U.S. dollars of an outstanding swap where dollars are received and a foreign currency is paid, then

$$V_{\text{swap}} = B_D - S_0 B_F$$

where B_F is the value, measured in the foreign currency, of the bond defined by the foreign cash flows on the swap and B_D is the value of the bond defined by the domestic cash flows on the swap, and S_0 is the spot exchange rate (expressed as number of dollars per unit of foreign currency). The value of a swap can therefore be determined from risk-free discount rates in the two currencies and the spot exchange rate.[13]

Similarly, the value of a swap where the foreign currency is received and dollars are paid is

$$V_{\text{swap}} = S_0 B_F - B_D$$

Example 7.7 illustrates the use of this formula.

Valuation as Portfolio of Forward Contracts

Each exchange of payments in a fixed-for-fixed currency swap is a forward foreign exchange contract. As shown in Section 5.7, forward foreign exchange contracts can be valued by assuming that forward rates are realized. The same assumptions can therefore be made for a currency swap. The forward exchange rates themselves can be calculated from equation (5.9). Example 7.8 illustrates this approach.

The value of a currency swap is normally close to zero initially. If the two principals are worth the same at the start of the swap, the value of the swap is also close to zero

[12] Usually it makes sense for the financial institution to bear the foreign exchange risk, because it is in the best position to hedge the risk.

[13] As in the case of interest rate swaps, the risk-free discount rate is sometimes calculated from LIBOR/swap rates and sometimes from OIS rates.

Example 7.7 Currency swap valuation in terms of bonds

Suppose that the term structure of risk-free interest rates is flat in both Japan and the United States. The Japanese rate is 4% per annum and the U.S. rate is 9% per annum (both with continuous compounding). Some time ago, a financial institution entered into a currency swap in which it receives 5% per annum in yen and pays 8% per annum in dollars once a year. The principals in the two currencies are \$10 million and 1,200 million yen. The swap will last for another three years, and the current exchange rate is 110 yen = \$1. The calculations are summarized in the following table (all amounts are in millions):

Time	*Cash flows on dollar bond (\$)*	*Present value (\$)*	*Cash flows on yen bond (yen)*	*Present value (yen)*
1	0.8	0.7311	60	57.65
2	0.8	0.6682	60	55.39
3	0.8	0.6107	60	53.22
3	10.0	7.6338	1,200	1,064.30
Total		9.6439		1,230.55

In this case, the cash flows from the dollar bond underlying the swap are as shown in the second column. The present value of the cash flows using the dollar discount rate of 9% are shown in the third column. The cash flows from the yen bond underlying the swap are shown in the fourth column of the table. The present value of the cash flows using the yen discount rate of 4% are shown in the final column of the table. The value of the dollar bond, B_D, is 9.6439 million dollars. The value of the yen bond is 1230.55 million yen. The value of the swap in dollars is therefore $(1{,}230.55/110) - 9.6439 = 1.5430$ million.

immediately after the initial exchange of principal. However, as in the case of interest rate swaps, this does not mean that each of the individual forward contracts underlying the swap has a value close to zero. It can be shown that, when interest rates in two currencies are significantly different, the payer of the high-interest currency is in the position where the forward contracts corresponding to the early exchanges of cash flows have negative values, and the forward contract corresponding to final exchange of principals has a positive value. The payer of the low-interest currency is in the opposite position; that is, the forward contracts corresponding to the early exchanges of cash flows have positive values and that corresponding to the final exchange has a negative value. These results are important when the credit risk in the swap is being evaluated.

7.14 OTHER CURRENCY SWAPS

Two other popular currency swaps are:

1. Fixed-for-floating, where a floating interest rate in one currency is exchanged for a fixed interest rate in another currency

Example 7.8 Currency swap valuation in terms of forward contracts

Consider again the situation described in Example 7.7. The Japanese risk-free rates are 4% per annum, while the U.S. risk-free rates are 9% per annum (both with continuous compounding). Some time ago, a financial institution entered into a currency swap in which it receives 5% per annum in yen and pays 8% per annum in dollars once a year. The principals in the two currencies are $10 million and 1,200 million yen. The swap will last for another three years, and the current exchange rate is 110 yen = $1. The calculations are summarized in the following table (all amounts are in millions):

Time	*Dollar cash flow*	*Yen cash flow*	*Forward exchange rate*	*Dollar value of yen cash flow*	*Net cash flow ($)*	*Present value*
1	−0.8	60	0.009557	0.5734	−0.2266	−0.2071
2	−0.8	60	0.010047	0.6028	−0.1972	−0.1647
3	−0.8	60	0.010562	0.6337	−0.1663	−0.1269
3	−10.0	1,200	0.010562	12.6746	+2.6746	2.0417
Total						1.5430

The financial institution pays $0.08 \times 10 = \$0.8$ million dollars and receives $1{,}200 \times 0.05 = 60$ million yen each year. In addition the dollar principal of $10 million is paid and the yen principal of 1,200 is received at the end of year 3. The current spot rate is 0.009091 dollar per yen. In this case, $r = 9\%$ and $r_f = 4\%$, so that the one-year forward rate is, from equation (5.9), $0.009091e^{(0.09-0.04)\times 1} = 0.009557$. The two- and three-year forward rates in the table are calculated similarly. The forward contracts underlying the swap can be valued by assuming that the forward rates are realized. If the one-year forward rate is realized, the value of yen cash flow at the end of year 1 will be $60 \times 0.009557 = 0.5734$ millions of dollars and the net cash flow at the end of year 1 will be $0.5734 - 0.8 = -0.2266$ millions of dollars. This has a present value of $-0.2266e^{-0.09\times 1} = -0.2071$ millions of dollars. This is the value of forward contract corresponding to the exchange of cash flows at the end of year 1. The value of the other forward contracts are calculated similarly. As shown in the table, the value of the swap is 1.5430. This is in agreement with the value we calculated in Example 7.7 by decomposing the swap into a long position in one bond and a short position in another.

2. Floating-for-floating, where a floating interest rate in one currency is exchanged for a floating interest rate in another currency.

An example of the first type of swap would be an exchange where Sterling LIBOR on a principal of £7 million is paid and 3% on a principal of $10 million is received with payments being made semiannually for 10 years. Similarly to a fixed-for-fixed currency swap, this would involve an initial exchange of principal in the opposite direction to the interest payments and a final exchange of principal in the same direction as the interest payments at the end of the swap's life. A fixed-for-floating swap can be regarded as a portfolio consisting of a fixed-for-fixed currency swap and a fixed-for-floating interest rate swap. For instance, the swap in our example can be regarded as (a) a swap where

3% on a principal of $10 million is received and (say) 4% on a principal of £7 million is paid plus (b) an interest rate swap where 4% is received and LIBOR is paid on a notional principal of £7 million.

To value the swap, we are considering we can calculate the value of the dollar payments in dollars by discounting them at the dollar risk-free rate. We can calculate the value of the sterling payments by (a) assuming that sterling LIBOR forward rates will be realized and discounting the cash flows at the sterling risk-free rate. The value of the swap is the difference between the values of the two sets of payments using current exchange rates.

An example of the second type of swap would be the exchange where sterling LIBOR on a principal of £7 million is paid and dollar LIBOR on a principal of $10 million is received. As in the other cases we have considered, this would involve an initial exchange of principal in the opposite direction to the interest payments and a final exchange of principal in the same direction as the interest payments at the end of the swap's life. A floating-for-floating swap can be regarded as a portfolio consisting of a fixed-for-fixed currency swap and two interest rate swaps, one in each currency. For instance, the swap in our example can be regarded as (a) a swap where 3% on a principal of $10 million is received and 4% on a principal of £7 million is paid plus (b) an interest rate swap where 4% is received and LIBOR is paid on a notional principal of £7 million plus (c) an interest rate swap where 3% is paid and LIBOR is received on a notional principal of $10 million.

A floating-for-floating swap can be valued by assuming that forward interest rates in each currency will be realized and discounting the cash flows at risk-free rates. The value of the swap is the difference between the values of the two sets of payments using current exchange rates.

7.15 CREDIT RISK

Contracts such as swaps that are private arrangements between two companies entail credit risks. Consider a financial institution that has entered into offsetting transactions with two companies (see Figure 7.4, 7.5, or 7.7). If neither party defaults, the financial institution remains fully hedged. A decline in the value of one transaction will always be offset by an increase in the value of the other transaction. However, there is a chance that one party will get into financial difficulties and default. The financial institution then still has to honor the contract it has with the other party.

Suppose that some time after the initiation of the transactions in Figure 7.4, the transaction with Microsoft has a positive value to the financial institution, whereas the transaction with Intel has a negative value. Suppose further that the financial institution has no other derivatives transactions with these companies. If Microsoft defaults, the financial institution is liable to lose the whole of the positive value it has in this contract. To maintain a hedged position, it would have to find a third party willing to take Microsoft's position. To induce the third party to take the position, the financial institution would have to pay the third party an amount roughly equal to the value of its contract with Microsoft prior to the default.

A financial institution clearly has credit-risk exposure from a swap when the value of the swap to the financial institution is positive. What happens when this value is negative and the counterparty gets into financial difficulties? In theory, the financial institution could realize a windfall gain, because a default would lead to it getting rid of a liability. In practice, it is likely that the counterparty would choose to sell the contract to a third party or rearrange its affairs in some way so that its positive value in the contract is not lost. The most realistic assumption for the financial institution is therefore as follows. If the counterparty goes bankrupt, there will be a loss if the value of the swap to the financial institution is positive, and there will be no effect on the financial institution's position if the value of the swap to the financial institution is negative. This situation is summarized in Figure 7.14.

In swaps, it is sometimes the case that the early exchanges of cash flows have positive values and the later exchanges have negative values. (This would be true in Figure 7.9a and in a currency swap where the interest paid is lower than the interest received.) These swaps are likely to have negative values for most of their lives and therefore entail less credit risk than swaps where the reverse is true.

Potential losses from defaults on a swap are much less than the potential losses from defaults on a loan with the same principal. This is because the value of the swap is usually only a small fraction of the value of the loan. Potential losses from defaults on a currency swap are greater than on an interest rate swap. The reason is that, because principal amounts in two different currencies are exchanged at the end of the life of a currency swap, a currency swap is liable to have a greater value at the time of a default than an interest rate swap.

It is important to distinguish between the credit risk and market risk to a financial institution in any contract. As discussed earlier, the credit risk arises from the possibility of a default by the counterparty when the value of the contract to the financial institution is positive. The market risk arises from the possibility that market variables such as interest rates and exchange rates will move in such a way that the value of a contract to the financial institution becomes negative.

One of the more bizarre stories in swap markets is outlined in Business Snapshot 7.2. It concerns the British Local Authority, Hammersmith and Fulham, and shows that in addition to bearing credit risk and market risk, banks trading swaps also sometimes bear legal risk.

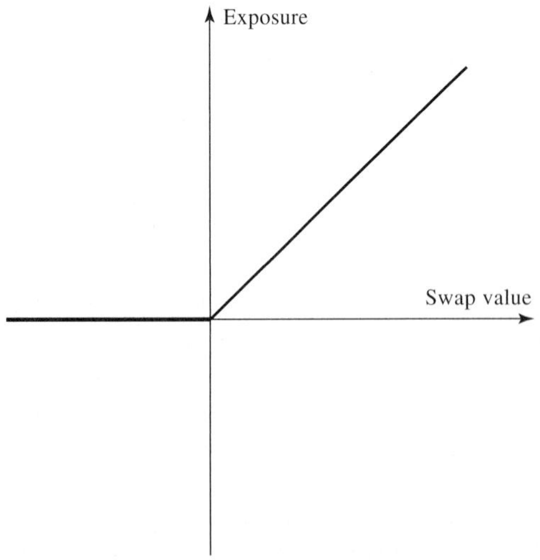

Figure 7.14 The credit exposure in a swap

Business Snapshot 7.2 The Hammersmith and Fulham story

Between 1987 to 1989 the London Borough of Hammersmith and Fulham in Great Britain entered into about 600 interest rate swaps and related instruments with a total notional principal of about 6 billion pounds. The transactions appear to have been entered into for speculative rather than hedging purposes. The two employees of Hammersmith and Fulham responsible for the trades had only a sketchy understanding of the risks they were taking and how the products they were trading worked.

By 1989, because of movements in sterling interest rates, Hammersmith and Fulham had lost several hundred million pounds on the swaps. To the banks on the other side of the transactions, the swaps were worth several hundred million pounds. The banks were concerned about credit risk. They had entered into offsetting swaps to hedge their interest rate risks. If Hammersmith and Fulham defaulted they would still have to honor their obligations on the offsetting swaps and would take a huge loss.

What happened was something a little different from a default. Hammersmith and Fulham's auditor asked to have the transactions declared void because Hammersmith and Fulham did not have the authority to enter into the transactions. The British courts agreed. The case was appealed and went all the way to the House of Lords, Britain's highest court. The final decision was that Hammersmith and Fulham did not have the authority to enter into the swaps, but that they ought to have the authority to do so in the future for risk management purposes. Needless to say, banks were furious that their contracts were overturned in this way by the courts.

Central Clearing

As explained in Chapter 2, in an attempt to reduce credit risk in over-the-counter markets, regulators require standardized over-the-counter derivatives to be cleared through central clearing parties (CCPs). The CCP acts as an intermediary between the two sides in a transaction. It requires initial margin and variation margin from both sides in the same way that these are required by futures clearing houses. LCH.Clearnet (formed by a merger of the London Clearing House and Paris-based Clearnet) is the largest CCP for interest rate swaps. It was clearing swaps with several trillion dollars of notional in 2012. It uses OIS discounting for its daily valuations.

Credit Default Swaps

A swap which has grown in importance since the year 2000 is a *credit default swap* (CDS). This is a swap that allows companies to hedge credit risks in the same way that they have hedged market risks for many years. A CDS is like an insurance contract that pays off if a particular company or country defaults. The company or country is known as the *reference entity*. The buyer of credit protection pays an insurance premium, known as the *CDS spread*, to the seller of protection for the life of the contract or until the reference entity defaults. Suppose that the notional principal of the CDS is $100 million and the CDS spread for a five-year deal is 120 basis points. The insurance premium would be 120 basis points applied to $100 million or $1.2 million per year. If the reference entity does not default during the five years, nothing is received in return for the insurance premiums. If reference entity does default and bonds issued by the reference entity are worth 40 cents per dollar of principal immediately after default, the seller of protection has to make a payment to the buyer of protection equal to \$60 million. The idea here is that, if the buyer of protection owned a portfolio of bonds issued by the reference entity with a principal of \$100 million, the insurance payoff would be sufficient to bring the value of the portfolio back up to \$100 million.

Credit default swaps are discussed in more detail in Chapter 23.

7.16 OTHER TYPES OF SWAP

In this chapter we have covered interest rate swaps where LIBOR is exchanged for a fixed rate of interest and currency swaps where a fixed rate of interest in one currency is exchanged for a fixed rate of interest in another currency. Many other types of swap are traded. We will discuss some of them Chapter 22. At this stage we provide an overview.

Variations on the Standard Interest Rate Swap

In fixed-for-floating interest rate swaps, LIBOR is the most common reference floating interest rate. In the examples in this chapter, the tenor (i.e., payment frequency) of LIBOR has been six months, but swaps where the tenor of LIBOR is one month, three months, and 12 months trade regularly. The tenor on the floating side does not have to match the tenor on the fixed side. (Indeed, as pointed out in footnote 3, the standard interest rate swap in the United States is one where there are quarterly LIBOR payments and semiannual fixed payments.) LIBOR is the most common floating rate, but others such as the commercial paper (CP) rate are occasionally used. Sometimes what are known as *basis swaps* are negotiated. For example, the three-month CP rate plus 10 basis points might be exchanged for three-month LIBOR with both being applied to the same principal. (This deal would allow a company to hedge its exposure when assets and liabilities are subject to different floating rates.)

The principal in a swap agreement can be varied throughout the term of the swap to meet the needs of a counterparty. In an *amortizing swap*, the principal reduces in a predetermined way. (This might be designed to correspond to the amortization schedule on a loan.) In a *step-up swap*, the principal increases in a predetermined way. (This might be designed to correspond to drawdowns on a loan agreement.) *Deferred swaps* or *forward swaps*, where the parties do not begin to exchange interest payments until some future date, can also be arranged. Sometimes swaps are negotiated where the principal to which the fixed payments are applied is different from the principal to which the floating payments are applied.

A *constant maturity swap* (CMS swap) is an agreement to exchange a LIBOR rate for a swap rate. An example would be an agreement to exchange six-month LIBOR applied to a certain principal for the 10-year swap rate applied to the same principal every six months for the next five years. A *constant maturity Treasury swap* (CMT swap) is a similar agreement to exchange a LIBOR rate for a particular Treasury rate (e.g., the 10-year Treasury rate).

In a *compounding swap* interest on one or both sides is compounded forward to the end of the life of the swap according to pre-agreed rules and there is only one payment date at the end of the life of the swap. In a *LIBOR-in-arrears* swap the LIBOR rate observed on a payment date is used to calculate the payment on that date. (As explained in Section 7.1, in a standard deal the LIBOR rate observed on one payment date is used to determine the payment on the next payment date.) In an *accrual swap* the interest on one side of the swap accrues only when the floating reference rate is in a certain range.

Other Currency Swaps

Sometimes a rate observed in one currency is applied to a principal amount in another currency. One such deal would be where three-month LIBOR observed in the United States is exchanged for three-month LIBOR in Britain with both rates being applied to a principal of 10 million British pounds. This type of swap is referred to as a *diff swap* or a *quanto*.

Equity Swaps

An *equity swap* is an agreement to exchange the total return (dividends and capital gains) realized on an equity index for either a fixed or a floating rate of interest. For example, the total return on the S&P 500 in successive six-month periods might be exchanged for LIBOR with both being applied to the same principal. Equity swaps can be used by portfolio managers to convert returns from a fixed or floating investment to the returns from investing in an equity index, and vice versa.

Options

Sometimes there are options embedded in a swap agreement. For example, in an *extendable swap*, one party has the option to extend the life of the swap beyond the specified period. In a *puttable swap*, one party has the option to terminate the swap early. Options on swaps, or *swaptions*, are also available. These provide one party with the right at a future time to enter into a swap where a predetermined fixed rate is exchanged for floating.

Commodity Swaps, Volatility Swaps, etc.

Commodity swaps are in essence a series of forward contracts on a commodity with different maturity dates and the same delivery prices. In a *volatility swap* there are a series of time periods. At the end of each period, one side pays a pre-agreed volatility while the other side pays the historical volatility realized during the period. Both volatilities are multiplied by the same notional principal in calculating payments.

Swaps are limited only by the imagination of financial engineers and the desire of corporate treasurers and fund managers for exotic structures. In Chapter 22, we will describe the famous 5/30 swap entered into between Procter and Gamble and Bankers Trust, where payments depended in a complex way on the 30-day commercial paper rate, a 30-year Treasury bond price, and the yield on a five-year Treasury bond.

SUMMARY

The two most common types of swap are interest rate swaps and currency swaps. In an interest rate swap, one party agrees to pay the other party interest at a fixed rate on a notional principal for a number of years. In return, it receives interest at a floating rate on the same notional principal for the same period of time. In a currency swap, one party agrees to pay interest on a principal amount in one currency. In return, it receives interest on a principal amount in another currency.

Principal amounts are not usually exchanged in an interest rate swap. In a currency swap, principal amounts are usually exchanged at both the beginning and the end of the life of the swap. For a party paying interest in the foreign currency, the foreign principal is received, and the domestic principal is paid at the beginning of the life of the swap. At the end of the life of the swap, the foreign principal is paid and the domestic principal is received.

An interest rate swap can be used to transform a floating-rate loan into a fixed-rate loan, or vice versa. It can also be used to transform a floating-rate investment to a fixed-rate investment, or vice versa. A currency swap can be used to transform a loan in one currency into a loan in another currency. It can also be used to transform an investment denominated in one currency into an investment denominated in another currency.

There are two ways of valuing interest rate and currency swaps. In the first, the swap is decomposed into a long position in one bond and a short position in another bond. In the second, it is regarded as a portfolio of forward contracts.

When a financial institution enters into a pair of offsetting swaps with different counterparties, it is exposed to credit risk. If one of the counterparties defaults when the financial institution has positive value in its swap with that counterparty, the financial institution loses money because it still has to honor its swap agreement with the other counterparty.

FURTHER READING

Baz, J., and M. Pascutti. "Alternative Swap Contracts Analysis and Pricing," *Journal of Derivatives*, (Winter 1996): 7–21.

Brown, K. C., and D. J. Smith. *Interest Rate and Currency Swaps: A Tutorial*. Association for Investment Management and Research, 1996.

Cooper, I., and A. Mello. "The Default Risk in Interest Rate Swaps," *Journal of Finance*, 46, 2 (1991): 597–620.

Dattatreya, R. E., and K. Hotta. *Advanced Interest Rate and Currency Swaps: State-of-the Art Products, Strategies, and Risk Management Applications*, Irwin, 1993.

Flavell, R. *Swaps and Other Instruments*. Chichester: Wiley, 2002.

Gupta, A., and M. G. Subrahmanyam. "An Empirical Examination of the Convexity Bias in the Pricing of Interest Rate Swaps," *Journal of Financial Economics*, 55, 2 (2000): 239–79.

Litzenberger, R. H. "Swaps: Plain and Fanciful," *Journal of Finance*, 47, 3 (1992): 831–50.

Minton, B. A. "An Empirical Examination of the Basic Valuation Models for Interest Rate Swaps," *Journal of Financial Economics*, 44, 2 (1997): 251–77.

Smith, D. J. "Valuing Interest Rate Swaps Using OIS Discounting," Working Paper, Boston University, 2012.

Sun, T., S. Sundaresan, and C. Wang. "Interest Rate Swaps: An Empirical Investigation," *Journal of Financial Economics*, 34, 1 (1993): 77–99.

Titman, S. "Interest Rate Swaps and Corporate Financing Choices," *Journal of Finance*, 47, 4 (1992): 1503–16.

Quiz (Answers at End of Book)

7.1. Companies A and B have been offered the following rates per annum on a \$20 million five-year loan:

	Fixed rate	*Floating rate*
Company A:	5.0%	LIBOR + 0.1%
Company B:	6.4%	LIBOR + 0.6%

Company A requires a floating-rate loan; company B requires a fixed-rate loan. Design a swap that will net a bank, acting as intermediary, 0.1% per annum and that will appear equally attractive to both companies.

7.2. A \$100 million interest rate swap has a remaining life of 10 months. Under the terms of the swap, six-month LIBOR is exchanged for 7% per annum (compounded semiannually). The average of the bid–offer rate being exchanged for six-month LIBOR in swaps of all maturities is currently 5% per annum with continuous compounding. The six-month LIBOR rate was 4.6% per annum two months ago. What is the current value of the swap to the party paying floating? What is its value to the party paying fixed? Use LIBOR discounting.

7.3. Company X wishes to borrow U.S. dollars at a fixed rate of interest. Company Y wishes to borrow Japanese yen at a fixed rate of interest. The amounts required by the two companies are roughly the same at the current exchange rate. The companies are subject to the following interest rates, which have been adjusted to reflect the impact of taxes:

	Yen	*Dollars*
Company X:	5.0%	9.6%
Company Y:	6.5%	10.0%

Design a swap that will net a bank, acting as intermediary, 50 basis points per annum. Make the swap equally attractive to the two companies and ensure that all foreign exchange risk is assumed by the bank.

7.4. Explain what a swap rate is. What is the relationship between swap rates and par yields?

7.5. A currency swap has a remaining life of 15 months. It involves exchanging interest at 10% on £20 million for interest at 6% on \$30 million once a year. The term structure of interest rates in both the United Kingdom and the United States is currently flat, and if the swap were negotiated today the interest rates exchanged would be 4% in dollars and 7% in sterling. All interest rates are quoted with annual compounding. The current exchange rate (dollars per pound sterling) is 1.5500. What is the value of the swap to the party paying sterling? What is the value of the swap to the party paying dollars?

7.6. Explain the difference between the credit risk and the market risk in a financial contract.

7.7. A corporate treasurer tells you that he has just negotiated a five-year loan at a competitive fixed rate of interest of 5.2%. The treasurer explains that he achieved the 5.2% rate by borrowing at six-month LIBOR plus 150 basis points and swapping LIBOR for 3.7%. He goes on to say that this was possible because his company has a comparative advantage in the floating-rate market. What has the treasurer overlooked?

Practice Questions (Answers in Solutions Manual/Study Guide)

7.8. Explain why a bank is subject to credit risk when it enters into two offsetting swap contracts.

7.9. Companies X and Y have been offered the following rates per annum on a \$5 million 10-year investment:

	Fixed rate	*Floating rate*
Company X:	8.0%	LIBOR
Company Y:	8.8%	LIBOR

Company X requires a fixed-rate investment and company Y requires a floating-rate investment. Design a swap that will net a bank, acting as intermediary, 0.2% per annum and will appear equally attractive to X and Y.

7.10. A financial institution has entered into an interest rate swap with company X. Under the terms of the swap, it receives 10% per annum and pays six-month LIBOR on a principal of \$10 million for five years. Payments are made every six months. Suppose that company X defaults on the sixth payment date (end of year 3) when the LIBOR/swap interest rate (with semiannual compounding) is 8% per annum for all maturities. What is the loss to the financial institution? Assume that six-month LIBOR was 9% per annum halfway through year 3. Use LIBOR discounting.

7.11. A financial institution has entered into a ten-year currency swap with company Y. Under the terms of the swap, the financial institution receives interest at 3% per annum in Swiss francs and pays interest at 8% per annum in U.S. dollars. Interest payments are exchanged once a year. The principal amounts are 7 million dollars and 10 million francs. Suppose that company Y declares bankruptcy at the end of year 6, when the exchange rate is \$0.80 per franc. What is the cost to the financial institution? Assume that, at the end of year 6, the interest rate is 3% per annum in Swiss francs and 8% per annum in U.S. dollars for all maturities. All interest rates are quoted with annual compounding.

7.12. Companies A and B face the following interest rates (adjusted for the differential impact of taxes):

	A	B
U.S. dollars (floating rate):	LIBOR + 0.5%	LIBOR + 1.0%
Canadian dollars (fixed rate):	5.0%	6.5%

Assume that A wants to borrow U.S. dollars at a floating rate of interest and B wants to borrow Canadian dollars at a fixed rate of interest. A financial institution is planning to arrange a swap and requires a 50-basis-point spread. If the swap is to appear equally attractive to A and B, what rates of interest will A and B end up paying?

7.13. After it hedges its foreign exchange risk using forward contracts, is the financial institution's average spread in Figure 7.11 likely to be greater than or less than 20 basis points? Explain your answer.

7.14. "Companies with high credit risks are the ones that cannot access fixed-rate markets directly. They are the companies that are most likely to be paying fixed and receiving floating in an interest rate swap." Assume that this statement is true. Do you think it increases or decreases the risk of a financial institution's swap portfolio? Assume that companies are most likely to default when interest rates are high.

7.15. Why is the expected loss from a default on a swap less than the expected loss from the default on a loan with the same principal?

7.16. A bank finds that its assets are not matched with its liabilities. It is taking floating-rate deposits and making fixed-rate loans. How can swaps be used to offset the risk?

7.17. Explain how you would value a swap that is the exchange of a floating rate in one currency for a fixed rate in another currency.

7.18. The LIBOR zero curve is flat at 5% (continuously compounded) out to 1.5 years. Swap rates for 2- and 3-year semiannual pay swaps are 5.4% and 5.6%, respectively. Estimate the LIBOR zero rates for maturities of 2.0, 2.5, and 3.0 years. (Assume that the 2.5-year swap rate is the average of the 2- and 3-year swap rates and use LIBOR discounting.)

7.19. OIS rates have been estimated as 3.4% for all maturities. The three-month LIBOR rate is 3.5%. For a six-month swap where payments are exchanged every three months the swap rate is 3.6%. All rates are expressed with quarterly compounding. What is the LIBOR forward rate for the three to six month period if OIS discounting is used?

Further Questions

7.20. (a) Company A has been offered the rates shown in Table 7.3. It can borrow for three years at 6.45%. What floating rate can it swap this fixed rate into? (b) Company B has been offered the rates shown in Table 7.3. It can borrow for five years at LIBOR plus 75 basis points. What fixed rate can it swap this floating rate into?

7.21. (a) Company X has been offered the rates shown in Table 7.3. It can invest for four years at 5.5%. What floating rate can it swap this fixed rate into? (b) Company Y has been offered the rates shown in Table 7.3. It can invest for ten years at LIBOR minus 50 basis points. What fixed rate can it swap this floating rate into?

7.22. The one-year LIBOR rate is 10% with annual compounding. A bank trades swaps where a fixed rate of interest is exchanged for 12-month LIBOR with payments being exchanged annually. Two- and three-year swap rates (expressed with annual compounding) are 11% and 12% per annum. Estimate the two- and three-year LIBOR zero rates when LIBOR discounting is used.

7.23. The one-year LIBOR zero rate is 3% and the LIBOR forward rate for the one- to two-year period is 3.2%. The three-year swap rate for a swap with annual payments is 3.2%. All rates are annually compounded. What is the LIBOR forward rate for the 2 to 3 year period if OIS discounting is used and the OIS zero rates for maturities of 1, 2, and 3 years are 2.5%, 2.7%, and 2.9%, respectively. What is the value of a three-year swap where 4% is received and LIBOR is paid on a principal of $100 million.

7.24. In an interest rate swap, a financial institution pays 10% per annum and receives three-month LIBOR in return on a notional principal of $100 million with payments being exchanged every three months. The swap has a remaining life of 14 months. The average of the bid and offer fixed rates currently being swapped for three-month LIBOR is 12% per annum for all maturities. The three-month LIBOR rate one month ago was 11.8% per annum. All rates are compounded quarterly. What is the value of the swap? Use LIBOR discounting.

7.25. Company A wishes to borrow U.S. dollars at a fixed rate of interest. Company B wishes to borrow sterling at a fixed rate of interest. They have been quoted the following rates per annum (adjusted for differential tax effects):

	Sterling	*U.S. dollars*
Company A:	11.0%	7.0%
Company B:	10.6%	6.2%

Design a swap that will net a bank, acting as intermediary, 10 basis points per annum and that will produce a gain of 15 basis points per annum for each of the two companies.

7.26. For all maturities, the U.S. dollar (USD) interest rate is 7% per annum and the Australian dollar (AUD) rate is 9% per annum. The current value of the AUD is 0.62 USD. In a swap agreement, a financial institution pays 8% per annum in AUD and receives 4% per annum in USD. The principals in the two currencies are $12 million USD and 20 million AUD. Payments are exchanged every year, with one exchange having just taken place. The swap will last two more years. What is the value of the swap to the financial institution? Assume all interest rates are continuously compounded.

7.27. Company X is based in the United Kingdom and would like to borrow $50 million at a fixed rate of interest for five years in U.S. funds. Because the company is not well known in the United States, this has proved to be impossible. However, the company has been quoted 12% per annum on fixed-rate five-year sterling funds. Company Y is based in the United States and would like to borrow the equivalent of $50 million in sterling funds for five years at a fixed rate of interest. It has been unable to get a quote but has been offered U.S. dollar funds at 10.5% per annum. Five-year government bonds currently yield 9.5% per annum in the United States and 10.5% in the United Kingdom. Suggest an appropriate currency swap that will net the financial intermediary 0.5% per annum.

CHAPTER 8 Securitization and the Credit Crisis of 2007

Derivatives such as forwards, futures, swaps, and options are concerned with transferring risk from one entity in the economy to another. The first seven chapters of this book have focused on forwards, futures, and swaps. Before moving on to discuss options, we consider another important way of transferring risk in the economy: securitization.

Securitization is of particular interest because of its role in the credit crisis (sometimes referred to as the "credit crunch") that started in 2007. The crisis had its origins in financial products created from mortgages in the United States, but rapidly spread from the United States to other countries and from financial markets to the real economy. Some financial institutions failed; others had to be rescued by national governments. There can be no question that the first decade of the twenty-first century was disastrous for the financial sector.

In this chapter, we examine the nature of securitization and its role in the crisis. In the course of the chapter, we will learn about the U.S. mortgage market, asset-backed securities, collateralized debt obligations, waterfalls, and the importance of incentives in financial markets.

8.1 SECURITIZATION

Traditionally, banks have funded their loans primarily from deposits. In the 1960s, U.S. banks found that they could not keep pace with the demand for residential mortgages with this type of funding. This led to the development of the mortgage-backed security (MBS) market. Portfolios of mortgages were created and the cash flows (interest and principal payments) generated by the portfolios were packaged as securities and sold to investors. The U.S. government created the Government National Mortgage Association (GNMA, also known as Ginnie Mae) in 1968. This organization guaranteed (for a fee) interest and principal payments on qualifying mortgages and created the securities that were sold to investors.

Thus, although banks originated the mortgages, they did not keep them on their balance sheets. Securitization allowed them to increase their lending faster than their

From Chapter 8 of *Fundamentals of Futures and Options Markets*, Eighth Edition. John C. Hull.

deposits were growing. GNMA's guarantee protected MBS investors against defaults by borrowers.[1]

In the 1980s, the securitization techniques developed for the mortgage market were applied to asset classes such as automobile loans and credit card receivables in the United States. Securitization also become popular in other parts of the world. As the securitization market developed, investors became comfortable with situations where they did not have a guarantee against defaults by borrowers.

ABSs

A securitization arrangement of the type used during the 2000 to 2007 period is shown in Figure 8.1. This is known as an *asset-backed security* or ABS. A portfolio of income-producing assets such as loans is sold by the originating banks to a special purpose vehicle (SPV) and the cash flows from the assets are then allocated to tranches. Figure 8.1 is simpler than the structures that were typically created because it has only three tranches (in practice, many more tranches were used). These are the senior tranche, the mezzanine tranche, and the equity tranche. The portfolio has a principal of \$100 million. This is divided as follows: \$80 million to the senior tranche, \$15 million to the mezzanine tranche, and \$5 million to the equity tranche. The senior tranche is promised a return of LIBOR plus 60 basis points, the mezzanine tranche is promised a return of LIBOR plus 250 basis points, and the equity tranche is promised a return of LIBOR plus 2,000 basis points.

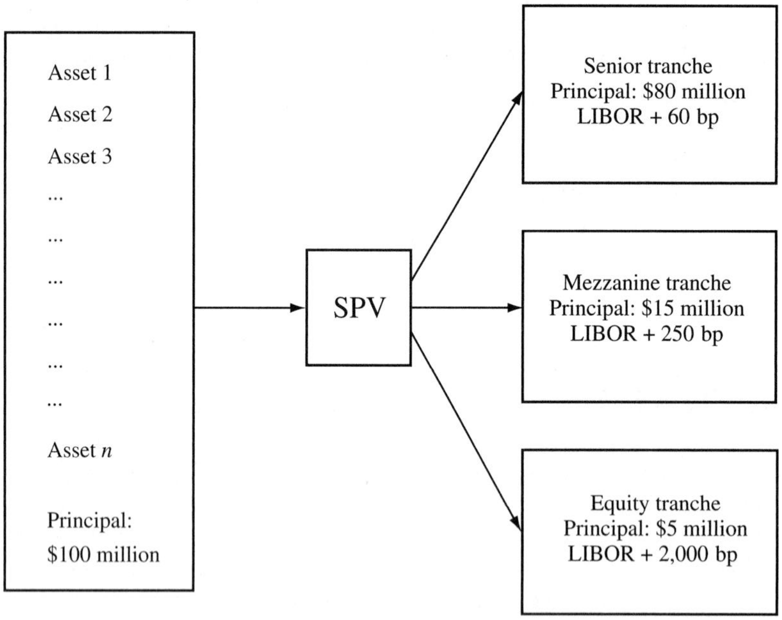

Figure 8.1 An asset-backed security (simplified); bp = basis points (1bp = 0.01%)

[1] However, MBS investors do face uncertainty about mortgage prepayments. Prepayments tend to be greatest when interest rates are low and the reinvestment opportunities open to investors are not particularly attractive. In the early days of MBSs, many MBS investors realized lower returns than they expected because they did not take this into account.

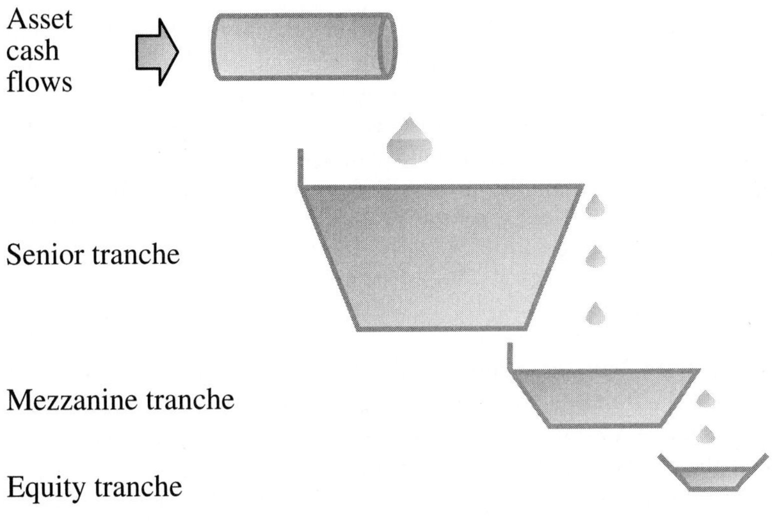

Figure 8.2 The waterfall in an asset-backed security

It sounds as though the equity tranche has the best deal, but this is not necessarily the case. The payments of interest and principal are not guaranteed. The equity tranche is more likely to lose part of its principal, and less likely to receive the promised interest payments on its outstanding principal, than the other tranches. Cash flows are allocated to tranches by specifying what is known as a waterfall. The general way a waterfall works is illustrated in Figure 8.2. A separate waterfall is applied to interest payments and the repayments of principal on the assets. Principal repayments are allocated to the senior tranche until its principal has been fully repaid. They are then allocated to mezzanine tranche until its principal has been fully repaid. Only after this has happened do principal repayments go to the equity tranche. Interest payments are allocated to the senior tranche until the senior tranche has received its promised return on its outstanding principal. Assuming that this promised return can be made, interest payments are then allocated to the mezzanine tranche. If the promised return to the mezzanine tranche can be made and cash flows are left over, they are allocated to the equity tranche.

The extent to which the tranches get their principal back depends on losses on the underlying assets. The effect of the waterfall is roughly as follows. The first 5% of losses are borne by the equity tranche. If losses exceed 5%, the equity tranche loses all its principal and some losses are borne by the principal of the mezzanine tranche. If losses exceed 20%, the mezzanine tranche loses all its principal and some losses are borne by the principal of the senior tranche.

There are therefore two ways of looking at an ABS. One is with reference to the waterfall in Figure 8.2. Cash flows go first to the senior tranche, then to the mezzanine tranche, and then to the equity tranche. The other is in terms of losses. Losses of principal are first borne by the equity tranche, then by the mezzanine tranche, and then by the senior tranche. Rating agencies such as Moody's, S&P, and Fitch played a key role in securitization. The ABS in Figure 8.1 is designed so that the senior tranche is rated AAA. The mezzanine tranche is typically rated BBB. The equity tranche is typically unrated.

The description of ABSs that we have given so far is somewhat simplified. Typically, more than three tranches with a wide range of ratings were created. In the waterfall rules, as we have described them, the allocation of cash flows to tranches is sequential in that they always flow first to the most senior tranche, then to the next most senior tranche, and so on. In practice, the rules are somewhat more complicated than this and are described in a legal document that is several hundred pages long. Another complication is that there was often some overcollateralization where the total principal of the tranches was less than the total principal of the underlying assets. Also, the weighted average return promised to the tranches was less than the weighted average return payable on the assets.[2]

ABS CDOs

Finding investors to buy the senior AAA-rated tranches of ABSs was usually not difficult, because the tranches promised returns that were very attractive when compared with the return on AAA-rated bonds. Equity tranches were typically retained by the originator of the assets or sold to a hedge fund.

Finding investors for mezzanine tranches was more difficult. This led to the creation of ABSs of ABSs. The way this was done is shown in Figure 8.3. Many different mezzanine tranches, created in the way indicated in Figure 8.1, are put in a portfolio and the risks associated with the cash flows from the portfolio are tranched out in the same way as the risks associated with cash flows from the assets are tranched out in Figure 8.1. The resulting structure is known as an *ABS CDO* or *Mezz ABS CDO*. In the example in Figure 8.3, the senior tranche of the ABS CDO accounts for 65% of the principal of the ABS mezzanine tranches, the mezzanine tranche of the ABS CDO accounts for 25% of the principal, and the equity tranche accounts for the remaining 10% of the principal. The structure is designed so that the senior tranche of the ABS CDO is given the highest credit rating of AAA. This means that the total of the AAA-rated instruments created in the example that is considered here is about 90% (80% plus 65% of 15%) of the principal of the underlying portfolios. This seems high but, if the securitization were carried further with an ABS being created from tranches of ABS CDOs (and this did happen), the percentage would be pushed even higher.

In the example in Figure 8.3, the AAA-rated tranche of the ABS can expect to receive its promised return and get its principal back if losses on the underlying portfolio of

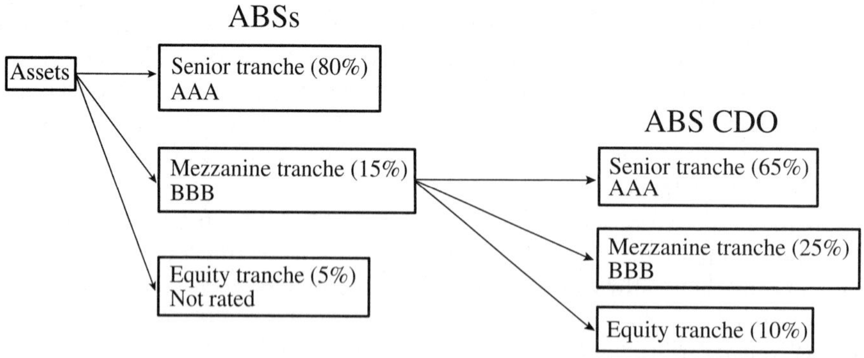

Figure 8.3 Creation of ABSs and an ABS CDO from portfoloios of assets (simplified)

[2] Both this feature and overcollateralization had the potential to make the structure very profitable for its creator.

Table 8.1 Estimated losses to AAA-rated tranches of ABS CDO in Figure 8.3

Losses on underlying assets	*Losses to mezzanine tranche of ABS*	*Losses to equity tranche of ABS CDO*	*Losses to mezzanine tranche of ABS CDO*	*Losses to senior tranche of ABS CDO*
10%	33.3%	100.0%	93.3%	0.0%
13%	53.3%	100.0%	100.0%	28.2%
17%	80.0%	100.0%	100.0%	69.2%
20%	100.0%	100.0%	100.0%	100.0%

assets is less than 20% because all losses of principal would then be absorbed by the more junior tranches. The AAA-rated tranche of the ABS CDO in Figure 8.3 is more risky. It will receive the promised return and get its principal back if losses on the underlying assets are 10.25% or less. This is because a loss of 10.25% means that mezzanine tranches of ABSs have to absorb losses equal to 5.25% of the ABS principal. As these tranches have a total principal equal to 15% of the ABS principal, they lose 5.25/15 or 35% of their principal. The equity and mezzanine tranches of the ABS CDO are then wiped out, but the senior tranche just manages to survive intact.

The senior tranche of the ABS CDO suffers losses if losses on the underlying portfolios are more than 10.25%. Consider, for example, the situation where losses are 17% on the underlying portfolios. Of the 17%, 5% is borne by the equity tranche of the ABS and 12% by the mezzanine tranche of the ABS. Losses on the mezzanine tranches are therefore 12/15 or 80% of their principal. The first 35% is absorbed by the equity and mezzanine tranches of the ABS CDO. The senior tranche of the ABS CDO therefore loses 45/65 or 69.2% of its value. These and other results are summarized in Table 8.1. Our calculations assume that all ABS portfolios have the same default rate.

8.2 THE U.S. HOUSING MARKET

Figure 8.4 gives the S&P/Case–Shiller composite-10 index for house prices in the U.S. between January 1987 and May 2012. This tracks house prices for ten metropolitan areas of the U.S. It shows that, in about the year 2000, house prices started to rise much faster than they had in the previous decade. The very low level of interest rates between 2002 and 2005 was an important contributory factor, but the bubble in house prices was largely fueled by mortgage-lending practices.

The 2000 to 2006 period was characterized by a huge increase in what is termed subprime mortgage lending. Subprime mortgages are mortgages that are considered to be significantly more risky than average. Before 2000, most mortgages classified as subprime were second mortgages. After 2000, this changed as financial institutions became more comfortable with the notion of a subprime first mortgage.

The Relaxation of Lending Standards

The relaxation of lending standards and the growth of subprime mortgages made house purchase possible for many families that had previously been considered to be not sufficiently creditworthy to qualify for a mortgage. These families increased the demand

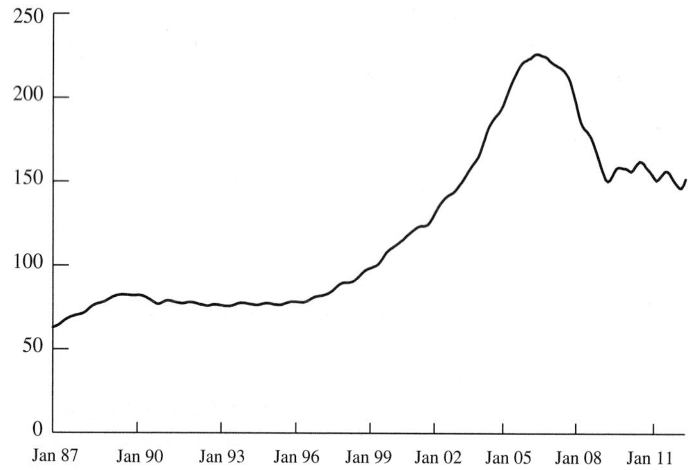

Figure 8.4 The S&P/Case–Shiller Composite-10 index of U.S. real estate prices, 1987–2012

for real estate and prices rose. To mortgage brokers and mortgage lenders, it was attractive to make more loans, particularly when higher house prices resulted. More lending meant bigger profits. Higher house prices meant that the lending was well covered by the underlying collateral. If the borrower defaulted, it was less likely that the resulting foreclosure would lead to a loss.

Mortgage brokers and mortgage lenders naturally wanted to keep increasing their profits. Their problem was that, as house prices rose, it was more difficult for first-time buyers to afford a house. In order to continue to attract new entrants to the housing market, they had to find ways to relax their lending standards even more—and this is exactly what they did. The amount lent as a percentage of the house price increased. Adjustable-rate mortgages (ARMS) were developed where there was a low "teaser" rate of interest that would last for two or three years and be followed by a rate that was much higher.[3] A typical teaser rate was about 6% and the interest rate after the end of the teaser rate period was typically six-month LIBOR plus 6%.[4] However, teaser rates as low as 1% or 2% have been reported. Lenders also became more cavalier in the way they reviewed mortgage applications. Indeed, the applicant's income and other information reported on the application form were frequently not checked.

Subprime Mortgage Securitization

Subprime mortgages were frequently securitized in the way indicated in Figures 8.1 to 8.3. The investors in tranches created from subprime mortgages usually had no guarantees that interest and principal would be paid. Securitization played a part in the

[3] If real estate prices increased, lenders expected the borrowers to prepay and take out a new mortgage at the end of the teaser rate period. However, prepayment penalties, often zero on prime mortgages, were quite high on subprime mortgages.

[4] A "2/28" ARM, for example, is an ARM where the rate is fixed for two years and then floats for the remaining 28 years.

crisis. The behavior of mortgage originators was influenced by their knowledge that mortgages would be securitized.[5] When considering new mortgage applications, the question was not "Is this a credit we want to assume?" Instead it was "Is this a mortgage we can make money on by selling it to someone else?"

When mortgages were securitized, the only information received about the mortgages by the buyers of the products that were created from them was the loan-to-value ratio (i.e., the ratio of the size of the loan to the assessed value of the house) and the borrower's FICO score.[6] Other information on the mortgage application form was considered irrelevant and, as already mentioned, was often not even checked by lenders. The most important thing for the lender was whether the mortgage could be sold to others—and this depended largely on the loan-to-value ratio and the applicant's FICO score.

It is interesting to note in passing that both the loan-to-value ratio and the FICO score were of doubtful quality. The property assessors who determined the value of a house at the time of a mortgage application sometimes succumbed to pressure from the lenders to come up with high values. Potential borrowers were sometimes counseled to take certain actions that would improve their FICO scores.[7]

Why was the government not regulating the behavior of mortgage lenders? The answer is that the U.S. government had since the 1990s been trying to expand home ownership and had been applying pressure to mortgage lenders to increase loans to low- and moderate-income people. Some state legislators, such as those in Ohio and Georgia, were concerned about what was going on and wanted to curtail predatory lending.[8] However, the courts decided that national standards should prevail.

A number of terms have been used to describe mortgage lending during the period leading up to the credit crunch. One is "liar loans" because individuals applying for a mortgage, knowing that no checks would be carried out, sometimes chose to lie on the application form. Another term used to describe some borrowers is "NINJA" (no income, no job, no assets).

The Bubble Bursts

All bubbles burst eventually and this one was no exception. In 2007, many mortgage holders found that they could no longer afford their mortgages when the teaser rates ended. This led to foreclosures and large numbers of houses coming on the market, which in turn led to a decline in house prices. Other mortgage holders, who had borrowed 100%, or close to 100%, of the cost of a house found that they had negative equity.

One of the features of the U.S. housing market is that mortgages are nonrecourse in many states. This means that, when there is a default, the lender is able to take possession of the house, but other assets of the borrower are off-limits. Consequently, the borrower has a free American-style put option. He or she can at any time sell the

[5] See B. J. Keys, T. Mukherjee, A. Seru, and V. Vig, "Did Securitization Lead to Lax Screening? Evidence from Subprime Loans," *Quarterly Journal of Economics*, 125, 1 (February 2010): 307–62

[6] FICO is a credit score developed by the Fair Isaac Corporation and is widely used in the U.S.. It ranges from 300 to 850.

[7] One such action might be to make regular payments on a new credit card for a few months.

[8] Predatory lending describes the situation where a lender deceptively convinces borrowers to agree to unfair and abusive loan terms.

house to the lender for the principal outstanding on the mortgage. This feature encouraged speculative activity and played a part in the cause of the bubble. Market participants realized belatedly how costly and destabilizing the put option could be. If the borrower had negative equity, the optimal decision was to exchange the house for the outstanding principal on the mortgage. The house was then sold by the lender, adding to the downward pressure on house prices.

It would be a mistake to assume that all mortgage defaulters were in the same position. Some were unable to meet mortgage payments and suffered greatly when they had to give up their homes. But many of the defaulters were speculators who bought multiple homes as rental properties and chose to exercise their put options. It was their tenants who suffered. There are also reports that some house owners (who were not speculators) were quite creative in extracting value from their put options. After handing the keys to their houses to the lender, they turned around and bought (sometimes at a bargain price) other houses that were in foreclosure. Imagine two people owning identical houses next to each other. Both have mortgages of $250,000. Both houses are worth $200,000 and in foreclosure can be expected to sell for $170,000. What is the owners' optimal strategy? The answer is that each person should exercise the put option and buy the neighbor's house.

The United States was not alone in having declining real estate prices. Prices declined in many other countries as well. Real estate prices in the United Kingdom were particularly badly affected.

The Losses

As foreclosures increased, the losses on mortgages also increased. It might be thought that a 35% reduction in house prices would lead to at most a 35% loss of principal on a defaulting mortgages. In fact, the losses were far greater than that. Houses in foreclosure were often in poor condition and sold for a small fraction of what their value was prior to the credit crisis. In 2008 and 2009, losses as high 75% were reported for mortgages on houses in foreclosure in some cases.

Investors in tranches that were formed from the mortgages incurred big losses. The value of the ABS tranches created from subprime mortgages was monitored by a series of indices known as ABX. These indices indicated that the tranches originally rated BBB had lost about 80% of their value by the end of 2007 and about 97% of their value by mid-2009. The value of the ABS CDO tranches created from BBB tranches was monitored by a series of indices known as TABX. These indices indicated that the tranches originally rated AAA lost about 80% of their value by the end of 2007 and were essentially worthless by mid-2009.

Financial institutions such as UBS, Merrill Lynch, and Citigroup had big positions in some of the tranches and incurred huge losses, as did the insurance giant AIG, which provided protection against losses on ABS CDO tranches that had originally been rated AAA. Many financial institutions had to be rescued with government funds. There have been few worse years in financial history than 2008. Bear Stearns was taken over by J. P. Morgan Chase; Merrill Lynch was taken over by Bank of America; Goldman Sachs and Morgan Stanley, which had formerly been investment banks, became bank holding companies with both commercial and investment banking interests; and Lehman Brothers was allowed to fail (see Business Snapshot 1.1).

The Credit Crisis

The losses on securities backed by residential mortgages led to a severe credit crisis. In 2006, banks were reasonably well capitalized, loans were relatively easy to obtain, and credit spreads were low. (The credit spread is the excess of the interest rate on a loan over the risk-free interest rate.) By 2008, the situation was totally different. The capital of banks had been badly eroded by their losses. They had become much more risk-averse and were reluctant to lend. Creditworthy individuals and corporations found borrowing difficult. Credit spreads had increased dramatically. The world experienced its worst recession in several generations. As discussed in Section 7.6, the LIBOR–OIS spread briefly reached 364 basis points in October 2008, indicating an extreme reluctance of banks to lend to each other. Another measure of the stress in financial markets is the TED spread. This is the excess of the three-month LIBOR interest rate over the three-month Treasury interest. In normal market conditions, it is 30 to 50 basis points. It reached over 450 basis points in October 2008.

8.3 WHAT WENT WRONG?

"Irrational exuberance" is a phrase coined by Alan Greenspan, Chairman of the Federal Reserve Board, to describe the behavior of investors during the bull market of the 1990s. It can also be applied to the period leading up the the credit crisis. Mortgage lenders, the investors in tranches of ABSs and ABS CDOs that were created from residential mortgages, and the companies that sold protection on the tranches assumed that the good times would last for ever. They thought that U.S. house prices would continue to increase. There might be declines in one or two areas, but the possibility of the widespread decline shown in Figure 8.4 was a scenario not considered by most people.

Many factors contributed to the crisis that started in 2007. Mortgage originators used lax lending standards. Products were developed to enable mortgage originators to profitably transfer credit risk to investors. Rating agencies moved from their traditional business of rating bonds, where they had a great deal of experience, to rating structured products, which were relatively new and for which there were relatively little historical data. The products bought by investors were complex and in many instances investors and rating agencies had inaccurate or incomplete information about the quality of the underlying assets. Investors in the structured products that were created thought they had found a money machine and chose to rely on rating agencies rather than forming their own opinions about the underlying risks. The return earned by the products rated AAA was high compared with the returns on bonds rated AAA.

Structured products such as those in Figures 8.1 and 8.3 are highly dependent on the default correlation between the underlying assets. Default correlation measures the tendency for different borrowers to default at about the same time. If the default correlation between the underlying assets in Figure 8.1 is low, the AAA-rated tranches are very unlikely to experience losses. As this default correlation increases, they become more vulnerable. The tranches of ABS CDOs in Figure 8.3 are even more heavily dependent on default correlation.

If mortgages exhibit moderate default correlation (as they do in normal times), there is very little chance of a high overall default rate and the AAA-rated tranches of both ABSs and ABS CDOs that are created from mortgages are fairly safe. However, as many investors found to their cost, default correlations tend to increase in stressed market conditions. This makes very high default rates possible.

There was a tendency to assume that a tranche with a particular rating could be equated to a bond with the that rating. The rating agencies published the criteria they used for rating tranches. S&P and Fitch rated a tranche so as to ensure that the probability of the tranche experiencing a loss was the same as the probability of a similarly rated bond experiencing a loss. Moody's rated a tranche so that the expected loss from the tranche was the the same as the expected loss from a similarly rated bond.[9] The procedures used by rating agencies were therefore designed to ensure that one aspect of the loss distributions of tranches and bonds were matched. However, other aspects of the distributions were liable to be quite different.

The differences between tranches and bonds were accentuated by the fact tranches were often quite thin. The AAA tranches often accounted for about 80% of the principal as in Figure 8.1, but it was not unusual for there to be 15 to 20 other tranches. Each of these tranches would be 1% or 2% wide. Such thin tranches are likely to either incur no losses or be totally wiped out. The chance of investors recovering part of their principal (as bondholders usually do) is small. Consider, for example, a BBB tranche that is responsible for losses in the range 5% to 6%, If losses on the underlying portfolio are less than 5%, the tranche is safe. If losses are greater than 6%, the tranche is wiped out. Only in the case where losses are between 5% and 6% is a partial recovery made by investors.

The difference between a thin BBB-rated tranche and a BBB-rated bond was overlooked by many investors. The difference makes the tranches of ABS CDOs created from the BBB-rated tranches of ABSs much riskier than tranches created in a similar way from BBB bonds. Losses on a portfolio of BBB bonds can reasonably be assumed to be unlikely to exceed 25% in even the most severe market conditions. Table 8.1 shows that 100% losses on a portfolio of BBB tranches can occur relatively easily—and this is even more true when the tranches are only 1% or 2% wide.

Regulatory Arbitrage

Many of the mortgages were originated by banks and it was banks that were the main investors in the tranches that were created from the mortgages. Why would banks choose to securitize mortgages and then buy the securitized products that were created? The answer concerns what is termed *regulatory arbitrage*. The regulatory capital banks were required to keep for the tranches created from a portfolio of mortgages was much less than the regulatory capital that would be required for the mortgages themselves.

Incentives

One of the lessons from the crisis is the importance of incentives. Economists use the term "agency costs" to describe the situation where incentives are such that the interests of two parties in a business relationship are not perfectly aligned. The process by which

[9] For a discussion of the criteria used by rating agencies and the reasonableness of the ratings given the criteria used, see J. Hull and A. White, "Ratings Arbitrage and Structured Products," *Journal of Derivatives*, 20, 1 (Fall 2012): 80–86, and "The Risk of Tranches Created from Mortgages," *Financial Analysts Journal*, 66, 5 (September/October 2010): 54–67.

mortgages were originated, securitized, and sold to investors was unfortunately riddled with agency costs.

The incentive of the originators of mortgages was to make loans that would be acceptable to the creators of the ABS and ABS CDO tranches. The incentive of the individuals who valued the houses on which the mortgages were written was to please the lender by providing as high a valuation as possible so that the loan-to-value ratio was as low as possible. (Pleasing the lender was likely to lead to more business from that lender.) The main concern of the creators of tranches was how the tranches would be rated. They wanted the volume of AAA-rated tranches that they created to be as high as possible and found ways of using the published criteria of rating agencies to achieve this. The rating agencies were paid by the issuers of the securities they rated and about half their income came from structured products.

Another source of agency costs concerns the incentives of the employees of financial institutions. Employee compensation falls into three categories: regular salary, the end-of-year bonus, and stock or stock options. Many employees at all levels of seniority in financial institutions, particularly traders, receive much of their compensation in the form of end-of-year bonuses. This form of compensation is focused on short-term performance. If an employee generates huge profits one year and is responsible for severe losses the next, the employee will often receive a big bonus the first year and will not have to return it the following year. (The employee might lose his or her job as a result of the second year losses, but even that is not a disaster. Financial institutions seem to be surprisingly willing to recruit individuals with losses on their résumés.)

Imagine you are an employee of a financial institution in 2006 responsible for investing in ABS CDOs created from mortgages. Almost certainly you would have recognized that there was a bubble in the US housing market and would expect that bubble to burst sooner or later. However, it is possible that you would decide to continue with your ABS CDO investments. If the bubble did not burst until after the end of 2006, you would still get a nice bonus at the end of 2006.

8.4 THE AFTERMATH

Prior to the crisis, over-the-counter derivatives markets were largely unregulated. This has changed. As mentioned in earlier chapters, there is now a requirement that most standardized over-the-counter derivatives be cleared through central clearing parties (CCPs). This means that they are treated similarly to derivatives such as futures that trade on exchanges. Banks will usually be members of one or more CCPs. When trading standardized derivatives, they will be required to post initial margin and variation margin with the CCP and will also be required to contribute to a default fund. For transactions that continue to be cleared bilaterally, collateral arrangements will be legislated rather than left to the judgement of the parties involved.

The bonuses paid by banks have come under more scrutiny and it is possible that in some jurisdictions there will be limits on the sizes of the bonuses that can be paid. The way bonuses are paid is changing. Before the crisis it was common for a trader's bonus for a year to be paid in full at the end of the year with no possibility of the bonus having to be returned. It is now more common for this bonus to be spread over several years and for it to be forfeited if subsequent results are poor.

Business Snapshot 8.1 The Basel Committee

As the activities of banks became more global in the 1980s, it became necessary for regulators in different countries to work together to determine an international regulatory framework. As a result the Basel Committee on Banking Supervision was formed. In 1988, it published a set of rules for the capital banks were required to keep for credit risk. These capital requirements have become known as Basel I. They were modified to accommodate the netting of transactions in 1995. In 1996 a new capital requirement for market risk was published. This capital requirement was implemented in 1998. In 1999 significant changes were proposed for the calculation of the capital requirements for credit risk and a capital requirement for operational risk was introduced. These rules are referred to as Basel II. Basel II is considerably more complicated than Basel I and its implementation was delayed until 2007 (later in some countries). During the credit crisis and afterwards the Basel committee introduced new regulatory requirements known as Basel II.5, which increased capital for market risk, and Basel III, which tightened capital requirements and introduced liquidity requirements.

The Dodd–Frank Wall Street Reform and Consumer Protection Act provides for more oversight of financial institutions and includes much new legislation affecting financial institutions. For example, proprietary trading and other similar activities of deposit-taking institutions are curtailed. (This is known as the "Volcker rule" because it was proposed by former Federal Reserve chairman Paul Volcker); every financial institution that is designated as systemically important has to prepare what is known as a "living will" mapping out how it can be safely wound up in the event of failure; issuers of securitized products are required (with some exceptions) to keep 5% of each product created.

Banks throughout the world are regulated by the Basel Committee on Banking Supervision.[10] Prior to the crisis, the committee implemented regulations known as Basel I and Basel II. These are summarized in Business Snapshot 8.1. Following the crisis, it has implemented what is known as "Basel II.5." This increases the capital requirements for market risk. Basel III was published in 2010 and will be implemented over a period lasting until 2019. It increases the amount of capital and quality of capital that banks are required to keep. It also requires banks to satisfy certain liquidity requirements. As discussed in Business Snapshot 4.3, one cause of problems during the crisis was the tendency of banks to place too much reliance on the use of short-term liabilities for long-term funding needs. The liquidity requirements are designed to make it more difficult for them to do this.

SUMMARY

Securitization is a process used by banks to create securities from loans and other income-producing assets. The securities are sold to investors. This removes the loans

[10] For more details on the work of the Basel Committee and bank regulatory requirements, see J. Hull, *Risk Management and Financial Institutions*, 3rd edition, Wiley, 2012.

from the banks' balance sheets and enables the banks to expand their lending faster than they would otherwise be able to. The first loans to be securitized were mortgages in the U.S. in the 1960s and 1970s. Investors who bought the mortgage-backed securities were not exposed to the risk of borrowers defaulting because the loans were backed by the Government National Mortgage Association. Later automobile loans, corporate loans, credit card receivables, and subprime mortgages were securitized. In many cases, investors in the securities created from these instruments did not have a guarantee against defaults.

Securitization played a part in the credit crisis that started in 2007. Tranches were created from subprime mortgages and new tranches were then created from these tranches. The origins of the crisis can be found in the U.S. housing market. The U.S. government was keen to encourage home ownership. Interest rates were low. Mortgage brokers and mortgage lenders found it attractive to do more business by relaxing their lending standards. Securitization meant that the investors bearing the credit risk were not usually the same as the original lenders. Rating agencies gave AAA ratings to the senior tranches that were created. There was no shortage of buyers for these AAA-rated tranches because their yields were higher than the yields on other AAA-rated securities. Banks thought the "good times" would continue and, because compensation plans focused their attention on short-term profits, chose to ignore the housing bubble and its potential impact on some very complicated products they were trading.

House prices rose as both first-time buyers and speculators entered the market. Some mortgages had included a low "teaser rate" for two or three years. After the teaser rate ended, there was a significant increase in the interest rate for some borrowers. Unable to meet the higher interest rate they had no choice but to default. This led to foreclosures and an increase in the supply of houses be sold. The price increases between 2000 and 2006 began to be reversed. Speculators and others who found that the amount owing on their mortgages was greater than the value of their houses (i.e., they had negative equity) defaulted. This accentuated the price decline.

Banks are paying a price for the crisis. New legislation and regulation will reduce their profitability. For example, capital requirements are being increased, liquidity regulations are being introduced, and OTC derivatives are being much more tightly regulated.

FURTHER READING

Gorton, G. "The Subprime Panic," *European Financial Management*, 15, 1 (January 2009): 10–46.

Hull, J. C. "The Financial Crisis of 2007: Another Case of Irrational Exuberance," in: *The Finance Crisis and Rescue: What Went Wrong? Why? What Lessons Can be Learned.* University of Toronto Press, 2008.

Hull, J. C., and A. White. "Ratings Arbitrage and Structured Products," *Journal of Derivatives*, 20, 1 (Fall 2012): 80–86.

Keys, B. J., T. Mukherjee, A. Seru, and V. Vig. "Did Securitization Lead to Lax Screening? Evidence from Subprime Loans," *Quarterly Journal of Economics*, 125, 1 (February 2010): 307–62.

Krinsman, A. N. "Subprime Mortgage Meltdown: How Did It Happen and How Will It End," *Journal of Structured Finance*, 13, 2 (Summer 2007): 13–19.

Mian, A., and A. Sufi. "The Consequences of Mortgage Credit Expansion: Evidence from the U.S. Mortgage Default Crisis," *Quarterly Journal of Economics*, 124, 4 (November 2010): 1449–96.

Zimmerman, T. "The Great Subprime Meltdown," *Journal of Structured Finance*, Fall 2007, 7–20.

Quiz (Answers at End of Book)

8.1. What was the role of GNMA (Ginnie Mae) in the mortgage-backed securities market of the 1970s?

8.2. Explain what is meant by (a) an ABS and (b) an ABS CDO.

8.3. What is a mezzanine tranche?

8.4. What is the waterfall in a securitization?

8.5. What are the numbers in Table 8.1 for a loss rate of (a) 12% and (b) 15%?

8.6. What is a subprime mortgage?

8.7. Why do you think the increase in house prices during the 2000 to 2007 period is referred to as a bubble?

Practice Questions (Answers in Solutions Manual/Study Guide)

8.8. Why did mortgage lenders frequently not check on information provided by potential borrowers on mortgage application forms during the 2000 to 2007 period?

8.9. How were the risks in ABS CDOs misjudged by the market?

8.10. What is meant by the term "agency costs"? How did agency costs play a role in the credit crisis?

8.11. How is an ABS CDO created? What was the motivation to create ABS CDOs?

8.12. Explain the impact of an increase in default correlation on the risks of the senior tranche of an ABS. What is its impact on the risks of the equity tranche?

8.13. Explain why the AAA-rated tranche of an ABS CDO is more risky than the AAA-rated tranche of an ABS.

8.14. Explain why the end-of-year bonus is sometimes referred to as "short-term compensation."

8.15. Add rows in Table 8.1 corresponding to losses on the underlying assets of (a) 2%, (b) 6%, (c) 12%, and (d) 18%.

Further Questions

8.16. Suppose that the principal assigned to the senior, mezzanine, and equity tranches is 70%, 20%, and 10% for both the ABS and the ABS CDO in Figure 8.3. What difference does this make to Table 8.1?

8.17. "Resecuritization was a badly flawed idea. AAA tranches created from the mezzanine tranches of ABSs are bound to have a higher probability of default than the AAA-rated tranches of ABSs." Discuss this point of view.

8.18. Suppose that mezzanine tranches of the ABS CDOs, similar to those in Figure 8.3, are resecuritized to form what is referred to as a "CDO squared." As in the case of tranches created from ABSs in Figure 8.3, 65% of the principal is allocated to a AAA tranche, 25% to a BBB tranche, and 10% to the equity tranche. How high does the loss percentage have to be on the underlying assets for losses to be experienced by a AAA-rated tranche that is created in this way. (Assume that every portfolio of assets that is used to create ABSs experiences the same loss rate.)

8.19. Investigate what happens as the width of the mezzanine tranche of the ABS in Figure 8.3 is decreased with the reduction of mezzanine tranche principal being divided equally between the equity and senior tranches. In particular, what is the effect on Table 8.1?

8.20. Suppose that the structure in Figure 8.1 is created in 2000 and lasts 10 years. There are no defaults on the underlying assets until the end of the eighth year when 17% of the principal is lost because of defaults during the credit crisis. No principal is lost in the final two years. There are no repayments of principal until the end. Evaluate the relative performance of the tranches. Assume a constant LIBOR rate of 3%. Consider both interest and principal payments.

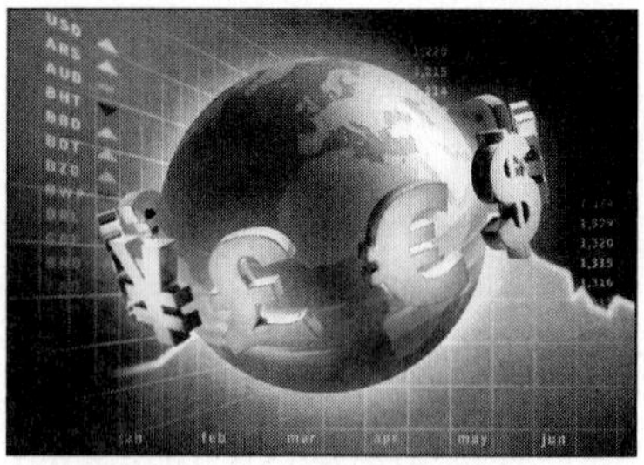

CHAPTER 9

Mechanics of Options Markets

The rest of this book is, for the most part, concerned with options. This chapter explains how options markets are organized, what terminology is used, how the contracts are traded, how margin requirements are set, and so on. Later chapters will examine such topics as trading strategies involving options, the determination of option prices, and the ways in which portfolios of options can be hedged. This chapter is concerned primarily with stock options. Details on the markets for currency options, index options, and futures options are provided in Chapters 15 and 16.

Options are fundamentally different from forward and futures contracts. An option gives the holder of the option the right to do something. The holder does not have to exercise this right. By contrast, in a forward or futures contract, the two parties have committed themselves to some action. It costs a trader nothing (except for the margin requirements) to enter into a forward or futures contract, whereas the purchase of an option requires an up-front payment.

When charts showing the gain or loss from option trading are produced, the usual practice is to ignore discounting, so that the profit is the final payoff minus the initial cost. The present chapter follows this practice.

9.1 TYPES OF OPTION

As mentioned in Chapter 1, there are two basic types of option. A *call option* gives the holder of the option the right to buy an asset by a certain date for a certain price. A *put option* gives the holder the right to sell an asset by a certain date for a certain price. The date specified in the contract is known as the *expiration date* or the *maturity date*. The price specified in the contract is known as the *exercise price* or the *strike price*.

Options can be either American or European, a distinction that has nothing to do with geographical location. *American options* can be exercised at any time up to the expiration date, whereas *European options* can be exercised only on the expiration date itself. Most of the options that are traded on exchanges are American. However, European options are generally easier to analyze than American options, and some of the properties of an American option are frequently deduced from those of its European counterpart.

Call Options

Example 9.1 considers the situation of an investor who buys a European call option with a strike price of \$100 to purchase 100 shares of a certain stock. Suppose that the current stock price is \$98, the expiration date of the option is in four months, and the price of an option to purchase one share is \$5. The initial investment is \$500. Because the option is European, the investor can exercise only on the expiration date. If the stock price on this date is less than \$100, the investor will clearly choose not to exercise. (There is no point in buying for \$100 a share that has a market value of less than \$100.) In these circumstances, the investor loses the whole of the initial investment of \$500. If the stock price is above \$100 on the expiration date, the option will be exercised. Suppose, for example, that the stock price is \$115. By exercising the option, the investor is able to buy 100 shares for \$100 per share. If the shares are sold immediately, the investor makes a gain of \$15 per share, or \$1,500, ignoring transactions costs. When the initial cost of the option is taken into account, the net profit to the investor is \$1,000.

Figure 9.1 shows how the investor's net profit or loss on an option to purchase one share varies with the final stock price in the example. It is important to realize that an investor sometimes exercises an option and makes a loss overall. Suppose that in the example the stock price is \$102 at the expiration of the option. The investor would exercise the option contract for a gain of $100 \times (\$102 - \$100) = \$200$ and realize a loss overall of \$300 when the initial cost of the option is taken into account. It is tempting to argue that the investor should not exercise the option in these circumstances. However, not exercising would lead to an overall loss of \$500, which is worse than the \$300 loss when the investor exercises. In general, call options should always be exercised at the expiration date if the stock price is above the strike price.

Put Options

Whereas the purchaser of a call option is hoping that the stock price will increase, the purchaser of a put option is hoping that it will decrease. Example 9.2 considers an investor who buys a European put option with a strike price of \$70 to sell 100 shares of a certain stock. Suppose that the current stock price is \$65, the expiration date of the

Example 9.1 Profit from call option

An investor buys a call option to purchase 100 shares.

Strike price = \$100
Current stock price = \$98
Price of an option to buy one share = \$5
The initial investment is $100 \times \$5 = \$500$

At the expiration of the option the stock price is \$115. At this time, the option is exercised for a gain of

$$(\$115 - \$100) \times 100 = \$1,500$$

When the initial cost of the option is taken into account, the net gain is

$$\$1,500 - \$500 = \$1,000$$

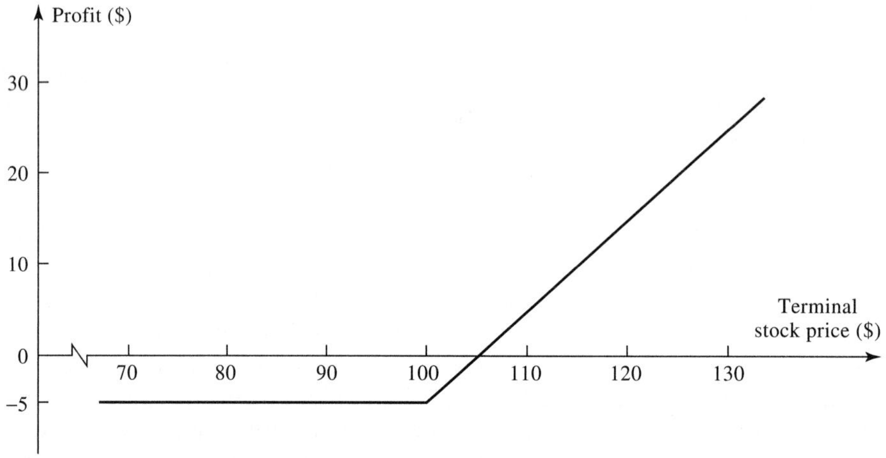

Figure 9.1 Profit from buying a European call option on one share of a stock. Option price = \$5; strike price = \$100

option is in three months, and the price of an option to sell one share is \$7. The initial investment is \$700. Because the option is European, it will be exercised only if the stock price is below \$70 on the expiration date. Suppose that the stock price is \$55 on this date. The investor can buy 100 shares for \$55 per share and, under the terms of the put option, sell the same shares for \$70 to realize a gain of \$15 per share, or \$1,500 (again, transactions costs are ignored). When the \$700 initial cost of the option is taken into account, the investor's net profit is \$800. There is no guarantee that the investor will make a gain. If the final stock price is above \$70, the put option expires worthless, and the investor loses \$700. Figure 9.2 shows the way in which the investor's profit or loss on an option to sell one share varies with the terminal stock price in this example.

Early Exercise

As already mentioned, exchange-traded stock options are generally American rather than European. This means that the investor in the foregoing examples would not have to

Example 9.2 Profit from put option

An investor buys a put option to sell 100 shares.

Strike price = \$70
Current stock price = \$65
Price of put option to sell one share = \$7

The initial investment is $100 \times \$7 = \$700$.

At the expiration of the option, the stock price is \$55. At this time, the investor buys 100 shares and, under the terms of the put option, sells them for \$70 per share to realize a gain of \$15 per share, or \$1,500 in total. When the initial cost of the option is taken into account, the net gain is

$$\$1{,}500 - \$700 = \$800$$

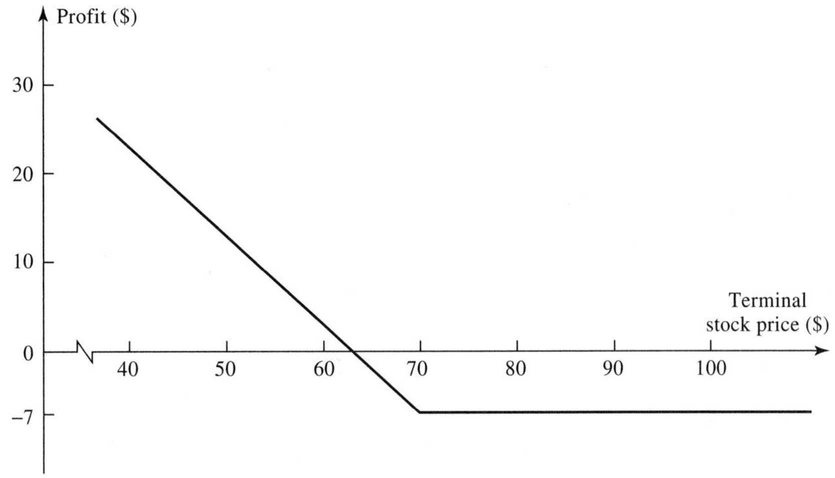

Figure 9.2 Profit from buying a European put option on one share of a stock. Option price = $7; strike price = $70

wait until the expiration date before exercising the option. We will see in later chapters that there are some circumstances under which it is optimal to exercise American options prior to the expiration date.

9.2 OPTION POSITIONS

There are two sides to every option contract. On one side is the investor who has taken the long position (i.e., has bought the option). On the other side is the investor who has taken a short position (i.e., has sold or *written* the option). The writer of an option receives cash up front, but has potential liabilities later. The writer's profit or loss is the reverse of that for the purchaser of the option. Figures 9.3 and 9.4 show the variation of

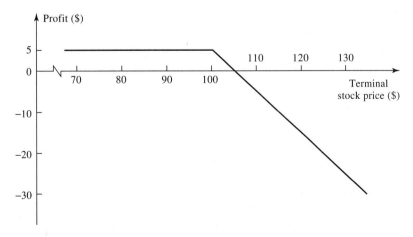

Figure 9.3 Profit from writing a European call option on one share of a stock. Option price = $5; strike price = $100

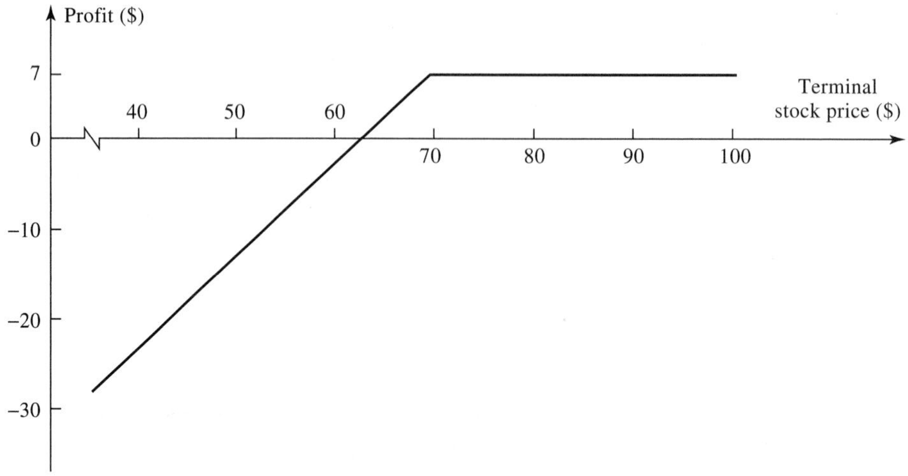

Figure 9.4 Profit from writing a European put option on one share of a stock. Option price = \$7; strike price = \$70

the profit or loss with the final stock price for writers of the options considered in Figures 9.1 and 9.2.

There are four types of option position:

1. A long position in a call option
2. A long position in a put option
3. A short position in a call option
4. A short position in a put option.

It is often useful to characterize a European option in terms of its payoff to the purchaser of the option. The initial cost of the option is not then included in the calculation. If K is the strike price and S_T is the final price of the underlying asset, the payoff from a long position in a European call option is

$$\max(S_T - K, 0)$$

This reflects the fact that the option will be exercised if $S_T > K$ and will not be exercised if $S_T \leqslant K$. The payoff to the holder of a short position in the European call option is

$$-\max(S_T - K, 0) = \min(K - S_T, 0)$$

The payoff to the holder of a long position in a European put option is

$$\max(K - S_T, 0)$$

and the payoff from a short position in a European put option is

$$-\max(K - S_T, 0) = \min(S_T - K, 0)$$

Figure 9.5 illustrates these payoffs.

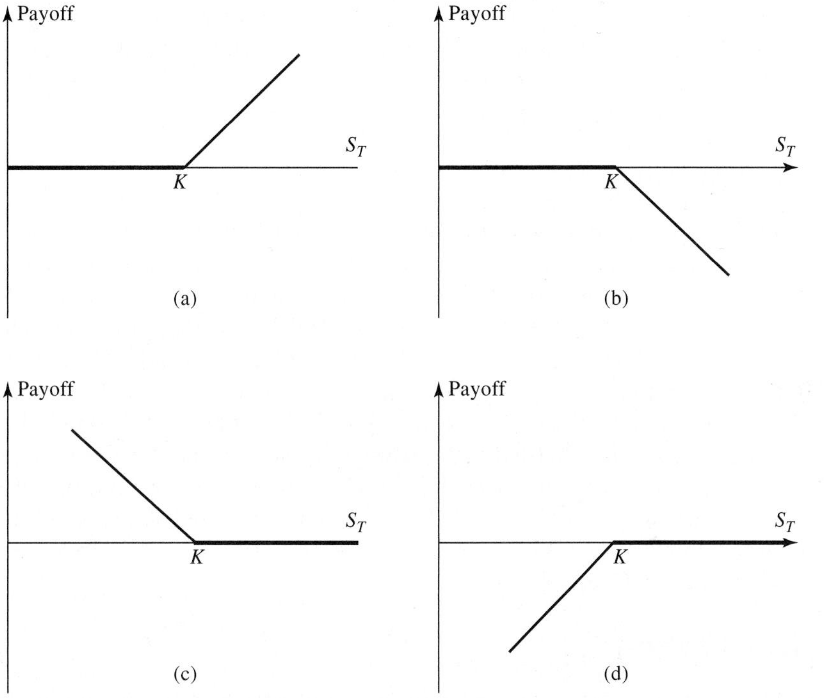

Figure 9.5 Payoffs from positions in European options: (a) long call, (b) short call, (c) long put, (d) short put. Strike price = K; price of asset at maturity = S_T

9.3 UNDERLYING ASSETS

In this section we provide a brief review of the trading of options on stocks, currencies, stock indices, and futures.

Stock Options

Most trading in stock options is on exchanges. In the United States the exchanges include the Chicago Board Options Exchange (www.cboe.com), NASDAQ OMX (www.nasdaqtrader.com), which acquired the Philadelphia Stock Exchange in 2008, NYSE Euronext (www.euronext.com), which acquired the American Stock Exchange in 2008, the International Securities Exchange (www.iseoptions.com), and the Boston Options Exchange (www.bostonoptions.com). Options trade on several thousand different stocks. One contract gives the holder the right to buy or sell 100 shares at the specified strike price. This contract size is convenient because the shares themselves are normally traded in lots of 100.

Foreign Currency Options

Most currency options trading is now in the over-the-counter market, but there is some exchange trading. Exchanges trading foreign currency options in the United States include NASDAQ OMX, which acquired the currency options business of the Philadelphia Stock Exchange in 2008. It offers European-style contracts on a variety of different currencies. One contract is to buy or sell 10,000 units of a foreign currency (1,000,000 units in the case of the Japanese yen) for US dollars. Foreign currency options contracts are discussed further in Chapter 15.

Index Options

Many different index options currently trade throughout the world in both the over-the-counter market and the exchange-traded market. The most popular exchange-traded contracts in the United States are those on the S&P 500 Index (SPX), the S&P 100 Index (OEX), the NASDAQ-100 Index (NDX), and the Dow Jones Industrial Index (DJX). All of these trade on the Chicago Board Options Exchange. Most of the contracts are European. An exception is the OEX contract on the S&P 100, which is American. One contract is to buy or sell 100 times the index at the specified strike price. Settlement is always in cash, rather than by delivering the portfolio underlying the index. Consider, for example, one call contract on an index with a strike price of 980. If it is exercised when the value of the index is 992, the writer of the contract pays the holder $(992 - 980) \times 100 = \$1{,}200$. Index options are discussed further in Chapter 15.

Futures Options

When an exchange trades a particular futures contract, it often also trades options on that contract. A futures option normally matures just before the delivery period in the futures contract. When a call option is exercised, the holder gains the excess of the futures price over the strike price. When a put option is exercised, the holder gains the excess of the strike price over the futures price. Futures options contracts are discussed further in Chapter 16.

9.4 SPECIFICATION OF STOCK OPTIONS

In the rest of this chapter, we will focus on stock options. As already mentioned, an exchange-traded stock option in the United States is an American-style option contract to buy or sell 100 shares of the stock. Details of the contract (the expiration date, the strike price, what happens when dividends are declared, how large a position investors can hold, and so on) are specified by the exchange.

Expiration Dates

One of the items used to describe a stock option is the month in which the expiration date occurs. Thus, a January call trading on IBM is a call option on IBM with an expiration date in January. The precise expiration date is the Saturday immediately following the third Friday of the expiration month. The last day on which options trade is the third Friday of the expiration month. An investor with a long position in an option normally has until 4:30 p.m. Central Time on that Friday to instruct a broker to exercise the option. The broker then has until 10:59 p.m. the next day to complete the paperwork notifying the exchange that exercise is to take place.

Stock options in the United States are on a January, February, or March cycle. The

January cycle consists of the months January, April, July, and October; the February cycle, the months February, May, August, and November; and the March cycle, the months March, June, September, and December. If the expiration date for the current month has not yet been reached, options trade with expiration dates in the current month, the following month, and the next two months in the cycle. If the expiration date of the current month has passed, options trade with expiration dates in the next month, the next-but-one month, and the next two months of the expiration cycle. For example, IBM is on a January cycle. At the beginning of January, options are traded with expiration dates in January, February, April, and July; at the end of January, they are traded with expiration dates in February, March, April, and July; at the beginning of May, they are traded with expiration dates in May, June, July, and October; and so on. When one option reaches expiration, trading in another is started. Longer-term options, known as LEAPS (long-term equity anticipation securities), also trade on many stocks in the United States stocks. These have expiration dates up to 39 months into the future. The expiration dates for LEAPS on stocks are always in January.

Strike Prices

The exchange normally chooses the strike prices at which options can be written so that they are spaced \$2.50, \$5, or \$10 apart. Typically the spacing is \$2.50 when the stock price is between \$5 and \$25, \$5 when the stock price is between \$25 and \$200, and \$10 for stock prices above \$200. As will be explained shortly, stock splits and stock dividends can lead to nonstandard strike prices.

When a new expiration date is introduced, the two or three strike prices closest to the current stock price are usually selected by the exchange. If the stock price moves outside the range defined by the highest and lowest strike price, trading is usually introduced in an option with a new strike price. To illustrate these rules, suppose that the stock price is \$84 when trading begins in the October options. Call and put options would probably first be offered with strike prices of \$80, \$85, and \$90. If the stock price rose above \$90, it is likely that a strike price of \$95 would be offered; if it fell below \$80, it is likely that a strike price of \$75 would be offered; and so on.

Terminology

For any given asset at any given time, many different option contracts may be trading. Consider a stock that has four expiration dates and five strike prices. If call and put options trade with every expiration date and every strike price, there are a total of 40 different contracts. All options of the same type (calls or puts) are referred to as an *option class*. For example, IBM calls are one class, whereas IBM puts are another class. An *option series* consists of all the options of a given class with the same expiration date and strike price. In other words, an option series refers to a particular contract that is traded. For example, IBM 70 October calls are an option series.

Options are referred to as *in the money*, *at the money*, or *out of the money*. If S is the stock price and K is the strike price, a call option is in the money when $S > K$, at the money when $S = K$, and out of the money when $S < K$. A put option is in the money when $S < K$, at the money when $S = K$, and out of the money when $S > K$. Clearly, an option will be exercised only when it is in the money. In the absence of transactions costs, an in-the-money option will always be exercised on the expiration date if it has not been exercised previously.

The *intrinsic value* of an option is defined as the maximum of zero and the value the option would have if it were exercised immediately. For a call option, the intrinsic value is therefore $\max(S - K, 0)$; for a put option, it is $\max(K - S, 0)$. An in-the-money American option must be worth at least as much as its intrinsic value because the holder can realize the intrinsic value by exercising immediately. Often it is optimal for the holder of an in-the-money American option to wait rather than exercise immediately. The option is then said to have *time value*. The total value of an option can be thought of as the sum of its intrinsic value and its time value.

Flex Options and Other Nonstandard Products

The Chicago Board Options Exchange (CBOE) offers *flex options* on equities and equity indices. These are options where the traders agree to nonstandard terms. These nonstandard terms can involve a strike price or an expiration date that is different from what is usually offered by the exchange. It can also involve the option being European rather than American. Flex options are an attempt by option exchanges to regain business from the over-the-counter markets. The exchange specifies a minimum size (e.g., 100 contracts) for flex option trades.

In addition to flex options, the CBOE trades a number of other nonstandard products. Examples are:

1. Options on exchange-traded funds.[1]
2. *Weeklys*. These are options that are created on a Thursday and expire on Friday of the following week.
3. *Binary options*. These are options that provide a fixed payoff of \$100 if the strike price is reached. For example, a binary call with a strike price of \$50 provides a payoff of \$100 if the price of the underlying stock exceeds \$50 on the expiry date; a binary put with a strike price of \$50 provides a payoff of \$100 if the price of the stock is below \$50 on the expiry date. Binary options are discussed further in Chapter 22.
4. *CEBOs*. These are credit event binary options, which provide a fixed payoff if a particular company (known as the reference entity) suffers a "credit event" by the maturity date. Credit events are defined as bankruptcy, failure to pay interest or principal on debt, and a restructuring of debt. Maturity dates are in December of a particular year, and payoffs, if any, are made on the maturity date. CEBOs are similar to credit default swaps which were discussed in Section 7.15 and will be covered in more detail in Chapter 23.
5. *DOOM options*. These are deep-out-of-the-money put options. Because they have a low strike price, they cost very little. They provide a payoff only if the price of the underlying asset plunges. DOOM options provide the same sort of protection as credit default swaps, which were discussed in Section 7.15 and will be covered in more detail in Chapter 23, and CEBOs, which have just been described.

[1] Exchange-traded funds (ETFs) have become a popular alternative to mutual funds for investors. They are traded like stocks and are designed so that their prices reflect the value of the assets of the fund closely.

Business Snapshot 9.1 Gucci Group's large dividend

When there is a large cash dividend (typically one more than 10% of the stock price) a committee of the Options Clearing Corporation (OCC) at the Chicago Board Options Exchange can decide to make adjustments to the terms of options traded on the exchange.

On May 28, 2003, Gucci Group N.V. (GUC) declared a cash dividend of 13.50 euros (approximately \$15.88) per common share and this was approved at the GUC annual shareholders meeting on July 16, 2003. The dividend was about 16% of the share price at the time it was declared. In this case the OCC committee decided to adjust the terms of options. The result was that the holder of a call contract paid 100 times the strike price on exercise and received \$1,588 of cash in addition to 100 shares; the holder of a put contract received 100 times the strike price on exercise and delivered \$1,588 of cash in addition to 100 shares.

Adjustments for large dividends are not always made. For example, Deutsche Terminbörse chose not to adjust the terms of options traded on that exchange when Daimler-Benz surprised the market on March 10, 1998, with a dividend equal to about 12% of its stock price.

Dividends and Stock Splits

The early over-the-counter options were dividend protected. If a company declared a cash dividend, the strike price for options on the company's stock was reduced on the ex-dividend day by the amount of the dividend. Exchange-traded options are not usually adjusted for cash dividends. In other words, when a cash dividend occurs, there are no adjustments to the terms of the option contract. An exception is sometimes made for large cash dividends (see Business Snapshot 9.1).

Exchange-traded options are adjusted for stock splits. A stock split occurs when the existing shares are "split" into more shares. For example, in a 3-for-1 stock split, three new shares are issued to replace each existing share. Because a stock split does not change the assets or the earning ability of a company, we should not expect it to have any effect on the wealth of the company's shareholders. All else being equal, the 3-for-1 stock split should cause the stock price to go down to one-third of its previous value. In general, an n-for-m stock split should cause the stock price to go down to m/n of its previous value. The terms of option contracts are adjusted to reflect expected changes in a stock price arising from a stock split. After an n-for-m stock split, the strike price is reduced to m/n of its previous value, and the number of shares covered by one contract is increased to n/m of its previous value. If the stock price declines in the way expected, the positions of both the writer and the purchaser of a contract remain unchanged. Example 9.3 provides an application of the rule.

Example 9.3 Impact on option terms of a stock split

Consider a call option to buy 100 shares of a company for \$30 per share. Suppose the company makes a 2-for-1 stock split. The terms of the option contract are then changed so that it gives the holder the right to purchase 200 shares for \$15 per share.

> **Example 9.4** Impact on option terms of a stock dividend
>
> Consider a put option to sell 100 shares of a company for \$15 per share. Suppose the company declares a 25% stock dividend. This is equivalent to a 5-for-4 stock split. The terms of the option contract are changed so that it gives the holder the right to sell 125 shares for \$12.

Stock options are adjusted for stock dividends. A stock dividend involves a company issuing more shares to its existing shareholders. For example, a 20% stock dividend means that investors receive one new share for each five already owned. A stock dividend, like a stock split, has no effect on either the assets or the earning power of a company. The stock price can be expected to go down as a result of a stock dividend. The 20% stock dividend is essentially the same as a 6-for-5 stock split. All else being equal, it should cause the stock price to decline to 5/6 of its previous value. The terms of an option are adjusted to reflect the expected price decline arising from a stock dividend in the same way as they are for that arising from a stock split. Example 9.4 provides an illustration.

Adjustments are also made for rights issues. The basic procedure is to calculate the theoretical price of the rights issue and then to reduce the strike price by this amount.

Position Limits and Exercise Limits

The Chicago Board Options Exchange often specifies a *position limit* for option contracts. This defines the maximum number of option contracts that an investor can hold on one side of the market. For this purpose, long calls and short puts are considered to be on the same side of the market. Also, short calls and long puts are considered to be on the same side of the market. The *exercise limit* usually equals the position limit. It defines the maximum number of contracts that can be exercised by any individual (or group of individuals acting together) in any period of five consecutive business days. Options on the largest and most frequently traded stocks have positions limits of 250,000 contracts. Smaller capitalization stocks have position limits of 200,000, 75,000, 50,000, or 25,000 contracts.

Position limits and exercise limits are designed to prevent the market from being unduly influenced by the activities of an individual investor or group of investors. However, whether the limits are really necessary is a controversial issue.

9.5 TRADING

Traditionally, exchanges have had to provide a large open area for individuals to meet and trade options. This has changed. Most derivatives exchanges are fully electronic, so that traders do not have to physically meet. The International Securities Exchange (www.iseoptions.com) launched the first all-electronic options market for equities in the United States in May 2000. Over 95% of the orders at the Chicago Board Options Exchange are handled electronically. The remainder are large or complex institutional orders that require the skills of floor traders.

Market Makers

Most options exchanges use market makers to facilitate trading. A market maker for a certain option is an individual who, when asked to do so, will quote both a bid and an offer price on the option. The bid is the price at which the market maker is prepared to buy, and the offer or asked is the price at which the market maker is prepared to sell. At the time the bid and the offer are quoted, the market maker does not know whether the trader who asked for the quotes wants to buy or sell the option. The offer is always higher than the bid, and the amount by which the offer exceeds the bid is referred to as the bid–offer spread. The exchange sets upper limits for the bid–offer spread. For example, it might specify that the spread be no more than \$0.25 for options priced at less than \$0.50, \$0.50 for options priced between \$0.50 and \$10, \$0.75 for options priced between \$10 and \$20, and \$1 for options priced over \$20.

The existence of the market maker ensures that buy and sell orders can always be executed at some price without any delays. Market makers therefore add liquidity to the market. The market makers themselves make their profits from the bid–offer spread. They use methods such as those that will be discussed in Chapter 17 to hedge their risks.

Offsetting Orders

An investor who has purchased an option can close out the position by issuing an offsetting order to sell the same option. Similarly, an investor who has written an option can close out the position by issuing an offsetting order to buy the same option. If, when an option contract is traded, neither investor is offsetting an existing position, the open interest increases by one contract. If one investor is offsetting an existing position and the other is not, the open interest stays the same. If both investors are offsetting existing positions, the open interest goes down by one contract.

9.6 COMMISSIONS

The types of orders that can be placed with a broker for options trading are similar to those for futures trading (see Section 2.8). A market order is to be executed immediately; a limit order specifies the least favorable price at which the order can be executed; and so on.

For a retail investor, commissions vary significantly from broker to broker. Discount brokers generally charge lower commissions than full-service brokers. The actual amount charged is often calculated as a fixed cost plus a proportion of the dollar amount of the trade. Table 9.1 shows the sort of schedule that might be offered by a discount broker. Using this schedule, the purchase of eight contracts when the option price is \$3 would cost $\$20 + (0.02 \times \$2{,}400) = \$68$ in commissions.

If an option position is closed out by entering into an offsetting trade, the commission must be paid again. If the option is exercised, the commission is the same as it would be if the investor placed an order to buy or sell the underlying stock.

Consider an investor who buys one call contract with a strike price of \$50 when the stock price is \$49. We suppose the option price is \$4.50, so that the cost of the contract is \$450. Under the schedule in Table 9.1, the purchase or sale of one contract always costs \$30 (both the maximum and minimum commission is \$30 for the first contract).

Table 9.1 A sample commission schedule for a discount broker

Dollar amount of trade	*Commission**
< \$2,500	\$20 + 0.02 of dollar amount
\$2,500 to \$10,000	\$45 + 0.01 of dollar amount
> \$10,000	\$120 + 0.0025 of dollar amount

* Maximum commission is \$30 per contract for the first five contracts plus \$20 per contract for each additional contract. Minimum commission is \$30 per contract for the first contract plus \$2 per contract for each additional contract.

Suppose that the stock price rises and the option is exercised when the stock reaches \$60. Assuming that the investor pays 0.75% commission to exercise the option and a further 0.75% commission to sell the stock, there is an additional cost of

$$2 \times 0.0075 \times \$60 \times 100 = \$90$$

The total commission paid is therefore \$120, and the net profit to the investor is

$$\$1{,}000 - \$450 - \$120 = \$430$$

Note that selling the option for \$10 instead of exercising it would save the investor \$60 in commissions. (The commission payable when an option is sold is only \$30 in our example.) As this example indicates, the commission system can push retail investors in the direction of selling options rather than exercising them.

A hidden cost in option trading (and in stock trading) is the market maker's bid–offer spread. Suppose that, in the example just considered, the bid price was \$4.00 and the offer price was \$4.50 at the time the option was purchased. We can reasonably assume that a "fair" price for the option is halfway between the bid and the offer price, or \$4.25. The cost to the buyer and to the seller of the market maker system is the difference between the fair price and the price paid. This is \$0.25 per option, or \$25 per contract.

9.7 MARGIN REQUIREMENTS

In the United States, when shares are purchased, an investor can either pay cash or borrow using a margin account (this is known as *buying on margin*). The initial margin is usually 50% of the value of the shares, and the maintenance margin is usually 25% of the value of the shares. The margin account operates similarly to that for a futures contract (see Chapter 2).[2]

When call or put options with maturities less than nine months are purchased, the option price must be paid in full. Investors are not allowed to buy options on margin because options already contain substantial leverage and buying on margin would raise this leverage to an unacceptable level. For options with maturities greater than nine months, investors can buy on margin, borrowing up to 25% of the option value.

[2] One difference is that, when there is a margin call, the investor is required to bring the balance in the margin account up to the maintenance margin level, not the initial margin level.

A trader who writes options is required to maintain funds in a margin account. Both the trader's broker and the exchange want to be satisfied that the trader will not default if the option is exercised. The amount of margin required depends on the trader's position.

Writing Naked Options

A *naked option* is an option that is not combined with an offsetting position in the underlying stock. The initial and maintenance margin for a written naked call option is the greater of the following two calculations:

1. A total of 100% of the proceeds of the sale plus 20% of the underlying share price less the amount if any by which the option is out of the money
2. A total of 100% of the option proceeds plus 10% of the underlying share price.

For a written naked put option, it is the greater of

1. A total of 100% of the proceeds of the sale plus 20% of the underlying share price less the amount if any by which the option is out of the money
2. A total of 100% of the option proceeds plus 10% of the exercise price.

Example 9.5 provides an illustration of the calculations. The 20% in the calculations is replaced by 15% for options on a broadly based stock index because a stock index is usually less volatile than the price of an individual stock.

A calculation similar to this one (but with the current market price replacing the proceeds of sale) is repeated every day. Funds can be withdrawn from the margin account when the calculation indicates that the margin required is less than the current balance in the margin account. When the calculation indicates that a greater margin is required, a margin call will be made.

Example 9.5 Margin calculations for a naked call option

An investor writes four naked call option contracts on a stock. The option price is \$5, the strike price is \$40, and the stock price is \$38. Because the option is \$2 out of the money, the first calculation gives

$$400 \times (5 + 0.2 \times 38 - 2) = \$4{,}240$$

The second calculation gives

$$400 \times (5 + 0.1 \times 38) = \$3{,}520$$

The initial and maintenance margin requirement is therefore \$4,240. Note that if the option had been a put, it would be \$2 in the money and the margin requirement would be

$$400 \times (5 + 0.2 \times 38) = \$5{,}040$$

In both cases the proceeds of the sale can be used to form part of the margin account.

Other Rules

In Chapter 11, we will examine option trading strategies such as covered calls, protective puts, spreads, combinations, straddles, and strangles. The CBOE has special rules for determining the margin requirements when these trading strategies are used. These are described in the *CBOE Margin Manual*, which is available on the CBOE website (www.cboe.com).

As an example of the rules, consider an investor who writes a covered call. This is a written call option when the shares that might have to be delivered are already owned. Covered calls are far less risky than naked calls, because the worst that can happen is that the investor is required to sell shares already owned at below their market value. No margin is required on the written option. However, the investor can borrow an amount equal to $0.5\min(S, K)$, rather than the usual $0.5S$, on the stock position.

9.8 THE OPTIONS CLEARING CORPORATION

The Options Clearing Corporation (OCC) performs much the same function for options markets as the clearinghouse does for futures markets (see Chapter 2). It guarantees that options writers will fulfill their obligations under the terms of options contracts and keeps a record of all long and short positions. The OCC has a number of members, and all options trades must be cleared through a member. If a broker is not itself a member of an exchange's OCC, it must arrange to clear its trades with a member. Members are required to have a certain minimum amount of capital and to contribute to a special fund that can be used if any member defaults on an option obligation.

The funds used to purchase an option must be deposited with the OCC by the morning of the business day folowing the trade. The writer of the option maintains a margin account with a broker, as described earlier. The broker maintains a margin account with the OCC member that clears its trades. The OCC member in turn maintains a margin account with the OCC. The margin requirements described in the previous section are the margin requirements imposed by the OCC on its members. A brokerage house may require a higher margin from its clients. However, it cannot require a lower margin.

Exercising an Option

When an investor notifies a broker to exercise an option, the broker in turn notifies the OCC member that clears its trades. This member then places an exercise order with the OCC. The OCC randomly selects a member with an outstanding short position in the same option. The member, using a procedure established in advance, selects a particular investor who has written the option. If the option is a call, this investor is required to sell stock at the strike price. If it is a put, the investor is required to buy stock at the strike price. The investor is said to be *assigned*. When an option is exercised, the open interest goes down by one.

At the expiration of the option, all in-the-money options should be exercised unless the transactions costs are so high as to wipe out the payoff from the option. Some brokers will automatically exercise options for their clients at expiration when it is in a client's interest to do so. Many exchanges also have rules for exercising options that are in the money at expiration.

9.9 REGULATION

Options markets are regulated in a number of different ways. Both the exchange and its Options Clearing Corporation have rules governing the behavior of traders. In addition, there are both federal and state regulatory authorities. In general, options markets have demonstrated a willingness to regulate themselves. There have been no major scandals or defaults by OCC members. Investors can have a high level of confidence in the way the market is run.

The Securities and Exchange Commission is responsible for regulating options markets in stocks, stock indices, currencies, and bonds at the federal level. The Commodity Futures Trading Commission is responsible for regulating markets for options on futures. The major options markets are in the states of Illinois and New York. These states actively enforce their own laws on unacceptable trading practices.

9.10 TAXATION

Determining the tax implications of option trading strategies can be tricky, and an investor who is in doubt about this should consult a tax specialist. In the United States, the general rule is that (unless the taxpayer is a professional trader) gains and losses from the trading of stock options are taxed as capital gains or losses. The way that capital gains and losses are taxed in the United States was discussed in Section 2.10. For both the holder and the writer of a stock option, a gain or loss is recognized when (a) the option expires unexercised, or (b) the option position is closed out. If the option is exercised, the gain or loss from the option is rolled into the position taken in the stock and recognized when the stock position is closed out. For example, when a call option is exercised, the party with a long position is deemed to have purchased the stock at the strike price plus the call price. This is then used as a basis for calculating this party's gain or loss when the stock is eventually sold. Similarly, the party with the short call position is deemed to have sold the stock at the strike price plus the call price. When a put option is exercised, the seller of the option is deemed to have bought stock for the strike price less the original put price and the purchaser of the option is deemed to have sold the stock for the strike price less the original put price.

Wash Sale Rule

One tax consideration in options trading in the United States is the wash sale rule. To understand this rule, imagine an investor who buys a stock when the price is $60 and plans to keep it for the long term. If the stock price drops to $40, the investor might be tempted to sell the stock and then immediately repurchase it so that the $20 loss is realized for tax purposes. To prevent this sort of thing, the tax authorities have ruled that when the repurchase is within 30 days of the sale (i.e., between 30 days before the sale and 30 days after the sale), any loss on the sale is not deductible. The disallowance also applies where, within the 61-day period, the taxpayer enters into an option or similar contract to acquire the stock. Thus, selling a stock at a loss and buying a call option within a 30-day period will lead to the loss being disallowed. The wash sale rule does not apply if the taxpayer is a dealer in stocks or securities and the loss is sustained in the ordinary course of business.

Constructive Sales

Prior to 1997, if a United States taxpayer shorted a security while holding a long position in a substantially identical security, no gain or loss was recognized until the short position was closed out. This means that short positions could be used to defer recognition of a gain for tax purposes. The situation was changed by the Tax Relief Act of 1997. An appreciated property is now treated as "constructively sold" when the owner does one of the following:

1. Enters into a short sale of the same or substantially identical property
2. Enters into a futures or forward contract to deliver the same or substantially identical property
3. Enters into one or more positions that eliminate substantially all of the loss and opportunity for gain.

It should be noted that transactions reducing only the risk of loss or only the opportunity for gain should not result in constructive sales. Therefore, an investor holding a long position in a stock can buy in-the-money put options on the stock without triggering a constructive sale.

Tax practitioners sometimes use options to minimize tax costs or maximize tax benefits (see the example in Business Snapshot 9.2). Tax authorities in many jurisdictions have proposed legislation designed to combat the use of derivatives for tax purposes. Before entering into any tax-motivated transaction, a corporate treasurer or private individual should explore in detail how the structure could be unwound in the event of legislative change and how costly this process could be.

9.11 WARRANTS, EMPLOYEE STOCK OPTIONS, AND CONVERTIBLES

Warrants are options issued by a financial institution or nonfinancial corporation. For example, a financial institution might issue put warrants on one million ounces of gold and then proceed to create a market for the warrants. To exercise the warrant, the holder would contact the financial institution. A common use of warrants by a nonfinancial corporation is at the time of a bond issue. The corporation issues call warrants on its own stock and then attaches them to the bond issue to make it more attractive to investors.

Employee stock options are call options issued to employees by their company to motivate them to act in the best interests of the company's shareholders (see Chapter 14). They are usually at the money at the time of issue. They are now expensed at fair market value on the company's income statement in most countries, making them a less attractive form of compensation than they used to be.

Convertible bonds, often simply referred to as *convertibles*, are bonds issued by a company that can be converted into equity at certain times using a predetermined exchange ratio. They are therefore bonds with an embedded call option on the company's stock.

One feature of warrants, employee stock options, and convertibles is that a predetermined number of options are issued. By contrast, the number of options on a particular stock that trade on the CBOE is not predetermined. As more people take

Business Snapshot 9.2 Tax planning using options

As a simple example of a possible tax planning strategy using options, suppose that Country A has a tax regime where the tax is low on interest and dividends and a high on capital gains, while Country B has a tax regime where tax is high on interest and dividends and low on capital gains. It is advantageous for a company to receive the income from a security in Country A and the capital gain, if there is one, in Country B. The company would like to keep capital losses in Country A where they can be used to offset capital gains on other items. All of this can be accomplished by arranging for a subsidiary company in Country A to have legal ownership of the security and for a subsidiary company in Country B to buy a call option on the security from the company in country A with the strike price of the option equal to the current value of the security. During the life of the option income from the security is earned in Country A. If the security price rises sharply the option will be exercised and the capital gain will be realized in Country B. If it falls sharply, the option will not be exercised and the capital loss will be realized in Country A.

positions in a particular option series, the number of options outstanding increases; as people close out positions, it declines. Warrants issued by a company on its own stock, employee stock options, and convertibles are different from exchange-traded options in another important way. When these instruments are exercised, the company issues more shares of its own stock and sells them to the option holder for the strike price. The exercise of the instruments therefore leads to an increase in the number of shares of the company's stock that are outstanding. By contrast, when an exchange-traded call option is exercised, the party with the short position buys in the market shares that have already been issued and sells them to the party with the long position for the strike price. The company whose stock underlies the option is not involved in any way.

9.12 OVER-THE-COUNTER OPTIONS MARKETS

Most of this chapter has focused on exchange-traded options markets. The over-the-counter market for options has become increasingly important since the early 1980s and is now larger than the exchange-traded market. As explained in Chapter 1, in the over-the-counter market, financial institutions, corporate treasurers, and fund managers trade over the phone. There is a wide range of assets underlying the options. Over-the-counter options on foreign exchange and interest rates are particularly popular. The chief potential disadvantage of the over-the-counter market is that the option writer may default. This means that the purchaser is subject to some credit risk. In an attempt to overcome this disadvantage, market participants usually require counterparties to post collateral. This was discussed in Section 2.5.

The instruments traded in the over-the-counter market are often structured by financial institutions to meet the precise needs of their clients. Sometimes this involves choosing exercise dates, strike prices, and contract sizes that are different from those offered by an exchange. In other cases the structure of the option is different from standard calls and puts. The option is then referred to as an *exotic option*. Chapter 22 describes a number of different types of exotic options.

SUMMARY

There are two types of options: calls and puts. A call option gives the holder the right to buy the underlying asset for a certain price by a certain date. A put option gives the holder the right to sell the underlying asset by a certain date for a certain price. There are four possible positions in options markets: a long position in a call, a short position in a call, a long position in a put, and a short position in a put. Taking a short position in an option is known as writing it. Options are currently traded on stocks, stock indices, foreign currencies, futures contracts, and other assets.

An exchange must specify the terms of the option contracts it trades. In particular, it must specify the size of the contract, the precise expiration time, and the strike price. In the United States one stock option contract gives the holder the right to buy or sell 100 shares. The expiration of a stock option contract is 10:59 p.m. Central Time on the Saturday immediately following the third Friday of the expiration month. Options with several different expiration months trade at any given time. Strike prices are at $2.5, $5, or $10 intervals, depending on the stock price. The strike price is generally fairly close to the stock price when trading in an option begins.

The terms of a stock option are not normally adjusted for cash dividends. However, they are adjusted for stock dividends, stock splits, and rights issues. The aim of the adjustment is to keep the positions of both the writer and the buyer of a contract unchanged.

Most options exchanges use market makers. These are individuals who are prepared to quote both a bid price (at which they are prepared to buy) and an offer price (at which they are prepared to sell). Market makers improve the liquidity of the market and ensure that there is never any delay in executing market orders. They themselves make a profit from the difference between their bid and offer prices (known as their bid–offer spread). The exchange has rules specifying upper limits for the bid–offer spread.

Writers of options have potential liabilities and are required to maintain margin with their brokers. If it is not a member of the Options Clearing Corporation, the broker will maintain a margin account with a firm that is a member. This firm will in turn maintain a margin account with the Options Clearing Corporation. The Options Clearing Corporation is responsible for keeping a record of all outstanding contracts, handling exercise orders, and so on.

Not all options are traded on exchanges. Many options are traded by phone in the over-the-counter market. An advantage of over-the-counter options is that they can be tailored by a financial institution to meet the particular needs of a corporate treasurer or fund manager.

FURTHER READING

Arzac, E. R. "PERCs, DECs, and Other Mandatory Convertibles," *Journal of Applied Corporate Finance*, 10, 1 (1997): 54–63.

Chicago Board Options Exchange. *Characteristics and Risks of Standardized Options*. Available online at: www.optionsclearing.com/about/publications/character-risks.jsp. First published 1994; last updated 2009.

McMillan, L. G. *McMillan on Options*, 2nd edn. Hoboken, NJ: Wiley, 2004.

Quiz (Answers at End of Book)

9.1. An investor buys a European put on a share for \$3. The stock price is \$42 and the strike price is \$40. Under what circumstances does the investor make a profit? Under what circumstances will the option be exercised? Draw a diagram showing the variation of the investor's profit with the stock price at the maturity of the option.

9.2. An investor sells a European call on a share for \$4. The stock price is \$47 and the strike price is \$50. Under what circumstances does the investor make a profit? Under what circumstances will the option be exercised? Draw a diagram showing the variation of the investor's profit with the stock price at the maturity of the option.

9.3. An investor sells a European call option with strike price of K and maturity T and buys a put with the same strike price and maturity. Describe the investor's position.

9.4. Explain why brokers require margin when clients write options but not when they buy options.

9.5. A stock option is on a February, May, August, and November cycle. What options trade on (a) April 1, and (b) May 30?

9.6. A company declares a 2-for-1 stock split. Explain how the terms change for a call option with a strike price of \$60.

9.7. "Employee stock options are different from regular exchange-traded stock options because they can change the company's capital structure." Explain this statement.

Practice Questions (Answers in Solutions Manual/Study Guide)

9.8. A corporate treasurer is designing a hedging program involving foreign currency options. What are the pros and cons of using (a) the NASDAQ OMX and (b) the over-the-counter market for trading?

9.9. Suppose that a European call option to buy a share for \$100.00 costs \$5.00 and is held until maturity. Under what circumstances will the holder of the option make a profit? Under what circumstances will the option be exercised? Draw a diagram illustrating how the profit from a long position in the option depends on the stock price at maturity of the option.

9.10. Suppose that a European put option to sell a share for \$60 costs \$8 and is held until maturity. Under what circumstances will the seller of the option (the party with the short position) make a profit? Under what circumstances will the option be exercised? Draw a diagram illustrating how the profit from a short position in the option depends on the stock price at maturity of the option.

9.11. Describe the terminal value of the following portfolio: a newly entered-into long forward contract on an asset and a long position in a European put option on the asset with the same maturity as the forward contract and a strike price that is equal to the forward price of the asset at the time the portfolio is set up. Show that the European put option has the same value as a European call option with the same strike price and maturity.

9.12. A trader buys a call option with a strike price of \$45 and a put option with a strike price of \$40. Both options have the same maturity. The call costs \$3 and the put costs \$4. Draw a diagram showing the variation of the trader's profit with the asset price.

9.13. Explain why an American option is always worth at least as much as a European option on the same asset with the same strike price and exercise date.

9.14. Explain why an American option is always worth at least as much as its intrinsic value.

9.15. Explain carefully the difference between writing a put option and buying a call option.

9.16. The treasurer of a corporation is trying to choose between options and forward contracts to hedge the corporation's foreign exchange risk. Discuss the advantages and disadvantages of each.

9.17. Consider an exchange-traded call option contract to buy 500 shares with a strike price of \$40 and maturity in four months. Explain how the terms of the option contract change when there is: (a) a 10% stock dividend; (b) a 10% cash dividend; and (c) a 4-for-1 stock split.

9.18. "If most of the call options on a stock are in the money, it is likely that the stock price has risen rapidly in the last few months." Discuss this statement.

9.19. What is the effect of an unexpected cash dividend on (a) a call option price and (b) a put option price?

9.20. Options on General Motors stock are on a March, June, September, and December cycle. What options trade on (a) March 1, (b) June 30, and (c) August 5?

9.21. Explain why the market maker's bid–offer spread represents a real cost to options investors.

9.22. A United States investor writes five naked call option contracts. The option price is \$3.50, the strike price is \$60.00, and the stock price is \$57.00. What is the initial margin requirement?

Further Questions

9.23. Calculate the intrinsic value and time value from the mid-market (average of bid and offer) prices the July 2012 call options in Table 1.2. Do the same for the July 2012 put options in Table 1.3. Assume in each case that the current mid-market stock price is \$561.40.

9.24. A trader has a put option contract to sell 100 shares of a stock for a strike price of \$60. What is the effect on the terms of the contract of:
(a) A \$2 dividend being declared
(b) A \$2 dividend being paid
(c) A 5-for-2 stock split
(d) A 5% stock dividend being paid.

9.25. A trader writes five naked put option contracts, with each contract being on 100 shares. The option price is \$10, the time to maturity is six months, and the strike price is \$64.
(a) What is the margin requirement if the stock price is \$58?
(b) How would the answer to (a) change if the rules for index options applied?
(c) How would the answer to (a) change if the stock price were \$70?
(d) How would the answer to (a) change if the trader is buying instead of selling the options?

9.26. The price of a stock is \$40. The price of a one-year European put option on the stock with a strike price of \$30 is quoted as \$7 and the price of a one-year European call option on the stock with a strike price of \$50 is quoted as \$5. Suppose that an investor buys 100 shares, shorts 100 call options, and buys 100 put options. Draw a diagram illustrating how the investor's profit or loss varies with the stock price over the next year. How does your answer change if the investor buys 100 shares, shorts 200 call options, and buys 200 put options?

9.27. "If a company does not do better than its competitors but the stock market goes up, executives do very well from their stock options. This makes no sense." Discuss this viewpoint. Can you think of alternatives to the usual employee stock option plan that take the viewpoint into account.

9.28. Use DerivaGem to calculate the value of an American put option on a non-dividend-paying stock when the stock price is \$30, the strike price is \$32, the risk-free rate is 5%, the volatility is 30%, and the time to maturity is 1.5 years. (Choose "Binomial American" for the Option Type and 50 time steps.)

(a) What is the option's intrinsic value?

(b) What is the option's time value?

(c) What would a time value of zero indicate? What is the value of an option with zero time value?

(d) Using a trial and error approach, calculate how low the stock price would have to be for the time value of the option to be zero.

9.29. On July 20, 2004, Microsoft surprised the market by announcing a \$3 dividend. The ex-dividend date was November 17, 2004, and the payment date was December 2, 2004. Its stock price at the time was about \$28. It also changed the terms of its employee stock options so that each exercise price was adjusted downward to

$$\text{Pre-dividend exercise price} \times \frac{\text{Closing price} - \$3.00}{\text{Closing price}}$$

The number of shares covered by each stock option outstanding was adjusted upward to

$$\text{Number of shares pre-dividend} \times \frac{\text{Closing Price}}{\text{Closing price} - \$3.00}$$

"Closing price" means the official NASDAQ closing price of a share of Microsoft common stock on the last trading day before the ex-dividend date.

Evaluate this adjustment. Compare it with the system used by exchanges to adjust for extraordinary dividends (see Business Snapshot 9.1).

CHAPTER 10

Properties of Stock Options

In this chapter, we look at the factors affecting stock option prices. A number of different arbitrage arguments are used to explore the relationships between European option prices, American option prices, and the underlying stock price. The most important of these relationships is put–call parity, which is a relationship between the price of a European call option, the price of a European put option, and the underlying stock price.

The chapter examines whether American options should be exercised early. It shows that it is never optimal to exercise an American call option on a non-dividend-paying stock prior to the option's expiration, but that under some circumstances the early exercise of an American put option on such a stock is optimal. When there are dividends, it can be optimal to exercise either calls or puts early.

10.1 FACTORS AFFECTING OPTION PRICES

There are six factors affecting the price of a stock option:

1. The current stock price, S_0
2. The strike price, K
3. The time to expiration, T
4. The volatility of the stock price, σ
5. The risk-free interest rate, r
6. The dividends that are expected to be paid.

In this section, we consider what happens to option prices when there is a change to one of these factors with all the other factors remaining fixed. The results are summarized in Table 10.1.

Figures 10.1 and 10.2 show how the price of a European call and put depends on the first five factors in the situation where $S_0 = 50$, $K = 50$, $r = 5\%$ per annum, $\sigma = 30\%$ per annum, $T = 1$ year, and there are no dividends. In this case the call price is 7.116 and the put price is 4.677.

Table 10.1 Summary of the effect on the price of a stock option of increasing one variable while keeping all others fixed*

Variable	*European call*	*European put*	*American call*	*American put*
Current stock price	+	−	+	−
Strike price	−	+	−	+
Time to expiration	?	?	+	+
Volatility	+	+	+	+
Risk-free rate	+	−	+	−
Dividends	−	+	−	+

* + indicates that an increase in the variable causes the option price to increase; − indicates that an increase in the variable causes the option price to decrease; ? indicates that the relationship is uncertain.

Stock Price and Strike Price

If a call option is exercised at some future time, the payoff will be the amount by which the stock price exceeds the strike price. Call options therefore become more valuable as the stock price increases and less valuable as the strike price increases. For a put option, the payoff on exercise is the amount by which the strike price exceeds the stock price. Put options, therefore, behave in the opposite way from call options. They become less valuable as the stock price increases and more valuable as the strike price increases. Figures 10.1a, b, c, d illustrate the way in which put and call prices depend on the stock price and strike price.

Time to Expiration

Consider next the effect of the expiration date. Both put and call American options become more valuable (or at least do not decrease in value) as the time to expiration increases. Consider two American options that differ only as far as the expiration date is concerned. The owner of the long-life option has all the exercise opportunities open to the owner of the short-life option—and more. The long-life option must therefore always be worth at least as much as the short-life option.

Although European put and call options usually become more valuable as the time to expiration increases (see, e.g., Figures 10.1e, f), this is not always the case. Consider two European call options on a stock: one with an expiration date in one month, the other with an expiration date in two months. Suppose that a very large dividend is expected in six weeks. The dividend will cause the stock price to decline, so that the short-life option could be worth more than the long-life option.[1]

Volatility

The precise way in which volatility is defined is discussed in Chapter 13. Roughly speaking, the *volatility* of a stock price is a measure of how uncertain we are about

[1] We assume that, when the life of the option is changed, the dividends on the stock and their timing remain unchanged.

future stock price movements. As volatility increases, the chance that the stock will do very well or very poorly increases. For the owner of a stock, these two outcomes tend to offset each other. However, this is not so for the owner of a call or put. The owner of a call benefits from price increases but has limited downside risk in the event of price decreases because the most the owner can lose is the price of the option. Similarly, the owner of a put benefits from price decreases, but has limited downside risk in the event

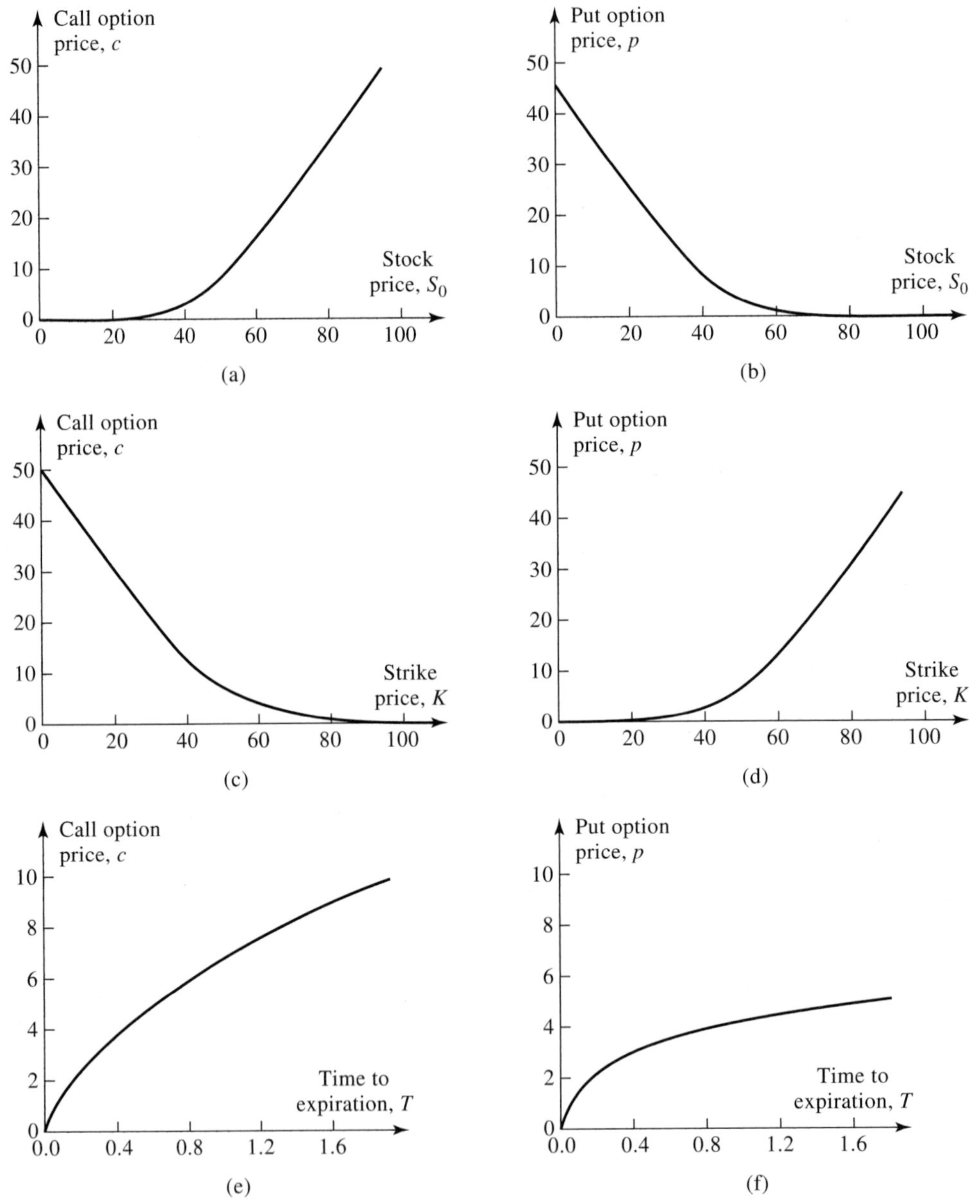

Figure 10.1 Effect of changes in stock price, strike price, and expiration date on option prices when $S_0 = 50$, $K = 50$, $r = 5\%$, $\sigma = 30\%$, and $T = 1$

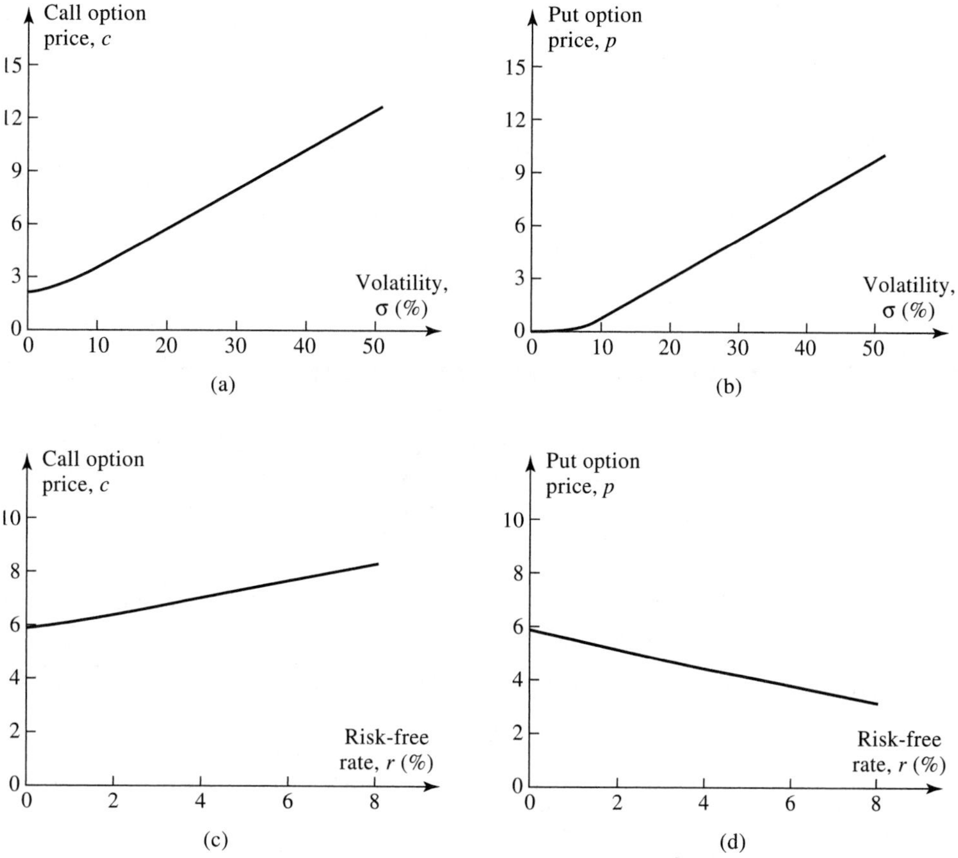

Figure 10.2 Effect of changes in volatility and risk-free interest rate on option prices when $S_0 = 50$, $K = 50$, $r = 5\%$, $\sigma = 30\%$, and $T = 1$

of price increases. The values of both calls and puts therefore increase as volatility increases (see Figures 10.2a, b).

Risk-Free Interest Rate

The risk-free interest rate affects the price of an option in a less clear-cut way. As interest rates in the economy increase, the expected return required by investors from the stock tends to increase. In addition, the present value of any future cash flow received by the holder of the option decreases. The combined impact of these two effects is to increase the value of call options and decrease the value of put options (see Figures 10.2c, d).

It is important to emphasize that we are assuming in Table 10.1 that interest rates change while all other variables stay the same. In particular, we are assuming in the table that interest rates change while the stock price remains the same. In practice, when interest rates rise (fall), stock prices tend to fall (rise). The combined effect of an interest rate increase and the accompanying stock price decrease can be to decrease the value of a call option and increase the value of a put option. Similarly, the combined effect of an interest rate decrease and the accompanying stock price increase can be to increase the value of a call option and decrease the value of a put option.

Dividends

Dividends have the effect of reducing the stock price on the ex-dividend date. This is bad news for the value of call options and good news for the value of put options. Consider a dividend whose ex-dividend date is during the life of an option. The value of the option is negatively related to the size of the dividend if the option is a call and positively related to the size of the dividend if the option is a put.

10.2 ASSUMPTIONS AND NOTATION

In this chapter we will make assumptions similar to those made when deriving forward and futures prices in Chapter 5. We assume that there are some market participants, such as large investment banks, for which the following statements are true:

1. There are no transactions costs.
2. All trading profits (net of trading losses) are subject to the same tax rate.
3. Borrowing and lending are possible at the risk-free interest rate.

We assume that these market participants are prepared to take advantage of arbitrage opportunities as they arise. As discussed in Chapters 1 and 5, this means that any available arbitrage opportunities disappear very quickly. For the purposes of our analyses, it is therefore reasonable to assume that there are no arbitrage opportunities.

We will use the following notation:

S_0: Current stock price
K: Strike price of option
T: Time to expiration of option
S_T: Stock price on the expiration date
r: Continuously compounded risk-free rate of interest for an investment maturing in time T
C: Value of American call option to buy one share
P: Value of American put option to sell one share
c: Value of European call option to buy one share
p: Value of European put option to sell one share.

It should be noted that r is the nominal rate of interest, not the real rate of interest. We can assume that $r > 0$. Otherwise, a risk-free investment would provide no advantages over cash. (Indeed, if $r < 0$, cash would be preferable to a risk-free investment.)

10.3 UPPER AND LOWER BOUNDS FOR OPTION PRICES

In this section we derive upper and lower bounds for option prices. These bounds do not depend on any particular assumptions about the factors mentioned in Section 10.1

(except $r > 0$). If an option price is above the upper bound or below the lower bound, there are profitable opportunities for arbitrageurs.

Upper Bounds

An American or European call option gives the holder the right to buy one share of a stock for a certain price. No matter what happens, the option can never be worth more than the stock. Hence, the stock price is an upper bound to the option price:

$$c \leqslant S_0 \quad \text{and} \quad C \leqslant S_0 \tag{10.1}$$

If these relationships were not true, an arbitrageur could easily make a riskless profit by buying the stock and selling the call option.

An American put option gives the holder the right to sell one share of a stock for K. No matter how low the stock price becomes, the option can never be worth more than K. Hence,

$$P \leqslant K \tag{10.2}$$

For European options, we know that at maturity the option cannot be worth more than K. It follows that it cannot be worth more than the present value of K today:

$$p \leqslant Ke^{-rT} \tag{10.3}$$

If this were not true, an arbitrageur could make a riskless profit by writing the option and investing the proceeds of the sale at the risk-free interest rate.

Lower Bound for Calls on Non-Dividend-Paying Stocks

A lower bound for the price of a European call option on a non-dividend-paying stock is

$$S_0 - Ke^{-rT}$$

We first look at a numerical example and then consider a more formal argument.

In Example 10.1, $S_0 = \$20$, $K = \$18$, $r = 10\%$ per annum, and $T = 1$ year, so that

$$S_0 - Ke^{-rT} = 20 - 18e^{-0.1} = 3.71$$

or \$3.71. The European call price is \$3.00, which is less than the theoretical minimum of \$3.71. An arbitrageur can short the stock and buy the call to provide a cash inflow of \$20.00 − \$3.00 = \$17.00. If invested for one year at 10% per annum, the \$17.00 grows to $17e^{0.1} = \$18.79$. At the end of the year, the option expires. If the stock price is greater than \$18.00, the arbitrageur exercises the option for \$18.00, closes out the short position, and makes a profit of

$$\$18.79 - \$18.00 = \$0.79$$

If the stock price is less than \$18.00, the stock is bought in market and the short position is closed out. The arbitrageur then makes an even greater profit. For example, if the stock price is \$17.00, the arbitrageur's profit is

$$\$18.79 - \$17.00 = \$1.79$$

Example 10.1 Call option price too low

A European call option on a non-dividend-paying stock with a strike price of \$18 and an expiration date in one year costs \$3. The stock price is \$20 and the risk-free interest rate is 10% per annum.

Action now

Buy the option for \$3
Short the stock to realize \$20
Invest \$17 for 1 year

Action in one year

If $S_T > 18$:	If $S_T < 18$:
Exercise option to buy stock for \$18	Buy stock for S_T
Use stock to close out short position	Use stock to close out short position
Receive \$18.79 from investment	Receive \$18.79 from investment
Net gain = \$0.79	Net gain = $18.79 - S_T$ (> \$0.79)

For a more formal argument, we consider the following two portfolios:

Portfolio A: one European call option plus a zero-coupon bond that provides a payoff of K at time T

Portfolio B: one share of the stock

In portfolio A, the zero-coupon bond will be worth K at time T. If $S_T > K$, the call option is exercised at maturity and portfolio A is worth S_T. If $S_T < K$, the call option expires worthless and the portfolio is worth K. Hence, at time T, portfolio A is worth

$$\max(S_T, K)$$

Portfolio B is worth S_T at time T. Hence, portfolio A is always worth as much as, and can be worth more than, portfolio B at the option's maturity. It follows that in the absence of arbitrage opportunities this must also be true today. The zero-coupon bond is worth Ke^{-rT} today. Hence,

$$c + Ke^{-rT} \geqslant S_0$$

or

$$c \geqslant S_0 - Ke^{-rT}$$

Because the worst that can happen to a call option is that it expires worthless, its value cannot be negative. This means that $c \geqslant 0$ and therefore

$$c \geqslant \max(S_0 - Ke^{-rT}, 0) \tag{10.4}$$

Example 10.2 provides an application of this formula.

Lower Bound for Puts on Non-Dividend-Paying Stocks

For a European put option on a non-dividend-paying stock, a lower bound for the price is

$$Ke^{-rT} - S_0$$

Example 10.2 Lower bound for call option

Consider a European call option on a non-dividend-paying stock when the stock price is \$51, the strike price is \$50, the time to maturity is six months, and the risk-free rate of interest is 12% per annum. In this case, $S_0 = 51$, $K = 50$, $T = 0.5$, and $r = 0.12$. From equation (10.4), a lower bound for the option price is $S_0 - Ke^{-rT}$, or

$$51 - 50e^{-0.12\times0.5} = \$3.91$$

Again, we first consider a numerical example and then look at a more formal argument. In Example 10.3, $S_0 = \$37$, $K = \$40$, $r = 5\%$ per annum, and $T = 0.5$ years, so that

$$Ke^{-rT} - S_0 = 40e^{-0.05\times0.5} - 37 = \$2.01$$

The European put price is \$1.00, which is less than the theoretical minimum of \$2.01. An arbitrageur can borrow \$38.00 for six months to buy both the put and the stock. At the end of the six months, the arbitrageur will be required to repay $38e^{0.05\times0.5} = \$38.96$. If the stock price is below \$40.00, the arbitrageur exercises the option to sell the stock for \$40.00, repays the loan, and makes a profit of

$$\$40.00 - \$38.96 = \$1.04$$

If the stock price is greater than \$40.00, the arbitrageur discards the option, sells the stock, and repays the loan for an even greater profit. For example, if the stock price is \$42.00, the arbitrageur's profit is

$$\$42.00 - \$38.96 = \$3.04$$

For a more formal argument, we consider the following two portfolios:

Portfolio C: one European put option plus one share

Portfolio D: an amount of cash equal to Ke^{-rT} (or equivalently a zero-coupon bond paying off K at time T)

Example 10.3 Put option price too low

A European put option on a non-dividend-paying stock with a strike price of \$40 and an expiration date in six months costs \$1. The stock price is \$37 and the risk-free interest rate is 5% per annum.

Action now

Borrow \$38 for six months
Buy the option for \$1
Buy the stock for \$37

Action in six months

If $S_T < 40$:	If $S_T > 40$:
Exercise the option to sell stock for \$40	Sell the stock for $+S_T$
Use \$38.96 to repay borrowings	Use \$38.96 to repay borrowings
Net gain = \$1.04	Net gain = $S_T - 38.96 > \$1.04$

Example 10.4 Lower bound for put option

Consider a European put option on a non-dividend-paying stock when the stock price is \$38, the exercise price is \$40, the time to maturity is three months, and the risk-free rate of interest is 10% per annum. In this case, $S_0 = 38$, $K = 40$, $T = 0.25$, and $r = 0.10$. From equation (10.5), a lower bound for the option price is $Ke^{-rT} - S_0$, or

$$40e^{-0.1\times0.25} - 38 = \$1.01$$

If $S_T < K$, the option in portfolio C is exercised at option maturity and the portfolio becomes worth K. If $S_T > K$, the put option expires worthless and the portfolio is worth S_T at this time. Hence, portfolio C is worth

$$\max(S_T,\ K)$$

in time T. Portfolio D is worth K in time T. Hence, portfolio C is always worth as much as, and can sometimes be worth more than, portfolio D in time T. It follows that in the absence of arbitrage opportunities portfolio C must be worth at least as much as portfolio D today. Hence,

$$p + S_0 \geqslant Ke^{-rT}$$

or

$$p \geqslant Ke^{-rT} - S_0$$

Because the worst that can happen to a put option is that it expires worthless, its value cannot be negative. This means that

$$p \geqslant \max(Ke^{-rT} - S_0,\ 0) \qquad \textbf{(10.5)}$$

Example 10.4 provides an application of this formula.

10.4 PUT–CALL PARITY

We now derive an important relationship between the prices of European put and call options that have the same strike price and time to maturity. Consider the following two portfolios that were used in the previous section:

Portfolio A: one European call option plus a zero-coupon bond that provides a payoff of K at time T

Portfolio C: one European put option plus one share of the stock

We continue to assume that the stock pays no dividends. The call and put options have the same strike price K and the same time to maturity T.

As discussed in the previous section, the zero-coupon bond in portfolio A will be worth K at time T. If the stock price S_T at time T proves to be above K, then the call option in portfolio A will be exercised. This means that portfolio A is worth $(S_T - K) + K = S_T$ at time T in these circumstances. If S_T proves to be less than K, then the call option in portfolio A will expire worthless and the portfolio will be worth K at time T.

Table 10.2 Values of Portfolio A and Portfolio C at time T

		$S_T > K$	$S_T < K$
Portfolio A	Call option	$S_T - K$	0
	Zero-coupon bond	K	K
	Total	S_T	K
Portfolio C	Put Option	0	$K - S_T$
	Share	S_T	S_T
	Total	S_T	K

In portfolio C, the share will be worth S_T at time T. If S_T proves to be below K, then the put option in portfolio C will be exercised. This means that portfolio C is worth $(K - S_T) + S_T = K$ at time T in these circumstances. If S_T proves to be greater than K, then the put option in portfolio C will expire worthless and the portfolio will be worth S_T at time T.

The situation is summarized in Table 10.2. If $S_T > K$, both portfolios are worth S_T at time T; if $S_T < K$, both portfolios are worth K at time T. In other words, both are worth

$$\max(S_T, K)$$

when the options expire at time T. Because they are European, the options cannot be exercised prior to time T. Since the portfolios have identical values at time T, they must have identical values today. If this were not the case, an arbitrageur could buy the less expensive portfolio and sell the more expensive one. Because the portfolios are guaranteed to cancel each other out at time T, this trading strategy would lock in an arbitrage profit equal to the difference in the values of the two portfolios.

The components of portfolio A are worth c and Ke^{-rT} today, and the components of portfolio C are worth p and S_0 today. Hence,

$$c + Ke^{-rT} = p + S_0 \quad \textbf{(10.6)}$$

This relationship is known as *put–call parity*. It shows that the value of a European call with a certain exercise price and exercise date can be deduced from the value of a European put with the same exercise price and exercise date, and vice versa.

To illustrate the arbitrage opportunities when equation (10.6) does not hold, suppose that the stock price is \$31, the exercise price is \$30, the risk-free interest rate is 10% per annum, the price of a three-month European call option is \$3, and the price of a three-month European put option is \$2.25. In this case,

$$c + Ke^{-rT} = 3 + 30e^{-0.1\times 3/12} = \$32.26$$
$$p + S_0 = 2.25 + 31 = \$33.25$$

Portfolio C is overpriced relative to portfolio A. An arbitrageur can buy the securities in portfolio A and short the securities in portfolio C. The strategy involves buying the call and shorting both the put and the stock, generating a positive cash flow of

$$-3 + 2.25 + 31 = \$30.25$$

up front. When invested at the risk-free interest rate, this amount grows to

$$30.25e^{0.1\times 0.25} = \$31.02$$

in three months. If the stock price at expiration of the option is greater than \$30, the call will be exercised. If it is less than \$30, the put will be exercised. In either case, the arbitrageur ends up buying one share for \$30. This share can be used to close out the short position. The net profit is therefore

$$\$31.02 - \$30.00 = \$1.02$$

For an alternative situation, suppose that the call price is \$3 and the put price is \$1. In this case,

$$c + Ke^{-rT} = 3 + 30e^{-0.1\times 3/12} = \$32.26$$
$$p + S_0 = 1 + 31 = \$32.00$$

Portfolio A is overpriced relative to portfolio C. An arbitrageur can short the securities in portfolio A and buy the securities in portfolio C to lock in a profit. The strategy involves shorting the call and buying both the put and the stock with an initial investment of

$$\$31 + \$1 - \$3 = \$29$$

When the investment is financed at the risk-free interest rate, a repayment of $29e^{0.1\times 0.25} = \$29.73$ is required at the end of the three months. As in the previous case, either the call or the put will be exercised. The short call and long put option position therefore leads to the stock being sold for \$30.00. The net profit is therefore

$$\$30.00 - \$29.73 = \$0.27$$

These examples are illustrated in Table 10.3. Business Snapshot 10.1 shows how options

Table 10.3 Arbitrage opportunities when put–call parity does not hold. Stock price = \$31; interest rate = 10%; call price = \$3. Both put and call have strike price of \$30 and three months to maturity

Three-month put price = \$2.25	*Three-month put price = \$1*
Action now:	*Action now*:
Buy call for \$3	Borrow \$29 for 3 months
Short put to realize \$2.25	Short call to realize \$3
Short the stock to realize \$31	Buy put for \$1
Invest \$30.25 for 3 months	Buy the stock for \$31
Action in 3 months if $S_T > 30$:	*Action in 3 months if* $S_T > 30$:
Receive \$31.02 from investment	Call exercised: sell stock for \$30
Exercise call to buy stock for \$30	Use \$29.73 to repay loan
Net profit = \$1.02	Net profit = \$0.27
Action in 3 months if $S_T < 30$:	*Action in 3 months if* $S_T < 30$:
Receive \$31.02 from investment	Exercise put to sell stock for \$30
Put exercised: buy stock for \$30	Use \$29.73 to repay loan
Net profit = \$1.02	Net profit = \$0.27

Business Snapshot 10.1 Put–call parity and capital structure

The pioneers of option pricing were Fischer Black, Myron Scholes, and Robert Merton. In the early 1970s they showed that options can be used to characterize the capital structure of a company. Today this analysis is widely used by financial institutions to assess a company's credit risk.

To illustrate the analysis, consider a company that has assets that are financed with zero-coupon bonds and equity. Suppose that the bonds mature in five years at which time a principal payment of K is required. The company pays no dividends. If the assets are worth more than K in five years, the equity holders choose to repay the bond holders. If the assets are worth less than K, the equity holders choose to declare bankruptcy and the bond holders end up owning the company.

The value of the equity in five years is therefore $\max(A_T - K, 0)$, where A_T is the value of the company's assets at that time. This shows that the equity holders have a five-year European call option on the assets of the company with a strike price of K. What about the bondholders? They get $\min(A_T, K)$ in five years. This is the same as $K - \max(K - A_T, 0)$. This shows that today the bonds are worth the present value of K minus the value of a five-year European put option on the assets with a strike price of K.

To summarize, if c and p are the values, respectively, of the call and put options on the company's assets, then

$$\text{Value of equity} = c$$

$$\text{Value of debt} = PV(K) - p$$

Denote the value of the assets of the company today by A_0. The value of the assets must equal the total value of the instruments used to finance the assets. This means that it must equal the sum of the value of the equity and the value of the debt, so that

$$A_0 = c + [PV(K) - p]$$

Rearranging this equation, we have

$$c + PV(K) = p + A_0$$

This is the put–call parity result in equation (10.6) for call and put options on the assets of the company.

and put–call parity can help us understand the positions of the debt holders and equity holders in a company.

American Options

Put–call parity holds only for European options. However, it is possible to derive some results for American option prices. It can be shown (see Problem 10.18) that, when there are no dividends,

$$S_0 - K \leqslant C - P \leqslant S_0 - Ke^{-rT} \qquad \textbf{(10.7)}$$

Example 10.5 provides an application of this equation.

Example 10.5 Relation between American call and put options

An American call option on a non-dividend-paying stock with exercise price \$20.00 and maturity in five months is worth \$1.50. Suppose that the current stock price is \$19.00 and the risk-free interest rate is 10% per annum. From equation (10.7), we have

$$19 - 20 \leqslant C - P \leqslant 19 - 20e^{-0.1\times 5/12}$$

or

$$1 \geqslant P - C \geqslant 0.18$$

showing that $P - C$ lies between \$1.00 and \$0.18. With C at \$1.50, P must lie between \$1.68 and \$2.50. In other words, upper and lower bounds for the price of an American put with the same strike price and expiration date as the American call are \$2.50 and \$1.68.

10.5 CALLS ON A NON-DIVIDEND-PAYING STOCK

In this section, we first show that it is never optimal to exercise an American call option on a non-dividend-paying stock before the expiration date.

To illustrate the general nature of the argument, consider an American call option on a non-dividend-paying stock with one month to expiration when the stock price is \$70 and the strike price is \$40. The option is deep in the money, and the investor who owns the option might well be tempted to exercise it immediately. However, if the investor plans to hold the stock obtained by exercising the option for more than one month, this is not the best strategy. A better course of action is to keep the option and exercise it at the end of the month. The \$40 strike price is then paid out one month later than it would be if the option were exercised immediately, so that interest is earned on the \$40 for one month. Because the stock pays no dividends, no income from the stock is sacrificed. A further advantage of waiting rather than exercising immediately is that there is some chance (however remote) that the stock price will fall below \$40 in one month. In this case the investor will not exercise in one month and will be glad that the decision to exercise early was not taken!

This argument shows that there are no advantages to exercising early if the investor plans to keep the stock for the remaining life of the option (one month, in this case). What if the investor thinks the stock is currently overpriced and is wondering whether to exercise the option and sell the stock? In this case, the investor is better off selling the option than exercising it.[2] The option will be bought by another investor who does want to hold the stock. Such investors must exist. Otherwise the current stock price would not be \$70. The price obtained for the option will be greater than its intrinsic value of \$30, for the reasons mentioned earlier.

For a more formal argument, we can use equation (10.4):

$$c \geqslant S_0 - Ke^{-rT}$$

[2] As an alternative strategy, the investor can keep the option and short the stock to lock in a better profit than \$10.

Because the owner of an American call has all the exercise opportunities open to the owner of the corresponding European call, we must have $C \geqslant c$. Hence,

$$C \geqslant S_0 - Ke^{-rT}$$

Given $r > 0$, it follows that $C > S_0 - K$ when $T > 0$. This means that the American call price C is always greater than the option's intrinsic value prior to maturity. If it were optimal to exercise at a particular time prior to maturity, C would equal the option's intrinsic value at that time. It follows that it can never be optimal to exercise early.

To summarize, there are two reasons an American call on a non-dividend-paying stock should not be exercised early. One relates to the insurance that it provides. A call option, when held instead of the stock itself, in effect insures the holder against the stock price falling below the strike price. Once the option has been exercised and the strike price has been exchanged for the stock price, this insurance vanishes. The other reason concerns the time value of money. From the perspective of the option holder, the later the strike price is paid out the better.

Bounds

Because American call options are never exercised early when there are no dividends, they are equivalent to European call options, so that $C = c$. From equations (10.1) and (10.4), it follows that upper and lower bounds are given by

$$\max(S_0 - Ke^{-rT},\, 0) \leqslant c,\ C \leqslant S_0$$

These bounds are illustrated in Figure 10.3.

The general way in which the call price varies with the stock price, S_0, is shown in Figure 10.4. As r or T or the stock price volatility increases, the line relating the call price to the stock price moves in the direction indicated by the arrows.

10.6 PUTS ON A NON-DIVIDEND-PAYING STOCK

It can be optimal to exercise an American put option on a non-dividend-paying stock early. Indeed, at any given time during its life, a put option should always be exercised early if it is sufficiently deep in the money.

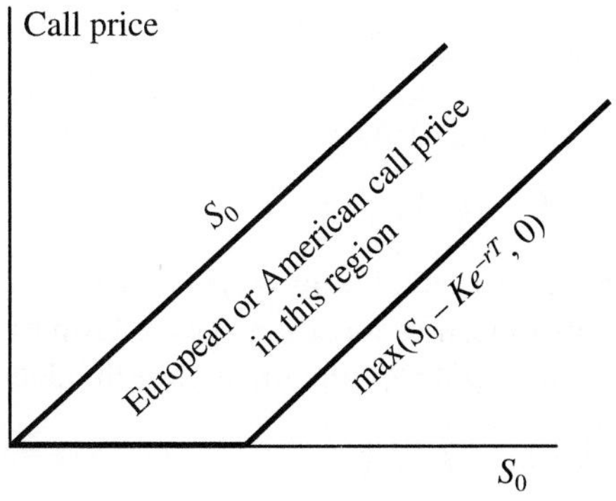

Figure 10.3 Bounds for European and American call options when there are no dividends

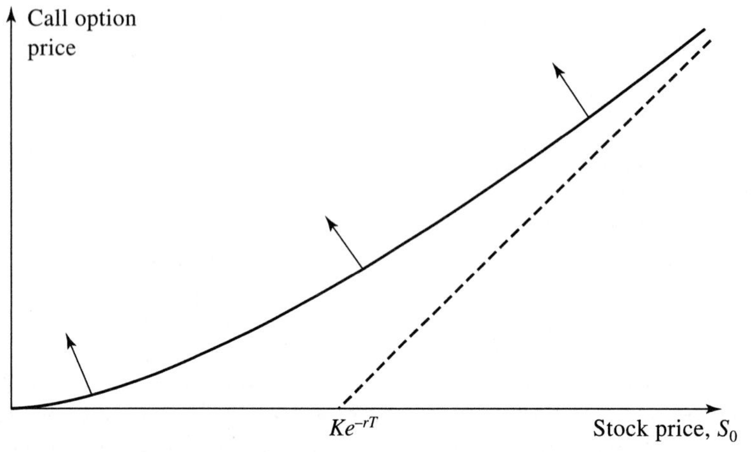

Figure 10.4 Variation of price of an American or European call option on a non-dividend-paying stock with the stock price S_0. Curve moves in the direction of the arrows when there is an increase in the interest rate, the time to maturity, or the stock price volatility

To illustrate, consider an extreme situation. Suppose that the strike price is \$10 and the stock price is virtually zero. By exercising immediately, an investor makes an immediate gain of \$10. If the investor waits, the gain from exercise might be less than \$10, but it cannot be more than \$10, because negative stock prices are impossible. Furthermore, receiving \$10 now is preferable to receiving \$10 in the future. It follows that the option should be exercised immediately.

Like a call option, a put option can be viewed as providing insurance. A put option, when held in conjunction with the stock, insures the holder against the stock price falling below a certain level. However, a put option is different from a call option in that it may be optimal for an investor to forgo this insurance and exercise early in order to realize the strike price immediately. In general, the early exercise of a put option becomes more attractive as S_0 decreases, as r increases, and as the volatility decreases.

Bounds

From equations (10.3) and (10.5), upper and lower bounds for a European put option when there are no dividends are given by

$$\max(Ke^{-rT} - S_0,\ 0) \leqslant p \leqslant Ke^{-rT}$$

For an American put option on a non-dividend-paying stock, the condition

$$P \geqslant \max(K - S_0,\ 0)$$

must apply because the option can be exercised at any time. This is a stronger condition than the one for a European put option in equation (10.5). Using the result in equation (10.2), bounds for an American put option on a non-dividend-paying stock are

$$\max(K - S_0,\ 0) \leqslant P \leqslant K$$

Figure 10.5 illustrates the bounds.

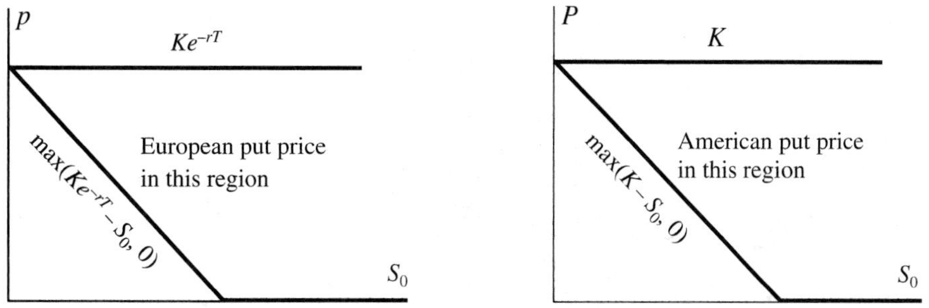

Figure 10.5 Bounds for European and American put options when there are no dividends

Figure 10.6 shows the general way in which the price of an American put option varies with S_0. As we argued earlier, provided that $r > 0$, it is always optimal to exercise an American put immediately when the stock price is sufficiently low. When early exercise is optimal, the value of the option is $K - S_0$. The curve representing the value of the put therefore merges into the put's intrinsic value, $K - S_0$, for a sufficiently small value of S_0. In Figure 10.6, this value of S_0 is shown as point A. The line relating the put price to the stock price moves in the direction indicated by the arrows when r decreases, when the volatility increases, and when T increases.

Because there are some circumstances when it is desirable to exercise an American put option early, it follows that an American put option is always worth more than the corresponding European put option. Furthermore, because an American put is sometimes worth its intrinsic value (see Figure 10.6), it follows that a European put option must sometimes be worth less than its intrinsic value. This means that the curve representing the relationship between the put price and the stock price for a European option must be below the corresponding curve for an American option.

Figure 10.7 shows the variation of the European put price with the stock price. Note that point B in Figure 10.7, at which the price of the option is equal to its intrinsic

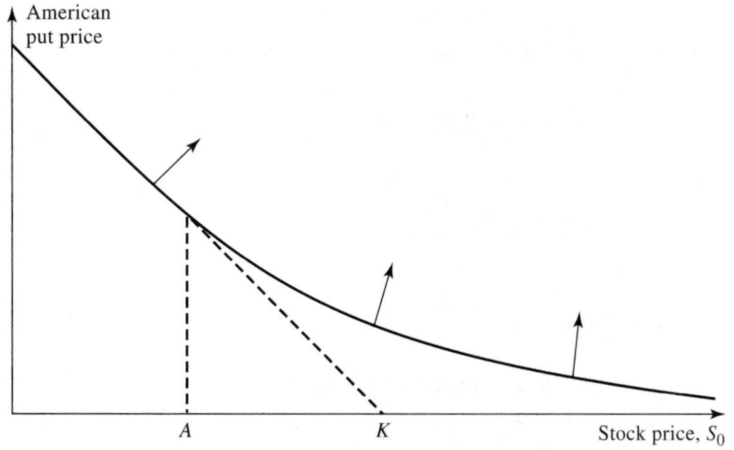

Figure 10.6 Variation of price of an American put option with stock price. Curve moves in the direction indicated by the arrows when the time to maturity or stock price volatility increases or when the interest rate decreases

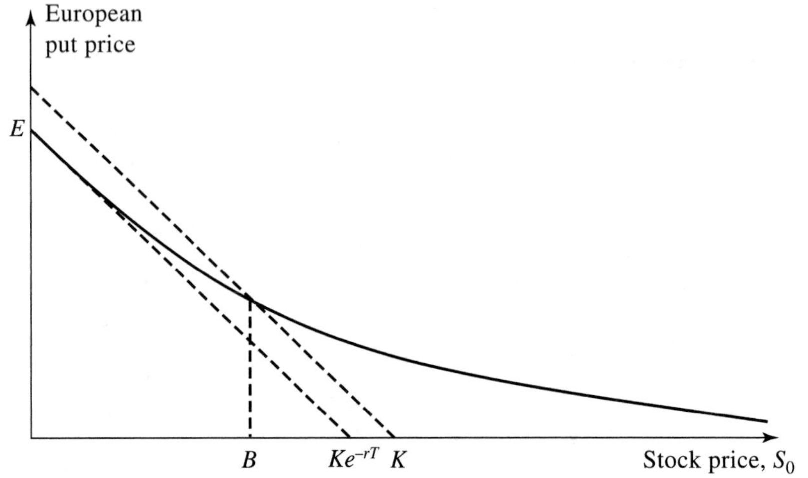

Figure 10.7 Variation of price of a European put option with the stock price

value, must represent a higher value of the stock price than point A in Figure 10.6 because the curve in Figure 10.7 is below that in Figure 10.6. Point E in Figure 10.7 is where $S_0 = 0$ and the European put price is Ke^{-rT}.

10.7 EFFECT OF DIVIDENDS

The results produced so far in this chapter have assumed that we are dealing with options on a non-dividend-paying stock. In this section we examine the impact of dividends. We assume that the dividends that will be paid during the life of the option are known. Most exchange-traded stock options have a life of less than one year, so this assumption is not too unreasonable in many situations. We will use D to denote the present value of the dividends during the life of the option. In the calculation of D, a dividend is assumed to occur at the time of its ex-dividend date.

Lower Bound for Calls and Puts

We can redefine portfolios A and B as follows:

Portfolio A: one European call option plus an amount of cash equal to $D + Ke^{-rT}$
Portfolio B: one share

A similar argument to the one used to derive equation (10.4) shows that

$$c \geqslant \max(S_0 - D - Ke^{-rT}, 0) \tag{10.8}$$

We can also redefine portfolios C and D as follows:

Portfolio C: one European put option plus one share
Portfolio D: an amount of cash equal to $D + Ke^{-rT}$

A similar argument to the one used to derive equation (10.5) shows that

$$p \geqslant \max(D + Ke^{-rT} - S_0,\ 0) \qquad \textbf{(10.9)}$$

Early Exercise

When dividends are expected, we can no longer assert that an American call option will not be exercised early. Sometimes it is optimal to exercise an American call immediately prior to an ex-dividend date. It is never optimal to exercise a call at other times. This point is discussed further in the Appendix to Chapter 13.

Put–Call Parity

Comparing the value at option maturity of the redefined portfolios A and C shows that, with dividends, the put–call parity result in equation (10.6) becomes

$$c + D + Ke^{-rT} = p + S_0 \qquad \textbf{(10.10)}$$

Dividends cause equation (10.7) to be modified (see Problem 10.19) to

$$S_0 - D - K \leqslant C - P \leqslant S_0 - Ke^{-rT} \qquad \textbf{(10.11)}$$

SUMMARY

There are six factors affecting the value of a stock option: the current stock price, the strike price, the expiration date, the stock price volatility, the risk-free interest rate, and the dividends expected during the life of the option. The value of a call generally increases as the current stock price, the time to expiration, the volatility, and the risk-free interest rate increase. The value of a call decreases as the strike price and expected dividends increase. The value of a put generally increases as the strike price, the time to expiration, the volatility, and the expected dividends increase. The value of a put decreases as the current stock price and the risk-free interest rate increase.

It is possible to reach some conclusions about the value of stock options without making any assumptions about the volatility of stock prices. For example, the price of a call option on a stock must always be worth less than the price of the stock itself. Similarly, the price of a put option on a stock must always be worth less than the option's strike price.

A European call option on a non-dividend-paying stock must be worth more than

$$\max(S_0 - Ke^{-rT},\ 0)$$

where S_0 is the stock price, K is the exercise price, r is the risk-free interest rate, and T is the time to expiration. A European put option on a non-dividend-paying stock must be worth more than

$$\max(Ke^{-rT} - S_0,\ 0)$$

When dividends with present value D will be paid, the lower bound for a European call option becomes

$$\max(S_0 - D - Ke^{-rT},\ 0)$$

and the lower bound for a European put option becomes

$$\max(Ke^{-rT} + D - S_0,\ 0)$$

Put–call parity is a relationship between the price, c, of a European call option on a stock and the price, p, of a European put option on a stock. For a non-dividend-paying stock, it is

$$c + Ke^{-rT} = p + S_0$$

For a dividend-paying stock, the put–call parity relationship is

$$c + D + Ke^{-rT} = p + S_0$$

Put–call parity does not hold for American options. However, it is possible to use arbitrage arguments to obtain upper and lower bounds for the difference between the price of an American call and the price of an American put.

In Chapter 13, we will carry the analyses in this chapter further by making specific assumptions about the probabilistic behavior of stock prices. This will enable us to derive exact pricing formulas for European stock options. In Chapters 12 and 18, we will see how numerical procedures can be used to price American options.

FURTHER READING

Black, F., and M. Scholes. "The Pricing of Options and Corporate Liabilities," *Journal of Political Economy*, 81 (May–June 1973): 637–59.

Broadie, M., and J. Detemple. "American Option Valuation: New Bounds, Approximations, and a Comparison of Existing Methods," *Review of Financial Studies*, 9, 4 (1996): 1211–50.

Merton, R. C. "On the Pricing of Corporate Debt: The Risk Structure of Interest Rates," *Journal of Finance*, 29, 2 (1974): 449–70.

Merton, R. C. "Theory of Rational Option Pricing," *Bell Journal of Economics and Management Science*, 4 (Spring 1973): 141–83.

Merton, R. C. "The Relationship between Put and Call Prices: Comment," *Journal of Finance*, 28 (March 1973): 183–84.

Stoll, H. R. "The Relationship between Put and Call Option Prices," *Journal of Finance*, 24 (December 1969): 801–24.

Quiz (Answers at End of Book)

10.1. List the six factors affecting stock option prices.

10.2. What is a lower bound for the price of a four-month call option on a non-dividend-paying stock when the stock price is \$28, the strike price is \$25, and the risk-free interest rate is 8% per annum?

10.3. What is a lower bound for the price of a one-month European put option on a non-dividend-paying stock when the stock price is \$12, the strike price is \$15, and the risk-free interest rate is 6% per annum?

10.4. Give two reasons that the early exercise of an American call option on a non-dividend-paying stock is not optimal. The first reason should involve the time value of money. The second reason should apply even if interest rates are zero.

10.5. "The early exercise of an American put is a trade-off between the time value of money and the insurance value of a put." Explain this statement.

10.6. Explain why an American call option on a dividend-paying stock is always worth at least as much as its intrinsic value. Is the same true of a European call option? Explain your answer.

10.7. The price of a non-dividend paying stock is \$19 and the price of a three-month European call option on the stock with a strike price of \$20 is \$1. The risk-free rate is 4% per annum. What is the price of a three-month European put option with a strike price of \$20?

Practice Questions (Answers in Solutions Manual/Study Guide)

10.8. Explain why the arguments leading to put–call parity for European options cannot be used to give a similar result for American options.

10.9. What is a lower bound for the price of a six-month call option on a non-dividend-paying stock when the stock price is \$80, the strike price is \$75, and the risk-free interest rate is 10% per annum?

10.10. What is a lower bound for the price of a two-month European put option on a non-dividend-paying stock when the stock price is \$58, the strike price is \$65, and the risk-free interest rate is 5% per annum?

10.11. A four-month European call option on a dividend-paying stock is currently selling for \$5. The stock price is \$64, the strike price is \$60, and a dividend of \$0.80 is expected in one month. The risk-free interest rate is 12% per annum for all maturities. What opportunities are there for an arbitrageur?

10.12. A one-month European put option on a non-dividend-paying stock is currently selling for \$2.50. The stock price is \$47, the strike price is \$50, and the risk-free interest rate is 6% per annum. What opportunities are there for an arbitrageur?

10.13. Give an intuitive explanation of why the early exercise of an American put becomes more attractive as the risk-free rate increases and volatility decreases.

10.14. The price of a European call that expires in six months and has a strike price of \$30 is \$2. The underlying stock price is \$29, and a dividend of \$0.50 is expected in two months and again in five months. The term structure is flat, with all risk-free interest rates being 10%. What is the price of a European put option that expires in six months and has a strike price of \$30?

10.15. Explain carefully the arbitrage opportunities in Problem 10.14 if the European put price is \$3.

10.16. The price of an American call on a non-dividend-paying stock is \$4. The stock price is \$31, the strike price is \$30, and the expiration date is in three months. The risk-free interest rate is 8%. Derive upper and lower bounds for the price of an American put on the same stock with the same strike price and expiration date.

10.17. Explain carefully the arbitrage opportunities in Problem 10.16 if the American put price is greater than the calculated upper bound.

10.18. Prove the result in equation (10.7). (*Hint*: For the first part of the relationship, consider (a) a portfolio consisting of a European call plus an amount of cash equal to K, and (b) a portfolio consisting of an American put option plus one share.)

10.19. Prove the result in equation (10.11). (*Hint*: For the first part of the relationship consider (a) a portfolio consisting of a European call plus an amount of cash equal to $D + K$, and (b) a portfolio consisting of an American put option plus one share.)

10.20. Consider a five-year call option on a non-dividend-paying stock granted to employees. The option can be exercised at any time after the end of the first year. Unlike a regular exchange-traded call option, the employee stock option cannot be sold. What is the likely impact of this restriction on the early exercise?

10.21. Use the DerivaGem software to verify that Figures 10.1 and 10.2 are correct.

Further Questions

10.22. Calls were traded on exchanges before puts. During the period of time when calls were traded but puts were not traded, how would you create a European put option on a non-dividend-paying stock synthetically?

10.23. The prices of European call and put options on a non-dividend-paying stock with 12 months to maturity, a strike price of \$120, and an expiration date in 12 months are \$20 and \$5, respectively. The current stock price is \$130. What is the implied risk-free rate?

10.24. A European call option and put option on a stock both have a strike price of \$20 and an expiration date in three months. Both sell for \$3. The risk-free interest rate is 10% per annum, the current stock price is \$19, and a \$1 dividend is expected in one month. Identify the arbitrage opportunity open to a trader.

10.25. Suppose that c_1, c_2, and c_3 are the prices of European call options with strike prices K_1, K_2, and K_3, respectively, where $K_3 > K_2 > K_1$ and $K_3 - K_2 = K_2 - K_1$. All options have the same maturity. Show that

$$c_2 \leqslant 0.5(c_1 + c_3)$$

(*Hint*: Consider a portfolio that is long one option with strike price K_1, long one option with strike price K_3, and short two options with strike price K_2.)

10.26. What is the result corresponding to that in Problem 10.25 for European put options?

10.27. Suppose that you are the manager and sole owner of a highly leveraged company. All the debt will mature in one year. If at that time the value of the company is greater than the face value of the debt, you will pay off the debt. If the value of the company is less than the face value of the debt, you will declare bankruptcy and the debt holders will own the company.
(a) Express your position as an option on the value of the company.
(b) Express the debt holders' position in terms of options on the value of the company.
(c) What can you do to increase the value of your position?

10.28. Consider an option on a stock when the stock price is \$41, the strike price is \$40, the risk-free rate is 6%, the volatility is 35%, and the time to maturity is one year. Assume that a dividend of \$0.50 is expected after six months.
(a) Use DerivaGem to value the option assuming it is a European call.

(b) Use DerivaGem to value the option assuming it is a European put.
(c) Verify that put–call parity holds.
(d) Explore, using DerivaGem, what happens to the price of the options as the time to maturity becomes very large. For this purpose, assume there are no dividends. Explain the results you get.

10.29. Consider a put option on a non-dividend-paying stock when the stock price is \$40, the strike price is \$42, the risk-free interest rate is 2%, the volatility is 25% per annum, and the time to maturity is three months. Use DerivaGem to determine the following:
(a) The price of the option if it is European (use Black–Scholes: European)
(b) The price of the option if it is American (use Binomial: American with 100 tree steps)
(c) Point B in Figure 10.7.

10.30. Section 10.1 gives an example of a situation where the value of a European call option decreases with the time to maturity. Give an example of a situation where the value of a European put option decreases with the time to maturity.

CHAPTER 11

Trading Strategies Involving Options

We discussed the profit pattern from an investment in a single option in Chapter 9. In this chapter we look at what can be achieved when an option is traded in conjunction with other assets. In particular, we examine the properties of portfolios consisting of (a) an option and a zero-coupon bond, (b) an option and the asset underlying the option, and (c) two or more options on the same asset.

A natural question is why a trader would want the profit patterns discussed here. The answer is that the choices a trader makes depend on the trader's judgment about how prices will move and the trader's willingness to take risks. Principal protected notes, discussed in Section 11.1, appeal to individuals who are risk-averse. They do not want to risk losing their principal, but have an opinion about whether a particular asset will increase or decrease in value and are prepared to let the return on principal depend on whether they are right. If a trader is willing to take rather more risk than this, he or she could choose a bull or bear spread, discussed in Section 11.3. Yet more risk would be taken with a straightforward long position in a call or put option.

Suppose that a trader feels there will be a big move in price of an asset, but does not know whether this will be up or down. There are a number of alternative trading strategies. A risk-averse trader might choose a reverse butterfly spread, discussed in Section 11.3, where there will be a small gain if the trader's hunch is correct and a small loss if it is not. A more aggressive investor might choose a straddle or strangle, discussed in Section 11.4, where potential gains and losses are larger.

In Chapter 10 we discussed put–call parity. Section 11.2 illustrates this result by showing how long (short) positions in calls can be converted into long (short) positions in puts, and vice versa. Section 11.3 discusses a related trading strategy involving what is known as a box spread where European calls and puts with two different strike prices are combined in a way that sometimes realizes an arbitrage profit.

11.1 PRINCIPAL-PROTECTED NOTES

Options are often used to create what are termed *principal-protected notes* for the retail market. These are products that appeal to conservative investors. The return earned by the investor depends on the performance of a stock, a stock index, or other risky asset, but the initial principal amount invested is not at risk. Example 11.1 illustrates how a simple principal-protected note can be created.

From Chapter 11 of *Fundamentals of Futures and Options Markets*, Eighth Edition. John C. Hull.

Example 11.1 Creation of a principal-protected note

Suppose that the 3-year interest rate is 6% with continuous compounding. This means that $1{,}000e^{-0.06\times 3} = \$835.27$ will grow to \$1,000 in 3 years. The difference between \$1,000 and \$835.27 is \$164.73. Suppose that a stock portfolio is worth \$1,000 and provides a dividend yield of 1.5% per annum. Suppose further that a 3-year at-the-money European call option on the stock portfolio can be purchased for less than \$164.73. (From DerivaGem, it can be verified that this will be the case if the volatility of the value of the portfolio is less than about 15%.) A bank can offer clients a \$1,000 investment opportunity consisting of:

1. A 3-year zero-coupon bond with a principal of \$1,000
2. A 3-year at-the-money European call option on the stock portfolio.

If the value of the portfolio increases the investor gets whatever \$1,000 invested in the portfolio would have grown to. (This is because the zero-coupon bond pays off \$1,000 and this equals the strike price of the option.) If the value of the portfolio goes down, the option has no value, but payoff from the zero-coupon bond ensures that the investor receives the original \$1,000 principal invested.

The attraction of a principal-protected note is that an investor is able to take a risky position without risking any principal. The worst that can happen is that the investor loses the chance to earn interest, or other income such as dividends, on the initial investment for the life of the note.

There are many variations on the product we have described. An investor who thinks that the price of an asset will decline can buy a principal-protected note consisting of a zero-coupon bond plus a put option. The investor's payoff in 3 years is then \$1,000 plus the payoff (if any) from the put option.

Is a principal-protected note a good deal from the retail investor's perspective? A bank will always build in a profit for itself when it creates a principal-protected note. This means that, in Example 11.1, the zero-coupon bond plus the call option will always cost the bank less than \$1,000. In addition, investors are taking the risk that the bank will not be in a position to make the payoff on the principal-protected note at maturity. (Some retail investors lost money on principal-protected notes created by Lehman Brothers when it failed in 2008.) In some situations, therefore, an investor will be better off if he or she buys the underlying option in the usual way and invests the remaining principal in a risk-free investment. However, this is not always the case. The investor is likely to face wider bid–offer spreads on the option than the bank and is likely to earn lower interest rates than the bank. It is therefore possible that the bank can add value for the investor while making a profit itself.

Now let us look at the principal-protected notes from the perspective of the bank. The economic viability of the structure in Example 11.1 depends critically on the level of interest rates and the volatility of the portfolio. If the interest rate is 3% instead of 6%, the bank has only $1{,}000 - 1{,}000e^{-0.03\times 3} = \$86.07$ with which to buy the call option. If interest rates are 6%, but the volatility is 25% instead of 15%, the price of the option would be about \$221. In either of these circumstances, the product described in Example 11.1 cannot be profitably created by the bank. However, there are a number of ways the bank can still create a viable 3-year product. For example, the strike price of the option can be increased so that the value of the portfolio has to rise by, say, 15% before the investor makes a gain; the investor's return could be capped; the return of the investor could depend on the average price of the asset instead of the final price; a knockout barrier could be specified. The derivatives involved in some of these alternatives will be discussed later in the book. (Capping the option corresponds to the creation of a bull spread for the investor and will be discussed later in this chapter.)

One way in which a bank can sometimes create a profitable principal-protected note when interest rates are low or volatilities are high is by increasing its life. Consider the situation in Example 11.1 when (a) the interest rate is 3% rather than 6% and (b) the stock portfolio has a volatility of 15% and provides a dividend yield of 1.5%. DerivaGem shows that a 3-year at-the-money European option costs about \$119. This is more than the funds available to purchase it ($1{,}000 - 1{,}000e^{-0.03\times3} = \$86.07$). A 10-year at-the-money option costs about \$217. This is less than the funds available to purchase it ($1{,}000 - 1{,}000e^{-0.03\times10} = \$259.18$), making the structure profitable. When the life is increased to 20 years, the option cost is about \$281, which is much less than the funds available to purchase it ($1{,}000 - 1{,}000e^{-0.03\times20} = \$451.19$), so that the structure is even more profitable.

A critical variable for the bank in our example is the dividend yield. The higher it is, the more profitable the product is for the bank. If the dividend yield were zero, the principal-protected note in Example 11.1 cannot be profitable for the bank no matter how long it lasts. (This follows from equation (10.4).)

11.2 STRATEGIES INVOLVING A SINGLE OPTION AND A STOCK

There are a number of different trading strategies involving a single option on a stock and the stock itself. The profits from these are illustrated in Figure 11.1. In this figure and in other figures throughout this chapter, the dashed line shows the relationship between profit and the stock price for the individual securities constituting the portfolio, whereas the solid line shows the relationship between profit and the stock price for the whole portfolio.

In Figure 11.1a, the portfolio consists of a long position in a stock plus a short position in a European call option. This is known as *writing a covered call*. The long stock position "covers" or protects the investor from the payoff on the short call that becomes necessary if there is a sharp rise in the stock price. In Figure 11.1b, a short position in a stock is combined with a long position in a call option. This is the reverse of writing a covered call. In Figure 11.1c, the investment strategy involves buying a European put option on a stock and the stock itself. The approach is referred to as a *protective put* strategy. In Figure 11.1d, a short position in a put option is combined with a short position in the stock. This is the reverse of a protective put.

The profit patterns in Figures 11.1a, b, c, d have the same general shape as the profit patterns discussed in Chapter 9 for short put, long put, long call, and short call, respectively. Put–call parity provides a way of understanding why this is so. From Chapter 10, the put–call parity relationship is

$$p + S_0 = c + Ke^{-rT} + D \tag{11.1}$$

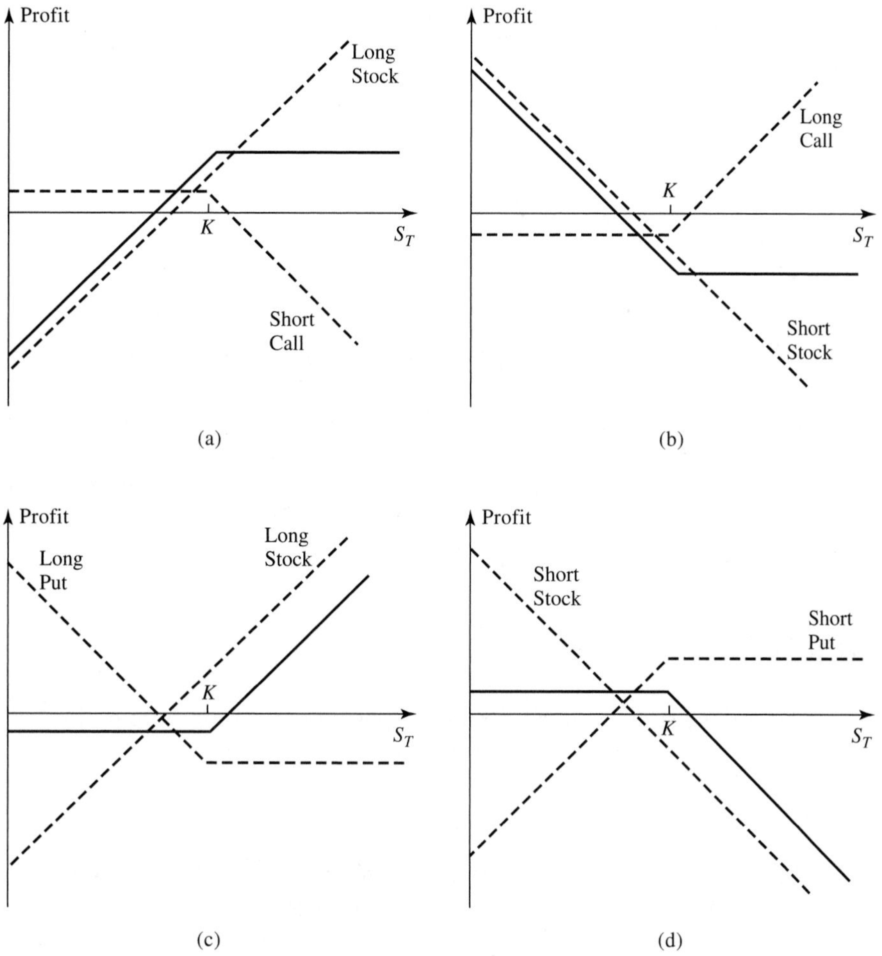

Figure 11.1 Profit patterns (a) long position in a stock combined with short position in a call; (b) short position in a stock combined with long position in a call; (c) long position in a put combined with long position in a stock; (d) short position in a put combined with short position in a stock

where p is the price of a European put, S_0 is the stock price, c is the price of a European call, K is the strike price of both call and put, r is the risk-free interest rate, T is the time to maturity of both call and put, and D is the present value of the dividends anticipated during the life of the options.

Equation (11.1) shows that a long position in a European put combined with a long position in the stock is equivalent to a long European call position plus a certain amount ($= Ke^{-rT} + D$) of cash. This explains why the profit pattern in Figure 11.1c is similar to the profit pattern from a long call position. The position in Figure 11.1d is the reverse of that in Figure 11.1c and therefore leads to a profit pattern similar to that from a short call position.

Equation (11.1) can be rearranged to become

$$S_0 - c = Ke^{-rT} + D - p$$

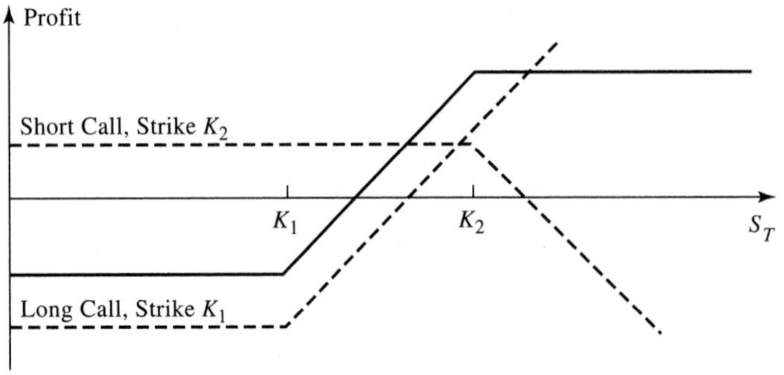

Figure 11.2 Profit from bull spread created using call options

This shows that a long position in a stock combined with a short position in a European call is equivalent to a short European put position plus a certain amount ($= Ke^{-rT} + D$) of cash. This explains why the profit pattern in Figure 11.1a is similar to that from a short put position. The position in Figure 11.1b is the reverse of that in Figure 11.1a and therefore leads to a profit pattern similar to that from a long put position.

11.3 SPREADS

A spread trading strategy involves taking a position in two or more options of the same type (i.e., two or more calls or two or more puts).

Bull Spreads

One of the most popular types of spreads is a *bull spread*. This can be created by buying a European call option on a stock with a certain strike price and selling a European call option on the same stock with a higher strike price. Both options have the same expiration date. The strategy is illustrated in Figure 11.2. The profits from the two option positions taken separately are shown by the dashed lines. The profit from the whole strategy is the sum of the profits given by the dashed lines and is indicated by the solid line. Because a call price always decreases as the strike price increases, the value of the option sold is always less than the value of the option bought. A bull spread, when created from calls, therefore requires an initial investment.

Suppose that K_1 is the strike price of the call option bought, K_2 is the strike price of the call option sold, and S_T is the stock price on the expiration date of the options. Table 11.1 shows the total payoff that will be realized from a bull spread in different circumstances. If the stock price does well and is greater than the higher strike price, the

Table 11.1 Payoff from a bull spread created using calls

Stock price range	*Payoff from long call option*	*Payoff from short call option*	*Total payoff*
$S_T \leqslant K_1$	0	0	0
$K_1 < S_T < K_2$	$S_T - K_1$	0	$S_T - K_1$
$S_T \geqslant K_2$	$S_T - K_1$	$K_2 - S_T$	$K_2 - K_1$

Example 11.2 Bull spread using call options

An investor buys for \$3 a three-month call with a strike price of \$30 and sells for \$1 a three-month call with a strike price of \$35. The payoff from this bull spread strategy is \$5 if the stock price is above \$35 and zero if it is below \$30. If the stock price is between \$30 and \$35, the payoff is the amount by which the stock price exceeds \$30. The cost of the strategy is \$3 − \$1 = \$2. The profit is therefore as follows:

Stock price range	*Profit*
$S_T \leqslant 30$	-2
$30 < S_T < 35$	$S_T - 32$
$S_T \geqslant 35$	$+3$

payoff is the difference between the two strike prices, or $K_2 - K_1$. If the stock price on the expiration date lies between the two strike prices, the payoff is $S_T - K_1$. If the stock price on the expiration date is below the lower strike price, the payoff is zero. The profit in Figure 11.2 is calculated by subtracting the initial investment from the payoff. Example 11.2 provides a numerical illustration of a bull spread using call options.

A bull spread strategy limits the investor's upside as well as downside risk. The strategy can be described by saying that the investor has a call option with a strike price equal to K_1 and has chosen to give up some upside potential by selling a call option with strike price K_2 ($K_2 > K_1$). In return for giving up the upside potential, the investor gets the price of the option with strike price K_2. Three types of bull spread can be distinguished:

1. Both calls are initially out of the money.
2. One call is initially in the money; the other call is initially out of the money.
3. Both calls are initially in the money.

The most aggressive bull spreads are those of type 1. They cost very little to set up and have a small probability of giving a relatively high payoff ($= K_2 - K_1$). As we move from type 1 to type 2 and from type 2 to type 3, the spreads become more conservative.

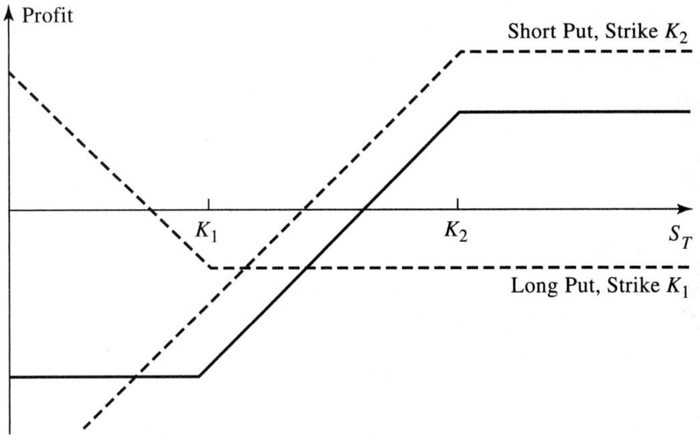

Figure 11.3 Profit from bull spread created using put options

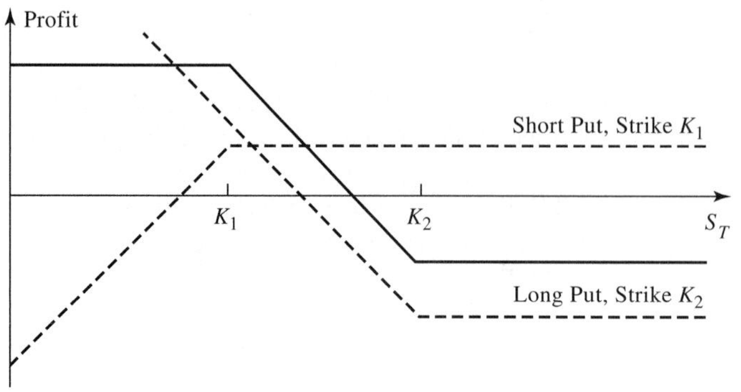

Figure 11.4 Profit from bear spread created using put options

Bull spreads can also be created by buying a European put with a low strike price and selling a European put with a high strike price, as illustrated in Figure 11.3. Unlike the bull spread created from calls, bull spreads created from puts involve a positive cash flow to the investor up front (ignoring margin requirements) and a payoff that is either negative or zero.

Bear Spreads

An investor who enters into a bull spread is hoping that the stock price will increase. By contrast, an investor who enters into a *bear spread* is hoping that the stock price will decline. Bear spreads can be created by buying a European put with one strike price and selling a European put with another strike price. The strike price of the option purchased is greater than the strike price of the option sold. (This is in contrast to a bull spread where the strike price of the option purchased is always less than the strike price of the option sold.) In Figure 11.4, the profit from the spread is shown by the solid line. A bear spread created from puts involves an initial cash outflow because the price of the put sold is less than the price of the put purchased. In essence, the investor has bought a put with a certain strike price and chosen to give up some of the profit potential by selling a put with a lower strike price. In return for the profit given up, the investor gets the price of the option sold.

Assume that the strike prices are K_1 and K_2, with $K_1 < K_2$. Table 11.2 shows the payoff that will be realized from a bear spread in different circumstances. If the stock price is greater than K_2, the payoff is zero. If the stock price is less than K_1, the payoff is $K_2 - K_1$. If the stock price is between K_1 and K_2, the payoff is $K_2 - S_T$. The profit is calculated by subtracting the initial cost from the payoff. Example 11.3 provides a numerical illustration.

Table 11.2 Payoff from a bear spread created with put options

Stock price range	*Payoff from long put option*	*Payoff from short put option*	*Total payoff*
$S_T \leqslant K_1$	$K_2 - S_T$	$S_T - K_1$	$K_2 - K_1$
$K_1 < S_T < K_2$	$K_2 - S_T$	0	$K_2 - S_T$
$S_T \geqslant K_2$	0	0	0

Example 11.3 Bear spread using put options

An investor buys for \$3 a three-month put with a strike price of \$35 and sells for \$1 a three-month put with a strike price of \$30. The payoff from this bear spread strategy is zero if the stock price is above \$35 and \$5 if it is below \$30. If the stock price is between \$30 and \$35, the payoff is $35 - S_T$. The options cost $\$3 - \$1 = \$2$ up front. The profit is therefore as follows:

Stock price range	*Profit*
$S_T \leqslant 30$	$+3$
$30 < S_T < 35$	$33 - S_T$
$S_T \geqslant 35$	-2

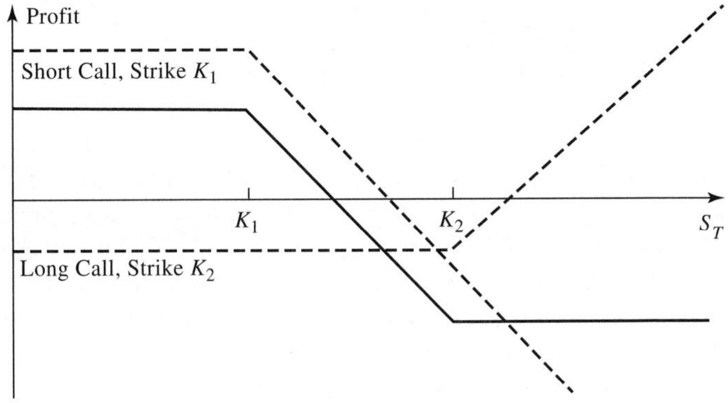

Figure 11.5 Profit from bear spread created using call options

Like bull spreads, bear spreads limit both the upside profit potential and the downside risk. Bear spreads can be created using calls instead of puts. The investor buys a call with a high strike price and sells a call with a low strike price, as illustrated in Figure 11.5. Bear spreads created with calls involve an initial cash inflow (ignoring margin requirements).

Box Spreads

A box spread is a combination of a bull call spread with strike prices K_1 and K_2 and a bear put spread with the same two strike prices. As shown in Table 11.3, the payoff

Table 11.3 Payoff from a box spread

Stock price range	*Payoff from bull call spread*	*Payoff from bear put spread*	*Total payoff*
$S_T \leqslant K_1$	0	$K_2 - K_1$	$K_2 - K_1$
$K_1 < S_T < K_2$	$S_T - K_1$	$K_2 - S_T$	$K_2 - K_1$
$S_T \geqslant K_2$	$K_2 - K_1$	0	$K_2 - K_1$

Business Snapshot 11.1 Losing money with box spreads

Suppose that a stock has a price of \$50 and a volatility of 30%. No dividends are expected and the risk-free rate is 8%. A trader offers you the chance to sell on the CBOE a two-month box spread where the strike prices are \$55 and \$60 for \$5.10. Should you do the trade?

The trade certainly sounds attractive. In this case, $K_1 = 55$, $K_2 = 60$, and the payoff is certain to be \$5 in two months. By selling the box spread for \$5.10 and investing the funds for two months, you would have more than enough funds to meet the \$5 payoff in two months. The theoretical value of the box spread today is $5 \times e^{-0.08\times 2/12} = \$4.93$.

Unfortunately there is a snag. CBOE stock options are American and the \$5 payoff from the box spread is calculated on the assumption that the options comprising the box are European. Option prices for this example (calculated using DerivaGem) are shown in the table below. A bull call spread where the strike prices are \$55 and \$60 costs $0.96 - 0.26 = \$0.70$. (This is the same for both European and American options because, as we saw in Chapter 10, the price of a European call is the same as the price of an American call when there are no dividends.) A bear put spread with the same strike prices costs $9.46 - 5.23 = \$4.23$ if the options are European and $10.00 - 5.44 = \$4.56$ if they are American. The combined value of both spreads if they are created with European options is $0.70 + 4.23 = \$4.93$. This is the theoretical box spread price calculated above. The combined value of buying both spreads if they are American is $0.70 + 4.56 = \$5.26$. Selling a box spread created with American options for \$5.10 would not be a good trade. You would realize this almost immediately as the trade involves selling a \$60 strike put and this would be exercised against you almost as soon as you sold it!

Option type	*Strike price*	*European option price*	*American option price*
Call	60	0.26	0.26
Call	55	0.96	0.96
Put	60	9.46	10.00
Put	55	5.23	5.44

from a box spread is always $K_2 - K_1$. The value of a box spread is therefore always the present value of this payoff or $(K_2 - K_1)e^{-rT}$. If it has a different value, there is an arbitrage opportunity. If the market price of the box spread is too low, it is profitable to buy the box. This involves buying a call with strike price K_1, buying a put with strike price K_2, selling a call with strike price K_2, and selling a put with strike price K_1. If the market price of the box spread is too high, it is profitable to sell the box. This involves buying a call with strike price K_2, buying a put with strike price K_1, selling a call with strike price K_1, and selling a put with strike price K_2.

It is important to realize that a box spread arbitrage only works with European options. Many of the options that trade on exchanges are American. As shown in Business Snapshot 11.1, inexperienced traders who treat American options as European are liable to lose money.

Butterfly Spreads

A *butterfly spread* involves positions in options with three different strike prices. It can be created by buying a European call option with a relatively low strike price, K_1, buying a European call option with a relatively high strike price, K_3, and selling two European call options with a strike price, K_2, halfway between K_1 and K_3. Generally K_2 is close to the current stock price. The pattern of profits from the strategy is shown in Figure 11.6. A butterfly spread leads to a profit if the stock price stays close to K_2, but gives rise to a small loss if there is a significant stock price move in either direction. It is therefore an appropriate strategy for an investor who feels that large stock price moves are unlikely. The strategy requires a small investment initially. The payoff from a butterfly spread is shown in Table 11.4.

Suppose that a certain stock is currently worth \$61. Consider an investor who feels that a significant price move in the next six months is unlikely. Suppose that the market prices of six-month European calls are as follows:

Strike price (\$)	*Call price* (\$)
55	10
60	7
65	5

The investor could create a butterfly spread by buying one call with a \$55 strike price, buying one call with a \$65 strike price, and selling two calls with a \$60 strike price. It costs $\$10 + \$5 - (2 \times \$7) = \$1$ to create the spread. If the stock price in six months is greater than \$65 or less than \$55, the total payoff is zero and the investor incurs a net loss of \$1. If the stock price is between \$56 and \$64, a profit is made. The maximum profit, \$4, occurs when the stock price in six months is \$60.

Butterfly spreads can be created using put options. The investor buys two European puts, one with a low strike price and one with a high strike price, and sells two European puts with an intermediate strike price, as shown in Figure 11.7. The butterfly spread in the example just considered would be created by buying two puts, one with a strike price of \$55 and one with a strike price of \$65, and selling two puts with a strike price of \$60. The

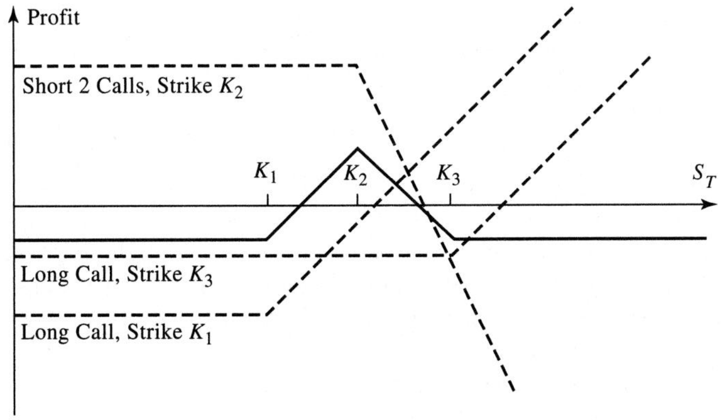

Figure 11.6 Profit from butterfly spread using call options

Table 11.4 Payoff from a butterfly spread

Stock price range	*Payoff from first long call*	*Payoff from second long call*	*Payoff from short calls*	*Total payoff**
$S_T \leqslant K_1$	0	0	0	0
$K_1 < S_T \leqslant K_2$	$S_T - K_1$	0	0	$S_T - K_1$
$K_2 < S_T < K_3$	$S_T - K_1$	0	$-2(S_T - K_2)$	$K_3 - S_T$
$S_T \geqslant K_3$	$S_T - K_1$	$S_T - K_3$	$-2(S_T - K_2)$	0

* These payoffs are calculated using the relationship $K_2 = 0.5(K_1 + K_3)$.

use of put options results in exactly the same spread as the use of call options. Put–call parity can be used to show that the initial investment is the same in both cases.

A butterfly spread can be sold or shorted by following the reverse strategy. Options are sold with strike prices of K_1 and K_3, and two options with the middle strike price K_2 are purchased. This strategy produces a modest profit if there is a significant movement in the stock price.

Calendar Spreads

Up to now we have assumed that the options used to create a spread all expire at the same time. We now move on to *calendar spreads* in which the options have the same strike price and different expiration dates.

A calendar spread can be created by selling a European call option with a certain strike price and buying a longer-maturity European call option with the same strike price. The longer the maturity of an option, the more expensive it usually is. A calendar spread therefore usually requires an initial investment. Profit diagrams for calendar spreads are usually produced so that they show the profit when the short-maturity option expires on the assumption that the long-maturity option position is closed out at that time. The profit pattern for a calendar spread produced from call options is shown in Figure 11.8. The pattern is similar to the profit from the butterfly spread in Figure 11.6. The investor makes a profit if the stock price at the expiration of the short-maturity option is close to the strike price of the short-maturity option. However, a loss is incurred when the stock price is significantly above or significantly below this strike price.

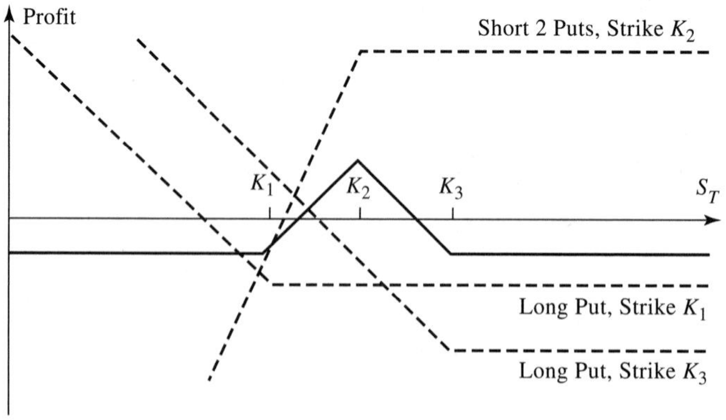

Figure 11.7 Profit from butterfly spread using put options

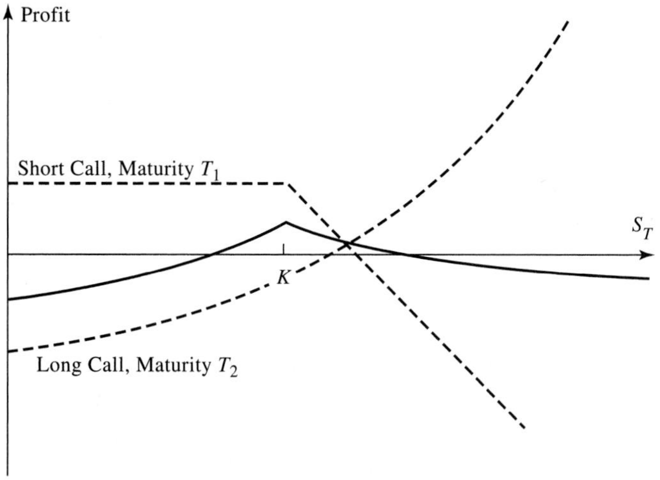

Figure 11.8 Profit from calendar spread created using two calls when $T_2 > T_1$, calculated at the time when the short maturity call expires

To understand the profit pattern from a calendar spread, first consider what happens if the stock price is very low when the short-maturity option expires. The short-maturity option is worthless and the value of the long-maturity option is close to zero. The investor therefore incurs a loss that is close to the cost of setting up the spread initially. Consider next what happens if the stock price, S_T, is very high when the short-maturity option expires. The short-maturity option costs the investor $S_T - K$, and the long-maturity option is worth a little more than $S_T - K$, where K is the strike price of the options. Again, the investor makes a net loss that is close to the cost of setting up the spread initially. If S_T is close to K, the short-maturity option costs the investor either a small amount or nothing at all. However, the long-maturity option is still quite valuable. In this case a significant net profit is made.

In a *neutral calendar spread*, a strike price close to the current stock price is chosen. A *bullish calendar spread* involves a higher strike price, whereas a *bearish calendar spread* involves a lower strike price.

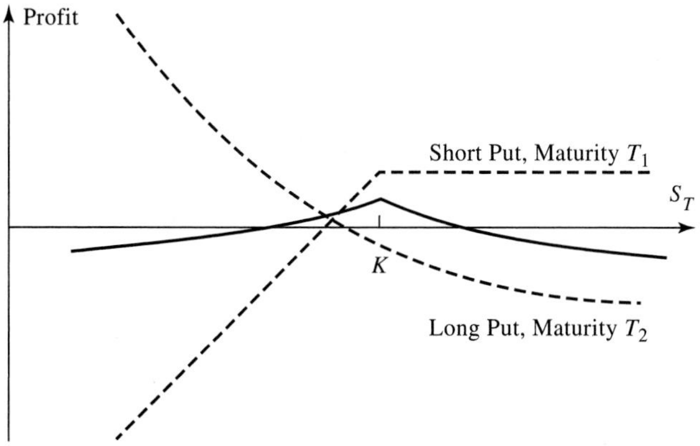

Figure 11.9 Profit from calendar spread created using two puts when $T_2 > T_1$, calculated at the time when the short maturity put expires

Calendar spreads can be created with put options as well as call options. The investor buys a long-maturity put option and sells a short-maturity put option. As shown in Figure 11.9, the profit pattern is similar to that obtained from using calls.

A *reverse calendar spread* is the opposite to that in Figures 11.8 and 11.9. The investor buys a short-maturity option and sells a long-maturity option. A small profit arises if the stock price at the expiration of the short-maturity option is well above or well below the strike price of the short-maturity option. However, a significant loss results if it is close to the strike price.

Diagonal Spreads

Bull, bear, and calendar spreads can all be created from a long position in one call and a short position in another call. In the case of bull and bear spreads, the calls have different strike prices and the same expiration date. In the case of calendar spreads, the calls have the same strike price and different expiration dates. In a *diagonal spread* both the expiration date and the strike price of the calls are different. This increases the range of profit patterns that are possible.

11.4 COMBINATIONS

A *combination* is an option trading strategy that involves taking a position in both calls and puts on the same stock. We will consider straddles, strips, straps, and strangles.

Straddle

One popular combination is a *straddle*, which involves buying a European call and put with the same strike price and expiration date. The profit pattern is shown in Figure 11.10. The strike price is denoted by K. If the stock price is close to this strike price at expiration of the options, the straddle leads to a loss. However, if there is a sufficiently large move in either direction, a significant profit will result. The payoff from a straddle is calculated in Table 11.5.

A straddle is appropriate when an investor is expecting a large move in a stock price but does not know in which direction the move will be. Consider an investor who feels that the price of a certain stock, currently valued at \$69 by the market, will move

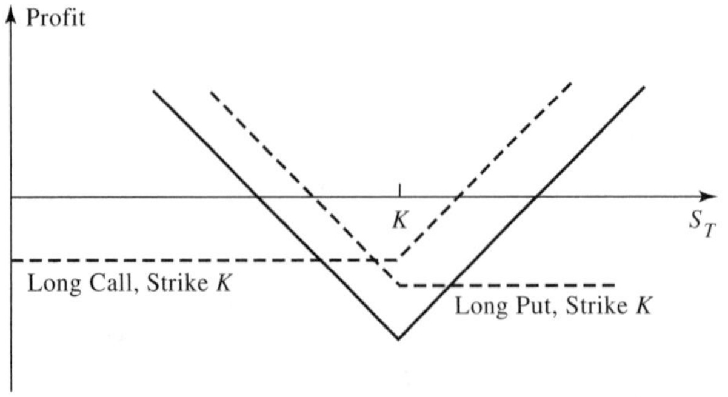

Figure 11.10 Profit from a straddle

Table 11.5 Payoff from a straddle

Range of stock price	*Payoff from call*	*Payoff from put*	*Total payoff*
$S_T \leqslant K$	0	$K - S_T$	$K - S_T$
$S_T > K$	$S_T - K$	0	$S_T - K$

significantly in the next three months. The investor could create a straddle by buying both a put and a call with a strike price of \$70 and an expiration date in three months. Suppose that the call costs \$4 and the put costs \$3. If the stock price stays at \$69, it is easy to see that the strategy costs the investor \$6 (an up-front investment of \$7 is required, the call expires worthless, and the put expires worth \$1). If the stock price moves to \$70, a loss of \$7 is experienced (this is the worst that can happen). However, if the stock price jumps up to \$90, a profit of \$13 is made; if the stock moves down to \$55, a profit of \$8 is made; and so on. As indicated in Business Snapshot 11.2 an investor should carefully consider whether the jump that he or she anticipates is already reflected in option prices before putting on a straddle trade.

The straddle in Figure 11.10 is sometimes referred to as a *bottom straddle* or straddle purchase. A *top straddle* or *straddle write* is the reverse position. It is created by selling a call and a put with the same exercise price and expiration date. It is a highly risky strategy. If the stock price on the expiration date is close to the strike price, a significant profit results. However, the loss arising from a large move is unlimited.

Strips and Straps

A *strip* consists of a long position in one European call and two European puts with the same strike price and expiration date. A *strap* consists of a long position in two European calls and one Euopean put with the same strike price and expiration date. The profit patterns from strips and straps are shown in Figure 11.11. In a strip the investor is betting that there will be a big stock price move and considers a decrease in the stock price to be more likely than an increase. In a strap the investor is also betting

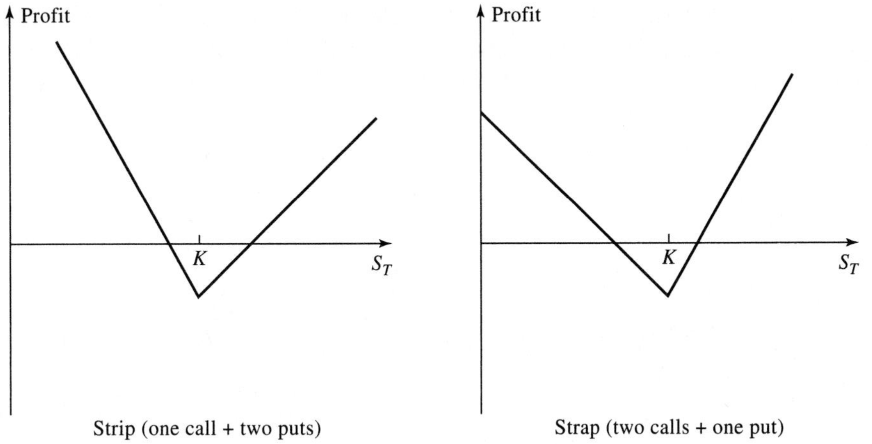

Figure 11.11 Profit from a strip and a strap

Business Snapshot 11.2 How to make money from trading straddles

Suppose that a big move is expected in a company's stock price because there is a takeover bid for the company or the outcome of a major lawsuit involving the company is about to be announced. Should you trade a straddle?

A straddle seems a natural trading strategy in this case. However, if your view of the company's situation is much the same as that of other market participants, this view will be reflected in the prices of options. Options on the stock will be significantly more expensive than options on a similar stock for which no jump is expected. The V-shaped profit pattern from the straddle in Figure 11.10 will have moved downward, so that a bigger move in the stock price is necessary for you to make a profit.

For a straddle to be an effective strategy, you must believe that there are likely to be big movements in the stock price and these beliefs must be different from those of most other investors. Market prices incorporate the beliefs of market participants. To make money from any investment strategy, you must take a view that is different from most of the rest of the market—and you must be right!

that there will be a big stock price move. However, in this case, an increase in the stock price is considered to be more likely than a decrease.

Strangles

In a *strangle*, sometimes called a *bottom vertical combination*, an investor buys a European put and a European call with the same expiration date and different strike prices. The profit pattern is shown in Figure 11.12. The call strike price, K_2, is higher than the put strike price, K_1. The payoff function for a strangle is calculated in Table 11.6.

A strangle is a similar strategy to a straddle. The investor is betting that there will be a large price move, but is uncertain whether it will be an increase or a decrease. Comparing Figures 11.12 and 11.10, we see that the stock price has to move farther in a strangle than in a straddle for the investor to make a profit. However, the downside risk if the stock price ends up at a central value is less with a strangle.

The profit pattern obtained with a strangle depends on how close together the strike prices are. The farther they are apart, the less the downside risk and the farther the stock price has to move for a profit to be realized.

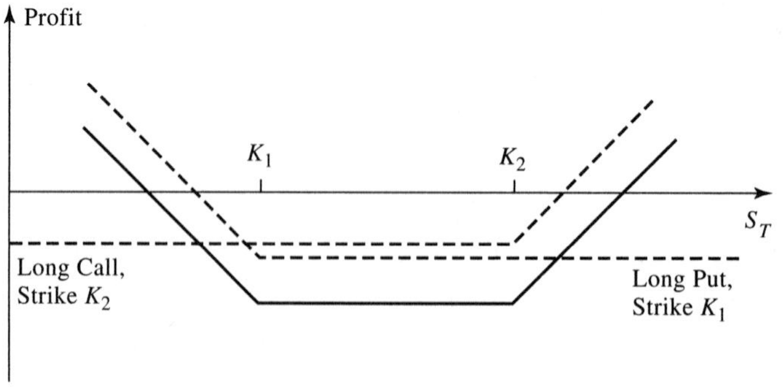

Figure 11.12 Profit from a strangle

Table 11.6 Payoff from a strangle

Range of stock price	*Payoff from call*	*Payoff from put*	*Total payoff*
$S_T \leqslant K_1$	0	$K_1 - S_T$	$K_1 - S_T$
$K_1 < S_T < K_2$	0	0	0
$S_T \geqslant K_2$	$S_T - K_2$	0	$S_T - K_2$

The sale of a strangle is sometimes referred to as a *top vertical combination.* It can be appropriate for an investor who feels that large stock price moves are unlikely. However, as with sale of a straddle, it is a risky strategy involving unlimited potential loss to the investor.

11.5 OTHER PAYOFFS

This chapter has demonstrated just a few of the ways in which options can be used to produce an interesting relationship between profit and stock price. If European options expiring at time T were available with every single possible strike price, any payoff function at time T could in theory be obtained. The easiest illustration of this involves butterfly spreads. Recall that a butterfly spread is created by buying options with strike prices K_1 and K_3 and selling two options with strike price K_2 where $K_1 < K_2 < K_3$ and $K_3 - K_2 = K_2 - K_1$. Figure 11.13 shows the payoff from a butterfly spread. The pattern could be described as a spike. As K_1 and K_3 move closer together, the spike becomes smaller. Through the judicious combination of a large number of very small spikes, any payoff function can be approximated.

SUMMARY

Principal-protected notes can be created from a zero-coupon bond and a European call option. They are attractive to some investors because the issuer of the product is able to guarantee that the purchaser will receive his or her principal back regardless of the performance of the asset underlying the option.

A number of common trading strategies involve a single option and the underlying stock. For example, writing a covered call involves buying the stock and selling a call

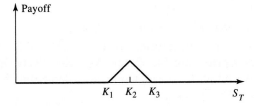

Figure 11.13 "Spike payoff" from a butterfly spread that can be used as a building block to create other payoffs

option on the stock; a protective put involves buying a put option and buying the stock. The former is similar to selling a put option; the latter is similar to buying a call option.

Spreads involve either taking a position in two or more calls or taking a position in two or more puts. A bull spread can be created by buying a call (put) with a low strike price and selling a call (put) with a high strike price. A bear spread can be created by buying a put (call) with a high strike price and selling a put (call) with a low strike price. A butterfly spread involves buying calls (puts) with a low and high strike price and selling two calls (puts) with some intermediate strike price. A calendar spread involves selling a call (put) with a short time to expiration and buying a call (put) with a longer time to expiration. A diagonal spread involves a long position in one option and a short position in another option such that both the strike price and the expiration date are different.

Combinations involve taking a position in both calls and puts on the same stock. A straddle combination involves taking a long position in a call and a long position in a put with the same strike price and expiration date. A strip consists of a long position in one call and two puts with the same strike price and expiration date. A strap consists of a long position in two calls and one put with the same strike price and expiration date. A strangle consists of a long position in a call and a put with different strike prices and the same expiration date. There are many other ways in which options can be used to produce interesting payoffs. It is not surprising that option trading has steadily increased in popularity and continues to fascinate investors.

FURTHER READING

Bharadwaj, A., and J. B. Wiggins. "Box Spread and Put–Call Parity Tests for the S&P Index LEAPS Markets," *Journal of Derivatives*, 8, 4 (Summer 2001): 62–71.

Chaput, J. S., and L. H. Ederington. "Option Spread and Combination Trading," *Journal of Derivatives*, 10, 4 (Summer 2003): 70–88.

McMillan, L. G. *McMillan on Options*, 2nd edn. Hoboken, NJ: Wiley, 2004.

Rendleman, R. J. "Covered Call Writing from an Expected Utility Perspective," *Journal of Derivatives*, 8, 3 (Spring 2001): 63–75.

Ronn, A. G., and E. I. Ronn. "The Box-Spread Arbitrage Conditions," *Review of Financial Studies*, 2, 1 (1989): 91–108.

Quiz (Answers at End of Book)

11.1. What is meant by a protective put? What position in call options is equivalent to a protective put?

11.2. Explain two ways in which a bear spread can be created.

11.3. When is it appropriate for an investor to purchase a butterfly spread?

11.4. Call options on a stock are available with strike prices of \$15, \$$17\frac{1}{2}$, and \$20 and expiration dates in three months. Their prices are \$4, \$2, and \$$\frac{1}{2}$, respectively. Explain how the options can be used to create a butterfly spread. Construct a table showing how profit varies with stock price for the butterfly spread.

11.5. What trading strategy creates a reverse calendar spread?

11.6. What is the difference between a strangle and a straddle?

11.7. A call option with a strike price of \$50 costs \$2. A put option with a strike price of \$45 costs \$3. Explain how a strangle can be created from these two options. What is the pattern of profits from the strangle?

Practice Questions (Answers in Solutions Manual/Study Guide)

11.8. Use put–call parity to relate the initial investment for a bull spread created using calls to the initial investment for a bull spread created using puts.

11.9. Explain how an aggressive bear spread can be created using put options.

11.10. Suppose that put options on a stock with strike prices \$30 and \$35 cost \$4 and \$7, respectively. How can the options be used to create (a) a bull spread and (b) a bear spread? Construct a table that shows the profit and payoff for both spreads.

11.11. Use put–call parity to show that the cost of a butterfly spread created from European puts is identical to the cost of a butterfly spread created from European calls.

11.12. A call with a strike price of \$60 costs \$6. A put with the same strike price and expiration date costs \$4. Construct a table that shows the profit from a straddle. For what range of stock prices would the straddle lead to a loss?

11.13. Construct a table showing the payoff from a bull spread when puts with strike prices K_1 and K_2 are used ($K_2 > K_1$).

11.14. An investor believes that there will be a big jump in a stock price, but is uncertain as to the direction. Identify six different strategies the investor can follow and explain the differences among them.

11.15. How can a forward contract on a stock with a particular delivery price and delivery date be created from options?

11.16. "A box spread comprises four options. Two can be combined to create a long forward position and two can be combined to create a short forward position." Explain this statement.

11.17. What is the result if the strike price of the put is higher than the strike price of the call in a strangle?

11.18. One Australian dollar is currently worth \$0.64. A one-year butterfly spread is set up using European call options with strike prices of \$0.60, \$0.65, and \$0.70. The risk-free interest rates in the United States and Australia are 5% and 4%, respectively, and the volatility of the exchange rate is 15%. Use the DerivaGem software to calculate the cost of setting up the butterfly spread position. Show that the cost is the same if European put options are used instead of European call options.

11.19. An index provides a dividend yield of 1% and has a volatility of 20%. The risk-free interest rate is 4%. How long does a principal-protected note, created as in Example 11.1, have to last for it to be profitable for the bank issuing it? Use DerivaGem.

Further Questions

11.20. A trader creates a bear spread by selling a six-month put option with a \$25 strike price for \$2.15 and buying a six-month put option with a \$29 strike price for \$4.75. What is the initial investment? What is the total payoff (excluding the initial investment) when the stock price in six months is (a) \$23, (b) \$28, and (c) \$33.

11.21. A trader sells a strangle by selling a European call option with a strike price of \$50 for \$3 and selling a European put option with a strike price of \$40 for \$4. For what range of prices of the underlying asset at maturity does the trader make a profit?

11.22. Three put options on a stock have the same expiration date and strike prices of \$55, \$60, and \$65. The market prices are \$3, \$5, and \$8, respectively. Explain how a butterfly spread can be created. Construct a table showing the profit from the strategy. For what range of stock prices would the butterfly spread lead to a loss?

11.23. A diagonal spread is created by buying a call with strike price K_2 and exercise date T_2 and selling a call with strike price K_1 and exercise date T_1 ($T_2 > T_1$). Draw a diagram showing the value of the spread at time T_1 when (a) $K_2 > K_1$ and (b) $K_2 < K_1$.

11.24. Draw a diagram showing the variation of an investor's profit and loss with the terminal stock price for a portfolio consisting of:
(a) One share and a short position in one call option
(b) Two shares and a short position in one call option
(c) One share and a short position in two call options
(d) One share and a short position in four call options.

In each case, assume the call option has an exercise price equal to the current stock price.

11.25. Suppose that the price of a non-dividend-paying stock is \$32, its volatility is 30%, and the risk-free rate for all maturities is 5% per annum. Use DerivaGem to calculate the cost of setting up the following positions. In each case provide a table showing the relationship between profit and final stock price. Ignore the impact of discounting.
(a) A bull spread using European call options with strike prices of \$25 and \$30 and a maturity of six months
(b) A bear spread using European put options with strike prices of \$25 and \$30 and a maturity of six months
(c) A butterfly spread using European call options with strike prices of \$25, \$30, and \$35 and a maturity of one year
(d) A butterfly spread using European put options with strike prices of \$25, \$30, and \$35 and a maturity of one year
(e) A straddle using options with a strike price of \$30 and a six-month maturity
(f) A strangle using options with strike prices of \$25 and \$35 and a six-month maturity.

11.26. What trading position is created from a long strangle and a short straddle when both have the same time to maturity? Assume that the strike price in the straddle is halfway between the two strike prices of the strangle.

11.27. Describe the trading position created in which a call option is bought with strike price K_2 and a put option is sold with strike price K_1 when both have the same time to maturity and $K_2 > K_1$. What does the position become when $K_1 = K_2$?

11.28. A bank decides to create a five-year principal-protected note on a non-dividend-paying stock by offering investors a zero-coupon bond plus a bull spread created from calls. The risk-free rate is 4% and the stock price volatility is 25%. The low-strike-price option in the bull spread is at the money. What is the maximum ratio of the high strike price to the low strike price in the bull spread. Use DerivaGem.

CHAPTER 12 Introduction to Binomial Trees

A useful and very popular technique for pricing an option involves constructing a *binomial tree*. This is a diagram that represents different possible paths that might be followed by the stock price over the life of the option. In this chapter we will take a first look at binomial trees and their relationship to an important principle known as risk-neutral valuation. The general approach adopted here is similar to that in an influential paper published by Cox, Ross, and Rubinstein in 1979.

The material in this chapter is important for a number of reasons. First, it explains the nature of the no-arbitrage arguments that are used for valuing options. Second, it explains the binomial tree numerical procedure that is widely used for valuing American options and other derivatives. Third, it introduces a very important principle, known as risk-neutral valuation.

The price of a European option given by the binomial tree numerical procedure converges to the price given by the famous Black–Scholes–Merton model as the number of steps converges to infinity. The proof of this is sketched out in the appendix to this chapter. The binomial tree numerical procedure is developed further in Chapter 18 and the Black–Scholes–Merton model is discussed further in Chapter 13.

12.1 A ONE-STEP BINOMIAL MODEL AND A NO-ARBITRAGE ARGUMENT

We start by considering a very simple situation. A stock price is currently \$20, and it is known that at the end of three months it will be either \$22 or \$18. We are interested in valuing a European call option to buy the stock for \$21 in three months. This option will have one of two values at the end of the three months. If the stock price turns out to be \$22, the value of the option will be \$1; if the stock price turns out to be \$18, the value of the option will be zero. The situation is illustrated in Figure 12.1.

It turns out that a relatively simple argument can be used to price the option in this example. The only assumption needed is that arbitrage opportunities do not exist. We set up a portfolio of the stock and the option in such a way that there is no uncertainty about the value of the portfolio at the end of the three months. We then argue that, because the portfolio has no risk, the return it earns must equal the risk-free interest

From Chapter 12 of *Fundamentals of Futures and Options Markets*, Eighth Edition. John C. Hull.

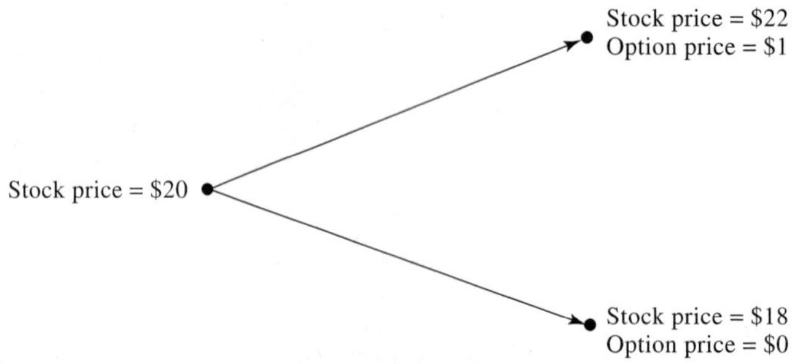

Figure 12.1 Stock price movements in numerical example

rate. This enables us to work out the cost of setting up the portfolio and therefore the option's price. Because there are two securities (the stock and the stock option) and only two possible outcomes, it is always possible to set up the riskless portfolio.

Consider a portfolio consisting of a long position in Δ shares of the stock and a short position in one call option. (Δ is the capital Greek letter "delta.") We calculate the value of Δ that makes the portfolio riskless. If the stock price moves up from \$20 to \$22, the value of the shares is 22Δ and the value of the option is 1, so that the total value of the portfolio is $22\Delta - 1$. If the stock price moves down from \$20 to \$18, the value of the shares is 18Δ and the value of the option is zero, so that the total value of the portfolio is 18Δ. The portfolio is riskless if the value of Δ is chosen so that the final value of the portfolio is the same for both alternatives. This means

$$22\Delta - 1 = 18\Delta$$

or

$$\Delta = 0.25$$

A riskless portfolio is therefore

Long: 0.25 shares

Short: 1 option

If the stock price moves up to \$22, the value of the portfolio is

$$22 \times 0.25 - 1 = 4.5$$

If the stock price moves down to \$18, the value of the portfolio is

$$18 \times 0.25 = 4.5$$

Regardless of whether the stock price moves up or down, the value of the portfolio is always 4.5 at the end of the life of the option. This shows that Δ (delta) is the number of shares necessary to hedge a short position in one option. It will be discussed further later in this chapter and in Chapter 17.

Riskless portfolios must, in the absence of arbitrage opportunities, earn the risk-free rate of interest. Suppose that in this case the risk-free rate is 12% per annum. It follows that the value of the portfolio today must be the present value of 4.5, or

$$4.5e^{-0.12\times 3/12} = 4.367$$

The value of the stock price today is known to be \$20. Suppose the option price is denoted by f. The value of the portfolio today is

$$20 \times 0.25 - f = 5 - f$$

It follows that

$$5 - f = 4.367$$

or

$$f = 0.633$$

This shows that, in the absence of arbitrage opportunities, the current value of the option must be 0.633. If the value of the option were more than 0.633, the portfolio would cost less than 4.367 to set up and would earn more than the risk-free rate. If the value of the option were less than 0.633, shorting the portfolio would provide a way of borrowing money at less than the risk-free rate.

A Generalization

We can generalize the no-arbitrage argument just presented by considering a stock whose price is S_0 and an option on the stock (or any derivative dependent on the stock) whose current price is f. We suppose that the option lasts for time T and that during the life of the option the stock price can either move up from S_0 to a new level, S_0u, or down from S_0 to a new level, S_0d ($u > 1$; $d < 1$). The proportional increase in the stock price when there is an up movement is $u - 1$; the proportional decrease when there is a down movement is $1 - d$. If the stock price moves up to S_0u, we suppose that the payoff from the option is f_u; if the stock price moves down to S_0d, we suppose the payoff from the option is f_d. The situation is illustrated in Figure 12.2.

As before, we imagine a portfolio consisting of a long position in Δ shares and a short position in one option. We calculate the value of Δ that makes the portfolio riskless. If there is an up movement in the stock price, the value of the portfolio at the end of the life of the option is

$$S_0u\Delta - f_u$$

If there is a down movement in the stock price, the value becomes

$$S_0d\Delta - f_d$$

The two are equal when

$$S_0u\Delta - f_u = S_0d\Delta - f_d$$

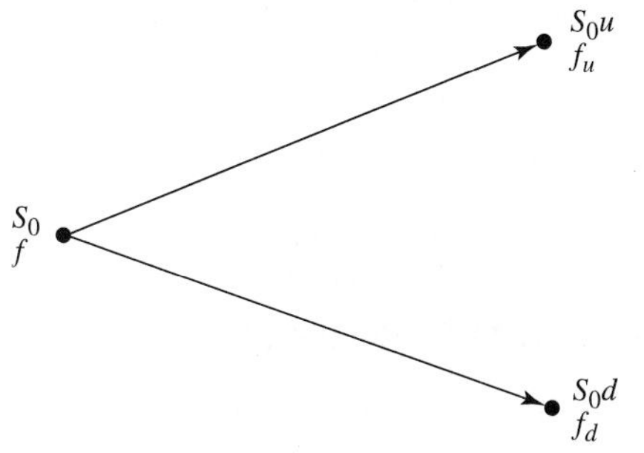

Figure 12.2 Stock and option prices in a general one-step tree

or

$$\Delta = \frac{f_u - f_d}{S_0 u - S_0 d} \tag{12.1}$$

In this case, the portfolio is riskless and for there to be no arbitrage opportunities it must earn the risk-free interest rate. Equation (12.1) shows that Δ is the ratio of the change in the option price to the change in the stock price as we move between the nodes at time T.

If we denote the risk-free interest rate by r, the present value of the portfolio is

$$(S_0 u\Delta - f_u)e^{-rT}$$

The cost of setting up the portfolio is

$$S_0\Delta - f$$

It follows that

$$S_0\Delta - f = (S_0 u\Delta - f_u)e^{-rT}$$

or

$$f = S_0\Delta(1 - ue^{-rT}) + f_u e^{-rT}$$

Substituting from equation (12.1) for Δ, we obtain

$$f = S_0\left(\frac{f_u - f_d}{S_0 u - S_0 d}\right)(1 - ue^{-rT}) + f_u e^{-rT}$$

or

$$f = \frac{f_u(1 - de^{-rT}) + f_d(ue^{-rT} - 1)}{u - d}$$

or

$$f = e^{-rT}[pf_u + (1 - p)f_d] \tag{12.2}$$

where

$$p = \frac{e^{rT} - d}{u - d} \tag{12.3}$$

Equations (12.2) and (12.3) enable an option to be priced when stock price movements are given by a one-step binomial model. The only assumption needed is that there are no arbitrage opportunities in the market.

In the numerical example considered previously (see Figure 12.1), $u = 1.1$, $d = 0.9$, $r = 0.12$, $T = 0.25$, $f_u = 1$, and $f_d = 0$. From equation (12.3),

$$p = \frac{e^{0.12\times 3/12} - 0.9}{1.1 - 0.9} = 0.6523$$

and, from equation (12.2),

$$f = e^{-0.12\times 0.25}(0.6523 \times 1 + 0.3477 \times 0) = 0.633$$

The result agrees with the answer obtained earlier in this section.

Irrelevance of the Stock's Expected Return

The option pricing formula in equation (12.2) does not involve the probabilities of the stock price moving up or down. For example, we get the same option price when the probability of an upward movement is 0.5 as we do when it is 0.9. This is surprising and seems counterintuitive. It is natural to assume that as the probability of an upward movement in the stock price increases, the value of a call option on the stock increases and the value of a put option on the stock decreases. This is not the case.

The key reason is that we are not valuing the option in absolute terms. We are calculating its value in terms of the price of the underlying stock. The probabilities of future up or down movements are already incorporated into the price of the stock. It turns out that we do not need to take them into account again when valuing the option in terms of the stock price.

12.2 RISK-NEUTRAL VALUATION

We are now in a position to introduce a very important principle in the pricing of derivatives known as *risk-neutral valuation*. This states that, when valuing a derivative, we can make the assumption that investors are *risk-neutral*. This assumption means investors do not increase the expected return they require from an investment to compensate for increased risk. A world where investors are risk-neutral is referred to as a *risk-neutral world*. The world we live in is, of course, not a risk-neutral world. The higher the risks investors take, the higher the expected returns they require. However, it turns out that assuming a risk-neutral world gives us the right option price for the world we live in, as well as for a risk-neutral world. Almost miraculously, it finesses the problem that we know hardly anything about the risk aversion of the buyers and sellers of options.

Risk-neutral valuation seems a surprising result when it is first encountered. Options are risky investments. Should not a person's risk preferences affect how they are priced? The answer is that, when we are pricing an option in terms of the price of the underlying stock, risk preferences are unimportant. As investors become more risk-averse, stock prices decline, but the formulas relating option prices to stock prices remain the same.

A risk-neutral world has two features that simplify the pricing of derivatives:

1. The expected return on a stock (or any other investment) is the risk-free rate.
2. The discount rate used for the expected payoff on an option (or any other instrument) is the risk-free rate.

Returning to equation (12.2), the parameter p should be interpreted as the probability of an up movement in a risk-neutral world, so that $1 - p$ is the probability of a down movement in this world. The expression

$$pf_u + (1 - p)f_d$$

is the expected future payoff from the option in a risk-neutral world and equation (12.2) states that the value of the option today is its expected future payoff in a risk-neutral world discounted at the risk-free rate. This is an application of risk-neutral valuation.

To prove the validity of our interpretation of p, we note that, when p is the probability of an up movement, the expected stock price $E(S_T)$ at time T is given by

$$E(S_T) = pS_0u + (1 - p)S_0d$$

or

$$E(S_T) = pS_0(u - d) + S_0d$$

Substituting from equation (12.3) for p gives

$$E(S_T) = S_0e^{rT} \tag{12.4}$$

This shows that the stock price grows, on average, at the risk-free rate when p is the probability of an up movement. In other words, the stock price behaves exactly as we would expect it to behave in a risk-neutral world when p is the probability of an up movement.

Risk-neutral valuation is a very important general result in the pricing of derivatives. It states that, when we assume the world is risk-neutral, we get the right price for a derivative in all worlds, not just in a risk-neutral one. We have shown that risk-neutral valuation is correct when a simple binomial model is assumed for how the price of the the stock evolves. It can be shown that the result is true regardless of the assumptions we make about the evolution of the stock price.

To apply risk-neutral valuation to the pricing of a derivative, we first calculate what the probabilities of different outcomes would be if the world were risk-neutral. We then calculate the expected payoff from the derivative and discount that expected payoff at the risk-free rate of interest.

The One-Step Binomial Example Revisited

We now return to the example in Figure 12.1 and show that risk-neutral valuation gives the same answer as no-arbitrage arguments. In Figure 12.1, the stock price is currently \$20 and will move either up to \$22 or down to \$18 at the end of three months. The option considered is a European call option with a strike price of \$21 and an expiration date in three months. The risk-free interest rate is 12% per annum.

We define p as the probability of an upward movement in the stock price in a risk-neutral world. We can calculate p from equation (12.3). Alternatively, we can argue that the expected return on the stock in a risk-neutral world must be the risk-free rate of 12%. This means that p must satisfy

$$22p + 18(1 - p) = 20e^{0.12\times3/12}$$

or

$$4p = 20e^{0.12\times3/12} - 18$$

That is, p must be 0.6523.

At the end of the three months, the call option has a 0.6523 probability of being worth 1 and a 0.3477 probability of being worth zero. Its expected value is therefore

$$0.6523 \times 1 + 0.3477 \times 0 = 0.6523$$

In a risk-neutral world this should be discounted at the risk-free rate. The value of the option today is therefore

$$0.6523e^{-0.12\times3/12}$$

or \$0.633. This is the same as the value obtained earlier, demonstrating that no-arbitrage arguments and risk-neutral valuation give the same answer.

Real World vs. Risk-Neutral World

It should be emphasized that p is the probability of an up movement in a risk-neutral world. In general this is not the same as the probability of an up movement in the real world. In our example $p = 0.6523$. When the probability of an up movement is 0.6523, the expected return on both the stock and the option is the risk-free rate of 12%. Suppose that in the real world the expected return on the stock is 16%, and q is the probability of an up movement in the real world. It follows that

$$22q + 18(1 - q) = 20e^{0.16\times 3/12}$$

so that $q = 0.7041$.

The expected payoff from the option in the real world is then

$$q \times 1 + (1 - q) \times 0$$

or 0.7041. Unfortunately, it is not easy to know the correct discount rate to apply to the expected payoff in the real world. The return the market requires on the stock is 16% and this is the discount rate that would be used for the expected cash flows from an investment in the stock. A position in a call option is riskier than a position in the stock. As a result, the discount rate to be applied to the payoff from a call option is greater than 16%, but we do not know how much greater than 16% it should be.[1] Using risk-neutral valuation is convenient because we know that in a risk-neutral world the expected return on all assets (and therefore the discount rate to use for all expected payoffs) is the risk-free rate.

12.3 TWO-STEP BINOMIAL TREES

We can extend the analysis to a two-step binomial tree such as that shown in Figure 12.3. Here the stock price starts at \$20 and in each of two time steps may go up by 10% or down by 10%. Each time step is three months long and the risk-free interest rate is 12% per annum. We consider a six-month option with a strike price of \$21.

The objective of the analysis is to calculate the option price at the initial node of the tree. This can be done by repeatedly applying the principles established earlier in the chapter. Figure 12.4 shows the same tree as Figure 12.3, but with both the stock price and the option price at each node. (The stock price is the upper number and the option price the lower.) The option prices at the final nodes of the tree are easily calculated. They are the payoffs from the option. At node D the stock price is 24.2 and the option price is $24.2 - 21 = 3.2$; at nodes E and F the option is out of the money and its value is zero.

At node C the option price is zero, because node C leads to either node E or node F and at both of these nodes the option price is zero. We calculate the option price at node B by focusing our attention on the part of the tree shown in Figure 12.5. Using the notation introduced earlier in the chapter, $u = 1.1$, $d = 0.9$, $r = 0.12$, and $T = 0.25$, so

[1] Because we know the correct value of the option is 0.633, we can deduce that the correct discount rate is 42.58%. This is because $0.633 = 0.7041e^{-0.4258\times 3/12}$.

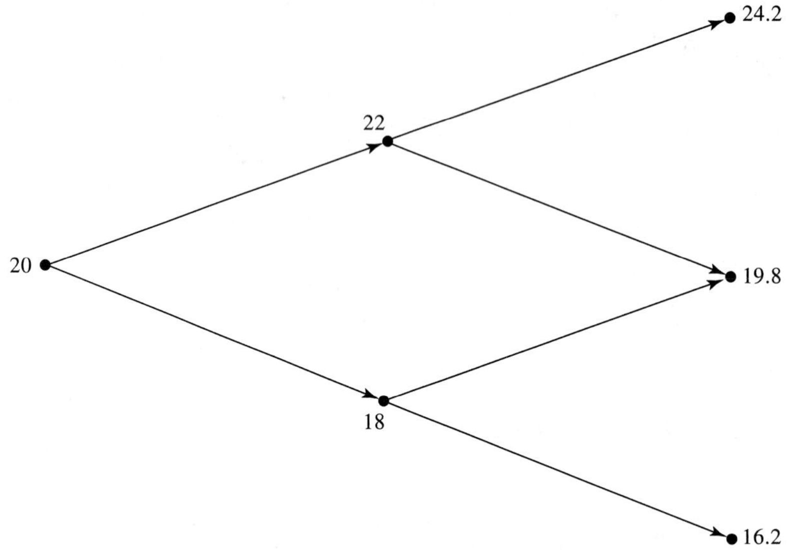

Figure 12.3 Stock prices in a two-step tree

that $p = 0.6523$ and equation (12.2) gives the value of the option at node B as

$$e^{-0.12\times 3/12}(0.6523 \times 3.2 + 0.3477 \times 0) = 2.0257$$

It remains for us to calculate the option price at the initial node A. We do so by focusing on the first step of the tree. We know that the value of the option at node B is 2.0257 and

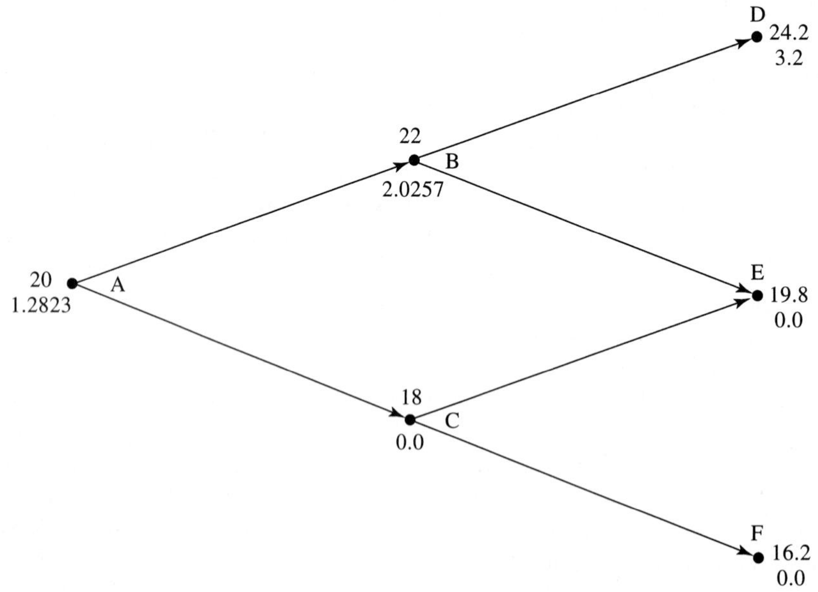

Figure 12.4 Stock and option prices in a two-step tree. The upper number at each node is the stock price; the lower number is the option price

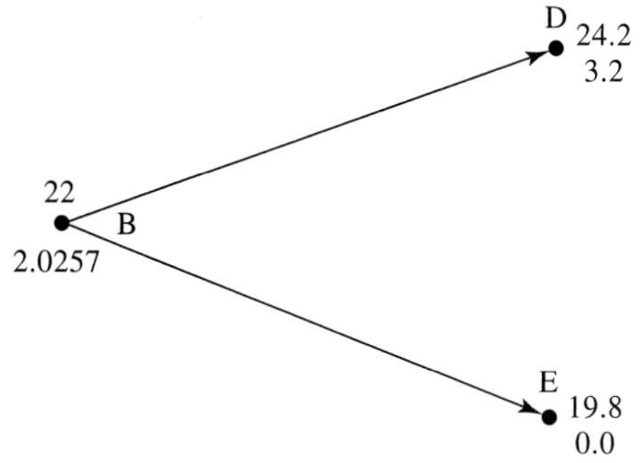

Figure 12.5 Evaluation of option price at node B of Figure 12.4

that at node C it is zero. Equation (11.2) therefore gives the value at node A as

$$e^{-0.12\times 3/12}(0.6523 \times 2.0257 + 0.3477 \times 0) = 1.2823$$

The value of the option is \$1.2823.

Note that this example was constructed so that u and d (the proportional up and down movements) were the same at each node of the tree and so that the time steps were of the same length. As a result, the risk-neutral probability, p, as calculated by equation (12.3) is the same at each node.

A Generalization

We can generalize the case of two time steps by considering the situation in Figure 12.6. The stock price is initially S_0. During each time step, it either moves up to u times its

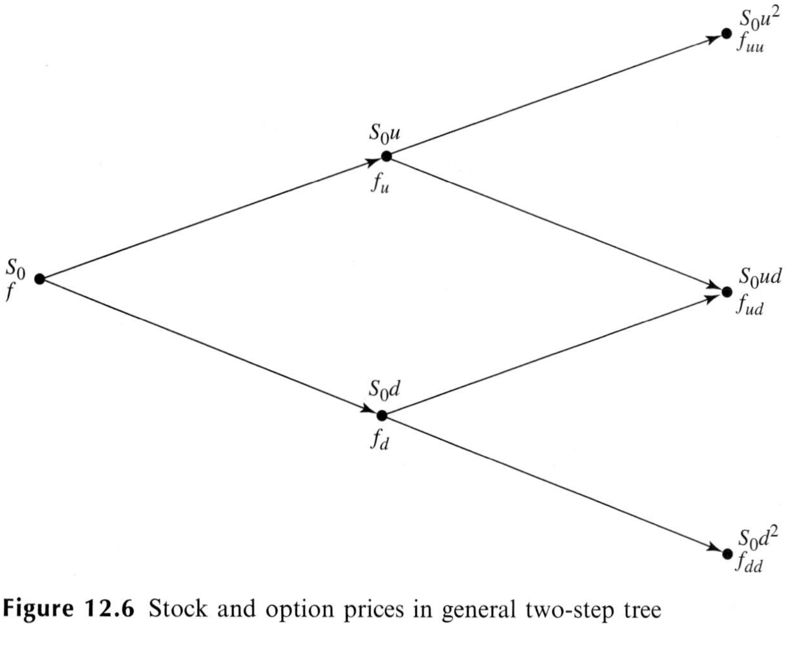

Figure 12.6 Stock and option prices in general two-step tree

initial value or moves down to d times its initial value. The notation for the value of the option is shown on the tree. (For example, after two up movements the value of the option is f_{uu}.) We suppose that the risk-free interest rate is r and the length of the time step is Δt years.

Because the length of a time step is now Δt rather than T, equations (12.2) and (12.3) become

$$f = e^{-r\Delta t}[pf_u + (1-p)f_d] \tag{12.5}$$

$$p = \frac{e^{r\Delta t} - d}{u - d} \tag{12.6}$$

Repeated application of equation (12.5) gives

$$f_u = e^{-r\Delta t}[pf_{uu} + (1-p)f_{ud}] \tag{12.7}$$

$$f_d = e^{-r\Delta t}[pf_{ud} + (1-p)f_{dd}] \tag{12.8}$$

$$f = e^{-r\Delta t}[pf_u + (1-p)f_d] \tag{12.9}$$

Substituting from equations (12.7) and (12.8) into (12.9), we get

$$f = e^{-2r\Delta t}[p^2 f_{uu} + 2p(1-p)f_{ud} + (1-p)^2 f_{dd}] \tag{12.10}$$

This is consistent with the principle of risk-neutral valuation mentioned earlier. The variables p^2, $2p(1-p)$, and $(1-p)^2$ are the probabilities that the upper, middle, and lower final nodes will be reached. The option price is equal to its expected payoff in a risk-neutral world discounted at the risk-free interest rate.

As we add more steps to the binomial tree, the risk-neutral valuation principle continues to hold. The option price is always equal to its expected payoff in a risk-neutral world, discounted at the risk-free interest rate.

12.4 A PUT EXAMPLE

The procedures described in this chapter can be used to price puts as well as calls. Consider a two-year European put with a strike price of \$52 on a stock whose current price is \$50. We suppose that there are two time steps of one year, and in each time step the stock price either moves up by a proportional amount of 20% or moves down by a proportional amount of 20%. We also suppose that the risk-free interest rate is 5%.

The tree is shown in Figure 12.7. In this case, $u = 1.2$, $d = 0.8$, $\Delta t = 1$, and $r = 0.05$. From equation (12.6), the value of the risk-neutral probability, p, is given by

$$p = \frac{e^{0.05\times 1} - 0.8}{1.2 - 0.8} = 0.6282$$

The possible final stock prices are: \$72, \$48, and \$32. In this case, $f_{uu} = 0$, $f_{ud} = 4$, and $f_{dd} = 20$. From equation (12.10),

$$f = e^{-2\times 0.05\times 1}(0.6282^2 \times 0 + 2 \times 0.6282 \times 0.3718 \times 4 + 0.3718^2 \times 20) = 4.1923$$

The value of the put is \$4.1923. This result can also be obtained using equation (12.5)

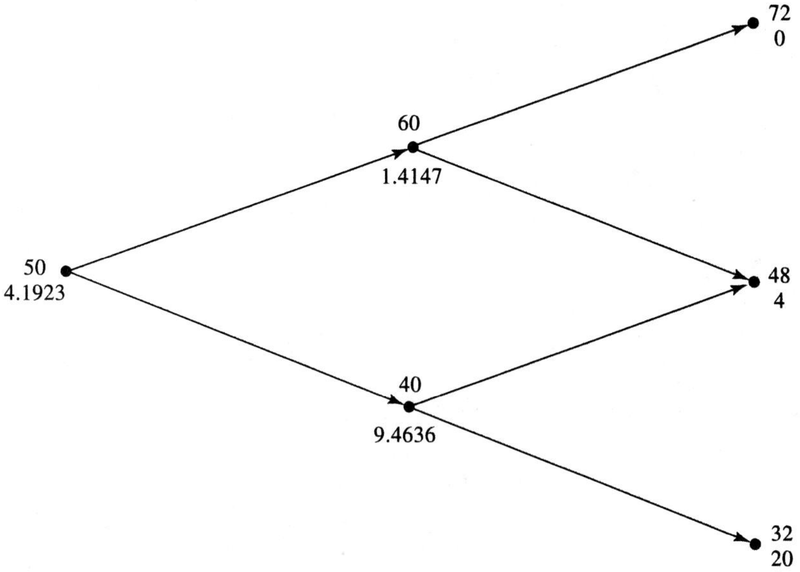

Figure 12.7 Use of two-step tree to value European put option. At each node the upper number is the stock price; the lower number is the option price

and working back through the tree one step at a time. Figure 12.7 shows the intermediate option prices that are calculated.

12.5 AMERICAN OPTIONS

Up to now all the options we have considered have been European. We now move on to consider how American options can be valued using binomial trees such as those in Figures 12.4 and 12.7. The procedure is to work back through the tree from the end to the beginning, testing at each node to see whether early exercise is optimal. The value of the option at the final nodes is the same as for the European option. At earlier nodes the value of the option is the greater of:

1. The value given by equation (12.5)
2. The payoff from early exercise.

Figure 12.8 shows how Figure 12.7 is affected if the option considered is American rather than European. The stock prices and their probabilities are unchanged. The values for the option at the final nodes are also unchanged. At node B, equation (12.2) gives the value of the option as 1.4147, whereas the payoff from early exercise is negative (= −8). Clearly early exercise is not optimal at node B, and the value of the option at this node is 1.4147. At node C, equation (12.5) gives the value of the option as 9.4636, whereas the payoff from early exercise is 12. In this case, early exercise is optimal and the value of the option at the node is 12. At the initial node A, the value given by equation (12.5) is

$$e^{-0.05\times 1}(0.6282 \times 1.4147 + 0.3718 \times 12.0) = 5.0894$$

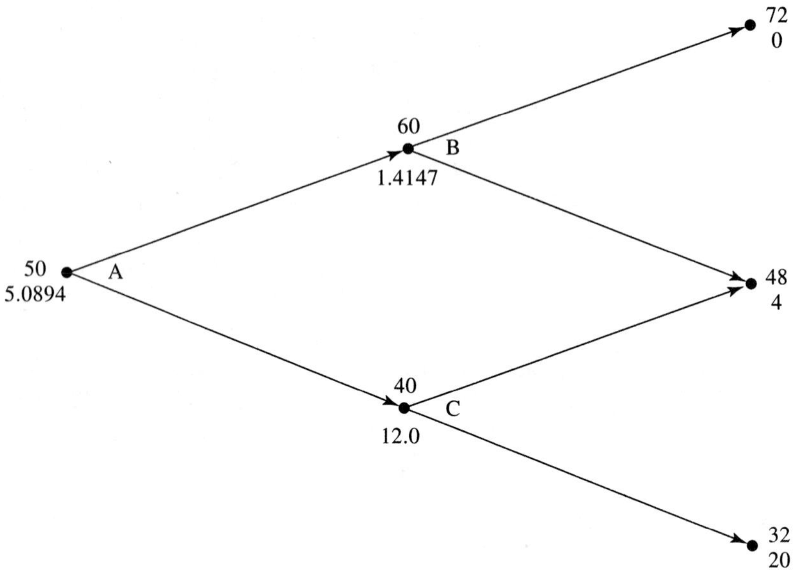

Figure 12.8 Use of two-step tree to value American put option. At each node the upper number is the stock price; the lower number is the option price

and the payoff from early exercise is 2. In this case, early exercise is not optimal. The value of the option is therefore \$5.0894.

12.6 DELTA

At this stage, it is appropriate to introduce *delta*, an important parameter (sometimes referred to as a "Greek letter" or "Greek") in the pricing and hedging of options.

The delta (Δ) of a stock option is the ratio of the change in the price of the stock option to the change in the price of the underlying stock. It is the number of units of the stock we should hold for each option shorted in order to create a riskless portfolio. It is the same as the Δ introduced earlier in this chapter. The construction of a riskless portfolio is sometimes referred to as *delta hedging*. The delta of a call option is positive, whereas the delta of a put option is negative.

From Figure 12.1, we can calculate the value of the delta of the call option being considered as

$$\frac{1-0}{22-18} = 0.25$$

This is because, when the stock price changes from \$18 to \$22, the option price changes from \$0 to \$1. (This is also the value of Δ calculated in Section 12.1.)

In Figure 12.4, the delta corresponding to stock price movements over the first time step is

$$\frac{2.0257-0}{22-18} = 0.5064$$

The delta for stock price movements over the second time step is

$$\frac{3.2 - 0}{24.2 - 19.8} = 0.7273$$

if there is an upward movement over the first time step, and

$$\frac{0 - 0}{19.8 - 16.2} = 0$$

if there is a downward movement over the first time step.

From Figure 12.7, delta is

$$\frac{1.4147 - 9.4636}{60 - 40} = -0.4024$$

at the end of the first time step and either

$$\frac{0 - 4}{72 - 48} = -0.1667 \quad \text{or} \quad \frac{4 - 20}{48 - 32} = -1.0000$$

at the end of the second time step.

The two-step examples show that delta changes over time. (In Figure 12.4, delta changes from 0.5064 to either 0.7273 or 0; in Figure 12.7, it changes from −0.4024 to either −0.1667 or −1.0000.) Thus, in order to maintain a riskless hedge using an option and the underlying stock, we need to adjust our holdings in the stock periodically. We will return to this feature of options in Chapters 13 and 17.

12.7 DETERMINING u AND d

Up to now we have assumed values for u and d. For example, in Figure 12.8, we assumed that $u = 1.2$ and $d = 0.8$. In practice, u and d are determined from the stock price volatility, σ. The formulas are

$$u = e^{\sigma\sqrt{\Delta t}} \tag{12.11}$$

$$d = \frac{1}{u} \tag{12.12}$$

where Δt is the length of one time step on the tree. These formulas will be explained further in Chapter 18. The complete set of equations defining the tree are equation (12.11) and equation (12.12), together with equation (12.6), which can be written

$$p = \frac{a - d}{u - d} \tag{12.13}$$

where

$$a = e^{r\Delta t} \tag{12.14}$$

Consider again the American put option in Figure 12.8, where the stock price is \$50, the strike price is \$52, the risk-free rate is 5%, the life of the option is two years, and there

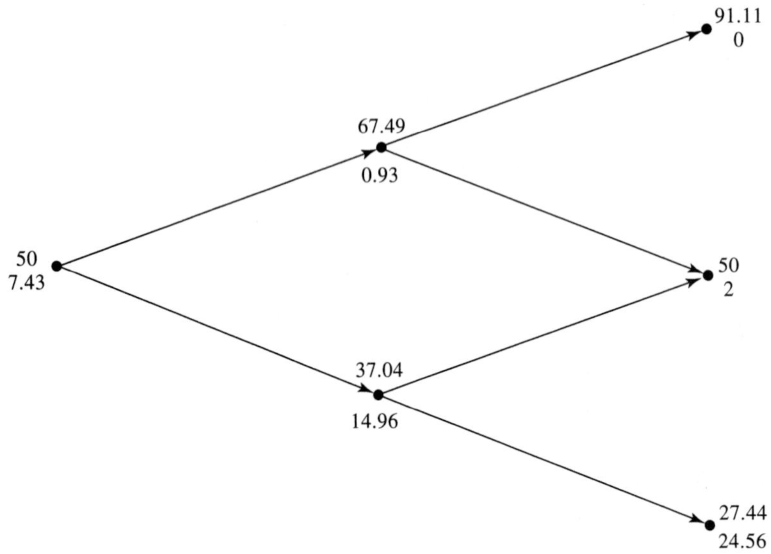

Figure 12.9 Two-step tree to value a two-year American put option when stock price is 50, strike price is 52, risk-free rate is 5%, and volatility is 30%

are two time steps. In this case, $\Delta t = 1$. Suppose that the volatility σ is 30%. Then, from equations (12.11) to (12.14), we have

$$u = e^{0.3\times 1} = 1.3499$$

$$d = \frac{1}{1.3499} = 0.7408$$

$$a = e^{0.05\times 1} = 1.0513$$

and

$$p = \frac{1.053 - 0.7408}{1.3499 - 0.7408} = 0.5097$$

The tree is shown in Figure 12.9. The value of the option is 7.43. (This is different from the value obtained in Figure 12.8 by assuming $u = 1.2$ and $d = 0.8$.) Note that the option is exercised at the end of the first step if the lower node is reached.

12.8 INCREASING THE NUMBER OF TIME STEPS

The binomial models presented so far have been unrealistically simple. Clearly an analyst can expect to obtain only a very rough approximation to an option price by assuming that stock price movements during the life of the option consist of one or two binomial steps.

When binomial trees are used in practice, the life of the option is typically divided into 30 or more time steps. In each time step there is a binomial stock price movement. With 30 time steps, there are 31 terminal stock prices and 2^{30}, or about 1 billion, possible stock price paths are implicitly considered.

The equations defining the tree are equations (12.11) to (12.14), regardless of the number of time steps. Suppose, for example, that there are five steps instead of two in the example we considered in Figure 12.9. The parameters would be $\Delta t = 2/5 = 0.4$, $r = 0.05$, and $\sigma = 0.3$. These give $u = e^{0.3\times\sqrt{0.4}} = 1.2089$, $d = 1/1.2089 = 0.8272$, $a = e^{0.05\times 0.4} = 1.0202$, and $p = (1.0202 - 0.8272)/(1.2089 - 0.8272) = 0.5056$.

As the number of time steps is increased (so that Δt becomes smaller), the binomial model makes the same assumptions about stock price behavior as the Black–Scholes–Merton model presented in the next chapter. As shown in the appendix to this chapter, the price given by the binomial model converges to the Black–Scholes–Merton price.

12.9 USING DerivaGem

The software accompanying this book, DerivaGem, is a useful tool for becoming comfortable with binomial trees. After loading the software in the way described at the end of this book, go to the Equity_FX_Index_Futures_Options worksheet. Choose Equity as the Underlying Type and select Binomial American as the Option Type. Enter the stock price, volatility, risk-free rate, time to expiration, exercise price, and tree steps as 50, 30%, 5%, 2, 52, and 2, respectively. Click on the *Put* button and then on *Calculate*. The price of the option is shown as 7.428 in the box labeled Price. Now click on *Display Tree* and you will see the equivalent of Figure 12.9. (The red numbers indicate the nodes where the option is exercised.)

Return to the Equity_FX_Index_Futures_Options worksheet and change the number of time steps to 5. Hit *Enter* and click on *Calculate*. You will find that the value of the option changes to 7.671. By clicking on *Display Tree* the five-step tree is displayed together with the values of u, d, a, and p we have just calculated.

DerivaGem can display trees that have up to 10 steps, but the calculations can be done for up to 500 steps. In our example, 500 steps gives the option price (to two decimal places) as 7.47. This is an accurate answer. By changing the Option Type to Binomial European, we can use the tree to value a European option. Using 500 time steps, the value of a European option with the same parameters as the American option is 6.76. (By changing the option type to Black–Scholes European, we can display the value of the option using the Black–Scholes–Merton formula that will be presented in the next chapter. This is also 6.76.) By changing the Underlying Type, we can consider options on assets other than stocks. We will now discuss these types of option.

12.10 OPTIONS ON OTHER ASSETS

We introduced options on indices, currencies, and futures contracts in Chapter 9 and will cover them in more detail in Chapters 15 and 16. It turns out that we can construct and use binomial trees for these options in exactly the same way as for options on stocks except that the equations for p change. As in the case of options on stocks, equation (12.2) applies so that the value at a node (before the possibility of early exercise is considered) is p times the value if there is an up movement plus $1 - p$ times the value if there is a down movement, discounted at the risk-free rate.

Options on Stocks Paying a Continuous Dividend Yield

Consider first a stock paying a known dividend yield at rate q. The total return from dividends and capital gains in a risk-neutral world is r. The dividends provide a return of q. Capital gains must therefore provide a return of $r - q$. If the stock starts at S_0, its expected value after one time step of length Δt must be $S_0 e^{(r-q)\Delta t}$. This means that

$$pS_0 u + (1 - p)S_0 d = S_0 e^{(r-q)\Delta t}$$

so that

$$p = \frac{e^{(r-q)\Delta t} - d}{u - d}$$

As in the case of options on non-dividend-paying stocks, we match volatility by setting $u = e^{\sigma\sqrt{\Delta t}}$ and $d = 1/u$. This means that we can use equations (12.11) to (12.14) except that we set $a = e^{(r-q)\Delta t}$ instead of $a = e^{r\Delta t}$.

Options on Stock Indices

When calculating a futures price for a stock index in Chapter 5, we assumed that the stocks underlying the index provided a dividend yield at rate q. We make a similar assumption here. The valuation of an option on a stock index is therefore very similar to the valuation of an option on a stock paying a known dividend yield. Example 12.1 illustrates this.

Options on Currencies

As pointed out in Section 5.10, a foreign currency can be regarded as an asset providing a yield at the foreign risk-free rate of interest, r_f. By analogy with the stock index case, we can construct a tree for options on a currency by using equations (12.11) to (12.14) and setting $a = e^{(r-r_f)\Delta t}$. Example 12.2 illustrates this.

Options on Futures

It costs nothing to take a long or a short position in a futures contract. It follows that in a risk-neutral world a futures price should have an expected growth rate of zero. (We discuss this point in more detail in Chapter 16.) As above, we define p as the probability of an up movement in the futures price, u as the amount by which the price is multiplied in an up movement, and d as the amount by which it is multiplied in a down movement. If F_0 is the initial futures price, the expected futures price at the end of one time step of length Δt should also be F_0. This means that

$$pF_0 u + (1 - p)F_0 d = F_0$$

so that

$$p = \frac{1 - d}{u - d}$$

and we can use equations (12.11) to (12.14) with $a = 1$. Example 12.3 illustrates this.

Example 12.1 Option on a stock index

A stock index is currently 810 and has a volatility of 20% and a dividend yield of 2%. The risk-free rate is 5%. The figure below shows the output from DerivaGem for valuing a European six-month call option with a strike price of 800 using a two-step tree. In this case,

$$\Delta t = 0.25, \quad u = e^{0.20\times\sqrt{0.25}} = 1.1052, \quad d = 1/u = 0.9048,$$

$$a = e^{(0.05-0.02)\times 0.25} = 1.0075, \quad p = \frac{1.0075 - 0.9048}{1.1052 - 0.9048} = 0.5126$$

The value of the option is 53.39.

DerivaGem Output:

At each node:
Upper value = Underlying Asset Price
Lower value = Option Price
Shading indicates where option is exercised

Strike price = 800
Discount factor per step = 0.9876
Time step, dt = 0.2500 years, 91.25 days
Growth factor per step, a = 1.0075
Probability of up move, p = 0.5126
Up step size, u = 1.1052
Down step size, d = 0.9048

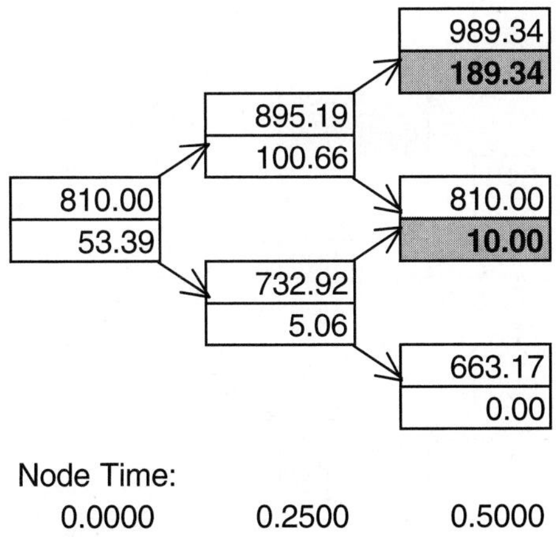

Example 12.2 Option on a foreign currency

The Australian dollar is currently worth 0.6100 U.S. dollars and this exchange rate has a volatility of 12%. The Australian risk-free rate is 7% and the U.S. risk-free rate is 5%. The figure below shows the output from DerivaGem for valuing a three-month American call option with a strike price of 0.6000 using a three-step tree. In this case,

$$\Delta t = 0.08333, \quad u = e^{0.12\times\sqrt{0.08333}} = 1.0352, \quad d = 1/u = 0.9660,$$

$$a = e^{(0.05-0.07)\times 0.08333} = 0.9983, \quad p = \frac{0.9983 - 0.9660}{1.0352 - 0.9660} = 0.4673$$

The value of the option is 0.019.

DerivaGem Output:

At each node:
Upper value = Underlying Asset Price
Lower value = Option Price
Shading indicates where option is exercised

Strike price = 0.6
Discount factor per step = 0.9958
Time step, dt = 0.0833 years, 30.42 days
Growth factor per step, a = 0.9983
Probability of up move, p = 0.4673
Up step size, u = 1.0352
Down step size, d = 0.9660

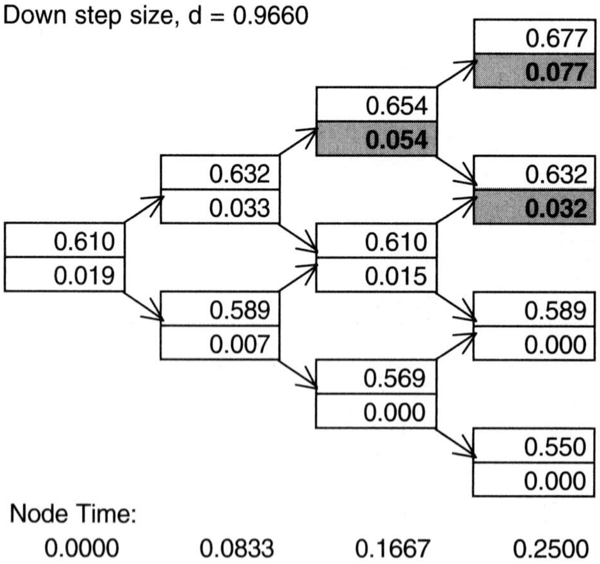

Example 12.3 Option on futures

A futures price is currently 31 and it has a volatility of 30%. The risk-free rate is 5%. The figure below shows the output from DerivaGem for valuing a nine-month American put option with a strike price of 30 using a three-step tree. In this case,

$$\Delta t = 0.25, \quad u = e^{0.3\sqrt{0.25}} = 1.1618, \quad d = 1/u = 1/1.1618 = 0.8607,$$

$$a = 1, \quad p = \frac{1 - 0.8607}{1.1618 - 0.8607} = 0.4626$$

The value of the option is 2.84.

DerivaGem Output:

At each node:
Upper value = Underlying Asset Price
Lower value = Option Price
Shading indicates where option is exercised

Strike price = 30
Discount factor per step = 0.9876
Time step, dt = 0.2500 years, 91.25 days
Growth factor per step, a = 1.000
Probability of up move, p = 0.4626
Up step size, u = 1.1618
Down step size, d = 0.8607

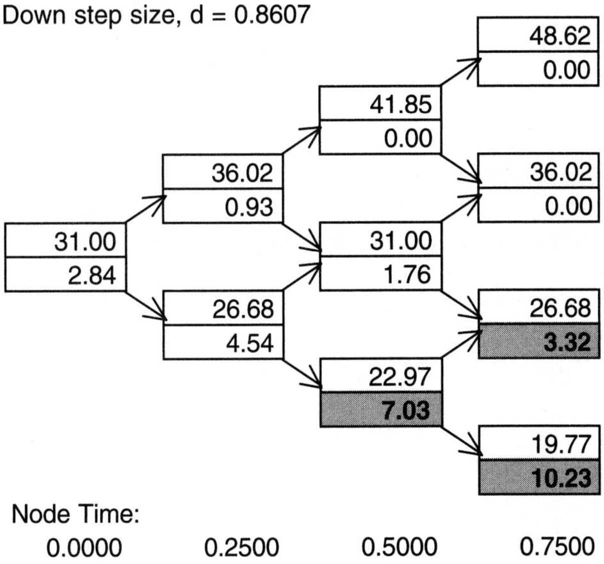

SUMMARY

This chapter has provided a first look at the valuation of options on stocks and other assets using trees. In the simple situation where movements in the price of a stock during the life of an option are governed by a one-step binomial tree, it is possible to set up a riskless portfolio consisting of a position in the stock option and a position in the stock. In a world with no arbitrage opportunities, riskless portfolios must earn the risk-free rate of interest. This enables the stock option to be priced in terms of the stock. It is interesting to note that no assumptions are required about the probabilities of up and down movements in the stock price at each node of the tree.

When stock price movements are governed by a multistep binomial tree, we can treat each binomial step separately and work back from the end of the life of the option to the beginning to obtain the current value of the option. Again only no-arbitrage arguments are used, and no assumptions are required about the probabilities of up and down movements in the stock price at each node.

An equivalent approach to valuing stock options involves risk-neutral valuation. This very important principle states that we can assume the world is risk neutral when valuing an option in terms of the underlying stock. This chapter has shown, through both numerical examples and algebra, that no-arbitrage arguments and risk-neutral valuation are equivalent and lead to the same option prices.

The delta of a stock option, Δ, considers the effect of a small change in the underlying stock price on the change in the option price. It is the ratio of the change in the option price to the change in the stock price. For a riskless position an investor should buy Δ shares for each option sold. An inspection of a typical binomial tree shows that delta changes during the life of an option. This means that to hedge a particular option position, we must change our holding in the underlying stock periodically.

Constructing binomial trees for valuing options on stock indices, currencies, futures contracts is very similar to doing so for valuing options on stocks. In Chapter 18, we will return to binomial trees and provide further details on how they are used in practice.

FURTHER READING

Coval, J. E., and T. Shumway. "Expected Option Returns," *Journal of Finance*, 56, 3 (2001), 983–1009.

Cox, J., S. Ross, and M. Rubinstein. "Option Pricing: A Simplified Approach," *Journal of Financial Economics*, 7 (October 1979): 229–64.

Rendleman, R., and B. Bartter. "Two State Option Pricing," *Journal of Finance*, 34 (1979): 1092–1110.

Shreve, S. *Stochastic Calculus for Finance,* I: *The Binomial Asset Pricing Model.* New York: Springer, 2005.

Quiz (Answers at End of Book)

12.1. A stock price is currently \$40. It is known that at the end of one month it will be either \$42 or \$38. The risk-free interest rate is 8% per annum with continuous compounding. What is the value of a one-month European call option with a strike price of \$39?

12.2. Explain the no-arbitrage and risk-neutral valuation approaches to valuing a European option using a one-step binomial tree.

12.3. What is meant by the delta of a stock option?

12.4. A stock price is currently \$50. It is known that at the end of six months it will be either \$45 or \$55. The risk-free interest rate is 10% per annum with continuous compounding. What is the value of a six-month European put option with a strike price of \$50?

12.5. A stock price is currently \$100. Over each of the next two six-month periods it is expected to go up by 10% or down by 10%. The risk-free interest rate is 8% per annum with continuous compounding. What is the value of a one-year European call option with a strike price of \$100?

12.6. For the situation considered in Problem 12.5, what is the value of a one-year European put option with a strike price of \$100? Verify that the European call and European put prices satisfy put–call parity.

12.7. What are the formulas for u and d in terms of volatility?

Practice Questions (Answers in Solutions Manual/Study Guide)

12.8. Consider the situation in which stock price movements during the life of a European option are governed by a two-step binomial tree. Explain why it is not possible to set up a position in the stock and the option that remains riskless for the whole of the life of the option.

12.9. A stock price is currently \$50. It is known that at the end of two months it will be either \$53 or \$48. The risk-free interest rate is 10% per annum with continuous compounding. What is the value of a two-month European call option with a strike price of \$49? Use no-arbitrage arguments.

12.10. A stock price is currently \$80. It is known that at the end of four months it will be either \$75 or \$85. The risk-free interest rate is 5% per annum with continuous compounding. What is the value of a four-month European put option with a strike price of \$80? Use no-arbitrage arguments.

12.11. A stock price is currently \$40. It is known that at the end of three months it will be either \$45 or \$35. The risk-free rate of interest with quarterly compounding is 8% per annum. Calculate the value of a three-month European put option on the stock with an exercise price of \$40. Verify that no-arbitrage arguments and risk-neutral valuation arguments give the same answers.

12.12. A stock price is currently \$50. Over each of the next two three-month periods it is expected to go up by 6% or down by 5%. The risk-free interest rate is 5% per annum with continuous compounding. What is the value of a six-month European call option with a strike price of \$51?

12.13. For the situation considered in Problem 12.12, what is the value of a six-month European put option with a strike price of \$51? Verify that the European call and European put prices satisfy put–call parity. If the put option were American, would it ever be optimal to exercise it early at any of the nodes on the tree?

12.14. A stock price is currently \$25. It is known that at the end of two months it will be either \$23 or \$27. The risk-free interest rate is 10% per annum with continuous compounding.

Suppose S_T is the stock price at the end of two months. What is the value of a derivative that pays off S_T^2 at this time?

12.15. Calculate u, d, and p when a binomial tree is constructed to value an option on a foreign currency. The tree step size is one month, the domestic interest rate is 5% per annum, the foreign interest rate is 8% per annum, and the volatility is 12% per annum.

12.16. The volatility of a non-dividend-paying stock whose price is \$78, is 30%. The risk-free rate is 3% per annum (continuously compounded) for all maturities. Calculate values for u, d, and p when a two-month time step is used. What is the value of a four-month European call option with a strike price of \$80 given by a two-step binomial tree. Suppose a trader sells 1,000 options (10 contracts). What position in the stock is necessary to hedge the trader's position at the time of the trade?

12.17. A stock index is currently 1,500. Its volatility is 18%. The risk-free rate is 4% per annum (continuously compounded) for all maturities and the dividend yield on the index is 2.5%. Calculate values for u, d, and p when a six-month time step is used. What is the value a 12-month American put option with a strike price of 1,480 given by a two-step binomial tree.

12.18. The futures price of a commodity is \$90. Use a three-step tree to value (a) a nine-month American call option with strike price \$93 and (b) a nine-month American put option with strike price \$93. The volatility is 28% and the risk-free rate (all maturities) is 3% with continuous compounding.

Further Questions

12.19. The current price of a non-dividend-paying biotech stock is \$140 with a volatility of 25%. The risk-free rate is 4%. For a three-month time step:
(a) What is the percentage up movement?
(b) What is the percentage down movement?
(c) What is the probability of an up movement in a risk-neutral world?
(d) What is the probability of a down movement in a risk-neutral world?
Use a two-step tree to value a six-month European call option and a six-month European put option. In both cases the strike price is \$150.

12.20. In Problem 12.19, suppose a trader sells 10,000 European call options. How many shares of the stock are needed to hedge the six-month European call for the first and second three-month period? For the second time period, consider both the case where the stock price moves up during the first period and the case where it moves down during the first period.

12.21. A stock price is currently \$50. It is known that at the end of six months it will be either \$60 or \$42. The risk-free rate of interest with continuous compounding is 12% per annum. Calculate the value of a six-month European call option on the stock with an exercise price of \$48. Verify that no-arbitrage arguments and risk-neutral valuation arguments give the same answer.

12.22. A stock price is currently \$40. Over each of the next two three-month periods it is expected to go up by 10% or down by 10%. The risk-free interest rate is 12% per annum with continuous compounding.

(a) What is the value of a six-month European put option with a strike price of \$42?
(b) What is the value of a six-month American put option with a strike price of \$42?

12.23. Using a "trial-and-error" approach, estimate how high the strike price has to be in Problem 12.22 for it to be optimal to exercise the put option immediately.

12.24. A stock price is currently \$30. During each two-month period for the next four months it will increase by 8% or decrease by 10%. The risk-free interest rate is 5%. Use a two-step tree to calculate the value of a derivative that pays off $[\max(30 - S_T, 0)]^2$, where S_T is the stock price in four months. If the derivative is American style, should it be exercised early?

12.25. Consider a European call option on a non-dividend-paying stock where the stock price is \$40, the strike price is \$40, the risk-free rate is 4% per annum, the volatility is 30% per annum, and the time to maturity is six months.
(a) Calculate u, d, and p for a two-step tree.
(b) Value the option using a two-step tree.
(c) Verify that DerivaGem gives the same answer.
(d) Use DerivaGem to value the option with 5, 50, 100, and 500 time steps.

12.26. Repeat Problem 12.25 for an American put option on a futures contract. The strike price and the futures price are \$50, the risk-free rate is 10%, the time to maturity is six months, and the volatility is 40% per annum.

12.27. A stock index is currently 990, the risk-free rate is 5%, and the dividend yield on the index is 2%. Use a three-step tree to value an 18-month American put option with a strike price of 1,000 when the volatility is 20% per annum. How much does the option holder gain by being able to exercise early? When is the gain made?

12.28. Calculate the value of nine-month American call option to buy 1 million units of a foreign currency using a three-step binomial tree. The current exchange rate is 0.79 and the strike price is 0.80 (both expressed as dollars per unit of the foreign currency). The volatility of the exchange rate is 12% per annum. The domestic and foreign risk-free rates are 2% and 5%, respectively. What position in the foreign currency is initially necessary to hedge the risk?

APPENDIX

Derivation of Black–Scholes–Merton Option Pricing Formula from Binomial Tree

One way of deriving the famous Black–Scholes–Merton result for valuing a European option on a non-dividend-paying stock is by allowing the number of time steps in the binomial tree to approach infinity. This appendix outlines the steps in the proof. The full proof is on the author's website:

www.rotman.utoronto.ca/~hull/BSMBinomialProof

Consider a tree with n time steps used to value a European call option with strike price K and life T. Each step is of length T/n. If there have been j upward movements and $n-j$ downward movements on the tree, the final stock price is $S_0u^jd^{n-j}$, where u is the proportional up movement, d is the proportional down movement, and S_0 is the initial stock price. The payoff from a European call option is then

$$\max(S_0u^jd^{n-j}-K,0)$$

From the properties of the binomial distribution, the probability of exactly j upward movements and $n-j$ downward movements is

$$\frac{n!}{(n-j)!\,j!}p^j(1-p)^{n-j}$$

It follows that the expected payoff from the call option is

$$\sum_{j=0}^{n}\frac{n!}{(n-j)!\,j!}p^j(1-p)^{n-j}\max(S_0u^jd^{n-j}-K,\,0)$$

Because the tree represents movements in a risk-neutral world, we can discount at this risk-free rate, r, to obtain the option price:

$$c=e^{-rT}\sum_{j=0}^{n}\frac{n!}{(n-j)!\,j!}p^j(1-p)^{n-j}\max(S_0u^jd^{n-j}-K,\,0) \qquad \textbf{(12A.1)}$$

Define α as the critical value of j so that when $j>\alpha$ the final stock price, $S_0u^jd^{n-j}$, is greater than K and when $j\leqslant\alpha$ it is less than or equal to K. Equation (12A.1) can be written as

$$c=e^{-rT}\sum_{j>\alpha}\frac{n!}{(n-j)!\,j!}p^j(1-p)^{n-j}(S_0u^jd^{n-j}-K)$$

For convenience, we define

$$U_1=\sum_{j>\alpha}\frac{n!}{(n-j)!\,j!}p^j(1-p)^{n-j}u^jd^{n-j} \qquad \textbf{(12A.2)}$$

and

$$U_2 = \sum_{j>\alpha} \frac{n!}{(n-j)!\, j!} p^j (1-p)^{n-j} \tag{12A.3}$$

so that

$$c = e^{-rT}(S_0 U_1 - K U_2) \tag{12A.4}$$

As is well known, the binomial distribution approaches a normal distribution as the number of trials approaches infinity. Using this result it can be shown that as n approaches infinity, U_1 tends to $N(d_1)e^{rT}$ and U_2 tends to $N(d_2)$, where

$$d_1 = \frac{\ln(S_0/K) + (r + \sigma^2/2)T}{\sigma\sqrt{T}}$$

$$d_2 = \frac{\ln(S_0/K) + (r - \sigma^2/2)T}{\sigma\sqrt{T}} = d_1 - \sigma\sqrt{T}$$

and N is the cumulative probability distribution function for a standard normal variable. Hence,

$$c = S_0 N(d_1) - K e^{-rT} N(d_2)$$

This is the Black–Scholes–Merton formula for the valuation of a European call option. It will be discussed in Chapter 13.

CHAPTER 13

Valuing Stock Options: The Black–Scholes–Merton Model

In the early 1970s, Fischer Black, Myron Scholes, and Robert Merton achieved a major breakthrough in the pricing of European stock options.[1] This involved the development of what has become known as the Black–Scholes or Black–Scholes–Merton model. This model has had a huge influence on the way in which traders price and hedge options. It has also been pivotal to the growth and success of financial engineering. An acknowledgment of the importance of the model came in 1997 when Myron Scholes and Robert Merton were awarded the Nobel prize for economics. Fischer Black died in 1995; otherwise, he would undoubtedly also have been one of the recipients of this prize.

How did Black, Scholes, and Merton make their breakthrough? Previous researchers had made similar assumptions to theirs and had correctly calculated the expected payoff from a European option. However, as explained in Section 12.2, it is difficult to know the correct discount rate to use for this payoff. Black and Scholes used the capital asset pricing model (see the appendix to Chapter 3) to determine the relationship between the market's required return on the option and the required return on the stock. This was not easy because the relationship depends on both the stock price and time. Merton's approach was different from that of Black and Scholes. His pricing model involved setting up a riskless portfolio consisting of the option and the underlying stock and arguing that the return on the portfolio over a short period of time must be the risk-free return. This is similar to what we did in Section 12.1—but more complicated because the portfolio changes continuously through time. Merton's approach is more general than that of Black and Scholes because it does not rely on the assumptions of the capital asset pricing model.

This chapter presents the Black–Scholes–Merton model for valuing European call and put options on a non-dividend-paying stock and discusses the assumptions on which it is based. It also considers more fully than in previous chapters the meaning of volatility and shows how volatility can be either estimated from historical data or

[1] See F. Black and M. Scholes, "The Pricing of Options and Corporate Liabilities," *Journal of Political Economy*, 81 (May/June 1973): 637–59; and R. C. Merton, "Theory of Rational Option Pricing," *Bell Journal of Economics and Management Science* 4 (Spring 1973): 141–83.

From Chapter 13 of *Fundamentals of Futures and Options Markets*, Eighth Edition. John C. Hull.

implied from option prices. Toward the end of the chapter we explain how the Black–Scholes–Merton results can be extended to deal with European call and put options on dividend-paying stocks.

13.1 ASSUMPTIONS ABOUT HOW STOCK PRICES EVOLVE

A stock option pricing model must make some assumptions about how stock prices evolve over time. If a stock price is $100 today, what is the probability distribution for the price in one day or in one week or in one year?

The Black–Scholes–Merton model considers a non-dividend-paying stock and assumes that the return on the stock in a short period of time is normally distributed. The returns in two different nonoverlapping periods are assumed to be independent. Define:

μ: Expected return on the stock

σ: Volatility of the stock price

The mean of the return in time Δt is $\mu\,\Delta t$. The standard deviation of the return is $\sigma\sqrt{\Delta t}$. The assumption underlying Black–Scholes–Merton is therefore that

$$\frac{\Delta S}{S} \sim \phi(\mu\,\Delta t, \sigma^2 \Delta t) \tag{13.1}$$

where ΔS is the change in the stock price S in time Δt, and $\phi(m, v)$ denotes a normal distribution with mean m and variance v. Note that it is the variance of the return, not its standard deviation, that is proportional to Δt.

When Δt is small, equation (13.1) shows that the percentage change in the stock price in time Δt is normal with standard deviation $\sigma\sqrt{\Delta t}$. Suppose that $\sigma = 0.3$, or 30% per annum, and the current stock price is $50. The standard deviation of the percentage change in the stock price in one week (= 1/52 years) is, to a good approximation,

$$30\% \times \sqrt{\frac{1}{52}} = 4.16\%$$

A one-standard-deviation move in the stock price in one week is therefore $\$50 \times 0.0416$, or $2.08.

During a short period of time, the standard deviation of the percentage change in a stock price is usually much greater than its expected percentage change. (For instance, in our example, if the expected return on the stock is, say, 15% per annum, the expected change in one week is 15%/52, or 0.29%, and the 4.16% standard deviation is over 14 times as great as this.) When calculating confidence levels for the future stock price, a commonly used short cut is to assume that the expected return is zero. There is a 95% probability that a normally distributed variable has a value within 1.96 standard deviations of the mean. In our example, it is therefore approximately true that there is a 95% chance that the change over one week is less that $1.96 \times 4.16\% = 8.2\%$ (i.e., between -8.2% and $+8.2\%$). Similarly, it is approximately true that there is a 95% chance that the dollar change will be less than $1.96 \times \$2.08 = \$4.08$.

The Lognormal Distribution

When longer time periods are considered, it is necessary to be more precise about the future stock price distribution. The assumption in equation (13.1) implies that the stock price at any future time has a *lognormal* distribution. The general shape of a lognormal distribution is shown in Figure 13.1. It can be contrasted with the more familiar normal distribution in Figure 13.2. Whereas a variable with a normal distribution can take any positive or negative value, a lognormally distributed variable is restricted to being positive. A normal distribution is symmetrical; a lognormal distribution is skewed with the mean, median, and mode all different.

A variable with a lognormal distribution has the property that its natural logarithm is normally distributed. The Black–Scholes–Merton assumption for stock prices therefore implies that $\ln S_T$ is normal, where S_T is the stock price at a future time T. The mean and standard deviation of $\ln S_T$ can be shown to be

$$\ln S_0 + \left(\mu - \frac{\sigma^2}{2}\right)T \quad \text{and} \quad \sigma\sqrt{T}$$

where S_0 is the current stock price. We can write this result as

$$\ln S_T \sim \phi\left[\ln S_0 + \left(\mu - \frac{\sigma^2}{2}\right)T,\ \sigma^2 T\right] \tag{13.2}$$

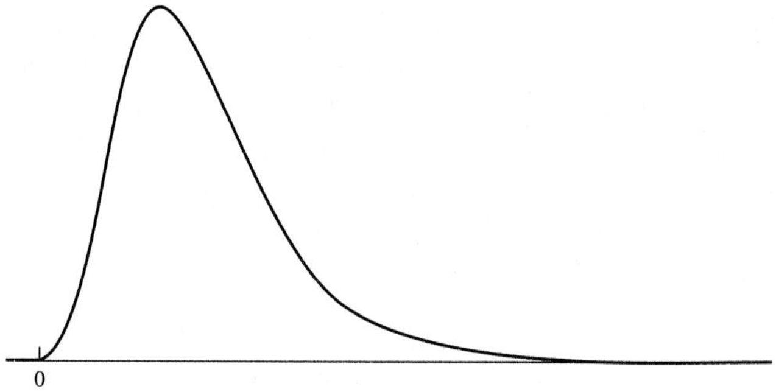

Figure 13.1 A lognormal distribution

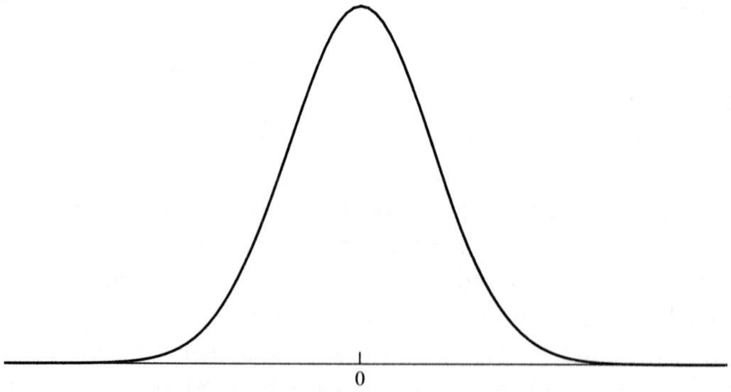

Figure 13.2 A normal distribution

The expected value (or mean) of S_T is

$$E(S_T) = S_0 e^{\mu T} \tag{13.3}$$

and the variance of S_T is

$$\text{var}(S_T) = S_0^2 e^{2\mu T}(e^{\sigma^2 T} - 1)$$

Example 13.1 provides an application of these equations.

From equation (13.2) and the properties of the normal distribution, we have

$$\ln S_T - \ln S_0 \sim \phi\left[\left(\mu - \frac{\sigma^2}{2}\right)T,\ \sigma^2 T\right]$$

or

$$\ln \frac{S_T}{S_0} \sim \phi\left[\left(\mu - \frac{\sigma^2}{2}\right)T,\ \sigma^2 T\right] \tag{13.4}$$

When $T = 1$, the expression $\ln(S_T/S_0)$ is the continuously compounded return provided by the stock in one year.[2] The mean and standard deviation of the continuously compounded return in one year are therefore $\mu - \sigma^2/2$ and σ, respectively. Example 13.2 shows how confidence limits for the return can be calculated.

We now consider in more detail the nature of the expected return and volatility parameter in the lognormal stock price model.

Example 13.1 Confidence limits, mean, and variance for a future stock price

Consider a stock with an initial price of \$40, an expected return of 16% per annum, and a volatility of 20% per annum. From equation (13.2), the probability distribution of the stock price, S_T, in six months is given by

$$\ln S_T \sim \phi\left[\ln 40 + \left(0.16 - \frac{0.2^2}{2}\right)0.5,\ 0.2^2 \times 0.5\right] \quad \text{or} \quad \ln S_T \sim \phi(3.759, 0.02)$$

There is a 95% probability that a normally distributed variable has a value within 1.96 standard deviations of its mean. In this case, the standard deviation is $\sqrt{0.02} = 0.141$. Hence, with 95% confidence, we have

$$3.759 - 1.96 \times 0.141 < \ln S_T < 3.759 + 1.96 \times 0.141$$

This implies

$$e^{3.759-1.96\times0.141} < S_T < e^{3.759+1.96\times0.141} \quad \text{or} \quad 32.55 < S_T < 56.56$$

Thus, there is a 95% probability that the stock price in six months will lie between 32.55 and 56.56. The mean and variance of S_T are

$$40e^{0.16\times0.5} = 43.33$$

and

$$40^2 e^{2\times0.16\times0.5}(e^{0.2\times0.2\times0.5} - 1) = 37.93$$

[2] We can distinguish between the continuously compounded return and the return with annual compounding. The former is $\ln(S_T/S_0)$; the latter is $(S_T - S_0)/S_0$.

Example 13.2 Confidence limits for stock price return

Consider a stock with an expected return of 17% per annum and a volatility of 20% per annum. The probability distribution for the rate of return (continuously compounded) realized over one year is normal, with mean

$$0.17 - \frac{0.2^2}{2} = 0.15$$

or 15% and standard deviation 20%. Because there is a 95% chance that a normally distributed variable will lie within 1.96 standard deviations of its mean, we can be 95% confident that the return realized over one year will be between $15 - 1.96 \times 20 = -24.2\%$ and $15 + 1.96 \times 20 = +54.2\%$.

13.2 EXPECTED RETURN

The expected return, μ, required by investors from a stock depends on the riskiness of the stock. The higher the risk, the higher the expected return. It also depends on the level of interest rates in the economy. The higher the level of interest rates, the higher the expected return required on any given stock. Fortunately, we do not have to concern ourselves with the determinants of μ in any detail. It turns out that the value of a stock option, when expressed in terms of the value of the underlying stock, does not depend on μ at all. Nevertheless, there is one aspect of the expected return from a stock that frequently causes confusion and needs to be explained.

Equation (13.1) shows that $\mu\,\Delta t$ is the expected percentage change in the stock price in a very short period of time, Δt. It is natural to assume from this that μ is the expected continuously compounded return on the stock over a longer period of time. However, this is not the case. Denote by R the continuously compounded return actually realized over a period of time of length T years. This satisfies

$$S_T = S_0 e^{RT}$$

so that

$$R = \frac{1}{T} \ln \frac{S_T}{S_0}$$

Equation (13.4) shows that the expected value, $E(R)$, of R is $\mu - \sigma^2/2$.

The reason why the expected continuously compounded return is different from μ is subtle, but important. Suppose we consider a very large number of very short periods of time of length Δt. Define S_i as the stock price at the end of the ith interval and ΔS_i as $S_{i+1} - S_i$. Under the assumptions we are making for stock price behavior (see equation (13.1)), the average of the returns on the stock in each interval is close to μ. In other words, $\mu\,\Delta t$ is close to the arithmetic mean of the $\Delta S_i/S_i$. However, the expected return over the whole period covered by the data, expressed with a compounding period of Δt, is close to the geometric mean of the $\Delta S_i/S_i$. This is $\mu - \sigma^2/2$, not μ.[3] Business Snapshot 13.1 provides a numerical example related to the mutual fund industry to illustrate this.

[3] The arguments in this section show that the term "expected return" is ambiguous. It can refer either to μ or to $\mu - \sigma^2/2$. Unless otherwise stated, it will be used to refer to μ throughout this book.

> **Business Snapshot 13.1** Mutual fund returns can be misleading
>
> The difference between μ and $\mu - \sigma^2/2$ is closely related to an issue in the reporting of mutual fund returns. Suppose that the following is a sequence of returns per annum reported by a mutual fund manager over the last five years (measured using annual compounding): 15%, 20%, 30%, −20%, 25%.
>
> The arithmetic mean of the returns, calculated by taking the sum of the returns and dividing by 5, is 14%. However, an investor would actually earn less than 14% per annum by leaving the money invested in the fund for five years. The dollar value of \$100 at the end of the five years would be
>
> $$100 \times 1.15 \times 1.20 \times 1.30 \times 0.80 \times 1.25 = \$179.40$$
>
> By contrast, a 14% return with annual compounding would give
>
> $$100 \times 1.14^5 = \$192.54$$
>
> The return that gives \$179.40 at the end of five years is 12.4%. This is because
>
> $$100 \times (1.124)^5 = 179.40$$
>
> What average return should the fund manager report? It is tempting for the manager to make a statement such as: "The average of the returns per year that we have realized in the last five years is 14%." Although true, this is misleading. It is much less misleading to say "The average return realized by someone who invested with us for the last five years is 12.4% per year." In some jurisdictions regulatory standards require fund managers to report returns the second way.
>
> This phenomenon is an example of a well-known result. The geometric mean of a set of numbers (not all the same) is always less than the arithmetic mean. In our example, the return multipliers each year are 1.15, 1.20, 1.30, 0.80, and 1.25. The arithmetic mean of these numbers is 1.140, but the geometric mean is only 1.124.

For a mathematical explanation of what is going on, we start with equation (13.3):

$$E(S_T) = S_0 e^{\mu T}$$

Taking logarithms, we get

$$\ln[E(S_T)] = \ln(S_0) + \mu T$$

It is now tempting to set $\ln[E(S_T)] = E[\ln(S_T)]$, so that $E[\ln(S_T)] - \ln(S_0) = \mu T$, or $E[\ln(S_T/S_0)] = \mu T$, which leads to $E(R) = \mu$. However, we cannot do this because ln is a nonlinear function. In fact, $\ln[E(S_T)] > E[\ln(S_T)]$, so that $E[\ln(S_T/S_0)] < \mu T$, which leads to $E(R) < \mu$. (As pointed out above, $E(R) = \mu - \sigma^2/2$.)

13.3 VOLATILITY

The volatility of a stock, σ, is a measure of our uncertainty about the returns provided by the stock. Stocks typically have volatilities between 15% and 50%.

From equation (13.4), the volatility of a stock price can be defined as the standard deviation of the return provided by the stock in one year when the return is expressed using continuous compounding.

It is approximately true that our uncertainty about a future stock price, as measured by its standard deviation, increases with the square root of how far ahead we are looking. For example, the standard deviation of the stock price in four weeks is approximately twice the standard deviation in one week.

13.4 ESTIMATING VOLATILITY FROM HISTORICAL DATA

A record of stock price movements can be used to estimate volatility. The stock price is usually observed at fixed intervals of time (e.g., every day, week, or month). We define:

$n+1$: Number of observations

S_i: Stock price at end of ith interval, where $i = 0, 1, \dots, n$

τ: Length of time interval in years

and let

$$u_i = \ln\left(\frac{S_i}{S_{i-1}}\right)$$

An estimate, s, of the standard deviation of the u_i is given by

$$s = \sqrt{\frac{1}{n-1}\sum_{i=1}^{n}(u_i - \bar{u})^2}$$

or

$$s = \sqrt{\frac{1}{n-1}\sum_{i=1}^{n}u_i^2 - \frac{1}{n(n-1)}\left(\sum_{i=1}^{n}u_i\right)^2}$$

where $\bar{u}$ is the mean of the u_i.[4] (See the appendix to Chapter 3.)

From equation (13.4), the standard deviation of the u_i is $\sigma\sqrt{\tau}$. The variable s is therefore an estimate of $\sigma\sqrt{\tau}$. It follows that σ itself can be estimated as $\hat{\sigma}$, where

$$\hat{\sigma} = \frac{s}{\sqrt{\tau}}$$

The standard error of this estimate can be shown to be approximately $\hat{\sigma}/\sqrt{2n}$. Example 13.3 illustrates the application of these formulas.

Choosing an appropriate value for n is not easy. More data generally lead to more accuracy, but σ does change over time and data that are too old may not be relevant for predicting the future volatility. A compromise that seems to work reasonably well is to use closing prices from daily data over the most recent 90 to 180 days. Alternatively, as a rule of thumb, we can set n equal to the number of days to which the volatility is to be applied. Thus, if the volatility estimate is to be used to value a two-year option, it is calculated from daily data over the last two years.

The foregoing analysis assumes that the stock pays no dividends. It can be adapted to accommodate dividend-paying stocks. The return, u_i, during a time interval that

[4] The value of $\bar{u}$ is often assumed to be zero when estimates of historical volatilities are made.

Example 13.3 Calculation of volatility from historical data

Table 13.1 shows a possible sequence of stock prices during 21 consecutive trading days. In this case, $n = 20$ and

$$\sum_{i=1}^{20} u_i = 0.09531 \quad \text{and} \quad \sum_{i=1}^{20} u_i^2 = 0.00326$$

and the estimate of the standard deviation of the daily return is

$$\sqrt{\frac{0.00326}{19} - \frac{0.09531^2}{20 \times 19}} = 0.01216$$

or 1.216%. Assuming that there are 252 trading days per year, $\tau = 1/252$ and the data give an estimate for the volatility per annum of $0.01216\sqrt{252} = 0.193$ or 19.3%. The standard error of this estimate is

$$\frac{0.193}{\sqrt{2 \times 20}} = 0.031$$

or 3.1% per annum.

includes an ex-dividend day is given by

$$u_i = \ln \frac{S_i + D}{S_{i-1}}$$

where D is the amount of the dividend. The return in other time intervals is still

$$u_i = \ln \frac{S_i}{S_{i-1}}$$

However, because tax factors play a part in determining returns around an ex-dividend date, it is probably best to discard altogether data for intervals that include an ex-dividend date when daily or weekly data is used.

Trading Days vs. Calendar Days

There is an important issue concerned with whether time should be measured in calendar days or trading days when volatility parameters are being estimated and used. As shown in Business Snapshot 13.2, research shows that volatility is much higher when the exchange is open for trading than when it is closed. As a result, practitioners tend to ignore days when the exchange is closed when estimating volatility from historical data and when calculating the life of an option. The volatility per annum is calculated from the volatility per trading day using the formula

$$\text{Volatility per annum} = \text{Volatility per trading day} \times \sqrt{\begin{matrix}\text{Number of trading} \\ \text{days per annum}\end{matrix}}$$

This is what we did when calculating volatility from the data in Table 13.1. The number of trading days in a year is usually assumed to be 252 for stocks.

Business Snapshot 13.2 What causes volatility?

It is natural to assume that the volatility of a stock is caused by new information reaching the market. This new information causes people to revise their opinions about the value of the stock. The price of the stock changes and volatility results. This view of what causes volatility is not supported by research.

With several years of daily stock price data, researchers can calculate:

1. The variance of stock price returns between the close of trading on one day and the close of trading on the next day when there are no intervening nontrading days.
2. The variance of the stock price returns between the close of trading on Friday and the close of trading on Monday.

The second variance is the variance of returns over a three-day period. The first is a variance over a one-day period. We might reasonably expect the second variance to be three times as great as the first variance. Fama (1965), French (1980), and French and Roll (1986) show that this is not the case. These three research studies estimate the second variance to be, respectively, 22%, 19%, and 10.7% higher than the first variance.

At this stage one might be tempted to argue that these results are explained by more news reaching the market when the market is open for trading. But research by Roll (1984) does not support this explanation. Roll looked at the prices of orange juice futures. By far the most important news for orange juice futures prices is news about the weather and news about the weather is equally likely to arrive at any time. When Roll did a similar analysis to that just described for stocks he found that the second (Friday-to-Monday) variance for orange juice futures is only 1.54 times the first variance.

The only reasonable conclusion from all this is that volatility is to a large extent caused by trading itself. (Traders usually have no difficulty accepting this conclusion!)

The life of an option is also usually measured using trading days rather than calendar days. It is calculated as T years, where

$$T = \frac{\text{Number of trading days until option maturity}}{252}$$

13.5 ASSUMPTIONS UNDERLYING BLACK–SCHOLES–MERTON

The assumptions made by Black, Scholes, and Merton when they derived their option pricing formula were as follows:

1. Stock price behavior corresponds to the lognormal model (developed earlier in this chapter) with μ and σ constant.
2. There are no transactions costs or taxes. All securities are perfectly divisible.
3. There are no dividends on the stock during the life of the option.
4. There are no riskless arbitrage opportunities.

Table 13.1 Computation of volatility

Day	*Closing stock price (\$),* S_i	*Price relative,* S_i/S_{i-1}	*Daily return,* $u_i = \ln(S_i/S_{i-1})$
0	20.00		
1	20.10	1.00500	0.00499
2	19.90	0.99005	−0.01000
3	20.00	1.00503	0.00501
4	20.50	1.02500	0.02469
5	20.25	0.98780	−0.01227
6	20.90	1.03210	0.03159
7	20.90	1.00000	0.00000
8	20.90	1.00000	0.00000
9	20.75	0.99282	−0.00720
10	20.75	1.00000	0.00000
11	21.00	1.01205	0.01198
12	21.10	1.00476	0.00475
13	20.90	0.99052	−0.00952
14	20.90	1.00000	0.00000
15	21.25	1.01675	0.01661
16	21.40	1.00706	0.00703
17	21.40	1.00000	0.00000
18	21.25	0.99299	−0.00703
19	21.75	1.02353	0.02326
20	22.00	1.01149	0.01143

5. Security trading is continuous.
6. Investors can borrow or lend at the same risk-free rate of interest.
7. The short-term risk-free rate of interest, r, is constant.

Some of these assumptions have been relaxed by other researchers. For example, variations on the Black–Scholes–Merton formula can be used when r and σ are functions of time and, as we shall see later in this chapter, the formula can be adjusted to take dividends into account.

13.6 THE KEY NO-ARBITRAGE ARGUMENT

The arguments that can be used to price options are analogous to the no-arbitrage arguments used in Chapter 12 when stock price changes were assumed to be binomial. A riskless portfolio consisting of a position in the option and a position in the underlying stock is set up. In the absence of arbitrage opportunities, the return from the portfolio must be the risk-free interest rate, r. This results in a differential equation that must be satisfied by the option.

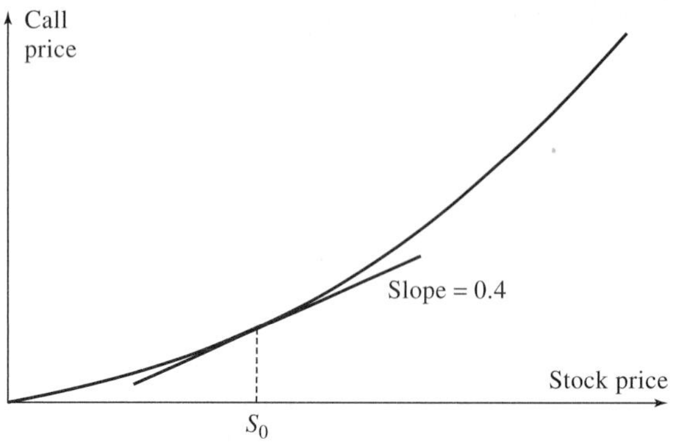

Figure 13.3 Relationship between call price and stock price. Current stock price is S_0

The reason a riskless portfolio can be set up is that the stock price and the option price are both affected by the same underlying source of uncertainty: stock price movements. In any short period of time, the price of a call option is perfectly positively correlated with the price of the underlying stock; the price of a put option is perfectly negatively correlated with the price of the underlying stock. In both cases, when an appropriate portfolio of the stock and the option is set up, the gain or loss from the stock position always offsets the gain or loss from the option position so that the overall value of the portfolio at the end of the short period of time is known with certainty.

Suppose, for example, that at some point in time the relationship between a small change in the stock price, ΔS, and the resultant small change in the price of a European call option, Δc, is given by

$$\Delta c = 0.4\Delta S$$

This means that the slope of the line representing the relationship between Δc and ΔS is 0.4, as indicated in Figure 13.3. A riskless portfolio would consist of:

1. A long position in 40 shares
2. A short position in 100 call options

Suppose that the stock price increases by 10 cents. The option price will increase by 4 cents and the $40 \times 0.10 = \$4$ gain on the shares is equal to the $100 \times 0.04 = \$4$ loss on the short option position.

There is one important difference between the analysis here and the analysis using a binomial model in Chapter 12. Here, the position that is set up is riskless for only a very short period of time. (Theoretically, it remains riskless only for an instantaneously short period of time.) To remain riskless, it must be frequently adjusted or *rebalanced*.[5] For example, the relationship between Δc and ΔS might change from $\Delta c = 0.4\,\Delta S$ today to $\Delta c = 0.5\,\Delta S$ tomorrow. (If so, an extra 0.1 shares must be purchased for each call option sold to maintain a riskless portfolio.) It is nevertheless true that the return from the riskless portfolio in any short period of time must be the risk-free interest rate. This can be used in conjunction with some stochastic calculus to produce the Black, Scholes, and Merton pricing formulas.

[5] We will examine the rebalancing of portfolios in more detail in Chapter 17.

13.7 THE BLACK–SCHOLES–MERTON PRICING FORMULAS

The Black–Scholes–Merton formulas for the prices of European calls and puts on non-dividend-paying stocks are[6]

$$c = S_0 N(d_1) - Ke^{-rT} N(d_2) \tag{13.5}$$

$$p = Ke^{-rT} N(-d_2) - S_0 N(-d_1) \tag{13.6}$$

where

$$d_1 = \frac{\ln(S_0/K) + (r + \sigma^2/2)T}{\sigma\sqrt{T}}$$

$$d_2 = \frac{\ln(S_0/K) + (r - \sigma^2/2)T}{\sigma\sqrt{T}} = d_1 - \sigma\sqrt{T}$$

The function $N(x)$ is the cumulative probability function for a standardized normal variable. In other words, it is the probability that a variable with a standard normal distribution will be less than x. It is illustrated in Figure 13.4. The remaining notation in equations (13.5) and (13.6) should be familiar. The variables c and p are the European call and put prices, S_0 is the stock price, K is the strike price, r is the risk-free interest rate (expressed with continuous compounding), T is the time to expiration, and σ is the volatility of the stock price. Because the American call price, C, equals the European call price, c, for a non-dividend-paying stock, equation (13.5) also gives the price of an American call. There is no exact analytic formula to value an American put, but binomial trees such as those introduced in Chapter 12 can be used.

In theory, the Black–Scholes formula is correct only if the short-term interest rate, r, is constant. In practice, the formula is usually used with the interest rate, r, being set equal to the risk-free interest rate on an investment that lasts for time T.

Properties of the Black–Scholes–Merton Formulas

A full proof of the Black–Scholes–Merton formulas is beyond the scope of this book. At this stage we show that the formulas have the right general properties by considering what happens when some of the parameters take extreme values.

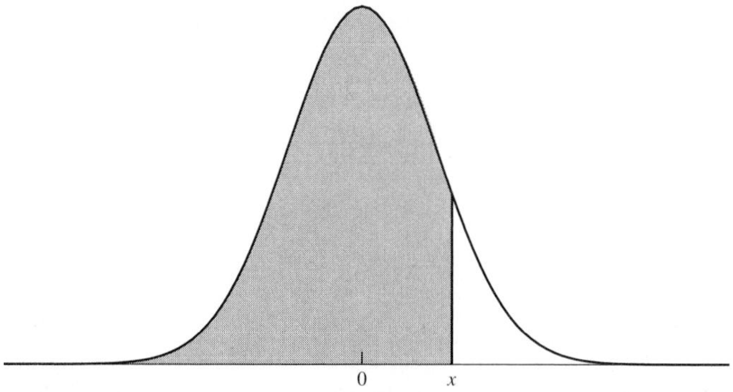

Figure 13.4 Shaded area represents $N(x)$

[6] The software, DerivaGem, that accompanies this book can be used to carry out Black–Scholes–Merton calculations for options on stocks, currencies, indices, and futures contracts.

When the stock price, S_0, becomes very large, a call option is almost certain to be exercised. It then becomes very similar to a forward contract with delivery price K. Therefore, from equation (5.5), we expect the call price to be

$$S_0 - Ke^{-rT}$$

This is, in fact, the call price given by equation (13.5) because, when S_0 becomes very large, both d_1 and d_2 become very large, and consequently $N(d_1)$ and $N(d_2)$ are both close to 1.0.

When the stock price becomes very large, the price of a European put option, p, approaches zero. This result is consistent with equation (13.6) because $N(-d_1)$ and $N(-d_2)$ are both close to zero when S_0 is large.

When the stock price becomes very small, both d_1 and d_2 become very large and negative. This means that $N(d_1)$ and $N(d_2)$ are then both very close to zero, and equation (13.5) gives a price close to zero for the call option. This is as expected. Also, $N(-d_1)$ and $N(-d_2)$ become close to 1, so that the price of the put option given by equation (13.6) is close to $Ke^{-rT} - S_0$. This is also as expected.

Example 13.4 illustrates the application of equations (13.5) and (13.6). The only difficulty is the computation of the cumulative normal distribution function, N. Tables for N are provided at the end of this book. It can also be evaluated using the NORMSDIST function in Excel.

Example 13.4 Using the Black–Scholes–Merton formulas

The stock price six months from the expiration of an option is \$42, the exercise price of the option is \$40, the risk-free interest rate is 10% per annum, and the volatility is 20% per annum. This means that $S_0 = 42$, $K = 40$, $r = 0.1$, $\sigma = 0.2$, $T = 0.5$,

$$d_1 = \frac{\ln(42/40) + (0.1 + 0.2^2/2) \times 0.5}{0.2\sqrt{0.5}} = 0.7693$$

$$d_2 = \frac{\ln(42/40) + (0.1 - 0.2^2/2) \times 0.5}{0.2\sqrt{0.5}} = 0.6278$$

$$c = 42N(0.7693) - 38.049N(0.6278)$$

$$p = 38.049N(-0.6278) - 42N(-0.7693)$$

Using Excel's NORMDIST function or the tables at the end of the book, we get

$$N(0.7693) = 0.7791, \quad N(-0.7693) = 0.2209$$

$$N(0.6278) = 0.7349, \quad N(-0.6278) = 0.2651$$

so that

$$c = 4.76 \quad \text{and} \quad p = 0.81$$

Ignoring the time value of money, the stock price has to rise by \$2.76 for the purchaser of the call to break even. Similarly, the stock price has to fall by \$2.81 for the purchaser of the put to break even.

Understanding $N(d_1)$ and $N(d_2)$

The term $N(d_2)$ in equation (13.5) has a fairly simple interpretation. It is the probability that a call option will be exercised in a risk-neutral world. The $N(d_1)$ term is not quite so easy to interpret. The expression $S_0N(d_1)e^{rT}$ is the expected stock price at time T in a risk-neutral world when stock prices less than the strike price are counted as zero. The strike price is only paid if the stock price is greater than K and as just mentioned this has a probability of $N(d_2)$. The expected payoff in a risk-neutral world is therefore

$$S_0N(d_1)e^{rT} - KN(d_2)$$

Present-valuing this from time T to time zero gives the Black–Scholes–Merton equation for a European call option:

$$c = S_0N(d_1) - Ke^{-rT}N(d_2)$$

For another way of understanding this, note that the Black–Scholes–Merton equation for the value of a European call option can be written as:

$$c = e^{-rT}N(d_2)[S_0e^{rT}N(d_1)/N(d_2) - K]$$

The terms here have the following interpretation:

e^{-rT}: Present value factor

$N(d_2)$: Probability of exercise

$e^{rT}N(d_1)/N(d_2)$: Expected percentage increase in stock if option is exercised

K: Strike price paid if option is exercised.

13.8 RISK-NEUTRAL VALUATION

A very important result in the pricing of derivatives is known as risk-neutral valuation. The principle was introduced in Chapter 12 and can be stated as follows:

> Any security dependent on other traded securities can be valued on the assumption that investors are risk neutral.

Note that risk-neutral valuation does not state that investors are risk neutral. What it does state is that derivatives such as options can be valued on the assumption that investors are risk neutral. It means that investors' risk preferences have no effect on the value of a stock option when it is expressed as a function of the price of the underlying stock. It explains why equations (13.5) and (13.6) do not involve the stock's expected return, μ. Risk-neutral valuation is a very powerful tool because in a risk-neutral world two particularly simple results hold:

1. The expected return from all investment assets is the risk-free interest rate.
2. The risk-free interest rate is the appropriate discount rate to apply to any expected future cash flow.

Options and other derivatives can be valued using risk-neutral valuation. The procedure is as follows:

1. Assume that the expected return from the underlying asset is the risk-free interest rate r (i.e., assume $\mu = r$).
2. Calculate the expected payoff.
3. Discount the expected payoff at the risk-free interest rate.

Application to Forward Contracts

This procedure can be used to derive the Black–Scholes–Merton formulas, but the mathematics is fairly complicated and will not be presented here. Instead, as an illustration, we will show how the procedure can be used to value a forward contract on a non-dividend-paying stock. (This contract has already been valued in Chapter 5 using a different approach.) We will make the assumption that interest rates are constant and equal to r.

Consider a long forward contract that matures at time T with delivery price K. The value of the contract at maturity is

$$S_T - K$$

The expected value of S_T was shown earlier in this chapter to be $S_0 e^{\mu T}$. In a risk-neutral world, it becomes $S_0 e^{rT}$. The expected payoff from the contract at maturity in a risk-neutral world is therefore

$$S_0 e^{rT} - K$$

Discounting at the risk-free rate r for time T gives the value, f, of the forward contract today as

$$f = e^{-rT}(S_0 e^{rT} - K) = S_0 - Ke^{-rT}$$

This is in agreement with the result in equation (5.5).

13.9 IMPLIED VOLATILITIES

The one parameter in the Black–Scholes–Merton pricing formulas that cannot be observed directly is the volatility of the stock price. Earlier in this chapter we saw how volatility can be estimated from a history of the stock price. We now show how to calculate what is known as an *implied volatility*. This is the volatility implied by an option price observed in the market.[7]

To illustrate the basic idea, suppose that the value of a European call option on a non-dividend-paying stock is 1.90 when $S_0 = 21$, $K = 20$, $r = 0.1$, and $T = 0.25$. The implied volatility is the value of σ that, when substituted into equation (13.5), gives $c = 1.90$. It is not possible to invert equation (13.5) so that σ is expressed as a function of S_0, K, r, T, and c, but an iterative search procedure can be used to find the implied σ. We could start by trying $\sigma = 0.20$. This gives a value of c equal to 1.76, which is too low. Because c is an increasing function of σ, a higher value of σ is required. We could next try a value of 0.30 for σ. This gives a value of c equal to 2.10, which is too high,

[7] Implied volatilities for European and American options on stocks, stock indices, foreign currencies, and futures can be calculated using the DerivaGem software supplied with this book.

and means that σ must lie between 0.20 and 0.30. Next, we try a value of 0.25 for σ. This also proves to be too high, showing that σ lies between 0.20 and 0.25. Proceeding in this way, we can halve the range for σ at each iteration and thereby calculate the correct value of σ to any required accuracy.[8] In this example, the implied volatility is 0.242, or 24.2% per annum.

Implied volatilities can be used to monitor the market's opinion about the volatility of a particular stock. Whereas historical volatilities (see Section 13.4) are "backward looking," implied volatilities are "forward looking." It is therefore not surprising that predictions of a stock's future volatility based on implied volatilities tend to be slightly better than those based on historical volatilities.

Traders often quote the implied volatility of an option rather than its price. This is convenient because the implied volatility tends to be less variable than the option price. The implied volatility of an option does depend on its strike price and time to maturity. As will be explained in Chapter 19, the implied volatilities of actively traded options are used by traders to estimate appropriate implied volatilities for other options.

The VIX Index

The CBOE publishes indices of implied volatility. The most popular index, the SPX VIX, is an index of the implied volatility of 30-day options on the S&P 500 calculated from a wide range of calls and puts.[9] It is sometimes referred to as the "fear factor." An index value of 15 indicates that the calculated implied volatility of 30-day options on the S&P 500 is about 15%. Trading in futures on the VIX started in 2004 and trading in options on the VIX started in 2006. One contract is on 1,000 times the index. Example 13.5 indicates how a futures trade on the VIX works.

Trading futures on the VIX index gives a different type of bet from trading options on the S&P 500. The future value of options on the S&P 500 depend on both the level of the S&P 500 and its volatility. By contrast, a futures contract on the VIX is a bet only on volatility. Figure 13.5 shows the VIX index between January 2004 and August 2012. Between the 2004 and mid-2007, it tended to stay between 10 and 20. It reached 30 during the second half of 2007 and a record 80 in October and November 2008 after Lehman's bankruptcy. By early 2010, it had declined to more normal levels, but it

Example 13.5 Trading VIX Futures

A trader buys an April futures contract on the VIX when the futures price is 18.5 (corresponding to a 30-day S&P 500 volatility of 18.5%) and closes out the contract when when the futures price is 19.3 (corresponding to a 30-day S&P 500 volatility of 19.3%). The trader makes a gain of

$$(19.3 - 18.5) \times 1,000 = 800$$

or \$800. As is usual with a futures contract, this gain is the cumulative result of daily gains and losses on the contract during the period it is held.

[8] This method is presented for illustration. Other, more powerful, procedures are usually used in practice.

[9] For a description of how the index is calculated see J. Hull, *Options, Futures, and Other Derivatives*, 8th edn. Upper Saddle River, NJ: Pearson, 2012, Chap. 24.

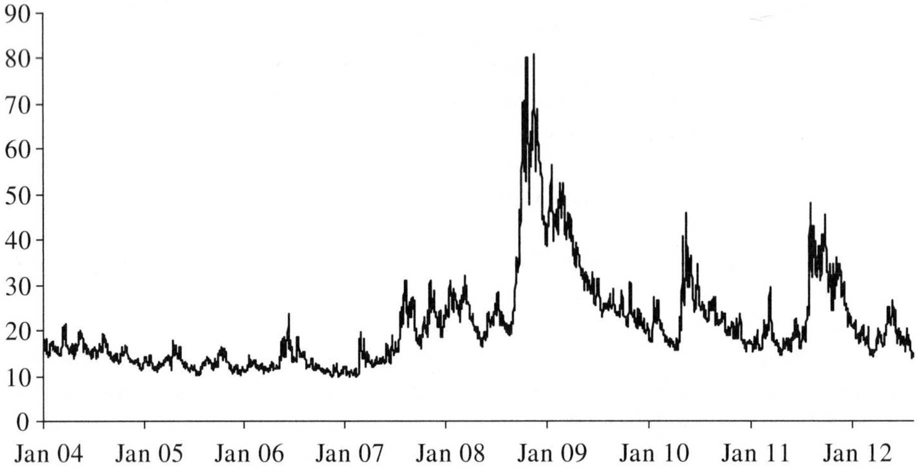

Figure 13.5 The VIX index: January 2004 to September 2012

spiked again in May 2010 and the second half of 2011 because of concerns about the European sovereign debt crisis.

13.10 DIVIDENDS

Up to now we have assumed that the stock on which the option is written pays no dividends. In practice, of course, many stocks do pay dividends. We now extend our results by assuming that the dividends paid on the stock during the life of an option can be predicted with certainty. When options last for relatively short periods of time (less than one year), the assumption is not too unreasonable. When options last for long periods of time, it is usual to assume that the dividend yield rather than the dollar amount of the dividend is known. Options can then be valued as described in Chapter 15.

The date on which the dividend is paid should be assumed to be the ex-dividend date. On this date the stock price declines by the amount of the dividend.[10] The effect is to reduce the value of calls and increase the value of puts.

European Options

European options can be analyzed by assuming that the stock price is the sum of two components: a riskless component that will be used to pay the known dividends during the life of the option and a risky component. The riskless component at any given time is the present value of all the dividends during the life of the option discounted from the ex-dividend dates to the present at the risk-free rate. The Black–Scholes–Merton formula is then correct if S_0 is set equal to the risky component. Operationally this

[10] For tax reasons the stock price may go down by somewhat less than the cash amount of the dividend. To take account of this phenomenon, we need to interpret the word *dividend* in the context of option pricing as the reduction in the stock price on the ex-dividend date caused by the dividend. Thus, if a dividend of $1 per share is anticipated and the share price normally goes down by 80% of the dividend on the ex-dividend date, the dividend should be assumed to be $0.80 for the purposes of the analysis.

Example 13.6 Using Black–Scholes–Merton when there are dividends

Consider a European call option on a stock with ex-dividend dates in two months and five months. The dividend on each ex-dividend date is expected to be \$0.50. The current share price is \$40, the exercise price is \$40, the stock price volatility is 30% per annum, the risk-free rate of interest is 9% per annum, and the time to maturity is six months. The present value of the dividends is

$$0.5e^{-0.09\times 2/12} + 0.5e^{-0.09\times 5/12} = 0.9741$$

The option price can therefore be calculated from the Black–Scholes–Merton formula with $S_0 = 40 - 0.9741 = 39.0259$, $K = 40$, $r = 0.09$, $\sigma = 0.3$, and $T = 0.5$:

$$d_1 = \frac{\ln(39.0259/40) + (0.09 + 0.3^2/2)\times 0.5}{0.3\sqrt{0.5}} = 0.2020$$

$$d_2 = \frac{\ln(39.0259/40) + (0.09 - 0.3^2/2)\times 0.5}{0.3\sqrt{0.5}} = -0.01012$$

Using the NORMDIST function in Excel gives

$$N(d_1) = 0.5800 \quad \text{and} \quad N(d_2) = 0.4959$$

and from equation (13.5) the call price is

$$39.0259 \times 0.5800 - 40e^{-0.09\times 0.5} \times 0.4959 = 3.67$$

or \$3.67.

means that the Black–Scholes–Merton formula can be used provided the stock price is reduced by the present value of all the dividends during the life of the option, the discounting being done from the ex-dividend dates at the risk-free rate. As already mentioned, a dividend is included in the calculations only if its ex-dividend date occurs during the life of the option. Example 13.6 illustrates the calculations.

With this procedure, σ in the Black–Scholes–Merton formula should be the volatility of the risky component of the stock price—not the volatility of the stock price itself. In practice, the two are usually assumed to be the same. In theory, the volatility of the risky component is approximately $S_0/(S_0 - D)$ times the volatility of the stock price, where D is the present value of the remaining dividends and S_0 is the stock price.

American Call Options

In Chapter 10, we saw that American call options should never be exercised early when the underlying stock pays no dividends. When dividends are paid, it is sometimes optimal to exercise at a time immediately before the stock goes ex-dividend. The reason is easy to understand. The dividend will make both the stock and the call option less valuable. If the dividend is sufficiently large and the call option is sufficiently in the money, it may be worth forgoing the remaining time value of the option in order to avoid the adverse effects of the dividend on the stock price.

Example 13.7 Using Black's approximation for an American call

Suppose that the option in Example 13.6 is American rather than European. The present value of the first dividend is given by

$$0.5e^{-0.09\times 2/12} = 0.4926$$

The value of the option on the assumption that it expires just before the final ex-dividend date can be calculated using the Black–Scholes–Merton formula, with $S_0 = 40 - 0.4926 = 39.5074$, $K = 40$, $r = 0.09$, $\sigma = 0.30$, and $T = 0.4167$. It is \$3.52. Black's approximation involves taking the greater of this value and the value of the option when it can be exercised only at the end of six months. From the previous example, we know that the latter is \$3.67. Black's approximation therefore gives the value of the American call as \$3.67.

In practice, call options are most likely to be exercised early immediately before the final ex-dividend date. The analysis in the appendix at the end of this chapter indicates why this is so and derives the conditions under which early exercise can be optimal. We now mention an approximate procedure suggested by Fischer Black for valuing American calls on dividend-paying stocks.

Black's Approximation

Black's approximation involves calculating the prices of two European options:

1. A European option that matures at the same time as the American option
2. A European option maturing just before the latest ex-dividend date that occurs during the life of the option

The strike price, initial stock price, risk-free interest rate, and volatility are the same as for the option under consideration. The American option price is set equal to the higher of these two European option prices. Example 13.7 illustrates the approach.

SUMMARY

The usual assumption in stock option pricing is that the price of a stock at some future time given its price today is lognormal. This in turn implies that the continuously compounded return from the stock in a period of time is normally distributed. Our uncertainty about future stock prices increases as we look further ahead. As a rough approximation, we can say that the standard deviation of the stock price is proportional to the square root of how far ahead we are looking.

To estimate the volatility, σ, of a stock price empirically, we need to observe the stock price at fixed intervals of time (e.g., every day, every week, or every month). For each time period, the natural logarithm of the ratio of the stock price at the end of the time period to the stock price at the beginning of the time period is calculated. The volatility is estimated as the standard deviation of these numbers divided by the square root of the length of the time period in years. Usually days when the exchanges are closed are ignored in measuring time for the purposes of volatility calculations.

Stock option valuation involves setting up a riskless portfolio of the option and the stock. Because the stock price and the option price both depend on the same underlying source of uncertainty, such a portfolio can always be created. The portfolio remains riskless for only a very short period of time. However, the return on a riskless portfolio must always be the risk-free interest rate if there are to be no arbitrage opportunities. It is this fact that enables the option price to be valued in terms of the stock price. The original Black–Scholes–Merton result gives the value of a European call or put option on a non-dividend-paying stock in terms of five variables: the stock price, the strike price, the risk-free interest rate, the volatility, and the time to expiration.

Surprisingly the expected return on the stock does not enter into the Black–Scholes–Merton equation. There is a general principle known as risk-neutral valuation, which states that any security dependent on other traded securities can be valued on the assumption that the world is risk neutral. The result proves to be very useful in practice. In a risk-neutral world the expected return from all securities is the risk-free interest rate, and the correct discount rate for expected cash flows is also the risk-free interest rate.

An implied volatility is the volatility that, when substituted into the Black–Scholes–Merton equation or its extensions, gives the market price of the option. Traders monitor implied volatilities. They often quote the implied volatility of an option rather than its price. They have developed procedures for using the volatilities implied by the prices of actively traded options to estimate the volatilities appropriate for other options.

The Black–Scholes–Merton results can be extended to cover European call and put options on dividend-paying stocks. One procedure is to use the Black–Scholes–Merton formula with the stock price reduced by the present value of the dividends anticipated during the life of the option and the volatility equal to the volatility of the stock price net of the present value of these dividends. Fischer Black has suggested an approximate way of valuing American call options on a dividend-paying stock. His approach involves setting the price equal to the greater of two European option prices. The first European option expires at the same time as the American option; the second expires immediately prior to the final ex-dividend date.

FURTHER READING

On the Black–Scholes–Merton model and its extensions

Black, F. "Fact and Fantasy in the Use of Options and Corporate Liabilities," *Financial Analysts Journal*, 31 (July/August 1975): 36–41, 61–72.

Black, F. "How We Came Up with the Option Pricing Formula," *Journal of Portfolio Management*, 15, 2 (1989): 4–8.

Black, F., and M. Scholes. "The Pricing of Options and Corporate Liabilities," *Journal of Political Economy*, 81 (May–June 1973): 637–59.

Hull, J. *Options, Futures, and Other Derivatives*, 8th edn. Upper Saddle River, NJ: Prentice Hall, 2012.

Merton, R. C. "Theory of Rational Option Pricing," *Bell Journal of Economics and Management Science*, 4 (Spring 1973): 141–83.

On the causes of volatility

Fama, E. F. "The Behavior of Stock Market Prices," *Journal of Business*, 38 (January 1965): 34–105.

French, K. R. "Stock Returns and the Weekend Effect," *Journal of Financial Economics*, 8 (March 1980): 55–69.

French, K. R., and R. Roll. "Stock Return Variances: The Arrival of Information and the Reaction of Traders," *Journal of Financial Economics*, 17 (September 1986): 5–26.

Roll, R. "Orange Juice and Weather," *American Economic Review*, 74, 5 (December 1984): 861–80.

Quiz (Answers at End of Book)

13.1. What does the Black–Scholes–Merton stock option pricing model assume about the probability distribution of the stock price in one year? What does it assume about the probability distribution of the continuously compounded rate of return on the stock during the year?

13.2. The volatility of a stock price is 30% per annum. What is the standard deviation of the percentage price change in one trading day?

13.3. Explain how risk-neutral valuation could be used to derive the Black–Scholes–Merton formulas.

13.4. Calculate the price of a three-month European put option on a non-dividend-paying stock with a strike price of \$50 when the current stock price is \$50, the risk-free interest rate is 10% per annum, and the volatility is 30% per annum.

13.5. What difference does it make to your calculations in the previous question if a dividend of \$1.50 is expected in two months?

13.6. What is meant by implied volatility? How would you calculate the volatility implied by a European put option price?

13.7. What is Black's approximation for valuing an American call option on a dividend-paying stock?

Practice Questions (Answers in Solutions Manual/Study Guide)

13.8. A stock price is currently \$40. Assume that the expected return from the stock is 15% and its volatility is 25%. What is the probability distribution for the rate of return (with continuous compounding) earned over a one-year period?

13.9. A stock price has an expected return of 16% and a volatility of 35%. The current price is \$38.

(a) What is the probability that a European call option on the stock with an exercise price of \$40 and a maturity date in six months will be exercised?

(b) What is the probability that a European put option on the stock with the same exercise price and maturity will be exercised?

13.10. Prove that, with the notation in the chapter, a 95% confidence interval for S_T is between

$$S_0e^{(\mu-\sigma^2/2)T-1.96\sigma\sqrt{T}} \quad \text{and} \quad S_0e^{(\mu-\sigma^2/2)T+1.96\sigma\sqrt{T}}$$

13.11. A portfolio manager announces that the average of the returns realized in each of the last 10 years is 20% per annum. In what respect is this statement misleading?

13.12. Assume that a non-dividend-paying stock has an expected return of μ and a volatility of σ. An innovative financial institution has just announced that it will trade a derivative that pays off a dollar amount equal to

$$\frac{1}{T}\ln\left(\frac{S_T}{S_0}\right)$$

at time T. The variables S_0 and S_T denote the values of the stock price at time zero and time T.

(a) Describe the payoff from this derivative.

(b) Use risk-neutral valuation to calculate the price of the derivative at time zero.

13.13. What is the price of a European call option on a non-dividend-paying stock when the stock price is \$52, the strike price is \$50, the risk-free interest rate is 12% per annum, the volatility is 30% per annum, and the time to maturity is three months?

13.14. What is the price of a European put option on a non-dividend-paying stock when the stock price is \$69, the strike price is \$70, the risk-free interest rate is 5% per annum, the volatility is 35% per annum, and the time to maturity is six months?

13.15. A call option on a non-dividend-paying stock has a market price of \$2.50. The stock price is \$15, the exercise price is \$13, the time to maturity is three months, and the risk-free interest rate is 5% per annum. What is the implied volatility?

13.16. Show that the Black–Scholes–Merton formula for a call option gives a price that tends to $\max(S_0 - K, 0)$ as $T \to 0$.

13.17. Explain carefully why Black's approach to evaluating an American call option on a dividend-paying stock may give an approximate answer even when only one dividend is anticipated. Does the answer given by Black's approach understate or overstate the true option value? Explain your answer.

13.18. Consider an American call option on a stock. The stock price is \$70, the time to maturity is eight months, the risk-free rate of interest is 10% per annum, the exercise price is \$65, and the volatility is 32%. A dividend of \$1 is expected after three months and again after six months. Use the results in the appendix to show that it can never be optimal to exercise the option on either of the two dividend dates. Use DerivaGem to calculate the price of the option.

13.19. A stock price is currently \$50 and the risk-free interest rate is 5%. Use the DerivaGem software to translate the following table of European call options on the stock into a table of implied volatilities, assuming no dividends. Are the option prices consistent with the assumptions underlying Black–Scholes–Merton?

	Maturity (months)		
Strike price (\$)	*3*	*6*	*12*
45	7.00	8.30	10.50
50	3.50	5.20	7.50
55	1.60	2.90	5.10

13.20. Show that the Black–Scholes–Merton formulas for call and put options satisfy put–call parity.

13.21. Show that the probability that a European call option will be exercised in a risk-neutral world is, with the notation introduced in this chapter, $N(d_2)$. What is an expression for the value of a derivative that pays off \$100 if the price of a stock at time T is greater than K?

Further Questions

13.22. If the volatility of a stock is 18% per annum, estimate the standard deviation of the percentage price change in (a) one day, (b) one week, and (c) one month.

13.23. A stock price is currently \$50. Assume that the expected return from the stock is 18% per annum and its volatility is 30% per annum. What is the probability distribution for the stock price in two years? Calculate the mean and standard deviation of the distribution. Determine the 95% confidence interval.

13.24. Suppose that observations on a stock price (in dollars) at the end of each of 15 consecutive weeks are as follows:

30.2, 32.0, 31.1, 30.1, 30.2, 30.3, 30.6, 33.0, 32.9, 33.0, 33.5, 33.5, 33.7, 33.5, 33.2

Estimate the stock price volatility. What is the standard error of your estimate?

13.25. A financial institution plans to offer a derivative that pays off a dollar amount equal to S_T^2 at time T, where S_T is the stock price at time T. Assume no dividends. Defining other variables as necessary use risk-neutral valuation to calculate the price of the derivative at time zero. (*Hint*: The expected value of S_T^2 can be calculated from the mean and variance of S_T given in Section 13.1.)

13.26. Consider an option on a non-dividend-paying stock when the stock price is \$30, the exercise price is \$29, the risk-free interest rate is 5% per annum, the volatility is 25% per annum, and the time to maturity is four months.
(a) What is the price of the option if it is a European call?
(b) What is the price of the option if it is an American call?
(c) What is the price of the option if it is a European put?
(d) Verify that put–call parity holds.

13.27. Assume that the stock in Problem 13.26 is due to go ex-dividend in 1.5 months. The expected dividend is 50 cents.
(a) What is the price of the option if it is a European call?
(b) What is the price of the option if it is a European put?
(c) Use the results in the appendix to this chapter to determine whether there are any circumstances under which the option is exercised early.

13.28. Consider an American call option when the stock price is \$18, the exercise price is \$20, the time to maturity is six months, the volatility is 30% per annum, and the risk-free interest rate is 10% per annum. Two equal dividends of 40 cents are expected during the life of the option, with ex-dividend dates at the end of two months and five months. Use Black's approximation and the DerivaGem software to value the option. Suppose now that the dividend is D on each ex-dividend date. Use the results in the Appendix to determine how high D can be without the American option being exercised early.

APPENDIX

The Early Exercise of American Call Options on Dividend-Paying Stocks

In Chapter 10, we saw that it is never optimal to exercise an American call option on a non-dividend-paying stock before the expiration date. A similar argument shows that the only times when a call option on a dividend-paying stock should be exercised are immediately before an ex-dividend date and on the expiration date. We assume that n ex-dividend dates are anticipated and that they are at times $t_1, t_2, \dots, t_n$, with $t_1 < t_2 < \cdots < t_n$. The dividends will be denoted by $D_1, D_2, \dots, D_n$, respectively.

We start by considering the possibility of early exercise immediately prior to the final ex-dividend date (i.e., at time t_n). If the option is exercised at time t_n, the investor receives

$$S(t_n) - K$$

where $S(t)$ denotes the stock price at time t.

If the option is not exercised, the stock price drops to $S(t_n) - D_n$. As shown in Chapter 10, a lower bound for the price of the option is then

$$S(t_n) - D_n - Ke^{-r(T-t_n)}$$

It follows that if

$$S(t_n) - D_n - Ke^{-r(T-t_n)} \geqslant S(t_n) - K$$

that is,

$$D_n \leqslant K(1 - e^{-r(T-t_n)}) \tag{13A.1}$$

it cannot be optimal to exercise at time t_n. On the other hand, if

$$D_n > K(1 - e^{-r(T-t_n)}) \tag{13A.2}$$

it can be shown that it is always optimal to exercise at time t_n for a sufficiently high value of $S(t_n)$. Inequality (13A.2) is most likely to be satisfied when the final ex-dividend date is fairly close to the maturity of the option (i.e., when $T - t_n$ is small) and the dividend is large.

Consider next time t_{n-1}, the penultimate ex-dividend date. If the option is exercised immediately prior to time t_{n-1}, the investor receives

$$S(t_{n-1}) - K$$

If the option is not exercised at time t_{n-1}, the stock price drops to $S(t_{n-1}) - D_{n-1}$ and the earliest subsequent time at which exercise could take place is t_n. A lower bound to the option price if it is not exercised at time t_{n-1} is

$$S(t_{n-1}) - D_{n-1} - Ke^{-r(t_n-t_{n-1})}$$

It follows that if

$$S(t_{n-1}) - D_{n-1} - Ke^{-r(t_n-t_{n-1})} \geqslant S(t_{n-1}) - K$$

or

$$D_{n-1} \leqslant K(1 - e^{-r(t_n-t_{n-1})})$$

Example 13A.1 Test of whether a call option should ever be exercised early

Example 13.6 considers an American call option where $S_0 = 40$, $K = 40$, $r = 0.09$, $\sigma = 0.30$, $t_1 = 0.1667$, $t_2 = 0.4167$, $T = 0.5$, $D_1 = D_2 = 0.5$, so that

$$K(1 - e^{-r(t_2-t_1)}) = 40(1 - e^{-0.09\times0.25}) = 0.89$$

Because this is greater than 0.5, it follows from inequality (13A.3) that the option should never be exercised on the first ex-dividend date. Also,

$$K(1 - e^{-r(T-t_2)}) = 40(1 - e^{-0.09\times0.08333}) = 0.30$$

Because this is less than 0.5, it follows from inequality (13A.1) that when the option is sufficiently deep in the money it should be exercised on the second ex-dividend date.

it is not optimal to exercise at time t_{n-1}. Similarly, for any $i < n$, if

$$D_i \leqslant K(1 - e^{-r(t_{i+1}-t_i)}) \qquad \textbf{(13A.3)}$$

it is not optimal to exercise immediately prior to time t_i. Example 13A.1 illustrates the use of these results.

The inequality (13A.3) is approximately equivalent to

$$D_i \leqslant Kr(t_{i+1} - t_i)$$

Assuming that K is fairly close to the current stock price, the dividend yield on the stock has to be either close to or above the risk-free rate of interest for the inequality not to be satisfied.

We can conclude from this analysis that, in many circumstances, the most likely time for the early exercise of an American call is the final ex-dividend date, t_n. Furthermore, if the inequality (13A.3) holds for $i = 1, 2, \ldots, n-1$ and the inequality (13A.1) also holds, then we can be certain that early exercise is never optimal.

CHAPTER 14

Employee Stock Options

Employee stock options are call options on a company's stock granted by the company to its employees. The options give the employees a stake in the fortunes of the company. If the company does well so that the company's stock price moves above the strike price, employees gain by exercising the options and then selling at the market price the stock they buy at the strike price.

Employee stock options have become very popular in the last 20 years. Many companies, particularly technology companies, feel that the only way they can attract and keep the best employees is to offer them very attractive stock option packages. Some companies grant options only to senior management; others grant them to people at all levels in the organization. Microsoft was one of the first companies to use employee stock options. All Microsoft employees were granted options and, as the company's stock price rose, it is estimated that over 10,000 of them became millionaires. In 2003, Microsoft announced that it would discontinue the use of options and award shares of Microsoft to employees instead. But many other companies throughout the world continue to be enthusiastic users of employee stock options.

Employee stock options are popular with start-up companies. Often these companies do not have the resources to pay key employees as much as they could earn with an established company and they solve this problem by supplementing the salaries of the employees with stock options. If the company does well and shares are sold to the public in an IPO, the options are likely to prove to be very valuable. Some newly formed companies have even granted options to students who worked for just a few months during their summer break—and in some cases this has led to windfalls of hundreds of thousands of dollars for the students!

This chapter explains how stock option plans work and how their popularity has been influenced by their accounting treatment. It discusses whether employee stock options help to align the interests of shareholders with those of top executives running a company. It also describes how these options are valued and looks at backdating scandals.

14.1 CONTRACTUAL ARRANGEMENTS

Employee stock options often last as long as 10 to 15 years. Very often the strike price is set equal to the stock price on the grant date so that the option is initially at the money.

From Chapter 14 of *Fundamentals of Futures and Options Markets*, Eighth Edition. John C. Hull.

The following are usually features of employee stock option plans:

1. There is a vesting period during which the options cannot be exercised. This vesting period can be as long as four years.
2. When employees leave their jobs (voluntarily or involuntarily) during the vesting period, they forfeit their options.
3. When employees leave (voluntarily or involuntarily) after the vesting period, they forfeit options that are out of the money and they have to exercise vested options that are in the money almost immediately.
4. Employees are not permitted to sell the options.
5. When an employee exercises options, the company issues new shares and sells them to the employee for the strike price.

The Early Exercise Decision

The fourth feature of employee stock option plans just mentioned has important implications. If employees, for whatever reason, want to realize a cash benefit from options that have vested, they must exercise the options and sell the underlying shares. They cannot sell the options to someone else. This leads to a tendency for employee stock options to be exercised earlier than similar regular exchange-traded or over-the-counter call options.

Consider a call option on a stock paying no dividends. In Section 10.5 we showed that, if it is a regular call option, it should never be exercised early. The holder of the option will always do better by selling the option rather than exercising it before the end of its life. However, the arguments we used in Section 10.5 are not applicable to employee stock options because they cannot be sold. The only way employees can realize a cash benefit from the options (or diversify their holdings) is by exercising the options and selling the stock. It is therefore not unusual for an employee stock option to be exercised well before it would be optimal to exercise the option if it were a regular exchange-traded or over-the-counter option.

Should an employee ever exercise his or her options before maturity and then keep the stock rather than selling it? Assume that the option's strike price is constant during the life of the option and the option can be exercised at any time. To answer the question we consider two options: the employee stock option and an otherwise identical regular option that can be sold in the market. We refer to the first option as option A and the second as option B. If the stock pays no dividends, we know that option B should never be exercised early. It follows that it is not optimal to exercise option A and keep the stock. If the employee wants to maintain a stake in his or her company, a better strategy is to keep the option. This delays paying the strike price and maintains the insurance value of the option, as described in Section 10.5. Only when it is optimal to exercise option B can it be a rational strategy for an employee to exercise option A before maturity and keep the stock.[1] As discussed in the appendix to Chapter 13, it is optimal to exercise option B only when a relatively high dividend is imminent.

In practice the early exercise behavior of employees varies widely from company to company. In some companies, there is a culture of not exercising early; in others,

[1] The only exception to this could be when an executive wants to own the stock for its voting rights.

employees tend to exercise options and sell the stock soon after the end of the vesting period, even if the options are only slightly in the money.

14.2 DO OPTIONS ALIGN THE INTERESTS OF SHAREHOLDERS AND MANAGERS?

For investors to have confidence in capital markets, it is important that the interests of shareholders and managers are reasonably well aligned. This means that managers should be motivated to make decisions that are in the best interests of shareholders. Managers are the agents of the shareholders and, as discussed in Chapter 8, economists use the term *agency costs* to describe the losses shareholders experience because managers do not act in their best interests. The prison sentences that are being served in the United States by some executives who chose to ignore the interests of their shareholders can be viewed as an attempt by the United States to signal to investors that, despite Enron and other scandals, it is determined to keep agency costs low.

Do employee stock options help align the interests of employees and shareholders? The answer to this question is not straightforward. There can be little doubt that they serve a useful purpose for a start-up company. The options are an excellent way for the main shareholders, who are usually also senior executives, to motivate employees to work long hours. If the company is successful and there is an IPO, the employees will do very well; but if the company is unsuccessful, the options will be worthless.

It is the options granted to the senior executives of publicly traded companies that are most controversial. It has been estimated that employee stock options account for about 50% of the remuneration of top executives in the United States. Executive stock options are sometimes referred to as an executive's "pay for performance." If the company's stock price goes up, so that shareholders make gains, the executive is rewarded. However, this overlooks the asymmetric payoffs of options. If the company does badly then the shareholders lose money, but all that happens to the executives is that they fail to make a gain. Unlike the shareholders, they do not experience a loss.[2] A better type of pay for performance involves the simpler strategy of giving stock to executives. The gains and losses of the executives then mirror those of other shareholders.

What temptations do stock options create for a senior executive? Suppose an executive plans to exercise a large number of stock options in three months and sell the stock. He or she might be tempted to time announcements of good news—or even move earnings from one quarter to another—so that the stock price increases just before the options are exercised. Alternatively, if at-the-money options are due to be granted to the executive in three months, the executive might be tempted to take actions that reduce the stock price just before the grant date. The type of behavior we are talking about here is of course totally unacceptable—and may well be illegal. But the backdating scandals, which are discussed later in this chapter, show that the way some executives have handled issues related to stock options leaves much to be desired.

Even when there is no impropriety of the type we have just mentioned, executive stock options are liable to have the effect of motivating executives to focus on short-term

[2] When options have moved out of the money, companies have sometimes replaced them with new at-the-money options. This practice known as "repricing" leads to the executive's gains and losses being even less closely tied to those of the shareholders.

profits at the expense of longer-term performance. In some cases they might even take risks they would not otherwise take (and risks that are not in the interests of the shareholders) because of the asymmetric payoffs of options. Managers of large funds worry that, because stock options are such a huge component of an executive's compensation, they are liable to be a big source of distraction. Senior management may spend too much time thinking about all the different aspects of their compensation and not enough time running the company!

A manager's inside knowledge and ability to affect outcomes and announcements is always liable to interact with his or her trading in a way that is to the disadvantage of other shareholders. One radical suggestion for mitigating this problem is to require executives to give notice to the market—perhaps one week's notice—of an intention to buy or sell their company's stock.[3] (Once the notice of an intention to trade had been given, it would be binding on the executive.) This allows the market to form its own conclusions about why the executive is trading. As a result, the price may increase before the executive buys and decrease before the executive sells.

14.3 ACCOUNTING ISSUES

An employee stock option represents a cost to the company and a benefit to the employee just like any other form of compensation. This point, which for many is self-evident, is actually quite controversial. Many corporate executives appear to believe that an option has no value unless it is in the money. As a result, they argue that an at-the-money option issued by the company is not a cost to the company. The reality is that, if options are valuable to employees, they must represent a cost to the company's shareholders—and therefore to the company. There is no free lunch. The cost to the company of the options arises from the fact that the company has agreed that, if its stock does well, it will sell shares to employees at a price less than that which would apply in the open market.

Prior to 1995 the cost charged to the income statement of a company when it issued stock options was the intrinsic value. Most options were at the money when they were first issued, so that this cost was zero. In 1995, accounting standard FAS 123 was issued. Many people expected it to require the expensing of options at their fair value. However, as a result of intense lobbying, the 1995 version of FAS 123 only encouraged companies to expense the fair value of the options they granted on the income statement. It did not require them to do so. If fair value was not expensed on the income statement, it had to be reported in a footnote to the company's accounts.

Accounting standards have now changed to require the expensing of stock options at their fair value on the income statement. In February 2004 the International Accounting Standards Board issued IAS 2 requiring companies to start expensing stock options in 2005. In December 2004 FAS 123 was revised to require the expensing of employee stock options in the United States starting in 2005.

The effect of the new accounting standards is to require options to be valued on the grant date and the valuation amount to be expensed on the income statement. Valuation at a later time than the grant date is not required. It can be argued that

[3] This would apply to the exercise of options because, if an executive wants to exercise options and sell the stock that is acquired, then he or she would have to give notice of intention to sell.

options should be revalued at financial year ends (or every quarter) until they are exercised or reach the end of their lives.[4] This would treat them in the same way as other derivative transactions entered into by the company. If the option became more valuable from one year to the next, there would then be an additional amount to be expensed. However, if it declined in value, there would be a positive impact on income. This approach would have a number of advantages. The cumulative charge to the company would reflect the actual cost of the options (either zero if the options are not exercised or the option payoff if they are exercised). Although the charge in any year would depend on the option pricing model used, the cumulative charge over the life of the option would not.[5] Arguably there would be much less incentive for the company to engage in the backdating practices described later in the chapter. The disadvantage usually cited for accounting in this way is that it is undesirable because it introduces volatility into the income statement.[6]

Nontraditional Option Plans

It is easy to understand why pre-2005 employee stock options tended to be at the money on the grant date and have strike prices that did not change during the life of the option. Any departure from this standard arrangement was likely to require the options to be expensed. Now that accounting rules have changed so that all options are expensed at fair value, many companies are considering alternatives to the standard arrangement.

One argument against the standard arrangement is that employees do well when the stock market goes up, even if their own company's stock price does less well than the market. One way of overcoming this problem is to tie the strike price of the options to the performance of the S&P 500. Suppose that on the option grant date the stock price is $30 and the S&P 500 is 1,500. The strike price would initially be set at $30. If the S&P 500 increased by 10% to 1,650, then the strike price would also increase by 10% to $33. If the S&P 500 moved down by 15% to 1,275, then the strike price would also move down by 15% to $25.50. The effect of this is that the company's stock price performance has to beat the performance of the S&P 500 to become in the money. As an alternative to using the S&P 500 as the reference index, the company could use an index of the prices of stocks in the same industrial sector as the company.

In another variation on the standard arrangement, the strike price increases through time in a predetermined way such that the shares of the stock have to provide a certain minimum return per year for the options to be in the money. In some cases profit targets are specified and the options vest only if the profit targets are met.[7]

---

[4] See J. Hull and A. White, "Accounting for Employee Stock Options: A Practical Approach to Handling the Valuation Issues," *Journal of Derivatives Accounting*, 1, 1 (2004): 3–9.

[5] Interestingly, if an option is settled in cash rather than by the company issuing new shares, it is subject to the accounting treatment proposed here. (However, there is no economic difference between an option that is settled in cash and one that is settled by selling new shares to the employee.)

[6] In fact the income statement is likely be less volatile if stock options are revalued. When the company does well, income is reduced by revaluing the executive stock options. When the company does badly, it is increased.

[7] This type of option is difficult to value because the payoff depends on reported accounting numbers as well as the stock price. Usually valuations assume that the profit targets will be achieved.

14.4 VALUATION

Accounting standards give companies quite a bit of latitude in choosing a method for valuing employee stock options. A frequently used simple approach is based on what is known as the option's *expected life*. This is the average time for which employees hold the option before it is exercised or expires. The expected life can be approximately estimated from historical data on the early exercise behavior of employees and reflects the vesting period, the impact of employees leaving the company, and the tendency we mentioned in Section 14.1 for employee stock options to be exercised earlier than regular options. The Black–Scholes–Merton model is used with the life of the option, T, set equal to the expected life. The volatility is usually estimated from several years of historical data as described in Section 13.4.

It should be emphasized that using the Black–Scholes–Merton formula in this way has no theoretical validity. There is no reason why the value of a European stock option with the time to maturity, T, set equal to the expected life should be approximately the same as the value of the American-style employee stock option in which we are interested. However, the results given by the model are not totally unreasonable. Companies, when reporting their employee stock option expense, will frequently mention the volatility and expected life used in their Black–Scholes–Merton computations. Example 14.1 describes how to value an employee stock option using this approach.

More sophisticated approaches, where the probability of exercise is estimated as a function of the stock price and time to maturity, are sometimes used. A binomial tree similar to the one in Chapter 12 is created, but with the calculations at each node being adjusted to reflect (a) whether the option has vested, (b) the probability of the employee leaving the company, and (c) the probability of the employee choosing to exercise.[8] Hull and White propose a simple rule where exercise takes place when the ratio of the stock price to the strike price reaches some multiple.[9] This requires only one parameter relating to early exercise (the multiple) to be estimated.

Example 14.1 A popular approach for valuing employee stock options

A company grants 1,000,000 options to its executives on November 1, 2013. The stock price on that date is \$30 and the strike price of the options is also \$30. The options last for 10 years and vest after 3 years. The company has issued similar at-the-money options for the last 10 years. The average time to exercise or expiry of these options is 4.5 years. The company therefore decides to use an "expected life" of 4.5 years. It estimates the long-term volatility of the stock price, using 5 years of historical data, to be 25%. The present value of dividends during the next 4.5 years is estimated to be \$4. The 4.5-year zero-coupon risk-free interest rate is 5%. The option is therefore valued using the Black–Scholes–Merton model (adjusted for dividends as described in Section 13.10) with $S_0 = 30 - 4 = 26$, $K = 30$, $r = 5\%$,

[8] For more details and an example, see J. Hull *Options, Futures, and Other Derivatives*, 8th edn. Pearson, 2012.

[9] See J. Hull and A. White, "How to Value Employee Stock Options," *Financial Analysts Journal*, 60, 1 (2004): 3–9. Software for implementing this approach is available at: www.rotman.utoronto.ca/~hull.

Business Snapshot 14.1 Employee stock options and dilution

Consider a company with 100,000 shares each worth $50. It surprises the market with an announcement that it is granting 100,000 stock options to its employees with a strike price of $50. If the market sees little benefit to the shareholders from the employee stock options in the form of reduced salaries and more highly motivated managers, the stock price will decline immediately after the announcement of the employee stock options. If the stock price declines to $45, the dilution cost to the current shareholders is $5 per share or $500,000 in total.

Suppose that the company does well so that by the end of three years the share price is $100. Suppose further that all the options are exercised at this point. The payoff to the employees is $50 per option. It is tempting to argue that there will be further dilution in that 100,000 shares worth $100 per share are now merged with 100,000 shares for which only $50 is paid, so that (a) the share price reduces to $75 and (b) the payoff to the option holders is only $25 per option. However, this argument is flawed. The exercise of the options is anticipated by the market and already reflected in the share price. The payoff from each option exercised is $50.

This example illustrates the general point that when markets are efficient the impact of dilution from employee stock options is reflected in the stock price as soon as they are announced and does not need to be taken into account again when the options are valued.

Dilution

The fact that a company issues new stock when an employee stock option is exercised leads to some dilution for existing stock holders because new shares are being sold to employees at below the current stock price. It is natural to assume that this dilution takes place at the time the option is exercised. However, this is not the case. Stock prices are diluted when the market first hears about a stock option grant. The possible exercise of options is anticipated and immediately reflected in the stock price. This point is emphasized by the example in Business Snapshot 14.1.

The stock price immediately after a grant is announced to the public reflects any dilution. Provided that this stock price is used in the valuation of the option, it is not necessary to adjust the option price for dilution. In many instances the market expects a company to make regular stock option grants and so the market price of the stock anticipates dilution even before the announcement is made.

14.5 BACKDATING SCANDALS

No discussion of employee stock options would be complete without mentioning backdating scandals. Backdating is the practice of marking a document with a date that precedes the current date.

Suppose that a company decides to grant at-the-money options to its employees on April 30 when the stock price is $50. If the stock price was $42 on April 3, it is tempting to behave as if the options were granted on April 3 and use a strike price of $42. This is legal provided that the company reports the options as $8 in the money on the date when the decision to grant the options is made, April 30. But it is illegal for the company to report

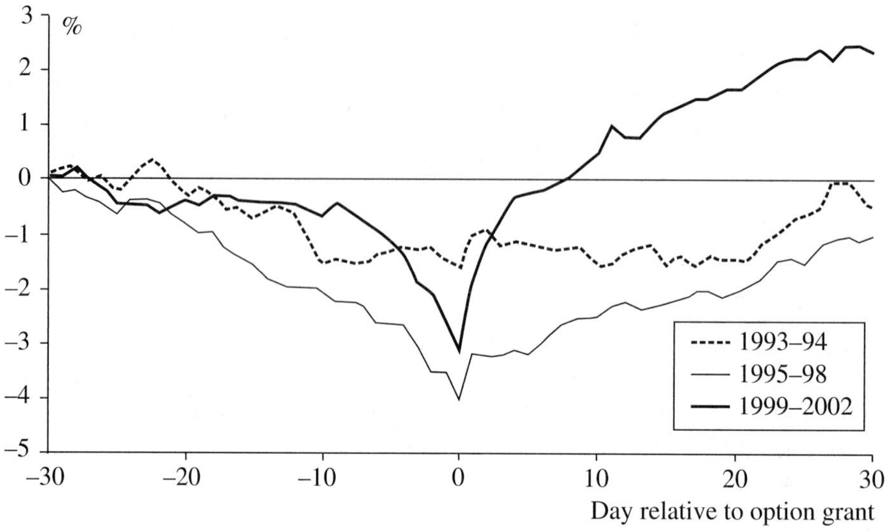

Figure 14.1 Erik Lie's results providing evidence of backdating (reproduced, with permission, from www.biz.uiowa.edu/faculty/elie/backdating.htm)

the options as at-the-money and granted on April 3. The value on April 3 of an option with a strike price of $42 is much less than its value on April 30. Shareholders are misled about the true cost of the decision to grant options if the company reports the options as granted on April 3.

How prevalent is backdating? To answer this question, researchers have investigated whether a company's stock price has, on average, a tendency to be low at the time of the grant date that the company reports. Early research by Yermack shows that stock prices tend to increase after reported grant dates.[10] Lie extended Yermack's work, showing that stock prices also tended to decrease before reported grant dates.[11] Furthermore he showed that the pre- and post-grant stock price patterns had become more pronounced over time. His results are summarized in Figure 14.1, which shows average abnormal returns around the grant date for the 1993–94, 1995–98, and 1999–2002 periods. (Abnormal returns are the returns after adjustments for returns on the market portfolio and the beta of the stock.) Standard statistical tests show that it is almost impossible for the patterns shown in Figure 14.1 to be observed by chance. This led both academics and regulators to conclude in 2002 that backdating had become a common practice. In August 2002 the SEC required option grants by public companies to be reported within two business days. Heron and Lie showed that this led to a dramatic reduction in the abnormal returns around the grant dates—particularly for those companies that complied with this requirement.[12] It might be argued that the patterns in Figure 14.1 are explained by managers simply choosing grant dates after bad news or before good news, but the Heron and Lie study provides compelling evidence that this is not the case.

[10] See D. Yermack, "Good timing: CEO stock option awards and company news announcements," *Journal of Finance*, 52 (1997), 449–476.

[11] See E. Lie, "On the timing of CEO stock option awards," *Management Science*, 51, 5 (May 2005), 802–12.

[12] See R. Heron and E. Lie, "Does backdating explain the stock price pattern around executive stock option grants," *Journal of Financial Economics*, 83, 2 (February 2007), 271–95.

Estimates of the number of companies that illegally backdated stock option grants in the United States vary widely. Tens and maybe hundreds of companies seem to have engaged in the practice. Many companies seem to have adopted the view that it was acceptable to backdate up to one month. Some CEOs resigned when their backdating practices came to light. In August 2007, Gregory Reyes of Brocade Communications Systems, Inc., became the first CEO to be tried for backdating stock option grants. Allegedly, Mr. Reyes said to a human resources employee: "It is not illegal if you do not get caught." In June 2010, he was sentenced to 18 months in prison and fined \$15 million. This was later reversed on appeal.

Companies involved in backdating have had to restate past financial statements and have been defendants in class action suits brought by shareholders who claim to have lost money as a result of backdating. For example, McAfee announced in December 2007 that it would restate earnings between 1995 and 2005 by \$137.4 million. In 2006, it set aside \$13.8 million to cover lawsuits.

SUMMARY

Executive compensation has increased very fast in the last 20 years and much of the increase has come from the exercise of stock options granted to the executives. Until 2005, at-the-money stock option grants were a very attractive form of compensation. They had no impact on the income statement and were very valuable to employees. Accounting standards now require options to be expensed.

There are a number of different approaches to valuing employee stock options. A common approach is to use the Black–Scholes–Merton model with the life of the option set equal to the expected time the option will remain unexercised.

Academic research has shown beyond doubt that many companies have engaged in the illegal practice of backdating stock option grants in order to reduce the strike price, while still contending that the options were at the money. The first prosecutions for this illegal practice were in 2007.

FURTHER READING

Carpenter, J., "The Exercise and Valuation of Executive Stock Options," *Journal of Financial Economics*, 48, 2 (May): 127–58.

Core, J. E., and W. R. Guay, "Stock Option Plans for Non-Executive Employees," *Journal of Financial Economics*, 61, 2 (2001): 253–87.

Heron, R., and E. Lie, "Does Backdating Explain the Stock Price Pattern around Executive Stock Option Grants," *Journal of Financial Economics*, 83, 2 (February 2007): 271–95.

Huddart, S., and M. Lang, "Employee Stock Option Exercises: An Empirical Analysis," *Journal of Accounting and Economics*, 21, 1 (February): 5–43.

Hull, J., and A. White, "How to Value Employee Stock Options," *Financial Analysts Journal,* 60, 1 (January/February 2004): 3–9.

Lie, E., "On the Timing of CEO Stock Option Awards," *Management Science*, 51, 5 (May 2005): 802–12.

Rubinstein, M., "On the Accounting Valuation of Employee Stock Options," *Journal of Derivatives*, 3, 1 (Fall 1996): 8–24.

Yermack, D., "Good Timing: CEO Stock Option Awards and Company News Announcements," *Journal of Finance*, 52 (1997): 449–76.

Quiz (Answers at End of Book)

14.1. Why was it attractive for companies to grant at-the-money stock options prior to 2005? What changed in 2005?

14.2. What are the main differences between a typical employee stock option and an American call option traded on an exchange or in the over-the-counter market?

14.3. Explain why employee stock options on a non-dividend-paying stock are frequently exercised before the end of their lives, whereas an exchange-traded call option on such a stock is never exercised early.

14.4. "Stock option grants are good because they motivate executives to act in the best interests of shareholders." Discuss this viewpoint.

14.5. "Granting stock options to executives is like allowing a professional footballer to bet on the outcome of games." Discuss this viewpoint.

14.6. Why did some companies backdate stock option grants in the US prior to 2002? What changed in 2002?

14.7. In what way would the benefits of backdating be reduced if a stock option grant had to be revalued at the end of each quarter?

Practice Questions (Answers in Solutions Manual/Study Guide)

14.8. Explain how you would do the analysis to produce a chart such as the one in Figure 14.1.

14.9. On May 31 a company's stock price is $70. One million shares are outstanding. An executive exercises 100,000 stock options with a strike price of $50. What is the impact of this on the stock price?

14.10. The notes accompanying a company's financial statements say: "Our executive stock options last 10 years and vest after 4 years. We valued the options granted this year using the Black–Scholes–Merton model with an expected life of 5 years and a volatility of 20%." What does this mean? Discuss the modeling approach used by the company.

14.11. A company has granted 500,000 options to its executives. The stock price and strike price are both $40. The options last for 12 years and vest after 4 years. The company decides to value the options using an expected life of 5 years and a volatility of 30% per annum. The company pays no dividends and the risk-free rate is 4%. What will the company report as an expense for the options on its income statement?

14.12. A company's CFO says: "The accounting treatment of stock options is crazy. We granted 10,000,000 at-the-money stock options to our employees last year when the stock price was $30. We estimated the value of each option on the grant date to be $5. At our year-end the stock price had fallen to $4, but we were still stuck with a $50 million charge to the P&L." Discuss.

Further Questions

14.13. A company has granted 2,000,000 options to its employees. The stock price and strike price are both \$60. The options last for 8 years and vest after 2 years. The company decides to value the options using an expected life of 6 years and a volatility of 22% per annum. Dividends on the stock are \$1 per year, payable halfway through each year, and the risk-free rate is 5%. What will the company report as an expense for the options on its income statement?

14.14. (a) Hedge funds earn a management fee plus an incentive fee that is a percentage of the profits, if any, that they generate (see Business Snapshot 1.3). How is a fund manager motivated to behave with this type of compensation package?

(b) "Granting options to an executive gives the executive the same type of compensation package as a hedge fund manager and motivates him or her to behave in the same way as a hedge fund manager." Discuss this statement.

CHAPTER 15

Options on Stock Indices and Currencies

Options on stock indices and currencies were introduced in Chapter 9. In this chapter we discuss them in more detail. We explain how they work and review some of the ways they can be used. In the second half of the chapter, the valuation results in Chapter 13 are extended to cover European options on a stock paying a known dividend yield. It is then argued that both stock indices and currencies are analogous to stocks paying dividend yields. This enables the results for options on a stock paying a dividend yield to be applied to these types of options as well.

15.1 OPTIONS ON STOCK INDICES

Several exchanges trade options on stock indices. Some of the indices track the movement of the market as a whole. Others are based on the performance of a particular sector (e.g., computer technology, oil and gas, transportation, or telecoms). Among the index options traded on the Chicago Board Options Exchange (CBOE) are American and European options on the S&P 100 (OEX and XEO), European options on the S&P 500 (SPX), European options on the Dow Jones Industrial Average (DJX), and European options on the Nasdaq 100 (NDX). In Chapter 9, we explained that the CBOE trades LEAPS and flex options on individual stocks. It also offers these option products on indices.

One index option contract is on 100 times the index. (Note that the Dow Jones index used for index options is 0.01 times the usually quoted Dow Jones index.) Index options are settled in cash. This means that, on exercise of the option, the holder of a call option contract receives $(S - K) \times 100$ in cash and the writer of the option pays this amount in cash, where S is the value of the index at the close of trading on the day of the exercise and K is the strike price. Similarly, the holder of a put option contract receives $(K - S) \times 100$ in cash and the writer of the option pays this amount in cash.

Portfolio Insurance

Portfolio managers can use index options to limit their downside risk. Suppose that the value of an index today is S_0. Consider a manager in charge of a well-diversified portfolio whose beta is 1.0. A beta of 1.0 implies that the returns from the portfolio mirror those

Example 15.1 Protecting the value of a portfolio that mirrors the S&P 500

A manager in charge of a portfolio worth \$500,000 is concerned that the market might decline rapidly during the next three months and would like to use index options as a hedge against the portfolio declining below \$450,000. The portfolio is expected to mirror closely the S&P 500, which is currently standing at 1,000.

The Strategy
The manager buys five put option contracts with a strike price of 900 on the S&P 500.

The Result
The index drops to 880.
The value of the portfolio drops to \$440,000.
There is a payoff of \$10,000 from the five put option contracts.

from the index. Assuming the dividend yield from the portfolio is the same as the dividend yield from the index, the percentage changes in the value of the portfolio can be expected to be approximately the same as the percentage changes in the value of the index. Because each contract is on 100 times the index. It follows that the value of the portfolio is protected against the possibility of the index falling below K if, for each $100S_0$ dollars in the portfolio, the manager buys one put option contract with strike price K. Suppose that the manager's portfolio is worth \$500,000 and the value of the index is 1,000. The portfolio is worth 500 times the index. The manager can obtain insurance against the value of the portfolio dropping below \$450,000 in the next three months by buying five three-month put option contracts on the index with a strike price of 900.

To illustrate how the insurance works, consider the situation where the index drops to 880 in three months. The portfolio will be worth about \$440,000. The payoff from the options will be $5 \times (900 - 880) \times 100 = \$10{,}000$, bringing the total value of the portfolio up to the insured value of \$450,000 (see Example 15.1).

When the Portfolio's Beta Is Not 1.0

If the portfolio's beta (β) is not 1.0, β put options must be purchased for each $100S_0$ dollars in the portfolio, where S_0 is the current value of the index. Suppose that the \$500,000 portfolio just considered has a beta of 2.0 instead of 1.0. We continue to assume that the index is 1,000. The number of put options required is

$$2.0 \times \frac{500{,}000}{1{,}000 \times 100} = 10$$

rather than 5 as before.

To calculate the appropriate strike price, the capital asset pricing model can be used (see the appendix to Chapter 3). Suppose that the risk free rate is 12%, the dividend yield on both the index and the portfolio is 4%, and protection is required against the value of the portfolio dropping below \$450,000 in the next three months. Under the capital asset pricing model, the expected excess return of a portfolio over the risk-free rate is assumed to equal beta times the excess return of the index portfolio over the risk-free rate. The model enables the expected value of the portfolio to be calculated for different values of the index at the end of three months. Table 15.1 shows the calculations for the case where

Table 15.1 Calculation of expected value of portfolio when the index is 1,040 in three months and $\beta = 2.0$

Value of index in three months:	1,040
Return from change in index:	40/1,000, or 4% per three months
Dividends from index:	$0.25 \times 4 = 1\%$ per three months
Total return from index:	$4 + 1 = 5\%$ per three months
Risk-free interest rate:	$0.25 \times 12 = 3\%$ per three months
Excess return from index over risk-free interest rate:	$5 - 3 = 2\%$ per three months
Expected excess return from portfolio over risk-free interest rate:	$2 \times 2 = 4\%$ per three months
Expected return from portfolio:	$3 + 4 = 7\%$ per three months
Dividends from portfolio:	$0.25 \times 4 = 1\%$ per three months
Expected increase in value of portfolio:	$7 - 1 = 6\%$ per three months
Expected value of portfolio:	$500,000 × 1.06 = $530,000

the index is 1,040. In this case, the expected value of the portfolio at the end of the three months is $530,000. Similar calculations can be carried out for other values of the index at the end of the three months. The results are shown in Table 15.2. The strike price for the options that are purchased should be the index level corresponding to the protection level required on the portfolio. In this case, the protection level is $450,000 and so the correct strike price for the 10 put option contracts that are purchased is 960.[1]

To illustrate how the insurance works, consider what happens if the value of the index falls to 880. As shown in Table 15.2, the value of the portfolio is then about $370,000. The put options pay off (960 − 880) × 10 × 100 = $80,000, and this is exactly what is necessary to move the total value of the portfolio manager's position up from $370,000 to the required level of $450,000 (see Example 15.2).

Table 15.2 Relationship between value of index and value of portfolio for $\beta = 2.0$

Value of index in three months	*Value of portfolio in three months ($)*
1,080	570,000
1,040	530,000
1,000	490,000
960	450,000
920	410,000
880	370,000

[1] Approximately 1% of $500,000, or $5,000, will be earned in dividends over the next three months. If we want the insured level of $450,000 to include dividends, we can choose a strike price corresponding to $445,000 rather than $450,000. This is 955.

Example 15.2 Protecting the value of a portfolio that has a beta of 2.0

A manager in charge of a portfolio worth \$500,000 is concerned that the market might decline rapidly during the next three months and would like to use index options as a hedge against the value of the portfolio declining below \$450,000. The portfolio has a beta of 2.0 and the S&P 500 is standing at 1000. The risk-free rate is 12% per annum and the dividend yield on both the index and the portfolio is 4% per annum.

The Strategy
The manager buys 10 put option contracts with a strike price of 960.

The Outcome
The index drops to 880.
The value of the portfolio drops to \$370,000.
There is a payoff of \$80,000 from the 10 put option contracts

Comparing Examples 15.1 and 15.2, we see that there are two reasons why the cost of hedging increases as the beta of a portfolio increases. More put options are required and they have a higher strike price.

15.2 CURRENCY OPTIONS

Currency options are primarily traded in the over-the-counter market. The advantage of this market is that large trades are possible, with strike prices, expiration dates, and other features tailored to meet the needs of corporate treasurers. Although currency options do trade on NASDAQ OMX in the United States, the exchange-traded market for these options is much smaller than the over-the-counter market.

An example of a European call option is a contract that gives the holder the right to buy one million euros with U.S. dollars at an exchange rate of 1.4000 U.S. dollars per euro. If the actual exchange rate at the maturity of the option is 1.4500, the payoff is $1{,}000{,}000 \times (1.4500 - 1.4000) = \$50{,}000$. Similarly, an example of a European put option is a contract that gives the holder the right to sell ten million Australian dollars for U.S. dollars at an exchange rate of 0.9000 U.S. dollars per Australian dollar. If the actual exchange rate at the maturity of the option is 0.8700, the payoff is $10{,}000{,}000 \times (0.9000 - 0.8700) = \$300{,}000$.

For a corporation wishing to hedge a foreign exchange exposure, foreign currency options are an alternative to forward contracts. A company due to receive sterling at a known time in the future can hedge its risk by buying put options on sterling that mature at that time. The hedging strategy guarantees that the exchange rate applicable to the sterling will not be less than the strike price, while allowing the company to benefit from any favorable exchange-rate movements. Similarly, a company due to pay sterling at a known time in the future can hedge by buying calls on sterling that mature at that time. This hedging strategy guarantees that the cost of the sterling will not be greater than a certain amount while allowing the company to benefit from favorable exchange-rate movements. Whereas a forward contract locks in the exchange rate for a future transaction, an option provides a type of insurance. This insurance is not free. It costs nothing to enter into a forward transaction, but options require a premium to be paid up front.

Range Forwards

A *range forward contract* is a variation on a standard forward contract for hedging foreign exchange risk. Consider a U.S. company that knows it will receive one million pounds sterling in three months. Suppose that the three-month forward exchange rate is 1.5200 dollars per pound. The company could lock in this exchange rate for the dollars it receives by entering into a short forward contract to sell one million pounds sterling in three months. This would ensure that the amount received for the one million pounds is $1,520,000.

An alternative is to buy a European put option with a strike price of K_1 and sell a European call option with a strike price K_2, where $K_1 < 1.5200 < K_2$. This is known as a short range forward contract. The payoff is shown in Figure 15.1a. In both cases the options are on one million pounds. If the exchange rate in three months proves to be less than K_1, the put option is exercised and as a result the company is able to sell the one million pounds at an exchange rate of K_1. If the exchange rate is between K_1 and K_2, neither option is exercised and the company gets the current exchange rate for the one million pounds. If the exchange rate is greater than K_2, the call option is exercised against the company with the result that the one million pounds is sold at an exchange rate of K_2. The exchange rate realized for the one million pounds is shown in Figure 15.2.

If the company knew it was due to pay rather than receive one million pounds in three months, it could sell a European put option with strike price K_1 and buy a European call option with strike price K_2. This is known as a long range forward contract and the payoff is shown in Figure 15.1b. If the exchange rate in three months proves to be less than K_1, the put option is exercised against the company and as a result the company buys the one million pounds it needs at an exchange rate of K_1. If the exchange rate is between K_1 and K_2, neither option is exercised and the company buys the one million pounds at the current exchange rate. If the exchange rate is greater than K_2, the call option is exercised and the company is able to buy the one million pounds at an exchange

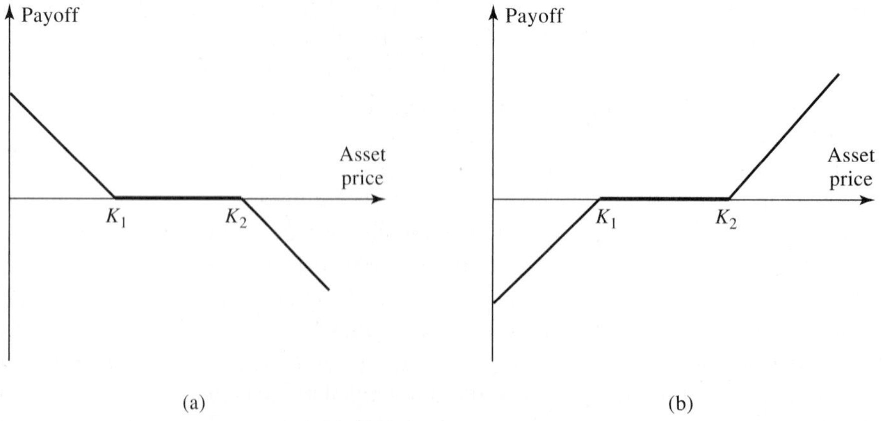

Figure 15.1 Payoffs from (a) short and (b) long range forward contract

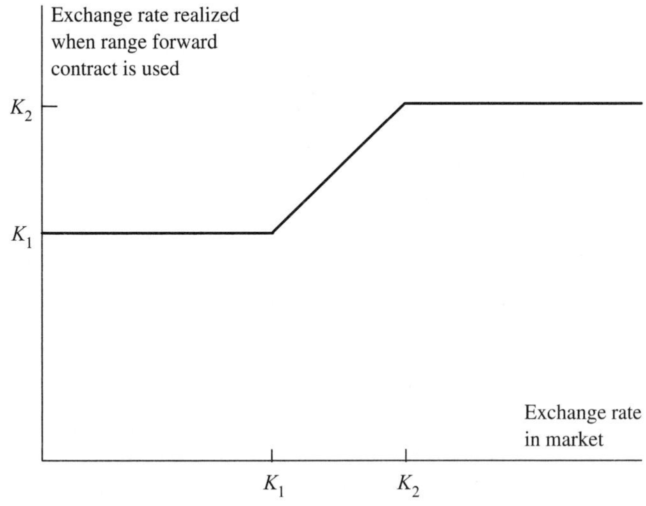

Figure15.2 Exchange rate realized when either (a) a short range forward contract is used to hedge a future foreign currency inflow or (b) a long range forward contract is used to hedge a future foreign currency outflow

rate of K_2. The exchange rate paid for the one million pounds is the same as that received for the one million pounds in the earlier example and is shown in Figure 15.2.

In practice, a range forward contract is set up so that the price of the put option equals the price of the call option. This means that it costs nothing to set up the range forward contract, just as it costs nothing to set up a regular forward contract. Suppose that the U.S. and British interest rates are both 5%, so that the spot exchange rate is 1.5200 (the same as the forward exchange rate). Suppose further that the exchange rate volatility is 14%. We can use DerivaGem to show that a European put with strike price 1.5000 to sell one pound in three months has the same price as a European call option with a strike price of 1.5413 to buy one pound in three months. (Both are worth 0.0325.) Setting $K_1 = 1.5000$ and $K_2 = 1.5413$ therefore leads to a contract with zero cost in our example.

In the limit, as the strike prices of the call and put options in a range forward contract are moved closer together, the range forward contract becomes a regular forward contract. A short range forward contract becomes a short forward contract and a long range forward contract becomes a long forward contract.

15.3 OPTIONS ON STOCKS PAYING KNOWN DIVIDEND YIELDS

In this section, we produce a simple rule that enables valuation results for European options on a non-dividend-paying stock to be extended so that they apply to European options on a stock paying a known dividend yield. Later, we show how this enables us to value options on stock indices and currencies.

Dividends cause stock prices to reduce on the ex-dividend date by the amount of the dividend payment. The payment of a dividend yield at rate q therefore causes the growth rate in the stock price to be less than it would otherwise be by an amount q. If, with a dividend yield of q, the stock price grows from S_0 today to S_T at time T, then in the absence of dividends it would grow from S_0 today to $S_T e^{qT}$ at time T. Alternatively, in the absence of dividends it would grow from $S_0 e^{-qT}$ today to S_T at time T.

This argument shows that we get the same probability distribution for the stock price at time T in each of the following two cases:

1. The stock starts at price S_0 and provides a dividend yield at rate q.
2. The stock starts at price $S_0 e^{-qT}$ and pays no dividends.

This leads to a simple rule. When valuing a European option lasting for time T on a stock paying a known dividend yield at rate q, we reduce the current stock price from S_0 to $S_0 e^{-qT}$ and then value the option as though the stock pays no dividends.[2]

Lower Bounds for Option Prices

As a first application of this rule, consider the problem of determining bounds for the price of a European option on a stock paying a dividend yield at rate q. Substituting $S_0 e^{-qT}$ for S_0 in equation (10.4), we see that a lower bound for the European call option price, c, is given by

$$c \geqslant \max(S_0 e^{-qT} - K e^{-rT},\ 0) \tag{15.1}$$

We can also prove this directly by considering the following two portfolios:

Portfolio A: one European call option plus an amount of cash equal to Ke^{-rT}

Portfolio B: e^{-qT} shares with dividends being reinvested in additional shares

To obtain a lower bound for a European put option, we can similarly replace S_0 by $S_0 e^{-qT}$ in equation (10.5) to get

$$p \geqslant \max(K e^{-rT} - S_0 e^{-qT},\ 0) \tag{15.2}$$

This result can also be proved directly by considering the following portfolios:

Portfolio C: one European put option plus e^{-qT} shares with dividends on the shares being reinvested in additional shares

Portfolio D: an amount of cash equal to Ke^{-rT}

Put–Call Parity

Replacing S_0 by $S_0 e^{-qT}$ in equation (10.6) we obtain put–call parity for an option on a stock paying a dividend yield at rate q:

$$c + Ke^{-rT} = p + S_0 e^{-qT} \tag{15.3}$$

This result can also be proved directly by considering the following two portfolios:

Portfolio A: one European call option plus an amount of cash equal to Ke^{-rT}

Portfolio C: one European put option plus e^{-qT} shares with dividends on the shares being reinvested in additional shares

[2] This rule is similar to the one in Section 13.10 for valuing a European option on a stock where the dollar amount of the dividend is known. In that case, the present value of the dividend was subtracted from the stock price. Here, the stock price is reduced by discounting it at the dividend yield rate.

Both portfolios are both worth $\max(S_T, K)$ at time T. They must therefore be worth the same today, and the put–call parity result in equation (15.3) follows. For American options, the put–call parity relationship is (see Problem 15.12)

$$S_0 e^{-qT} - K \leqslant C - P \leqslant S_0 - Ke^{-rT}$$

Pricing Formulas

By replacing S_0 by $S_0 e^{-qT}$ in the Black–Scholes–Merton formulas (13.5) and (13.6), we obtain the price c of a European call and the price p of a European put on a stock paying a dividend yield at rate q as

$$c = S_0 e^{-qT} N(d_1) - Ke^{-rT} N(d_2) \tag{15.4}$$

$$p = Ke^{-rT} N(-d_2) - S_0 e^{-qT} N(-d_1) \tag{15.5}$$

Since

$$\ln \frac{S_0 e^{-qT}}{K} = \ln \frac{S_0}{K} - qT$$

it follows that d_1 and d_2 are given by

$$d_1 = \frac{\ln(S_0/K) + (r - q + \sigma^2/2)T}{\sigma\sqrt{T}}$$

$$d_2 = \frac{\ln(S_0/K) + (r - q - \sigma^2/2)T}{\sigma\sqrt{T}} = d_1 - \sigma\sqrt{T}$$

These results were first derived by Merton.[3] As discussed in Chapter 13, the word *dividend* should, for the purposes of option valuation, be defined as the reduction in the stock price on the ex-dividend date arising from any dividends declared. If the dividend yield rate is known but not constant during the life of the option, equations (15.4) and (15.5) are still true, with q equal to the average annualized dividend yield during the option's life.

15.4 VALUATION OF EUROPEAN STOCK INDEX OPTIONS

In valuing index futures in Chapter 5, we assumed that the index could be treated as an asset paying a known yield. In valuing index options, we make similar assumptions. This means that inequalities (15.1) and (15.2) provide a lower bound for European index options; equation (15.3) is the put–call parity result for European index options; equations (15.4) and (15.5) can be used to value European options on an index; and the binomial tree approach can be used for American options. In all cases, S_0 is equal to the value of the index, σ is equal to the volatility of the index, and q is equal to the average annualized dividend yield on the index during the life of the option. An application of the valuation formulas is given in Example 15.3.

---

[3] See R.C. Merton, "Theory of Rational Option Pricing," *Bell Journal of Economics and Management Science*, 4 (Spring 1973): 141–83.

Example 15.3 Valuation of stock index option

Consider a European call option on the S&P 500 that is two months from maturity. The current value of the index is 930, the exercise price is 900, the risk-free interest rate is 8% per annum, and the volatility of the index is 20% per annum. Dividend yields of 0.2% and 0.3% are expected in the first month and the second month, respectively. In this case $S_0 = 930$, $K = 900$, $r = 0.08$, $\sigma = 0.2$, and $T = 2/12$. The total dividend yield during the option's life is $0.2 + 0.3 = 0.5\%$. This corresponds to 3% per annum. Hence, $q = 0.03$ and

$$d_1 = \frac{\ln(930/900) + (0.08 - 0.03 + 0.2^2/2) \times 2/12}{0.2\sqrt{2/12}} = 0.5444$$

$$d_2 = \frac{\ln(930/900) + (0.08 - 0.03 - 0.2^2/2) \times 2/12}{0.2\sqrt{2/12}} = 0.4628$$

$$N(d_1) = 0.7069, \qquad N(d_2) = 0.6782$$

so that the call price, c, is given by equation (15.4) as

$$c = 930 \times 0.7069e^{-0.03\times 2/12} - 900 \times 0.6782e^{-0.08\times 2/12} = 51.83$$

One contract would cost $5,183.

The calculation of q should include only dividends for which the ex-dividend dates occur during the life of the option. In the United States ex-dividend dates tend to occur during the first week of February, May, August, and November. At any given time, the correct value of q is therefore likely to depend on the life of the option. This is even more true for some indices created from stocks trading in other countries. In Japan, for example, all companies tend to use the same ex-dividend dates.

If the absolute amount of the dividend that will be paid on the stocks underlying the index (rather than the dividend yield) is assumed to be known, an alternative valuation approach is to use the basic Black–Scholes–Merton formulas with the initial stock price being reduced by the present value of the dividends. This is the approach recommended in Chapter 13 for a stock paying known dividends. However, it may be difficult to implement for a broadly based stock index because it requires a knowledge of the dividends expected on every stock underlying the index.

It is sometimes argued that, in the long run, the return from investing in a well-diversified portfolio of stocks is almost certain to beat the return from a bond portfolio. If this were so, a long-dated put option on the stock portfolio where the strike price equaled the future value of the bond portfolio less dividends on the stock portfolio would not cost very much. In fact, as indicated by Business Snapshot 15.1, it is quite expensive.

Using Forward Prices

Define F_0 as the forward price of the index for a contract with maturity T. As shown by equation (5.3), $F_0 = S_0e^{(r-q)T}$. This means that the equations for the European call

Business Snapshot 15.1 Can we guarantee that stocks will beat bonds in the long run?

It is often said that if you are a long-term investor you should buy stocks rather than bonds. Consider a U.S. fund manager who is trying to persuade investors to buy, as a long-term investment, an equity fund that is expected to mirror the S&P 500. The manager might be tempted to offer purchasers of the fund a guarantee that their return will be at least as good as the return on risk-free bonds over the next 10 years. Historically stocks have outperformed bonds in the United States over almost any 10-year period. It appears that the fund manager would not be giving much away.

In fact, this type of guarantee is surprisingly expensive. Suppose that an equity index is 1,000 today, the dividend yield on the index is 1% per annum, the volatility of the index is 15% per annum, and the 10-year risk-free rate is 5% per annum. To outperform bonds, the stocks underlying the index must earn more than 5% per annum. The dividend yield will provide 1% per annum. The capital gains on the stocks must therefore provide 4% per annum. This means that we require the index level to be at least $1{,}000e^{0.04\times 10} = 1{,}492$ in 10 years.

A guarantee that the return on \$1,000 invested in the index will be greater than the return on \$1,000 invested in bonds over the next 10 years is therefore equivalent to the right to sell the index for 1,492 in 10 years. This is a European put option on the index and can be valued from equation (15.5) with $S_0 = 1{,}000$, $K = 1{,}492$, $r = 5\%$, $\sigma = 15\%$, $T = 10$, and $q = 1\%$. The value of the put option is 169.7. This shows that the guarantee contemplated by the fund manager is worth about 17% of the fund—hardly something that should be given away!

price, c, and the European put price, p, in equations (15.4) and (15.5) can be written

$$c = F_0 e^{-rT} N(d_1) - K e^{-rT} N(d_2) \qquad \textbf{(15.6)}$$

$$p = K e^{-rT} N(-d_2) - F_0 e^{-rT} N(-d_1) \qquad \textbf{(15.7)}$$

where

$$d_1 = \frac{\ln(F_0/K) + \sigma^2 T/2}{\sigma\sqrt{T}}$$

$$d_2 = \frac{\ln(F_0/K) - \sigma^2 T/2}{\sigma\sqrt{T}}$$

Once the forward prices of the index for a number of different maturity dates have been obtained, the term structure of forward prices can be estimated, and other options can be valued using equations (15.6) and (15.7). The advantage of using these equations is that the dividend yield on the index does not need to be estimated.

Implied Dividend Yields

If estimates of the dividend yield are required (e.g., because an American option is being valued), calls and puts with the same strike price and time to maturity can again be used. From equation (15.3),

$$q = -\frac{1}{T}\ln\frac{c - p + Ke^{-rT}}{S_0}$$

For a particular strike price and time to maturity, the estimates of q calculated from this equation are liable to be unreliable. But when the results from many matched pairs of calls and puts are combined, a clearer picture of the dividend yield being assumed by the market emerges.

15.5 VALUATION OF EUROPEAN CURRENCY OPTIONS

To value currency options, we define S_0 as the spot exchange rate. To be precise, S_0 is the value of one unit of the foreign currency in U.S. dollars. As explained in Section 5.10, a foreign currency is analogous to a stock paying a known dividend yield. The owner of foreign currency receives a yield equal to the risk-free interest rate, r_f, in the foreign currency. Inequalities (15.1) and (15.2), with q replaced by r_f, provide bounds for the European call price, c, and the European put price, p:

$$c \geqslant \max(S_0 e^{-r_f T} - Ke^{-rT}, 0)$$

$$p \geqslant \max(Ke^{-rT} - S_0 e^{-r_f T}, 0)$$

Equation (15.3), with q replaced by r_f, provides the put–call parity result for European currency options:

$$c + Ke^{-rT} = p + S_0 e^{-r_f T}$$

Finally, equations (15.4) and (15.5) provide the pricing formulas for European currency options when q is replaced by r_f:

$$c = S_0 e^{-r_f T} N(d_1) - Ke^{-rT} N(d_2) \qquad \textbf{(15.8)}$$

$$p = Ke^{-rT} N(-d_2) - S_0 e^{-r_f T} N(-d_1) \qquad \textbf{(15.9)}$$

where

$$d_1 = \frac{\ln(S_0/K) + (r - r_f + \sigma^2/2)T}{\sigma\sqrt{T}}$$

$$d_2 = \frac{\ln(S_0/K) + (r - r_f - \sigma^2/2)T}{\sigma\sqrt{T}} = d_1 - \sigma\sqrt{T}$$

Example 15.4 shows how these formulas are to calculate implied volatilities for

Example 15.4 Implied volatility for a currency option

Consider a four-month European call option on the British pound. Suppose that the current exchange rate is 1.6000, the exercise price is 1.6000, the risk-free interest rate in the United States is 8% per annum, the risk-free interest rate in Britain is 11% per annum, and the option price is 4.3 cents. In this case, $S_0 = 1.6$, $K = 1.6$, $r = 0.08$, $r_f = 0.11$, $T = 0.3333$, and $c = 0.043$. The implied volatility can be calculated by trial and error. A volatility of 20% gives an option price of 0.0639; a volatility of 10% gives an option price of 0.0285; and so on. The implied volatility is 14.1%.

currency options. Both r and r_f are the rates for a maturity T. Put and call options on a currency are symmetrical in that a put option to sell currency A for currency B at a strike price K is the same as a call option to buy K units of currency B with currency A at a strike price of $1/K$.

Using Forward Exchange Rates

Since banks and other financial institutions trade forward foreign exchange contracts actively, forward exchange rates are often used for valuing currency options.

From equation (5.9), the forward rate, F_0, for a maturity T is given by $F_0 = S_0 e^{(r-r_f)T}$. This relationship allows equations (15.8) and (15.9) to be simplified to

$$c = e^{-rT}[F_0 N(d_1) - KN(d_2)] \tag{15.10}$$

$$p = e^{-rT}[KN(-d_2) - F_0 N(-d_1)] \tag{15.11}$$

where

$$d_1 = \frac{\ln(F_0/K) + \sigma^2 T/2}{\sigma\sqrt{T}}$$

$$d_2 = \frac{\ln(F_0/K) - \sigma^2 T/2}{\sigma\sqrt{T}} = d_1 - \sigma\sqrt{T}$$

Note that, for equations (15.10) and (15.11) to be correct, the maturities of the forward contract and the option must be the same.

Equations (15.10) and (15.11) are the same as equations (15.6) and (15.7). They enable the price of a European option on the spot price of an asset to be calculated from forward or futures prices. As we shall see in Chapter 16, they are a particular case of what is known as Black's model.

15.6 AMERICAN OPTIONS

As described in Chapter 12, binomial trees can be used to value American options on indices and currencies. As in the case of American options on a non-dividend-paying stock, the parameter determining the size of up movements, u, is set equal to $e^{\sigma\sqrt{\Delta t}}$, where σ is the volatility and Δt is the length of time steps. The parameter determining the size of down movements, d, is set equal to $1/u$, or $e^{-\sigma\sqrt{\Delta t}}$. For a non-dividend-paying stock, the probability of an up movement is

$$p = \frac{a - d}{u - d} \tag{15.12}$$

where $a = e^{r\Delta t}$. For options on indices and currencies, the formula for p is the same, but a is defined differently. In the case of options on an index,

$$a = e^{(r-q)\Delta t} \tag{15.13}$$

where q is the dividend yield on the index. In the case of options on a currency,

$$a = e^{(r-r_f)\Delta t}$$

where r_f is the foreign risk-free rate. Example 12.1 in Section 12.10 shows how a two-step tree can be constructed to value an option on an index. Example 12.2 shows how a three-step tree can be constructed to value an option on a currency. Further examples of the use of binomial trees to value options on indices and currencies are given in Chapter 18.

In some circumstances, it is optimal to exercise American currency and index options prior to maturity. Thus, American currency and index options are worth more than their European counterparts. In general, call options on high-interest currencies and put options on low-interest currencies are the most likely to be exercised prior to maturity. (The reason is that a high-interest currency is expected to depreciate and a low-interest currency is expected to appreciate.) Also, call options on indices with high dividend yields and put options on indices with low dividend yields are most likely to be exercised early.

SUMMARY

The index options that trade on exchanges are settled in cash. On exercise of an index call option, the holder receives 100 times the amount by which the index exceeds the strike price. Similarly, on exercise of an index put option contract, the holder receives 100 times the amount by which the strike price exceeds the index. Index options can be used for portfolio insurance. If the value of the portfolio mirrors the index, it is appropriate to buy one put option contract for each $100S_0$ dollars in the portfolio, where S_0 is the value of the index. If the portfolio does not mirror the index, β put option contracts should be purchased for each $100S_0$ dollars in the portfolio, where β is the beta of the portfolio calculated using the capital asset pricing model. The strike price of the put options purchased should reflect the level of insurance required.

Most currency options are traded in the over-the-counter market. They can be used by corporate treasurers to hedge foreign exchange exposure. For example, a U.S. corporate treasurer who knows that the company will be receiving sterling at a certain time in the future can hedge by buying put options that mature at that time. Similarly, a U.S. corporate treasurer who knows that the company will be paying sterling at a certain time in the future can hedge by buying call options that mature at that time. Currency options can also be used to create a range forward contract. This is a zero-cost contract that can be used to provide downside protection while giving up some of the upside for a company with a foreign exchange exposure.

The Black–Scholes–Merton formula for valuing European options on a non-dividend-paying stock can be extended to cover European options on a stock paying a known dividend yield. The extension can be used to value European options on stock indices and currencies because:

1. A stock index is analogous to a stock paying a dividend yield. The dividend yield is the dividend yield on the stocks that make up the index.
2. A foreign currency is analogous to a stock paying a dividend yield. The foreign risk-free interest rate plays the role of the dividend yield.

Binomial trees can be used to value American options on stock indices and foreign currencies.

FURTHER READING

Amin, K., and R. A. Jarrow. "Pricing Foreign Currency Options under Stochastic Interest Rates," *Journal of International Money and Finance*, 10 (1991): 310–29.

Biger, N., and J. C. Hull. "The Valuation of Currency Options," *Financial Management*, 12 (Spring 1983): 24–28.

Bodie, Z. "On the Risk of Stocks in the Long Run," *Financial Analysts Journal*, 51, 3 (1995): 18–22.

Garman, M. B., and S. W. Kohlhagen. "Foreign Currency Option Values," *Journal of International Money and Finance*, 2 (December 1983): 231–37.

Giddy, I. H., and G. Dufey. "Uses and Abuses of Currency Options," *Journal of Applied Corporate Finance*, 8, 3 (1995): 49–57.

Grabbe, J. O. "The Pricing of Call and Put Options on Foreign Exchange," *Journal of International Money and Finance*, 2 (December 1983): 239–53.

Jorion, P. "Predicting Volatility in the Foreign Exchange Market," *Journal of Finance* 50, 2(1995): 507–28.

Merton, R. C. "Theory of Rational Option Pricing," *Bell Journal of Economics and Management Science*, 4 (Spring 1973): 141–83.

Quiz (Answers at End of Book)

15.1. A portfolio is currently worth \$10 million and has a beta of 1.0. An index is currently standing at 800. Explain how a put option on the index with a strike price of 700 can be used to provide portfolio insurance.

15.2. "Once we know how to value options on a stock paying a dividend yield, we know how to value options on stock indices and currencies." Explain this statement.

15.3. A stock index is currently 300, the dividend yield on the index is 3% per annum, and the risk-free interest rate is 8% per annum. What is a lower bound for the price of a six-month European call option on the index when the strike price is 290?

15.4. A currency is currently worth \$0.80. Over each of the next two months it is expected to increase or decrease in value by 2%. The domestic and foreign risk-free interest rates are 6% and 8%, respectively. What is the value of a two-month European call option with a strike price of \$0.80?

15.5. Explain how corporations can use range forward contracts to hedge their foreign exchange risk when they are due to receive a certain amount of a foreign currency in the future.

15.6. Calculate the value of a three-month at-the-money European call option on a stock index when the index is at 250, the risk-free interest rate is 10% per annum, the volatility of the index is 18% per annum, and the dividend yield on the index is 3% per annum.

15.7. Calculate the value of an eight-month European put option on a currency with a strike price of 0.50. The current exchange rate is 0.52, the volatility of the exchange rate is 12%, the domestic risk-free interest rate is 4% per annum, and the foreign risk-free interest rate is 8% per annum.

Practice Questions (Answers in Solutions Manual/Study Guide)

15.8. Show that the formula in equation (15.9) for a put option to sell one unit of currency A for currency B at strike price K gives the same value as equation (15.8) for a call option to buy K units of currency B for currency A at strike price $1/K$.

15.9. A foreign currency is currently worth \$1.50. The domestic and foreign risk-free interest rates are 5% and 9%, respectively. Calculate lower bounds for the values of six-month European and American call options on the currency with a strike price of \$1.40.

15.10. Consider a stock index currently standing at 250. The dividend yield on the index is 4% per annum, and the risk-free rate is 6% per annum. A three-month European call option on the index with a strike price of 245 is currently worth \$10. What is the value of a three-month put option on the index with a strike price of 245?

15.11. An index currently stands at 696 and has a volatility of 30% per annum. The risk-free rate of interest is 7% per annum and the index provides a dividend yield of 4% per annum. Calculate the value of a three-month European put with an exercise price of 700.

15.12. Show that, if C is the price of an American call with exercise price K and maturity T on a stock paying a dividend yield of q, and P is the price of an American put on the same stock with the same strike price and exercise date, then $S_0e^{-qT} - K < C - P < S_0 - Ke^{-rT}$, where S_0 is the stock price, r is the risk-free rate, and $r > 0$. [*Hint*: To obtain the first half of the inequality, consider possible values of:

Portfolio A: a European call option plus an amount K invested at the risk-free rate
Portfolio B: an American put option plus e^{-qT} of stock with dividends being reinvested in the stock

To obtain the second half of the inequality, consider possible values of:

Portfolio C: an American call option plus an amount Ke^{-rT} invested at the risk-free rate
Portfolio D: a European put option plus one stock with dividends being reinvested in the stock.]

15.13. Show that a European call option on a currency has the same price as the corresponding European put option on the currency when the forward price equals the strike price.

15.14. Would you expect the volatility of a stock index to be greater or less than the volatility of a typical stock? Explain your answer.

15.15. Does the cost of portfolio insurance increase or decrease as the beta of a portfolio increases? Explain your answer.

15.16. Suppose that a portfolio is worth \$60 million and the S&P 500 is at 1200. If the value of the portfolio mirrors the value of the index, what options should be purchased to provide protection against the value of the portfolio falling below \$54 million in one year's time?

15.17. Consider again the situation in Problem 15.16. Suppose that the portfolio has a beta of 2.0, the risk-free interest rate is 5% per annum, and the dividend yield on both the portfolio and the index is 3% per annum. What options should be purchased to provide protection against the value of the portfolio falling below \$54 million in one year's time?

15.18. An index currently stands at 1,500. European call and put options with a strike price of 1,400 and time to maturity of six months have market prices of 154.00 and 34.25, respectively. The six-month risk-free rate is 5%. What is the implied dividend yield?

15.19. A total return index tracks the return, including dividends, on a certain portfolio. Explain how you would value (a) forward contracts and (b) European options on the index.

15.20. What is the put–call parity relationship for European currency options?

15.21. Can an option on the yen–euro exchange rate be created from two options, one on the dollar–euro and the other on the dollar–yen exchange rate? Explain your answer.

15.22. Prove the results in equations (15.1), (15.2), and (15.3) using the portfolios indicated.

Further Questions

15.23. The Dow Jones Industrial Average on January 12, 2007, was 12,556 and the price of the March 126 call was \$2.25. Use the DerivaGem software to calculate the implied volatility of this option. Assume the risk-free rate was 5.3% and the dividend yield was 3%. The option expires on March 20, 2007. Estimate the price of a March 126 put. What is the volatility implied by the price you estimate for this option? (Note that options are on the Dow Jones index divided by 100.)

15.24. A stock index currently stands at 300 and has a volatility of 20%. The risk-free interest rate is 8% and the dividend yield on the index is 3%. Use a three-step binomial tree to value a six-month put option on the index with a strike price of 300 if it is (a) European and (b) American?

15.25. Suppose that the spot price of the Canadian dollar is U.S. \$0.95 and that the Canadian dollar/U.S. dollar exchange rate has a volatility of 8% per annum. The risk-free rates of interest in Canada and the United States are 4% and 5% per annum, respectively. Calculate the value of a European call option to buy one Canadian dollar for U.S. \$0.95 in nine months. Use put–call parity to calculate the price of a European put option to sell one Canadian dollar for U.S. \$0.95 in nine months. What is the price of a call option to buy U.S. \$0.95 with one Canadian dollar in nine months?

15.26. The spot price of an index is 1,000 and the risk-free rate is 4%. The prices of three-month European call and put options when the strike price is 950 are 78 and 26. Estimate (a) the dividend yield and (b) the implied volatility.

15.27. The USD/euro exchange rate is 1.3000 and the exchange rate volatility is 15%. A U.S. company will receive 1 million euros in three months. The euro and USD risk-free rates are 5% and 4%, respectively. The company decides to use a range forward contract with the lower strike price equal to 1.2500.
(a) What should the higher strike price be to create a zero-cost contract?
(b) What position in calls and puts should the company take?
(c) Show that your answer to (a) does not depend on interest rates provided that the interest rate differential between the two currencies, $r - r_f$, remains the same.

15.28. In Business Snapshot 15.1, what is the cost of a guarantee that the return on the fund will not be negative over the next 10 years?

15.29. The one-year forward price of the Mexican peso is \$0.0750 per MXN. The U.S. risk-free rate is 1.25%. The exchange rate volatility is 13%. What is the value of one-year European call and put options with a strike price of 0.0800.

CHAPTER 16 Futures Options

The options we have considered so far provide the holder with the right to buy or sell a certain asset by a certain date for a certain price. They are sometimes termed *options on spot* or *spot options* because, when the options are exercised, the sale or purchase of the asset at the agreed-on price takes place immediately. In this chapter we move on to consider *options on futures*, also known as *futures options*. In these contracts, exercise of the option gives the holder a position in a futures contract.

The Commodity Futures Trading Commission in the United States authorized the trading of options on futures on an experimental basis in 1982. Permanent trading was approved in 1987, and since then the popularity of the contract with investors has grown very fast.

In this chapter we consider how futures options work and the differences between these options and spot options. We examine how futures options can be priced using either binomial trees or formulas similar to those produced by Black, Scholes, and Merton for stock options. We also explore the relative pricing of futures options and spot options.

16.1 NATURE OF FUTURES OPTIONS

A futures option is the right, but not the obligation, to enter into a futures contract at a certain futures price by a certain date. Specifically, a call futures option is the right to enter into a long futures contract at a certain price; a put futures option is the right to enter into a short futures contract at a certain price. Futures options are generally American; that is, they can be exercised any time during the life of the contract.

As we will now illustrate, the effective payoff from a call futures option is $\max(F - K, 0)$ and the effective payoff from a put futures option is $\max(K - F, 0)$, where F is the futures price at the time of exercise and K is the strike price. Consider first the position of an investor who has bought a July call futures option on gold with a strike price of \$1,800 per ounce. The asset underlying one contract is 100 ounces of gold. As with other exchange-traded option contracts, the investor is required to pay for the option at the time the contract is entered into. If the call futures option is exercised, the investor obtains a long futures contract, and there is a cash settlement to reflect the investor entering into the futures contract at the strike price. Suppose that the July futures price at

From Chapter 16 of *Fundamentals of Futures and Options Markets*, Eighth Edition. John C. Hull.

Example 16.1 Mechanics of call futures options

An investor buys a July call futures option contract on gold. The contract size is 100 ounces. The strike price is 1,800.

The Exercise Decision

The investor exercises when the July gold futures price is 1,840 and the most recent settlement price is 1,838.

The Outcome

1. The investor receives a cash amount equal to (1,838 − 1,800) × 100 = $3,800.
2. The investor receives a long futures contract.
3. The investor closes out the long futures contract immediately for a gain of (1,840 − 1,838) × 100 = $200.
4. Total payoff = $4,000.

the time the option is exercised is 1,840 and the most recent settlement price for the July futures contract is 1,838. The investor receives a cash amount equal to the excess of the most recent settlement price over the strike price. This amount, (1,838 − 1,800) × 100 = $3,800 in our example, is added to the investor's margin account.

As shown in Example 16.1, if the investor closes out the July futures contract immediately, the gain on the futures contract is $(1,840 - 1,838) \times 100$, or $200. The total payoff from exercising the futures option contract is then $4,000. This corresponds to the July futures price at the time of exercise less the strike price. If the investor keeps the futures contract, the usual margin requirements for futures apply.

The investor who sells (or writes) a call futures option receives the option premium, but takes the risk that the contract will be exercised. When the contract is exercised, this investor assumes a short futures position. An amount equal to $F - K$ is deducted from the investor's margin account, where F is the most recent settlement price. The exchange clearinghouse arranges for this sum to be transferred to the investor on the other side of the transaction who chose to exercise the option.

Put futures options work analogously to call options. Example 16.2 considers an investor who buys a September put futures option on corn with a strike price of 300 cents

Example 16.2 Mechanics of put futures options

An investor buys a September put futures option contract on corn. The contract size is 5,000 bushels. The strike price is 300 cents.

The Exercise Decision

The investor exercises when the September corn futures price is 280 and the most recent settlement price is 279.

The Outcome

1. The investor receives a cash amount of (3.00 − 2.79) × 5,000 = $1,050.
2. The investor receives a short futures contract.
3. The investor closes out the short futures position immediately for a loss of (2.80 − 2.79) × 5,000 = $50.
4. Total payoff = $1,000.

per bushel. Each contract is on 5,000 bushels of corn. If the put futures option is exercised, the investor obtains a short futures contract plus a cash settlement. Suppose the contract is exercised when the September futures price is 280 cents and the most recent settlement price is 279 cents. The investor receives a cash amount equal to the excess of the strike price over the most recent settlement price. The cash amount received, $(3.00 - 2.79) \times 5{,}000 = \$1{,}050$ in our example, is added to the investor's margin account. If the investor closes out the futures contract immediately, the loss on the short futures contract is $(2.80 - 2.79) \times 5{,}000 = \$50$. The total payoff from exercising the futures option contract is then \$1,000. This corresponds to the strike price minus the futures price at the time of exercise. As in the case of call futures, the usual margin requirements apply if the investor decides to keep the futures position.

The investor on the other side of the transaction (i.e., the investor who sold the put futures option) obtains a long futures position when the option is exercised, and the excess of the strike price over the most recent settlement price is deducted from the investor's margin account.

Expiration Months

Futures options are referred to by the delivery month of the underlying futures contract—not by the expiration month of the option. As mentioned earlier, most futures options are American. The expiration date of a futures option contract is usually on, or a few days before, the earliest delivery date of the underlying futures contract. (For example, the CME Group Treasury bond futures option expires on the latest Friday that precedes by at least five business days the end of the month before the futures delivery month.) An exception is the CME Group mid-curve Eurodollar contract where the futures contract expires either one or two years after the options contract.

Popular contracts trading in the United States are those on corn, soybeans, cotton, sugar-world, crude oil, natural gas, gold, Treasury bonds, Treasury notes, five-year Treasury notes, 30-day federal funds, Eurodollars, one-year and two-year mid-curve Eurodollars, Euribor, Eurobunds, and the S&P 500.

16.2 REASONS FOR THE POPULARITY OF FUTURES OPTIONS

It is natural to ask why people choose to trade options on futures rather than options on the underlying asset. The main reason appears to be that a futures contract is, in many circumstances, more liquid and easier to trade than the underlying asset. Furthermore, a futures price is known immediately from trading on the futures exchange, whereas the spot price of the underlying asset may not be so readily available.

Consider Treasury bonds. The market for Treasury bond futures is much more active than the market for any particular Treasury bond. Also, a Treasury bond futures price is known immediately from exchange trading. By contrast, the current market price of a bond can be obtained only by contacting one or more dealers. It is not surprising that investors would rather take delivery of a Treasury bond futures contract than Treasury bonds.

Futures on commodities are also often easier to trade than the commodities themselves. For example, it is much easier and more convenient to make or take delivery of a live-cattle futures contract than it is to make or take delivery of the cattle themselves.

An important point about a futures option is that exercising it does not usually lead to delivery of the underlying asset, as in most circumstances the underlying futures contract is closed out prior to delivery. Futures options are therefore normally eventually settled in cash. This is appealing to many investors, particularly those with limited capital who may find it difficult to come up with the funds to buy the underlying asset when an option on spot is exercised. Another advantage sometimes cited for futures options is that futures and futures options are traded side by side in the same exchange. This facilitates hedging, arbitrage, and speculation. It also tends to make the markets more efficient. A final point is that futures options entail lower transactions costs than spot options in many situations.

16.3 EUROPEAN SPOT AND FUTURES OPTIONS

The payoff from a European call option with strike price K on the spot price of an asset is

$$\max(S_T - K,\ 0)$$

where S_T is the spot price at the option's maturity. The payoff from a European call option with the same strike price on the futures price of the asset is

$$\max(F_T - K,\ 0)$$

where F_T is the futures price at the option's maturity. If the futures contract matures at the same time as the option, then $F_T = S_T$ and the two options are equivalent. Similarly, a European futures put option is worth the same as its spot put option counterpart when the futures contract matures at the same time as the option.

Most of the futures options that trade are American-style. However, as we shall see, it is useful to study European futures options because the results that are obtained can be used to value the corresponding European spot options.

16.4 PUT–CALL PARITY

In Chapter 10 we derived a put–call parity relationship for European stock options. We now consider a similar argument to derive a put–call parity relationship for European futures options. Consider European call and put futures options, both with strike price K and time to expiration T. We can form two portfolios:

Portfolio A: a European call futures option plus an amount of cash equal to Ke^{-rT}

Portfolio B: a European put futures option plus a long futures contract plus an amount of cash equal to F_0e^{-rT}, where F_0 is the futures price

In portfolio A, the cash can be invested at the risk-free rate, r, and grows to K at time T. Let F_T be the futures price at maturity of the option. If $F_T > K$, the call option in portfolio A is exercised and portfolio A is worth F_T. If $F_T \leqslant K$, the call is not exercised and portfolio A is worth K. The value of portfolio A at time T is therefore

$$\max(F_T,\ K)$$

In portfolio B, the cash can be invested at the risk-free rate to grow to F_0 at time T. The put option provides a payoff of $\max(K - F_T,\ 0)$. The futures contract provides a payoff of $F_T - F_0$.[1] The value of portfolio B at time T is therefore

$$F_0 + (F_T - F_0) + \max(K - F_T,\ 0) = \max(F_T,\ K)$$

Because the two portfolios have the same value at time T and European options cannot be exercised early, it follows that they are worth the same today. The value of portfolio A today is

$$c + Ke^{-rT}$$

where c is the price of the call futures option. The daily settlement process ensures that the futures contract in portfolio B is worth zero today. Portfolio B is therefore worth

$$p + F_0e^{-rT}$$

where p is the price of the put futures option. Hence

$$c + Ke^{-rT} = p + F_0e^{-rT} \tag{16.1}$$

The difference between this put–call parity relationship and the one for a non-dividend-paying stock in equation (10.6) is that the stock price, S_0, is replaced by the discounted futures price, F_0e^{-rT}. For American futures options, the relationship is (see Problem 16.19)

$$F_0e^{-rT} - K < C - P < F_0 - Ke^{-rT} \tag{16.2}$$

As shown in Section 16.3, when the underlying futures contract matures at the same time as the option, European futures and spot options are the same. Equation (16.1) therefore gives a relationship between the price of a call option on the spot price, the price of a put option on the spot price, and the futures price when both options mature at the same time as the futures contract. Example 16.3 illustrates this.

Example 16.3 Put–call parity using futures prices

Suppose that the price of a European call option on spot silver for delivery in six months is \$0.56 per ounce when the exercise price is \$8.50. Assume that the silver futures price for delivery in six months is currently \$8.00, and the risk-free interest rate for an investment that matures in six months is 10% per annum. From a rearrangement of equation (16.1), the price of a European put option on spot silver with the same maturity and exercise date as the call option is

$$0.56 + 8.50e^{-0.1\times 6/12} - 8.00e^{-0.1\times 6/12} = 1.04$$

[1] This analysis assumes that a futures contract is like a forward contract and settled at the end of its life rather than on a day-to-day basis.

16.5 BOUNDS FOR FUTURES OPTIONS

The put–call parity relationship in equation (16.1) provides bounds for European call and put options. Because the price of a put, p, cannot be negative, it follows from equation (16.1) that

$$c + Ke^{-rT} \geqslant F_0 e^{-rT}$$

or

$$c \geqslant \max[(F_0 - K)e^{-rT}, 0] \quad \textbf{(16.3)}$$

Similarly, because the price of a call option cannot be negative, it follows from equation (16.1) that

$$Ke^{-rT} \leqslant F_0 e^{-rT} + p$$

or

$$p \geqslant \max[(K - F_0)e^{-rT}, 0] \quad \textbf{(16.4)}$$

These bounds are similar to the ones derived for European stock options in Chapter 10. The prices of European call and put options are very close to their lower bounds when the options are deep in the money. To see why this is so, we return to the put–call parity relationship in equation (16.1). When a call option is deep in the money, the corresponding put option is deep out of the money. This means that p is very close to zero. The difference between c and its lower bound equals p, so that the price of the call option must be very close to its lower bound. A similar argument applies to put options.

Because American futures options can be exercised at any time, we must have

$$C \geqslant \max(F_0 - K, 0)$$

and

$$P \geqslant \max(K - F_0, 0)$$

Thus, assuming interest rates are positive, the lower bound for an American option price is always higher than the lower bound for the corresponding European option price. There is always some chance that an American futures option will be exercised early.

16.6 VALUATION OF FUTURES OPTIONS USING BINOMIAL TREES

This section examines, more formally than in Chapter 12, how binomial trees can be used to price futures options. A key difference between futures options and stock options is that there are no up-front costs when a futures contract is entered into.

Suppose that the current futures price is 30 and that it will move either up to 33 or down to 28 over the next month. We consider a one-month call option on the futures with a strike price of 29 and ignore daily settlement. The situation is as indicated in Figure 16.1. If the futures price proves to be 33, the payoff from the option is 4 and the value of the futures contract is 3. If the futures price proves to be 28, the payoff from the option is zero and the value of the futures contract is −2.[2]

[2] There is an approximation here in that the gain or loss on the futures contract is not realized at time T. It is realized day by day between time 0 and time T. However, as the length of the time step in a binomial tree becomes shorter, the approximation becomes better.

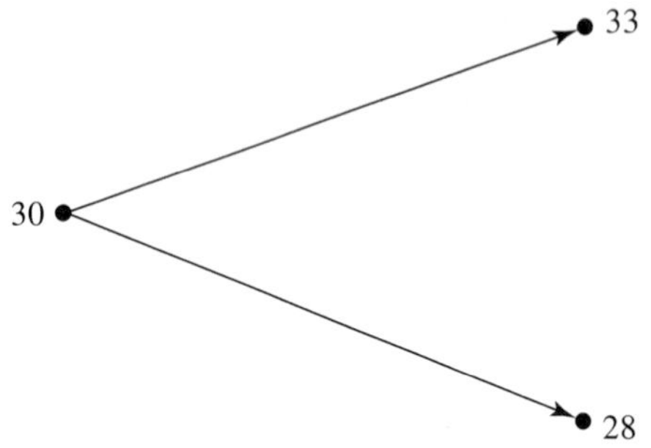

Figure 16.1 Futures price movements in the numerical example

To set up a riskless hedge, we consider a portfolio consisting of a short position in one options contract and a long position in Δ futures contracts. If the futures price moves up to 33, the value of the portfolio is $3\Delta - 4$; if it moves down to 28, the value of the portfolio is -2Δ. The portfolio is riskless when these are the same, that is, when

$$3\Delta - 4 = -2\Delta$$

or $\Delta = 0.8$.

For this value of Δ, we know the portfolio will be worth $3 \times 0.8 - 4 = -1.6$ in one month. Assume a risk-free interest rate of 6%. The value of the portfolio today must be

$$-1.6e^{-0.06\times 1/12} = -1.592$$

The portfolio consists of one short option and Δ futures contracts. Because the value of the futures contract today is zero, the value of the option today must be 1.592.

A Generalization

We can generalize this analysis by considering a futures price that starts at F_0 and is anticipated to rise to F_0u or move down to F_0d over the time period T. We consider an option maturing at time T and suppose that its payoff is f_u if the futures price moves up and f_d if it moves down. The situation is summarized in Figure 16.2.

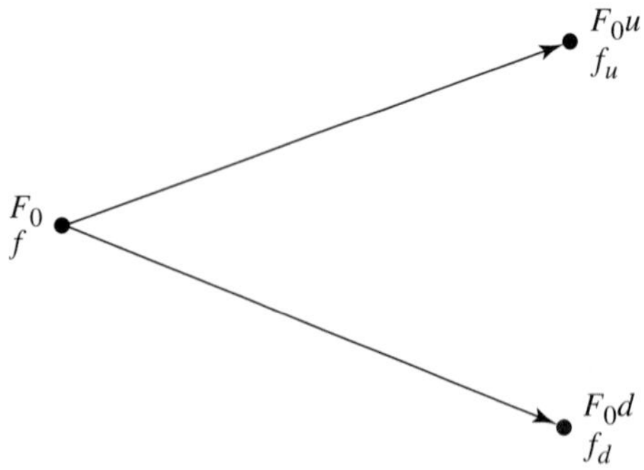

Figure 16.2 Futures price and option price in a general situation

The riskless portfolio in this case consists of a short position in one option combined with a long position in Δ futures contracts, where

$$\Delta = \frac{f_u - f_d}{F_0 u - F_0 d}$$

The value of the portfolio at time T is then always

$$(F_0 u - F_0)\Delta - f_u$$

Denoting the risk-free interest rate by r, we obtain the value of the portfolio today as

$$[(F_0 u - F_0)\Delta - f_u]e^{-rT}$$

Another expression for the present value of the portfolio is $-f$, where f is the value of the option today. It follows that

$$-f = [(F_0 u - F_0)\Delta - f_u]e^{-rT}$$

Substituting for Δ and simplifying reduces this equation to

$$f = e^{-rT}[pf_u + (1-p)f_d] \qquad \textbf{(16.5)}$$

where

$$p = \frac{1-d}{u-d} \qquad \textbf{(16.6)}$$

This agrees with the result in Section 12.10.

In the numerical example considered previously (see Figure 16.1), $u = 1.1$, $d = 0.9333$, $r = 0.06$, $T = 1/12$, $f_u = 4$, and $f_d = 0$. From equation (16.6),

$$p = \frac{1 - 0.9333}{1.1 - 0.9333} = 0.4$$

and, from equation (16.5),

$$f = e^{-0.06\times 1/12}[0.4 \times 4 + 0.6 \times 0] = 1.592$$

This result agrees with the answer obtained for this example earlier.

Multistep Trees

Multistep binomial trees are used to value American-style futures options in much the same way that they are used to value options on stocks. This is explained in Section 12.10. The parameter defining up movements in the futures price is $u = e^{\sigma\sqrt{\Delta t}}$, where σ is the volatility of the futures price and Δt is the length of one time step. The probability of an up movement in the future price is that in equation (16.6):

$$p = \frac{1-d}{u-d}$$

Example 12.3 illustrates the use of multistep binomial trees for valuing a futures option. Example 18.1 in Chapter 18 provides a further illustration.

16.7 A FUTURES PRICE AS AN ASSET PROVIDING A YIELD

There is a general result that makes the analysis of futures options analogous to the analysis of options on a stock paying a dividend yield. This result is that futures prices behave in the same way as a stock paying a dividend yield equal to the domestic risk-free rate r.

One clue that this might be so is given by comparing equation (16.6) with equations (15.12) and (15.13). The equations are identical when we set $q = r$. Another clue is that the lower bounds for futures options prices and the put–call parity relationship for futures options prices are the same as those for options on a stock paying a dividend yield at rate q when the stock price is replaced by the futures price and $q = r$.

We can understand the general result by noting that a futures contract requires zero investment. In a risk-neutral world, the expected profit from holding a position in an investment that costs zero to set up must be zero. Hence the expected payoff from a futures contract in a risk-neutral world must be zero. It follows that the expected growth rate of the futures price in a risk-neutral world must be zero. A stock paying a dividend at rate q grows at an expected rate of $r - q$ in a risk-neutral world. If we set $q = r$, the expected growth rate of the stock price is zero, making it analogous to a futures price.

16.8 BLACK'S MODEL FOR VALUING FUTURES OPTIONS

Fischer Black provided a model for valuing futures options in a paper published in 1976. The model is known as *Black's model*. The underlying assumption is that futures prices have the same lognormal property that we assumed for stock prices in Chapter 13. The European call price, c, and the European put price, p, for a futures option are given by equations (15.4) and (15.5) with S_0 replaced by F_0 and $q = r$:

$$c = e^{-rT}[F_0 N(d_1) - KN(d_2)] \tag{16.7}$$

$$p = e^{-rT}[KN(-d_2) - F_0 N(-d_1)] \tag{16.8}$$

where

$$d_1 = \frac{\ln(F_0/K) + \sigma^2 T/2}{\sigma\sqrt{T}}$$

$$d_2 = \frac{\ln(F_0/K) - \sigma^2 T/2}{\sigma\sqrt{T}} = d_1 - \sigma\sqrt{T}$$

σ is the volatility of the futures price, and T is the time to maturity of the option (not the futures). Example 16.4 illustrates these formulas.

16.9 USING BLACK'S MODEL INSTEAD OF BLACK–SCHOLES–MERTON

The results in Section 16.3 show that European futures options and European spot options are equivalent when the option contract matures at the same time as the futures contract. Black's model, equations (16.7) and (16.8), therefore provides a way of

Example 16.4 Valuation of a European futures option

Consider a European put futures option on a commodity. The time to the option's maturity is four months, the current futures price is \$60, the exercise price is \$60, the risk-free interest rate is 9% per annum, and the volatility of the futures price is 25% per annum. In this case, $F_0 = 60$, $K = 60$, $r = 0.09$, $T = 4/12$, $\sigma = 0.25$, and $\ln(F_0/K) = 0$, so that

$$d_1 = \frac{\sigma\sqrt{T}}{2} = 0.07216, \quad d_2 = -\frac{\sigma\sqrt{T}}{2} = -0.07216$$

$$N(-d_1) = 0.4712, \quad N(-d_2) = 0.5288$$

and the put price p is given by

$$p = e^{-0.09\times 4/12}(60 \times 0.5288 - 60 \times 0.4712) = 3.35$$

or \$3.35.

calculating the value of European options on the spot price of a asset. This is illustrated in Example 16.5.

Traders like to use Black's model rather than Black–Scholes–Merton to value European spot options. It has fairly general applicability. The underlying can be a consumption or investment asset and it can provide income to the holder. The variable F_0 in equations (16.7) and (16.8) is set equal to either the futures or the forward price of the underlying asset for a contract maturing at the same time as the option. Traders keep track of the forward or futures curve for the assets on which they trade options. This is a curve showing the forward or futures price as a function of the maturity of the contract. They interpolate as necessary. Suppose, for example, that they know that the one- and two-year forward prices of an asset are 860 and 880, respectively. They would value a

Example 16.5 Valuing a spot option using futures prices

Consider a six-month European call option on the spot price of gold, that is, an option to buy one ounce of gold in six months. The strike price is \$1,800, the six-month futures price of gold is \$1,860, the risk-free rate of interest is 5% per annum, and the volatility of the futures price is 20%. The option is the same as a six-month European option on the six-month futures contract. The value of the option is therefore given by equation (16.7) as

$$e^{-0.05\times 0.5}[1{,}860N(d_1) - 1{,}800N(d_2)]$$

where

$$d_1 = \frac{\ln(1{,}860/1{,}800) + 0.2^2 \times 0.5/2}{0.2 \times \sqrt{0.5}} = 0.3026$$

$$d_2 = \frac{\ln(1{,}860/1{,}800) - 0.2^2 \times 0.5/2}{0.2 \times \sqrt{0.5}} = 0.1611$$

It is \$132.56.

1.25-year option by assuming that the 1.25-year forward price (and therefore the value of F_0 that is used) is 865.

Equations (15.11) and (15.12) are examples of Black's model being used to value European options on the spot value of a currency. In this case, Black's model avoids the need to estimate the foreign risk-free interest rate explicitly because all the information needed about the foreign risk-free rate is in F_0. Equations (15.6) and (15.7) are examples of Black's model being used to value a European option on the spot value of an equity index in terms of futures or forward prices for the index. In this case, the dividends paid by the portfolio underlying the index do not have to be estimated explicitly because all the information needed about dividends is in F_0. In general, the big advantage of Black's model is that it avoids the need to estimate the income, storage cost, or convenience yield for the underlying asset. The futures or forward price that is used in the model incorporates the market's estimate of these quantities.

16.10 AMERICAN FUTURES OPTIONS vs. AMERICAN SPOT OPTIONS

Traded futures options are in practice usually American. Assuming that the risk-free rate of interest, r, is positive, there is always some chance that it will be optimal to exercise an American futures option early. American futures options are therefore worth more than their European counterparts.

It is not generally true that an American futures option is worth the same as the corresponding American spot option when the futures and options contracts have the same maturity.[3] Suppose, for example, that there is a normal market with futures prices consistently higher than spot prices prior to maturity. An American call futures option must be worth more than the corresponding American spot call option. The reason is that in some situations the futures option will be exercised early, in which case it will provide a greater profit to the holder. Similarly, an American put futures option must be worth less than the corresponding American spot put option. If there is an inverted market with futures prices consistently lower than spot prices, the reverse must be true. American call futures options are worth less than the corresponding American spot call option, whereas American put futures options are worth more than the corresponding American spot put option.

The differences just described between American futures options and American spot options hold true when the futures contract expires later than the options contract as well as when the two expire at the same time. In fact, the later the futures contract expires the greater the differences tend to be.

16.11 FUTURES-STYLE OPTIONS

Some exchanges trade what are termed *futures-style options*. These are futures contracts on the payoff from an option. Normally a trader who buys (sells) an option, whether on

[3] The spot option "corresponding" to a futures option is defined here as one with the same strike price and the same expiration date.

the spot price of an asset or on the futures price of an asset, pays (receives) cash up front. By contrast, traders who buy or sell a futures-style option post margin in the same way that they do on a regular futures contract (see Chapter 2). The contract is settled daily as with any other futures contract and the final settlement price is the payoff from the option. Just as a futures contract is a bet on what the future price of an asset will be, a futures-style option is a bet on what the payoff from an option will be.[4] If interest rates are constant, a futures contract on an option payoff is the same as a forward contract on the option payoff. It follows from this that the futures price for a futures-style option is the price that would be paid for the option if payment were made in arrears. It is therefore the value of a regular option compounded forward at the risk-free rate.

From equations (16.7) and (16.8), this means that the futures price in a call futures style option is

$$F_0N(d_1) - KN(d_2)$$

and the futures price in a put futures-style option is

$$KN(-d_2) - F_0N(-d_1)$$

where d_1 and d_2 are defined as in equations (16.7) and (16.8). These formulas do not depend on the level of interest rates.

An American futures-style option can be exercised early, in which case there is an immediate final settlement at the option's intrinsic value. As it turns out, it is never optimal to exercise an American futures-style option on a futures contract early because the futures price of the option is always greater than the intrinsic value. This type of American futures-style option can therefore be treated as though it were the corresponding European futures-style option.

SUMMARY

Futures options require delivery of the underlying futures contract on exercise. When a call is exercised, the holder acquires a long futures position plus a cash amount equal to the excess of the futures price over the strike price. Similarly, when a put is exercised the holder acquires a short position plus a cash amount equal to the excess of the strike price over the futures price. The futures contract that is delivered usually expires slightly later than the option.

A futures price behaves in the same way as a stock that provides a dividend yield equal to the risk-free rate, r. This means that the results produced in Chapter 15 for options on stock paying a dividend yield apply to futures options if we replace the stock price by the futures price and set the dividend yield equal to the risk-free interest rate. Pricing formulas for European futures options were first produced by Fischer Black in 1976. They assume that the futures price is lognormally distributed at the option's expiration.

---

[4] For a more detailed discussion of futures-style options, see D. Lieu, "Option Pricing with Futures-Style Margining," *Journal of Futures Markets*, 10, 4 (1990): 327–38. For pricing when interest rates are stochastic, see R.-R. Chen and L. Scott, "Pricing Interest Rate Futures Options with Futures-Style Margining," *Journal of Futures Markets*, 13, 1 (1993): 15–22.

If the expiration dates for the option and futures contracts are the same, a European futures option is worth exactly the same as the corresponding European spot option. This result is often used to value European options on the spot price of an asset. The result is not true of American options. If the futures market is normal, an American call futures is worth more than the corresponding American spot call option, while an American put futures is worth less than the corresponding American spot put option. If the futures market is inverted, the reverse is true.

FURTHER READING

Black, F. "The Pricing of Commodity Contracts," *Journal of Financial Economics*, 3 (1976): 167–79.

Hilliard, J. E., and J. Reis. "Valuation of Commodity Futures and Options under Stochastic Convenience Yields, Interest Rates, and Jump Diffusions in the Spot," *Journal of Financial and Quantitative Analysis*, 33, 1 (March 1998): 61–86.

Miltersen, K. R., and E. S. Schwartz. "Pricing of Options on Commodity Futures with Stochastic Term Structures of Convenience Yields and Interest Rates," *Journal of Financial and Quantitative Analysis*, 33, 1 (March 1998): 33–59.

Quiz (Answers at End of Book)

16.1. Explain the difference between a call option on yen and a call option on yen futures.

16.2. Why are options on bond futures more actively traded than options on bonds?

16.3. "A futures price is like a stock paying a dividend yield." What is the dividend yield?

16.4. A futures price is currently 50. At the end of six months it will be either 56 or 46. The risk-free interest rate is 6% per annum. What is the value of a six-month European call option on the futures with a strike price of 50?

16.5. How does the put–call parity formula for a futures option differ from put–call parity for an option on a non-dividend-paying stock?

16.6. Consider an American futures call option where the futures contract and the option contract expire at the same time. Under what circumstances is the futures option worth more than the corresponding American option on the underlying asset?

16.7. Calculate the value of a five-month European put futures option when the futures price is \$19, the strike price is \$20, the risk-free interest rate is 12% per annum, and the volatility of the futures price is 20% per annum.

Practice Questions (Answers in Solutions Manual/Study Guide)

16.8. Suppose you buy a put option contract on October gold futures with a strike price of \$1,800 per ounce. Each contract is for the delivery of 100 ounces. What happens if you exercise when the October futures price is \$1,760?

16.9. Suppose you sell a call option contract on April live cattle futures with a strike price of 90 cents per pound. Each contract is for the delivery of 40,000 pounds. What happens if the contract is exercised when the futures price is 95 cents?

16.10. Consider a two-month call futures option with a strike price of 40 when the risk-free interest rate is 10% per annum. The current futures price is 47. What is a lower bound for the value of the futures option if it is (a) European and (b) American?

16.11. Consider a four-month put futures option with a strike price of 50 when the risk-free interest rate is 10% per annum. The current futures price is 47. What is a lower bound for the value of the futures option if it is (a) European and (b) American?

16.12. A futures price is currently 60 and its volatility is 30%. The risk-free interest rate is 8% per annum. Use a two-step binomial tree to calculate the value of a six-month European call option on the futures with a strike price of 60. If the call were American, would it ever be worth exercising it early?

16.13. In Problem 16.12, what value does the binomial tree give for a six-month European put option on futures with a strike price of 60? If the put were American, would it ever be worth exercising it early? Verify that the call prices calculated in Problem 16.12 and the put prices calculated here satisfy put–call parity relationships.

16.14. A futures price is currently 25, its volatility is 30% per annum, and the risk-free interest rate is 10% per annum. What is the value of a nine-month European call on the futures with a strike price of 26?

16.15. A futures price is currently 70, its volatility is 20% per annum, and the risk-free interest rate is 6% per annum. What is the value of a five-month European put on the futures with a strike price of 65?

16.16. Suppose that a one-year futures price is currently 35. A one-year European call option and a one-year European put option on the futures with a strike price of 34 are both priced at 2 in the market. The risk-free interest rate is 10% per annum. Identify an arbitrage opportunity.

16.17. "The price of an at-the-money European call futures option always equals the price of a similar at-the-money European put futures option." Explain why this statement is true.

16.18. Suppose that a futures price is currently 30. The risk-free interest rate is 5% per annum. A three-month American call futures option with a strike price of 28 is worth 4. Calculate bounds for the price of a three-month American put futures option with a strike price of 28.

16.19. Show that, if C is the price of an American call option on a futures contract when the strike price is K and the maturity is T, and P is the price of an American put on the same futures contract with the same strike price and exercise date, then

$$F_0e^{-rT} - K < C - P < F_0 - Ke^{-rT}$$

where F_0 is the futures price and r is the risk-free rate. Assume that $r > 0$ and that there is no difference between forward and futures contracts. (*Hint*: Use an analogous approach to that indicated for Problem 15.12.)

16.20. Calculate the price of a three-month European call option on the spot value of silver. The three-month futures price is \$12, the strike price is \$13, the risk-free rate is 4% and the volatility of the price of silver is 25%.

Further Questions

16.21. A futures price is currently 40. It is known that at the end of three months the price will be either 35 or 45. What is the value of a three-month European call option on the futures with a strike price of 42 if the risk-free interest rate is 7% per annum?

16.22. The futures price of an asset is currently 78 and the risk-free rate is 3%. A six-month put on the futures with a strike price of 80 is currently worth 6.5. What is the value of a six-month call on the futures with a strike price of 80 if both the put and call are European? What is the range of possible values of the six-month call with a strike price of 80 if both put and call are American?

16.23. Use a three-step tree to value an American put futures option when the futures price is 50, the life of the option is 9 months, the strike price is 50, the risk-free rate is 3%, and the volatility is 25%.

16.24. Calculate the implied volatility of soybean futures prices from the following information concerning a European put on soybean futures:

Current futures price	525
Exercise price	525
Risk-free rate	6% per annum
Time to maturity	5 months
Put price	20

16.25. It is February 4. July call options on corn futures with strike prices of 260, 270, 280, 290, and 300 cost 26.75, 21.25, 17.25, 14.00, and 11.375, respectively. July put options with these strike prices cost 8.50, 13.50, 19.00, 25.625, and 32.625, respectively. The options mature on June 19, the current July corn futures price is 278.25, and the risk-free interest rate is 1.1%. Calculate implied volatilities for the options using DerivaGem. Comment on the results you get.

16.26. Calculate the price of a six-month European put option on the spot value of the S&P 500. The six-month forward price of the index is 1,400, the strike price is 1,450, the risk-free rate is 5%, and the volatility of the index is 15%.

16.27. The strike price of a futures option is 550 cents, the risk-free interest rate is 3%, the volatility of the futures price is 20%, and the time to maturity of the option is 9 months. The futures price is 500 cents.

(a) What is the price of the option if it is a European call?
(b) What is the price of the option if it is a European put?
(c) Verify that put–call parity holds.
(d) What is the futures price for a futures-style option if it is a call?
(e) What is the futures price for a futures-style option if it is a put?

CHAPTER 17 The Greek Letters

A financial institution that sells an option to a client in the over-the-counter market is faced with the problem of managing its risk. If the option happens to be the same as one that is traded on an exchange, the financial institution can neutralize its exposure by buying on the exchange the same option as it has sold. But when the option has been tailored to the needs of a client and does not correspond to the standardized products traded by exchanges, hedging the exposure is more difficult.

In this chapter we discuss some of the alternative approaches to this problem. We cover what are commonly referred to as the "Greek letters," or simply the "Greeks." Each Greek letter measures a different dimension to the risk in an option position and the aim of a trader is to manage the Greeks so that all risks are acceptable. The analysis presented in this chapter is applicable to market makers in options on an exchange as well as to over-the-counter traders working for financial institutions.

Toward the end of the chapter, we will consider the creation of options synthetically. This turns out to be very closely related to the hedging of options. Creating an option position synthetically is essentially the same task as hedging the opposite option position. For example, creating a long call option synthetically is the same as hedging a short position in the call option.

17.1 ILLUSTRATION

In the next few sections, we use as an example the position of a financial institution that has sold for \$300,000 a European call option on 100,000 shares of a non-dividend-paying stock. We assume that the stock price is \$49, the strike price is \$50, the risk-free interest rate is 5% per annum, the stock price volatility is 20% per annum, the time to maturity is 20 weeks (0.3846 years), and the expected return from the stock is 13% per annum.[1] With our usual notation, this means that

$$S_0 = 49, \quad K = 50, \quad r = 0.05, \quad \sigma = 0.20, \quad T = 0.3846, \quad \mu = 0.13$$

The Black–Scholes–Merton price of the option is about \$240,000 (\$2.40 for an option

[1] As shown in Chapters 12 and 13, the expected return is irrelevant to the pricing of an option. It is given here because it can have some bearing on the effectiveness of a hedging scheme.

to buy one share). The financial institution has therefore sold the option for \$60,000 more than its theoretical value. But it is faced with the problem of hedging the risks.[2]

17.2 NAKED AND COVERED POSITIONS

One strategy open to the financial institution is to do nothing. This is sometimes referred to as a *naked position*. It is a strategy that works well if the stock price is below \$50 at the end of the 20 weeks. The option then costs the financial institution nothing and it makes a profit of \$300,000. A naked position works less well if the call is exercised because the financial institution then has to buy 100,000 shares at the market price prevailing in 20 weeks to cover the call. The cost to the financial institution is 100,000 times the amount by which the stock price exceeds the strike price. For example, if after 20 weeks the stock price is \$60, the option costs the financial institution \$1,000,000. This is considerably greater than the \$300,000 charged for the option.

As an alternative to a naked position, the financial institution can adopt a *covered position*. This involves buying 100,000 shares as soon as the option has been sold. If the option is exercised, this strategy works well, but in other circumstances it could lead to a significant loss. For example, if the stock price drops to \$40, the financial institution loses \$900,000 on its stock position. This is considerably greater than the \$300,000 charged for the option.[3]

Neither a naked position nor a covered position provides a good hedge. If the assumptions underlying the Black–Scholes–Merton formula hold, the cost to the financial institution should always be \$240,000 on average for both approaches.[4] But on any one occasion the cost is liable to range from zero to over \$1,000,000. A good hedge would ensure that the cost is always close to \$240,000.

17.3 A STOP-LOSS STRATEGY

One interesting hedging procedure that is sometimes proposed involves a *stop-loss strategy*. To illustrate the basic idea, consider an institution that has written a call option with strike price K to buy one unit of a stock. The hedging procedure involves buying one unit of the stock as soon as its price rises above K and selling it as soon as its price falls below K. The objective is to hold a naked position whenever the stock price is less than K and a covered position whenever the stock price is greater than K. The procedure is designed to ensure that at time T the institution owns the stock if the option closes in the money and does not own it if the option closes out of the money. The strategy appears to produce payoffs that are the same as the payoffs on the option. In the situation illustrated in Figure 17.1, it involves buying the stock at time t_1, selling

---

[2] A call option on a non-dividend-paying stock is a convenient example with which to develop our ideas. The points that will be made apply to other types of options and to other derivatives.

[3] Put–call parity shows that the exposure from writing a covered call is the same as the exposure from writing a naked put.

[4] More precisely, the present value of the expected cost is \$240,000 for both approaches assuming that appropriate risk-adjusted discount rates are used.

it at time t_2, buying it at time t_3, selling it at time t_4, buying it at time t_5, and delivering it at time T.

As usual, we denote the initial stock price by S_0. The cost of setting up the hedge initially is S_0 if $S_0 > K$ and zero otherwise. It seems as though the total cost, Q, of writing and hedging the option is equal to the initial intrinsic value of the option:

$$Q = \max(S_0 - K, 0) \tag{17.1}$$

This is because all purchases and sales subsequent to time zero are made at price K. If this were in fact correct, the hedging procedure would work perfectly in the absence of transactions costs. Furthermore, the cost of hedging the option would always be less than its Black–Scholes–Merton price. Thus, an investor could earn riskless profits by writing options and hedging them.

There are two reasons why equation (17.1) is incorrect. The first is that the cash flows to the hedger occur at different times and must be discounted. The second is that purchases and sales cannot be made at exactly the same price K. This second point is critical. If we assume a risk-neutral world with zero interest rates, we can justify ignoring the time value of money. But we cannot legitimately assume that both purchases and sales are made at the same price. If markets are efficient, the hedger cannot know whether, when the stock price equals K, it will continue above or below K.

As a practical matter, purchases must be made at a price $K + \epsilon$ and sales must be made at a price $K - \epsilon$, for some small positive number, ϵ. Thus, every purchase and subsequent sale involves a cost (apart from transaction costs) of 2ϵ. A natural response on the part of the hedger is to monitor price movements more closely so that ϵ is reduced. Assuming that stock prices change continuously, ϵ can be made arbitrarily small by monitoring the stock prices closely. But as ϵ is made smaller, trades tend to occur more frequently. Thus,

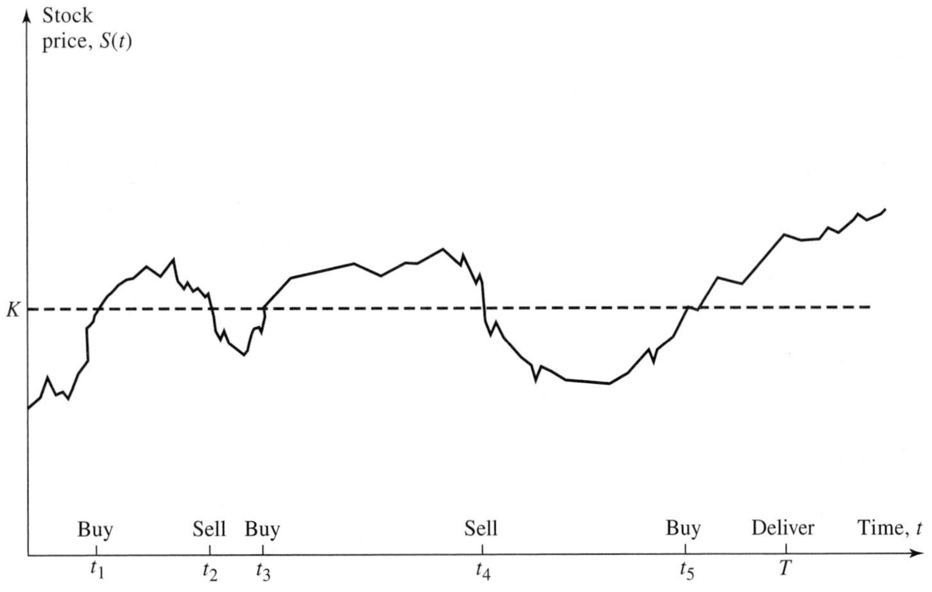

Figure 17.1 A stop-loss strategy

Table 17.1 Performance of stop-loss strategy. (The performance measure is the ratio of the standard deviation of the cost of writing the option and hedging it to the theoretical price of the option.)

Δt (weeks):	5	4	2	1	0.5	0.25
Hedge performance:	1.02	0.93	0.82	0.77	0.76	0.76

the lower cost per trade is offset by the increased frequency of trading. As $\epsilon \to 0$, the expected number of trades tends to infinity.

A stop-loss strategy, although superficially attractive, does not work particularly well as a hedging procedure. Consider its use for an out-of-the-money option. If the stock price never reaches the strike price of K, the hedging procedure costs nothing. If the path of the stock price crosses the strike price level many times, the procedure is quite expensive. Monte Carlo simulation can be used to assess the overall performance of stop-loss hedging. This involves randomly sampling paths for the stock price and observing the results of using the procedure. Table 17.1 shows the results for the option considered in Section 17.1. It assumes that the stock price is observed at the end of time intervals of length Δt.[5] The hedge performance measure is the ratio of the standard deviation of the cost of hedging the option to the Black–Scholes–Merton price of the option. Each result is based on 1,000 sample paths for the stock price and has a standard error of about 2%. It appears to be impossible to produce a value for the hedge performance measure below 0.70 regardless of how small Δt is made.

17.4 DELTA HEDGING

Most traders use more sophisticated hedging procedures than those mentioned so far. These involve calculating measures such as delta, gamma, and vega. In this section we consider the role played by delta.

The *delta* of an option, Δ, was introduced in Chapter 12. It is defined as the rate of change of the option price with respect to the price of the underlying asset. It is the slope of the curve that relates the option price to the underlying asset price. Suppose that the delta of a call option on a stock is 0.6. This means that when the stock price changes by a small amount, the option price changes by about 60% of that amount. Figure 17.2 shows the relationship between a call price and the underlying stock price. When the stock price corresponds to point A, the option price corresponds to point B, and Δ is the slope of the line indicated. In general, the delta of a call equals $\Delta c/\Delta S$, where ΔS is a small change in the stock price and Δc the resulting change in the call price.

Suppose that, in Figure 17.2, the stock price is \$100 and the option price is \$10. Consider a trader working for a financial institution who sells 20 call option contracts

[5] The precise hedging rule used was as follows. If the stock price moves from below K to above K in a time interval of length Δt, it is bought at the end of the interval. If it moves from above K to below K in the time interval, it is sold at the end of the interval. Otherwise, no action is taken.

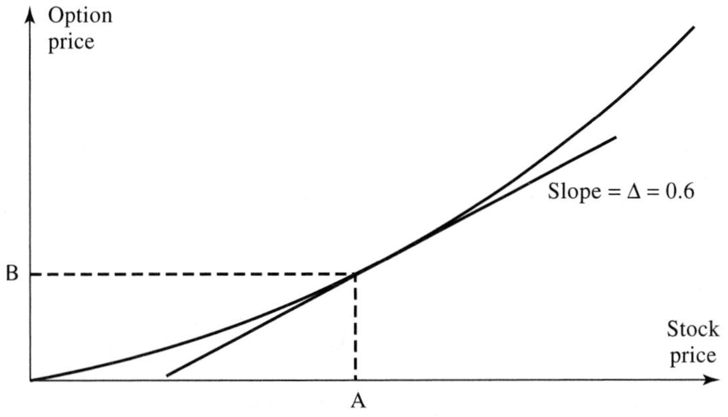

Figure 17.2 Calculation of delta

on a stock—that is, options on 2,000 shares. The trader's position could be hedged by buying $0.6 \times 2{,}000 = 1{,}200$ shares. The gain (loss) on the stock position would then tend to offset the loss (gain) on the option position. For example, if the stock price goes up by \$1 (producing a gain of \$1,200 on the shares purchased), the option price will tend to go up by $0.6 \times \$1 = \$0.60$ (producing a loss of \$1,200 on the options written); if the stock price goes down by \$1 (producing a loss of \$1,200 on the shares purchased), the option price will tend to go down by \$0.60 (producing a gain of \$1,200 on the options written).

In this example, the delta of the trader's short position in 2,000 options (i.e., 20 contracts) is $0.6 \times (-2{,}000) = -1{,}200$. The trader loses $1{,}200\Delta S$ on the option position when the stock price increases by ΔS. The delta of one share of the stock is 1.0, so that the long position in 1,200 shares has a delta of +1,200. The delta of the trader's overall position is, therefore, zero. The delta of the stock position offsets the delta of the option position. A position with a delta of zero is referred to as *delta neutral*.

It is important to realize that, because the delta of an option does not remain constant, the investor's position remains delta hedged (or delta neutral) for only a relatively short period of time. The hedge has to be adjusted periodically. This is known as *rebalancing*. In our example, at the end of one day the stock price might increase to \$110. As indicated by Figure 17.2, an increase in the stock price leads to an increase in delta. Suppose that delta rises from 0.60 to 0.65. An extra $0.05 \times 2{,}000 = 100$ shares would then have to be purchased to maintain the hedge. This is illustrated in Example 17.1.

The delta-hedging procedure just described is an example of *dynamic hedging*. It can be contrasted with *static hedging*, where a hedge is set up initially and never adjusted. Static hedging is sometimes also referred to as *hedge and forget*. Delta is closely related to the Black–Scholes–Merton analysis. As explained in Chapter 13, Merton showed that it is possible to set up a riskless portfolio consisting of a position in an option on a stock and a position in the stock. Expressed in terms of Δ, the portfolio is

$$\begin{cases} -1: & \text{option} \\ +\Delta: & \text{shares of the stock} \end{cases}$$

Using our new terminology, we can say that Merton valued options by setting up a

Example 17.1 Use of delta hedging

A trader working for a financial institution sells 20 call option contracts (2,000 options) on a certain stock. The option price is \$10, the stock price is \$100, and the option's delta is 0.6. The delta of the option position is $0.6 \times -2{,}000 = -1{,}200$.

First Hedge
The trader buys 1,200 shares to create a delta-neutral position.

Price Change
During the next day, the stock price increases to \$110 and the delta changes to 0.65. The delta of the option position changes to $0.65 \times -2{,}000 = -1{,}300$.

Hedge Rebalancing
The trader buys a further 100 shares to maintain delta neutrality.

delta-neutral position and arguing that the return on the position should be the risk-free interest rate.

Delta of European Stock Options

For a European call option on a non-dividend-paying stock, it can be shown that

$$\Delta\,(\text{call}) = N(d_1)$$

where d_1 is defined as for equation (13.5) and $N(x)$ is the cumulative distribution function for a standard normal distribution. Example 17.2 illustrates this formula. The formula gives the delta of a long position in one call option. The delta of a short position in one call option is $-N(d_1)$. Using delta hedging for a long option position involves maintaining a short position in $N(d_1)$ shares for each option purchased. Similarly, using delta hedging for a short option position involves maintaining a long position in $N(d_1)$ shares for each option sold.

For a European put option on a non-dividend-paying stock, delta is given by

$$\Delta\,(\text{put}) = N(d_1) - 1$$

Delta is negative, which means that a long position in a put option should be hedged with a long position in the underlying stock, and a short position in a put option should be hedged with a short position in the underlying stock. Figure 17.3 shows the

Example 17.2 Delta of a stock option

Consider a call option on a non-dividend-paying stock where the stock price is \$49, the strike price is \$50, the risk-free rate is 5%, the time to maturity is 20 weeks (= 0.3846 years), and the volatility is 20%. In this case, we have

$$d_1 = \frac{\ln(49/50) + (0.05 + 0.2^2/2) \times 0.3846}{0.2 \times \sqrt{0.3846}} = 0.0542$$

Delta is $N(d_1)$, or 0.522. When the stock price changes by ΔS, the option price changes by $0.522\Delta S$.

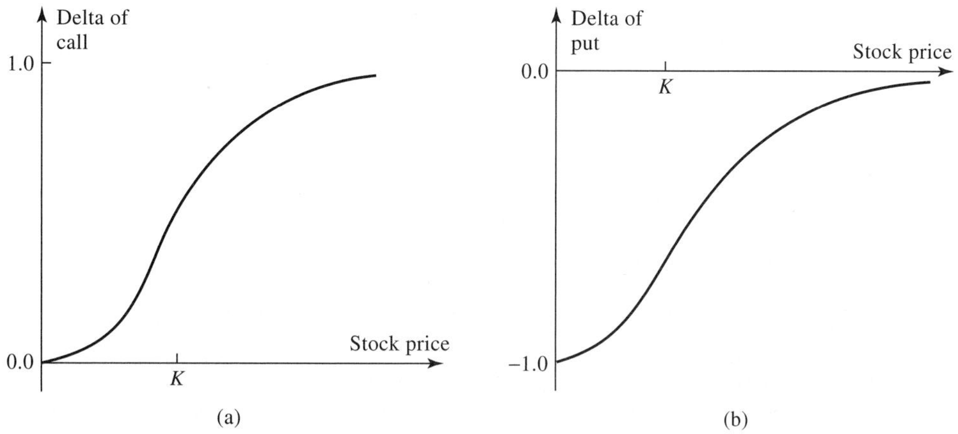

Figure 17.3 Variation of delta with stock price for (a) call option and (b) put option on a non-dividend-paying stock

variation of the delta of a call option and a put option with the stock price. Figure 17.4 shows the variation of delta with the time to maturity for in-the-money, at-the-money, and out-of-the-money call options.

Dynamic Aspects of Delta Hedging

Tables 17.2 and 17.3 provide two examples of the operation of delta hedging for the example in Section 17.1. The hedge is assumed to be adjusted or rebalanced weekly. The initial value of the delta of the option being sold can be calculated from the data in

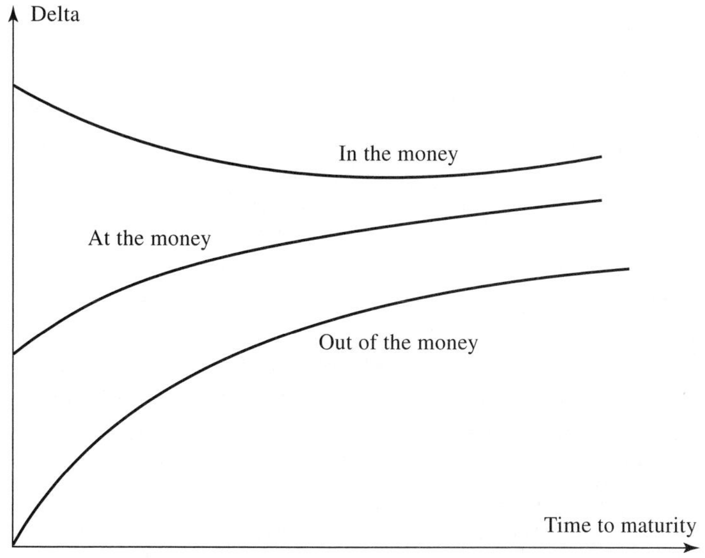

Figure 17.4 Typical patterns for variation of delta with time to maturity for a call option

Table 17.2 Simulation of delta hedging. Option closes in the money and cost of hedging is $263,300

Week	*Stock price*	*Delta*	*Shares purchased*	*Cost of shares purchased ($000)*	*Cumulative cost including interest ($000)*	*Interest cost ($000)*
0	49.00	0.522	52,200	2,557.8	2,557.8	2.5
1	48.12	0.458	(6,400)	(308.0)	2,252.3	2.2
2	47.37	0.400	(5,800)	(274.7	1,979.8	1.9
3	50.25	0.596	19,600	984.9	2,966.6	2.9
4	51.75	0.693	9,700	502.0	3,471.5	3.3
5	53.12	0.774	8,100	430.3	3,905.1	3.8
6	53.00	0.771	(300)	(15.9)	3,893.0	3.7
7	51.87	0.706	(6,500)	(337.2)	3,559.5	3.4
8	51.38	0.674	(3,200)	(164.4)	3,398.5	3.3
9	53.00	0.787	11,300	598.9	4,000.7	3.8
10	49.88	0.550	(23,700)	(1,182.2)	2,822.3	2.7
11	48.50	0.413	(13,700)	(664.4)	2,160.6	2.1
12	49.88	0.542	12,900	643.5	2,806.2	2.7
13	50.37	0.591	4,900	246.8	3,055.7	2.9
14	52.13	0.768	17,700	922.7	3,981.3	3.8
15	51.88	0.759	(900)	(46.7)	3,938.4	3.8
16	52.87	0.865	10,600	560.4	4,502.6	4.3
17	54.87	0.978	11,300	620.0	5,126.9	4.9
18	54.62	0.990	1,200	65.5	5,197.3	5.0
19	55.87	1.000	1,000	55.9	5,258.2	5.1
20	57.25	1.000	0	0.0	5,263.3	

Section 17.1 as 0.522 (see Example 17.2). The delta of the financial institution's initial short option position is $0.522 \times -100{,}000 = -52{,}200$. This means that, as soon as the option is written, 52,200 shares must be purchased for a cost of $49 \times 52{,}200 = \$2{,}557{,}800$. We assume this money is borrowed and the rate of interest is 5%. An interest cost of approximately $2,500 is therefore incurred in the first week.

In Table 17.2, the stock price falls by the end of the first week to $48.12. The delta of the option declines to 0.458, so that the new delta of the option position is $0.458 \times -100{,}000 = -45{,}800$. This means that 6,400 of the shares purchased at week 0 must be sold to maintain the hedge. The strategy realizes $308,000 in cash, and the cumulative borrowings at the end of Week 1 are reduced to $2,252,300. During the second week, the stock price reduces to $47.37, delta declines again, and so on. Toward the end of the life of the option, it becomes apparent that the option will be exercised and the delta of the option approaches 1.0. By Week 20, therefore, the hedger has a fully covered position. The hedger receives $5 million for the stock held, so that the total cost of writing the option and hedging it is $263,300.

Table 17.3 illustrates an alternative sequence of events such that the option closes out of the money. As it becomes clear that the option will not be exercised, delta approaches zero. By Week 20, the hedger has a naked position and has incurred costs totaling $256,600.

In Tables 17.2 and 17.3, the costs of hedging the option, when discounted to the beginning of the period, are close to, but not exactly the same as, the Black–Scholes–Merton price of $240,000. If the hedge worked perfectly, the cost of hedging would, after discounting, be exactly equal to the Black–Scholes–Merton price for every simulated stock price path. The reason for the variation in the cost of delta hedging is that the hedge is rebalanced only once a week. As rebalancing takes place more frequently, the variation in the cost of hedging is reduced. Of course, the examples in Tables 17.2 and 17.3 are idealized in that they assume the volatility is constant and there are no transaction costs.

Table 17.4 shows statistics on the performance of delta hedging obtained from 1,000 random stock price paths in our example. As in Table 17.1, the performance measure is the ratio of the standard deviation of the cost of hedging the option to the Black–Scholes–Merton price of the option. It is clear that delta hedging is a great improvement over a stop-loss strategy. Unlike a stop-loss strategy, the performance of delta-hedging strategy gets steadily better as the hedge is monitored more frequently.

Delta hedging aims to keep the value of the financial institution's position as close to unchanged as possible. Initially, the value of the written option is $240,000. In the situation depicted in Table 17.2, the value of the option can be calculated as $414,500 in Week 9. Thus, the financial institution has lost $174,500 on its short option position. Its

Table 17.3 Simulation of delta hedging. Option closes out of the money and cost of hedging = $256,600

Week	*Stock price*	*Delta*	*Shares purchased*	*Cost of shares purchased ($000)*	*Cumulative cost including interest ($000)*	*Interest cost ($000)*
0	49.00	0.522	52,200	2,557.8	2,557.8	2.5
1	49.75	0.568	4,600	228.9	2,789.2	2.7
2	52.00	0.705	13,700	712.4	3,504.3	3.4
3	50.00	0.579	(12,600)	(630.0)	2,877.7	2.8
4	48.38	0.459	(12,000)	(580.6)	2,299.9	2.2
5	48.25	0.443	(1,600)	(77.2)	2,224.9	2.1
6	48.75	0.475	3,200	156.0	2,383.0	2.3
7	49.63	0.540	6,500	322.6	2,707.9	2.6
8	48.25	0.420	(12,000)	(579.0)	2,131.5	2.1
9	48.25	0.410	(1,000)	(48.2)	2,085.4	2.0
10	51.12	0.658	24,800	1,267.8	3,355.2	3.2
11	51.50	0.692	3,400	175.1	3,533.5	3.4
12	49.88	0.542	(15,000)	(748.2)	2,788.7	2.7
13	49.88	0.538	(400)	(20.0)	2,771.4	2.7
14	48.75	0.400	(13,800)	(672.7)	2,101.4	2.0
15	47.50	0.236	(16,400)	(779.0)	1,324.4	1.3
16	48.00	0.261	2,500	120.0	1,445.7	1.4
17	46.25	0.062	(19,900)	(920.4)	526.7	0.5
18	48.13	0.183	12,100	582.4	1,109.6	1.1
19	46.63	0.007	(17,600)	(820.7)	290.0	0.3
20	48.12	0.000	(700)	(33.7)	256.6	

Table 17.4 Performance of delta hedging. The performance measure is the ratio of the standard deviation of the cost of writing the option and hedging it to the theoretical price of the option

Time between hedge rebalancing (weeks):	5	4	2	1	0.5	0.25
Performance measure:	0.43	0.39	0.26	0.19	0.14	0.09

cash position, as measured by the cumulative cost, is $1,442,900 worse in Week 9 than in Week 0. The value of the shares held has increased from $2,557,800 to $4,171,100. The net effect of all this is that the value of the financial institution's position has changed by only $4,100 between Week 0 and Week 9.

Where the Cost Comes From

The delta-hedging procedure in Tables 17.2 and 17.3 creates the equivalent of a long position in the option synthetically. This neutralizes the short position the financial institution created by writing the option. As the tables illustrate, delta hedging a short position generally involves selling stock just after the price has gone down and buying stock just after the price has gone up. It might be termed a buy-high, sell-low trading strategy! The present value of the expected cost is the option price, or $240,000. This comes from the average difference between the price at which stock is purchased and the price at which it is sold.

Delta of a Portfolio

The delta of a portfolio of options or other derivatives dependent on a single asset whose price is S is given by

$$\frac{\Delta\Pi}{\Delta S}$$

where ΔS is a small change in the price of the asset and $\Delta\Pi$ is the resultant change in the value of the portfolio.

The delta of the portfolio can be calculated from the deltas of the individual options in the portfolio. If a portfolio consists of a quantity w_i of option i $(1 \leqslant i \leqslant n)$, the delta of the portfolio is given by

$$\Delta = \sum_{i=1}^{n} w_i \Delta_i$$

where Δ_i is the delta of the ith option. The formula can be used to calculate the position in the underlying asset necessary to make the delta of the portfolio zero. When this position has been taken, the portfolio is referred to as being *delta neutral*.

Suppose a financial institution has the following three positions in options on a stock:

1. A long position in 100,000 call options with strike price $55 and an expiration date in three months. The delta of each option is 0.533.
2. A short position in 200,000 call options with strike price $56 and an expiration date in five months. The delta of each option is 0.468.

3. A short position in 50,000 put options with strike price \$56 and an expiration date in two months. The delta of each option is −0.508.

The delta of the whole portfolio is

$$100{,}000 \times 0.533 - 200{,}000 \times 0.468 - 50{,}000 \times (-0.508) = -14{,}900$$

This means that the portfolio can be made delta neutral by buying 14,900 shares.

Transaction Costs

Derivatives dealers usually rebalance their positions once a day to maintain delta neutrality. When a dealer has a small number of options on a particular asset, this is liable to be prohibitively expensive because of the transaction costs incurred on trades. For a large portfolio of options, it is more feasible. Only one trade in the underlying asset is necessary to zero out delta for the whole portfolio. The hedging transactions costs are absorbed by the profits on many different trades.

17.5 THETA

The *theta* of a portfolio of options, Θ, is the rate of change of the value of the portfolio with respect to the passage of time with all else remaining the same. Specifically,

$$\Theta = \frac{\Delta\Pi}{\Delta t}$$

where $\Delta\Pi$ is change in the value of the portfolio when an amount of time Δt passes with all else remaining the same. Theta is sometimes referred to as the *time decay* of the portfolio. For a European call option on a non-dividend-paying stock, it can be shown from the Black–Scholes–Merton formula that

$$\Theta\,(\text{call}) = -\frac{S_0 N'(d_1)\sigma}{2\sqrt{T}} - rKe^{-rT}N(d_2)$$

where d_1 and d_2 are defined as for equation (13.5) and

$$N'(x) = \frac{1}{\sqrt{2\pi}}e^{-x^2/2} \qquad \textbf{(17.2)}$$

is the probability density function for a standard normal distribution.

For a European put option on the stock,

$$\Theta\,(\text{put}) = -\frac{S_0 N'(d_1)\sigma}{2\sqrt{T}} + rKe^{-rT}N(-d_2)$$

Since $N(-d_2) = 1 - N(d_2)$, the theta of a put exceeds the theta of the corresponding call by rKe^{-rT}. Example 17.3 provides an application of the formulas.

In these formulas, time is measured in years. Usually, when theta is quoted, time is measured in days, so that theta is the change in the portfolio value when one day passes with all else remaining the same. We can either measure theta "per calendar day" or "per trading day." To obtain the theta per calendar day, the formula for theta must be

Example 17.3 Theta of a stock option

As in Example 17.2, consider a call option on a non-dividend-paying stock where the stock price is \$49, the strike price is \$50, the risk-free rate is 5%, the time to maturity is 20 weeks (= 0.3846 years), and the volatility is 20%. In this case, $S_0 = 49$, $K = 50$, $r = 0.05$, $\sigma = 0.2$, and $T = 0.3846$. The option's theta is

$$-\frac{S_0 N'(d_1)\sigma}{2\sqrt{T}} - rKe^{-rT}N(d_2) = -4.31$$

The theta is $-4.31/365 = -0.0118$ per calendar day, or $-4.31/252 = -0.0171$ per trading day.

divided by 365; to obtain theta per trading day, it must be divided by 252. (DerivaGem measures theta per calendar day.)

Theta is usually negative for an option.[6] This is because as time passes, with all else remaining the same, the option tends to become less valuable. The variation of Θ with stock price for a call option on a stock is shown in Figure 17.5. When the stock price is very low, theta is close to zero. For an at-the-money call option, theta is large and negative. As the stock price becomes larger, theta tends to $-rKe^{-rT}$. Figure 17.6 shows typical patterns for the variation of Θ with the time to maturity for in-the-money, at-the-money, and out-of-the-money call options.

Theta is not the same type of hedge parameter as delta. There is uncertainty about the future stock price, but there is no uncertainty about the passage of time. It makes sense to hedge against changes in the price of the underlying asset, but it does not make any sense to hedge against the passage of time. In spite of this, many traders regard theta as a useful descriptive statistic for a portfolio. This is because, as we shall see later, in a delta-neutral portfolio theta is a proxy for gamma.

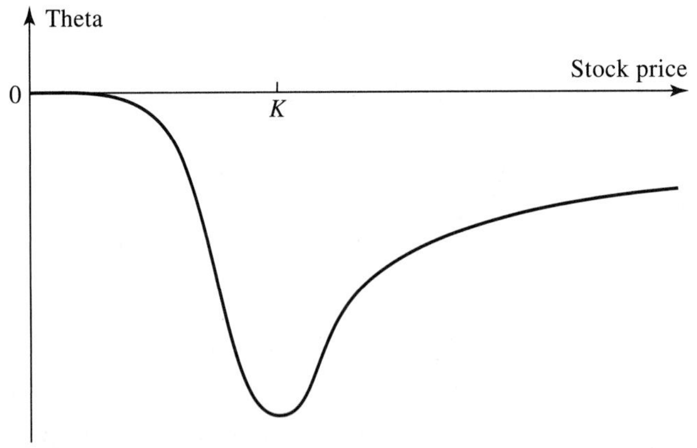

Figure 17.5 Variation of theta of a European call option with stock price

[6] An exception to this could be an in-the-money European put option on a non-dividend-paying stock or an in-the-money European call option on a currency with a very high interest rate.

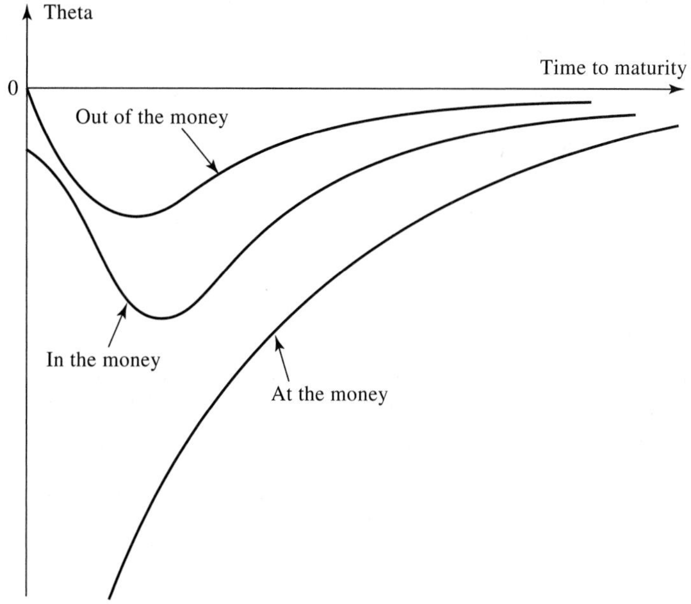

Figure 17.6 Typical patterns for variation of theta of a European call option with time to maturity

17.6 GAMMA

The *gamma*, Γ, of a portfolio of options on an underlying asset is the rate of change of the portfolio's delta with respect to the price of the underlying asset. If gamma is small, delta changes slowly, and adjustments to keep a portfolio delta neutral need to be made only relatively infrequently. However, if gamma is highly negative or highly positive, delta is very sensitive to the price of the underlying asset. It is then quite risky to leave a delta-neutral portfolio unchanged for any length of time. Figure 17.7 illustrates this point. When the stock price moves from S to S', delta hedging assumes that the option price moves from C to C', when in fact it moves from C to C''. The difference between C'

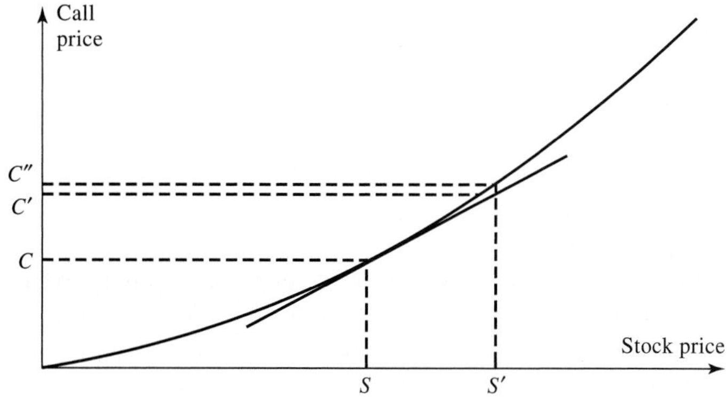

Figure 17.7 Hedging error introduced by nonlinearity

Example 17.4 Impact of gamma on change in value of a delta-neutral portfolio

Suppose that the gamma of a delta-neutral portfolio of options on an asset is $-10{,}000$. Equation (17.3) shows that, if a jump of $+2$ or -2 in the price of the asset occurs (without any time passing), there is an unexpected decrease in the value of the portfolio of approximately $0.5 \times 10{,}000 \times 2^2 = \$20{,}000$.

and C'' leads to a hedging error. The size of the error depends on the curvature of the relationship between the option price and the stock price. Gamma measures this curvature.

Suppose that ΔS is the change in the price of an underlying asset in a small interval of time, Δt, and $\Delta \Pi$ is the corresponding change in the price of the portfolio. For a delta-neutral portfolio, it is approximately true that

$$\Delta \Pi = \Theta \, \Delta t + \tfrac{1}{2} \Gamma \, \Delta S^2 \tag{17.3}$$

where Θ is the theta of the portfolio. Example 17.4 provides an application of this formula.

Figure 17.8 shows the nature of this relationship between $\Delta \Pi$ and ΔS for a delta-neutral portfolio. It shows that when gamma is positive, the portfolio declines in value if there is no change in S but increases in value if there is a large positive or negative change in S. When gamma is negative, the reverse is true: the portfolio increases in value if there is no change in S but decreases in value if there is a large positive or negative change in S. As the absolute value of gamma increases, the sensitivity of the value of the portfolio to ΔS increases.

Making a Portfolio Gamma Neutral

A position in the underlying asset has zero gamma and cannot be used to change the gamma of a portfolio. What is required is a position in an instrument such as an option that is not linearly dependent on the underlying asset.

Suppose that a delta-neutral portfolio has a gamma equal to Γ, and a traded option has a gamma equal to Γ_T. If the number of traded options added to the portfolio is w_T, then the gamma of the portfolio is

$$w_T \Gamma_T + \Gamma$$

Hence, the position in the traded option necessary to make the portfolio gamma neutral is $-\Gamma/\Gamma_T$. Including the traded option is likely to change the delta of the portfolio, so the position in the underlying asset then has to be changed to maintain delta neutrality. Note that the portfolio is gamma neutral only for a short period of time. As time passes, gamma neutrality can be maintained only if the position in the traded option is adjusted so that it is always equal to $-\Gamma/\Gamma_T$.

Making a portfolio gamma neutral as well as delta neutral can be regarded as a correction for the hedging error illustrated in Figure 17.7. Delta neutrality provides protection against relatively small stock price moves between rebalancing. Gamma neutrality provides protection against larger movements in this stock price between hedge rebalancing. Suppose that a portfolio is delta neutral and has a gamma of $-3{,}000$. The delta and gamma of a particular traded call option are 0.62 and 1.50,

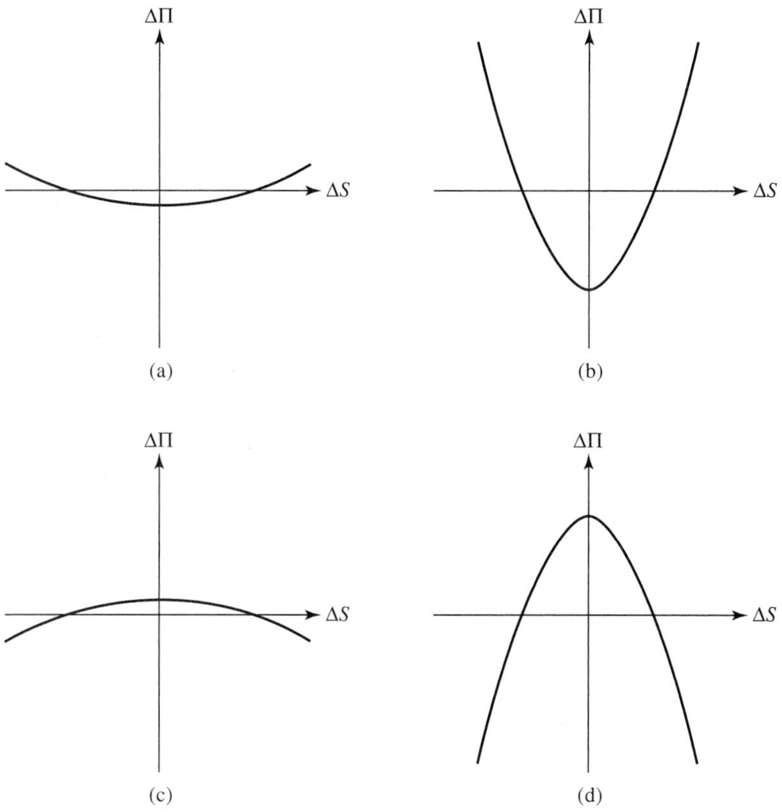

Figure 17.8 Relationship between $\Delta\Pi$ and ΔS in time Δt for a delta-neutral portfolio: (a) slightly positive gamma, (b) large positive gamma, (c) slightly negative gamma, and (d) large negative gamma

respectively. The portfolio can be made gamma neutral by including in the portfolio a long position of

$$\frac{3{,}000}{1.5} = 2{,}000$$

in the call option. However, the delta of the portfolio will then change from zero to $2{,}000 \times 0.62 = 1{,}240$. Therefore, 1,240 units of the underlying asset must be sold from the portfolio to keep it delta neutral. See Example 17.5 for a summary of this trading strategy.

Example 17.5 Making a portfolio gamma and delta neutral

A trader's portfolio is delta neutral and has a gamma of −3,000. The delta and gamma of a particular traded call option are 0.62 and 1.50, respectively. The trader wants to make the portfolio gamma neutral as well as delta neutral. He or she can:

1. Make portfolio gamma neutral buying 2,000 options (20 contracts).
2. Sell 1,240 units of the underlying asset to maintain delta neutrality.

Example 17.6 Gamma of a stock option

As in Example 17.2, consider a call option on a non-dividend-paying stock where the stock price is \$49, the strike price is \$50, the risk-free rate is 5%, the time to maturity is 20 weeks (= 0.3846 years), and the volatility is 20%. In this case, $S_0 = 49$, $K = 50$, $r = 0.05$, $\sigma = 0.2$, and $T = 0.3846$. The option's gamma is

$$\frac{N'(d_1)}{S_0\sigma\sqrt{T}} = 0.066$$

When the stock price changes by ΔS, the delta of the option changes by $0.066\Delta S$.

Calculation of Gamma

For a European call or put option on a non-dividend-paying stock, the gamma is given by

$$\Gamma = \frac{N'(d_1)}{S_0\sigma\sqrt{T}}$$

where d_1 is defined as for equation (13.5) and $N'(x)$ is as given by equation (17.2). Example 17.6 provides an application of this formula. The gamma of a long option position is always positive and varies with S_0 in the way indicated in Figure 17.9. The variation of gamma with time to maturity for out-of-the-money, at-the-money, and in-the-money options is shown in Figure 17.10. For an at-the-money option, gamma increases as the time to maturity decreases. Short-life at-the-money options have very high gammas, which means that the value of the option holder's position is highly sensitive to jumps in the stock price.

17.7 RELATIONSHIP BETWEEN DELTA, THETA, AND GAMMA

The Black–Scholes–Merton analysis can be used to show that the Greek letters for a portfolio of calls, puts, and other financial instruments dependent on an asset paying

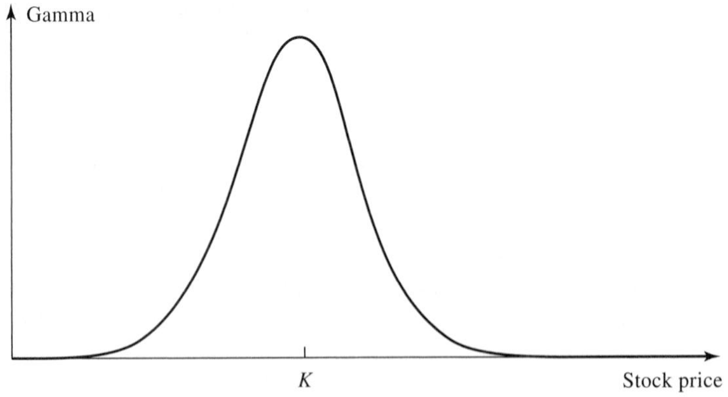

Figure 17.9 Variation of gamma with stock price for an option

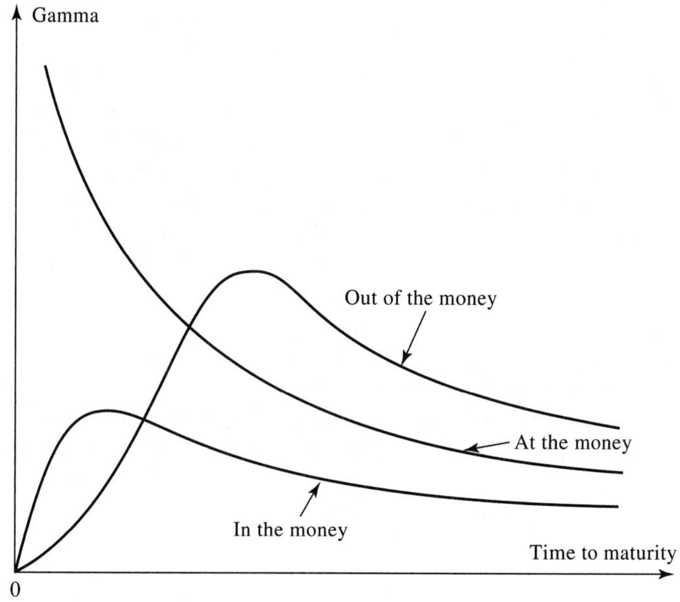

Figure 17.10 Variation of gamma with time to maturity for a stock option

no dividends must satisfy

$$\Theta + rS_0\Delta + \tfrac{1}{2}\sigma^2 S_0^2 \Gamma = r\Pi \tag{17.4}$$

where S_0 is the asset price and Π is the value of the portfolio.

For a delta-neutral portfolio, $\Delta = 0$, so that

$$\Theta + \tfrac{1}{2}\sigma^2 S_0^2 \Gamma = r\Pi$$

This shows that when Θ is large and positive, gamma of a portfolio tends to be large and negative, and vice versa. This is consistent with the way Figure 17.8 has been drawn and explains why theta is sometimes regarded as a proxy for gamma in a delta-neutral portfolio.

17.8 VEGA

Up to now we have implicitly assumed that the volatility of the asset underlying a derivative is constant. In practice, volatilities change over time. This means that the value of a derivative is liable to change because of movements in volatility as well as because of changes in the asset price and the passage of time.

The *vega* of a portfolio of derivatives, $\mathcal{V}$, is the rate of change of the value of the portfolio with respect to the volatility of the underlying asset.[7] If vega is highly positive or highly negative, the portfolio's value is very sensitive to small changes in volatility. If it is close to zero, volatility changes have relatively little impact on the value of the portfolio.

A position in the underlying asset has zero vega. However, the vega of a portfolio can

[7] Vega is the name given to one of the "Greek letters" in option pricing, but it is not one of the letters in the Greek alphabet.

Example 17.7 Making a portfolio delta, gamma, and vega neutral

Consider a portfolio that is delta neutral, with a gamma of −5,000 and a vega of −8,000. The options shown in the table below can be traded. The portfolio can be made vega neutral by including a long position in 4,000 of Option 1. This would increase delta to 2,400 and require that 2,400 units of the asset be sold to maintain delta neutrality. The gamma of the portfolio would change from −5,000 to −3,000.

	Delta	*Gamma*	*Vega*
Portfolio	0	−5,000	−8,000
Option 1	0.6	0.5	2.0
Option 2	0.5	0.8	1.2

To make the portfolio gamma and vega neutral, both Option 1 and Option 2 can be used. If w_1 and w_2 are the quantities of Option 1 and Option 2 that are added to the portfolio, we require

$$-5{,}000 + 0.5w_1 + 0.8w_2 = 0$$
$$-8{,}000 + 2.0w_1 + 1.2w_2 = 0$$

The solution to these equations is $w_1 = 400$, $w_2 = 6{,}000$. The portfolio can therefore be made gamma and vega neutral by including 400 of Option 1 and 6,000 of Option 2. The delta of the portfolio after the addition of the positions in the two traded options is $400 \times 0.6 + 6{,}000 \times 0.5 = 3{,}240$. Hence, 3,240 units of the asset would have to be sold to maintain delta neutrality.

be changed, similarly to the way gamma can be changed, by adding a position in a traded option. If $\mathcal{V}$ is the vega of the portfolio and $\mathcal{V}_T$ is the vega of a traded option, a position of $-\mathcal{V}/\mathcal{V}_T$ in the traded option makes the portfolio instantaneously vega neutral. Unfortunately, a portfolio that is gamma neutral will not in general be vega neutral, and vice versa. If a hedger requires a portfolio to be both gamma and vega neutral, at least two traded derivatives dependent on the underlying asset must usually be used. This is illustrated in Example 17.7.

For a European call or put option on a non-dividend-paying stock, vega is given by

$$\mathcal{V} = S_0\sqrt{T}\,N'(d_1)$$

Example 17.8 Vega of a stock option

As in Example 17.2, consider a call option on a non-dividend-paying stock where the stock price is \$49, the strike price is \$50, the risk-free rate is 5%, the time to maturity is 20 weeks (= 0.3846 years), and the volatility is 20%. In this case, $S_0 = 49$, $K = 50$, $r = 0.05$, $\sigma = 0.2$, and $T = 0.3846$. The option's vega is

$$S_0\sqrt{T}N'(d_1) = 12.1$$

Thus a 1% (0.01) increase in the volatility from (20 to 21%) increases the value of the option by approximately $0.01 \times 12.1 = 0.121$.

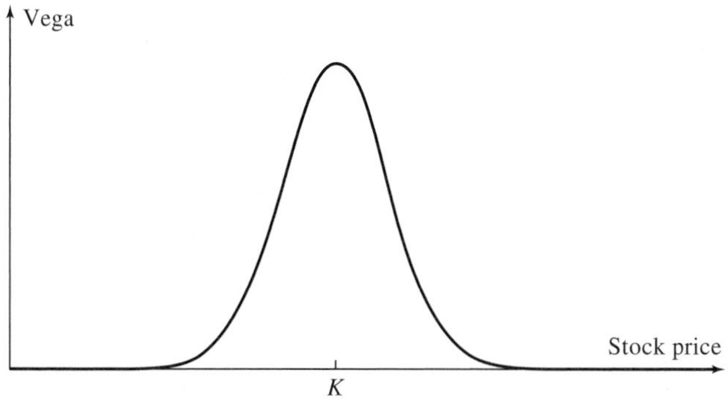

Figure 17.11 Variation of vega with stock price for an option

where d_1 is defined as for equation (13.5). The formula for $N'(x)$ is given in equation (17.2). Example 17.8 provides an application of this formula. The vega of a long position in a European or American option is always positive. The general way in which vega varies with S_0 is shown in Figure 17.11.

Calculating vega from the Black–Scholes–Merton model may seem strange because one of the assumptions underlying the model is that volatility is constant. It would be theoretically more correct to calculate vega from a model in which volatility is assumed to be stochastic. However, it turns out that the vega calculated from a stochastic volatility model is very similar to the Black–Scholes–Merton vega, so the practice of calculating vega from a model in which volatility is constant works reasonably well.[8]

Gamma neutrality protects against large changes in the price of the underlying asset between hedge rebalancing. Vega neutrality protects against a variable σ. As might be expected, whether it is best to use an available traded option for vega or gamma hedging depends on the time between hedge rebalancing and the volatility of the volatility.[9]

17.9 RHO

The *rho* of a portfolio of options is the rate of change of the value of the portfolio with respect to the interest rate. It measures the sensitivity of the value of a portfolio to a change in the interest rate when all else remains the same. For a European call option on a non-dividend-paying stock,

$$\text{rho (call)} = KTe^{-rT}N(d_2)$$

where d_2 is defined as for equation (13.5). For a European put option,

$$\text{rho (put)} = -KTe^{-rT}N(-d_2)$$

Example 17.9 provides an application of these formulas.

[8] See J. C. Hull and A. White, "The Pricing of Options on Assets with Stochastic Volatilities," *Journal of Finance*, 42 (June 1987): 281–300; J. C. Hull and A. White, "An Analysis of the Bias in Option Pricing Caused by a Stochastic Volatility," *Advances in Futures and Options Research*, 3 (1988): 27–61.

[9] For a discussion of this issue, see J. C. Hull and A. White. "Hedging the Risks from Writing Foreign Currency Options," *Journal of International Money and Finance*, 6 (June 1987): 131–52.

Example 17.9 Rho of a stock option

As in Example 17.2, consider a call option on a non-dividend-paying stock where the stock price is \$49, the strike price is \$50, the risk-free rate is 5%, the time to maturity is 20 weeks (= 0.3846 years), and the volatility is 20%. In this case, $S_0 = 49$, $K = 50$, $r = 0.05$, $\sigma = 0.2$, and $T = 0.3846$. The option's rho is

$$KTe^{-rT}N(d_2) = 8.91$$

This means that a 1% (0.01) increase in the risk-free rate (from 5 to 6%) increases the value of the option by approximately $0.01 \times 8.91 = 0.0891$.

17.10 THE REALITIES OF HEDGING

In an ideal world, traders working for financial institutions would be able to rebalance their portfolios very frequently in order to maintain all Greek letters equal to zero. In practice, this is not possible. When managing a large portfolio dependent on a single underlying asset, traders usually make delta zero, or close to zero, at least once a day by trading the underlying asset. Unfortunately, a zero gamma and a zero vega are less easy to achieve, because it is difficult to find options or other nonlinear derivatives that can be traded in the volume required at competitive prices. Business Snapshot 17.1 provides a discussion of how dynamic hedging is organized in practice.

There are big economies of scale in trading derivatives. Maintaining delta neutrality for a small number of options on an asset by trading daily is usually not economically feasible. The trading costs per option being hedged are high.[10] But when a derivatives dealer maintains delta neutrality for a large portfolio, the trading costs per option being hedged are likely to be much more reasonable.

17.11 SCENARIO ANALYSIS

In addition to monitoring risks such as delta, gamma, and vega, option traders often also carry out a scenario analysis. The analysis involves calculating the gain or loss on their portfolio over a specified period under a variety of different scenarios. The time period chosen is likely to depend on the liquidity of the instruments. The scenarios can be either chosen by management or generated by a model.

Consider a bank with a portfolio of options on a foreign currency. There are two main variables on which the value of the portfolio depends. These are the exchange rate and the exchange rate volatility. Suppose that the exchange rate is currently 1.0000 and its volatility is 10% per annum. The bank could calculate a table such as Table 17.5 showing the profit or loss experienced during a two-week period under different scenarios. This table considers seven different exchange rates and three different volatilities. Because a one-standard-deviation move in the exchange rate during a

[10] The trading costs arise from the fact that each day the hedger buys some of the underlying asset at the offer price or sells some of the underlying asset at the bid price.

Business Snapshot 17.1 Dynamic hedging in practice

In a typical arrangement at a financial institution, the responsibility for a portfolio of derivatives dependent on a particular underlying asset is assigned to one trader or to a group of traders working together. For example, one trader at Goldman Sachs might be assigned responsibility for all derivatives dependent on the value of the Australian dollar. A computer system calculates the value of the portfolio and Greek letters for the portfolio. Limits are defined for each Greek letter and special permission is required if a trader wants to exceed a limit at the end of a trading day.

The delta limit is often expressed as the equivalent maximum position in the underlying asset. For example, the delta limit of Goldman Sachs for a stock might be $1 million. If the stock price is $50, this means that the absolute value of delta as we have calculated it can be no more than 20,000. The vega limit is usually expressed as a maximum dollar exposure per 1% change in the volatility.

As a matter of course, options traders make themselves delta neutral—or close to delta neutral—at the end of each day. Gamma and vega are monitored, but are not usually managed on a daily basis. Financial institutions often find that their business with clients involves writing options and that as a result they accumulate negative gamma and vega. They are then always looking out for opportunities to manage their gamma and vega risks by buying options at competitive prices.

There is one aspect of an options portfolio that mitigates problems of managing gamma and vega somewhat. Options are often close to the money when they are first sold so that they have relatively high gammas and vegas. But after some time has elapsed, the underlying asset price has often changed enough for them to become deep out of the money or deep in the money. Their gammas and vegas are then very small and of little consequence. A nightmare scenario for an options trader is where written options remain very close to the money as the maturity date is approached.

two-week period is about 0.02, the exchange rate moves considered are approximately zero, one, two, and three standard deviations.

In Table 17.5 the greatest loss is in the lower right corner of the table. The loss corresponds to the volatility increasing to 12% and the exchange rate moving up to 1.06. Usually the greatest loss in such a table occurs at one of the corners, but this is not always so. Consider, for example, the situation where a bank's portfolio consists of a short position in a butterfly spread (see Section 11.3). The greatest loss will be experienced if the exchange rate stays where it is.

Table 17.5 Profit or loss realized in two weeks under different scenarios (millions of dollars)

Volatility	*Exchange rate*						
	0.94	*0.96*	*0.98*	*1.00*	*1.02*	*1.04*	*1.06*
8%	+102	+55	+25	+6	−10	−34	−80
10%	+80	+40	+17	+2	−14	−38	−85
12%	+60	+25	+9	−2	−18	−42	−90

17.12 EXTENSION OF FORMULAS

The formulas produced so far for delta, theta, gamma, vega, and rho have been for an option on a non-dividend-paying stock. Table 17.6 shows how they change when the stock pays a continuous dividend yield at rate q. The expressions for d_1 and d_2 are as for equations (15.4) and (15.5). By setting q equal to the dividend yield on an index, we obtain the Greek letters for European options on indices. By setting q equal to the foreign risk-free rate, we obtain the Greek letters for European options on a currency. By setting $q = r$, we obtain delta, gamma, theta, and vega for European options on a futures contract. The rho for a call futures option is $-cT$ and the rho for a European put futures option is $-pT$.

In the case of currency options, there are two rhos corresponding to the two interest rates. The rho corresponding to the domestic interest rate is given by the formula in Table 17.6 (with d_2 as for equation (15.8)). The rho corresponding to the foreign interest rate for a European call on a currency is

$$\text{rho (call, foreign rate)} = -Te^{-r_f T} S_0 N(d_1)$$

For a European put, it is

$$\text{rho (put, foreign rate)} = Te^{-r_f T} S_0 N(-d_1)$$

with d_1 as for equation (15.8). The calculation of Greek letters for American options is discussed in Chapter 18.

Delta of Forward Contracts

The concept of delta can be applied to financial instruments other than options. Consider a forward contract on a non-dividend-paying stock. Equation (5.5) shows that the value of a forward contract is $S_0 - Ke^{-rT}$, where K is the delivery price and T is the forward contract's time to maturity. When the price of the stock changes by ΔS, with all else remaining the same, the value of a forward contract on the stock also changes by ΔS. The delta of a long forward contract on one share of the stock is therefore always 1.0. This

Table 17.6 Greek letters for European options on an asset that provides a yield at rate q

Greek letter	*Call option*	*Put option*
Delta	$e^{-qT}N(d_1)$	$e^{-qT}[N(d_1) - 1]$
Gamma	$\dfrac{N'(d_1)e^{-qT}}{S_0\sigma\sqrt{T}}$	$\dfrac{N'(d_1)e^{-qT}}{S_0\sigma\sqrt{T}}$
Theta	$-S_0N'(d_1)\sigma e^{-qT}/(2\sqrt{T})$ $+ qS_0N(d_1)e^{-qT} - rKe^{-rT}N(d_2)$	$-S_0N'(d_1)\sigma e^{-qT}/(2\sqrt{T})$ $- qS_0N(-d_1)e^{-qT} + rKe^{-rT}N(-d_2)$
Vega	$S_0\sqrt{T}N'(d_1)e^{-qT}$	$S_0\sqrt{T}N'(d_1)e^{-qT}$
Rho	$KTe^{-rT}N(d_2)$	$-KTe^{-rT}N(-d_2)$

means that a long forward contract on one share can be hedged by shorting one share; a short forward contract on one share can be hedged by purchasing one share.[11]

For an asset providing a dividend yield at rate q, equation (5.7) shows that the forward contract's delta is e^{-qT}. For the delta of a forward contract on a stock index, q is set equal to the dividend yield on the index in this expression. For the delta of a forward foreign exchange contract, it is set equal to the foreign risk-free rate, r_f.

Delta of a Futures Contract

From equation (5.1), the futures price for a contract on an investment asset that provides no income is $S_0 e^{rT}$, where T is the time to maturity of the futures contract, S_0 is the price of the asset today, and r is the risk-free rate. This shows that when the price of the stock changes by ΔS, with all else remaining the same, the futures price changes by $\Delta S\, e^{rT}$. The delta of a futures contract on an investment asset providing no income is therefore e^{rT}. For a futures position on an asset providing a dividend yield at rate q, equation (5.3) shows similarly that delta is $e^{(r-q)T}$.

It is interesting that the impact of daily settlement is to make the deltas of futures and forward contracts slightly different. This is true even when interest rates are constant and the forward price equals the futures price. (This is related to the point made in Business Snapshot 5.2.)

Sometimes a futures contract is used to achieve a delta-neutral position. Define:

T: Maturity of futures contract

H_A: Required position in asset for delta hedging

H_F: Alternative required position in futures contracts for delta hedging

If the underlying asset is a non-dividend-paying stock, the analysis we have just given shows that

$$H_F = e^{-rT} H_A \tag{17.5}$$

When the underlying asset pays a dividend yield q,

$$H_F = e^{-(r-q)T} H_A \tag{17.6}$$

For a stock index, we set q equal to the dividend yield on the index; for a currency, we

Example 17.10 Using futures to hedge a currency portfolio

Suppose that a portfolio of currency options held by a U.S. bank can be made delta neutral with a short position of 458,000 pounds sterling. Risk-free rates are 4% in the U.S. and 7% in the U.K. From equation (17.7), hedging using nine-month currency futures requires a short futures position

$$e^{-(0.04-0.07)\times 9/12} \times 458{,}000$$

or £468,442. Since each futures contract is for the purchase or sale of £62,500, seven contracts would be shorted. (Seven is the nearest whole number to 468,442/62,500.)

[11] These are hedge-and-forget schemes. Since delta is always 1.0, no changes need to be made to the position in the stock during the life of the contract.

set it equal to the foreign risk-free rate, r_f, so that

$$H_F = e^{-(r-r_f)T} H_A \tag{17.7}$$

Example 17.10 illustrates the use of this formula.

17.13 CREATING OPTIONS SYNTHETICALLY FOR PORTFOLIO INSURANCE

A portfolio manager is often interested in acquiring a put option on his or her portfolio. This provides protection against market declines while preserving the potential for a gain if the market does well. One approach (discussed in Chapter 15) is to buy put options on a market index such as the S&P 500. An alternative is to create the options synthetically.

Creating an option synthetically involves maintaining a position in the underlying asset (or futures on the underlying asset) so that the delta of the position is equal to the delta of the required option. The position necessary to create an option synthetically is the reverse of that necessary to hedge it. This is because the procedure for hedging an option involves the creation of an equal and opposite option synthetically.

There are two reasons why it may be more attractive for the portfolio manager to create the required put option synthetically than to buy it in the market. The first is that options markets do not always have the liquidity to absorb the trades required by managers of large funds. The second is that fund managers often require strike prices and exercise dates that are different from those available in exchange-traded options markets.

The synthetic option can be created from trading the portfolio or from trading in index futures contracts. We first examine the creation of a put option by trading the portfolio. From Table 17.6, the delta of a European put on the portfolio is

$$\Delta = e^{-qT}[N(d_1) - 1] \tag{17.8}$$

where, with our usual notation,

$$d_1 = \frac{\ln(S_0/K) + (r - q + \sigma^2/2)T}{\sigma\sqrt{T}}$$

S_0 is the value of the portfolio, K the strike price, r the risk-free rate, q the dividend yield on the portfolio, σ the volatility of the portfolio, and T the life of the option.

To create the put option synthetically, the fund manager should ensure that at any given time a proportion

$$e^{-qT}[1 - N(d_1)]$$

of the stocks in the original portfolio has been sold and the proceeds invested in riskless assets. As the value of the original portfolio declines, the delta of the put given by equation (17.8) becomes more negative and the proportion of the original portfolio sold must be increased. As the value of the original portfolio increases, the delta of the put becomes less negative and the proportion of the original portfolio sold must be decreased (i.e., some of the original portfolio must be repurchased). This is illustrated by Example 17.11.

Example 17.11 Portfolio insurance trading strategy

A portfolio is worth \$90 million. To protect against market downturns the managers of the portfolio require a six-month European put option on the portfolio with a strike price of \$87 million. The risk-free rate is 9% per annum, the dividend yield is 3% per annum, and the volatility of the portfolio is 25% per annum. The S&P 500 index stands at 900. As the portfolio is considered to mimic the S&P 500 fairly closely, one alternative discussed in Section 15.1 is to buy 1,000 put option contracts on the S&P 500 with a strike price of 870. Another alternative is to create the required option synthetically. In this case, $S_0 = 90$ million, $K = 87$ million, $r = 0.09$, $q = 0.03$, $\sigma = 0.25$, and $T = 0.5$, so that

$$d_1 = \frac{\ln(90/87) + (0.09 - 0.03 + 0.25^2/2)0.5}{0.25\sqrt{0.5}} = 0.4499$$

and the delta of the required option is

$$e^{-qT}[N(d_1) - 1] = -0.3215$$

This shows that 32.15% of the portfolio should be sold initially and invested in risk-free assets to match the delta of the required option. The amount of the portfolio sold must be monitored frequently. For example, if the value of the portfolio reduces to \$88 million after one day, the delta of the required option changes to −0.3679 and a further 4.64% of the original portfolio should be sold and invested in risk-free assets. If the value of the portfolio increases to \$92 million, the delta of the required option changes to −0.2787 and 4.28% of the original portfolio should be repurchased.

Using this strategy to create portfolio insurance means that at any given time funds are divided between the stock portfolio on which insurance is required and riskless assets. As the value of the stock portfolio increases, riskless assets are sold and the position in the stock portfolio is increased. As the value of the stock portfolio declines, the position in the stock portfolio is decreased and riskless assets are purchased. The cost of the insurance arises from the fact that the portfolio manager is always selling after a decline in the market and buying after a rise in the market.

Use of Index Futures

Using index futures to create options synthetically can be preferable to using the underlying stocks because the transaction costs associated with trades in index futures are generally lower than those associated with the corresponding trades in the underlying stocks. The dollar amount of the futures contracts shorted as a proportion of the value of the portfolio should from equations (17.6) and (17.8) be

$$e^{-qT}e^{-(r-q)T^*}[1 - N(d_1)] = e^{q(T^*-T)}e^{-rT^*}[1 - N(d_1)]$$

where T^* is the maturity time of the futures contract. If the portfolio is worth A_1 times the index and each index futures contract is on A_2 times the index, the number of

Example 17.12 Portfolio insurance using futures

Suppose that in Example 17.11 futures contracts on the S&P 500 maturing in nine months are used to create the option synthetically. In this case, initially $T = 0.5$, $T^* = 0.75$, $A_1 = 100{,}000$, and $d_1 = 0.4499$. Each index futures contract is on 250 times the index, so $A_2 = 250$. The number of futures contracts shorted should be

$$e^{q(T^*-T)}e^{-rT^*}[1 - N(d_1)]\frac{A_1}{A_2} = 122.95$$

or 123 rounding to the nearest whole number. As time passes and index changes, the position in futures contracts must be adjusted.

futures contracts shorted at any given time should be

$$e^{q(T^*-T)}e^{-rT^*}[1 - N(d_1)]\frac{A_1}{A_2}$$

Example 17.12 illustrates the use of this formula.

Up to now we have assumed that the portfolio mirrors the index. As discussed in Section 15.1, the hedging procedure can be adjusted to deal with other situations. The strike price for the options used should be the expected level of the market index when the portfolio's value reaches its insured value. The number of index options used should be β times the number of options that would be required if the portfolio had a beta of 1.0. The volatility of portfolio can be assumed to be its beta times the volatility of an appropriate well-diversified index.

17.14 STOCK MARKET VOLATILITY

We discussed in Chapter 13 the issue of whether volatility is caused solely by the arrival of new information or whether trading itself generates volatility. Portfolio insurance strategies such as those just described have the potential to increase volatility. When the market declines, they cause portfolio managers either to sell stock or to sell index futures contracts. Either action may accentuate the decline (see Business Snapshot 17.2). The sale of stock is liable to drive down the market index further in a direct way. The sale of index futures contracts is liable to drive down futures prices. This creates selling pressure on stocks via the mechanism of index arbitrage (see Chapter 5), so that the market index is liable to be driven down in this case as well. Similarly, when the market rises, the portfolio insurance strategies cause portfolio managers either to buy stock or to buy futures contracts. This may accentuate the rise.

In addition to formal portfolio insurance trading strategies, we can speculate that many investors consciously or subconsciously follow portfolio insurance rules of their own. For example, an investor may enter the market when it is rising but will sell when it is falling to limit the downside risk.

Whether portfolio insurance trading strategies (formal or informal) affect volatility depends on how easily the market can absorb the trades that are generated by portfolio insurance. If portfolio insurance trades are a very small fraction of all trades, there is

Business Snapshot 17.2 Was portfolio insurance to blame for the crash of 1987?

On Monday, October 19, 1987, the Dow Jones Industrial Average dropped by more than 20%. Many people feel that portfolio insurance played a major role in this crash.

In October 1987 between $60 billion and $90 billion of equity assets were subject to portfolio insurance trading rules where put options were created synthetically in the way discussed in Section 17.13. During the period Wednesday, October 14, 1987, to Friday, October 16, 1987, the market declined by about 10% with much of this decline taking place on Friday afternoon. The trading rules should have generated at least $12 billion of equity or index futures sales as a result of this decline. In fact, portfolio insurers had time to sell only $4 billion and they approached the following week with huge amounts of selling already dictated by their models. It is estimated that on Monday, October 19, sell programs by three portfolio insurers accounted for almost 10% of the sales on the New York Stock Exchange, and that portfolio insurance sales amounted to 21.3% of all sales in index futures markets. It is likely that the decline in equity prices was exacerbated by investors other than portfolio insurers selling heavily because they anticipated the actions of portfolio insurers.

Because the market declined so fast and the stock exchange systems were overloaded, many portfolio insurers were unable to execute the trades generated by their models and failed to obtain the protection they required. Needless to say, the popularity of portfolio insurance schemes has declined significantly since 1987. One of the morals of this story is that it is dangerous to follow a particular trading strategy—even a hedging strategy—when many other market participants are doing the same thing.

likely to be no effect. As portfolio insurance becomes more popular, it is liable to have a destabilizing effect on the market.

SUMMARY

Financial institutions offer a variety of option products to their clients. Often the options do not correspond to the standardized products traded by exchanges. The financial institutions are then faced with the problem of hedging their exposure. Naked and covered positions leave them subject to an unacceptable level of risk. One course of action that is sometimes proposed is a stop-loss strategy. This involves holding a naked position when an option is out of the money and converting it to a covered position as soon as the option moves into the money. Although superficially attractive, the strategy does not provide a good hedge.

The delta, Δ, of an option is the rate of change of its price with respect to the price of the underlying asset. Delta hedging involves creating a position with zero delta (sometimes referred to as a delta-neutral position). Because the delta of the underlying asset is 1.0, one way of hedging is to take a position of $-\Delta$ in the underlying asset for each long option being hedged. The delta of an option changes over time. This means that the position in the underlying asset has to be frequently adjusted.

Once an option position has been made delta neutral, the next stage is often to look at its gamma. The gamma of an option is the rate of change of its delta with respect to the price of the underlying asset. It is a measure of the curvature of the relationship between the option price and the asset price. The impact of this curvature on the performance of delta hedging can be reduced by making an option position gamma neutral. If Γ is the gamma of the position being hedged, this reduction is usually achieved by taking a position in a traded option that has a gamma of $-\Gamma$.

Delta and gamma hedging are both based on the assumption that the volatility of the underlying asset is constant. In practice, volatilities do change over time. The vega of an option or an option portfolio measures the rate of change of its value with respect to volatility. A trader who wishes to hedge an option position against volatility changes can make the position vega neutral. As with the procedure for creating gamma neutrality, this usually involves taking an offsetting position in a traded option. If the trader wishes to achieve both gamma and vega neutrality, two traded options are usually required.

Two other measures of the risk of an option position are theta and rho. Theta measures the rate of change of the value of the position with respect to the passage of time, with all else remaining constant. Rho measures the rate of change of the value of the position with respect to the interest rate, with all else remaining constant.

In practice, option traders usually rebalance their portfolios at least once a day to maintain delta neutrality. It is usually not feasible to maintain gamma and vega neutrality on a regular basis. Typically a trader monitors these measures. If they get too large, either corrective action is taken or trading is curtailed.

Portfolio managers are sometimes interested in creating put options synthetically for the purposes of insuring an equity portfolio. They can do so either by trading the portfolio or by trading index futures on the portfolio. Trading the portfolio involves splitting the portfolio between equities and risk-free securities. As the market declines, more is invested in risk-free securities; as the market increases, more is invested in equities. Trading index futures involves keeping the equity portfolio intact and selling index futures. As the market declines, more index futures are sold; as it rises, fewer are sold. This type of portfolio insurance works well under normal conditions. On Monday, October 19, 1987, when the Dow Jones Industrial Average dropped very sharply, it worked badly. Portfolio insurers were unable to sell either stocks or index futures fast enough to protect their positions.

FURTHER READING

Taleb, N. N. *Dynamic Hedging: Managing Vanilla and Exotic Options*. New York: Wiley, 1996.

Quiz (Answers at End of Book)

17.1. Explain how a stop-loss hedging trading rule can be implemented for the writer of an out-of-the-money call option. Why does it provide a relatively poor hedge?

17.2. What does it mean to assert that the delta of a call option is 0.7? How can a short position in 1,000 call options be made delta neutral when the delta of each option is 0.7?

17.3. Calculate the delta of an at-the-money six-month European call option on a non-dividend-paying stock when the risk-free interest rate is 10% per annum and the stock price volatility is 25% per annum.

17.4. Can the vega of a derivatives portfolio be changed by taking a position in the underlying asset? Explain your answer.

17.5. What is meant by the gamma of an option position? What are the risks in the situation where the gamma of a position is highly negative and the delta is zero?

17.6. "The procedure for creating an option position synthetically is the reverse of the procedure for hedging the option position." Explain this statement.

17.7. Explain why portfolio insurance may have played a part in the stock market crash of October 19, 1987.

Practice Questions (Answers in Solutions Manual/Study Guide)

17.8. What does it mean to assert that the theta of an option position is -0.1 when time is measured in years? If a trader feels that neither a stock price nor its implied volatility will change, what type of option position is appropriate?

17.9. The Black–Scholes–Merton price of an out-of-the-money call option with an exercise price of \$40 is \$4. A trader who has written the option plans to use a stop-loss strategy. The trader's plan is to buy at \$40.10 and to sell at \$39.90. Estimate the expected number of times the stock will be bought or sold.

17.10. Suppose that a stock price is currently \$20 and that a call option with an exercise price of \$25 is created synthetically using a continually changing position in the stock. Consider the following two scenarios:
(a) Stock price increases steadily from \$20 to \$35 during the life of the option.
(b) Stock price oscillates wildly, ending up at \$35.
Which scenario would make the synthetically created option more expensive? Explain your answer.

17.11. What is the delta of a short position in 1,000 European call options on silver futures? The options mature in eight months, and the futures contract underlying the option matures in nine months. The current nine-month futures price is \$8 per ounce, the exercise price of the options is \$8, the risk-free interest rate is 12% per annum, and the volatility of silver is 18% per annum.

17.12. In Problem 17.11, what initial position in nine-month silver futures is necessary for delta hedging? If silver itself is used, what is the initial position? If one-year silver futures are used, what is the initial position? Assume no storage costs for silver.

17.13. A company uses delta hedging to hedge a portfolio of long positions in put and call options on a currency. Which of the following would give the most favorable result?
(a) A virtually constant spot rate
(b) Wild movements in the spot rate.
Explain your answer.

17.14. Repeat Problem 17.13 for a financial institution with a portfolio of short positions in put and call options on a currency.

17.15. A financial institution has just sold 1,000 seven-month European call options on the Japanese yen. Suppose that the spot exchange rate is 0.80 cent per yen, the exercise price is 0.81 cent per yen, the risk-free interest rate in the United States is 8% per annum, the risk-free interest rate in Japan is 5% per annum, and the volatility of the yen is 15% per annum. Calculate the delta, gamma, vega, theta, and rho of the financial institution's position. Interpret each number.

17.16. Under what circumstances is it possible to make a European option on a stock index both gamma neutral and vega neutral by adding a position in one other European option?

17.17. A fund manager has a well-diversified portfolio that mirrors the performance of the S&P 500 and is worth \$360 million. The value of the S&P 500 is 1,200, and the portfolio manager would like to buy insurance against a reduction of more than 5% in the value of the portfolio over the next six months. The risk-free interest rate is 6% per annum. The dividend yield on both the portfolio and the S&P 500 is 3%, and the volatility of the index is 30% per annum.

(a) If the fund manager buys traded European put options, how much would the insurance cost?

(b) Explain carefully alternative strategies open to the fund manager involving traded European call options, and show that they lead to the same result.

(c) If the fund manager decides to provide insurance by keeping part of the portfolio in risk-free securities, what should the initial position be?

(d) If the fund manager decides to provide insurance by using nine-month index futures, what should the initial position be?

17.18. Repeat Problem 17.17 on the assumption that the portfolio has a beta of 1.5. Assume that the dividend yield on the portfolio is 4% per annum.

17.19. Show by substituting for the various terms in equation (17.4) that the equation is true for:

(a) A single European call option on a non-dividend-paying stock

(b) A single European put option on a non-dividend-paying stock

(c) Any portfolio of European put and call options on a non-dividend-paying stock.

17.20. Suppose that \$70 billion of equity assets are the subject of portfolio insurance schemes. Assume that the schemes are designed to provide insurance against the value of the assets declining by more than 5% within one year. Making whatever estimates you find necessary, use the DerivaGem software to calculate the value of the stock or futures contracts that the administrators of the portfolio insurance schemes will attempt to sell if the market falls by 23% in a single day.

17.21. Does a forward contract on a stock index have the same delta as the corresponding futures contract? Explain your answer.

17.22. A bank's position in options on the dollar–euro exchange rate has a delta of 30,000 and a gamma of −80,000. Explain how these numbers can be interpreted. The exchange rate (dollars per euro) is 0.90. What position would you take to make the position delta neutral? After a short period of time, the exchange rate moves to 0.93. Estimate the new delta. What additional trade is necessary to keep the position delta neutral? Assuming the bank did set up a delta-neutral position originally, has it gained or lost money from the exchange-rate movement?

Further Questions

17.23. Consider a one-year European call option on a stock when the stock price is \$30, the strike price is \$30, the risk-free rate is 5%, and the volatility is 25% per annum. Use the DerivaGem software to calculate the price, delta, gamma, vega, theta, and rho of the option. Verify that delta is correct by changing the stock price to \$30.1 and recomputing the option price. Verify that gamma is correct by recomputing the delta for the situation where the stock price is \$30.1. Carry out similar calculations to verify that vega, theta, and rho are correct. Use the DerivaGem software to plot the option price, delta, gamma, vega, theta, and rho against the stock price for the stock option.

17.24. A financial institution has the following portfolio of over-the-counter options on sterling:

Type	*Position*	*Delta of option*	*Gamma of option*	*Vega of option*
Call	−1,000	0.50	2.2	1.8
Call	−500	0.80	0.6	0.2
Put	−2,000	−0.40	1.3	0.7
Call	−500	0.70	1.8	1.4

A traded option is available with a delta of 0.6, a gamma of 1.5, and a vega of 0.8.

(a) What position in the traded option and in sterling would make the portfolio both gamma neutral and delta neutral?

(b) What position in the traded option and in sterling would make the portfolio both vega neutral and delta neutral?

17.25. Consider again the situation in Problem 17.24. Suppose that a second traded option with a delta of 0.1, a gamma of 0.5, and a vega of 0.6 is available. How could the portfolio be made delta, gamma, and vega neutral?

17.26. A deposit instrument offered by a bank guarantees that investors will receive a return during a six-month period that is the greater of (a) zero and (b) 40% of the return provided by a market index. An investor is planning to put \$100,000 in the instrument. Describe the payoff as an option on the index. Assuming that the risk-free rate of interest is 8% per annum, the dividend yield on the index is 3% per annum, and the volatility of the index is 25% per annum, is the product a good deal for the investor?

17.27. Use DerivaGem to check that equation (17.4) is satisfied for the option considered in Section 17.1. (*Note*: DerivaGem produces a value of theta "per calendar day." The theta in equation (17.4) is "per year.")

17.28. Use the DerivaGem Application Builder functions to reproduce Table 17.2. (Note that in Table 17.2 the stock position is rounded to the nearest 100 shares.) Calculate the gamma and theta of the position each week. Calculate the change in the value of the portfolio each week and check whether equation (17.3) is approximately satisfied. (*Note*: DerivaGem produces a value of theta "per calendar day." The theta in equation (17.3) is "per year.")

CHAPTER 18

Binomial Trees in Practice

As we have seen in Chapters 13, 15, and 16, the Black–Scholes–Merton model and its extensions can be used to value European call and put options on stocks, stock indices, currencies, and futures contracts. For American options we rely on binomial trees. In this chapter we cover, more completely than in Chapter 12, how binomial trees are used in practice. In particular, we explain how the binomial tree methodology can be used to value American options on a range of different underlying assets including dividend-paying stocks and how it can be used to calculate the Greek letters that were introduced in Chapter 17. The DerivaGem software that accompanies this book can be used to carry out the calculations described in the chapter and to display the binomial trees that are used.

18.1 THE BINOMIAL MODEL FOR A NON-DIVIDEND-PAYING STOCK

The binomial tree methodology for handling American-style options was first proposed by Cox, Ross, and Rubinstein.[1] Consider the evaluation of an option on a non-dividend-paying stock. We start by dividing the life of the option into a large number of small time intervals of length Δt. We assume that in each time interval the stock price moves from its initial value of S to one of two new values, Su and Sd. This model is illustrated in Figure 18.1. In general, $u > 1$ and $d < 1$. The movement from S to Su is, therefore, an "up" movement and the movement from S to Sd is a "down" movement. The probability of an up movement will be denoted by p. The probability of a down movement is $1 - p$.

Risk-Neutral Valuation

The risk-neutral valuation principle, discussed in Chapters 12 and 13, states that any security dependent on a stock price can be valued on the assumption that the world is

[1] See J.C. Cox, S.A. Ross, and M. Rubinstein, "Option Pricing: A Simplified Approach," *Journal of Financial Economics*, 7 (October 1979), 229–64.

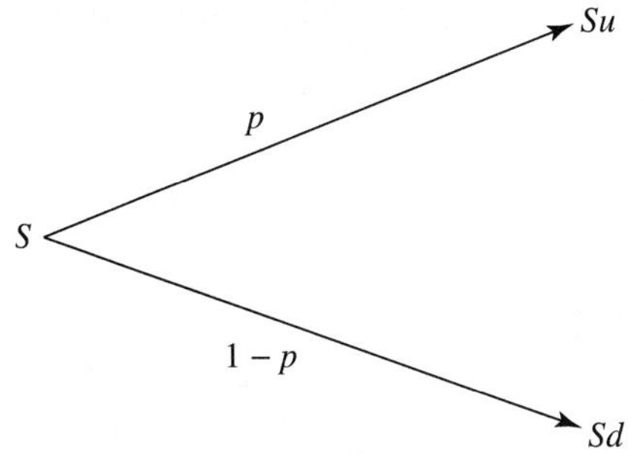

Figure 18.1 Stock price movements in time Δt under the binomial model

risk neutral. This means that, for the purposes of valuing an option (or any other derivative), we can assume the following:

1. The expected return from all traded securities is the risk-free interest rate.
2. Future cash flows can be valued by discounting their expected values at the risk-free interest rate.

We will make use of this result when using a binomial tree.

Determination of p, u, and d

We design the tree to represent the behavior of a stock price in a risk-neutral world. The parameters p, u, and d must give correct values for the mean and variance of the stock price return during a time interval Δt in this world. The expected return from a stock is the risk-free interest rate, r. Hence, the expected value of the stock price at the end of a time interval Δt is $Se^{r\Delta t}$, where S is the stock price at the beginning of the time interval. To match the mean stock price return with the tree, we therefore need

$$Se^{r\Delta t} = pSu + (1 - p)Sd \qquad \textbf{(18.1)}$$

or

$$e^{r\Delta t} = pu + (1 - p)d \qquad \textbf{(18.2)}$$

The variance of a variable Q is defined as $E(Q^2) - E(Q)^2$, where E denotes expected value. Defining R as the proportional change in the asset price in time Δt, there is a probability p that $1 + R$ is u and a probability $1 - p$ that $1 + R$ is d. It follows that the variance of $1 + R$ is $pu^2 + (1 - p)d^2 - [pu + (1 - p)d]^2$. Because adding a constant to a variable makes no difference to its variance, the variance of $1 + R$ is the same as the variance of R. As explained in Section 13.1, this is $\sigma^2\Delta t$. Hence,

$$\sigma^2\Delta t = pu^2 + (1 - p)d^2 - [pu + (1 - p)d]^2 \qquad \textbf{(18.3)}$$

Equations (18.2) and (18.3) impose two conditions on p, u, and d. A third condition used by Cox, Ross, and Rubinstein is

$$u = \frac{1}{d}$$

When Δt is small, equations (18.2), (18.3), and this equation are satisfied by

$$p = \frac{a - d}{u - d} \tag{18.4}$$

$$u = e^{\sigma\sqrt{\Delta t}} \tag{18.5}$$

$$d = e^{-\sigma\sqrt{\Delta t}} \tag{18.6}$$

where

$$a = e^{r\Delta t} \tag{18.7}$$

The variable a is sometimes referred to as the *growth factor*. Equations (18.4) to (18.7) are consistent with equations (12.11) to (12.14) in Chapter 12.

The Tree of Stock Prices

Figure 18.2 shows the complete tree of stock prices that is considered when the binomial model is used and there are four time steps. At time zero, the stock price, S_0, is known. At time Δt, there are two possible stock prices, S_0u and S_0d; at time $2\Delta t$, there are three possible stock prices, S_0u^2, S_0, and S_0d^2; and so on. In general, at time $i\,\Delta t$, we consider $i + 1$ stock prices. These are

$$S_0u^jd^{i-j} \quad (j = 0, 1, \ldots, i)$$

Note that the relationship $u = 1/d$ is used in computing the stock price at each node of the tree in Figure 18.2. For example, the asset price when $j = 2$ and $i = 3$ is $S_0u^2d = S_0u$. Note also that the tree recombines in the sense that an up movement followed by a down movement leads to the same stock price as a down movement followed by an up movement.

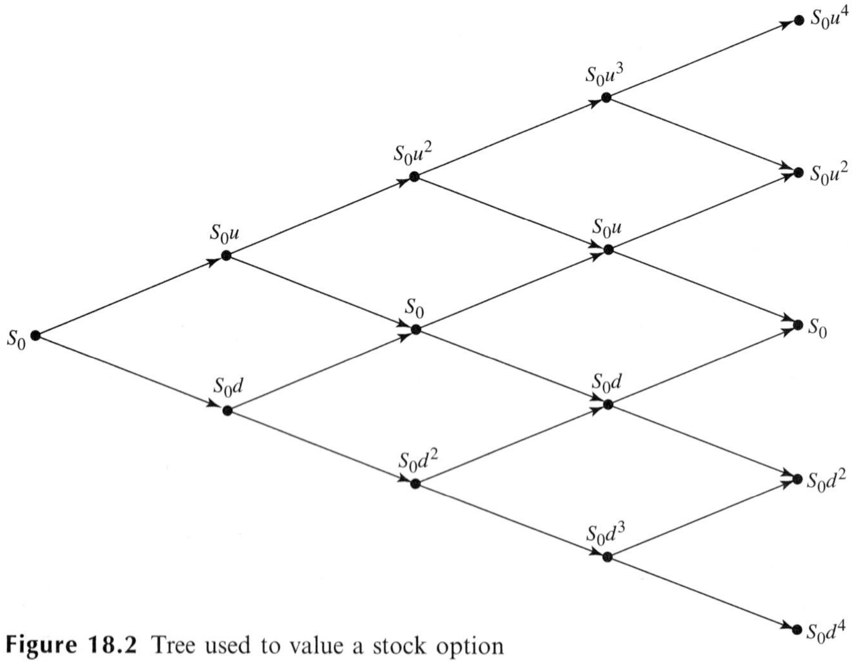

Figure 18.2 Tree used to value a stock option

Working Backward through the Tree

Options are evaluated by starting at the end of the tree (time T) and working backward, a procedure known as *backwards induction*. The value of the option is known at time T. For example, a put option is worth $\max(K - S_T, 0)$ and a call option is worth $\max(S_T - K, 0)$, where S_T is the stock price at time T and K is the strike price. Because a risk-neutral world is assumed, the value at each node at time $T - \Delta t$ can be calculated as the expected value at time T discounted at rate r for a time period Δt. Similarly, the value at each node at time $T - 2\Delta t$ can be calculated as the expected value at time $T - \Delta t$ discounted for a time period Δt at rate r, and so on. If the option is American, it is necessary to check at each node to see whether early exercise is preferable to holding the option for a further time period Δt. Eventually, by working back through all the nodes, we obtain the value of the option at time zero.

Illustration

We now illustrate the procedure with a five-step tree. Consider an American put option on a non-dividend-paying stock when the stock price is \$50, the strike price is \$50, the risk-free interest rate is 10% per annum, the life is five months, and the volatility is 40% per annum. With our usual notation, this means that $S_0 = 50$, $K = 50$, $r = 0.10$, $\sigma = 0.40$, and $T = 0.4167$. We divide the life of the option into five intervals of length one month for the purposes of constructing a binomial tree. Then $\Delta t = 1/12$ and, using equations (18.4) to (18.7),

$$u = e^{\sigma\sqrt{\Delta t}} = 1.1224, \qquad d = e^{-\sigma\sqrt{\Delta t}} = 0.8909, \qquad a = e^{r\Delta t} = 1.0084$$

$$p = \frac{a - d}{u - d} = 0.5073, \qquad 1 - p = 0.4927$$

Figure 18.3 shows the binomial tree (produced using DerivaGem). At each node there are two numbers. The top one shows the stock price at the node; the lower one shows the value of the option at the node. The probability of an up movement is always 0.5073; the probability of a down movement is always 0.4927.

The stock price at the jth ($j = 0, 1, \dots, i$) node at time $i\,\Delta t$ ($i = 0, 1, \dots, 5$) is calculated as $S_0 u^j d^{i-j}$. For example, the stock price at node A ($i = 4, j = 1$) (i.e., the second node up at the end of the fourth time step) is $50 \times 1.1224 \times 0.8909^3 = \$39.69$.

The option prices at the final nodes are calculated as $\max(K - S_T, 0)$. For example, the option price at node G is $50.00 - 35.36 = 14.64$. The option prices at the penultimate nodes are calculated from the option prices at the final nodes. First, we assume no exercise of the option at a node. This means that the option price is calculated as the present value of the expected option price one time step later. For example, at node E, the option price is calculated as

$$(0.5073 \times 0 + 0.4927 \times 5.45)e^{-0.10 \times 1/12} = 2.66$$

whereas at node A it is calculated as

$$(0.5073 \times 5.45 + 0.4927 \times 14.64)e^{-0.10 \times 1/12} = 9.90$$

We then check to see if early exercise is preferable to waiting. At node E, early exercise

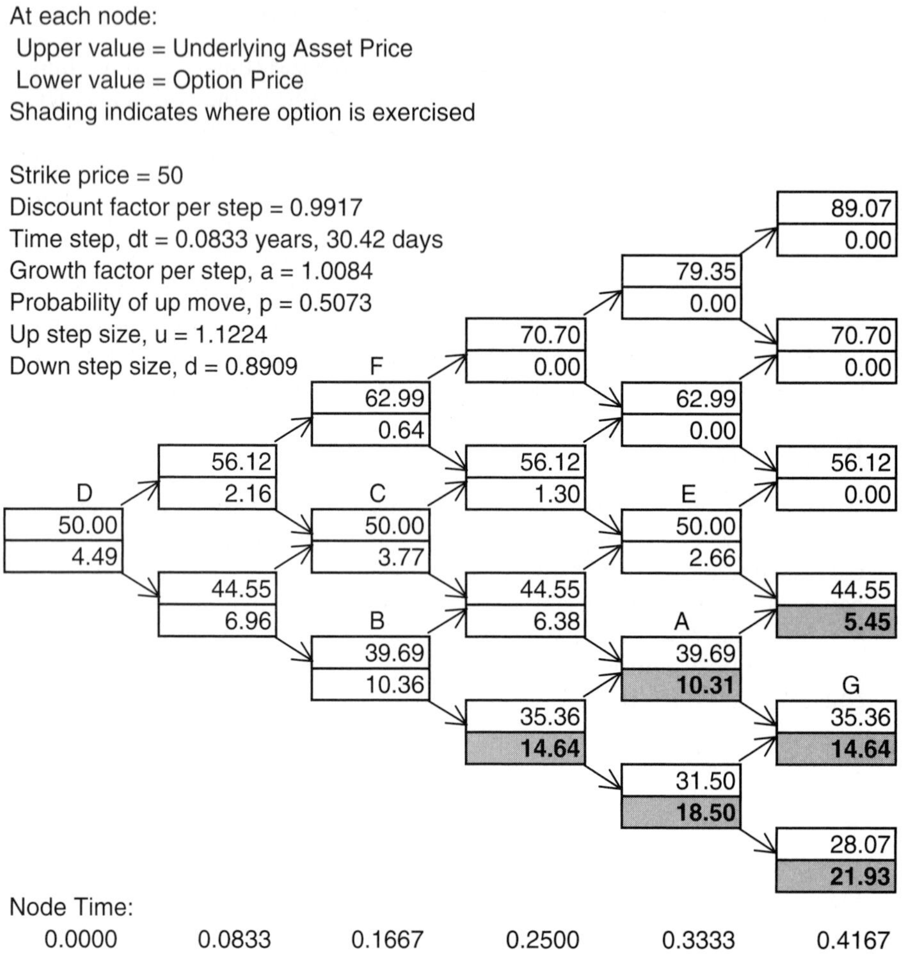

Figure 18.3 Binomial tree from DerivaGem for American put on non-dividend-paying stock

would give a value for the option of zero because both the stock price and strike price are \$50. Clearly, it is best to wait. The correct value for the option at node E is, therefore, \$2.66. At node A, it is a different story. If the option is exercised, it is worth \$50.00 − \$39.69, or \$10.31. This is more than \$9.90. If node A is reached, the option should, therefore, be exercised and the correct value for the option at node A is \$10.31.

Option prices at earlier nodes are calculated in a similar way. Note that it is not always best to exercise an option early when it is in the money. Consider node B. If the option is exercised, it is worth \$50.00 − \$39.69, or \$10.31. However, if it is not exercised, it is worth

$$(0.5073 \times 6.38 + 0.4927 \times 14.64)e^{-0.10\times 1/12} = 10.36$$

The option should, therefore, not be exercised at this node, and the correct option value at the node is \$10.36.

Working back through the tree, we find the value of the option at the initial node to be \$4.49. This is our numerical estimate for the option's current value. In practice, a smaller value of Δt, and many more nodes, would be used. DerivaGem shows that with 30, 50, and 100 time steps we get values for the option of 4.263, 4.272, and 4.278, respectively.

Expressing the Approach Algebraically

Suppose that the life of an American put option on a non-dividend-paying stock is divided into N subintervals of length Δt. We will refer to the jth node at time $i\,\Delta t$ as the (i, j) node, where $0 \leqslant i \leqslant N$ and $0 \leqslant j \leqslant i$. Define $f_{i,j}$ as the value of the option at the (i, j) node. The stock price at the (i, j) node is $S_0 u^j d^{i-j}$. Because the value of an American put at its expiration date is $\max(K - S_T, 0)$, we know that

$$f_{N,j} = \max(K - S_0 u^j d^{N-j}, 0) \quad (j = 0, 1, \ldots, N)$$

There is a probability, p, of moving from the (i, j) node at time $i\,\Delta t$ to the $(i+1, j+1)$ node at time $(i+1)\Delta t$, and a probability $1-p$ of moving from the (i, j) node at time $i\,\Delta t$ to the $(i+1, j)$ node at time $(i+1)\Delta t$. Assuming no early exercise, risk-neutral valuation gives

$$f_{i,j} = e^{-r\Delta t}[p f_{i+1,j+1} + (1-p) f_{i+1,j}]$$

for $0 \leqslant i \leqslant N-1$ and $0 \leqslant j \leqslant i$. When early exercise is possible, this value for $f_{i,j}$ must be compared with the option's intrinsic value, and we obtain

$$f_{i,j} = \max\{K - S_0 u^j d^{i-j},\ e^{-r\Delta t}[p f_{i+1,j+1} + (1-p) f_{i+1,j}]\}$$

Note that, because the calculations start at time T and work backward, the value at time $i\,\Delta t$ captures not only the effect of early exercise possibilities at time $i\,\Delta t$, but also the effect of early exercise at subsequent times.

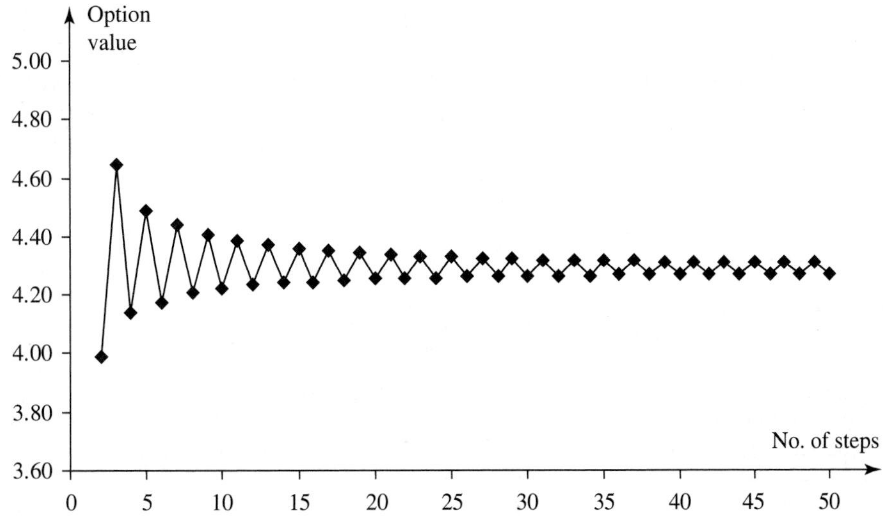

Figure 18.4 Convergence of option price calculated from a binomial tree

In the limit as Δt tends to zero, an exact value for the American put is obtained. In practice, $N = 30$ usually gives reasonable results. Figure 18.4 shows the convergence of the option price in the example we have been considering. (This figure was calculated using the Application Builder functions provided with the DerivaGem software. See Sample Application A.)

If a call rather than a put is being valued, the value at the final node is $\max(S_T - K, 0)$, so that

$$f_{N,j} = \max(S_0 u^j d^{N-j} - K, 0) \quad (j = 0, 1, \dots, N)$$

Also, when early exercise is possible, the expression for $f_{i,j}$ must reflect the payoff from a call rather than a put, so that

$$f_{i,j} = \max\{S_0 u^j d^{i-j} - K, e^{-r\Delta t}[p f_{i+1,j+1} + (1-p) f_{i+1,j}]\}$$

Estimating Delta and Other Greek Letters

It will be recalled that the delta, Δ, of an option is the rate of change of its price with respect to the underlying stock price. It can be calculated as

$$\frac{\Delta f}{\Delta S}$$

where ΔS is a small change in the stock price and Δf is the corresponding small change in the option price. At time Δt, we have an estimate $f_{1,1}$ for the option price when the stock price is $S_0 u$ and an estimate $f_{1,0}$ for the option price when the stock price is $S_0 d$. This means that, when $\Delta S = S_0 u - S_0 d$, we have $\Delta f = f_{1,1} - f_{1,0}$. An estimate of Δ at time Δt is therefore

$$\Delta = \frac{f_{1,1} - f_{1,0}}{S_0 u - S_0 d} \tag{18.8}$$

To determine gamma, Γ, we note that there are two estimates of Δ at time $2\Delta t$. When the stock price is $(S_0 u^2 + S_0)/2$ (halfway between the second and third node at time $2\Delta t$), delta is $(f_{2,2} - f_{2,1})/(S_0 u^2 - S_0)$; when the stock price is $(S_0 + S_0 d^2)/2$ (halfway between the first and second node at time $2\Delta t$), delta is $(f_{2,1} - f_{2,0})/(S_0 - S_0 d^2)$. The difference between the two stock prices is h, where

$$h = 0.5(S_0 u^2 - S_0 d^2)$$

Gamma is the change in delta divided by h, or

$$\Gamma = \frac{[(f_{2,2} - f_{2,1})/(S_0 u^2 - S_0)] - [(f_{2,1} - f_{2,0})/(S_0 - S_0 d^2)]}{h} \tag{18.9}$$

These procedures provide estimates of delta at time Δt and of gamma at time $2\Delta t$. In practice, they are usually used as estimates of delta and gamma at time zero as well.[2]

[2] If slightly more accuracy is required for delta and gamma, we can start the binomial tree at time $-2\Delta t$ and assume that the stock price is S_0 at this time. This leads to the option price being calculated for three different stock prices at time zero.

A further hedge parameter that can be obtained directly from the tree is theta, Θ. This is the rate of change of the option price with time when all else is kept constant. The value of the option at time zero, when the stock price is S_0, is $f_{0,0}$. The value of the option at time $2\Delta t$, when the stock price is S_0, is $f_{2,1}$. An estimate of theta is therefore

$$\Theta = \frac{f_{2,1} - f_{0,0}}{2\Delta t} \tag{18.10}$$

Vega can be calculated by making a small change, $\Delta\sigma$, in the volatility and constructing a new tree to obtain a new value of the option (the number of time steps should be kept the same). The estimate of vega is

$$\mathcal{V} = \frac{f^* - f}{\Delta\sigma}$$

where f and f^* are the estimates of the option price from the original and the new tree, respectively. Rho can be calculated similarly.

As an illustration, consider the tree in Figure 18.3. In this case, $f_{1,0} = 6.96$ and $f_{1,1} = 2.16$. Equation (18.8) gives an estimate of delta of

$$\frac{2.16 - 6.96}{56.12 - 44.55} = -0.41$$

From equation (18.9), an estimate of the gamma of the option can be obtained from the values at nodes B, C, and F as

$$\frac{[(0.64 - 3.77)/(62.99 - 50.00)] - [(3.77 - 10.36)/(50.00 - 39.69)]}{11.65} = 0.03$$

From equation (18.10), an estimate of the theta of the option can be obtained from the values at nodes D and C as

$$\frac{3.77 - 4.49}{0.1667} = -4.3 \text{ per year}$$

or -0.012 per calendar day. These are, of course, only rough estimates. They become progressively better as the number of time steps on the tree is increased. Using 50 time steps, DerivaGem provides estimates of -0.414, 0.033, and -0.0117 for delta, gamma, and theta, respectively.

18.2 USING THE BINOMIAL TREE FOR OPTIONS ON INDICES, CURRENCIES, AND FUTURES CONTRACTS

As shown in Section 12.10, the binomial tree approach to valuing options on non-dividend-paying stocks can easily be adapted to valuing American calls and puts on a stock paying a continuous dividend yield at rate q.

Because the dividends provide a return of q, the stock price itself must, on average, in a risk-neutral world provide a return of $r - q$. Hence, equation (18.1) becomes

$$Se^{(r-q)\Delta t} = pSu + (1 - p)Sd$$

so that

$$e^{(r-q)\Delta t} = pu + (1 - p)d$$

Example 18.1 Tree for option on index futures

Consider a four-month American call option on index futures. The current futures price is 300, the exercise price is 300, the risk-free interest rate is 8% per annum, and the volatility of the index is 30% per annum. We divide the life of the option into four one-month intervals for the purposes of constructing the tree. In this case, $F_0 = 300$, $K = 300$, $r = 0.08$, $\sigma = 0.3$, $T = 4/12$, and $\Delta t = 1/12$. Because a futures contract is analogous to a stock paying dividends at a continuous rate r, q should be set equal to r in equation (18.11). This gives $a = 1$. The other parameters necessary to construct the tree are

$$u = e^{\sigma\sqrt{\Delta t}} = 1.0905, \quad d = \frac{1}{u} = 0.9170, \quad p = \frac{a-d}{u-d} = 0.4784, \quad 1-p = 0.5216$$

The tree is shown in the figure below (the upper number is the futures price; the lower number is the option price). The estimated value of the option is 19.16. More accuracy is obtained with more steps. With 50 time steps DerivaGem gives a value of 20.18; with 100 time steps it gives a value of 20.22.

DerivaGem Output:

At each node:
Upper value = Underlying Asset Price
Lower value = Option Price
Shading indicates where option is exercised

Strike price = 300
Discount factor per step = 0.9934
Time step, dt = 0.0833 years, 30.42 days
Growth factor per step, a = 1.0000
Probability of up move, p = 0.4784
Up step size, u = 1.0905
Down step size, d = 0.9170

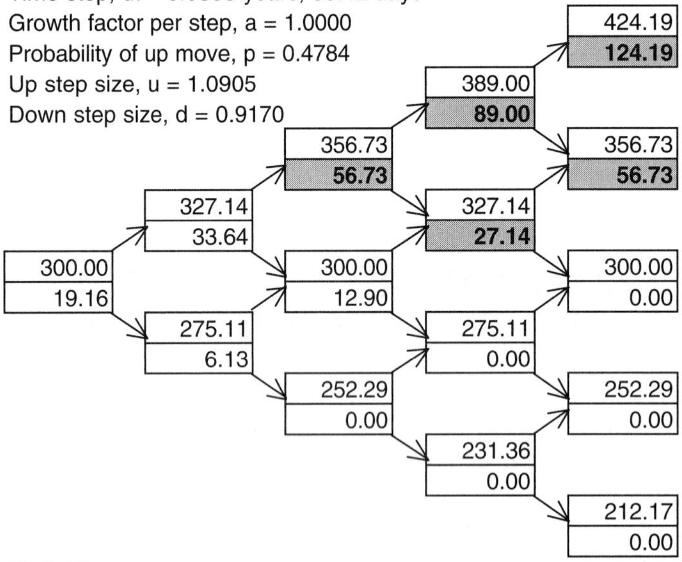

Node Time:
0.0000 0.0833 0.1667 0.2500 0.3333

Example 18.2 Tree for option on currency

Consider a one-year American put option on the British pound (GBP). The current exchange rate (USD per GBP) is 1.6100, the strike price is 1.6000, the U.S. risk-free interest rate is 8% per annum, the sterling risk-free interest rate is 9% per annum, and the volatility of the sterling exchange rate is 12% per annum. In this case, $S_0 = 1.61$, $K = 1.60$, $r = 0.08$, $r_f = 0.09$, $\sigma = 0.12$, and $T = 1.0$. We divide the life of the option into four three-month periods for the purposes of constructing the tree, so that $\Delta t = 0.25$. In this case, $q = r_f$ and equation (18.11) gives

$$a = e^{(0.08-0.09)\times 0.25} = 0.9975$$

The other parameters necessary to construct the tree are:

$$u = e^{\sigma\sqrt{\Delta t}} = 1.0618, \quad d = \frac{1}{u} = 0.9418, \quad p = \frac{a-d}{u-d} = 0.4642, \quad 1-p = 0.5358$$

The tree is shown in the figure below (the upper number is the exchange rate; the lower number is the option price). The estimated value of the option is \$0.0710. Using 50 time steps, DerivaGem gives the value of the option as 0.0738; with 100 time steps, it also gives the value 0.0738.

DerivaGem Output:

At each node:
Upper value = Underlying Asset Price
Lower value = Option Price
Shading indicates where option is exercised

Strike price = 1.6
Discount factor per step = 0.9802
Time step, dt = 0.2500 years, 91.25 days
Growth factor per step, a = 0.9975
Probability of up move, p = 0.4642
Up step size, u = 1.0618
Down step size, d = 0.9418

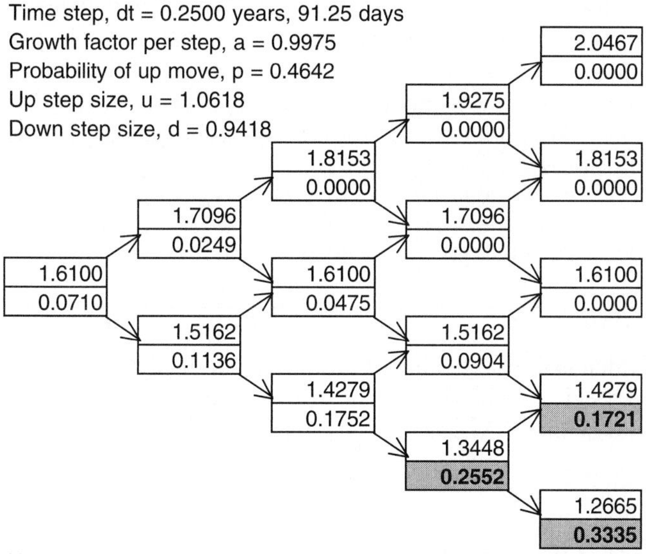

Node Time:
0.0000 0.2500 0.5000 0.7500 1.0000

The parameters p, u, and d must satisfy this equation and equation (18.3). Equations (18.4), (18.5), and (18.6) are still correct but with

$$a = e^{(r-q)\Delta t} \tag{18.11}$$

The binomial tree numerical procedure can therefore be used exactly as before with this new value of a.

We showed in Chapters 15 and 16 that stock indices, currencies, and futures contracts can for the purposes of option evaluation be considered as stocks paying continuous dividend yields. In the case of a stock index, the relevant dividend yield is the dividend yield on the stock portfolio underlying the index; in the case of a currency, it is the foreign risk-free interest rate; in the case of a futures contract, it is the domestic risk-free interest rate. Examples 18.1 and 18.2 illustrate this.

18.3 THE BINOMIAL MODEL FOR A DIVIDEND-PAYING STOCK

We now move on to the more tricky issue of how the binomial model can be used for a stock paying discrete dividends. As in Chapter 13, the word "dividend" will for the purposes of our discussion be used to refer to the reduction in the stock price on the ex-dividend date as a result of the dividend.

Known Dividend Yield

For long-life stock options, it is sometimes assumed for convenience that there is a known continuous dividend yield of q on the stock. The options can then be valued in the same way as options on a stock index. For more accuracy, known dividend yields can be assumed to be paid discretely. Suppose first that a single dividend will be paid at a certain time and that it will be a proportion δ of the stock price at that time. The parameters u, d, and p can be calculated as though no dividends are expected. The tree takes the form shown in Figure 18.5 and can be analyzed in a way that is analogous to that just described. If the time $i\,\Delta t$ is prior to the stock going ex-dividend, the nodes on the tree correspond to stock prices

$$S_0 u^j d^{i-j} \quad (j = 0, 1, \dots, i)$$

If the time $i\,\Delta t$ is after the stock goes ex-dividend, the nodes correspond to stock prices

$$S_0(1-\delta)u^j d^{i-j} \quad (j = 0, 1, \dots, i)$$

Several known dividends during the life of an option can be dealt with similarly. If δ_i is the total dividend yield associated with all ex-dividend dates between time zero and time $i\,\Delta t$, the nodes at time $i\,\Delta t$ correspond to stock prices

$$S_0(1-\delta_i)u^j d^{i-j}$$

Known Dollar Dividend

In some situations, particularly when the life of the option is short, it is more realistic to assume that the dollar amount of the dividend rather than the dividend yield is known in advance. If the volatility of the stock, σ, is assumed constant, the tree takes the form shown in Figure 18.6. It does not recombine, which means that the number of nodes that have to be evaluated is liable to become very large. Suppose that there is only one dividend, that the ex-dividend date, τ, is between $k\Delta t$ and $(k+1)\Delta t$, and that the dollar amount of the dividend is D. When $i \leqslant k$, the nodes on the tree at time $i\,\Delta t$ correspond to stock prices

$$S_0 u^j d^{i-j} \quad (j = 0, 1, 2, \dots, i)$$

as before. When $i = k+1$, the nodes on the tree correspond to stock prices

$$S_0 u^j d^{i-j} - D \quad (j = 0, 1, 2, \dots, i)$$

When $i = k+2$, the nodes on the tree correspond to stock prices

$$(S_0 u^j d^{i-1-j} - D)u \quad \text{and} \quad (S_0 u^j d^{i-1-j} - D)d$$

for $j = 0, 1, 2, \dots, i-1$, so that there are $2i$ rather than $i+1$ nodes. At time $(k+m)\Delta t$, there are $m(k+2)$ rather than $k+m+1$ nodes. The number of nodes expands even faster when there are several ex-dividend dates during the option's life.

The node-proliferation problem can be solved by assuming, as in the analysis of European options in Chapter 13, that the stock price has two components: a part that is uncertain and a part that is the present value of all future dividends during the life of the option. Suppose that there is only one ex-dividend date, τ, during the life of the option and that $k\Delta t \leqslant \tau \leqslant (k+1)\Delta t$. The value of the uncertain component, S^*, at

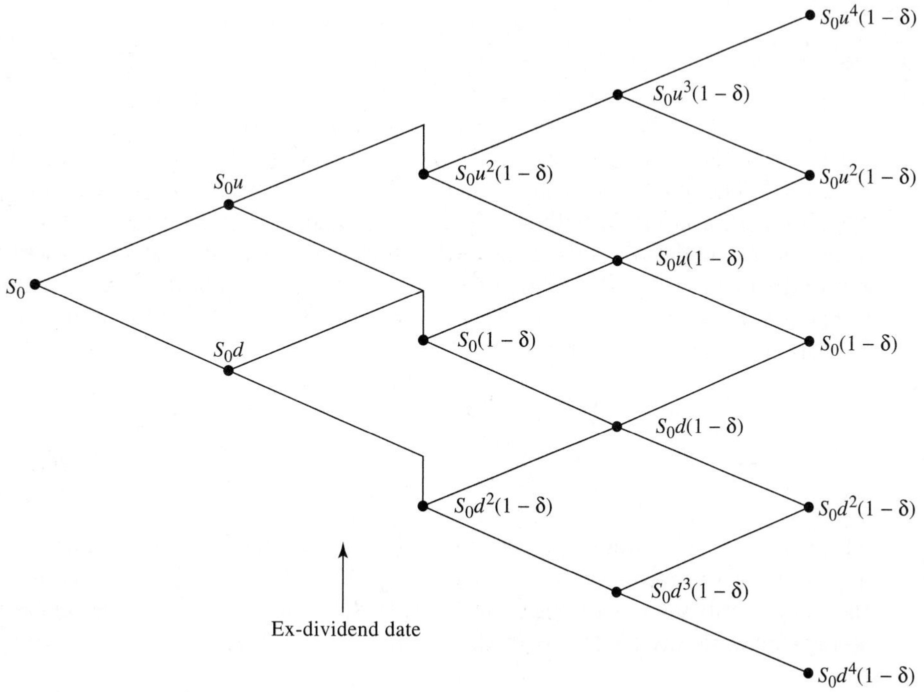

Figure 18.5 Tree when stock pays a known dividend yield at one particular time

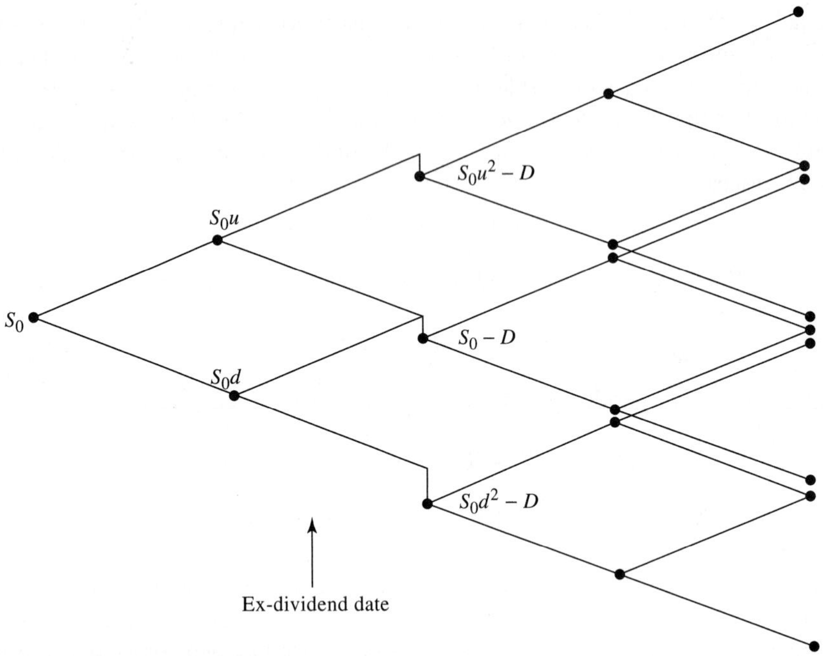

Figure 18.6 Tree when dollar amount of dividend is assumed known and volatility is assumed constant

time $i\,\Delta t$ is given by

$$S^* = S \quad \text{when } i\,\Delta t > \tau$$

and

$$S^* = S - De^{-r(\tau - i\,\Delta t)} \quad \text{when } i\,\Delta t \leqslant \tau$$

where D is the dividend. Define σ^* as the volatility of S^* and assume that σ^* is constant.[3] The parameters p, u, and d can be calculated from equations (18.4), (18.5), (18.6), and (18.7) with σ replaced by σ^*, and a tree can be constructed in the usual way to model S^*. By adding to the stock price at each node the present value of future dividends (if any), the tree can be converted into another tree that models S. Suppose that S_0^* is the value of S^* at time zero. At time $i\,\Delta t$, the nodes on this tree correspond to the stock prices

$$S_0^* u^j d^{i-j} + De^{-r(\tau - i\,\Delta t)} \quad (j = 0, 1, \dots, i)$$

when $i\,\Delta t < \tau$ and

$$S_0^* u^j d^{i-j} \quad (j = 0, 1, \dots, i)$$

when $i\,\Delta t > \tau$. This approach, which has the advantage of being consistent with the approach for European options in Section 13.10, succeeds in achieving a situation where the tree recombines so that there are $i + 1$ nodes at time $i\,\Delta t$. It can be generalized in a straightforward way to deal with the situation where there are several dividends. The

[3] In theory, σ^* is slightly greater than σ, the volatility of S. In practice, implied volatilities are used and no distinction is usually made between the two.

Example 18.3 Tree for option on a dividend-paying stock

Consider a five-month American put option on a stock that is expected to pay a single dividend of \$2.06 during the life of the option. The initial stock price is \$52, the strike price is \$50, the risk-free interest rate is 10% per annum, the volatility is 40% per annum, and the ex-dividend date is in 3.5 months.

We first construct a tree to model S^*, the stock price less the present value of future dividends during the life of the option. Initially, the present value of the dividend is $2.06 \times e^{-0.1 \times 3.5/12} = 2.00$. The initial value of S^* is therefore 50. Assuming that the 40% per annum volatility refers to S^*, Figure 18.3 provides a binomial tree for S^*. (S^* has the same initial value and volatility as the stock price on which Figure 18.3 was based.) Adding the present value of the dividend at each node leads to the figure below, which is a binomial tree for S. The probabilities at each node are, as in Figure 18.3, 0.5073 for an up movement and 0.4927 for a down movement. Working back through the tree in the usual way gives the option price as \$4.44 (50 steps give 4.202; 100 steps give 4.212).

DerivaGem Output:

At each node:
Upper value = Underlying Asset Price
Lower value = Option Price
Shading indicates where option is exercised

Strike price = 50
Discount factor per step = 0.9917
Time step, dt = 0.0833 years, 30.42 days
Growth factor per step, a = 1.0084
Probability of up move, p = 0.5073
Up step size, u = 1.1224
Down step size, d = 0.8909

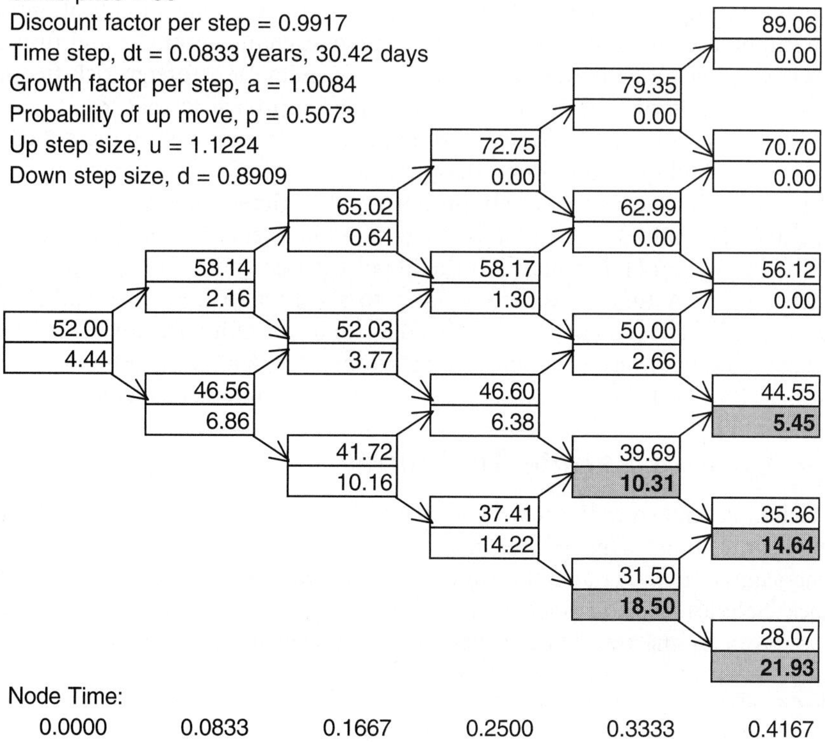

approach is illustrated in Example 18.3. As indicated earlier, for long-life options a known dividend yield rather than a known dollar dividend is often assumed.

18.4 EXTENSIONS OF THE BASIC TREE APPROACH

We now explain two ways in which the binomial tree approach can be extended.

Time-Dependent Interest Rates and Volatilities

Up to now we have been assuming that interest rates are constant. When the term structure is steeply upward or downward sloping and American options are being valued, this may not be a satisfactory assumption. It is more appropriate to assume that the interest rate for a period of length Δt in the future equals the current forward interest rate for that period. We can accommodate this assumption by setting

$$a = e^{f(t)\Delta t} \tag{18.12}$$

for nodes at time t where $f(t)$ is the forward rate between times t and $t + \Delta t$. This does not change the geometry of the tree because u and d do not depend on a. The probabilities on the branches emanating from nodes at time t are as before:[4]

$$p = \frac{a - d}{u - d} \quad \text{and} \quad 1 - p = \frac{u - a}{u - d}$$

The rest of the way in which we use the tree is the same as before, except that when discounting from time $t + \Delta t$ to time t we use $f(t)$. A similar modification of the basic tree can be used to value index options, foreign exchange options, and futures options. In these applications the dividend yield on an index or a foreign risk-free rate can be made a function of time by following a similar approach to that just described.

Making the volatility σ a function of time in a binomial tree is more difficult. Suppose $\sigma(t)$ is the volatility used to price an option with a life of t. One approach is to make the length of each time step inversely proportional to the average variance rate during the time step. The values of u and d are then the same everywhere and the tree recombines. Define the $V = \sigma(T)^2 T$, where T is the life of the tree and define t_i as the end of the ith time step. For N time steps, we choose t_i to satisfy $\sigma(t_i)^2 t_i = iV/N$ and set $u = e^{\sqrt{V/N}}$ with $d = 1/u$. The parameter p is defined as for a constant volatility. This procedure can be combined with the procedure just mentioned for dealing with non-constant interest rates, so that both interest rates and volatilities are time-dependent.

The Control Variate Technique

A technique known as the *control variate technique* can be used for the evaluation of an American option.[5] This involves using the same tree to calculate both the value of the American option, f_{A}, and the value of the corresponding European option, f_{E}. The Black–Scholes–Merton price of the European option, f_{BSM}, is also calculated. The error given by the tree in the pricing of the European option, $f_{\mathrm{BSM}} - f_{\mathrm{E}}$, is assumed

[4] For a sufficiently large number of time steps, these probabilities are always positive.

[5] See J.C. Hull and A. White, "The Use of the Control Variate Technique in Option Pricing," *Journal of Financial and Quantitative Analysis* 23 (September 1988): 237–51.

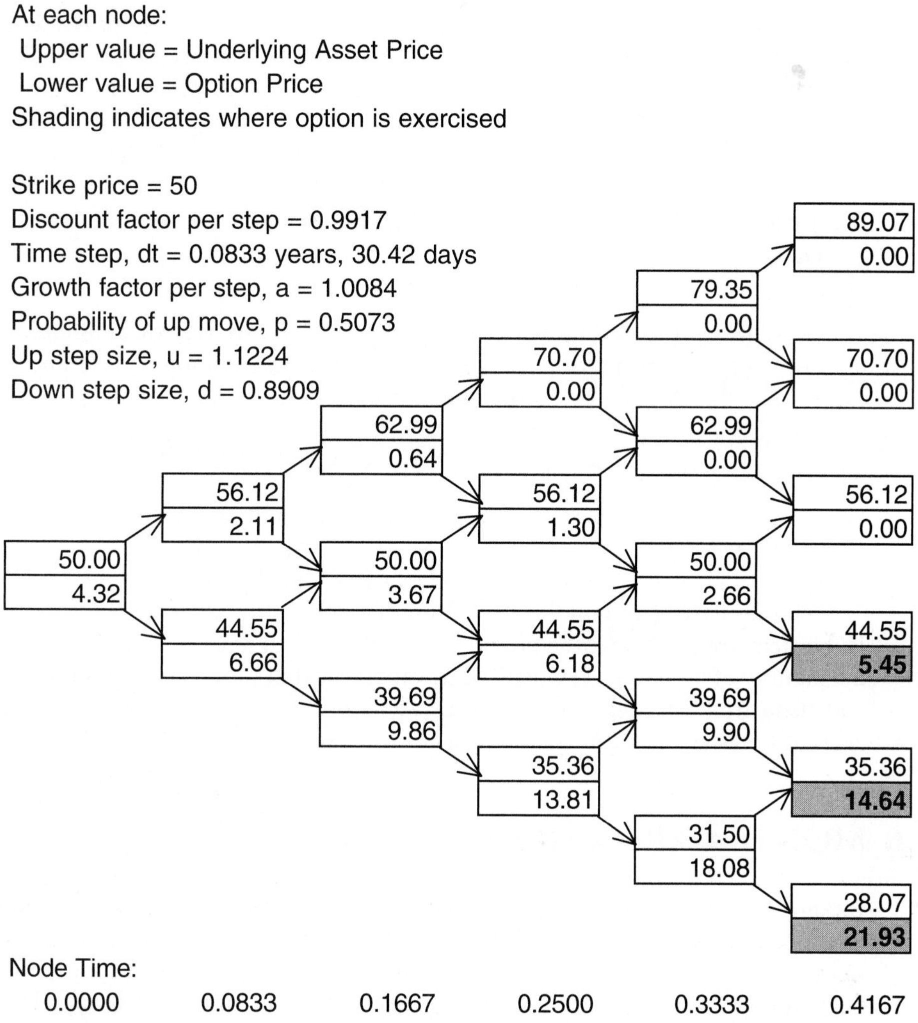

Figure 18.7 Tree produced by DerivaGem for European version of option in Figure 18.3. At each node, the upper number is the stock price and the lower number is the option price

equal to that given by the tree in the pricing of the American option. This gives the estimate of the price of the American option to be

$$f_A + (f_{BSM} - f_E)$$

To illustrate this approach, Figure 18.7 values the option in Figure 18.3 on the assumption that it is European. The price obtained, f_E, is \$4.32. From the Black–Scholes–Merton formula, the true European price of the option, f_{BSM}, is \$4.08. The estimate of the American price, f_A, in Figure 18.3 is \$4.49. The control variate estimate of the American price is therefore

$$4.49 + (4.08 - 4.32) = 4.25$$

A good estimate of the American price, calculated using 100 steps, is 4.278. The control variate approach does, therefore, produce a considerable improvement over the basic tree estimate of 4.49 in this case. In effect, it uses the tree to calculate the difference between the European and the American price rather than the American price itself.

18.5 ALTERNATIVE PROCEDURE FOR CONSTRUCTING TREES

The Cox, Ross, and Rubinstein approach is not the only way of building a binomial tree. Instead of imposing the assumption $u = 1/d$ on equations (18.2) and (18.3), we can set $p = 0.5$. A solution to the equations for small Δt is then

$$u = e^{(r-\sigma^2/2)\Delta t+\sigma\sqrt{\Delta t}}, \quad d = e^{(r-\sigma^2/2)\Delta t-\sigma\sqrt{\Delta t}}$$

When the stock provides a continuous dividend yield at rate q, the variable r becomes $r - q$ in these formulas. This allows trees with $p = 0.5$ to be built for options on indices, foreign exchange, and futures. The procedure is illustrated in Example 18.4.

This alternative tree-building procedure has the advantage over the Cox, Ross, and Rubinstein approach that the probabilities are always 0.5 regardless of the value of σ or the number of time steps.[6] A small disadvantage is that the calculation of delta, gamma, and theta from the tree is not quite as accurate because the values of the underlying asset at times Δt and $2\Delta t$ are no longer centered at S_0.

18.6 MONTE CARLO SIMULATION

Binomial trees can be used in conjunction with a procedure known as *Monte Carlo simulation* for valuing derivatives. Once the tree has been constructed, we randomly sample paths through it. Instead of working backward from the end of the tree to the beginning, we work forward through the tree. The basic procedure is as follows. At the first node we sample a random number between 0 and 1. If the number lies between 0 and p, we take the upper branch; if it lies between p and 1, we take the lower branch. We repeat this procedure at the node that is then reached and at all subsequent nodes that are reached until we get to the end of the tree. We then calculate the payoff on the option for the particular path sampled. This completes the first trial. We carry out many more trials by repeating the whole procedure. Our estimate of the value of the option is the arithmetic average of the payoffs from all the trials discounted at the risk-free interest rate. Example 18.5 provides an illustration.

Monte Carlo simulation, as just described, cannot easily be used for American options, because we have no way of knowing whether early exercise is optimal when a certain node is reached. It can be used to value European options so that a check is provided on the pricing formulas for these options. It can also be used to price some of the exotic options we will discuss in Chapter 22 (e.g. Asian options and lookback options).

---

[6] In the unusual situation that time steps are so large that $\sigma < |(r-q)\sqrt{\Delta t}|$, the Cox, Ross, and Rubinstein tree gives negative probabilities. The alternative procedure described here does not have that drawback.

Example 18.4 Alternative tree construction

A nine-month American call option on a foreign currency has a strike price of 0.7950 (USD per unit of foreign currency). The current exchange rate is 0.7900, the domestic risk-free interest rate is 6% per annum, the foreign risk-free interest rate is 10% per annum, and the volatility of the exchange rate is 4% per annum. In this case, $S_0 = 0.79$, $K = 0.795$, $r = 0.06$, $r_f = 0.10$, $\sigma = 0.04$, and $T = 0.75$. We divide the life of the option into three-month periods for the purposes of constructing the tree so that $\Delta t = 0.25$. We set the probabilities on each branch to 0.5 and

$$u = e^{(0.06-0.10-0.0016/2)0.25+0.04\sqrt{0.25}} = 1.0098$$

$$d = e^{(0.06-0.10-0.0016/2)0.25-0.04\sqrt{0.25}} = 0.9703$$

The tree for the exchange rate is shown in the figure below. The tree gives the value of the option as 0.0026.

At each node:
Upper value = Underlying Asset Price
Lower value = Option Price
Shading indicates where option is exercised

Strike price = 0.795
Discount factor per step = 0.9851
Time step, dt = 0.2500 years, 91.25 days

Probability of up move, p = 0.5000

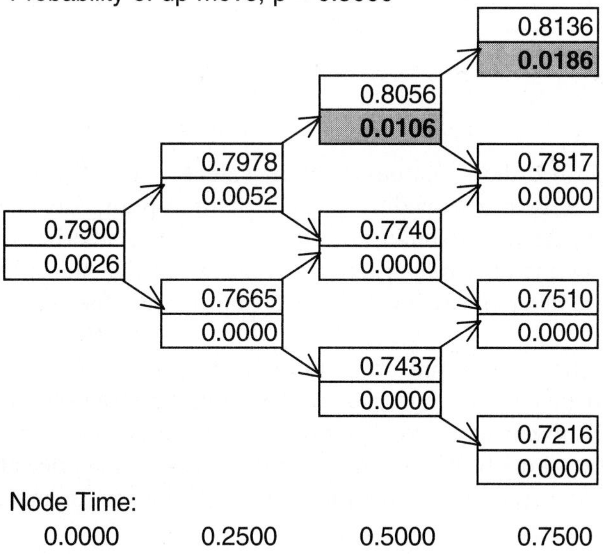

Example 18.5 Using Monte Carlo simulation with a tree

Suppose that the tree in Figure 18.3 is used to value an option that pays off $\max(S_{ave} - 50, 0)$ where S_{ave} is the average stock price during the five months (with the first and last stock price being included in the average). This is known as an Asian option. When ten simulation trials are used, one possible result is shown in the following table (U = up movement; D = down movement):

Trial	*Path*	*Average stock price*	*Option payoff*
1	UUUUD	64.98	14.98
2	UUUDD	59.82	9.82
3	DDDUU	42.31	0.00
4	UUUUU	68.04	18.04
5	UUDDU	55.22	5.22
6	UDUUD	55.22	5.22
7	DDUDD	42.31	0.00
8	UUDDU	55.22	5.22
9	UUUDU	62.25	12.25
10	DDUUD	45.56	0.00
Average			7.08

The option payoff is the amount by which the average stock price exceeds \$50. The value of the option is calculated as the average payoff discounted at the risk-free rate. In this case, the average payoff is \$7.08 and the risk-free rate is 10%, and so the calculated value is $7.08e^{-0.1\times5/12} = 6.79$. (This illustrates the method. In practice we would have to use more time steps on the tree and many more simulation trials to get an accurate answer.)

SUMMARY

This chapter has described how options can be valued using the binomial tree approach. This approach involves dividing the life of the option into a number of small intervals of length Δt and assuming that an asset price at the beginning of an interval can lead to only one of two alternative asset prices at the end of the interval. One of these alternative asset prices involves an up movement; the other involves a down movement.

The sizes of the up movements and down movements, and their associated probabilities, are chosen so that the change in the asset price has the correct mean and standard deviation for a risk-neutral world. Option prices are calculated by starting at the end of the tree and working backward. At the end of the tree, the price of an option is its intrinsic value. At earlier nodes on the tree, the value of an option, if it is American, must be calculated as the greater of

1. The value it has if exercised immediately
2. The value it has if held for a further period of time of length Δt.

If it is exercised at a node, the value of the option is its intrinsic value. If it is held for a further period of length Δt, the value of the option is its expected value at the end of the time period Δt discounted at the risk-free rate.

Delta, gamma, and theta can be estimated directly from the values of the option at the various nodes of the tree. Vega can be estimated by making a small change to the volatility and recomputing the value of the option using a similar tree. Rho can similarly be estimated by making a small change to the interest rate and recomputing the tree.

The binomial tree approach can handle options on stocks paying continuous dividend yields. Because stock indices, currencies, and most futures contracts can be regarded as analogous to stocks paying continuous yields, binomial trees can handle options on these assets as well.

When the binomial tree approach is used to value options on a stock paying known dollar dividends, it is convenient to use the tree to model the stock price less the present value of all future dividends during the life of the option. This keeps the number of nodes on the tree from becoming unmanageable and is consistent with the way European options on dividend-paying stocks are valued.

The computational efficiency of the binomial model can be improved by using the control variate technique. This involves valuing both the American option that is of interest and the corresponding European option using the same tree. The error in the price of the European option is used as an estimate of the error in the price of the American option.

FURTHER READING

Boyle, P. P. "Options: A Monte Carlo Approach," *Journal of Financial Economics*, 4 (1977): 323–28.

Boyle, P. P., M. Broadie, and P. Glasserman. "Monte Carlo Methods for Security Pricing," *Journal of Economic Dynamics and Control*, 21 (1997): 1267–1322.

Cox, J. C., S. A. Ross, and M. Rubinstein. "Option Pricing: A Simplified Approach," *Journal of Financial Economics*, 7 (October 1979): 229–64.

Figlewski, S., and B. Gao. "The Adaptive Mesh Model: A New Approach to Efficient Option Pricing," *Journal of Financial Economics*, 53 (1999), 313–51.

Hull, J. C., and A. White. "The Use of the Control Variate Technique in Option Pricing," *Journal of Financial and Quantitative Analysis*, 23 (September 1988): 237–51.

Longstaff, F. A. and E. S. Schwartz. "Valuing American Options by Simulation: A Least Squares Approach," *Review of Financial Studies*, 14, 1 (2001): 113–47.

Rendleman, R., and B. Bartter. "Two State Option Pricing," *Journal of Finance*, 34 (1979): 1092–1110.

Quiz (Answers at End of Book)

18.1. Which of the following can be estimated for an American option by constructing a single binomial tree: delta, gamma, vega, theta, rho?

18.2. The probability for an up-movement on a binomial tree is $(a - d)/(u - d)$. Explain how the growth factor a is calculated for (a) a non-dividend-paying stock, (b) a stock index, (c) a foreign currency, and (d) a futures contract.

18.3. Calculate the price of a three-month American put option on a non-dividend-paying stock when the stock price is \$60, the strike price is \$60, the risk-free interest rate is 10% per annum, and the volatility is 45% per annum. Use a binomial tree with a time step of one month.

18.4. Explain how the control variate technique is implemented.

18.5. Calculate the price of a nine-month American call option on corn futures when the current futures price is 198 cents, the strike price is 200 cents, the risk-free interest rate is 8% per annum, and the volatility is 30% per annum. Use a binomial tree with a time step of three months.

18.6. "For a dividend-paying stock the tree for the stock price does not recombine, but the tree for the stock price less the present value of future dividends does recombine." Explain.

18.7. Explain the problem in using Monte Carlo simulation to value an American option.

Practice Questions (Answers in Solutions Manual/Study Guide)

18.8. Consider an option that pays off the amount by which the final stock price exceeds the average stock price achieved during the life of the option. Can this be valued from a binomial tree using backwards induction?

18.9. A nine-month American put option on a non-dividend-paying stock has a strike price of \$49. The stock price is \$50, the risk-free rate is 5% per annum, and the volatility is 30% per annum. Use a three-step binomial tree to calculate the option price.

18.10. Use a three-time-step tree to value a nine-month American call option on wheat futures. The current futures price is 400 cents, the strike price is 420 cents, the risk-free rate is 6%, and the volatility is 35% per annum. Estimate the delta of the option from your tree.

18.11. A three-month American call option on a stock has a strike price of \$20. The stock price is \$20, the risk-free rate is 3% per annum, and the volatility is 25% per annum. A dividend of \$2 is expected in 1.5 months. Use a three-step binomial tree to calculate the option price.

18.12. A one-year American put option on a non-dividend-paying stock has an exercise price of \$18. The current stock price is \$20, the risk-free interest rate is 15% per annum, and the volatility of the stock is 40% per annum. Use the DerivaGem software with four three-month time steps to estimate the value of the option. Display the tree and verify that the option prices at the final and penultimate nodes are correct. Use DerivaGem to value the European version of the option. Use the control variate technique to improve your estimate of the price of the American option.

18.13. A two-month American put option on a stock index has an exercise price of 480. The current level of the index is 484, the risk-free interest rate is 10% per annum, the dividend yield on the index is 3% per annum, and the volatility of the index is 25% per annum. Divide the life of the option into four half-month periods and use the binomial tree approach to estimate the value of the option.

18.14. How would you use the control variate approach to improve the estimate of the delta of an American option when the binomial tree approach is used?

18.15. How would you use the binomial tree approach to value an American option on a stock index when the dividend yield on the index is a function of time?

Further Questions

18.16. An American put option to sell a Swiss franc for dollars has a strike price of \$0.80 and a time to maturity of one year. The volatility of the Swiss franc is 10%, the dollar interest rate is 6%, the Swiss franc interest rate is 3%, and the current exchange rate is 0.81. Use a tree with three time steps to value the option. Estimate the delta of the option from your tree.

18.17. A one-year American call option on silver futures has an exercise price of \$9.00. The current futures price is \$8.50, the risk-free rate of interest is 12% per annum, and the volatility of the futures price is 25% per annum. Use the DerivaGem software with four three-month time steps to estimate the value of the option. Display the tree and verify that the option prices at the final and penultimate nodes are correct. Use DerivaGem to value the European version of the option. Use the control variate technique to improve your estimate of the price of the American option.

18.18. A six-month American call option on a stock is expected to pay dividends of \$1 per share at the end of the second month and the fifth month. The current stock price is \$30, the exercise price is \$34, the risk-free interest rate is 10% per annum, and the volatility of the part of the stock price that will not be used to pay the dividends is 30% per annum. Use the DerivaGem software with the life of the option divided into 100 time steps to estimate the value of the option. Compare your answer with that given by Black's approximation (see Section 13.10).

18.19. The DerivaGem Application Builder functions enable you to investigate how the prices of options calculated from a binomial tree converge to the correct value as the number of time steps increases (see Figure 18.4 and Sample Application A in DerivaGem). Consider a put option on a stock index where the index level is 900, the strike price is 900, the risk-free rate is 5%, the dividend yield is 2%, and the time to maturity is 2 years:
   (a) Produce results similar to Sample Application A on convergence for the situation where the option is European and the volatility of the index is 20%.
   (b) Produce results similar to Sample Application A on convergence for the situation where the option is American and the volatility of the index is 20%.
   (c) Produce a chart showing the pricing of the American option when the volatility is 20% as a function of the number of time steps when the control variate technique is used.
   (d) Suppose that the price of the American option in the market is 85.0. Produce a chart showing the implied volatility estimate as a function of the number of time steps.

18.20. Estimate delta, gamma, and theta from the tree in Example 18.1. Explain how each can be interpreted.

18.21. How much is gained from exercising early at the lowest node at the nine-month point in Example 18.2?

18.22. A four-step Cox–Ross–Rubinstein binomial tree is used to price a one-year American put option on an index when the index level is 500, the strike price is 500, the dividend yield is 2%, the risk-free rate is 5%, and the volatility is 25% per annum. What is the option price, delta, gamma, and theta? Explain how you would calculate vega and rho.

CHAPTER 19 Volatility Smiles

How close are the market prices of options to those predicted by the Black–Scholes–Merton model? Do traders really use the Black–Scholes–Merton model when determining a price for an option? Are the probability distributions of asset prices really lognormal? In this chapter we answer these questions. We explain that traders do use the Black–Scholes–Merton model—but not in exactly the way that Black, Scholes, and Merton originally intended. This is because they allow the volatility used to price an option to depend on its strike price and time to maturity.

A plot of the implied volatility of an option as a function of its strike price is known as a *volatility smile*. In this chapter we describe the volatility smiles that traders use in equity and foreign currency markets. We explain the relationship between a volatility smile and the probability distribution being assumed for the future asset price. We also discuss how option traders vary volatility with option maturity and how they use volatility surfaces as pricing tools.

The appendix to this chapter uses put–call parity to show that the implied volatility of a European call option must be the same as that of a European put option when both have the same strike price and time to maturity. This is convenient. It means that the volatility smile for European call options must be the same as that for European put options. The implied volatility of an American option is in most cases very similar to that of a European option with the same strike price and time to maturity. As a result, we can say that the volatility smiles we will present apply—at least approximately—to all European and American options with a particular time to maturity.

19.1 FOREIGN CURRENCY OPTIONS

The volatility smile for foreign currency options has the general form shown in Figure 19.1. The implied volatility is relatively low for at-the-money options, but becomes progressively higher as an option moves either into the money or out of the money.

The volatility smile in Figure 19.1 corresponds to the probability distribution shown by the solid line in Figure 19.2. We will refer to this as the *implied distribution*. A lognormal distribution with the same mean and standard deviation as the implied

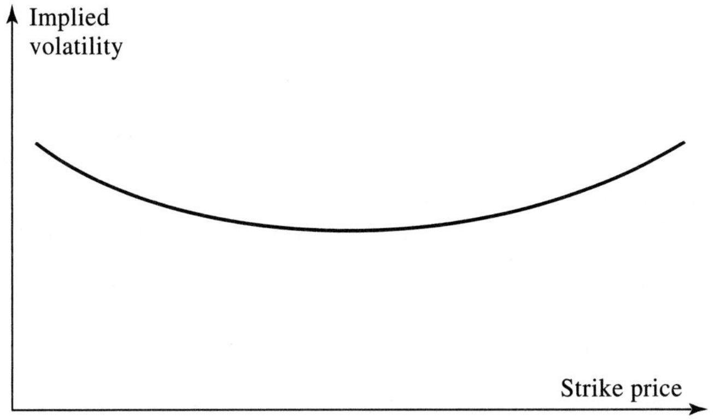

Figure 19.1 Volatility smile for foreign currency options

distribution is shown by the dashed line in Figure 19.2. It can be seen that the implied distribution has heavier tails than the lognormal distribution.[1]

To see that Figures 19.1 and 19.2 are consistent with each other, consider first a deep-out-of-the-money call option with a high strike price of K_2. This option pays off only if the exchange rate proves to be above K_2. Figure 19.2 shows that the probability of this is higher for the implied probability distribution than for the lognormal distribution. We therefore expect the implied distribution to give a relatively high price for the option. A relatively high price leads to a relatively high implied volatility—and this is exactly

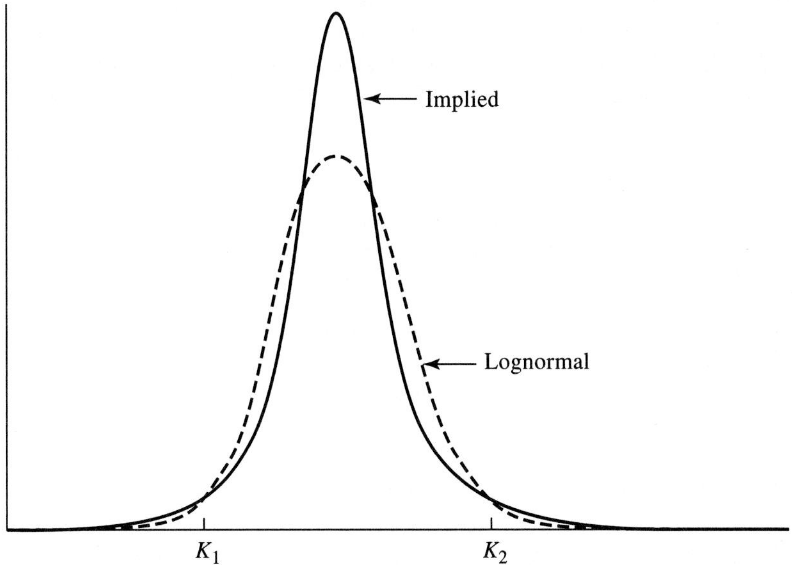

Figure 19.2 Implied distribution and lognormal distribution for foreign currency options

[1] This is known as kurtosis. Note that, in addition to having a heavier tail, the implied distribution is more "peaked." Both small and large movements in the exchange rate are more likely than with the lognormal distribution. Intermediate movements are less likely.

what we observe in Figure 19.1 for the option. The two figures are therefore consistent with each other for high strike prices. Consider next a deep-out-of-the-money put option with a low strike price of K_1. This option pays off only if the exchange rate proves to be below K_1. Figure 19.2 shows that the probability of this is also higher for the implied probability distribution than for the lognormal distribution. We therefore expect the implied distribution to give a relatively high price, and a relatively high implied volatility, for this option as well. Again, this is exactly what we observe in Figure 19.1.

Empirical Results

We have just shown that the volatility smile used by traders for foreign currency options implies that they consider that the lognormal distribution understates the probability of extreme movements in exchange rates. To test whether they are right, Table 19.1 examines the daily movements in 12 different exchange rates over a 10-year period.[2] The first step in the production of the table is to calculate the standard deviation of daily percentage change in each exchange rate. The next stage is to note how often the actual percentage change exceeded one standard deviation, two standard deviations, and so on. The final stage is to calculate how often this would have happened if the percentage changes had been normally distributed. (The lognormal model implies that percentage changes are almost exactly normally distributed over a one-day time period.)

Daily changes exceed three standard deviations on 1.34% of days. The lognormal model predicts that this should happen on only 0.27% of days. Daily changes exceed four, five, and six standard deviations on 0.29%, 0.08%, and 0.03% of days, respectively. The lognormal model predicts that we should hardly ever observe this happening. The table therefore provides evidence to support the existence of heavy tails (Figure 19.2) and the volatility smile used by traders (Figure 19.1). Business Snapshot 19.1 shows how you could have made money if you had done the analysis in Table 19.1 ahead of the rest of the market.

Table 19.1 Percent of days when daily exchange rate moves are greater than one, two, . . . , six standard deviations (S.D. = standard deviation of daily change)

	Real world	*Lognormal model*
> 1 S.D.	25.04	31.73
> 2 S.D.	5.27	4.55
> 3 S.D.	1.34	0.27
> 4 S.D.	0.29	0.01
> 5 S.D.	0.08	0.00
> 6 S.D.	0.03	0.00

[2] The results in this table are taken from J. C. Hull and A. White, "Value at Risk When Daily Changes in Market Variables Are Not Normally Distributed," *Journal of Derivatives*, 5, no. 3 (Spring 1998): 9–19.

Business Snapshot 19.1 Making money from foreign currency options

Black, Scholes, and Merton in their option pricing model assume that the underlying's asset price has a lognormal distribution at future times. This is equivalent to the assumption that asset price changes over a short period of time, such as one day, are normally distributed. Suppose that most market participants are comfortable with the Black–Scholes–Merton assumptions for exchange rates. You have just done the analysis in Table 19.1 and know that the lognormal assumption is not a good one for exchange rates. What should you do?

The answer is that you should buy deep-out-of-the-money call and put options on a variety of different currencies and wait. These options will be relatively inexpensive and more of them will close in the money than the lognormal model predicts. The present value of your payoffs will on average be much greater than the cost of the options.

In the mid-1980s, a few traders knew about the heavy tails of foreign exchange probability distributions. Everyone else thought that the lognormal assumption of Black–Scholes–Merton was reasonable. The few traders who were well informed followed the strategy we have described—and made lots of money. By the late 1980s everyone realized that foreign currency options should be priced with a volatility smile and the trading opportunity disappeared.

Reasons for the Smile in Foreign Currency Options

Why are exchange rates not lognormally distributed? Two of the conditions for an asset price to have a lognormal distribution are:

1. The volatility of the asset is constant.
2. The price of the asset changes smoothly with no jumps.

Neither of these conditions is satisfied for an exchange rate. The volatility of an exchange rate is far from constant, and exchange rates frequently exhibit jumps.[3] The effect of both nonconstant volatility and jumps is that extreme outcomes become more likely.

The impact of jumps and nonconstant volatility depends on the option maturity. As the maturity of the option is increased, the percentage impact of a nonconstant volatility on prices becomes more pronounced, but its percentage impact on implied volatility usually becomes less pronounced. The percentage impact of jumps on both prices and the implied volatility becomes less pronounced as the maturity of the option is increased.[4] The result of all this is that the volatility smile becomes less pronounced as option maturity increases.

19.2 EQUITY OPTIONS

The volatility smile for equity options has been studied by Rubinstein (1985), Rubinstein (1994), and Jackwerth and Rubinstein (1996). Prior to 1987, there was no marked

[3] Sometimes the jumps are in response to the actions of central banks.

[4] When we look at sufficiently long-dated options, jumps tend to get "averaged out," so that the exchange rate distribution when there are jumps is almost indistinguishable from that obtained when the exchange rate changes smoothly.

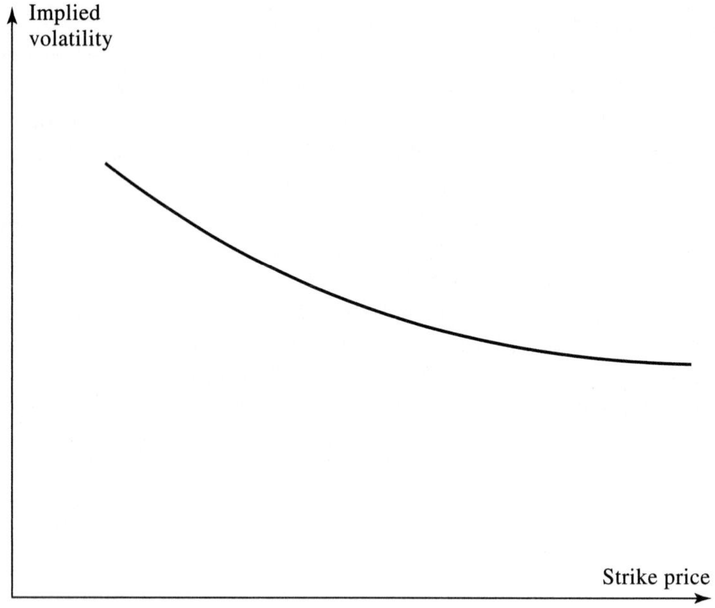

Figure 19.3 Volatility smile for equities

volatility smile. Since 1987 the volatility smile used by traders to price equity options (both those on individual stocks and those on stock indices) has had the general form shown in Figure 19.3. This is sometimes referred to as a *volatility skew*. The volatility decreases as the strike price increases. The volatility used to price an option with a low strike price (i.e., a deep-out-of-the-money put or a deep-in-the-money call) is significantly higher than that used to price an option with a high strike price (i.e., a deep-in-the-money put or a deep-out-of-the-money call).

The volatility smile for equity options corresponds to the implied probability distribution given by the solid line in Figure 19.4. A lognormal distribution with the same

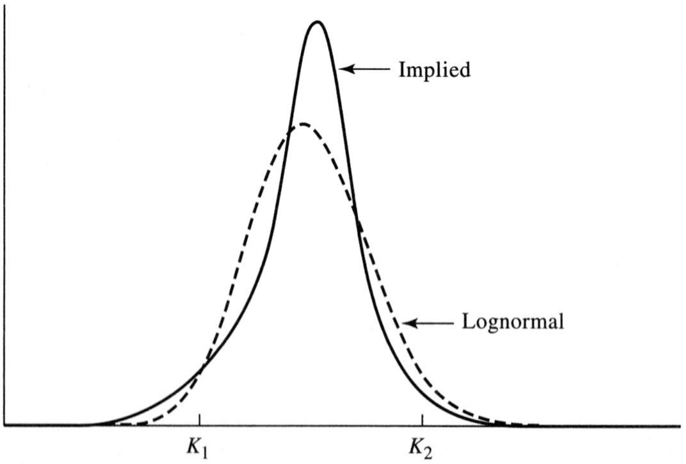

Figure 19.4 Implied distribution and lognormal distribution for equity options

Business Snapshot 19.2 Crashophobia

It is interesting that the pattern for equities in Figure 19.3 has existed only since the stock market crash of October 1987. Prior to October 1987, implied volatilities were much less dependent on strike price. This has led Mark Rubinstein to suggest that one reason for the equity volatility smile may be "crashophobia." Traders are concerned about the possibility of another crash similar to October 1987, and they price options accordingly.

There is some empirical support for this explanation. Declines in the S&P 500 tend to be accompanied by a steepening of the skew. When the S&P 500 increases, the skew tends to become less steep.

mean and standard deviation as the implied distribution is represented by the dotted line. It can be seen that the implied distribution has a heavier left tail and less heavy right tail than the lognormal distribution.

To see that Figures 19.3 and 19.4 are consistent with each other, we proceed as for Figures 19.1 and 19.2 and consider options that are deep out of the money. From Figure 19.4, a deep-out-of-the-money call with a strike price of K_2 has a lower price when the implied distribution is used than when the lognormal distribution is used. This is because the option pays off only if the stock price proves to be above K_2, and the probability of this is lower for the implied probability distribution than for the lognormal distribution. We therefore expect the implied distribution to give a relatively low price for the option. A relatively low price leads to a relatively low implied volatility—and this is exactly what we observe in Figure 19.3 for the option. Consider next a deep-out-of-the-money put option with a strike price of K_1. This option pays off only if the stock price proves to be below K_1. Figure 19.4 shows that the probability of this is higher for the implied probability distribution than for the lognormal distribution. We therefore expect the implied distribution to give a relatively high price, and a relatively high implied volatility, for this option. Again, this is exactly what we observe in Figure 19.3.

The Reason for the Smile in Equity Options

One possible explanation for the smile in equity options concerns leverage. As a company's equity declines in value, the company's leverage increases. This means that the equity becomes more risky and its volatility increases. As a company's equity increases in value, leverage decreases. The equity then becomes less risky and its volatility decreases. This argument suggests that we can expect the volatility of a stock to be a decreasing function of the stock price and is consistent with Figures 19.3 and 19.4. Another explanation is "crashophobia" (see Business Snapshot 19.2).

19.3 THE VOLATILITY TERM STRUCTURE AND VOLATILITY SURFACES

Traders allow the implied volatility to depend on time to maturity as well as strike price. Implied volatility tends to be an increasing function of maturity when short-dated volatilities are historically low. This is because there is then an expectation that volatilities

Table 19.2 Volatility surface

Option maturity	*Strike price*				
	0.90	*0.95*	*1.00*	*1.05*	*1.10*
1 month	14.2	13.0	12.0	13.1	14.5
3 months	14.0	13.0	12.0	13.1	14.2
6 months	14.1	13.3	12.5	13.4	14.3
1 year	14.7	14.0	13.5	14.0	14.8
2 years	15.0	14.4	14.0	14.5	15.1
5 years	14.8	14.6	14.4	14.7	15.0

will increase. Similarly, volatility tends to be a decreasing function of maturity when short-dated volatilities are historically high. This is because there is then an expectation that volatilities will decrease.

Volatility surfaces combine volatility smiles with the volatility term structure to tabulate the volatilities appropriate for pricing an option with any strike price and any maturity. An example of a volatility surface that might be used for foreign currency options is shown in Table 19.2. (The current exchange rate is assumed to be 1.00.) In this table, the volatility smile becomes less pronounced as the option maturity increases. As mentioned earlier, this is what is observed for currency options. It is also what is observed for options on most other assets.

One dimension of a volatility surface is strike price; the other is time to maturity. The main body of the volatility surface shows implied volatilities calculated from the Black–Scholes–Merton model. At any given time, some of the entries in the volatility surface are likely to correspond to options for which reliable market data are available. The implied volatilities for these options are calculated directly from their market prices and entered into the table. The rest of the volatility surface is typically determined using some form of interpolation.

When a new option has to be valued, financial engineers look up the appropriate volatility in the table. For example, when valuing a nine-month option with a strike price of 1.05, a financial engineer would interpolate between 13.4 and 14.0 to obtain a volatility of 13.7%. This is the volatility that would be used in the Black–Scholes–Merton formula or in a binomial tree. When valuing a 1.5-year option with a strike price of 0.925, a two-dimensional interpolation would be used to give an implied volatility of 14.525%.

Define T as the time to maturity, S_0 as the asset price, and F_0 as the forward price of the asset. Sometimes the volatility smile is defined as the relationship between the implied volatility and K/S_0 rather than between the implied volatility and K. A more sophisticated approach is to relate the implied volatility to

$$\frac{1}{\sqrt{T}}\ln\frac{K}{F_0}$$

The smile is then usually much less dependent on the time to maturity.[5]

[5] For a discussion of this approach, see S. Natenberg, *Option Pricing and Volatility: Advanced Trading Strategies and Techniques*, 2nd edn. McGraw-Hill, 1994; R. Tompkins, *Options Analysis: A State of the Art Guide to Options Pricing*, Burr Ridge, IL: Irwin, 1994. Empirical evidence supporting this approach is in T. Daglish, J. Hull, and W. Suo, "Volatility Surfaces: Theory, Rules of Thumb, and Empirical Evidence," *Quantitative Finance*, 7, 5 (October 2007), 507–24.

The Role of the Model

How important is an option-pricing model if traders are prepared to use a different volatility for every deal? It can be argued that the Black–Scholes–Merton model is no more than a sophisticated interpolation tool used by traders for ensuring that an option is priced consistently with the market prices of other actively traded options. If traders stopped using Black–Scholes–Merton and switched to another plausible model, the volatility surface would change and the shape of the smile would change. But arguably, the dollar prices quoted in the market would not change appreciably. Of course, the model used can affect Greek letters and are important for pricing in situations where similar derivatives do not trade.

19.4 WHEN A SINGLE LARGE JUMP IS ANTICIPATED

We now consider an example of how an unusual volatility smile could arise in equity markets. Suppose that a stock price is currently \$50 and an important news announcement in a few days is expected to either increase the stock price by \$8 or reduce it by \$8. (This announcement might concern the outcome of a takeover attempt or the verdict in an important lawsuit.)

The probability distribution of the stock price in, say, one month might then consist of a mixture of two lognormal distributions, the first corresponding to favorable news, and the second to unfavorable news. The situation is illustrated in Figure 19.5. The solid line shows the mixture-of-lognormals distribution for the stock price in one month; the dashed line shows a lognormal distribution with the same mean and standard deviation as this distribution.

The true probability distribution is bimodal (certainly not lognormal). One easy way to investigate the general effect of a bimodal stock price distribution is to consider the extreme case where there are only two possible future stock prices. This is what we will now do. Suppose that the stock price is currently \$50 and that it is known that in one month it will be either \$42 or \$58. Suppose further that the risk-free rate is 12% per

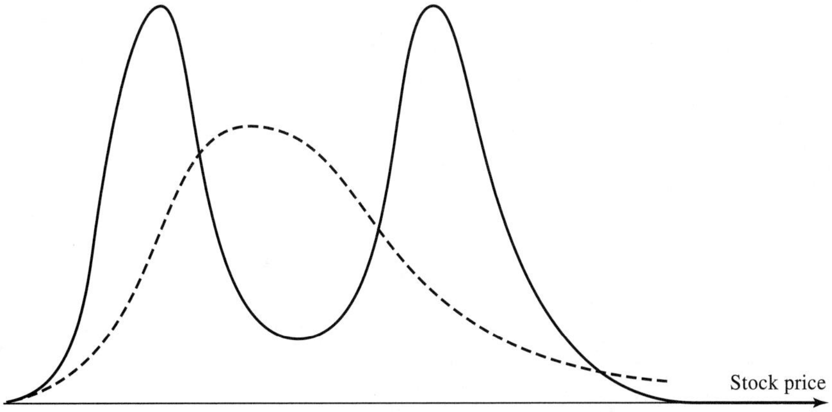

Figure 19.5 Effect of a single large jump. The solid line is the true distribution; the dashed line is the lognormal distribution

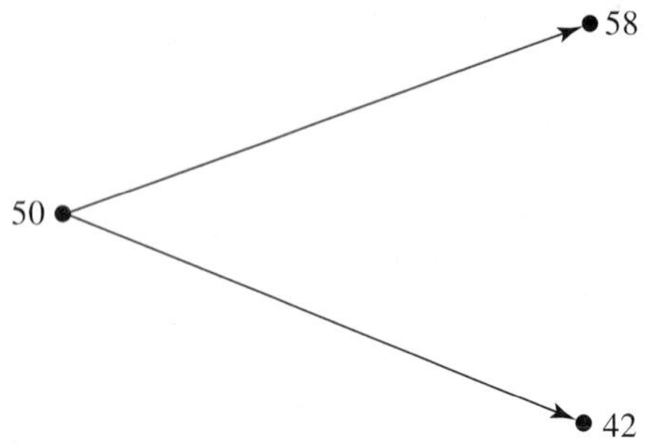

Figure 19.6 Change in stock price in one month

annum. The situation is illustrated in Figure 19.6. Options can be valued using the binomial model from Chapters 12 and 18. In this case, $u = 1.16$, $d = 0.84$, $a = 1.0101$, and $p = 0.5314$. The results from valuing a range of different options are shown in Table 19.3. The first column shows alternative strike prices; the second shows prices of one-month European call options; the third shows the prices of one-month European put option prices; and the fourth shows implied volatilities. (As shown in the appendix to this chapter, the implied volatility of a European put option is the same as that of a European call option when they have the same strike price and maturity.) Figure 19.7 displays the volatility smile from Table 19.3. It is actually a "frown" (the opposite of that observed for currencies) with volatilities declining as we move out of or into the money. The volatility implied from an option with a strike price of 50 will overprice an option with a strike price of 44 or 56.

SUMMARY

The Black–Scholes–Merton model and its extensions assume that the probability distribution of the underlying asset at any given future time is lognormal. This assumption is not the one made by traders. They assume the probability distribution

Table 19.3 Implied volatilities in situation where it is known that the stock price will move from \$50 to either \$42 or \$58

Strike price (\$)	*Call price (\$)*	*Put price (\$)*	*Implied volatility (%)*
42	8.42	0.00	0.0
44	7.37	0.93	58.8
46	6.31	1.86	66.6
48	5.26	2.78	69.5
50	4.21	3.71	69.2
52	3.16	4.64	66.1
54	2.10	5.57	60.0
56	1.05	6.50	49.0
58	0.00	7.42	0.0

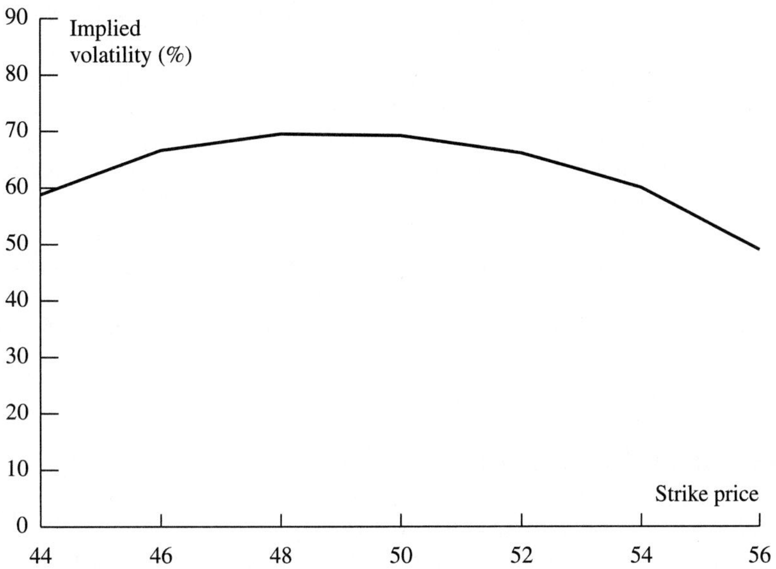

Figure 19.7 Volatility smile for situation in Table 19.3

of an equity price has a heavier left tail and less heavy right tail than the lognormal distribution. They also assume that the probability distribution of an exchange rate has a heavier right tail and a heavier left tail than the lognormal distribution.

Traders use volatility smiles to allow for nonlognormality. The volatility smile defines the relationship between the implied volatility of an option and its strike price. For equity options, the volatility smile tends to be downward sloping. This means that out-of-the-money puts and in-the-money calls tend to have high implied volatilities whereas out-of-the-money calls and in-the-money puts tend to have low implied volatilities. For foreign currency options, the volatility smile is U-shaped. Both out-of-the-money and in-the-money options have higher implied volatilities than at-the-money options.

Often traders also use a volatility term structure. The implied volatility of an option then depends on its life. When volatility smiles and volatility term structures are combined, they produce a volatility surface. This defines implied volatility as a function of both the strike price and the time to maturity.

FURTHER READING

Bakshi, G., C. Cao, and Z. Chen. "Empirical Performance of Alternative Option Pricing Models," *Journal of Finance*, 52, no. 5 (December 1997): 2004–49.

Bates, D. S. "Post-'87 Crash Fears in the S&P Futures Market," *Journal of Econometrics*, 94 (Jan./Feb. 2000): 181–238.

Daglish, T., J. Hull, and W. Suo. "Volatility Surfaces: Theory, Rules of Thumb, and Empirical Evidence," *Quantitative Finance*, 7, 5 (2007): 507–24.

Derman, E. "Regimes of Volatility," *Risk*, April 1999: 55–59.

Ederington, L., and W. Guan. "Why Are Those Options Smiling," *Journal of Derivatives*, 10, 2 (2002): 9–34.

Jackwerth, J. C., and M. Rubinstein. "Recovering Probability Distributions from Option Prices," *Journal of Finance*, 51 (December 1996): 1611–31.

Melick, W. R., and C. P. Thomas. "Recovering an Asset's Implied Probability Density Function from Option Prices: An Application to Crude Oil during the Gulf Crisis," *Journal of Financial and Quantitative Analysis*, 32, no. 1 (March 1997): 91–115.

Rubinstein, M. "Nonparametric Tests of Alternative Option Pricing Models Using All Reported Trades and Quotes on the 30 Most Active CBOE Option Classes from August 23, 1976, through August 31, 1978," *Journal of Finance*, 40 (June 1985): 455–80.

Xu, X., and S. J. Taylor. "The Term Structure of Volatility Implied by Foreign Exchange Options," *Journal of Financial and Quantitative Analysis*, 29 (1994): 57–74.

Quiz (Answers at End of Book)

19.1. What volatility smile is likely to be observed when:
 (a) Both tails of the stock price distribution are less heavy than those of the lognormal distribution?
 (b) The right tail is heavier, and the left tail is less heavy, than that of a lognormal distribution?

19.2. What volatility smile is observed for equities?

19.3. What volatility smile is likely to be caused by jumps in the underlying asset price? Is the pattern likely to be more pronounced for a two-year rather than a three-month option?

19.4. A European call and put option have the same strike price and time to maturity. The call has an implied volatility of 30% and the put has implied volatility of 25%. What trades would you do?

19.5. Explain carefully why a distribution with a heavier left tail and less heavy right tail than the lognormal distribution gives rise to a downward sloping volatility smile.

19.6. The market price of a European call is \$3.00 and its price given by Black–Scholes–Merton model with a volatility of 30% is \$3.50. The price given by this Black–Scholes–Merton model for a European put option with the same strike price and time to maturity is \$1.00. What should the market price of the put option be? Explain the reasons for your answer.

19.7. Explain what is meant by crashophobia.

Practice Questions (Answers in Solutions Manual/Study Guide)

19.8. A stock price is currently \$20. Tomorrow, news is expected to be announced that will either increase the price by \$5 or decrease the price by \$5. What are the problems in using Black–Scholes–Merton to value one-month options on the stock?

19.9. What volatility smile is likely to be observed for six-month options when the volatility is uncertain and positively correlated to the stock price?

19.10. What problems do you think would be encountered in testing a stock option pricing model empirically?

19.11. Suppose that a central bank's policy is to allow an exchange rate to fluctuate between 0.97 and 1.03. What pattern of implied volatilities for options on the exchange rate would you expect to see?

19.12. Option traders sometimes refer to deep-out-of-the-money options as being options on volatility. Why do you think they do this?

19.13. A European call option on a certain stock has a strike price of \$30, a time to maturity of one year, and an implied volatility of 30%. A European put option on the same stock has a strike price of \$30, a time to maturity of one year, and an implied volatility of 33%. What is the arbitrage opportunity open to a trader? Does the arbitrage work only when the lognormal assumption underlying Black–Scholes–Merton holds? Explain the reasons for your answer carefully.

19.14. Suppose that the result of a major lawsuit affecting a company is due to be announced tomorrow. The company's stock price is currently \$60. If the ruling is favorable to the company, the stock price is expected to jump to \$75. If it is unfavorable, the stock is expected to jump to \$50. What is the risk-neutral probability of a favorable ruling? Assume that the volatility of the company's stock will be 25% for six months after the ruling if the ruling is favorable and 40% if it is unfavorable. Use DerivaGem to calculate the relationship between implied volatility and strike price for six-month European options on the company today. The company does not pay dividends. Assume that the six-month risk-free rate is 6%. Consider call options with strike prices of \$30, \$40, \$50, \$60, \$70, and \$80.

19.15. An exchange rate is currently 0.8000. The volatility of the exchange rate is quoted as 12% and interest rates in the two countries are the same. Using the lognormal assumption, estimate the probability that the exchange rate in three months will be (a) less than 0.7000, (b) between 0.7000 and 0.7500, (c) between 0.7500 and 0.8000, (d) between 0.8000 and 0.8500, (e) between 0.8500 and 0.9000, and (f) greater than 0.9000. Based on the volatility smile usually observed in the market for exchange rates, which of these estimates would you expect to be too low and which would you expect to be too high?

19.16. The price of a stock is \$40. A six-month European call option on the stock with a strike price of \$30 has an implied volatility of 35%. A six-month European call option on the stock with a strike price of \$50 has an implied volatility of 28%. The six-month risk-free rate is 5% and no dividends are expected. Explain why the two implied volatilities are different. Use DerivaGem to calculate the prices of the two options. Use put–call parity to calculate the prices of six-month European put options with strike prices of \$30 and \$50. Use DerivaGem to calculate the implied volatilities of these two put options.

19.17. "The Black–Scholes–Merton model is used by traders as an interpolation tool." Discuss this view.

19.18. Using Table 19.2, calculate the implied volatility a trader would use for an 8-month option with a strike price of 1.04.

Further Questions

19.19. A company's stock is selling for \$4. The company has no outstanding debt. Analysts consider the liquidation value of the company to be at least \$300,000 and there are 100,000 shares outstanding. What volatility smile would you expect to see?

19.20. A company is currently awaiting the outcome of a major lawsuit. This is expected to be known within one month. The stock price is currently \$20. If the outcome is positive, the stock price is expected to be \$24 at the end of one month. If the outcome is negative, it is expected to be \$18 at this time. The one-month risk-free interest rate is 8% per annum.
(a) What is the risk-neutral probability of a positive outcome?
(b) What are the values of one-month call options with strike prices of \$19, \$20, \$21, \$22, and \$23?
(c) Use DerivaGem to calculate a volatility smile for one-month call options.
(d) Verify that the same volatility smile is obtained for one-month put options.

19.21. A futures price is currently \$40. The risk-free interest rate is 5%. Some news is expected tomorrow that will cause the volatility over the next three months to be either 10% or 30%. There is a 60% chance of the first outcome and a 40% chance of the second outcome. Use DerivaGem to calculate a volatility smile for three-month options.

19.22. Data for a number of foreign currencies are provided on the author's website:

http://www.rotman.utoronto.ca/~hull/data

Choose a currency and use the data to produce a table similar to Table 19.1.

19.23. Data for a number of stock indices are provided on the author's website:

http://www.rotman.utoronto.ca/~hull/data

Choose an index and test whether a three standard deviation down movement happens more often than a three standard deviation up movement.

19.24. Consider a European call and a European put with the same strike price and time to maturity. Show that they change in value by the same amount when the volatility increases from a level, σ_1, to a new level, σ_2 within a short period of time. (*Hint*: Use put–call parity.)

19.25. Using Table 19.2, calculate the implied volatility a trader would use for an 11-month option with a strike price of 0.98.

APPENDIX

Why the Put Volatility Smile Is the Same As the Call Volatility Smile

Put–call parity, which we explained in Chapters 10 and 15, is an important relationship between the price, c, of a European call and the price, p, of a European put:

$$p + S_0 e^{-qT} = c + Ke^{-rT} \tag{19A.1}$$

The call and the put have the same strike price, K, and time to maturity, T. The variable S_0 is the price of the underlying asset today, r is the risk-free interest rate for maturity T, and q is the yield on the asset.

A key feature of the put–call parity relationship is that it is based on a relatively simple arbitrage argument. It does not require any assumption about the future probability distribution of the asset price. It is true both when the asset price distribution is lognormal and when it is not lognormal.

Suppose that, for a particular value of the volatility, $p_{\rm bsm}$ and $c_{\rm bsm}$ are the values of European put and call options calculated using the Black–Scholes–Merton model. Suppose further that $p_{\rm mkt}$ and $c_{\rm mkt}$ are the market values of these options. Because put–call parity holds for the Black–Scholes–Merton model, we must have

$$p_{\rm bsm} + S_0 e^{-qT} = c_{\rm bsm} + Ke^{-rT}$$

In the absence of arbitrage opportunities it holds for market prices too, so that

$$p_{\rm mkt} + S_0 e^{-qT} = c_{\rm mkt} + Ke^{-rT}$$

Subtracting the second of these two equations from the first, we obtain

$$p_{\rm bsm} - p_{\rm mkt} = c_{\rm bsm} - c_{\rm mkt} \tag{19A.2}$$

This shows that the dollar pricing error when the Black–Scholes–Merton model is

Example 19A.1 Implied volatilities for puts and calls

The value of a foreign currency is \$0.60. The risk-free interest rate is 5% per annum in the United States and 10% per annum for the foreign currency. The market price of a European call option on the foreign currency with a maturity of one year and a strike price of \$0.59 is 0.0236. DerivaGem shows that the implied volatility of the call is 14.5%. For there to be no arbitrage, the put–call parity relationship in equation (19A.1) must apply with q equal to the foreign risk-free rate. The price, p, of a European put option with a strike price of \$0.59 and maturity of one year therefore satisfies

$$p + 0.60e^{-0.10\times 1} = 0.0236 + 0.59e^{-0.05\times 1}$$

so that $p = 0.0419$. DerivaGem shows that, when the put has this price, its implied volatility is also 14.5%, as expected.

used to price a European put option should be exactly the same as the dollar pricing error when it is used to price a European call option with the same strike price and time to maturity.

Suppose that the implied volatility of the put option is 22%. This means that $p_{\text{bsm}} = p_{\text{mkt}}$ when a volatility of 22% is used in the Black–Scholes–Merton model. From equation (19A.2), it follows that $c_{\text{bsm}} = c_{\text{mkt}}$ when this volatility is used. The implied volatility of the call, therefore, is also 22%. This argument shows that the implied volatility of a European call option is always the same as the implied volatility of a European put option when the two have the same strike price and maturity date. To put this another way, for a given strike price and maturity, the correct volatility to use in conjunction with the Black–Scholes–Merton model to price a European call should always be the same as that used to price a European put. This is also approximately true for American options. It follows that when traders refer to the relationship between implied volatility and strike price, or to the relationship between implied volatility and maturity, they do not need to state whether they are talking about calls or puts. The relationship is the same for both. This result is illustrated in Example 19A.1.

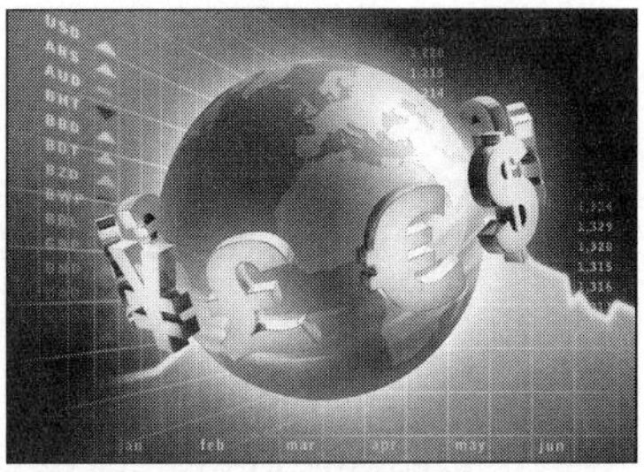

CHAPTER 20 Value at Risk

In Chapter 17, we examined measures such as delta, gamma, and vega for describing different aspects of the risk in a portfolio consisting of options and other financial assets. A financial institution usually calculates each of these measures each day for every market variable to which it is exposed. Often there are hundreds, or even thousands, of these market variables. A delta–gamma–vega analysis, therefore, leads to a very large number of different risk measures being produced each day. These risk measures provide valuable information for the financial institution's traders, but they are of limited use to senior management.

Value at risk (VaR) is an attempt to provide a single number summarizing the total risk in a portfolio of financial assets for senior management. It has become widely used by corporate treasurers and fund managers as well as by financial institutions. Bank regulators also use VaR in determining the capital a bank is required to keep for the risks it is bearing.

In this chapter, we explain the VaR measure and describe the two main approaches for calculating it. These are known as the *historical simulation* approach and the *model-building* approach.

20.1 THE VaR MEASURE

When using the value-at-risk (VaR) measure, an analyst is interested in making a statement of the following form:

> I am X percent certain that there will not be a loss of more than V dollars in the next N days.

Here, V is the VaR of the portfolio. It is a function of two parameters: the time horizon, N days, and the confidence level, X percent. It is the loss level over N days that has a probability of only $(100 - X)$ percent of being exceeded. Bank regulators require banks to calculate VaR for market risk with $N = 10$ and $X = 99$ (see Business Snapshot 20.1).

When N days is the time horizon and X percent is the confidence level, VaR is the loss corresponding to the $(100 - X)$th percentile of the distribution of the gain in the value of the portfolio over the next N days, with losses being counted as negative gains.

Business Snapshot 20.1 How bank regulators use VaR

The Basel Committee on Bank Supervision is a committee of the world's bank regulators that meets regularly in Basel, Switzerland. In 1988 it published what has become known as Basel I. This is an agreement between the regulators on how the capital a bank is required to hold for credit risk should be calculated. Later the Basel Committee published *The 1996 Amendment* which was implemented in 1998 and required banks to hold capital for market risk as well as credit risk. The Amendment distinguishes between a bank's trading book and its banking book. The banking book consists primarily of loans and is not usually revalued on a regular basis for managerial and accounting purposes. The trading book consists of the myriad of different instruments that are traded by the bank (stocks, bonds, swaps, forward contracts, options, etc.) and is normally revalued daily.

The 1996 Amendment calculates capital for the trading book using the VaR measure with $N = 10$ and $X = 99$. This means that it focuses on the revaluation loss over a 10-day period that is expected to be exceeded only 1% of the time. The capital the bank is required to hold is k times this VaR measure (with an adjustment for what are termed specific risks). The multiplier k is chosen on a bank-by-bank basis by the regulators and must be at least 3.0. For a bank with excellent well-tested VaR estimation procedures, it is likely that k will be set equal to the minimum value of 3.0. For other banks it may be higher.

Basel I has been followed by Basel II, Basel II.5, and Basel III. Basel II (which was implemented in most parts of the world in about 2007) uses VaR with a one-year time horizon and a 99.9% confidence level for calculating capital for credit risk and operational risk. Basel II.5 (which was implemented in 2012) revised the way market risk capital is calculated. One of the changes involves what is known as *stressed VaR*. This is a VaR measure based on how market variables have moved during a particularly adverse time period. Basel III is increasing the amount of capital that banks are required to hold and the proportion of that capital that must be equity.

Interestingly, in May 2012, the Basel committee issued a discussion paper indicating that it is considering switching from VaR to expected shortfall for market risk.

Alternatively it is the loss corresponding to the Xth percentile of the distribution of the loss in value of the portfolio over the next N days, with gains being counted as negative losses. For example, when $N = 5$ and $X = 97$, VaR is the third percentile of the distribution of gains in the value of the portfolio, or the 97th percentile of the distribution of losses, over the next five days. VaR is illustrated in Figures 20.1 and 20.2.

VaR is an attractive measure because it is easy to understand. In essence, it asks the simple question "How bad can things get?" This is the question all senior managers want answered. They are very comfortable with the idea of compressing all the Greek letters for all the market variables underlying a portfolio into a single number.

If we accept that it is useful to have a single number to describe the risk of a portfolio, an interesting question is whether VaR is the best alternative. Some researchers have argued that VaR may tempt traders to choose a portfolio with a return distribution similar to that in Figure 20.2. The portfolios in Figures 20.1 and 20.2 have the same VaR, but the portfolio in Figure 20.2 is much riskier because potential losses are much larger.

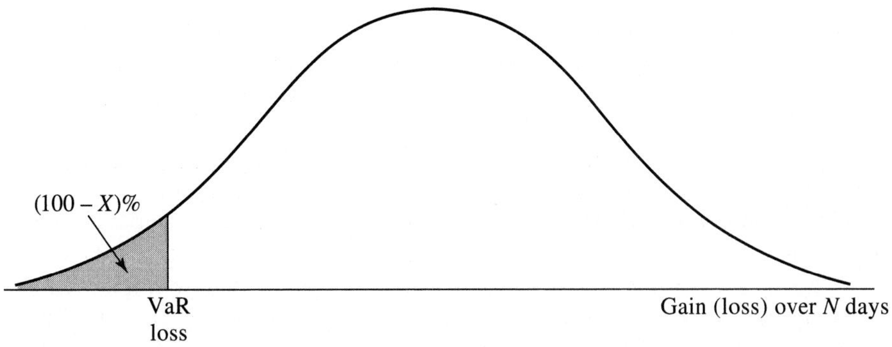

Figure 20.1 Calculation of VaR from the probability distribution of changes in the portfolio value; confidence level is X percent. Gains in portfolio value are positive; losses are negative

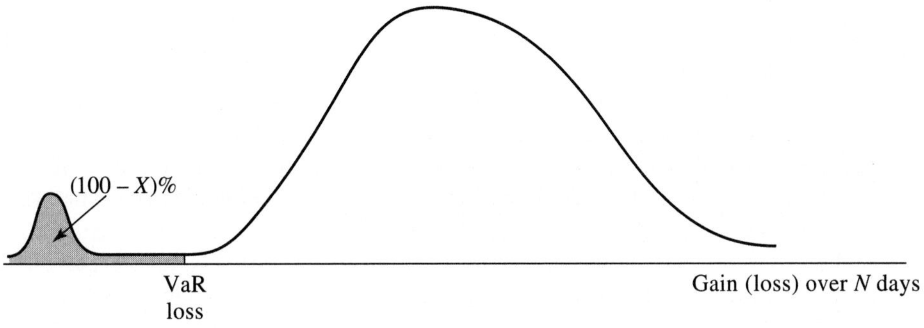

Figure 20.2 Alternative situation to Figure 20.1; VaR is the same, but the potential loss is larger

A measure that deals with the problem we have just mentioned is *expected shortfall*.[1] Whereas VaR asks the question "How bad can things get?", expected shortfall asks: "If things do get bad, how much can the company expect to lose?" Expected shortfall is the expected loss during an N-day period conditional on the loss being worse than the VaR loss. For example, with $X = 99$ and $N = 10$, expected shortfall is the average amount the company loses over a 10-day period when the loss is worse than the 10-day 99% VaR.

VaR has traditionally been the most popular measure of risk for regulators and many risk managers (see Business Snapshot 20.1). In the rest of this chapter, we focus on market risk and discuss alternative ways VaR can be measured.

The Time Horizon

VaR has two parameters: the time horizon, N, measured in days, and the confidence level, X. In practice, analysts almost invariably set $N = 1$ in the first instance when

[1] This measure, which is also known as *tail loss* or *conditional VaR* (C-VaR), was suggested by P. Artzner, F. Delbaen, J.M. Eber, and D. Heath, "Coherent Measures of Risk," *Mathematical Finance*, 9 (1999): 203–28. These authors define certain properties that a good risk measure should have and show that the standard VaR measure does not have all of them. For a more detailed discussion of the expected shortfall, see J. Hull, *Risk Management and Financial Institutions*, 3rd edition, 2012, Hoboken: Wiley.

market risk VaR is being calculated. This is because there is not usually enough data available to estimate directly the behavior of market variables over periods of time longer than one day. The usual (approximate) assumption is

$$N\text{-day VaR} = 1\text{-day VaR} \times \sqrt{N}$$

This formula is exactly true when the changes in the value of the portfolio on successive days have independent identical normal distributions with mean zero.

Business Snapshot 20.1 explains that the 1996 amendment to Basel I required a bank's capital for market risk to be at least three times the 10-day 99% VaR. Given the way a 10-day VaR is calculated, this capital level is $3 \times \sqrt{10} = 9.49$ times the 1-day 99% VaR.

20.2 HISTORICAL SIMULATION

Historical simulation is one popular way of estimating VaR. It involves using past data as a guide to what will happen in the future. Suppose that we want to calculate VaR for a portfolio using a one-day time horizon, a 99% confidence level, and 501 days of data. (As already explained, the time horizon and confidence level are those typically used for a market risk VaR calculation; 501 is a popular choice for the number of days of data used because, as we shall see, it leads to 500 scenarios being created.) The first step is to identify the market variables affecting the portfolio. These will typically be exchange rates, interest rates, commodity prices, and so on. All prices are measured in the domestic currency. For example, one market variable for a German bank is likely to be the S&P 500 measured in euros. Data are then collected on movements in these market variables over the most recent 501 days. This provides 500 alternative scenarios for what can happen between today and tomorrow. Denote the first day for which we have data as Day 0, the second day as Day 1, and so on. Scenario 1 is where the percentage changes in the values of all variables are the same as they were between Day 0 and Day 1, Scenario 2 is where they are the same as between Day 1 and Day 2, and so on. For each scenario, the dollar change in the value of the portfolio between today and tomorrow is calculated. This defines a probability distribution for daily loss (gains are negative losses) in the value of our portfolio. The 99th percentile of the distribution can be estimated as the fifth-highest loss.[2] The estimate of VaR is the loss when we are at this 99th percentile point. We are 99% certain that we will not take a loss greater than the VaR estimate if the changes in market variables in the last 501 days are representative of what will happen between today and tomorrow.

To express the approach algebraically, define v_i as the value of a market variable on Day i and suppose that today is Day n. The ith scenario in the historical simulation approach assumes that the value of the market variable tomorrow will be

$$\text{Value under } i\text{th scenario} = v_n \frac{v_i}{v_{i-1}}$$

[2] There are alternatives here. A case can be made for using the fifth-highest loss, the sixth-highest loss, or an average of the two. In Excel's PERCENTILE function, when there are n observations and k is an integer, the $k/(n-1)$ percentile is the observation ranked $k+1$. Other percentiles are calculated using linear interpolation.

Illustration: Investment in Four Stock Indices

To illustrate the calculations underlying the approach, suppose that an investor in the U.S. owns, on September 25, 2008, a portfolio worth \$10 million consisting of investments in four stock indices: the Dow Jones Industrial Average (DJIA) in the U.S., the FTSE 100 in the U.K., the CAC 40 in France, and the Nikkei 225 in Japan. The value of the investment in each index on September 25, 2008, is shown in Table 20.1. An Excel spreadsheet containing 501 days of historical data on the closing prices of the four indices together with exchange rates and a complete set of VaR calculations is on the author's website:[3]

www.rotman.utoronto.ca/~hull/Fundamentals/VaRExample

Because we are considering a U.S. investor, the values of the FTSE 100, CAC 40, and Nikkei 225 must be measured in U.S. dollars. For example, the FTSE 100 was 5,823.40 on August 10, 2008, when the exchange rate was 1.8918 USD per GBP. This means that, measured in U.S. dollars, it was $5{,}823.40 \times 1.8918 = 11{,}016.71$. An extract from the data with all the indices measured in U.S. dollars is shown in Table 20.2.

September 25, 2008, is an interesting date to choose in evaluating an equity investment. The turmoil in credit markets, which started in August 2007, was over a year old. Equity prices had been declining for several months. Volatilities were increasing. Lehman Brothers had filed for bankruptcy ten days earlier. The Treasury Secretary's \$700 billion Troubled Asset Relief Program (TARP) had not yet been passed by the United States Congress.

Table 20.3 shows the values of the indices (measured in U.S. dollars) on September 26, 2008, for the scenarios considered. Scenario 1 (the first row in Table 20.3) shows the values of indices on September 26, 2008, assuming that their percentage changes between September 25 and September 26, 2008, are the same as they were between August 7 and August 8, 2006; Scenario 2 (the second row in Table 20.3) shows the values of market variables on September 26, 2008, assuming these percentage changes are the same as those between August 8 and August 9, 2006; and so on. In general, Scenario i assumes that the percentage changes in the indices between September 25 and September 26 are the same as they were between Day $i-1$ and Day i for $1 \leqslant i \leqslant 500$. The 500 rows in Table 20.3 are the 500 scenarios considered.

Table 20.1 Investment portfolio used for VaR calculations

Index	*Portfolio value (\$000s)*
DJIA	4,000
FTSE 100	3,000
CAC 40	1,000
Nikkei 225	2,000
Total	10,000

[3] To keep the example as straightforward as possible, only days when all four indices traded were included in the compilation of the data. This is why the 501 items of data extend from August 7, 2006 to September 25, 2008. An alternative would be to try and estimate data for days that were not U.S. holidays. Dividends have been ignored to keep the example simple.

Table 20.2 U.S. dollar equivalent of stock indices for historical simulation calculation

Day	*Date*	*DJIA*	*FTSE 100*	*CAC 40*	*Nikkei 225*
0	Aug. 7, 2006	11,219.38	11,131.84	6,373.89	131.77
1	Aug. 8, 2006	11,173.59	11,096.28	6,378.16	134.38
2	Aug. 9, 2006	11,076.18	11,185.35	6,474.04	135.94
3	Aug. 10, 2006	11,124.37	11,016.71	6,357.49	135.44
⋮	⋮	⋮	⋮	⋮	⋮
499	Sept. 24, 2008	10,825.17	9,438.58	6,033.93	114.26
500	Sept. 25, 2008	11,022.06	9,599.90	6,200.40	112.82

The DJIA was 11,022.06 on September 25, 2008. On August 8, 2006, it was 11,173.59, down from 11,219.38 on August 7, 2006. Therefore the value of the DJIA under Scenario 1 is

$$11{,}022.06 \times \frac{11{,}173.59}{11{,}219.38} = 10{,}977.08$$

Similarly, the values of the FTSE 100, the CAC 40, and the Nikkei 225 are 9,569.23, 6,204.55, and 115.05, respectively. Therefore the value of the portfolio under Scenario 1 is (in \$000s)

$$4{,}000 \times \frac{10{,}977.08}{11{,}022.06} + 3{,}000 \times \frac{9{,}569.23}{9{,}599.90} + 1{,}000 \times \frac{6{,}204.55}{6{,}200.40} + 2{,}000 \times \frac{115.05}{112.82} = 10{,}014.334$$

The portfolio therefore has a gain of \$14,334 under Scenario 1. A similar calculation is carried out for the other scenarios. A histogram for the losses (with gains being negative losses) is shown in Figure 20.3. (The bars on the histogram represent losses (\$000s) in the ranges 450 to 550, 350 to 450, 250 to 350, and so on.)

The losses for the 500 different scenarios are then ranked. An extract from the results of doing this is shown in Table 20.4. The worst scenario is number 494 (where the loss is \$477,841). The one-day 99% value at risk can be estimated as the fifth-worst loss. This is \$253,385.

Table 20.3 Scenarios generated for September 26, 2008, using data in Table 20.2

Scenario number	*DJIA*	*FTSE 100*	*CAC 40*	*Nikkei 225*	*Portfolio value (\$000s)*	*Loss (\$000s)*
1	10,977.08	9,569.23	6,204.55	115.05	10,014.334	−14.334
2	10,925.97	9,676.96	6,293.60	114.13	10,027.481	−27.481
3	11,070.01	9,455.16	6,088.77	112.40	9,946.736	53.264
⋮	⋮	⋮	⋮	⋮	⋮	
499	10,831.43	9,383.49	6,051.94	113.85	9,857.465	142.535
500	11,222.53	9,763.97	6,371.45	111.40	10,126.439	−126.439

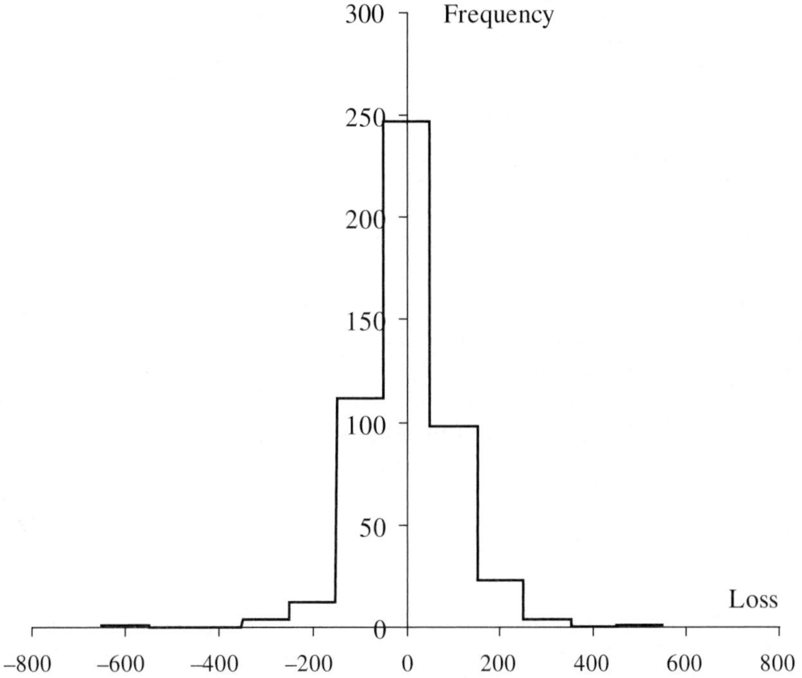

Figure 20.3 Histogram of losses for the scenarios considered between September 25 and September 26, 2008

Table 20.4 Losses ranked from highest to lowest for 500 scenarios

Scenario number	*Loss ($)*
494	477,841
339	345,435
349	282,204
329	277,041
487	253,385
227	217,974
131	202,256
238	201,389
473	191,269
306	191,050
477	185,127
495	184,450
376	182,707
237	180,105
365	172,224
⋮	⋮

As explained in Section 20.1, the ten-day 99% VaR is usually calculated as $\sqrt{10}$ times the one-day 99% VaR. In this case the ten-day VaR would therefore be

$$\sqrt{10} \times 253{,}385 = 801{,}274$$

or \$801,274.

Each day the VaR estimate in our example would be updated using the most recent 501 days of data. Consider, for example, what happens on September 26, 2008 (Day 501). We find out new values for all the market variables and are able to calculate a new value for our portfolio. We then go through the procedure we have outlined to calculate a new VaR. Data on the market variables from August 8, 2006, to September 26, 2008 (Day 1 to Day 501) are used in the calculation. (This gives us the required 500 observations on the percentage changes in market variables; the August 7, 2006, Day 0, values of the market variables are no longer used.) Similarly, on the next trading day September 29, 2008 (Day 502), data from August 9, 2006, to September 29, 2008 (Day 2 to Day 502) are used to determine VaR, and so on.

In practice, a financial institution's portfolio is, of course, considerably more complicated than the one we have considered here. It is likely to consist of thousands or even millions of positions. Some of the bank's positions are typically in forward contracts, options, and other derivatives. The VaR on any given day is calculated on the assumption that the portfolio will remain unchanged over the next business day. In practice, of course, the portfolio changes from day to day. If a bank's trading leads to a riskier porfolio, the 10-day 99% VaR typically increases; if it leads to a less risky portfolio, VaR typically decreases.

The market variables that have to be considered in a VaR calculation include exchange rates, commodity prices, and interest rates. In the case of interest rates, a bank typically needs several term structures of zero-coupon interest rates in a number of different currencies in order to value its portfolio. The market variables that are considered are the ones from which these term structures are calculated (see Chapter 4 for the calculation of the term structure of zero rates). There might be as many as ten market variables for each zero curve to which the bank is exposed.

20.3 MODEL-BUILDING APPROACH

The main alternative to historical simulation is the model-building approach (sometimes also called the variance–covariance approach). Before getting into the details of the approach, it is appropriate to mention one issue concerned with the units for measuring volatility.

Daily Volatilities

In option pricing, time is usually measured in years and the volatility of an asset is usually quoted as a "volatility per year". When using the model-building approach to calculate VaR for market risk, time is usually measured in days and the volatility of an asset is usually quoted as a "volatility per day."

What is the relationship between the volatility per year used in option pricing and the volatility per day used in VaR calculations? Let us define σ_{year} as the volatility per year of a certain asset and σ_{day} as the equivalent volatility per day of the asset. Assuming

252 trading days in a year, equation (13.4) gives the standard deviation of the continuously compounded return on the asset in one year as either σ_{year} or $\sigma_{\text{day}}\sqrt{252}$. It follows that

$$\sigma_{\text{year}} = \sigma_{\text{day}}\sqrt{252}$$

or

$$\sigma_{\text{day}} = \frac{\sigma_{\text{year}}}{\sqrt{252}}$$

so that daily volatility is about 6% of annual volatility.

The volatility σ_{day} is approximately equal to the standard deviation of the percentage change in the asset price in one trading day. For the purposes of calculating VaR, we assume exact equality. The daily volatility of an asset price (or any other variable) is therefore defined as equal to the standard deviation of the percentage change in one trading day.

Our discussion in the next few sections assumes that estimates of daily volatilities and correlations are available. Later sections discuss how the estimates can be produced.

Single-Asset Case

We now consider how VaR is calculated using the model-building approach in a very simple situation where the portfolio consists of a position in a single stock. The portfolio we consider is one consisting of \$10 million in shares of Microsoft. We suppose that $N = 10$ and $X = 99$, so that we are interested in the loss level over 10 days that we are 99% confident will not be exceeded. Initially, we consider a one-day time horizon.

Assume that the volatility of Microsoft is 2% per day (corresponding to about 32% per year). Because the size of the position is \$10 million, the standard deviation of daily changes in the value of the position is 2% of \$10 million, or \$200,000.

It is customary in the model-building approach to assume that the expected change in a market variable over the time period considered is zero. This is not exactly true, but it is a reasonable assumption. The expected change in the price of a market variable over a short time period is generally small when compared with the standard deviation of the change. Suppose, for example, that Microsoft has an expected return of 20% per annum. Over a one-day period, the expected return is 0.20/252, or about 0.08%, much less than the 2% standard deviation of the return. Over a 10-day period, the expected return is 0.08×10, or about 0.8%, whereas the standard deviation of the return is $2\sqrt{10}$, or about 6.3%.

So far, we have established that the change in the value of the portfolio of Microsoft shares over a one-day period has a standard deviation of \$200,000 and (at least approximately) a mean of zero. We assume that the change is normally distributed.[4] From the Excel NORMSINV function, $N(-2.326) = 0.01$. This means that there is a 1% probability that a normally distributed variable will decrease in value by more than 2.326 standard deviations. Equivalently, it means that we are 99% certain that a normally distributed variable will not decrease in value by more than 2.326 standard deviations.

[4] To be consistent with the option pricing assumption in Chapter 13, we could assume that the price of Microsoft is lognormal tomorrow. Because one day is such a short period of time, this is almost indistinguishable from the assumption we do make—that the change in the stock price between today and tomorrow is normal.

Therefore the one-day 99% VaR for our portfolio consisting of a \$10 million position in Microsoft is

$$2.326 \times 200{,}000 = \$465{,}300$$

As discussed earlier, the N-day VaR is calculated as $\sqrt{N}$ times the one-day VaR. The 10-day 99% VaR for Microsoft is therefore

$$465{,}300 \times \sqrt{10} = \$1{,}471{,}300$$

Consider next a portfolio consisting of a \$5 million position in AT&T, and suppose the daily volatility of AT&T is 1% (approximately 16% per year). A similar calculation to that for Microsoft shows that the standard deviation of the change in the value of the portfolio in one day is

$$5{,}000{,}000 \times 0.01 = 50{,}000$$

Assuming the change is normally distributed, the one-day 99% VaR is

$$50{,}000 \times 2.326 = \$116{,}300$$

and the 10-day 99% VaR is

$$116{,}300 \times \sqrt{10} = \$367{,}800$$

Two-Asset Case

Now consider a portfolio consisting of both \$10 million of Microsoft shares and \$5 million of AT&T shares. We suppose that the returns on the two shares have a bivariate normal distribution with a correlation of 0.3. A standard result in statistics tells us that, if two variables X and Y have standard deviations equal to σ_X and σ_Y, with the coefficient of correlation between them being equal to ρ, then the standard deviation of $X + Y$ is given by

$$\sigma_{X+Y} = \sqrt{\sigma_X^2 + \sigma_Y^2 + 2\rho\sigma_X\sigma_Y}$$

To apply this result, we set X equal to the change in the value of the position in Microsoft over a one-day period and Y equal to the change in the value of the position in AT&T over a one-day period, so that

$$\sigma_X = 200{,}000, \qquad \sigma_Y = 50{,}000$$

Therefore the standard deviation of the change in the value of the portfolio consisting of both stocks over a one-day period is

$$\sqrt{200{,}000^2 + 50{,}000^2 + 2 \times 0.3 \times 200{,}000 \times 50{,}000} = 220{,}200$$

The change is normally distributed and the mean change is assumed to be zero. So the one-day 99% VaR is

$$220{,}200 \times 2.326 = \$512{,}300$$

The 10-day 99% VaR is $\sqrt{10}$ times this or \$1,620,100. The calculations are summarized in Example 20.1.

Example 20.1 Calculation of VaR in a simple situation

A company has a portfolio consisting of \$10 million invested in Microsoft and \$5 million invested in AT&T. The daily volatility of Microsoft is 2%, the daily volatility of AT&T is 1%, and the coefficient of correlation between the returns from Microsoft and AT&T is 0.3.

Calculation of VaR

1. The standard deviation of the change in value of the Microsoft position per day is $10{,}000{,}000 \times 0.02 = \$200{,}000$.
2. The standard deviation of the change in value of the AT&T position per day is $5{,}000{,}000 \times 0.01 = \$50{,}000$.
3. The standard deviation of the change in the portfolio value per day is therefore:

$$\sqrt{200{,}000^2 + 50{,}000^2 + 2 \times 0.3 \times 200{,}000 \times 50{,}000} = 220{,}200$$

4. The one-day 99% VaR is therefore:

$$220{,}200 \times 2.326 = \$512{,}300$$

5. The 10-day 99% VaR is $\sqrt{10} \times 512{,}300$, or \$1,620,100.

The Benefits of Diversification

In the example we have just considered:

1. The 10-day 99% VaR for the portfolio of Microsoft shares is \$1,471,300.
2. The 10-day 99% VaR for the portfolio of AT&T shares is \$367,800.
3. The 10-day 99% VaR for the portfolio of both Microsoft and AT&T shares is \$1,620,100.

The amount

$$(1{,}471{,}300 + 367{,}800) - 1{,}620{,}100 = \$219{,}000$$

represents the benefits of diversification. If Microsoft and AT&T were perfectly correlated, the VaR for the portfolio of both Microsoft and AT&T would equal the VaR for the Microsoft portfolio plus the VaR for the AT&T portfolio. Less than perfect correlation leads to some of the risk being "diversified away."[5]

20.4 GENERALIZATION OF LINEAR MODEL

The examples we have just considered are simple illustrations of the use of the linear model for calculating VaR. Suppose that we have a portfolio worth P consisting of n assets with an amount α_i being invested in asset i ($1 \leqslant i \leqslant n$). Define Δx_i as the return on asset i in one day. The dollar change in the value of our investment in asset i in one

[5] Harry Markowitz was one of the first researchers to study the benefits of diversification to a portfolio manager. He was awarded a Nobel prize for this research in 1990. See H. Markowitz, "Portfolio Selection," *Journal of Finance* 7, no. 1 (March 1952): 77–91.

day is $\alpha_i\,\Delta x_i$ and

$$\Delta P = \sum_{i=1}^{n} \alpha_i\,\Delta x_i \tag{20.1}$$

where ΔP is the dollar change in the value of the whole portfolio in one day.

In the example considered in the previous section, \$10 million was invested in the first asset (Microsoft) and \$5 million was invested in the second asset (AT&T), so that (in millions of dollars) $\alpha_1 = 10$, $\alpha_2 = 5$, and

$$\Delta P = 10\Delta x_1 + 5\Delta x_2$$

If we assume that the Δx_i in equation (20.1) are multivariate normal, then ΔP is normally distributed. To calculate VaR, we therefore need to calculate only the mean and standard deviation of ΔP. We assume, as discussed in the previous section, that the expected value of each Δx_i is zero. This implies that the mean of ΔP is zero.

To calculate the standard deviation of ΔP, we define σ_i as the daily volatility of the ith asset and ρ_{ij} as the coefficient of correlation between returns on asset i and asset j. This means that σ_i is the standard deviation of Δx_i, and ρ_{ij} is the coefficient of correlation between Δx_i and Δx_j. The variance of ΔP, which we will denote by σ_P^2, is given by

$$\sigma_P^2 = \sum_{i=1}^{n}\sum_{j=1}^{n} \rho_{ij}\,\alpha_i\,\alpha_j\,\sigma_i\,\sigma_j \tag{20.2}$$

This equation can also be written as

$$\sigma_P^2 = \sum_{i=1}^{n} \alpha_i^2\sigma_i^2 + 2\sum_{i=1}^{n}\sum_{j<i} \rho_{ij}\,\alpha_i\,\alpha_j\,\sigma_i\,\sigma_j$$

The standard deviation of the change over N days is $\sigma_P\sqrt{N}$, and the 99% VaR for an N-day time horizon is $2.33\sigma_P\sqrt{N}$.

The portfolio return in one day is $\Delta P/P$. From equation (20.2), the variance of this is

$$\sum_{i=1}^{n}\sum_{j=1}^{n} \rho_{ij}\,w_i\,w_j\,\sigma_i\,\sigma_j$$

where $w_i = \alpha_i/P$ is the weight of the ith investment in the portfolio. This version of equation (20.2) is the one usually used by portfolio managers.

In the example considered in the previous section, $\sigma_1 = 0.02$, $\sigma_2 = 0.01$, and $\rho_{12} = 0.3$. As already noted, $\alpha_1 = 10$ and $\alpha_2 = 5$, so that

$$\sigma_P^2 = 10^2 \times 0.02^2 + 5^2 \times 0.01^2 + 2 \times 10 \times 5 \times 0.3 \times 0.02 \times 0.01 = 0.0485$$

and $\sigma_P = 0.2202$. This is the standard deviation of the change in the portfolio value per day (in millions of dollars). The ten-day 99% VaR is $2.326 \times 0.2202 \times \sqrt{10} =$ \$1.62 million. This agrees with the calculation in the previous section.

Correlation and Covariance Matrices

A correlation matrix is a matrix where the entry in the ith row and jth column is the correlation ρ_{ij} between variable i and j. It is shown in Table 20.5. Since a variable is always perfectly correlated with itself, the diagonal elements of the correlation matrix are 1. Furthermore, because $\rho_{ij} = \rho_{ji}$, the correlation matrix is symmetric. The correlation matrix, together with the daily standard deviations of the variables, enables the portfolio variance to be calculated using equation (20.2).

Instead of working with correlations and volatilities, analysts often use variances and covariances. The daily variance var_i of variable i is the square of its daily volatility:

$$\text{var}_i = \sigma_i^2$$

The covariance cov_{ij} between variable i and variable j is the product of the daily volatility of variable i, the daily volatility of variable j, and the correlation between i and j:

$$\text{cov}_{ij} = \sigma_i \sigma_j \rho_{ij}$$

The equation for the variance of the portfolio in equation (20.2) can be written

$$\sigma_P^2 = \sum_{i=1}^{n} \sum_{j=1}^{n} \text{cov}_{ij}\, \alpha_i \alpha_j \tag{20.3}$$

In a *covariance matrix*, the entry in the ith row and jth column is the covariance between variable i and variable j. As just mentioned, the covariance between a variable and itself is its variance. The diagonal entries in the matrix are therefore variances (see Table 20.6). For this reason, the covariance matrix is sometimes called the *variance–covariance matrix*. (Like the correlation matrix, it is symmetric.) Using matrix notation,

Table 20.5 A correlation matrix: ρ_{ij} is the correlation between variable i and variable j

$$\begin{bmatrix} 1 & \rho_{12} & \rho_{13} & \cdots & \rho_{1n} \\ \rho_{21} & 1 & \rho_{23} & \cdots & \rho_{2n} \\ \rho_{31} & \rho_{32} & 1 & \cdots & \rho_{3n} \\ \vdots & \vdots & \vdots & \vdots & \vdots \\ \rho_{n1} & \rho_{n2} & \rho_{n3} & \cdots & 1 \end{bmatrix}$$

Table 20.6 A variance–covariance matrix: cov_{ij} is the covariance between variable i and variable j. Diagonal entries are variance: $\text{cov}_{ii} = \text{var}_i$

$$\begin{bmatrix} \text{var}_1 & \text{cov}_{12} & \text{cov}_{13} & \cdots & \text{cov}_{1n} \\ \text{cov}_{21} & \text{var}_2 & \text{cov}_{23} & \cdots & \text{cov}_{2n} \\ \text{cov}_{31} & \text{cov}_{32} & \text{var}_3 & \cdots & \text{cov}_{3n} \\ \vdots & \vdots & \vdots & \vdots & \vdots \\ \text{cov}_{n1} & \text{cov}_{n2} & \text{cov}_{n3} & \cdots & \text{var}_n \end{bmatrix}$$

the equation for the variance of the portfolio in equation (20.3) becomes

$$\sigma_P^2 = \boldsymbol{\alpha}^{\mathsf{T}} C \boldsymbol{\alpha}$$

where $\boldsymbol{\alpha}$ is the (column) vector whose ith element is α_i, C is the variance–covariance matrix, and $\boldsymbol{\alpha}^{\mathsf{T}}$ is the transpose of $\boldsymbol{\alpha}$.

The variances and covariances are generally calculated from historical data. We will illustrate this later in the chapter for the four-index example introduced in Section 20.2.

Handling Interest Rates

It is out of the question in the model-building approach to define a separate market variable for every single bond price or interest rate to which a company is exposed. Some simplifications are necessary. The usual approach is to choose as market variables the prices of zero-coupon bonds with standard maturities: 1 month, 3 months, 6 months, 1 year, 2 years, 5 years, 7 years, 10 years, and 30 years. For the purposes of calculating VaR, the cash flows from instruments in the portfolio are mapped into cash flows occurring on the standard maturity dates. Consider a \$1 million position in a Treasury bond lasting 1.2 years that pays a coupon of 6% semiannually. Coupons are paid in 0.2, 0.7, and 1.2 years, and the principal is paid in 1.2 years. This bond is therefore, in the first instance, regarded as a \$30,000 position in 0.2-year zero-coupon bond plus a \$30,000 position in a 0.7-year zero-coupon bond plus a \$1.03 million position in a 1.2-year zero-coupon bond. The position in the 0.2-year bond is then replaced by an approximately equivalent position in 1-month and 3-month zero-coupon bonds; the position in the 0.7-year bond is replaced by an approximately equivalent position in 6-month and 1-year zero-coupon bonds; and the position in the 1.2-year bond is replaced by an approximately equivalent position in 1-year and 2-year zero-coupon bonds. The result is that the position in the 1.2-year coupon-bearing bond is, for VaR purposes, regarded as a position in zero-coupon bonds having maturities of 1 month, 3 months, 6 months, 1 year, and 2 years.

This procedure is known as *cash-flow mapping*. One way of doing it is explained on www.rotman.utoronto.ca/~hull/Fundamentals/cashflowmapping. Note that cash-flow mapping is not necessary when the historical simulation approach is used. This is because the complete term structure of interest rates can be estimated using the bootstrap method for each of the scenarios considered.

Applications of the Linear Model

The simplest application of the linear model is to a portfolio with no derivatives consisting of positions in stocks, bonds, foreign exchange, and commodities. In this case the change in the value of the portfolio is linearly dependent on the percentage changes in the prices of the assets comprising the portfolio. As already mentioned, for the purposes of VaR calculations, all asset prices are measured in the domestic currency. The market variables considered by a large bank in the United States are therefore likely to include the value of the Nikkei 225 index in dollars, the price of a 10-year sterling zero-coupon bond measured in dollars, and so on.

An example of a derivative that can be handled by the linear model is a forward contract to buy a foreign currency. Suppose the contract matures at time T. It can be regarded as the exchange of a foreign zero-coupon bond maturing at time T for a domestic zero-coupon bond maturing at time T. For the purposes of calculating VaR, the forward contract is therefore treated as a long position in the foreign bond combined with a short position in the domestic bond. Each bond can be handled using the cash-flow mapping procedure outlined above.

Consider next an interest rate swap. As explained in Chapter 7, this can be regarded as the exchange of a floating-rate bond for a fixed-rate bond. The fixed-rate bond is a regular coupon-bearing bond. The floating-rate bond is worth par just after the next payment date. It can be regarded as a zero-coupon bond with a maturity date equal to the next payment date. Therefore, the interest rate swap reduces to a portfolio of long and short positions in bonds and can be handled using the cash-flow mapping procedure outlined above.

The Linear Model and Options

We now consider how we might try to use the linear model when there are options. Consider first a portfolio consisting of options on a single stock whose current price is S. Suppose that the delta of the position (calculated in the way described in Chapter 17) is δ.[6] Because δ is the rate of change of the value of the portfolio with S, it is approximately true that

$$\delta = \frac{\Delta P}{\Delta S}$$

so that

$$\Delta P = \delta\,\Delta S \tag{20.4}$$

where ΔS is the dollar change in the stock price in one day and ΔP is, as usual, the dollar change in the portfolio in one day. Define Δx as the percentage change in the stock price in one day:

$$\Delta x = \frac{\Delta S}{S}$$

It follows that an approximate relationship between ΔP and Δx is

$$\Delta P = S\delta\,\Delta x$$

When we have a position in several underlying market variables that includes options, we can derive an approximate linear relationship between ΔP and the Δx_i similarly. This relationship is

$$\Delta P = \sum_{i=1}^{n} S_i\delta_i\,\Delta x_i \tag{20.5}$$

where S_i is the value of the ith market variable and δ_i is the delta of the portfolio with respect to the ith market variable. This corresponds to equation (20.1):

$$\Delta P = \sum_{i=1}^{n} w_i\,\Delta x_i$$

with $w_i = S_i\delta_i$. Equation (20.2) or (20.3) can therefore be used to calculate the standard deviation of ΔP. This is illustrated in Example 20.2.

[6] Normally we denote the delta and gamma of a portfolio by Δ and Γ. In this section and the next one, we use the lower case Greek letters δ and γ to avoid overworking Δ.

Example 20.2 Using the linear model for options

A portfolio consists of options on Microsoft and AT&T. The options on Microsoft have a delta of 1,000, and the options on AT&T have a delta of 20,000. The Microsoft share price is \$120, and the AT&T share price is \$30. From equation (20.5), it is approximately true that

$$\Delta P = 120 \times 1{,}000 \times \Delta x_1 + 30 \times 20{,}000 \times \Delta x_2$$

or

$$\Delta P = 120{,}000\Delta x_1 + 600{,}000\Delta x_2$$

where Δx_1 and Δx_2 are the returns from Microsoft and AT&T in one day and ΔP is the resultant change in the value of the portfolio. (The portfolio is assumed to be equivalent to an investment of \$120,000 in Microsoft and \$600,000 in AT&T.) Assuming that the daily volatility of Microsoft is 2% and the daily volatility of AT&T is 1%, and the correlation between the daily changes is 0.3, the standard deviation of ΔP (in thousands of dollars) is

$$\sqrt{(120 \times 0.02)^2 + (600 \times 0.01)^2 + 2 \times 120 \times 0.02 \times 600 \times 0.01 \times 0.3} = 7.099$$

Because $N(-1.645) = 0.05$, the 5-day 95% value at risk is

$$1.645 \times \sqrt{5} \times 7{,}099 = \$26{,}110$$

20.5 QUADRATIC MODEL

When a portfolio includes options, the linear model is an approximation. It does not take account of the gamma of the portfolio. As discussed in Chapter 17, delta is defined as the rate of change of the portfolio value with respect to an underlying market variable and gamma is defined as the rate of change of the delta with respect to the market variable. Gamma measures the curvature of the relationship between the portfolio value and an underlying market variable.

Figure 20.4 shows the impact of a nonzero gamma on the probability distribution of the value of the portfolio. When gamma is positive, the probability distribution of ΔP

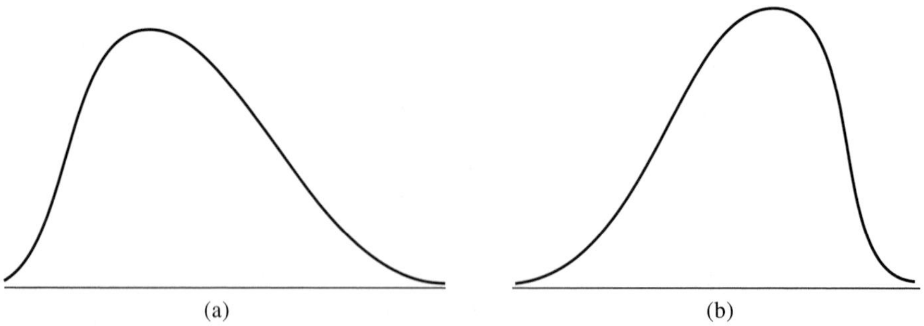

Figure 20.4 Probability distribution for value of portfolio: (a) positive gamma, (b) negative gamma

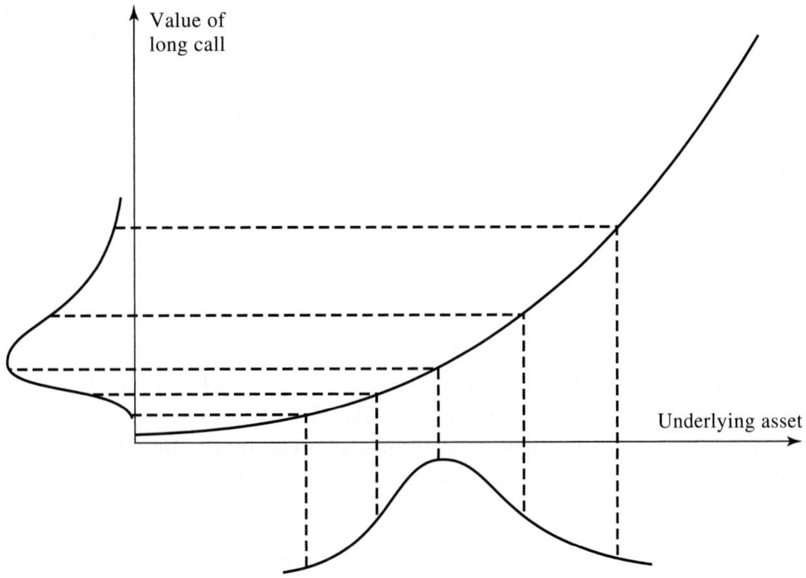

Figure 20.5 Translation of normal probability distribution for asset into probability distribution for value of a long call on asset

tends to be positively skewed; when gamma is negative, it tends to be negatively skewed. Figures 20.5 and 20.6 illustrate the reason for this result. Figure 20.5 shows the relationship between the value of a long call option and the price of the underlying asset. A long call is an example of an option position with positive gamma. The figure shows that, when the probability distribution for the price of the underlying asset at the end of one day is normal, the probability distribution for the option price

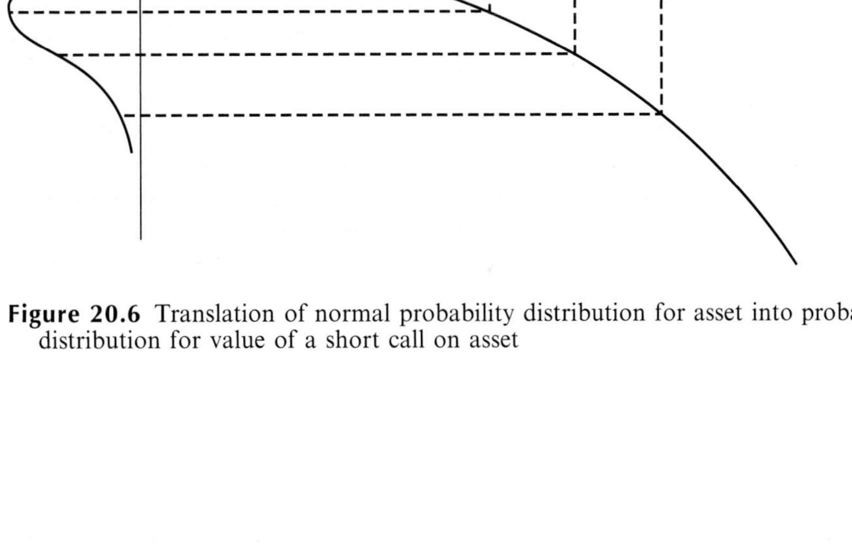

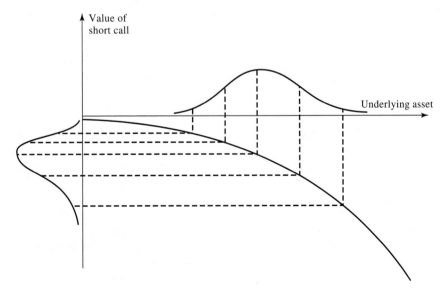

Figure 20.6 Translation of normal probability distribution for asset into probability distribution for value of a short call on asset

is positively skewed.[7] Figure 20.6 shows the relationship between the value of a short call position and the price of the underlying asset. A short call position has a negative gamma. In this case we see that a normal distribution for the price of the underlying asset at the end of one day gets mapped into a negatively skewed distribution for the value of the option position.

The VaR for a portfolio is critically dependent on the left tail of the probability distribution of ΔP. For example, when the confidence level used is 99%, the VaR is calculated as the value in the left tail below which there is only 1% of the distribution. As indicated in Figures 20.4a and 20.5, a positive gamma portfolio tends to have a less heavy left tail than the normal distribution. If the distribution of ΔP is normal, the calculated VaR tends to be too high. Similarly, as indicated in Figures 20.4b and 20.6, a negative gamma portfolio tends to have a heavier left tail than the normal distribution. If the distribution of ΔP is normal, the calculated VaR tends to be too low.

For a more accurate estimate of VaR than that given by the linear model, both delta and gamma measures can be used to relate ΔP to the Δx_i. Consider a portfolio dependent on a single asset whose price is S. Suppose that the delta of a portfolio is δ and its gamma is γ. An improvement over the approximation in equation (20.4) is

$$\Delta P = \delta\,\Delta S + \tfrac{1}{2}\gamma(\Delta S)^2$$

Setting

$$\Delta x = \frac{\Delta S}{S}$$

reduces this to

$$\Delta P = S\delta\,\Delta x + \tfrac{1}{2}S^2\gamma(\Delta x)^2 \tag{20.6}$$

A similar quadratic equation relating ΔP to the Δx_i applies when there is more than one market variable. One approach to calculating VaR is to use Monte Carlo simulation. This is similar to the historical simulation approach described in Section 20.2, except that alternative movements in market variables are sampled from an assumed multivariate distribution instead of being calculated from historical data.

In the case of both historical simulation and Monte Carlo simulation, a quadratic approximation similar to equation (20.6) is often used to save computation time.

20.6 ESTIMATING VOLATILITIES AND CORRELATIONS

The model-building approach requires daily volatilities for all market variables and correlations between each pair of market variables. We now consider how these can be obtained.

In this section, we define σ_n as the volatility per day of a market variable on day n, as estimated at the end of day $n-1$. (This is a change of notation. Earlier in this chapter, σ_n was used to denote the volatility of the nth variable.) The square of the volatility, σ_n^2, on day n is the *variance rate*. The standard approach to estimating σ_n from historical data is described in Section 13.4. Suppose that the value of the market variable at the

[7] As mentioned in footnote 4, we can use the normal distribution as an approximation to the lognormal distribution in VaR calculations.

end of day i is S_i. The variable u_i is defined as the continuously compounded return during day i (between the end of day $i-1$ and the end of day i):

$$u_i = \ln\frac{S_i}{S_{i-1}}$$

An unbiased estimate σ_n^2 of the variance rate per day, using the most recent m observations on the u_i, is given by

$$\sigma_n^2 = \frac{1}{m-1}\sum_{i=1}^{m}(u_{n-i}-\bar{u})^2 \qquad \textbf{(20.7)}$$

where $\bar{u}$ is the mean of the u_i:

$$\bar{u} = \frac{1}{m}\sum_{i=1}^{m}u_{n-i}$$

For the purposes of monitoring volatility, the formula in equation (20.7) is usually changed in a number of ways:

1. u_i is defined as the percentage change in the market variable between the end of day $i-1$ and the end of day i, so that[8]

$$u_i = \frac{S_i - S_{i-1}}{S_{i-1}} \qquad \textbf{(20.8)}$$

2. $\bar{u}$ is assumed to be zero.[9]
3. $m-1$ is replaced by m.

These three changes make very little difference to the variance estimates that are calculated. They result in equation (20.7) being replaced by

$$\sigma_n^2 = \frac{1}{m}\sum_{i=1}^{m}u_{n-i}^2 \qquad \textbf{(20.9)}$$

where u_i is given by equation (20.8).

EWMA

Equation (20.9) gives equal weight to $u_{n-1}^2, u_{n-2}^2, \ldots, u_{n-m}^2$. Given that the objective is to monitor the current level of volatility, it is appropriate to give more weight to recent data. A model that does this is

$$\sigma_n^2 = \sum_{i=1}^{m}\alpha_i u_{n-i}^2 \qquad \textbf{(20.10)}$$

The variable α_i is the amount of weight given to the observation i days ago. The α's are

[8] This is consistent with the point made in Section 20.3 about the way that volatility is defined for the purposes of VaR calculations.

[9] As explained in Section 20.3, this assumption usually has very little effect on estimates of the variance because the expected change in a variable in one day is very small when compared with the standard deviation of changes. As an alternative to the assumption, we can define u_i as the realized return minus the expected return on day i.

positive. Because we wish to give less weight to older observations, $\alpha_i < \alpha_j$ when $i > j$. The weights must sum to unity, so that

$$\sum_{i=1}^{m} \alpha_i = 1$$

The exponentially weighted moving average (EWMA) model is a particular case of the model in equation (20.10) where the weights, α_i, decrease exponentially as we move back through time. Specifically, $\alpha_{i+1} = \lambda \alpha_i$, where λ is a constant between zero and one.

It turns out that this weighting procedure leads to a particularly simple formula for updating volatility estimates. The formula is

$$\sigma_n^2 = \lambda \sigma_{n-1}^2 + (1 - \lambda) u_{n-1}^2 \qquad \textbf{(20.11)}$$

The estimate σ_n of the volatility of a variable for day n (made at the end of day $n - 1$) is calculated from σ_{n-1} (the estimate that was made at the end of day $n - 2$) and u_{n-1} (the most recent daily percent change in the variable). Example 20.3 provides an application of equation (20.11).

To understand why equation (20.11) corresponds to weights that decrease exponentially, we substitute for σ_{n-1}^2, to get

$$\sigma_n^2 = \lambda[\lambda \sigma_{n-2}^2 + (1 - \lambda) u_{n-2}^2] + (1 - \lambda) u_{n-1}^2$$

or

$$\sigma_n^2 = (1 - \lambda)(u_{n-1}^2 + \lambda u_{n-2}^2) + \lambda^2 \sigma_{n-2}^2$$

Substituting in a similar way for σ_{n-2}^2 gives

$$\sigma_n^2 = (1 - \lambda)(u_{n-1}^2 + \lambda u_{n-2}^2 + \lambda^2 u_{n-3}^2) + \lambda^3 \sigma_{n-3}^2$$

Continuing in this way, we obtain

$$\sigma_n^2 = (1 - \lambda) \sum_{i=1}^{m} \lambda^{i-1} u_{n-i}^2 + \lambda^m \sigma_{n-m}^2$$

For large m, the term $\lambda^m \sigma_{n-m}^2$ is sufficiently small to be ignored, so that equation (20.11) is the same as equation (20.10) with $\alpha_i = (1 - \lambda)\lambda^{i-1}$. The weights for the u_i decline at rate λ as we move back through time. Each weight is λ times the previous weight.

The EWMA approach has the attractive feature that relatively little data need to be stored. At any given time, only the current estimate of the variance rate and the most recent observation on the value of the market variable need be remembered. When a new observation on the value of the market variable is obtained, a new u^2 is calculated and equation (20.11) is used to update the estimate of the variance rate. The old estimate of the variance rate and the old value of the market variable can then be discarded.

The EWMA approach is designed to track changes in the volatility. Suppose there is a big move in the market variable on day $n - 1$, so that u_{n-1}^2 is large. From equation (20.11), this causes σ_n, the estimate of the daily volatility for day n, to move upward. The value of λ governs how responsive the estimate of the daily volatility is to the most recent observation on the daily change. A low value of λ leads to a great deal of weight being given to the u_{n-1}^2 when σ_n is calculated. In this case, the estimates produced for the volatility on successive days are themselves highly volatile. A high value of λ (i.e., a value

Example 20.3 Updating volatility using EWMA

The EWMA parameter λ is 0.90, the volatility estimated for day $n-1$ is 1% per day, and the change in the market variable during day $n-1$ is 2%. In this case, $\sigma_{n-1}^2 = 0.01^2 = 0.0001$ and $u_{n-1}^2 = 0.02^2 = 0.0004$. Equation (20.11) gives

$$\sigma_n^2 = 0.9 \times 0.0001 + 0.1 \times 0.0004 = 0.00013$$

The estimate σ_n of the volatility for day n, therefore, is $\sqrt{0.00013}$, or 1.14% per day. Note that the expected value of u_{n-1}^2 is σ_{n-1}^2 or 0.0001. In this example, the realized value of u_{n-1}^2 is greater than the expected value, and as a result the volatility estimate increases. If the realized value of u_{n-1}^2 had been less than its expected value, the estimate of the volatility would have decreased.

close to 1.0) produces estimates of the daily volatility that respond relatively slowly to new information provided by the daily changes.

Correlations

Consider two different market variables, U and V. We define u_i and v_i as the percentage changes in U and V between the end of day $i-1$ and the end of day i:

$$u_i = \frac{U_i - U_{i-1}}{U_{i-1}}, \qquad v_i = \frac{V_i - V_{i-1}}{V_{i-1}}$$

where U_i and V_i are the values of U and V at the end of day i. We also define:

$\sigma_{u,n}$: Daily volatility of variable U, estimated for day n

$\sigma_{v,n}$: Daily volatility of variable V, estimated for day n

cov_n: Estimate of covariance between daily changes in U and V for day n

As mentioned earlier, the covariance is the coefficient of correlation times the product of the volatilities. As a result, the estimate of the correlation between U and V for day n is

$$\frac{\text{cov}_n}{\sigma_{u,n}\sigma_{v,n}}$$

Using equal weights and assuming that the means of u_i and v_i are zero, equation (20.8) shows that the variance rates of U and V can be estimated from the most recent m observations as

$$\sigma_{u,n}^2 = \frac{1}{m}\sum_{i=1}^{m} u_{n-i}^2 \quad \text{and} \quad \sigma_{v,n}^2 = \frac{1}{m}\sum_{i=1}^{m} v_{n-i}^2$$

A similar estimate for the covariance between U and V is

$$\text{cov}_n = \frac{1}{m}\sum_{i=1}^{m} u_{n-i}v_{n-i} \qquad \textbf{(20.12)}$$

An alternative is an EWMA model similar to equation (20.11). The formula for

Example 20.4 Updating correlation using EWMA

The EWMA parameter λ is 0.95 and the estimate of the correlation between two variables U and V on day $n-1$ is 0.6. The estimate of the volatilities of U and V on day $n-1$ are 1% and 2%, respectively. The actual changes in U and V on day $n-1$ are 0.5% and 2.5%, respectively. In this case, from the relationship between correlation and covariance, the estimate of the covariance between the U and V on day $n-1$ is

$$0.6 \times 0.01 \times 0.02 = 0.00012$$

The variance and covariance for day n are calculated as follows:

$$\sigma_{u,n}^2 = 0.95 \times 0.01^2 + 0.05 \times 0.005^2 = 0.00009625$$
$$\sigma_{v,n}^2 = 0.95 \times 0.02^2 + 0.05 \times 0.025^2 = 0.00041125$$
$$\text{cov}_n = 0.95 \times 0.00012 + 0.05 \times 0.005 \times 0.025 = 0.00012025$$

The new volatility of U is $\sqrt{0.00009625} = 0.981\%$ and the new volatility of V is $\sqrt{0.00041125} = 2.028\%$. The new coefficient of correlation between U and V is

$$\frac{0.00012025}{0.00981 \times 0.02028} = 0.6044$$

updating the covariance estimate is then

$$\text{cov}_n = \lambda\,\text{cov}_{n-1} + (1-\lambda)u_{n-1}v_{n-1} \tag{20.13}$$

A similar analysis to that presented for the EWMA volatility model shows that the weights given to observations on the $u_i v_i$ decline as we move back through time. The lower the value of λ, the greater the weight that is given to recent observations. Example 20.4 provides an application of equation (20.13).

Example Involving Four Stock Indices

We now return to the example considered in Section 20.2. This involved a portfolio on September 25, 2008, consisting of a \$4 million investment in the Dow Jones Industrial Average, a \$3 million investment in the FTSE 100, a \$1 million investment in the CAC 40, and a \$2 million investment in the Nikkei 225. Daily returns were collected over 500 days ending on September 25, 2008. Data and all calculations presented here can be found at: www.rotman.utoronto.ca/~hull/Fundamentals/VaRExample.

Table 20.7 Correlation matrix on September 25, 2008, calculated by giving equal weight to the last 500 daily returns: variable 1 is DJIA; variable 2 is FTSE 100; variable 3 is CAC 40; variable 4 is Nikkei 225

$$\begin{bmatrix} 1 & 0.489 & 0.496 & -0.062 \\ 0.489 & 1 & 0.918 & 0.201 \\ 0.496 & 0.918 & 1 & 0.211 \\ -0.062 & 0.201 & 0.211 & 1 \end{bmatrix}$$

Table 20.8 Covariance matrix on September 25, 2008, calculated by giving equal weight to the last 500 daily returns: variable 1 is DJIA; variable 2 is FTSE 100; variable 3 is CAC 40; variable 4 is Nikkei 225

$$\begin{bmatrix} 0.0001227 & 0.0000768 & 0.0000767 & -0.0000095 \\ 0.0000768 & 0.0002010 & 0.0001817 & 0.0000394 \\ 0.0000767 & 0.0001817 & 0.0001950 & 0.0000407 \\ -0.0000095 & 0.0000394 & 0.0000407 & 0.0001909 \end{bmatrix}$$

The correlation matrix that would be calculated on September 25, 2008, by giving equal weight to the last 500 returns is shown in Table 20.7. The FTSE 100 and CAC 40 are very highly correlated. The Dow Jones Industrial Average is moderately highly correlated with both the FTSE 100 and the CAC 40. The correlation of the Nikkei 225 with other indices is less high.

The covariance matrix for the equal-weight case is shown in Table 20.8. From equation (20.3), this matrix gives the variance of the portfolio losses ($000s) as 8,761.833. The standard deviation is the square root of this, or 93.60. The one-day 99% VaR is therefore $2.33 \times 93.60 = 217{,}757$, or $217,757. This compares with $253,385, calculated using the historical simulation approach in Section 20.2.

Use of EWMA

Instead of calculating variances and covariances by giving equal weight to all observed returns, we now use the exponentially weighted moving average method with $\lambda = 0.94$. This gives the variance–covariance matrix in Table 20.9.[10] From equation (20.3), the variance of portfolio losses ($000s) is 40,995.765. The standard deviation is the square root of this, or 202.474. The one-day 99% VaR is therefore

$$2.33 \times 202.474 = 471.025$$

or $471,025. This is over twice as high as the value given when returns are equally weighted. Tables 20.10 and 20.11 show the reasons. The standard deviation of a portfolio consisting of long positions in securities increases with the standard deviations of security returns and also with the correlations between security returns. Table 20.10 shows that the estimated daily standard deviations are much higher when EWMA is

Table 20.9 Covariance matrix on September 25, 2008, calculated using the EWMA method with $\lambda = 0.94$: variable 1 is DJIA; variable 2 is FTSE 100; variable 3 is CAC 40; variable 4 is Nikkei 225

$$\begin{bmatrix} 0.0004801 & 0.0004303 & 0.0004257 & -0.0000396 \\ 0.0004303 & 0.0010314 & 0.0009630 & 0.0002095 \\ 0.0004257 & 0.0009630 & 0.0009535 & 0.0001681 \\ -0.0000396 & 0.0002095 & 0.0001681 & 0.0002541 \end{bmatrix}$$

[10] In the EWMA calculations, the variance is initially set equal to the population variance. But all reasonable starting variances give essentially the same result because in this case all we are interested in is the final variance.

Table 20.10 Volatilities (% per day) using equal weighting and EWMA

	DJIA	*FTSE 100*	*CAC 40*	*Nikkei 225*
Equal weighting:	1.11	1.42	1.40	1.38
EWMA:	2.19	3.21	3.09	1.59

used than when data are equally weighted. This is because volatilities were much higher during the period immediately preceding September 25, 2008, than during the rest of the 500 days covered by the data. Comparing Table 20.11 with Table 20.7, we see that correlations had also increased.[11]

20.7 COMPARISON OF APPROACHES

We have discussed two methods for estimating VaR: the historical simulation approach and the model-building approach. The advantages of the model-building approach are that results can be produced very quickly and it can easily be used in conjunction with volatility updating procedures such as EWMA. The main disadvantage of the model-building approach is that it assumes that the market variables have a multivariate normal distribution. In practice, daily changes in market variables often have distributions that are quite different from normal (see, for example, Table 19.1). It is also the case that the model-building approach tends to give poor results for low-delta portfolios.

The historical simulation approach has the advantage that historical data determine the joint probability distribution of the market variables. It also avoids the need for cash-flow mapping. The main disadvantages of historical simulation are that it is computationally slow and does not easily allow volatility updating to be used.

20.8 STRESS TESTING AND BACK TESTING

In addition to calculating VaR, financial institutions carry out what is known as *stress testing*. This involves estimating how a portfolio would have performed under extreme market conditions. The extreme conditions can be generated by senior management or from historical data.

For example, to test the impact of an extreme movement in U.S. equity prices, a company might set the percentage changes in all market variables equal to those on

Table 20.11 Correlation matrix on September 25, 2008, calculated using the EWMA method: variable 1 is DJIA; variable 2 is FTSE 100; variable 3 is CAC 40; variable 4 is Nikkei 225

$$\begin{bmatrix} 1 & 0.611 & 0.629 & -0.113 \\ 0.611 & 1 & 0.971 & 0.409 \\ 0.629 & 0.971 & 1 & 0.342 \\ -0.113 & 0.409 & 0.342 & 1 \end{bmatrix}$$

[11] This is an example of the phenomenon that correlations tend to increase in adverse market conditions.

October 19, 1987, when the S&P 500 moved by 22.3 standard deviations. If this is considered to be too extreme, the company might choose January 8, 1988, when the S&P 500 moved by 6.8 standard deviations. To test the effect of extreme movements in U.K. interest rates, the company might set the percentage changes in all market variables equal to those on April 10, 1992, when 10-year bond yields moved by 7.7 standard deviations.

Stress testing can be considered as a way of taking into account extreme events that do occur from time to time but are virtually impossible according to the probability distributions assumed for market variables. A 5-standard-deviation daily move in a market variable is one such extreme event. Under the assumption of a normal distribution, it happens about once every 7,000 years, but, in practice, it is not uncommon to see a 5-standard-deviation daily move once or twice every 10 years.

Following the credit crisis that started in 2007, regulators have proposed the calculation of what is referred to as *stressed VaR*. This is VaR based on how market variables moved during a stressed period of one year (such as 2008).

Whatever the method used for calculating VaR, an important reality check is *back testing*. It involves testing how well the VaR estimates would have performed in the past. Suppose that we are calculating a one-day 99% VaR. Back testing would involve looking at how often the loss in a day exceeded the one-day 99% VaR calculated for that day. If this happened on about 1% of the days, we can feel reasonably comfortable with the methodology for calculating VaR. If it happened on, say, 7% of days, the methodology is suspect.

SUMMARY

A value at risk (VaR) calculation is aimed at making a statement of the form: "We are X percent certain that we will not lose more than V dollars in the next N days." The variable V is the VaR, X percent is the confidence level, and N days is the time horizon.

One approach to calculating VaR is historical simulation. This involves creating a database consisting of the daily movements in all market variables over a period of time. The first simulation trial assumes that the percentage changes in each market variable are the same as those on the first day covered by the database; the second simulation trial assumes that the percentage changes are the same as those on the second day; and so on. The change ΔP in the portfolio value is calculated for each simulation trial, and the VaR is calculated as the appropriate percentile of the probability distribution of ΔP.

An alternative is the model-building approach. This is relatively straightforward if two assumptions can be made:

1. The change in the value of the portfolio (ΔP) is linearly dependent on percentage changes in the market variables.
2. The percentage changes in the market variables are multivariate normally distributed.

The probability distribution of ΔP is then normal, and there are analytic formulas for relating the standard deviation of ΔP to the volatilities and correlations of the underlying market variables. The VaR can be calculated from well-known properties of the normal distribution.

When a portfolio includes options, ΔP is not linearly related to the percentage changes in the market variables and is not normally distributed. The calculation of VaR using the model building approach is then more difficult and may involve Monte Carlo simulation.

When the model-building approach is used, volatilities and correlations are usually updated daily. A popular approach is the exponentially weighted moving average method. In this the weights given to observations decline as they become older. The weight given to data from i days ago is λ times the weight given to data from $i-1$ days ago for some parameter λ between zero and one.

FURTHER READING

Artzner P., F. Delbaen, J. M. Eber, and D. Heath. "Coherent Measures of Risk," *Mathematical Finance*, 9 (1999): 203–28.

Basak, S., and A. Shapiro. "Value-at-Risk-Based Risk Management: Optimal Policies and Asset Prices," *Review of Financial Studies*, 14, 2 (2001): 371–405.

Beder, T. "VaR: Seductive But Dangerous," *Financial Analysts Journal*, 51, 5 (1995): 12–24.

Boudoukh, J., M. Richardson, and R. Whitelaw. "The Best of Both Worlds," *Risk*, May 1998: 64–67.

Dowd, K. *Beyond Value at Risk: The New Science of Risk Management*. New York: Wiley, 1998.

Duffie, D., and J. Pan. "An Overview of Value at Risk," *Journal of Derivatives*, 4, 3 (Spring 1997): 7–49.

Embrechts, P., C. Kluppelberg, and T. Mikosch. *Modeling Extremal Events for Insurance and Finance*. New York: Springer, 1997.

Frye, J. "Principals of Risk: Finding VAR through Factor-Based Interest Rate Scenarios," in *VAR: Understanding and Applying Value at Risk*, pp. 275–88. London: Risk Publications, 1997.

Hendricks, D. "Evaluation of Value-at-Risk Models Using Historical Data," *Economic Policy Review*, Federal Reserve Bank of New York, 2 (April 1996): 39–69.

Hopper, G. "Value at Risk: A New Methodology for Measuring Portfolio Risk," *Business Review*, Federal Reserve Bank of Philadelphia, July/Aug. 1996: 19–29.

Hua, P., and P. Wilmott, "Crash Courses," *Risk*, June 1997: 64–67.

Hull, J. C., and A. White. "Value at Risk When Daily Changes in Market Variables Are Not Normally Distributed," *Journal of Derivatives*, 5 (Spring 1998): 9–19.

Hull, J. C., and A. White. 'Incorporating Volatility Updating into the Historical Simulation Method for Value at Risk," *Journal of Risk*, 1, 1 (1998): 5–19.

Jackson, P., D. J. Maude, and W. Perraudin. "Bank Capital and Value at Risk," *Journal of Derivatives*, 4, 3 (Spring 1997): 73–90.

Jamshidian, F., and Y. Zhu. "Scenario Simulation Model: Theory and Methodology," *Finance and Stochastics*, 1 (1997): 43–67.

Jorion, P. *Value at Risk*. 3rd edn. McGraw-Hill, 2007.

Longin, F. M. "Beyond the VaR," *Journal of Derivatives*, 8, 4 (Summer 2001): 36–48.

Marshall, C., and M. Siegel. "Value at Risk: Implementing a Risk Measurement Standard," *Journal of Derivatives*, 4, 3 (Spring 1997): 91–111.

McNeil, A. J. "Extreme Value Theory for Risk Managers," in: *Internal Modeling and CAD II*. London: Risk Books, 1999. See also: www.math.ethz.ch/~mcneil.

Neftci, S. "Value at Risk Calculations, Extreme Events and Tail Estimation," *Journal of Derivatives*, 7, 3 (Spring 2000): 23–38.

Rich, D. "Second Generation VaR and Risk-Adjusted Return on Capital," *Journal of Derivatives*, 10, 4 (Summer 2003): 51–61.

Quiz (Answers at End of Book)

20.1. Explain the historical simulation method for calculating VaR.

20.2. Explain the exponentially weighted moving average (EWMA) model for estimating volatility from historical data.

20.3. The most recent estimate of the daily volatility of an asset is 1.5%, and the price of the asset at the close of trading yesterday was \$30.00. The parameter λ in the EWMA model is 0.94. Suppose that the price of the asset at the close of trading today is \$30.50. How will this cause the volatility to be updated by the EWMA model?

20.4. Consider a position consisting of a \$300,000 investment in asset A and a \$500,000 investment in asset B. Assume that the daily volatilities of the assets are 1.8% and 1.2%, respectively, and that the coefficient of correlation between their returns is 0.3. What is the five-day 95% value at risk for the portfolio?

20.5. A financial institution owns a portfolio of options on the U.S. dollar/sterling exchange rate. The delta of the portfolio is 56.0. The current exchange rate is 1.5000. Derive an approximate linear relationship between the change in the portfolio value and the percentage change in the exchange rate. If the daily volatility of the exchange rate is 0.7%, estimate the 10-day 99% VaR.

20.6. Suppose you know that the gamma of the portfolio in the previous quiz question is 16.2. How does this change your estimate of the relationship between the change in the portfolio value and the percentage change in the exchange rate?

20.7. Suppose a company has a portfolio consisting of positions in stocks, bonds, foreign exchange, and commodities. Assume there are no derivatives. Explain the assumptions underlying (a) the historical simulation and (b) the model-building approach for calculating VaR.

Practice Questions (Answers in Solutions Manual/Study Guide)

20.8. A company uses an EWMA model for forecasting volatility. It decides to change the parameter λ from 0.95 to 0.85. Explain the likely impact on the forecasts.

20.9. Explain the difference between value at risk and expected shortfall.

20.10. Consider a position consisting of a \$100,000 investment in asset A and a \$100,000 investment in asset B. Assume that the daily volatilities of both assets are 1% and that the coefficient of correlation between their returns is 0.3. What is the five-day 99% value at risk for the portfolio?

20.11. The volatility of a certain market variable is 30% per annum. Calculate a 99% confidence interval for the size of the percentage daily change in the variable.

20.12. Explain how an interest rate swap is mapped into a portfolio of zero-coupon bonds with standard maturities for the purposes of a VaR calculation.

20.13. Explain why the linear model can provide only approximate estimates of VaR for a portfolio containing options.

20.14. Some time ago a company entered into a forward contract to buy £1 million for \$1.5 million. The contract now has six months to maturity. The daily volatility of a six-month zero-coupon sterling bond (when its price is translated to dollars) is 0.06% and the daily volatility of a six-month zero-coupon dollar bond is 0.05%. The correlation between returns from the two bonds is 0.8. The current exchange rate is 1.53. Calculate the standard deviation of the change in the dollar value of the forward contract in one day. What is the 10-day 99% VaR? Assume that the six-month interest rate in both sterling and dollars is 5% per annum with continuous compounding.

20.15. The most recent estimate of the daily volatility of the U.S. dollar–sterling exchange rate is 0.6%, and the exchange rate at 4 p.m. yesterday was 1.5000. The parameter λ in the EWMA model is 0.9. Suppose that the exchange rate at 4 p.m. today proves to be 1.4950. How would the estimate of the daily volatility be updated?

20.16. Suppose that the daily volatilities of asset A and asset B calculated at close of trading yesterday are 1.6% and 2.5%, respectively. The prices of the assets at close of trading yesterday were \$20 and \$40, and the estimate of the coefficient of correlation between the returns on the two assets made at the close of trading yesterday was 0.25. The parameter λ used in the EWMA model is 0.95.
(a) Calculate the current estimate of the covariance between the assets.
(b) On the assumption that the prices of the assets at close of trading today are \$20.5 and \$40.5, update the correlation estimate.

20.17. Suppose that the daily volatility of the FTSE 100 stock index (measured in sterling) is 1.8% and the daily volatility of the USD/GBP exchange rate is 0.9%. Suppose further that the correlation between the FTSE 100 and the USD/GBP exchange rate is 0.4. What is the volatility of the FTSE 100 when it is translated to U.S. dollars? Assume that the USD/GBP exchange rate is expressed as the number of U.S. dollars per pound sterling. [*Hint*: When $Z = XY$, the percentage daily change in Z is approximately equal to the percentage daily change in X plus the percentage daily change in Y.]

20.18. Suppose that in Problem 20.17 the correlation between the S&P 500 index (measured in dollars) and the FTSE 100 index (measured in sterling) is 0.7, the correlation between the S&P 500 index (measured in dollars) and the USD/GBP exchange rate is 0.3, and the daily volatility of the S&P 500 index is 1.6%. What is the correlation between the S&P 500 index (measured in dollars) and the FTSE 100 index when it is translated to dollars? [*Hint*: For three variables X, Y, and Z, the covariance between $X + Y$ and Z equals the covariance between X and Z plus the covariance between Y and Z.]

20.19. The one-day 99% VaR is calculated for the four-index example in Section 20.2 as \$253,385. Look at the underlying spreadsheets on the author's website and calculate: (a) the one-day 95% VaR and (b) the one-day 97% VaR.

20.20. Use the spreadsheets on the author's website to calculate the one-day 99% VaR, using the basic methodology in Section 20.2, if the four-index portfolio considered in Section 20.2 is equally divided between the four indices.

20.21. At the end of Section 20.6, the VaR for the four-index example was calculated using the model-building approach. How does the VaR calculated change if the investment is \$2.5 million in each index? Carry out calculations when (a) volatilities and correlations are estimated using the equally weighted model and (b) when they are estimated using the EWMA model with $\lambda = 0.94$. Use the spreadsheets on the author's website.

20.22. What is the effect of changing λ from 0.94 to 0.97 in the EWMA calculations in the four-index example at the end of Section 20.6. Use the spreadsheets on the author's website.

Further Questions

20.23. Consider a position consisting of a \$300,000 investment in gold and a \$500,000 investment in silver. Suppose that the daily volatilities of these two assets are 1.8% and 1.2%, respectively, and that the coefficient of correlation between their returns is 0.6. What is the 10-day 97.5% value at risk for the portfolio? By how much does diversification reduce the VaR?

20.24. Consider a portfolio of options on a single asset. Suppose that the delta of the portfolio is 12, the value of the asset is \$10, and the daily volatility of the asset is 2%. Estimate the one-day 95% VaR for the portfolio from the delta. Suppose next that the gamma of the portfolio is −2.6. Derive a quadratic relationship between the change in the portfolio value and the percentage change in the underlying asset price in one day.

20.25. A bank has written a call option on one stock and a put option on another stock. For the first option, the stock price is 50, the strike price is 51, the volatility is 28% per annum, and the time to maturity is nine months. For the second option, the stock price is 20, the strike price is 19, the volatility is 25% per annum, and the time to maturity is one year. Neither stock pays a dividend, the risk-free rate is 6% per annum, and the correlation between stock price returns is 0.4. Calculate a 10-day 99% VaR using DerivaGem and the linear model.

20.26. Suppose that the price of gold at close of trading yesterday was \$600, and its volatility was estimated as 1.3% per day. The price at the close of trading today is \$596. Update the volatility estimate using the EWMA model with $\lambda = 0.94$.

20.27. Suppose that in Problem 20.26 the price of silver at the close of trading yesterday was \$16, its volatility was estimated as 1.5% per day, and its correlation with gold was estimated as 0.8. The price of silver at the close of trading today is unchanged at \$16. Update the volatility of silver and the correlation between silver and gold using the EWMA model with $\lambda = 0.94$.

20.28. An Excel spreadsheet containing daily data on a number of different exchange rates and stock indices can be downloaded from the author's website:

`http://www.rotman. utoronto.ca/~hull/data`

Choose one exchange rate and one stock index. Estimate the value of λ in the EWMA model that minimizes the value of

$$\sum_i (v_i - \beta_i)^2$$

where v_i is the variance forecast made at the end of day $i - 1$ and β_i is the variance calculated from data between day i and $i + 25$. Use Excel's Solver tool. Set the variance forecast at the end of the first day equal to the square of the return on that day to start the EWMA calculations.

20.29. A common complaint of risk managers is that the model-building approach (either linear or quadratic) does not work well when delta is close to zero. Test what happens when delta is close to zero in using Sample Application E in the DerivaGem Applications. [You can do this by experimenting with different option positions and adjusting the position in the underlying to give a delta of zero.] Explain the results you get.

20.30. Suppose that the portfolio considered in Section 20.2 has (in $000s) 3,000 in DJIA, 3,000 in FTSE, 1,000 in CAC 40 and 3,000 in Nikkei 225. Use the spreadsheet on the author's website to calculate what difference this makes to the one-day 99% VaR that is calculated in Section 20.2.

20.31. The calculations for the four-index example at the end of Section 20.6 assume that the investments in the DJIA, FTSE 100, CAC 40, and Nikkei 225 are $4 million, $3 million, $1 million, and $2 million, respectively. How does the VaR calculated change if the investments are $3 million, $3 million, $1 million, and $3 million, respectively? Carry out calculations when (a) volatilities and correlations are estimated using the equally weighted model and (b) when they are estimated using the EWMA model. What is the effect of changing λ from 0.94 to 0.90 in the EWMA calculations? Use the spreadsheets on the author's website.

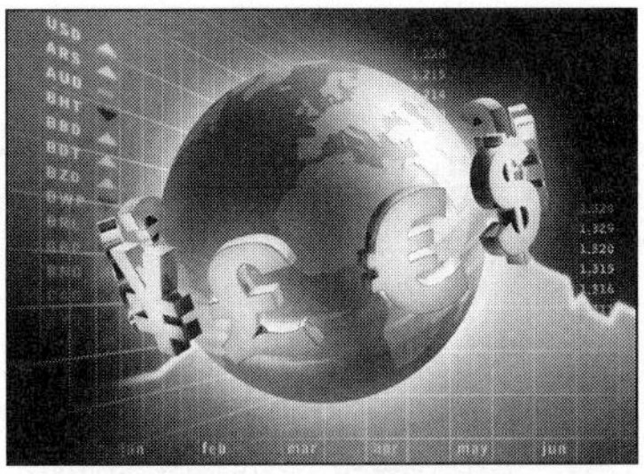

CHAPTER 21

Interest Rate Options

Interest rate options are options whose payoffs are dependent in some way on the level of interest rates. During the 1980s and 1990s they became increasingly popular. Many different types of interest rate options now trade very actively both in the over-the-counter market and on exchanges. This chapter discusses some of the products and how they are used. It explains two popular exchange-traded instruments: Treasury bond futures options and Eurodollar futures options. It also describes the standard market models that are used for pricing three popular over-the-counter instruments: European bond options, interest rate caps and floors, and European swap options. These models are in the spirit of the original Black–Scholes–Merton model for European stock options and are based on the assumption that a key market variable will be lognormally distributed at a future time.

21.1 EXCHANGE-TRADED INTEREST RATE OPTIONS

Among the most actively traded interest rate options offered by exchanges in the United States are those on Treasury bond futures, Treasury note futures, and Eurodollar futures.

Treasury bond futures options are traded by the CME Group and are options to enter into Treasury bond futures contracts. As mentioned in Chapter 6, one Treasury bond futures contract is for the delivery of \$100,000 of Treasury bonds. The price of a Treasury bond futures option is quoted as a percentage of the face value of the underlying Treasury bonds to the nearest sixty-fourth of 1%. Suppose the quote for the March call futures option on a Treasury bond is 2-06, or $2\frac{6}{64}\%$ of the bond principal, when the strike price is 110. This means that one contract costs \$2,093.75. On exercise, it provides a payoff equal to 1,000 times the excess of the bond futures quote over 110. Options on 10-year Treasury note futures work similarly to options on Treasury bond futures. Options on 5-year and 2-year Treasury note futures also work similarly except that prices are quoted to one half of one sixty-fourth of 1%.

Options on Eurodollar futures are traded by the CME Group and are options to enter into Eurodollar futures contracts. As explained in Chapter 6, when the Eurodollar futures quote changes by one basis point, or 0.01, there is a gain or loss on a Eurodollar futures contract of \$25. Similarly, in the pricing of options on Eurodollar futures, one basis point represents \$25. Suppose the quote for a June put option with a strike price

From Chapter 21 of *Fundamentals of Futures and Options Markets*, Eighth Edition. John C. Hull.

Example 21.1 A Eurodollar futures option trade

It is February and the futures price for the June Eurodollar contract is 93.82. (This corresponds to a three-month Eurodollar interest rate of 6.18% per annum.) The price of a call option on the contract with a strike price of 94.00 is quoted at the CME as 20 basis points. This option could be attractive to an investor who thinks interest rates will decline. Suppose that short-term interest rates do drop by about 100 basis points and the investor exercises the call when the Eurodollar futures price is 94.78. (This corresponds to a three-month Eurodollar interest rate of 5.22% per annum.) The payoff is $25 \times (9{,}478 - 9{,}400) = \$1{,}950$. The cost of the contract is $20 \times 25 = \$500$. The investor's profit is therefore \$1,450.

of 96.25 is 59 basis points. One contract costs $59 \times \$25 = \$1{,}475$. On exercise, it provides a payoff equal to \$25 times the number of basis points by which 96.25 exceeds the June futures quote.

Interest rate futures option contracts work in the same way as the other futures options contracts discussed in Chapter 16. In addition to a cash payoff, a call option holder obtains a long position in the futures contract when the option is exercised and the call option writer obtains a corresponding short position. A put option holder obtains a short position in the futures contract when the option is exercised and the put option writer obtains the corresponding long position.

Interest rate futures prices increase when bond prices increase (i.e., when interest rates fall). They decrease when bond prices decrease (i.e., when interest rates rise). An investor who thinks that short-term interest rates will rise can speculate by buying put options on Eurodollar futures, whereas an investor who thinks the rates will fall can speculate by buying call options on Eurodollar futures (see Example 21.1). An investor who thinks that long-term interest rates will rise can speculate by buying put options on Treasury note futures or Treasury bond futures, whereas an investor who thinks the rates will fall can speculate by buying call options on these instruments (see Example 21.2).

Bond futures options and Eurodollar futures options are American. The easiest valuation approach is to use a binomial tree in the way described in Chapters 12, 16,

Example 21.2 A Treasury bond futures option trade

It is August and the futures price for the December Treasury bond contract is 96-09 (or $96\frac{9}{32} = 96.28125$). The yield on long-term government bonds is about 6.4% per annum. An investor who feels that this yield will fall by December might choose to buy December calls with a strike price of 98. Assume that the price of these calls is 1-04 (or $1\frac{4}{64} = 1.0625\%$ of the principal). If long-term rates fall to 6% per annum and the Treasury bond futures price rises to 100-00, the investor will make a net profit per \$100 of bond futures of

$$100.00 - 98.00 - 1.0625 = 0.9375$$

Because one option contract is for the purchase or sale of instruments with a face value of \$100,000 and quotes are per \$100 of principal, the investor would make a profit of \$937.50 per option contract bought.

and 18. When bond futures options are valued, the bond futures price is modeled by the tree and the volatility parameter used is the volatility of the bond futures price. In the case of Eurodollar futures, analysts often use the tree to model 100 minus the futures price. A call (put) Eurodollar futures option with a strike price of 96 is then regarded as a put (call) option on 100 minus the Eurodollar futures price with a strike price of 4, and the volatility used is the volatility of 100 minus the futures price.

21.2 EMBEDDED BOND OPTIONS

Some bonds contain embedded call and put options. For example, a *callable bond* contains provisions that allow the issuing firm to buy back the bond at a predetermined price at certain times in the future. The holder of such a bond has sold a call option to the issuer. The strike price or call price in the option is the predetermined price that must be paid by the issuer to the holder to buy back the bond. Callable bonds usually cannot be called for the first few years of their life. (This is known as a *lock-out period.*) After that the call price is usually a decreasing function of time. For example, a ten-year callable bond might have no call privileges for the first two years. After that the issuer might have the right to buy the bond back at a price of \$110.00 in years 3 and 4 of its life, at a price of \$107.50 in years 5 and 6, at a price of \$106.00 in years 7 and 8, and at a price of \$103.00 in years 9 and 10. The value of the call option is reflected in the quoted yields on bonds. Bonds with call features generally offer higher yields than bonds with no call features.

A *puttable bond* contains provisions that allow the holder to demand early redemption at a predetermined price at certain times in the future. The holder of such a bond has purchased a put option on the bond as well as the bond itself. Because the put option increases the value of the bond to the holder, bonds with put features provide lower yields than bonds with no put features. A simple example of a puttable bond is a ten-year retractable bond in which the holder has the right to be repaid at the end of five years.

A number of instruments other than bonds have embedded bond options. For example, the early redemption privilege on fixed-rate deposits is equivalent to a put option on a bond. The prepayment privilege on a fixed-rate loan is equivalent to a call option on a bond. Also, a loan commitment made by a bank or other financial institution is a put option on a bond. Suppose, for example, that a bank quotes a five-year interest rate of 3% per annum to a potential borrower and states that the rate is good for the next two months. The client has in effect obtained the right to sell a five-year bond with a 3% coupon to the financial institution for its face value any time within the next two months. The option will be exercised if rates increase.

21.3 BLACK'S MODEL

Since the Black–Scholes–Merton model was first published in 1973, it has become a very popular tool. As explained in Chapters 15 and 16, the model has been extended so that it can be used to value options on foreign exchange, options on indices, and options on futures contracts. As outlined in Chapter 19, traders have found flexible ways of using the model to reflect market prices. It is not surprising, therefore, that the model has been extended so that it covers interest rate derivatives.

The extension of the Black–Scholes–Merton model that is most widely used in the interest rate area is Black's model.[1] This was originally developed for valuing options on commodity futures, but as explained in Section 16.8, by setting the maturity of the futures contract equal to that of the option, it can also be used to value European options on spot prices. In this chapter, we show how Black's model is used for over-the-counter interest rate options.

Consider a European call option on a variable V. We define:

T: Time to maturity of the option (years)

F: Futures price of V for a contract maturing at time T

F_0: Value of F at time zero

F_T: Value of F at time T

K: Strike price of the option

r: T-year risk-free rate used for discounting (LIBOR or OIS, see Chapter 7)

σ: Volatility of F

V_T: Value of V at time T

The option pays off $\max(V_T - K, 0)$ at time T. Because the futures contract matures at time T, $F_T = V_T$ and we can also regard the option as paying off $\max(F_T - K, 0)$ at time T. As shown in Chapter 16, Black's model gives the value, c, of the option at time zero as

$$c = e^{-rT}[F_0 N(d_1) - KN(d_2)] \tag{21.1}$$

where

$$d_1 = \frac{\ln(F_0/K) + \sigma^2 T/2}{\sigma\sqrt{T}}$$

$$d_2 = \frac{\ln(F_0/K) - \sigma^2 T/2}{\sigma\sqrt{T}} = d_1 - \sigma\sqrt{T}$$

The value, p, of the corresponding put option is given by

$$p = e^{-rT}[KN(-d_2) - F_0 N(-d_1)] \tag{21.2}$$

Extension of Black's Model

We can extend Black's model by allowing the time when the payoff is made to be different from T. Assume that the payoff on the option is calculated from the value of the variable V at time T, but that the payoff is delayed until time T^* where $T^* \geqslant T$. In this case, it is necessary to discount the payoff from time T^* instead of from time T. We define r^* as the interest rate for maturity T^*, and equations (21.1) and (21.2) become

$$c = e^{-r^*T^*}[F_0 N(d_1) - KN(d_2)] \tag{21.3}$$

$$p = e^{-r^*T^*}[KN(-d_2) - F_0 N(-d_1)] \tag{21.4}$$

[1] See F. Black "The Pricing of Commodity Contracts," *Journal of Financial Economics*, 3 (March 1976): 167–79.

where

$$d_1 = \frac{\ln(F_0/K) + \sigma^2 T/2}{\sigma\sqrt{T}}$$

$$d_2 = \frac{\ln(F_0/K) - \sigma^2 T/2}{\sigma\sqrt{T}} = d_1 - \sigma\sqrt{T}$$

How the Model Is Used

When Black's model is used to price European interest rate options trading in the over-the-counter market, the variable F_0 in equations (21.1) to (21.4) is usually set equal to the forward price of V rather than its futures price. Recall from Chapter 5 that futures prices and forward prices are equal when interest rates are assumed to be constant, but different when they are assumed to evolve unpredictably. When we are dealing with an option on an interest-rate-dependent variable, the assumption that F_0 is a forward price is therefore questionable. However, it turns out (at least for the products considered in this chapter) that this assumption exactly offsets another assumption that is usually made when Black's model is used. This is that interest rates are constant for the purposes of discounting. When used to value interest rate options, Black's model therefore has a stronger theoretical basis than sometimes supposed.[2]

21.4 EUROPEAN BOND OPTIONS

A European bond option is an option to buy or sell a bond for a certain price, K, at a certain time, T. European bond options are often valued using equations (21.1) and (21.2) with V equal to the bond price. The variable σ is the volatility of the forward bond price, F, so that $\sigma\sqrt{T}$ is the standard deviation of the logarithm of the bond price at time T.

As explained in Chapter 5, F_0 can be calculated from today's spot bond price, B, using the formula

$$F_0 = (B - I)e^{rT} \tag{21.5}$$

where I is the present value of the coupons that will be paid during the life of the option and r is the interest rate for a maturity T. In this formula both the spot bond price and the forward bond price are cash prices rather than quoted prices. (The relationship between cash and quoted bond prices is explained in Chapter 6; the cash price is the quoted price plus accrued interest.) Traders refer to the quoted price of a bond as the "clean price" and the cash price as the "dirty price."

The strike price, K, in equations (21.1) and (21.2) should be the dirty (i.e., cash) strike price. If a particular contract defines the strike price as the cash amount that is exchanged for the bond when the option is exercised, K should be set equal to this strike price. If, as is more common, the strike price is the clean price applicable when the option is exercised, K should be set equal to the strike price plus accrued interest at the expiration date of the option. Example 21.3 provides an illustration of this.

[2] For an explanation of this, see J. C. Hull, *Options, Futures, and Other Derivatives*, 8th edn. Upper Saddle River, NJ: Pearson, 2012, Chapters 27 and 28.

Example 21.3 Valuation of a bond option

Consider a 10-month European call option on a 9.75-year bond with a face value of \$1,000. (When the option matures, the bond will have 8 years and 11 months remaining.) Suppose that the current cash bond price is \$960, the strike price is \$1,000, the 10-month risk-free interest rate is 10% per annum, and the forward bond price volatility is 9% per annum. The bond pays coupons semiannually at a rate of 10% per year, and coupon payments of \$50 are expected in 3 months and 9 months. (This means that the accrued interest is \$25 and the quoted bond price is \$935.) We suppose that the 3-month and 9-month risk-free interest rates are 9.0% and 9.5% per annum, respectively. The present value of the coupon payments is therefore

$$50e^{-0.09\times0.25} + 50e^{-0.095\times0.75} = 95.45$$

or \$95.45. The bond forward price, from equation (21.5), is given by

$$F_0 = (960 - 95.45)e^{0.1\times10/12} = 939.68$$

(a) If the strike price is the cash price that would be paid for the bond on exercise, the parameters for equation (21.1) are $F_0 = 939.68$, $K = 1000$, $r = 0.1$, $\sigma = 0.09$, and $T = 0.8333$. The price of the call option is \$9.49.

(b) If the strike price is the quoted price that would be paid for the bond on exercise, one-month's accrued interest must be added to K, because the maturity of the option is one month after a coupon date. This produces a value for K of

$$1{,}000 + 100 \times 0.08333 = 1{,}008.33$$

The values for the other parameters in equation (21.1) are unchanged ($F_0 = 939.68$, $r = 0.1$, $\sigma = 0.09$, and $T = 0.8333$). The price of the option is \$7.97.

Yield Volatilities

The volatilities that are quoted for bond options are often yield volatilities rather than price volatilities. The duration concept, introduced in Chapter 6, is used by the market to convert a quoted yield volatility into a price volatility. Suppose that D is the modified duration of the bond underlying the option at the option maturity, as defined in Section 6.4. The relationship between the change in the forward bond price, F, and its yield, y_F, at the maturity of the option is

$$\frac{\Delta F}{F} \approx -D\,\Delta y_F$$

or

$$\frac{\Delta F}{F} \approx -Dy_F\frac{\Delta y_F}{y_F}$$

Volatility is a measure of the standard deviation of percentage changes in the value of a variable. This equation therefore suggests that the volatility of the forward bond price, σ, used in Black's model can be approximately related to the volatility of the forward bond

Example 21.4 Bond option valuation using yield volatilities

Consider a European put option on a 10-year bond with a principal of 100. The coupon is 8% per year payable semiannually. The life of the option is 2.25 years and the strike price of the option is 115. The forward yield volatility is 20%. The zero curve is flat at 5% with continuous compounding. The DerivaGem software accompanying this book shows that the quoted price of the bond is 122.82. The price of the option when the strike price is a quoted price is \$2.36. When the strike price is a cash price, the price of the option is \$1.74. (Note that earlier versions of DerivaGem give slightly different prices because they assume 365 days per year and round times to the nearest whole number of days.)

yield, σ_y, by

$$\sigma = Dy_0\sigma_y \tag{21.6}$$

where y_0 is the initial value of y_F. When a yield volatility is quoted for a European bond option, the implicit assumption is usually that it will be converted to a price volatility using equation (21.6), and that this volatility will then be used in conjunction with equation (21.1) or (21.2) to obtain the option's price. Suppose that the bond underlying a call option will have a modified duration of five years at option maturity, the forward yield is 8%, and the forward yield volatility quoted by a broker is 20%. This means that the market price of the option corresponding to the broker quote is the price given by equation (21.1) when the volatility variable, σ, is

$$5 \times 0.08 \times 0.2 = 0.08$$

or 8% per annum.

The Bond_Options worksheet of the DerivaGem software accompanying this book can be used to price European bond options using Black's model by selecting Black-European as the Pricing Model. The user inputs a yield volatility, which is handled in the way just described. The strike price can be the cash or quoted strike price. This is illustrated in Example 21.4.

21.5 INTEREST RATE CAPS

A popular interest rate option offered by financial institutions in the over-the-counter market is an *interest rate cap*. Interest rate caps can best be understood by first considering a floating rate note where the interest rate is reset periodically equal to LIBOR. The time between resets is known as the *tenor*. Suppose the tenor is three months. The interest rate on the note for the first three months is the initial three-month LIBOR rate; the interest rate for the next three months is set equal to the three-month LIBOR rate prevailing in the market at the three-month point; and so on.

An interest rate cap is designed to provide insurance against the rate of interest on the floating-rate note rising above a certain level. This level is known as the *cap rate*. The operation of the cap is illustrated schematically in Figure 21.1. Suppose that the principal amount is \$10 million, the life of the cap is five years, and the cap rate is 5%. (Because the tenor is three months, this cap rate is expressed with quarterly

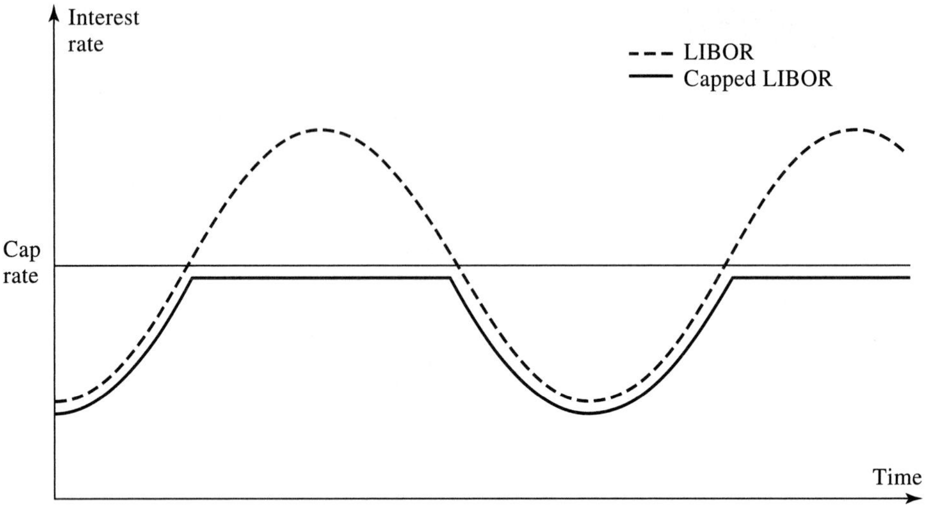

Figure 21.1 Effect of a cap in providing insurance against LIBOR rising above the cap rate

compounding.) Suppose that on a particular reset date the three-month LIBOR interest rate is 6%. The floating rate note would require

$$0.25 \times 0.06 \times \$10{,}000{,}000 = \$150{,}000$$

of interest to be paid three months later. With a three-month LIBOR rate of 5% the interest payment would be

$$0.25 \times 0.05 \times \$10{,}000{,}000 = \$125{,}000$$

The cap therefore provides a payoff of \$25,000 (= \$150,000 − \$125,000).[3] Note that the payoff does not occur on the reset date when the 6% is observed. It occurs three months later. This reflects the usual time lag between an interest rate being observed and the corresponding payment being required.

If a corporation obtains a floating-rate loan where the rate of interest is linked to LIBOR, a cap can be used to limit the interest paid. For example, if the floating rate on a loan is LIBOR plus 30 basis points and the loan lasts for five years, the cap we have just considered would ensure that the rate paid is never higher than 5.30%. At each reset date during the life of the cap we observe LIBOR. If LIBOR is less than 5%, there is no payoff from the cap three months later. If LIBOR is greater than 5%, the payoff is one-quarter of the excess applied to the principal of \$10 million. This is summarized in Example 21.5.

Note that caps are usually defined so that the initial LIBOR rate, even if it is greater than the cap rate, does not lead to a payoff on the first reset date. In our example, the cap lasts for five years. Therefore there is a total of 19 reset dates (at times 0.25, 0.50, 0.75, ..., 4.75 years) and 19 potential payoffs from the caps (at times 0.50, 0.75, 1.00, ..., 5.00 years).

[3] This calculation assumes exactly one quarter of a year between reset dates. In practice, the calculation takes account of the exact number of days between reset dates using a specified day count convention.

Example 21.5 Use of an interest rate cap

A company entering into a five-year \$10 million floating-rate loan agreement is concerned about possible increases in interest rates. The rate on the loan is 3-month LIBOR plus 30 basis points.

To hedge its exposure, the company buys a five-year LIBOR interest rate cap with a cap rate of 5% per annum and a \$10 million principal from a financial institution. This has the effect of ensuring that the interest rate paid by the company in any three-month period is never more than 5.3% per annum.

The Cap as a Portfolio of Interest Rate Options

Consider a cap with a principal of L and a cap rate of R_K. Suppose that the reset dates are $t_1, t_2, \dots, t_n$ and the corresponding payment dates are $t_2, t_3, \dots, t_{n+1}$. Define R_k as the LIBOR interest rate for the period between time t_k and t_{k+1} observed at time t_k $(1 \leqslant k \leqslant n)$. The cap leads to a payoff at time t_{k+1} of

$$L\delta_k \max(R_k - R_K,\ 0) \tag{21.7}$$

where $\delta_k = t_{k+1} - t_k$.[4]

The expression in equation (21.7) is the payoff from a call option on the LIBOR rate observed at time t_k with the payoff occurring at time t_{k+1}. The cap is a portfolio of n such call options. These call options are known as *caplets*.

Floors and Collars

Interest rate floors are defined analogously to caps. A *floor* provides a payoff when the interest rate on the underlying floating-rate note falls below a certain rate. With the notation already introduced, a floor provides a payoff at time t_{k+1} $(k = 1, 2, \dots, n)$ of

$$L\delta_k \max(R_K - R_k,\ 0)$$

Analogously to an interest rate cap, an interest rate floor is a portfolio of put options on interest rates. Each of the individual options comprising a floor is known as a *floorlet*.

An interest rate collar (sometimes called a floor–ceiling agreement) is an instrument designed to guarantee that the interest rate on the underlying LIBOR floating-rate note always lies between two levels. A *collar* is a combination of a long position in a cap and a short position in a floor. It is usually constructed so that the price of the cap is initially equal to the price of the floor. The cost of entering into the collar is then zero.

As explained in Business Snapshot 21.1, there is a put–call parity relationship between caps and floors.

---

[4] In this equation, both R_k and R_K are expressed with a compounding frequency equal to the frequency of resets. For example, if there are four reset dates per year, they are quarterly compounded. The presentation here is simplified in that it assumes that interest rates are measured using an actual/actual day count. In the United States, LIBOR is quoted using an actual/360 day count. This means that δ_k must be calculated using this day count. For example, if t_k is May 1 and t_{k+1} is August 1, then there are 92 (actual) days between May 1 and August 1 and $\delta_k = 92/360 = 0.2556$.

Business Snapshot 21.1 Put–call parity for caps and floors

There is a put–call parity relationship between the prices of caps and floors. This is

$$\text{Value of cap} = \text{Value of floor} + \text{Value of swap}$$

In this relationship, the cap and floor have the same strike price, R_K. The swap is an agreement to receive LIBOR and pay a fixed rate of R_K with no exchange of payments on the first reset date. All three instruments have the same life and the same frequency of payments.

To see that the result is true, consider a long position in the cap combined with a short position in the floor. The cap provides a cash flow of LIBOR − R_K for periods when LIBOR is greater than R_K. The short floor provides a cash flow of

$$-(R_K - \text{LIBOR}) = \text{LIBOR} - R_K$$

for periods when LIBOR is less than R_K. There is therefore a cash flow of LIBOR − R_K in all circumstances. This is the cash flow on the swap. It follows that the value of the cap minus the value of the floor must equal the value of the swap.

Note that swaps are usually structured so that LIBOR at time zero determines a payment on the first reset date. Caps and floors are usually structured so that there is no payoff on the first reset date. This is why put–call parity involves a nonstandard swap where there is no payment on the first reset date.

Valuation of Caps and Floors

A caplet that provides a payoff at time t_{k+1} based on the rate at time t_k is usually valued by using Black's model in Section 21.3 with $V = R_k$. (This means the rate underlying the caplet is assumed to be lognormal.) Because the payoff is at time t_{k+1} rather than t_k, equation (21.3) provides the value of this caplet as

$$L\delta_k e^{-r_{k+1}t_{k+1}}[F_k N(d_1) - R_K N(d_2)] \tag{21.8}$$

where r_{k+1} is the continuously compounded risk-free rate for a maturity t_{k+1},

$$d_1 = \frac{\ln(F_k/R_K) + \sigma_k^2 t_k/2}{\sigma_k\sqrt{t_k}}$$

$$d_2 = \frac{\ln(F_k/R_K) - \sigma_k^2 t_k/2}{\sigma_k\sqrt{t_k}} = d_1 - \sigma_k\sqrt{t_k}$$

Here, F_k is the forward LIBOR interest rate for the period between time t_k and t_{k+1}, and σ_k is the volatility of F_k (so that $\sigma_k\sqrt{t_k}$ is the standard deviation of $\ln R_k$). Example 21.6 provides an application of equation (21.8).

The value of the corresponding floorlet is, from equation (21.4),

$$L\delta_k e^{-r_{k+1}t_{k+1}}[R_K N(-d_2) - F_k N(-d_1)] \tag{21.9}$$

Note that R_K and F_k are expressed with a compounding frequency equal to the frequency of resets in these equations, while r_{k+1} is expressed with continuous compounding.

Example 21.6 Valuation of a caplet

Consider a contract that caps LIBOR on \$10 million at 8% per annum (with quarterly compounding) for three months starting in one year. This is a caplet and could be one element of a cap. Suppose that the LIBOR/swap zero curve is flat at 7% per annum with quarterly compounding and the volatility of the three-month forward rate underlying the caplet is 20% per annum. The continuously compounded zero rate for all maturities is 6.9395%. Assuming LIBOR is used as the risk-free rate in equation (21.8), $F_k = 0.07$, $\delta_k = 0.25$, $L = 10$, $R_K = 0.08$, $r_{k+1} = 0.069394$, $\sigma_k = 0.20$, $t_k = 1.0$, and $t_{k+1} = 1.25$. Also,

$$d_1 = \frac{\ln(0.07/0.08) + 0.2^2 \times 1/2}{0.20 \times 1} = -0.5677$$

$$d_2 = d_1 - 0.20 = -0.7677$$

so that the caplet price (in \$ million) is

$$0.25 \times 10 \times e^{-0.069395 \times 1.25}[0.07N(-0.5677) - 0.08N(-0.7677)] = \$0.005162$$

The DerivaGem software accompanying this book agrees with this price. Earlier versions give slightly different prices because they assume 365 days per year and round times to the nearest whole number of days.)

Each caplet of a cap must be valued separately using equation (21.8). Similarly, each floorlet of a floor must be valued using equation (21.9). One approach is to use a different volatility for each caplet (or floorlet). The volatilities are then referred to as *spot volatilities*.[5] An alternative approach is to use the same volatility for all the caplets (floorlets) comprising any particular cap (floor), but to vary this volatility according to the life of the cap (floor). The volatilities used are then referred to as *flat volatilities*. The volatilities quoted in the market are usually flat volatilities. However, many traders like to estimate spot volatilities because this allows them to identify underpriced and overpriced caplets and floorlets. The put (call) options on Eurodollar futures that are traded by the CME Group (see Section 21.1) are similar to caplets (floorlets). The implied spot volatilities for caplets and floorlets on three-month LIBOR are frequently compared with those calculated from the prices of Eurodollar futures options.

Figure 21.2 shows a typical pattern for spot volatilities and flat volatilities as a function of maturity. (In the case of a spot volatility, the maturity is the maturity of a caplet or floorlet; in the case of a flat volatility, it is the maturity of a cap or floor.) The flat volatilities are akin to cumulative averages of the spot volatilities and therefore exhibit less variability. As indicated by Figure 21.2, a "hump" in the volatilities at about the two- to three-year point is usually observed. This hump is observed both when the volatilities are implied from option prices and when they are calculated from historical data. There is no general agreement on the reason for the existence of the hump. One possible explanation is as follows. Rates at the short end of the zero curve are controlled by central banks. By contrast, two- and three-year interest rates are determined to a large

[5] The term *forward volatilities* is sometimes also used to describe these volatilities.

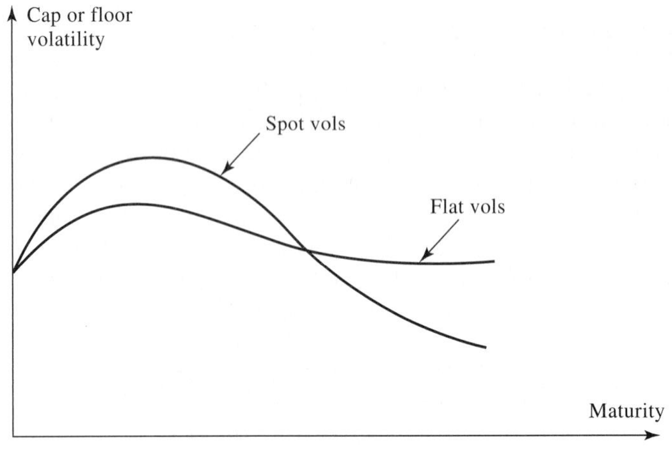

Figure 21.2 The implied volatility hump

extent by the activities of traders. These traders may be overreacting to the changes they observe in the short rate and causing the volatility of these rates to be higher than the volatility of short rates. For maturities beyond two to three years, the mean reversion of interest rates, which will be discussed later in this chapter, causes volatilities to decline.

Interdealer brokers provide tables of flat implied volatilities for caps and floors. The instruments underlying the quotes are usually "at the money." This is defined as a situation where the cap/floor rate equals the swap rate for a swap that has the same payment dates as the cap. Table 21.1 shows typical broker quotes for the U.S. dollar market. The tenor of the cap is three months, and the cap life varies from one year to ten years. The volatilities are flat volatilities rather than spot volatilities. The data exhibits the type of "hump" shown in Figure 21.2.

Using DerivaGem

The DerivaGem software accompanying this book can be used to price interest rate caps and floors using Black's model and LIBOR discounting. In the Cap_and_Swap_Option

Table 21.1 Typical broker flat volatility quotes for U.S. dollar caps and floors (percent per annum)

Life (years)	*Cap bid*	*Cap offer*	*Floor bid*	*Floor offer*
1	18.00	20.00	18.00	20.00
2	23.25	24.25	23.75	24.75
3	24.00	25.00	24.50	25.50
4	23.75	24.75	24.25	25.25
5	23.50	24.50	24.00	25.00
7	21.75	22.75	22.00	23.00
10	20.00	21.00	20.25	21.25

Business Snapshot 21.2 Swaptions and bond options

As explained in Chapter 7, an interest rate swap can be regarded as an agreement to exchange a fixed-rate bond for a floating-rate bond. At the start of a swap, the value of the floating-rate bond always equals the principal amount of the swap. It follows that a swaption can be regarded as an option to exchange a fixed-rate bond for the principal amount of the swap.

A swaption is therefore a type of bond option. If a swaption gives the holder the right to pay fixed and receive floating, it is a put option on the fixed-rate bond with strike price equal to the principal. If a swaption gives the holder the right to pay floating and receive fixed, it is a call option on the fixed-rate bond with a strike price equal to the principal.

worksheet, select Cap/Floor as the Underlying Type and Black-European as the Pricing Model. The LIBOR zero curve is input using continuously compounded rates. The inputs include the start date and the end date of the period covered by the cap, the flat volatility, and the cap settlement frequency (i.e., the tenor). The software calculates the payment dates by working back from the end of period covered by the cap to the beginning. The initial caplet/floorlet is assumed to cover a period of length between 0.5 and 1.5 times a regular period. Suppose, for example, that the period covered by the cap is 1.95 years to 2.80 years and the settlement frequency is quarterly. There are three caplets covering the periods 2.55 years to 2.80 years, 2.30 years to 2.55 years, 1.95 years to 2.30 years.

21.6 EUROPEAN SWAP OPTIONS

Swap options, or *swaptions*, are options on interest rate swaps and are an increasingly popular type of interest rate option. They give the holder the right, but not the obligation, to enter into a specified interest rate swap at a certain time in the future. Large financial institutions that offer interest rate swap contracts to their corporate clients are often also prepared to sell them swaptions or buy swaptions from them. As shown in Business Snapshot 21.2, a swaption can be viewed as a type of bond option.

To give an example of how a swaption might be used, consider a company which knows that in six months it will enter into a five-year floating-rate loan agreement and that it will wish to swap the floating-interest payments for fixed-interest payments to convert the loan into a fixed-rate loan. (See Chapter 7 for a discussion of how swaps can be used in this way.) At a cost, the company could enter into a swaption giving it the right to receive six-month LIBOR and pay a certain fixed rate of interest (say, 3% per annum) for a five-year period starting in six months. If the fixed rate on a regular five-year swap in six months turns out to be less than 3% per annum, the company will choose not to exercise the swaption and will enter into a swap agreement in the usual way. However, if the fixed rate turns out to be greater than 3% per annum, the company will choose to exercise the swaption and will obtain a swap at more favorable terms than those available in the market.

When used in the way just described, swaptions provide companies that are planning future borrowings with protection against interest rate increases. Swaptions are an alternative to forward swaps (sometimes called *deferred swaps*). Forward swaps involve no up-front cost, but have the disadvantage that they obligate the company to enter into a swap agreement. With a swaption, the company is able to benefit from favorable interest rate movements while acquiring protection from unfavorable interest rate movements. The difference between a swaption and a forward swap is analogous to the difference between an option on a foreign currency and a forward contract on the currency.

Valuation of European Swaptions

Consider a swaption where we have the right to pay a rate R_K and receive LIBOR on a swap that will last n years starting in T years. We suppose that there are m payments per year on the swap and that the principal is L.

As explained in Chapter 7, the *swap rate* for a particular maturity at a particular time is the fixed rate that would be exchanged for LIBOR in a newly issued swap with that maturity. Suppose that the swap rate for an n-year swap starting at time T is R. (Both R and R_K are expressed with a compounding frequency of m times per year.) By comparing the cash flows on a swap where the fixed rate is R to the cash flows on a swap where the fixed rate is R_K, we see that the payoff from the swaption consists of a series of cash flows equal to

$$\frac{L}{m}\max(R - R_K,\ 0)$$

The cash flows are received m times per year for the n years of the life of the swap. Suppose that the swap payment dates are $t_1, t_2, \dots, t_{mn}$, measured in years from today. (It is approximately true that $t_i = T + i/m$.) Each cash flow is the payoff from a call option on R with strike price R_K.

In the standard market model for valuing swaptions, V in Section 21.3 is set equal to R. From equation (21.3), the value of the cash flow received at time t_i is

$$\frac{L}{m}e^{-r_i t_i}[F_0 N(d_1) - R_K N(d_2)]$$

where

$$d_1 = \frac{\ln(F_0/R_K) + \sigma^2 T/2}{\sigma\sqrt{T}}$$

$$d_2 = \frac{\ln(F_0/R_K) - \sigma^2 T/2}{\sigma\sqrt{T}} = d_1 - \sigma\sqrt{T}$$

Here F_0 is the forward swap rate, r_i is the continuously compounded risk-free zero rate for a maturity of t_i, and σ is the volatility of the forward swap rate.

The total value of the swaption is

$$\sum_{i=1}^{mn}\frac{L}{m}e^{-r_i t_i}[F_0 N(d_1) - R_K N(d_2)]$$

If we define A as the value of a contract that pays $1/m$ at times t_i $(1 \leqslant i \leqslant mn)$ so that

$$A = \frac{1}{m}\sum_{i=1}^{mn} e^{-r_i t_i}$$

Example 21.7 Valuation of a swaption

Suppose that the LIBOR yield curve is flat at 6% per annum with continuous compounding and this is used as the risk-free zero curve. Consider a swaption that gives the holder the right to pay 6.2% in a 3-year swap starting in 5 years. Payments are made semiannually and the principal is \$100 million. In this case,

$$A = \tfrac{1}{2}\left(e^{-0.06\times 5.5} + e^{-0.06\times 6} + e^{-0.06\times 6.5} + e^{-0.06\times 7} + e^{-0.06\times 7.5} + e^{-0.06\times 8}\right) = 2.0035$$

A rate of 6% per annum with continuous compounding translates into 6.09% with semiannual compounding. It follows that in this example $F_0 = 0.0609$, $R_K = 0.062$, $T = 5$. If the volatility of the forward swap rate is 20%, $\sigma = 0.2$ and

$$d_1 = \frac{\ln(0.0609/0.062) + 0.2^2 \times 5/2}{0.2\sqrt{5}} = 0.1836$$

$$d_2 = d_1 - 0.2\sqrt{5} = -0.2636$$

From equation (21.10) the value of the swaption is (in \$ million)

$$100 \times 2.0035 \times [0.0609 \times N(0.1836) - 0.062 \times N(-0.2636)] = 2.07$$

or \$2.07. (This is in agreement with the price given by DerivaGem.)

then the value of the swaption becomes[6]

$$LA[F_0 N(d_1) - R_K N(d_2)] \tag{21.10}$$

Example 21.7 provides an application of this formula.

If the swaption gives the holder the right to receive a fixed rate of R_K instead of paying it, the payoff from the swaption is

$$\frac{L}{m}\max(R_K - R,\ 0)$$

This is a put option on R. As before, the payoffs are received at times t_i $(1 \leqslant i \leqslant mn)$. Equation (21.4) gives the value of the swaption as

$$LA[R_K N(-d_2) - F_0 N(-d_1)] \tag{21.11}$$

The DerivaGem software provides an implementation of equations (21.10) and (21.11)

---

[6] Here, F_0 and R_K are measured with a compounding frequency corresponding to the frequency of payments on the swap. For example, if payments are twice a year, then they are measured with semiannual compounding. The formula for A is simplified in that it assumes payments are made at intervals of exactly $1/m$ years. To be more precise, we should define the A in equations (21.10) and (21.11) as

$$A = \sum_{i=1}^{mn} a_i P(0, t_i)$$

where $P(0, t)$ is the price of a zero-coupon bond maturing at time t and a_i is the time between t_{i-1} and t_i measured with the day count convention specified in the contract ($t_0 = T$). For example, if t_{i-1} is March 1 and t_i is September 1 and the day count is specified as actual/365, then $a_i = 184/365 = 0.5041$.

Table 21.2 Typical broker quotes for U.S. European swaptions (mid-market volatilities % per annum)

	Swap length (years)						
Expiration	*1*	*2*	*3*	*4*	*5*	*7*	*10*
1 month	17.75	17.75	17.75	17.50	17.00	17.00	16.00
3 months	19.50	19.00	19.00	18.00	17.50	17.00	16.00
6 months	20.00	20.00	19.25	18.50	18.75	17.75	16.75
1 year	22.50	21.75	20.50	20.00	19.50	18.25	16.75
2 years	22.00	22.00	20.75	19.50	19.75	18.25	16.75
3 years	21.50	21.00	20.00	19.25	19.00	17.75	16.50
4 years	20.75	20.25	19.25	18.50	18.25	17.50	16.00
5 years	20.00	19.50	18.50	17.75	17.50	17.00	15.50

assuming LIBOR discounting is used. In the Cap_and_Swap_Options worksheet select Swap Option as the Underlying Type and Black-European as the Pricing Model.

Interdealer brokers provide tables of implied volatilities for European swaptions. The instruments underlying the quotes are usually "at the money" in the sense that the strike swap rate equals the forward swap rate. Table 21.2 shows typical broker quotes provided for the U.S. dollar market. The tenor of the underlying swaps (i.e., the frequency of resets on the floating rate) is six months. The life of the option is shown on the vertical scale. This varies from one month to five years. The life of the underlying swap at the maturity of the option is shown on the horizontal scale. This varies from one year to ten years. The volatilities in the extreme left column of the table correspond to instruments that are similar to caps. They exhibit the hump discussed earlier. As we move to the columns corresponding to options on longer-lived swaps, the hump persists, but it becomes less pronounced.

21.7 TERM STRUCTURE MODELS

The European bond option pricing model that we have presented assumes that a bond price at some future time is lognormally distributed; the cap pricing model assumes that an interest rate at some future time is lognormally distributed; the European swap option pricing model assumes that a swap rate at some future time is lognormally distributed. These assumptions are not consistent with each other. This makes it difficult for traders to compare the way the market prices different types of instruments.

A related disadvantage of the models is that they cannot easily be extended to value instruments other than those for which they were designed. For example, Black's model for valuing a European swap option cannot easily be extended to value American swap options. A more sophisticated approach to valuing interest rate derivative securities involves constructing a *term structure model*. This is a model that describes the probabilistic behavior of the term structure of interest rates. Term structure models are more complicated than those used to describe the movements of a stock price or currency. This is because they are concerned with movements in a whole zero-coupon

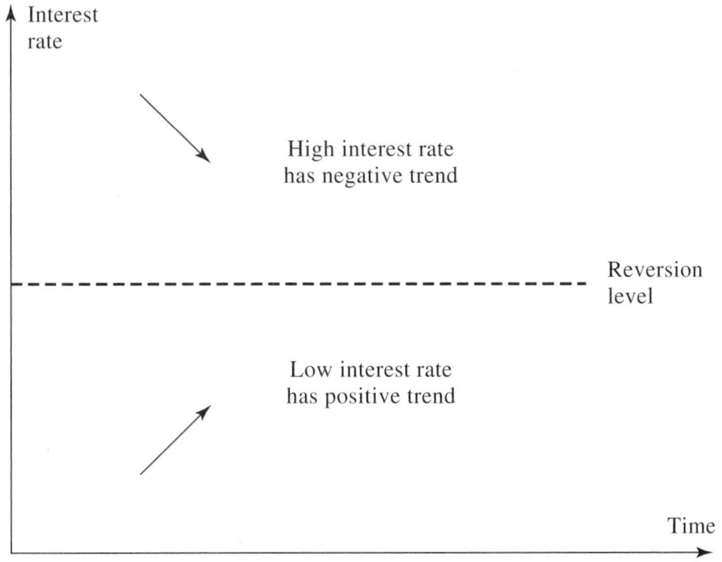

Figure 21.3 Mean reversion

yield curve, not with changes to a single variable. As time passes, all interest rates do not necessarily change by the same amount so that the shape of the yield curve is liable to change.

Explaining how term structure models are constructed is beyond the scope of this book. But it is worth noting one property of an interest rate that distinguishes it from a stock price or an exchange rate—or indeed the price of any investment asset. A short-term interest rate (say, the three-month rate) appears to exhibit a property known as *mean reversion*. It tends to be pulled back to some long-run average level. When the short-term interest rate is very high, it tends to move down; when it is very low, it tends to move up. For example, if the three-month interest rate in the United States reaches 15%, the next movement is more likely to be down than up; if it reaches 1%, the next movement is more likely to be up than down. This is illustrated in Figure 21.3.

If a stock price exhibited mean reversion, there would be an obvious trading strategy: buy the stock when its price is at a historic low; sell the stock when its price is at a historic high. Mean-reverting three-month interest rates do not provide a similar trading strategy. This is because an interest rate is not the price of a security that can be traded. There is no traded instrument whose price is always equal to the three-month rate.

SUMMARY

Interest rate options arise in practice in many different ways. For example, options on Treasury bond futures, Treasury note futures, and Eurodollar futures are actively traded by exchanges. Many traded bonds include features that are options. The loans and deposit instruments offered by financial institutions often contain embedded options.

Three popular over-the-counter instruments are bond options, interest caps and floors, and swap options. A bond option is an option to buy or sell a particular bond. An interest rate cap (floor) provides a payoff when a floating rate of interest rises above (falls below) the strike rate. A swap option is an option to enter into a swap, where a specified fixed rate will be exchanged for floating, at a particular time in the future. Black's model is the model used by the market for valuing these instruments. In the case of bond options, the probability distribution of the underlying bond is assumed to be lognormal. In the case of caps and floors, the underlying interest rates are assumed to be lognormal. In the case of swap options, the underlying swap rate is assumed to be lognormal.

FURTHER READING

Black, F. "The Pricing of Commodity Contracts," *Journal of Financial Economics*, 3 (1976): 167–79.

Black, F., E. Derman, and W. Toy. "A One-Factor Model of Interest Rates and Its Application to Treasury Bond Options," *Financial Analysts Journal*, (January/February 1990): 33–39.

Black, F., and P. Karasinski. "Bond and Option Pricing When Short Rates Are Lognormal," *Financial Analysts Journal*, (July/August 1991): 52–59.

Brace A., D. Gatarek, and M. Musiela. "The Market Model of Interest Rate Dynamics," *Mathematical Finance*, 7, 2 (1997): 127–55.

Cox, J. C., J. E. Ingersoll, and S. A. Ross. "A Theory of the Term Structure of Interest Rates," *Econometrica*, 53 (1985): 385–407.

Heath, D., R. Jarrow, and A. Morton. "Bond Pricing and the Term Structure of Interest Rates: A New Methodology," *Econometrica*, 60 (1992): 77–105.

Ho, T. S. Y., and S. B. Lee. "Term Structure Movements and Pricing Interest Rate Contingent Claims," *Journal of Finance*, 41 (December 1986): 1011–29.

Hull, J. C. *Options, Futures, and Other Derivatives*, 8th edn. Upper Saddle River, NJ: Pearson, 2012.

Hull, J. C., and A. White. "Pricing Interest Rate Derivative Securities," *Review of Financial Studies*, 3, 4 (1990): 573–92.

Hull, J. C., and A. White. "Using Hull–White Interest Rate Trees," *Journal of Derivatives*, (Spring 1996): 26–36.

James, J., and N. Webber. *Interest Rate Modeling*. Chichester, UK: Wiley, 2000.

Jamshidian, F. "LIBOR and Swap Market Models and Measures," *Finance and Stochastics*, 1 (1997): 293–330.

Miltersen, K., K. Sandmann, and D. Sondermann, "Closed Form Solutions for Term Structure Derivatives with Lognormal Interest Rates," *Journal of Finance*, 52, 1 (March 1997): 409–30.

Rebonato, R. *Interest Rate Option Models*. 2nd edn. New York: Wiley, 1998.

Vasicek, O. A. "An Equilibrium Characterization of the Term Structure," *Journal of Financial Economics*, 5(1977): 177–88.

Quiz (Answers at End of Book)

21.1. A company caps three-month LIBOR at 10% per annum. The principal amount is $20 million. On a reset date three-month LIBOR is 12% per annum. What payment would this lead to under the cap? When would the payment be made?

21.2. Explain the features of (a) callable and (b) puttable bonds.

21.3. Explain why a swaption can be regarded as a type of bond option.

21.4. Use Black's model to value a 1-year European put option on a 10-year bond. The current cash price of the bond is \$125, the strike price is \$110, the 1-year risk-free interest rate is 10% per annum, the bond's forward price volatility is 8% per annum, and the present value of the coupons that will be paid during the life of the option is \$10.

21.5. Suppose you buy a Eurodollar call futures option contract with a strike price of 97.25. You exercise when the underlying Eurodollar futures price is 98.12. What is the payoff?

21.6. Calculate the price of an option that caps the 3-month rate starting in 18 months' time at 13% (quoted with quarterly compounding) on a principal amount of \$1,000. The forward interest rate for the period in question is 12% per annum (quoted with quarterly compounding), the 21-month risk-free interest rate (continuously compounded) is 11.5% per annum, and the volatility of the forward rate is 12% per annum.

21.7. What are the advantages of term structure models over Black's model for valuing interest rate derivatives?

Practice Questions (Answers in Solutions Manual/Study Guide)

21.8. A bank uses Black's model to price European bond options. Suppose that an implied price volatility for a 5-year option on a bond maturing in 10 years is used to price a 9-year option on the bond. Would you expect the resultant price to be too high or too low? Explain your answer.

21.9. Consider a 4-year European call option on a bond that will mature in 5 years. The 5-year bond price is \$105, the price of a 4-year bond with the same coupon as the 5-year bond is \$102, the strike price of the option is \$100, the 4-year risk-free interest rate is 10% per annum (continuously compounded), and the volatility of the forward price of the bond underlying the option is 2% per annum. What is the present value of the principal in the 4-year bond? What is the present value of the coupons in the 4-year bond? What is the forward price of the bond underlying the option? What is the value of the option?

21.10. If the yield volatility for a 5-year put option on a bond maturing in 10 years time is specified as 22%, how should the option be valued? Assume that, based on today's interest rates, the modified duration of the bond at the maturity of the option will be 4.2 years and the forward yield on the bond is 7%.

21.11. A corporation knows that in three months it will have \$5 million to invest for 90 days at LIBOR minus 50 basis points and wishes to ensure that the rate obtained will be at least 6.5%. What position in exchange-traded interest rate options should the corporation take?

21.12. Explain carefully how you would use (a) spot volatilities and (b) flat volatilities to value a 5-year cap.

21.13. What other instrument is the same as a 5-year zero-cost collar in which the strike price of the cap equals the strike price of the floor? What does the common strike price equal?

21.14. Suppose that the 1-year, 2-year, 3-year, 4-year and 5-year LIBOR/swap zero rates are 6%, 6.4%, 6.7%, 6.9%, and 7%. The price of a 5-year semiannual cap with a principal of \$100 at a cap rate of 8% is \$3. Use DerivaGem (with LIBOR discounting) to determine:
(a) The 5-year flat volatility for caps and floors
(b) The floor rate in a zero-cost 5-year collar when the cap rate is 8%.

21.15. Show that $V_1 + f = V_2$, where V_1 is the value of a swaption to pay a fixed rate of R_K and receive LIBOR between times T_1 and T_2, f is the value of a forward swap to receive a fixed rate of R_K and pay LIBOR between times T_1 and T_2, and V_2 is the value of a swaption to receive a fixed rate of R_K between times T_1 and T_2. Deduce that $V_1 = V_2$ when R_K equals the current forward swap rate.

21.16. Explain why there is an arbitrage opportunity if the implied Black (flat) volatility for a cap is different from that for a floor. Do the broker quotes in Table 21.1 present an arbitrage opportunity?

21.17. Suppose that zero rates are as in Problem 21.14. Use DerivaGem (with LIBOR discounting) to determine the value of an option to pay a fixed rate of 6% and receive LIBOR on a five-year swap starting in one year. Assume that the principal is \$100 million, payments are exchanged semiannually, and the swap rate volatility is 21%.

Further Questions

21.18. Consider an eight-month European put option on a Treasury bond that currently has 14.25 years to maturity. The bond principal is \$1,000. The current cash bond price is \$910, the exercise price is \$900, and the volatility of the forward bond price is 10% per annum. A coupon of \$35 will be paid by the bond in three months. The risk-free interest rate is 8% for all maturities up to one year. Use Black's model to determine the price of the option. Consider both the case where the strike price corresponds to the cash price of the bond and the case where it corresponds to the quoted price.

21.19. Use the DerivaGem software to value a five-year collar that guarantees that the maximum and minimum interest rates on a LIBOR-based loan (with quarterly resets) are 7% and 5%, respectively. The LIBOR zero curve (continuously compounded) is currently flat at 6% and is used for discounting. The flat volatility is 20%. Assume that the principal is \$100.

21.20. Suppose that the LIBOR yield curve is flat at 8% with annual compounding and is used for discounting. A swaption gives the holder the right to receive 7.6% in a 5-year swap starting in 4 years. Payments are made annually. The volatility of the forward swap rate is 25% per annum and the principal is \$1 million. Use Black's model to price the swaption. Compare your answer to that given by DerivaGem.

21.21. Calculate the price of a cap on the 3-month LIBOR rate in 9 months' time for a principal amount of \$1,000. Use Black's model and the following information:

Quoted 9-month Eurodollar futures price = 92
Interest rate volatility implied by a 9-month Eurodollar option = 15% per annum
The 12-month risk-free interest rate with continuous compounding = 7.5% per annum
Cap rate = 8% per annum.

21.22. Use the DerivaGem software to value a European swaption that gives you the right in 2 years to enter into a 5-year swap in which you pay a fixed rate of 6% and receive floating. Cash flows are exchanged semiannually on the swap. The continuously compounded 1-year, 2-year, 5-year, and 10-year LIBOR/swap zero rates (which are also used for discounting) are 5%, 6%, 6.5%, and 7%, respectively. Assume a principal of \$100 and a volatility of 15% per annum. Give an example of how the swaption might be used by a corporation. What bond option is equivalent to the swaption?

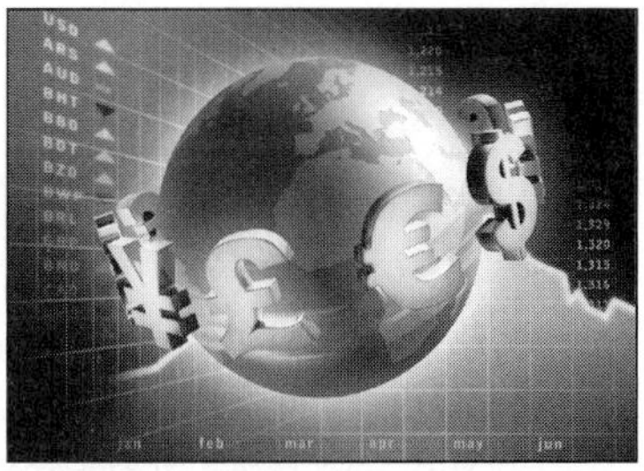

CHAPTER 22 Exotic Options and Other Nonstandard Products

The derivatives we have covered in the first 21 chapters of this book are what are termed *plain vanilla products*. They have standard well-defined properties and trade actively. Their prices or implied volatilities are quoted by exchanges or by interdealer brokers on a regular basis. One of the exciting features of the over-the-counter derivatives market is the number of nonstandard (or exotic) products that have been created by financial engineers. Although they are usually a relatively small part of its portfolio, these exotic products are important to a derivatives dealer such as an investment bank because they are generally much more profitable than plain vanilla products.

Exotic products are developed for a number of reasons. Sometimes they meet a genuine hedging need in the market; sometimes there are tax, accounting, legal, or regulatory reasons why corporate treasurers or fund managers find exotic products attractive; sometimes the products are designed to reflect a corporate treasurer's or fund manager's view on potential future movements in particular market variables; occasionally an exotic product is designed by a derivatives dealer to appear more attractive than it is to an unwary corporate treasurer or fund manager.

In this chapter, we start by considering variations on the standard call and put options that we have covered in earlier chapters. We then look at mortgage-backed securities, which have become an important feature of the U.S. interest rate derivatives market. Finally, we describe some nonstandard swap products. The objective of this chapter is to give a flavor for the range of instruments that have been developed. It does not provide a complete list of such instruments.

22.1 EXOTIC OPTIONS

In this section, we describe a number of different types of exotic options that are offered on underlying assets such as stocks, stock indices, and currencies. We use a categorization similar to that in an excellent series of articles written by Eric Reiner and Mark Rubinstein for *Risk* magazine in 1991 and 1992. Asian, barrier, binary, chooser, compound, and lookback options can be valued using DerivaGem.[1]

[1] The procedures used by the market to value all the options described in this section are covered in J. C. Hull, *Options, Futures, and Other Derivatives*, 8th edn. Upper Saddle River, NJ: Pearson, 2012, Chapter 25.

From Chapter 22 of *Fundamentals of Futures and Options Markets*, Eighth Edition. John C. Hull.

Packages

A *package* is a portfolio consisting of standard European calls, standard European puts, forward contracts, cash, and the underlying asset itself. We discussed a number of different types of packages in Chapter 11: bull spreads, bear spreads, butterfly spreads, calendar spreads, straddles, strangles, and so on.

Often a package is structured by financial engineers so that it has zero cost initially. An example is a *range forward contract*. This was explained in Chapter 15. It consists of a long call and a short put or a short call and a long put, with the call strike price greater than the put strike price.

Nonstandard American Options

In a standard American option, exercise can take place at any time during the life of the option, and the exercise price is always the same. The American options that are traded in the over-the-counter market do not always have these features. For example:

1. Early exercise may be restricted to certain dates. The instrument is then known as a *Bermudan option*—Bermuda being between Europe and America!
2. Early exercise may be allowed during only part of the life of the option.
3. The strike price may change during the life of the option.

The warrants issued by corporations on their own stock often have some or all of these features. For example, in a seven-year warrant, exercise might be possible on particular dates during years 3 to 7, with the strike price being \$30 during years 3 and 4, \$32 during the next two years, and \$33 during the final year.

Nonstandard American options can usually be valued using a binomial tree. At each node, the test (if any) for early exercise is adjusted to reflect the terms of the option.

Gap Options

A gap call option is a European call options that pays off $S_T - K_1$ when $S_T > K_2$. The difference between a gap call option and a regular call option with a strike price of K_2 is that the payoff when $S_T > K_2$ is increased by $K_2 - K_1$. (This increase is positive or negative depending on whether $K_2 > K_1$ or $K_1 > K_2$.)

A gap call option can be valued by a small modification to the Black–Scholes–Merton formula. With our usual notation, the value is

$$S_0 e^{-qT} N(d_1) - K_1 e^{-rT} N(d_2) \qquad \textbf{(22.1)}$$

where

$$d_1 = \frac{\ln(S_0/K_2) + (r - q + \sigma^2/2)T}{\sigma\sqrt{T}}$$

$$d_2 = d_1 - \sigma\sqrt{T}$$

The price in this formula is greater than the price given by the Black–Scholes–Merton formula for a regular call option with strike price K_2 by

$$(K_2 - K_1)e^{-rT} N(d_2)$$

To understand this difference, note that the probability that the option will be exercised

Example 22.1 A gap option in insurance

An asset is currently worth \$500,000. Over the next year, it is expected to have a volatility of 20%. The risk-free rate is 5%, and no income is expected. Suppose that an insurance company agrees to buy the asset for \$400,000 if its value has fallen below \$400,000 at the end of one year. The payout will be $400{,}000 - S_T$ whenever the value of the asset is less than \$400,000. The insurance company has provided a regular put option where the policyholder has the right to sell the asset to the insurance company for \$400,000 in one year. This can be valued using equation (13.6), with $S_0 = 500{,}000$, $K = 400{,}000$, $r = 0.05$, $\sigma = 0.2$, $T = 1$. The value is \$3,436.

Suppose next that the cost of transferring the asset is \$50,000 and this cost is borne by the policyholder. The option is then exercised only if the value of the asset is less than \$350,000. In this case, the cost to the insurance company is $K_1 - S_T$ when $S_T < K_2$, where $K_2 = 350{,}000$, $K_1 = 400{,}000$, and S_T is the price of the asset in one year. This is a gap put option. The value is given by equation (22.2), with $S_0 = 500{,}000$, $K_1 = 400{,}000$, $K_2 = 350{,}000$, $r = 0.05$, $q = 0$, $\sigma = 0.2$, $T = 1$. It is \$1,896. Recognizing the costs to the policyholder of making a claim reduces the cost of the policy to the insurance company by about 45% in this case.

is $N(d_2)$ and, when it is exercised, the payoff to the holder of the gap option is greater than that to the holder of the regular option by $K_2 - K_1$.

For a gap put option, the payoff is $K_1 - S_T$ when $S_T < K_2$. The value of the option is

$$K_1 e^{-rT} N(-d_2) - S_0 e^{-qT} N(-d_1) \quad \textbf{(22.2)}$$

where d_1 and d_2 are defined as for equation (22.1).

Example 22.1 shows how a gap option might arise in insurance.

Forward Start Options

Forward start options are options that will start at some time in the future. Employee stock options, which were discussed in Chapter 14, can be viewed as a type of forward start option. In a typical stock option plan, a company promises that it will grant at-the-money options to employees at certain times in the future.

When the underlying asset provides no income, an at-the-money forward start option is (using the assumptions underlying the Black–Scholes–Merton model) worth the same as a regular at-the-money option with the same life. For example, an at-the-money option that will start in three years and mature in five years is worth the same as a two-year at-the-money option initiated today (see Problem 22.13).

Cliquet Options

A cliquet option (which is also called a ratchet or strike reset option) is a series of call or put options with rules for determining the strike price. Suppose that the reset dates are at times $\tau, 2\tau, \ldots, (n-1)\tau$, with $n\tau$ being the end of the cliquet's life. A simple structure would be as follows. The first option has a strike price K (which might equal the initial asset price) and lasts between times 0 and τ; the second option provides a payoff at time 2τ with a strike price equal to the value of the asset at time τ; the third option provides a payoff at time 3τ with a strike price equal to the value of the asset at time 2τ; and so on. This is a regular option plus $n - 1$ forward start options.

Compound Options

Compound options are options on options. There are four main types of compound options: a call on a call, a put on a call, a call on a put, and a put on a put. Compound options have two strike prices and two exercise dates. Consider, for example, a call on a call. On the first exercise date, T_1, the holder of the compound option is entitled to pay the first strike price, K_1, and receive a call option. The call option gives the holder the right to buy the underlying asset for the second strike price, K_2, on the second exercise date, T_2. The compound option will be exercised on the first exercise date only if the value of the second option on that date is greater than the first strike price. Compound options tend to be much more sensitive to volatility than plain vanilla options.

Chooser Options

A *chooser* option (sometimes referred to as an *as you like it* option) has the feature that, after a specified period of time, the holder can choose whether the option is a call or a put. Suppose that the time when the choice is made is T_1. The value of the chooser option at this time is

$$\max(c, p)$$

where c is the value of the call underlying the option and p is the value of the put underlying the option.

If the options underlying the chooser option are both European and have the same strike price, put–call parity can be used to provide a valuation formula. Suppose that S_1 is the underlying asset price at time T_1, K is the strike price, T_2 is the maturity of the options, r is the risk-free interest rate, and q is the dividend yield on the asset. Put–call parity implies that

$$\begin{aligned}\max(c, p) &= \max(c,\ c + Ke^{-r(T_2-T_1)} - S_1e^{-q(T_2-T_1)}) \\ &= c + e^{-q(T_2-T_1)}\max(0,\ Ke^{-(r-q)(T_2-T_1)} - S_1)\end{aligned}$$

This shows that the chooser option is a package consisting of:

1. A call option with strike price K and maturity T_2
2. $e^{-q(T_2-T_1)}$ put options with strike price $Ke^{-(r-q)(T_2-T_1)}$ and maturity T_1

As such, it can readily be valued.

Barrier Options

Barrier options are options where the payoff depends on whether the underlying asset's price reaches a certain level during a certain period of time. A number of different types of barrier options regularly trade in the over-the-counter market. They are attractive to some market participants because they are less expensive than the corresponding regular options. Barrier options can be classified as either *knock-out options* or *knock-in options*. A knock-out option ceases to exist when the underlying asset price reaches a certain level; a knock-in option comes into existence only when the underlying asset price reaches a certain level.

There are four types of knock-out options. An *up-and-out call* option is a regular European call option that ceases to exist as soon as the asset price reaches a barrier level. The barrier level is greater than the asset price at the time the option is initiated. A *down-and-out call* is defined similarly except that the barrier level is below the asset price at the time the option is initiated. An *up-and-out put* and *down-and-out put* are defined similarly.

There are similarly four types of knock-in options. An *up-and-in call* option is a regular European call option that starts to exist as soon as the asset price reaches a barrier level. The barrier level is greater than the asset price when the option is initiated. A *down-and-in call* is similar except that the barrier level is below the asset price when the option is initiated. An *up-and-in put* and a *down-and-in put* are defined analogously. There are relationships between the prices of barrier options and regular options. For example, the price of a down-and-out call option plus the price of a down-and-in call option must equal the price of a regular European option (when strike prices, times to maturity, and barrier levels are the same). Similarly, the price of a down-and-out put option plus the price of a down-and-in put option must equal the price of a regular European option.

Barrier options often have quite different properties from regular options. For example, sometimes vega is negative. Consider an up-and-out call option when the asset price is close to the barrier level. As volatility increases, the probability that the barrier will be hit increases. As a result, a volatility increase causes a price decrease.

In determining whether a barrier is hit, sometimes the price is observed on a more or less continuous basis.[2] On other occasions the terms on the contract state that the price is observed periodically (e.g., once a day at 12 noon).

One disadvantage of the barrier options we have considered so far is that a "spike" in the asset price can cause the option to be knocked in or out. An alternative structure is a *Parisian option*, where the asset price has to be above or below the barrier for a period of time for the option to be knocked in or out. For example, a down-and-out Parisian put option with a strike price equal to 90% of the initial asset price and a barrier at 75% of the initial asset price might specify that the option is knocked out if the asset price is below the barrier for 50 days. (The 50 days might be a "continuous period of 50 days" or "any 50 days during the option's life.") Parisian options are more difficult to value that regular barrier options.[3] Monte Carlo simulation is one approach that can be used.

Binary Options

Binary options are options with discontinuous payoffs. A simple example of a binary option is a *cash-or-nothing call*. This pays off nothing if the asset price ends up below the strike price at time T and pays a fixed amount, Q, if it ends up above the strike price. In a risk-neutral world, the probability of the asset price being above the strike price at the maturity of an option is, with our usual notation, $N(d_2)$. The value of a

[2] One way to track whether a barrier is reached from below (above) is to send a limit order to an exchange to sell (buy) the asset at the barrier price and see whether the order is filled.

[3] See, for example, M. Chesney, J. Cornwall, M. Jeanblanc-Picqué, G. Kentwell, and M. Yor, "Parisian Pricing," *Risk*, 10, 1 (1997): 77–79.

cash-or-nothing call is therefore $Qe^{-rT}N(d_2)$. A *cash-or-nothing put* is defined analogously to a cash-or-nothing call. It pays off Q if the asset price is below the strike price and nothing if it is above the strike price. The value of a cash-or-nothing put is $Qe^{-rT}N(-d_2)$.

Another type of binary option is an *asset-or-nothing call.* This pays off nothing if the underlying asset price ends up below the strike price and pays the asset price if it ends up above the strike price. With our usual notation, the value of an asset-or-nothing call is $S_0e^{-qT}N(d_1)$. An *asset-or-nothing put* pays off nothing if the underlying asset price ends up above the strike price and the asset price if it ends up below the strike price. The value of an asset-or-nothing put is $S_0e^{-qT}N(-d_1)$.

A regular European call option is equivalent to a long position in an asset-or-nothing call and a short position in a cash-or-nothing call where the cash payoff in the cash-or-nothing call equals the strike price. Similarly, a regular European put option is equivalent to a long position in a cash-or-nothing put and a short position in an asset-or-nothing put where the cash payoff on the cash-or-nothing put equals the strike price.

Lookback Options

The payoffs from lookback options depend on the maximum or minimum asset price reached during the life of the option. The payoff from a *floating lookback call* is the amount that the final asset price exceeds the minimum asset price achieved during the life of the option. The payoff from a *floating lookback put* is the amount by which the maximum asset price achieved during the life of the option exceeds the final asset price.

A floating lookback call is a way that the holder can buy the underlying asset at the lowest price achieved during the life of the option. Similarly, a floating lookback put is a way that the holder can sell the underlying asset at the highest price achieved during the life of the option. The underlying asset in a lookback option is often a commodity. The frequency with which the asset price is observed for the purposes of computing the maximum or minimum is important and must be specified in the contract.

In a *fixed lookback option*, a strike price is specified. For a call, the payoff is the same as for a regular option except that the final asset price is replaced by the maximum asset price realized over the life of the option; for a put, the payoff is the same as for a regular option except that the final asset price is replaced by the minimum asset price realized over the life of the option.

Shout Options

A *shout option* is a European option where the holder can "shout" to the writer at one time during its life. At the end of the life of the option, the option holder receives either the usual payoff from a European option or the intrinsic value at the time of the shout, whichever is greater. Suppose the strike price is \$50 and the holder of a call shouts when the price of the underlying asset is \$60. If the final asset price is less than \$60, the holder receives a payoff of \$10. If it is greater than \$60, the holder receives the excess of the final asset price over \$50.

A shout option has some of the same features as a lookback option, but is considerably less expensive. It can be valued by noting that, if the option is shouted at a time τ when the asset price is S_τ, the payoff from the option is

$$\max(0,\ S_T - S_\tau) + (S_\tau - K)$$

where, as usual, K is the strike price and S_T is the asset price at time T. The value at time τ if the option is shouted is therefore the present value of $S_\tau - K$ (received at time T) plus the value of a European option with strike price S_τ. This allows a binomial tree to be used to value the option. As we roll back through the the tree, we test whether shouting is optimal at each node.

Asian Options

Asian options are options where the payoff depends on the arithmetic average of the price of the underlying asset during the life of the option. The payoff from an *average price call* is $\max(0, S_{\text{ave}} - K)$ and that from an *average price put* is $\max(0, K - S_{\text{ave}})$, where S_{ave} is the average price of the underlying asset. Average price options are less expensive than regular options and are arguably more appropriate than regular options for meeting some of the needs of corporate treasurers. Suppose that a U.S. corporate treasurer expects to receive a cash flow of 100 million Australian dollars spread evenly over the next year from the company's Australian subsidiary. The treasurer is likely to be interested in an option that guarantees that the average exchange rate realized during the year is above some level. An average price put option can achieve this more effectively than regular put options. We discussed a way binomial trees can be used in conjunction with Monte Carlo simulation to value Asian options at the end of Chapter 18.

Another type of Asian option is an average strike option. An *average strike call* pays off $\max(0, S_T - S_{\text{ave}})$ and an *average strike put* pays off $\max(0, S_{\text{ave}} - S_T)$. Average strike options can guarantee that the average price paid for an asset in frequent trading over a period of time is not greater than the final price. Alternatively, it can guarantee that the average price received for an asset in frequent trading over a period of time is not less than the final price.

Options to Exchange One Asset for Another

Options to exchange one asset for another (sometimes referred to as *exchange options*) arise in various contexts. An option to buy yen with Australian dollars is, from the point of view of a U.S. investor, an option to exchange one foreign currency asset for another foreign currency asset. A stock tender offer is an option to exchange shares in one stock for shares in another stock.

An option to obtain the better or worse of two assets is closely related to an exchange option. It is a position in one of the assets combined with an option to exchange it for the other asset:

$$\min(U_T, V_T) = V_T - \max(V_T - U_T, 0)$$

$$\max(U_T, V_T) = U_T + \max(V_T - U_T, 0)$$

Options Involving Several Assets

Options involving two or more risky assets are sometimes referred to as *rainbow options*. One example is the bond futures contract traded on the CBOT described in Chapter 6. The party with the short position is allowed to choose between a large number of different bonds when making delivery.

Probably the most common example of an option involving several assets is a *basket option*. This is an option where the payoff is dependent on the value of a portfolio (or basket) of assets. The assets are usually either individual stocks or stock indices or currencies. Basket option prices depend on both the volatilities of the assets' prices and the correlations between them. The latter are usually estimated from historical data.

22.2 AGENCY MORTGAGE-BACKED SECURITIES

One feature of the United States interest rate derivatives market that we mentioned in Chapter 8 is the active trading in *mortgage-backed securities*. A mortgage-backed security (MBS) is created when a financial institution decides to sell part of its residential mortgage portfolio to investors. The mortgages are put into a pool and investors acquire a stake in the pool by buying units. The units are known as mortgage-backed securities. A secondary market is usually created for the units so that investors can sell them to other investors as desired. An investor who owns units representing X percent of a certain pool is entitled to X percent of the principal and interest cash flows received from the mortgages in the pool.

The mortgages underlying an agency MBS (unlike those considered in Chapter 8) are guaranteed by a government-related agency, such as the Government National Mortgage Association (GNMA) or the Federal National Mortgage Association (FNMA), so that investors are protected against defaults. This makes an agency MBS sound like a regular fixed-income security issued by the government. However, there is a critical difference between an agency MBS and a regular fixed-income investment. The mortgages in an MBS pool have prepayment privileges and these can be quite valuable to the householder. In the United States mortgages typically last for 30 years and can be prepaid at any time. This means that the householder has a 30-year American-style option to put the mortgage back to the lender at its face value.

Prepayments on mortgages occur for a variety of reasons. Sometimes interest rates have fallen and the owner of the house decides to refinance at a lower rate of interest. On other occasions, a mortgage is prepaid simply because the house is being sold. A critical element in valuing an agency MBS is the determination of the *prepayment function*. This function describes expected prepayments on the underlying pool of mortgages at a particular time in terms of interest rates and other relevant variables.

A prepayment function is very unreliable as a predictor of actual prepayment experience for an individual mortgage. When many similar mortgage loans are combined in the same pool, there is a "law of large numbers" effect at work, and prepayments can be predicted from an analysis of historical data more accurately. As already mentioned, prepayments are not always motivated by pure interest rate considerations. Nevertheless, prepayments tend to be more likely when interest rates are low than when they are high. This means that investors should require a higher rate of interest on an agency MBS than on other fixed-income securities because there is a tendency for the cash received from prepayments to be reinvested at low rates.

Collateralized Mortgage Obligations

The simplest type of agency MBS is a *pass-through*. All investors receive the same return and bear the same prepayment risk. Not all mortgage-backed securities work in this way. In a *collateralized mortgage obligation* (CMO), there are a number of tranches or classes, and rules are developed for determining how principal repayments are channeled to different classes. Different classes bear different amounts of prepayment risk. The CMO structure is therefore similar in concept to the ABS structure considered in Chapter 8, but investors bear no default risk.

As an example of a CMO, consider an agency MBS with investors divided into three classes: class A, class B, and class C. All the principal repayments (both those that are scheduled and those that are prepayments) are channeled to class A investors until investors in this class have been completely paid off. Principal repayments are then channeled to class B investors until these investors have been completely paid off. Finally, principal repayments are channeled to class C investors. In this situation class A investors bear the most prepayment risk. Class A securities can be expected to last less long than class B securities, which in turn can be expected to last less long than class C securities.

The objective of this type of structure is to create classes of securities that are more attractive to institutional investors than those created by a simpler pass-through MBS. The prepayment risks assumed by the different classes depend on the par value in each class. For example, class C bears very little prepayment risk if the par values in classes A, B, and C are 400, 300, and 100, respectively. It bears rather more prepayment risk if the par values in the classes are 100, 200, and 500.

IOs and POs

In a *stripped MBS*, principal payments are separated from interest payments. All principal payments are channeled to one class of security, known as a *principal only* (PO). All interest payments are channeled to another class of security, known as an *interest only* (IO). Both IOs and POs are risky investments. As prepayment rates increase, a PO becomes more valuable and an IO becomes less valuable. As prepayment rates decrease, the reverse happens. In a PO, a fixed amount of principal is returned to the investor, but the timing is uncertain. A high rate of prepayments on the underlying pool leads to the principal being received early (which is, of course, good news for the holder of the PO). A low rate of prepayments on the underlying pool delays the return of the principal and reduces the yield provided by the PO. In an IO, the total of the cash flows received by the investor is not certain. The higher the rate of prepayments, the lower the total cash flows received by the investor, and vice versa.

22.3 NONSTANDARD SWAPS

We discussed plain vanilla interest rate swaps in Chapter 7. These are agreements to exchange interest at the LIBOR rate for interest at a fixed rate. Business Snapshot 7.1 in Chapter 7 gives a confirmation for a hypothetical plain vanilla swap. In this section we describe a number of nonstandard swap agreements.[4]

Variations on the Vanilla Deal

Many interest rate swaps involve relatively minor changes being made to the plain vanilla structure discussed in Chapter 7. In some swaps the notional principal changes with time in a predetermined way. Swaps where the notional principal is an increasing function of

[4] The valuation of many of the swaps described here is described in J.C. Hull, *Options, Futures, and Other Derivatives*, 8th edn. Upper Saddle River, NJ: Pearson, 2012, Chapter 32.

Business Snapshot 22.1 Hypothetical confirmation for nonstandard swap

Trade date	5-January-2013
Effective date	11-January-2013
Business day convention (all dates)	Following business day
Holiday calendar	U.S.
Termination date	11-January-2018
Fixed Amounts	
Fixed-rate payer	Microsoft
Fixed-rate notional principal	USD 100 million
Fixed-rate	6% per annum
Fixed-rate day count convention	Actual/365
Fixed-rate payment dates	Each 11-July and 11-January, commencing 11-July, 2013, up to and including 11-January, 2018
Floating Amounts	
Floating-rate payer	Goldman Sachs
Floating-rate notional principal	USD 120 million
Floating rate	USD 1 month LIBOR
Floating-rate day count convention	Actual/360
Floating-rate payment dates	11-July, 2013, and the 11th of each month thereafter, up to and including 11-January, 2018

time are known as *step-up swaps*. Swaps where the notional principal is a decreasing function of time are known as *amortizing swaps*. Step-up swaps could be useful for a construction company that intends to borrow increasing amounts of money at floating rates to finance a particular project and wants to swap to fixed-rate funding. An amortizing swap could be used by a company that has fixed-rate borrowings with a certain prepayment schedule and wants to swap them to borrowings at a floating rate.

The principal can be different on the two sides of a swap. Also the frequency of payment can be different. This is illustrated by the hypothetical swap between Microsoft and Goldman Sachs in Business Snapshot 22.1 where the notional principal is \$120 million on the floating side and \$100 million on fixed side. Payments are made every month on the floating side and every six months on the fixed side.

The floating reference rate for a swap is not always LIBOR. In some swaps, for instance, it is the commercial paper (CP) rate. A *basis swap* involves exchanging cash flows calculated using one floating reference rate for those calculated using another floating reference rate, for example a swap where the three-month CP rate plus 10 basis points is exchanged for three-month LIBOR with both being applied to a principal of \$100 million. A basis swap could be used for risk management by a financial institution whose assets and liabilities are dependent on different floating reference rates.

Compounding Swaps

Another variation on the plain vanilla swap is a *compounding swap*. A confirmation for a compounding swap is in Business Snapshot 22.2. In this example there is only one

Business Snapshot 22.2 Hypothetical confirmation for compounding swap

Trade date	5-January-2013
Effective date	11-January-2013
Holiday calendar	U.S.
Business day convention (all dates)	Following business day
Termination date	11-January-2018
Fixed Amounts	
Fixed-rate payer	Microsoft
Fixed-rate notional principal	USD 100 million
Fixed rate	6% per annum
Fixed-rate day count convention	Actual/365
Fixed-rate payment date	11-January, 2018
Fixed-rate compounding	Applicable at 6.3%
Fixed-rate compounding dates	Each 11-July and 11-January, commencing 11-July, 2013, up to and including 11-July, 2017
Floating Amounts	
Floating-rate payer	Goldman Sachs
Floating-rate notional principal	USD 100 million
Floating rate	USD 6 month LIBOR plus 20 basis points
Floating-rate day count convention	Actual/360
Floating-rate payment date	11-January, 2018
Floating-rate compounding	Applicable at LIBOR plus 10 basis points
Floating-rate compounding dates	Each 11-July and 11-January, commencing 11-July, 2013, up to and including 11-July, 2017

payment date for both the floating-rate payments and the fixed-rate payments. This is at the end of the life of the swap. The floating rate of interest is LIBOR plus 20 basis points. Instead of being paid, the interest is compounded forward until the end of the life of the swap at a rate of LIBOR plus 10 basis points. The fixed rate of interest is 6%. Instead of being paid this interest is compounded forward at a fixed rate of interest of 6.3% until the end of the swap.

Currency Swaps

We introduced currency swaps in Chapter 7. They enable an interest rate exposure in one currency to be swapped for an interest rate exposure in another currency. Usually two principals are specified, one in each currency. The principals are exchanged at both the beginning and the end of the life of the swap, as described in Section 7.12.

Suppose that the currencies involved in a currency swap are U.S. dollars (USD) and British pounds (GBP). In a fixed-for-fixed currency swap, a fixed rate of interest is specified in each currency. The payments on one side are determined by applying the fixed rate of interest in USD to the USD principal; the payments on the other side are determined by applying the fixed rate of interest in GBP to the GBP principal.

Another popular type of currency swap is floating-for-floating. In this the payments on one side are determined by applying USD LIBOR (possibly with a spread added) to the USD principal; similarly the payments on the other side are determined by applying GBP LIBOR (possibly with a spread added) to the GBP principal. A third type of swap is a cross-currency interest rate swap where a floating rate in one currency is exchanged for a fixed rate in another currency.

Valuation and Convexity Adjustments

In Chapter 7 we explained that plain vanilla interest rate and currency swaps can be valued by assuming that interest rates in the future will equal the corresponding forward interest rates observed in the market today. The nonstandard swaps we have discussed so far can also be valued in this way. However, the next three types of swaps that we will discuss cannot. They are valued by assuming that interest rates in the future will equal the corresponding forward interest rates observed in the market today plus an adjustment. The adjustment is known as a *convexity adjustment*.[5]

LIBOR-in-Arrears Swap

A plain vanilla interest rate swap is designed so that the floating rate of interest observed on one payment date is paid on the next payment date. An alternative instrument that is sometimes traded is a *LIBOR-in-arrears swap*. In this, the floating rate paid on a payment date equals the rate observed on the payment date itself.

CMS Swaps

A constant maturity swap (CMS) is an interest rate swap where the floating rate equals the swap rate for a swap with a certain life. For example, the floating payments on a CMS swap might be made every six months at a rate equal to the five-year swap rate. Usually there is a lag so that the payment on a particular payment date is equal to the swap rate observed on the previous payment date. Suppose that rates are set at times $t_0, t_1, t_2, \dots$, payments are made at times $t_1, t_2, t_3, \dots$, and L is the notional principal. The floating payment at time t_{i+1} is $\delta_i L s_i$, where $\delta_i = t_{i+1} - t_i$ and s_i is the five-year swap rate at time t_i.

Differential Swaps

A *differential swap*, sometimes referred to as a *diff swap*, is an interest rate swap where a floating interest rate is observed in one currency and applied to a principal in another currency. For example, a swap might involve the payments going one way being calculated as USD LIBOR applied to a USD principal and the payments going the other way being calculated as GBP LIBOR (plus or minus a spread) being applied to the same USD principal. Diff swaps are sometimes also referred to as *quantos*.

A diff swap is a "pure interest rate play." This distinguishes it from a regular floating-for-floating currency swap. The company paying GBP in our diff swap example gains if GBP LIBOR decreases relative to USD LIBOR and loses if the reverse happens. The

[5] For a discussion of these types of convexity adjustments, see J.C. Hull, *Options, Futures, and Other Derivatives*, 8th edn. Upper Saddle River, NJ: Pearson, 2012, Chapter 29.

Business Snapshot 22.3 Hypothetical confirmation for equity swap

Trade date	5-January-2013
Effective date	11-January-2013
Business day convention (all dates)	Following business day
Holiday calendar	U.S.
Termination date	11-January-2018
Equity Amounts	
Equity payer	Microsoft
Equity principal	USD 100 million
Equity index	Total Return S&P 500 index
Equity payment	$100(I_1 - I_0)/I_0$, where I_1 is the index level on the payment date and I_0 is the index level on the immediately preceding payment date. In the case of the first payment date, I_0 is the index level on 11 January, 2013
Equity payment dates	Each 11-July and 11-January, commencing 11-July, 2013, up to and including 11-January, 2018
Floating Amounts	
Floating-rate payer	Goldman Sachs
Floating-rate notional principal	USD 100 million
Floating-rate	USD 6 month LIBOR
Floating-rate day count convention	Actual/360
Floating-rate payment dates	Each 11-July and 11-January, commencing 11-July, 2013, up to and including 11-January, 2018

payoff from a currency swap where GBP floating is exchanged for USD floating depends on exchange-rate movements as well as on interest rate movements in the two countries.

Equity Swaps

In an equity swap one party promises to pay the return on an equity index applied to a notional principal and the other promises to pay a fixed or floating return on the notional principal. Equity swaps enable fund managers to increase or reduce their exposure to an index without buying and selling stock. An equity swap is a convenient way of packaging a series of forward contracts on an equity index to meet the needs of the market.

The equity index is usually a total return index where dividends are reinvested in the stocks comprising the index. A confirmation for an equity swap is in Business Snapshot 22.3. In this, Microsoft pays the six-month return on the S&P 500 to Goldman Sachs and Goldman Sachs pays six-month LIBOR to Microsoft. The principal on either side of the swap is $100 million and payments are made every six months.

Accrual Swaps

Accrual swaps are swaps where the interest on one side accrues only when the floating reference rate is within a certain range. Sometimes the range remains fixed during the entire life of the swap; sometimes it is reset periodically.

As a simple example of an accrual swap, consider a deal where a fixed rate of 6% is exchanged for three-month LIBOR every quarter. The principal is \$10 million and the fixed rate accrues only on days when three-month LIBOR is below 8% per annum. Define n_1 as the number of days in a quarter that the three-month LIBOR is below 8% and n_2 is the number of days in the year. The payment made at the end of the quarter is

$$10{,}000{,}000 \times 0.06 \times \frac{n_1}{n_2}$$

For example, when $n_1 = 25$ and $n_2 = 365$, the payment is \$41,096. In a regular swap the payment would be about $0.25 \times 0.06 \times 10{,}000{,}000$ or \$150,000.

Compared with a regular swap, the fixed-rate payer saves $10{,}000{,}000 \times 0.06/365 =$ \$1,644 for each day interest rates are above 8%. The fixed-rate payer's position can therefore be considered equivalent to a regular swap plus a series of binary options, one for each day of the life of the swap.

Cancelable Swaps

A cancelable swap is a plain vanilla interest rate swap where one side has the option to terminate on one or more payment dates. Terminating a swap is the same as entering into the offsetting (opposite) swap. Consider a swap between Microsoft and Goldman Sachs. If Microsoft has the option to cancel, it can regard the swap as a regular swap plus a long position in an option to enter into the offsetting swap. If Goldman Sachs has the cancelation option, Microsoft has a regular swap plus a short position in an option to enter into the same swap.

If there is only one termination date, a cancelable swap is the same as a regular swap plus a position in a European swap option. Consider, for example, a ten-year swap where Microsoft will receive 6% and pay LIBOR. Suppose that Microsoft has the option to terminate at the end of six years. The swap is a regular ten-year swap to receive 6% and pay LIBOR plus long position in a six-year European option to enter into a four-year swap where 6% is paid and LIBOR is received. (The latter is referred to as a 6×4 European option.) The standard market model for valuing European swap options was described in Chapter 21.

When the swap can be terminated on a number of different payment dates, it is a regular swap option plus a Bermudan-style swap option. Consider, for example, the situation where Microsoft has entered into a five-year swap with semiannual payments where 6% is received and LIBOR is paid. Suppose that the counterparty has the option to terminate on the swap on payment dates between year 2 and year 5. The swap is regular swap plus a short position in a Bermudan-style swap option where the Bermudan style swap option is an option to enter into a swap that matures in five years and involves a fixed payment at 6% being received and a floating payment at LIBOR being paid. The swap option can be exercised on any payment date between year 2 and year 5.

Sometimes compounding swaps are cancelable. Typically the confirmation agreement states that on termination the floating rate payer pays the compounded value of the floating amounts up to the termination date and the fixed rate payer pays the compounded value of the fixed payments up to the termination date.

Index Amortizing Swaps

A swap that was very popular in the United States in the mid-1990s is an *index amortizing rate swap* (sometimes also called an *indexed principal swap*). With this swap, the principal reduces in a way dependent on the level of interest rates. The lower the interest rate, the greater the reduction in the principal. The fixed side of an indexed amortizing swap was originally designed to mirror approximately the return obtained by an investor from an agency mortgage-backed security. To an investor, the swap then has the effect of exchanging the return on the mortgage-backed security for a floating-rate return.

Commodity Swaps

Commodity swaps are now becoming increasingly popular. A company that consumes 100,000 barrels of oil per year could agree to pay $8 million each year for the next 10 years and to receive in return 100,000S, where S is the current market price of oil per barrel. The agreement would in effect lock in the company's oil cost at $80 per barrel. An oil producer might agree to the opposite exchange, thereby locking in the price it realized for its oil at $80 per barrel.

Volatility and Variance Swaps

A *volatility swap* is an agreement to exchange the realized volatility of an asset over a period for a prespecified fixed volatility. The difference between the two volatilities is multiplied by a specified notional principal to determine the payoff. The realized volatility is usually calculated as described in Section 13.4, with the assumption that the mean return $\bar{u}$ is zero. A *variance swap* is similarly an agreement to exchange the realized variance rate (i.e., the square of the volatility) over a period for a prespecified variance rate. Again, the difference between the two variance rates is multiplied by a specified notional principal to determine the payoff.

Like trades in the VIX index (see Section 13.9), volatility and variance swaps provide payoffs that depend only on volatility. The VIX index payoffs depend on implied volatility, while the payoffs from volatility and variance swaps depend on the volatility actually observed. Volatility swaps can be contrasted with options. The former are "pure plays" on realized volatility; the value of the latter depend on other factors in addition to volatility.

Other Swaps

Swaps can be engineered in many other ways. Some swaps have payoffs that are calculated in quite bizarre ways. An example is a deal entered into between Procter & Gamble and Bankers Trust in 1993 (see Business Snapshot 22.4). The details of this transaction are in the public domain because it later became the subject of litigation.[6]

[6] See D. J. Smith, "Aggressive Corporate Finance: A Close Look at the Procter and Gamble–Bankers Trust Leveraged Swap," *Journal of Derivatives* 4, No. 4 (Summer 1997): 67–79.

Business Snapshot 22.4 Procter & Gamble's bizarre deal

A particularly bizarre swap is the so-called "5/30" swap entered into between Bankers Trust (BT) and Procter & Gamble (P&G) on November 2, 1993. This was a five-year swap with semiannual payments. The notional principal was $200 million. BT paid P&G 5.30% per annum. P&G paid BT the average 30-day commercial paper (CP) rate minus 75 basis points plus a spread. The average CP rate was calculated by taking observations on the 30-day CP rate each day during the preceding accrual period and averaging them.

The spread was zero for the first payment date (May 2, 1994). For the remaining nine payment dates, it was

$$\max\left[0, \frac{98.5\left(\dfrac{5\,\text{yr CMT\%}}{5.78\%}\right) - (30\,\text{yr TSY price})}{100}\right]$$

In this expression, five-year CMT is the constant maturity Treasury yield (i.e., the yield on a five-year Treasury note, as reported by the Federal Reserve). The 30-year TSY price is the midpoint of the bid and offer cash bond prices for the 6.25% Treasury bond maturing on August 2023. Note that the spread calculated from the formula is a decimal interest rate. It is not measured in basis points. If the formula gives 0.1 and the average CP rate is 6%, the rate paid by P&G is 15.25%.

P&G were hoping that the spread would be zero and the deal would enable them to exchange fixed-rate funding at 5.30% for funding at 75 basis points less than the commercial paper rate. In fact, interest rates rose sharply in early 1994, bond prices fell, and the swap proved very, very expensive. (See Problem 22.20.)

SUMMARY

Exotic options are options with rules governing the payoffs that are not as straightforward as those for standard options. They provide corporate treasurers and fund managers with a wide range of alternatives for achieving their objectives. Some exotic options are nothing more than portfolios of regular European and American calls and puts. Others are much more complicated.

Mortgage-backed securities are created when a financial institution decides to sell part of its residential portfolio of mortgages to investors. The mortgages are put in a pool and investors acquire a stake in the pool by buying units. The mortgages are guaranteed against defaults by a government agency, but investors are subject to prepayment risk. Often the return from a pool of mortgages is split into a number of components with different properties in an attempt to meet the needs of different types of investors.

Swaps have proved to be very versatile financial instruments, and many variations on the plain vanilla fixed-for-floating deal now exist. Some such as step-up swaps, amortizing swaps, compounding swaps, LIBOR in arrears swaps, diff swaps, and CMS swaps involve changes to the way payments are calculated or their timing. Others such as accrual swaps and cancelable swaps have embedded options.

FURTHER READING

Boyle, P.P., and S.H. Lau. "Bumping Up against the Barrier with the Binomial Method," *Journal of Derivatives*, 1, 4 (Summer 1994): 6–14.

Broadie, M., P. Glasserman, and S.G. Kou. "A Continuity Correction for Discrete Barrier Options," *Mathematical Finance*, 7, 4 (October 1997): 325–49.

Broadie, M., P. Glasserman, and S.G. Kou. "Connecting Discrete and Continuous Path-Dependent Options," *Finance and Stochastics*, 2 (1998): 1–28.

Chance, D., and D. Rich. "The Pricing of Equity Swap and Swaptions," *Journal of Derivatives*, 5, 4 (Summer 1998): 19–31.

Clewlow, L., and C. Strickland. *Exotic Options: The State of the Art*. London: Thomson, 1997.

Conze, A., and S. Viswanathan. "Path Dependent Options: The Case of Lookback Options," *Journal of Finance*, 46 (1991): 1893–1907.

Demeterfi, K., E. Derman, M. Kamal, and J. Zou. "A Guide to Volatility and Variance Swaps," *Journal of Derivatives*, 6, 4 (Summer 1999): 9–32.

Forster, D.M. "The State of the Law after Procter & Gamble vs Bankers Trust," *Derivatives Quarterly*, 3, 2 (1996): 8–17.

Geske, R. "The Valuation of Compound Options," *Journal of Financial Economics*, 7 (1979): 63–81.

Goldman B., H. Sosin, and M.A. Gatto. "Path Dependent Options: Buy at the Low, Sell at the High," *Journal of Finance*, 34 (December 1979): 1111–27.

Hull, J.C. *Options, Futures, and Other Derivatives*, 8th edn. Upper Saddle River, NJ: Pearson, 2012.

Hull, J.C., and A. White. "Efficient Procedures for Valuing European and American Path-Dependent Options," *Journal of Derivatives*, (Fall 1993): 21–31.

Laatch, F.E. "Tax Clienteles, Arbitrage, and the Pricing of Total Return Swaps," *Journal of Derivatives*, 8, 2 (Winter 2000): 37–46.

Margrabe, W. "The Value of an Option to Exchange One Asset for Another," *Journal of Finance*, 33 (March 1978): 177–86.

Rubinstein, M. "Pay Now, Choose Later," *Risk* (February 1991), 44–47.

Rubinstein, M. "Options for the Undecided," *Risk* (April 1991), 70–73.

Rubinstein, M. "Two in One," *Risk* (May 1991), 49.

Rubinstein, M. "One for Another," *Risk* (July/August 1991), 30–32.

Rubinstein, M. "Somewhere Over the Rainbow." *Risk* (November 1991), 63–66.

Rubinstein, M. "Double Trouble," *Risk* (December 1991 / January 1992), 53–56.

Rubinstein, M., and E. Reiner. "Breaking Down the Barriers," *Risk*, (September 1991), 28–35.

Rubinstein, M., and E. Reiner. "Unscrambling the Binary Code," *Risk* (October 1991), 75–83.

Smith D.J. "Aggressive Corporate Finance: A Close Look at the Procter and Gamble–Bankers Trust Leveraged Swap," *Journal of Derivatives*, 4, 4 (Summer 1997): 67–79.

Stulz, R. "Options on the Minimum or Maximum of Two Assets," *Journal of Financial Economics*, 10 (1982): 161–85.

Turnbull, S.M., and L.M. Wakeman. "A Quick Algorithm for Pricing European Average Options," *Journal of Financial and Quantitative Analysis*, 26 (September 1991): 377–89.

Quiz (Answers at End of Book)

22.1. Explain the difference between a forward start option and a chooser option.

22.2. What is the value of a cash-or-nothing call that promises to pay $100 if the price of a non-dividend-paying stock is above \$50 in three months? The current stock price is \$50, the risk-free rate is 4%, and the stock price volatility is 20%.

22.3. List eight types of barrier options.

22.4. How does an equity swap work?

22.5. Explain why IOs and POs have opposite sensitivities to the rate of prepayments.

22.6. Explain the relationship between a cancelable swap and a swap option.

22.7. The Canadian dollar LIBOR rate is 2% higher than the U.S. LIBOR rate for all maturities. A trader thinks that the spread between three-month U.S. LIBOR and three-month Canadian LIBOR will widen, but is unsure about how the exchange rate between the U.S. dollar and Canadian dollar will move. Explain how the trader could use a diff swap. Why would the trader prefer a diff swap to a floating-for-floating currency swap?

Practice Questions (Answers in Solutions Manual/Study Guide)

22.8. Describe the payoff from a portfolio consisting of a floating lookback call and a floating lookback put with the same maturity.

22.9. Consider a chooser option where the holder has the right to choose between a European call and a European put at any time during a two-year period. The maturity dates and strike prices for the calls and puts are the same regardless of when the choice is made. Is it ever optimal to make the choice before the end of the two-year period? Explain your answer.

22.10. Suppose that c_1 and p_1 are the prices of a European average price call and a European average price put with strike price K and maturity T, c_2 and p_2 are the prices of a European average strike call and European average strike put with maturity T, and c_3 and p_3 are the prices of a regular European call and a regular European put with strike price K and maturity T. Show that $c_1 + c_2 - c_3 = p_1 + p_2 - p_3$.

22.11. The text derives a decomposition of a particular type of chooser option into a call maturing at time T_2 and a put maturing at time T_1. By using put–call parity to obtain an expression for c instead of p, derive an alternative decomposition into a call maturing at time T_1 and a put maturing at time T_2.

22.12. Explain why a down-and-out put is worth zero when the barrier is greater than the strike price.

22.13. Prove that an at-the-money forward start option on a non-dividend-paying stock that will start in three years and mature in five years is worth the same as a two-year at-the-money option starting today.

22.14. Suppose that the strike price of an American call option on a non-dividend-paying stock grows at rate g. Show that if g is less than the risk-free rate, r, it is never optimal to exercise the call early.

22.15. Answer the following questions about compound options:

(a) What put–call parity relationship exists between the price of a European call on a call and a European put on a call?

(b) What put–call parity relationship exists between the price of a European call on a put and a European put on a put?

22.16. Does a floating lookback call become more valuable or less valuable as we increase the frequency with which we observe the asset price in calculating the minimum?

22.17. Does a down-and-out call become more valuable or less valuable as we increase the frequency with which we observe the asset price in determining whether the barrier has been crossed? What is the answer to the same question for a down-and-in call?

22.18. Explain why a regular European call option is the sum of a down-and-out European call and a down-and-in European call.

22.19. What is the value of a derivative that pays off \$100 in six months if the S&P 500 index is greater than 1,000 and zero otherwise? Assume that the current level of the index is 960, the risk-free rate is 8% per annum, the dividend yield on the index is 3% per annum, and the volatility of the index is 20%.

22.20. Estimate the interest rate paid by P&G on the 5/30 swap in Business Snapshot 22.4 if (a) the CP rate is 6.5% and the Treasury yield curve is flat at 6% and (b) the CP rate is 7.5% and the Treasury yield curve is flat at 7%.

Further Questions

22.21. Use DerivaGem to calculate the value of:
(a) A regular European call option on a non-dividend-paying stock where the stock price is \$50, the strike price is \$50, the risk-free rate is 5% per annum, the volatility is 30%, and the time to maturity is one year
(b) A down-and-out European call which is as in (a) with the barrier at \$45
(c) A down-and-in European call which is as in (a) with the barrier at \$45.

Show that the option in (a) is worth the sum of the values of the options in (b) and (c).

22.22. What is the value in dollars of a derivative that pays off £10,000 in one year provided that the dollar–sterling exchange rate is greater than 1.5000 at that time? The current exchange rate is 1.4800. The dollar and sterling interest rates are 4% and 8% per annum, respectively. The volatility of the exchange rate is 12% per annum.

22.23. Consider an up-and-out barrier call option on a non-dividend-paying stock when the stock price is 50, the strike price is 50, the volatility is 30%, the risk-free rate is 5%, the time to maturity is one year, and the barrier is 80. Use DerivaGem to value the option and graph the relationship between (a) the option price and the stock price, (b) the option price and the time to maturity, and (c) the option price and the volatility. Provide an intuitive explanation for the results you get. Show that the delta, theta, and vega for an up-and-out barrier call option can be either positive or negative.

22.24. Suppose that the LIBOR zero rate is flat at 5% with annual compounding. In a five-year swap, company X pays a fixed rate of 6% and receives LIBOR annually on a principal of \$100 million. The volatility of the two-year swap rate in three years is 20%.
(a) What is the value of the swap?
(b) Use DerivaGem to calculate the value of the swap if company X has the option to cancel after three years.
(c) Use DerivaGem to calculate the value of the swap if the counterparty has the option to cancel after three years.
(d) What is the value of the swap if either side can cancel at the end of three years?

22.25. Outperformance certificates (also called "sprint certificates," "accelerator certificates," or "speeders") are offered to investors by many European banks as a way of investing in a company's stock. The initial investment equals the stock price, S_0. If the stock price goes up between time 0 and time T, the investor gains k times the increase at time T, where k is a constant greater than 1.0. However, the stock price used to calculate the gain at time T is capped at some maximum level M. If the stock price goes down, the investor's loss is equal to the decrease. The investor does not receive dividends.

(a) Show that an outperformance certificate is a package.

(b) Calculate using DerivaGem the value of a one-year outperformance certificate when the stock price is 50 euros, $k = 1.5$, $M = 70$ euros, the risk-free rate is 5%, and the stock price volatility is 25%. Dividends equal to 0.5 euros are expected in 2 months, 5 months, 8 months, and 11 months.

22.26. What is the relationship between a regular call option, a binary call option, and a gap call option?

CHAPTER 23 Credit Derivatives

An important development in derivatives markets since the late 1990s has been the growth of credit derivatives. In 2000, the total notional principal for outstanding credit derivatives contracts was about \$800 billion. By 2011, this had risen to about \$30 trillion. Credit derivatives are contracts where the payoff depends on the creditworthiness of one or more companies or countries. This chapter explains how credit derivatives work and how they are valued.

Credit derivatives allow companies to trade credit risks in much the same way that they trade market risks. Banks and other financial institutions used to be in the position where they could do little once they had assumed a credit risk except wait (and hope for the best). Now they can actively manage their portfolios of credit risks, keeping some and entering into credit derivatives contracts to protect themselves from others. As indicated in Business Snapshot 23.1, banks have been the biggest buyers of credit protection and insurance companies have been the biggest sellers.

Credit derivatives can be categorized as "single-name" or "multi-name." The most popular single-name credit derivative is a credit default swap (CDS). The payoff from this instrument depends on the creditworthiness of one company or country. There are two sides to the contract: the buyer and seller of protection. There is a payoff from the seller of protection to the buyer of protection if the specified entity (company or country) defaults on its obligations. The most popular multi-name credit derivative is a collateralized debt obligation (CDO). In this, a portfolio of debt instruments is specified and a structure is created where the cash flows from the portfolio are channelled to different categories of investors. Chapter 8 described how ABSs and ABS CDOs were created from residential mortgages during the period leading up to the credit crisis. This chapter shows how the same type of structure can be created by pooling the credit risks of companies or countries. Multi-name credit derivatives have increased in popularity relative to single-name credit derivatives. Between 2004 and 2011, their share of the credit derivatives market rose from about 20% to about 40%.

This chapter starts by explaining how credit default swaps work and how they are valued. It then covers the trading of forwards and options on credit default swaps and total return swaps. It explains credit indices, basket credit default swaps, and synthetic collateralized debt obligations.

From Chapter 23 of *Fundamentals of Futures and Options Markets*, Eighth Edition. John C. Hull.

Business Snapshot 23.1 Who Bears the Credit Risk?

Traditionally banks have been in the business of making loans and then bearing the credit risk that the borrower will default. However, banks have for some time been reluctant to keep loans on their balance sheets. This is because, after the capital required by regulators has been accounted for, the average return earned on loans is often less attractive than that on other assets. In the late 1990s and early 2000s, banks made extensive use of credit derivatives to shift the credit risk in their loans to other parts of the financial system.

If banks have been net buyers of credit protection, who have been net sellers? The answer is insurance companies. Insurance companies are not regulated in the same way as banks and as a result are sometimes more willing to bear credit risks than banks.

The result of all this is that the financial institution bearing the credit risk of a loan is often different from the financial institution that did the original credit checks. As the credit crisis starting in 2007 has shown, this is not always good for the overall health of the financial system.

23.1 CREDIT DEFAULT SWAPS

The most popular credit derivative is a *credit default swap* (CDS). This was introduced in Chapter 7. It is a contract that provides insurance against the risk of a default by particular company. The company is known as the *reference entity* and a default by the company is known as a *credit event*. The buyer of the insurance obtains the right to sell bonds issued by the company for their face value when a credit event occurs and the seller of the insurance agrees to buy the bonds for their face value when a credit event occurs.[1] The total face value of the bonds that can be sold is known as the credit default swap's *notional principal*.

The buyer of the CDS makes periodic payments to the seller until the expiry of the CDS or until a credit event occurs. These payments are normally made in arrears every quarter, but transactions where payments are made every month, every 6 months, or every 12 months also occur and sometimes payments are made in advance. The settlement in the event of a default is either physical delivery of the bonds or a cash payment.

An example will help to illustrate how a typical deal is structured. Suppose that two parties enter into a 5-year credit default swap on March 20, 2014. Assume that the notional principal is $100 million and the buyer agrees to pay 90 basis points per annum for protection against default by the reference entity, with payments being made quarterly in arrears.

The CDS is shown in Figure 23.1. If the reference entity does not default (i.e., there is no credit event), the buyer receives no payoff and pays 22.5 basis points (a quarter of 90 basis points) on $100 million on June 20, 2014, and every quarter thereafter until March 20, 2019. The amount paid each quarter is $0.00225 \times 100{,}000{,}000$, or $225,000.[2] If there is a credit event, a substantial payoff is likely. Suppose that the buyer notifies the

[1] The face value (or par value) of a coupon-bearing bond is the principal amount that the issuer repays at maturity if it does not default.

[2] The quarterly payments are liable to be slightly different from $225,000 because of the application of the day count conventions described in Chapter 6.

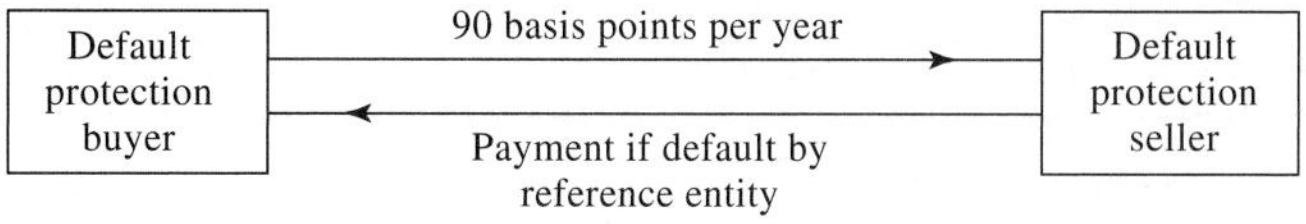

Figure 23.1 Credit default swap

seller of a credit event on May 20, 2017 (2 months into the fourth year). If the contract specifies physical settlement, the buyer has the right to sell bonds issued by the reference entity with a face value of \$100 million for \$100 million. If, as is now usual, there is cash settlement, an auction process is used to determine the mid-market value of the cheapest deliverable bond several days after the credit event. Suppose the auction indicates that this bond is worth \$35 per \$100 of face value. The cash payoff would be \$65 million.

The regular payments from the buyer of protection to the seller of protection cease when there is a credit event. However, because these payments are made in arrears, a final accrual payment by the buyer is usually required. In our example, where there is a default on May 20, 2017, the buyer would be required to pay to the seller the amount of the annual payment accrued between March 20, 2017, and May 20, 2017 (approximately \$150,000), but no further payments would be required.

The total amount paid per year, as a percent of the notional principal, to buy protection (90 basis points in our example) is known as the *CDS spread.* Large banks are market makers in the credit default swap market. When quoting on a new 5-year credit default swap on a company, a market maker might bid 250 basis points and offer 260 basis points. This means that the market maker is prepared to buy protection by paying 250 basis points per year (i.e., 2.5% of the principal per year) and to sell protection for 260 basis points per year (i.e., 2.6% of the principal per year).

Many different companies and countries are reference entities for CDSs. As mentioned, payments are usually made quarterly in arrears. Maturities of 5 years are most popular, but other maturities such as 1, 2, 3, 7, and 10 years are not uncommon. Usually contracts mature on one of the following standard dates: March 20, June 20, September 20, and December 20 and payments are made on these dates. As a result, the actual time to maturity of a contract when it is initiated is close to, but not exactly the same as, the number of years to maturity that is specified. Suppose you call a dealer on November 15, 2014, to buy 5-year protection on a company. The contract would probably last until December 20, 2019. Your first payment would be due on December 20, 2014, and would equal an amount covering the November 15, 2014, to December 20, 2014, period.[3] A key aspect of a CDS contract is the definition of a credit event (i.e., a default). Usually a credit event is defined as a failure to make a payment as it becomes due, a restructuring of debt, or a bankruptcy. Restructuring is sometimes excluded in North American contracts, particularly in situations where the yield on the company's debt is high. More information on the CDS market is given in Business Snapshot 23.2.

Recovery Rate

When a company goes bankrupt, those who are owed money by the company file claims against the company. Sometimes there is a reorganization in which these creditors agree to a partial payment of their claims. In other cases, the assets of the

[3] If the time to the first standard date is less than 1 month, then the first payment is typically made on the second standard payment date; otherwise it is made on the first standard payment date.

Business Snapshot 23.2 The CDS Market

In 1998 and 1999, the International Swaps and Derivatives Association (ISDA) developed a standard contract for trading credit default swaps in the over-the-counter market. Since then the market has grown very fast. A CDS contract is like an insurance contract in many ways, but there is one key difference. An insurance contract provides protection against losses on an asset that is owned. In the case of a CDS, the underlying asset does not have to be owned.

During the credit turmoil that started in August 2007, regulators became very concerned about systemic risk (see Business Snapshot 1.2). They felt that credit default swaps were a source of vulnerability for financial markets. The danger is that a default by one financial institution might lead to big losses by its counterparties in CDS transactions and further defaults by other financial institutions. Regulatory concerns were fueled by troubles at insurance giant AIG. This was a big seller of protection on the AAA-rated tranches created from mortgages (see Chapter 8). The protection proved to have a large negative value to AIG and large positive values to the financial institutions which were its counterparties. AIG was bailed out by the US government and its counterparties avoided credit losses.

Regulatory concerns have led to the development of clearing houses for CDS trades (and other over-the-counter derivatives) between financial institutions (see Sections 1.3 and 2.5). The clearing house requires market participants to post margin on their CDS trades in much the same way that traders post margin on futures contracts.

During 2007 and 2008, trading ceased in many types of credit derivatives, but CDSs continued to trade actively (although the cost of protection increased dramatically). The advantage of CDSs over some other credit derivatives is that the way they work is straightforward. Other credit derivatives, such as those created from the securitization of household mortgages (see Chapter 8), lack this transparency.

It is not uncommon for the volume of CDSs on a company to be greater than its debt. Cash settlement of contracts is then clearly necessary. When Lehman defaulted in September 2008, there was about \$400 billion of CDS contracts and \$155 billion of Lehman debt outstanding. The payout to the buyers of protection (determined by an auction process) was 91.375% of principal.

company are sold by a liquidator and the proceeds are used to meet the claims as far as possible. Some claims typically have priority over other claims and are met more fully.

The recovery rate for a bond is normally defined as the price at which the bond trades about 30 days after default, as a percent of its face value. Table 23.1 provides historical data on the average recovery rates for different types of bonds in the United States. The average recovery rate varied from 51.5% for bonds that are both senior to other lenders and secured to 24.7% for those that rank after other lenders.

Given the way the recovery is defined, the payoff from a CDS can be written as $L(1 - R)$, where L is the notional principal and R is the recovery rate.

Credit Default Swaps and Bond Yields

A CDS can be used to hedge a position in a corporate bond. Suppose that an investor buys a 5-year corporate bond yielding 7% per year for its face value and at the same

Table 23.1 Recovery rates on corporate bonds as a percentage of face value, 1982–2011 (*Source*: Moody's)

Class	*Average recovery rate* (%)
Senior secured	51.5
Senior unsecured	36.8
Senior subordinated	30.9
Subordinated	31.5
Junior subordinated	24.7

time enters into a 5-year CDS to buy protection against the issuer of the bond defaulting. Suppose that the CDS spread is 200 basis points, or 2%, per annum. The effect of the CDS is to convert the corporate bond to a risk-free bond (at least approximately). If the bond issuer does not default the investor earns 5% per year when the CDS spread is netted against the corporate bond yield. If the bond does default the investor earns 5% up to the time of the default. Under the terms of the CDS, the investor is then able to exchange the bond for its face value. This face value can be invested at the risk-free rate for the remainder of the 5 years.

This shows that the excess of an n-year bond yield over the risk-free rate should approximately equal the n-year CDS spread. If it is markedly more than this, an investor can earn more than the risk-free rate by buying the corporate bond and buying protection. If it is markedly less than this, an investor can borrow at less than the risk-free rate by shorting the corporate bond and selling CDS protection. The relevant risk-free rate in these calculations is usually assumed to be the LIBOR/swap rate.

The CDS–bond basis is defined as

$$\text{CDS–bond basis} = \text{CDS spread} - \text{Excess of bond yield over risk-free rate}$$

The arbitrage argument given above suggests that this should be close to zero. Prior to the 2007 credit crisis, it was on average slightly positive. During the crisis, it tended to be negative and became highly negative for a short period of time in January 2009.

The Cheapest-to-Deliver Bond

Usually a CDS specifies that a number of different bonds can be delivered in the event of a default. The bonds typically have the same seniority, but they may not sell for the same percentage of face value immediately after a default.[4] This gives the holder of a CDS a cheapest-to-deliver bond option. As already mentioned, an auction process is usually used to determine the value of the cheapest-to-deliver bond and, therefore, the payoff to the buyer of protection.

[4] There are a number of reasons for this. The claim that is made in the event of a default is typically equal to the bond's face value plus accrued interest. Bonds with high accrued interest at the time of default therefore tend to have higher prices immediately after default. Also the market may judge that in the event of a reorganization of the company some bond holders will fare better than others.

23.2 VALUATION OF CREDIT DEFAULT SWAPS

The CDS spread for a particular reference entity can be calculated from default probability estimates. We will illustrate how this is done with a simple example.

Suppose that the probability of a reference entity defaulting during a year conditional on no earlier default is 2%. Table 23.2 shows survival probabilities and unconditional default probabilities (i.e., default probabilities as seen at time zero) for each of the 5 years. The probability of a default during the first year is 0.02 and the probability the reference entity will survive until the end of the first year is 0.98. The probability of a default during the second year is $0.02 \times 0.98 = 0.0196$ and the probability of survival until the end of the second year is $0.98 \times 0.98 = 0.9604$. The probability of default during the third year is $0.02 \times 0.9604 = 0.0192$, and so on.

We will assume that defaults always happen halfway through a year and that payments on the credit default swap are made once a year, at the end of each year. We also assume that the risk-free interest rate is 5% per annum with continuous compounding and the recovery rate is 40%. There are three parts to the calculation. These are shown in Tables 23.3, 23.4, and 23.5.

Table 23.3 shows the calculation of the present value of the expected payments made on the CDS assuming that payments are made at the rate of s per year and the notional principal is \$1. For example, there is a 0.9412 probability that the third payment of s is made. The expected payment is therefore $0.9412s$ and its present value is $0.9412se^{-0.05\times 3} = 0.8101s$. The total present value of the expected payments is $4.0704s$.

Table 23.4 shows the calculation of the present value of the expected payoff assuming a notional principal of \$1. As mentioned earlier, we are assuming that defaults always happen halfway through a year. For example, there is a 0.0192 probability of a payoff halfway through the third year. Given that the recovery rate is 40%, the expected payoff at this time is $0.0192 \times 0.6 \times 1 = 0.0115$. The present value of the expected payoff is $0.0115e^{-0.05\times 2.5} = 0.0102$. The total present value of the expected payoffs is \$0.0511.

As a final step, Table 23.5 considers the accrual payment made in the event of a default. For example, there is a 0.0192 probability that there will be a final accrual payment halfway through the third year. The accrual payment is $0.5s$. The expected accrual payment at this time is therefore $0.0192 \times 0.5s = 0.0096s$. Its present value is $0.0096se^{-0.05\times 2.5} = 0.0085s$. The total present value of the expected accrual payments is $0.0426s$.

Table 23.2 Unconditional annual default probabilities and survival probabilities.

Time (years)	*Default probability*	*Survival probability*
1	0.0200	0.9800
2	0.0196	0.9604
3	0.0192	0.9412
4	0.0188	0.9224
5	0.0184	0.9039

Table 23.3 Calculation of the present value of expected payments. Payment = s per annum.

Time (years)	*Probability of survival*	*Expected payment*	*Discount factor*	*PV of expected payment*
1	0.9800	0.9800s	0.9512	0.9322s
2	0.9604	0.9604s	0.9048	0.8690s
3	0.9412	0.9412s	0.8607	0.8101s
4	0.9224	0.9224s	0.8187	0.7552s
5	0.9039	0.9039s	0.7788	0.7040s
Total				4.0704s

From Tables 23.3 and 23.5, the present value of the expected payments is

$$4.0704s + 0.0426s = 4.1130s$$

From Table 23.4, the present value of the expected payoff is 0.0511. Equating the two gives

$$4.1130s = 0.0511$$

or $s = 0.0124$. The mid-market CDS spread for the 5-year deal we have considered should be 0.0124 times the principal or 124 basis points per year.

These calculations assume that defaults happen only at points midway between payment dates. This simple assumption usually gives good results, but can easily be relaxed.

Marking to Market a CDS

A CDS, like most other swaps, is marked to market daily. It may have a positive or negative value. Suppose, for example the credit default swap in our example had been negotiated some time ago for a spread of 150 basis points. The present value of the payments by the buyer would be $4.1130 \times 0.0150 = 0.0617$ and the present value of the payoff would be 0.0511 as above. The value of swap to the seller would therefore be

Table 23.4 Calculation of the present value of expected payoff. Notional principal = \$1.

Time (years)	*Probability of default*	*Recovery rate*	*Expected payoff (\$)*	*Discount factor*	*PV of expected payoff (\$)*
0.5	0.0200	0.4	0.0120	0.9753	0.0117
1.5	0.0196	0.4	0.0118	0.9277	0.0109
2.5	0.0192	0.4	0.0115	0.8825	0.0102
3.5	0.0188	0.4	0.0113	0.8395	0.0095
4.5	0.0184	0.4	0.0111	0.7985	0.0088
Total					0.0511

Table 23.5 Calculation of the present value of accrual payment

Time (years)	*Probability of default*	*Expected accrual payment*	*Discount factor*	*PV of expected accrual payment*
0.5	0.0200	0.0100s	0.9753	0.0097s
1.5	0.0196	0.0098s	0.9277	0.0091s
2.5	0.0192	0.0096s	0.8825	0.0085s
3.5	0.0188	0.0094s	0.8395	0.0079s
4.5	0.0184	0.0092s	0.7985	0.0074s
Total				0.0426s

0.0617 − 0.0511, or 0.0106 times the principal. Similarly the mark-to-market value of the swap to the buyer of protection would be −0.0106 times the principal.

Default Probabilities

A key step in valuing credit default swaps is the estimation of default probabilities. The conditional default probability for a period of time is the probability that there will be a default during that period conditional on no earlier default. The unconditional default probability for the time period is the probability as seen today that a default will happen during the time period. If we assume that a company will eventually default, the unconditional default probabilities for all future time periods must add up to one. The same is not true of conditional default probabilities. In our example, Table 23.2 converts conditional default probabilities to unconditional default probabilities. The *hazard rate* $h(t)$ at a future time t is defined so that $h(t)\,\Delta t$ is the conditional probability of default between times t and $t + \Delta t$ for a small Δt. The probability of a default by time t is $1 - \exp(-\bar{h}t)$, where $\bar{h}$ is the average hazard rate between time zero and time t.

The DerivaGem software can be used to calculate credit spreads from hazard rates. The hazard rate can be input as a constant or a step function. Using the formula just given, the default rate of 2% per year in Table 23.2 corresponds to a hazard rate of 2.02%. Substituting a hazard rate of 2.02%, an interest rate of 5%, annual payments, and a recovery rate of 40% into the DerivaGem CDSs worksheet, we get a spread of 124 basis points, which agrees with the calculation in Tables 2.3 to 2.5.

In practice, default probabilities are frequently implied from the prices of actively traded CDSs and then used to price less actively traded CDSs. They are also sometimes implied from bond prices or asset swaps. (The latter are instruments that provide a direct measure of the excess of a bond yield over the LIBOR/swap rate.)

Suppose that we change the example in Tables 23.3 to 23.5 so that we do not know the default probabilities. Instead we know that the mid-market CDS spread for a newly issued five-year CDS is 100 basis points per year. We can reverse-engineer our calculations to conclude that the implied default probability per year (conditional on no earlier default) is 1.61% per year.[5]

[5] The DerivaGem CDS worksheet can be employed to do this. It gives the hazard rate as 1.626%. This is equivalent to a conditional default probability of 1.61% per year in Table 23.2. If spreads for several CDS swaps are available, DerivaGem calculates a step function for the hazard rate that matches them.

Using either quoted CDS spreads or quoted bond prices to estimate implied default probabilities requires an estimate of the recovery rate. The same recovery rate is typically used to (a) estimate implied default probabilities and (b) value credit default swaps. The net result of this is the value of a CDS (or the estimate of a CDS spread) is not very sensitive to the recovery rate. This is because implied probabilities of default are approximately proportional to $1/(1 - R)$ and the payoffs from a CDS are proportional to $1 - R$, so that the expected payoff is almost independent of R.

The default probabilities implied from CDS spreads or bond prices are *risk-neutral default probabilities*. These are the correct default probabilities to use when valuing a credit derivative.[6] It is tempting to estimate default probabilities from the historical data on defaults provided by rating agencies. However, the latter are "*real-world*" default probabilities and are not correct for valuing derivatives. Risk-neutral default probabilities are markedly higher than real-world default probabilities. Companies that make the mistake of using historical default data for valuing credit default swaps are likely to find that selling protection appears very attractive.

Why are real-world default probabilities inappropriate for valuing credit derivatives? A financial institution that sells credit protection is exposing itself to some systematic (nondiversifiable) risk. When the economy does badly more companies default and payoffs on CDSs increase. The financial institution needs to base its premiums on more than real-world default probabilities in order to be adequately compensated for bearing this systematic risk.

Binary Credit Default Swaps

A binary credit default swap is structured similarly to a regular credit default swap except that the payoff is a fixed dollar amount. Suppose that, in the example we have considered in Tables 23.2 to 23.5, the payoff is \$1, instead of $1 - R$ dollars and the swap spread is s. Tables 23.2, 23.3, and 23.5 are the same. Table 23.4 is replaced by Table 23.6. The CDS spread for a new binary CDS is given by

$$4.1130s = 0.0852$$

so that the CDS spread, s, is 0.0207 or 207 basis points.

Table 23.6 Calculation of the present value of expected payoff from a binary credit default swap. Principal = \$1.

Time (years)	*Probability of default*	*Expected payoff (\$)*	*Discount factor*	*PV of expected payoff (\$)*
0.5	0.0200	0.0200	0.9753	0.0195
1.5	0.0196	0.0196	0.9277	0.0182
2.5	0.0192	0.0192	0.8825	0.0170
3.5	0.0188	0.0188	0.8395	0.0158
4.5	0.0184	0.0184	0.7985	0.0147
Total				0.0852

[6] This is because we are using risk-neutral valuation to value the CDS. We estimate expected cash flows in a risk-neutral world and discount them at the risk-free rate.

In the case of a regular CDS we pointed out that there is very little sensitivity to the recovery rate provided the same recovery rate is used to estimate default probabilities and to value the CDS. The same is not true of a binary CDS.

Basket Credit Default Swaps

In a *basket credit default swap*, there are a number of reference entities. An *add-up basket* CDS provides a payoff when any of the reference entities default. A *first-to-default* CDS provides a payoff only when the first default occurs. A *second-to-default* CDS provides a payoff only when the second default occurs. More generally, an *nth-to-default* CDS provides a payoff only when the nth default occurs. Payoffs are calculated in the same way as for a regular CDS. After the relevant default has occurred, there is a settlement. The swap then terminates and there are no further payments by either party.

The default correlation between two companies is a measure of their tendency to default at about the same time. An nth-to-default swap is more complicated to value than a regular credit default swap because it depends on the default correlation between the reference entities in the basket. For example, the higher the default correlation, the lower the CDS spread on a first-to-default swap.

The Future of the CDS Market

Some people think the CDS market will eventually be as big as the interest rate swap market; others are less optimistic. As pointed out in Business Snapshot 23.3, there is a potential asymmetric information problem in the CDS market that is not present in other over-the-counter derivatives markets. We now move on to consider other credit derivatives.

23.3 TOTAL RETURN SWAPS

A *total return swap* is an agreement to exchange the total return on a bond (or any portfolio of assets) for LIBOR plus a spread. The total return includes coupons, interest, and the gain or loss on the asset over the life of the swap.

An example of a total return swap is a five-year agreement with a notional principal of $100 million to exchange the total return on a corporate bond for LIBOR plus 25 basis points. This is illustrated in Figure 23.2. On coupon payment dates the payer pays the coupons earned on an investment of $100 million in the bond. The receiver pays interest at a rate of LIBOR plus 25 basis points on a principal of $100 million. (LIBOR is set on one coupon date and paid on the next as in a plain vanilla interest rate swap.) At the end of the life of the swap, there is a payment reflecting the change in value of the bond. For example, if the bond increases in value by 10% over the life of the swap, the payer is required to pay $10 million (= 10% of $100 million) at the end of the five years. Similarly, if the bond decreases in value by 15%, the receiver is required to pay $15 million at the end of the five years. If there is a default on the bond, the swap is usually terminated and the receiver makes a final payment equal to the excess of $100 million over the market value of the bond.

If the notional principal is added to both sides at the end of the life of the swap, the total return swap can be characterized as follows. The payer pays the cash flows on an

> **Business Snapshot 23.3** Is the CDS market a fair game?
>
> There is one important difference between credit default swaps and the other over-the-counter derivatives that we have considered in this book. The other over-the-counter derivatives depend on interest rates, exchange rates, equity indices, commodity prices, and so on. There is no reason to assume that any one market participant has better information than other market participants about these variables.
>
> Credit default swaps spreads depend on the probability that a particular company will default during a particular period of time. Arguably some market participants have more information to estimate this probability than others. A financial institution that works closely with a particular company by providing advice, making loans, and handling new issues of securities is likely to have more information about the creditworthiness of the company than another financial institution that has no dealings with the company. Economists refer to this as an *asymmetric information* problem.
>
> Whether asymmetric information will curtail the expansion of the credit default swap market remains to be seen. Financial institutions emphasize that the decision to buy protection against the risk of default by a company is normally made by a risk manager and is not based on any special information that may exist elsewhere in the financial institution about the company.

investment of \$100 million in the 5% corporate bond. The receiver pays the cash flows on a \$100 million bond paying LIBOR plus 25 basis points. If the payer owns the bond, the total return swap allows it to pass the credit risk on the bond to the receiver. If it does not own the bond the total return swap allows it to take a short position in the bond.

Total return swaps are often used as a financing tool. One scenario that could lead to the swap in Figure 23.2 is as follows. The receiver wants financing to invest \$100 million in the reference bond. It approaches the payer (which is likely to be a financial institution) and agrees to the swap. The payer then invests \$100 million in the bond. This leaves the receiver in the same position as it would have been if it had borrowed money at LIBOR plus 25 basis points to buy the bond. The payer retains ownership of the bond for the life of the swap and faces less credit risk than it would have done if it had lent money to the receiver to finance the purchase of the bond, with the bond being used as collateral for the loan. If the receiver defaults, the payer does not have the legal problems of trying to realize on its collateral. Total return swaps are similar to repos (see Section 4.1) in that they are structured to minimize credit risk when securities are being financed.

The spread over LIBOR received by the payer is compensation for bearing the risk that the receiver will default. The payer will lose money if the receiver defaults at a time when the reference bond's price has declined. The spread therefore depends on the credit quality of the receiver, the credit quality of the bond issuer, and the correlation between the two.

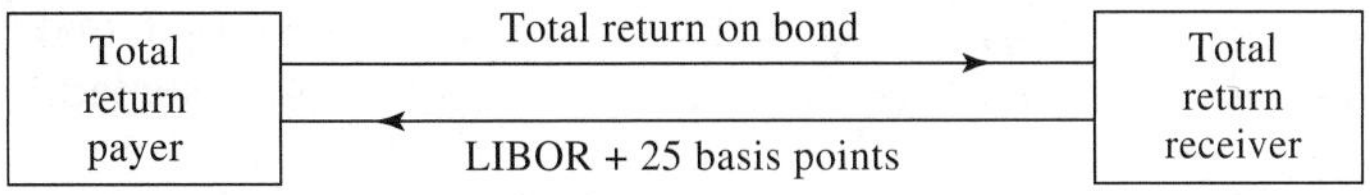

Figure 23.2 Total return swap

There are a number of variations on the standard deal we have described. Sometimes, instead of there being a cash payment for the change in value of the bond, there is physical settlement where the payer exchanges the underlying asset for the notional principal at the end of the life of the swap. Sometimes the change-in-value payments are made periodically rather than all at the end. The swap then has similarities to an equity swap (see Section 22.3).

23.4 CDS FORWARDS AND OPTIONS

A forward credit default swap is the obligation to buy or sell a particular credit default swap on a particular reference entity at a particular future time T. If the reference entity defaults before time T, the forward contract ceases to exist. Thus a bank could enter into a forward contract to sell five-year protection on a company for 280 basis points starting in one year. If the company defaults during the next year the bank's obligation under the forward contract ceases to exist.

A credit default swap option is an option to buy or sell a particular credit default swap on a particular reference entity at a particular future time T. For example, an investor could negotiate the right to buy five-year protection on a company starting in one year for 280 basis points. This is a call option. If the five-year CDS spread for the company in one year turns out to be more than 280 basis points the option will be exercised; otherwise it will not be exercised. The cost of the option would be paid up front. Similarly an investor might negotiate the right to sell five-year protection on a company for 280 basis points starting in one year. This is a put option. If the five-year CDS spread for the company in one year turns out to be less than 280 basis points the option will be exercised; otherwise it will not be exercised. Again the cost of the option would be paid up front. Like CDS forwards, CDS options are usually structured so that they will cease to exist if the reference entity defaults before option maturity.

23.5 CREDIT INDICES

Participants in credit markets have developed indices to track credit default swap spreads. In 2004 there were agreements between different producers of indices that led to some consolidation. Two important standard portfolios used by index providers are:

1. CDX NA IG, a portfolio of 125 investment grade companies in North America
2. iTraxx Europe, a portfolio of 125 investment grade names in Europe

These portfolios are updated on March 20 and September 20 each year. Companies that are no longer investment grade are dropped from the portfolios and new investment grade companies are added.[7]

Suppose that the 5-year CDX NA IG index is quoted by a market maker as bid 65 basis points, offer 66 basis points. (This is referred to as the index spread.) Roughly

[7] On September 20, 2012, the Series 18 iTraxx Europe portfolio and the Series 19 CDX NA IG portfolio were defined. The series numbers indicate that, by the end of September 2012, the iTraxx Europe portfolio had been updated 17 times and the CDX NA IG portfolio had been updated 18 times.

speaking, this means that a trader can buy CDS protection on all 125 companies in the index for 66 basis points per company. Suppose a trader wants \$800,000 of protection on each company. The total cost is $0.0066 \times 800{,}000 \times 125$, or \$660,000 per year. The trader can similarly sell \$800,000 of protection on each of the 125 companies for a total of \$650,000 per annum. When a company defaults, the protection buyer receives the usual CDS payoff and the annual payment is reduced by $660{,}000/125 = \$5{,}280$. There is an active market in buying and selling CDS index protection for maturities of 3, 5, 7, and 10 years. The maturities for these types of contracts on the index are usually December 20 and June 20. (This means that a "5-year" contract actually lasts between $4\frac{3}{4}$ and $5\frac{1}{4}$ years.) Roughly speaking, the index is the average of the CDS spreads on the companies in the underlying portfolio.[8]

23.6 THE USE OF FIXED COUPONS

The precise way in which standard CDS and CDS index transactions work is a little more complicated than has been described up to now. For each underlying and each maturity, a coupon and a recovery rate are specified. A price is calculated from the quoted spread using the following procedure:

1. Assume four payments per year, made in arrears.
2. Imply a hazard rate from the quoted spread. This involves calculations similar to those in Section 23.2. An iterative search is used to determine the hazard rate that leads to the quoted spread.
3. Calculate a duration D for the CDS payments. This is the number that the spread is multiplied by to get the present value of the spread payments. (In the example in Section 23.2, it is 4.1130.)
4. The price P is given by $P = 100 - 100 \times D \times (S - C)$, where S is the spread and C is the coupon expressed in decimal form.

When a trader buys protection the trader pays $100 - P$ per \$100 of the total remaining notional and the seller of protection receives this amount. (If $100 - P$ is negative, the buyer of protection receives money and the seller of protection pays money.) The buyer of protection then pays the coupon times the remaining notional on each payment date. (On a CDS, the remaining notional is the original notional until default and zero thereafter. For a CDS index, the remaining notional is the number of names in the index that have not yet defaulted multiplied by the principal per name.) The payoff when there is a default is calculated in the usual way. This arrangement facilitates trading because the regular quarterly payments made by the buyer of protection are independent of the spread at the time the buyer enters into the contract.

[8] More precisely, the index is slightly lower than the average of the credit default swap spreads for the companies in the portfolio. To understand the reason for this consider a portfolio consisting of two companies, one with a spread of 1,000 basis points and the other with a spread of 10 basis points. To buy protection on the companies would cost slightly less than 505 basis points per company. This is because the 1,000 basis points is not expected to be paid for as long as the 10 basis points and should therefore carry less weight. Another complication for CDX NA IG, but not iTraxx Europe, is that the definition of default applicable to the index includes restructuring, whereas the definition for CDS contracts on the underlying companies often does not.

Example 23.1 How fixed coupons work

Suppose that the iTraxx Europe index quote is 34 basis points and the coupon is 40 basis points for a contract lasting exactly 5 years, with both quotes being expressed using a actual/360 day count. (This is the usual day count convention in CDS and CDS index markets.) The equivalent actual/actual quotes are 0.345% for the index and 0.406% for the coupon. Suppose that the yield curve is flat at 4% per year (actual/actual, continuously compounded). The specified recovery rate is 40%. With four payments per year in arrears, the implied hazard rate is 0.5717%. The duration is 4.447 years. The price is therefore

$$100 - 100 \times 4.447 \times (0.00345 - 0.00406) = 100.27$$

Consider a contract where protection is \$1 million per name. Initially, the seller of protection would pay the buyer \$1,000,000 × 125 × 0.0027. Thereafter, the buyer of protection would make quarterly payments in arrears at an annual rate of \$1,000,000 × 0.00406 × n, where n is the number of companies that have not defaulted. When a company defaults, the payoff is calculated in the usual way and there is an accrual payment from the buyer to the seller calculated at the rate of 0.406% per year on \$1 million.

23.7 COLLATERALIZED DEBT OBLIGATIONS

We discussed asset backed securities (ABSs) in Chapter 8. In that chapter our prime concern was with ABSs where the underlying assets were residential mortgages. An ABS where the underlying assets are corporate bonds is known as a *collateralized debt obligation*, or CDO. A waterfall similar to that indicated in Figure 8.2 is defined for the interest and principal payments on the bonds. The precise rules underlying the waterfall are complicated, but are designed so that if one tranche is more senior to another it is more likely to receive promised interest payments and repayments of bond principal.

Synthetic CDOs

A CDO created from a bond portfolio is known as a *cash CDO*. In an important market development, it was recognized that a long position in a corporate bond has the same risk as the seller of protection (i.e., the party with a short position) in a CDS. Instead of buying a portfolio of bonds, the originator of a CDO can short CDSs. A CDO created in this way is known as a *synthetic CDO*. Both the CDS spread payments that are received on the portfolio of short CDSs and the payments that have to be made when defaults occur are distributed to tranches.

The rules for allocating cash flows to tranches in synthetic CDOs are more standard than in cash CDOs. Figure 23.3 shows a simple structure. The most junior tranche is responsible for the payoffs on the credit default swaps until they have reached 5% of the total notional principal underlying the CDOs; the second most junior tranche is responsible for the payoffs between 5% and 15% of the total notional principal; and so on. The income from the credit default swaps is distributed to the tranches in a way that reflects the risk they are bearing. In the example, Tranche 4 gets 800 basis points on

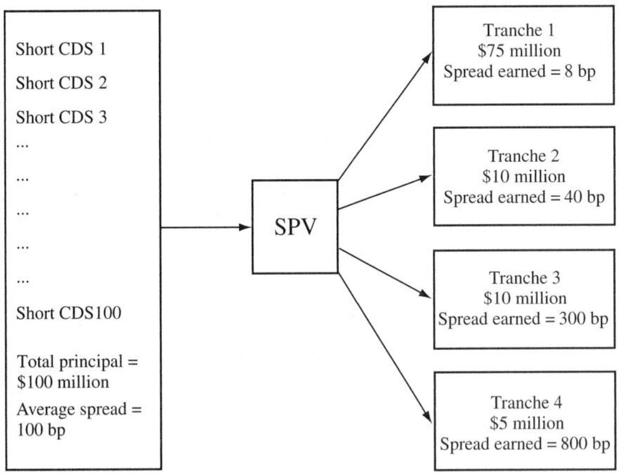

Figure 23.3 The structure of a synthetic CDO

its remaining principal; Tranche 3 gets 300 basis points on its remaining principal; and so on. The principal declines as defaults for which the tranche is responsible occur. For example, at a time when when payoffs on the CDSs total $8 million, the most junior tranche has lost all its principal and earns no interest; the principal of the second most junior tranche has reduced from $10 million to $7 million and the 300 basis point is earned on only $7 million. Synthetic CDOs are sometimes referred to as unfunded structures since the tranche-holders do not invest anything. They receive periodic protection payments and cover losses due to default as they occur.[9]

Standard Portfolios and Single-Tranche Trading

In Section 23.5, we discussed CDS indices such as CDX NA IG and iTraxx Europe. These track credit spreads on investment grade bonds in North America and Europe, respectively. The market uses the portfolios underlying these indices to define standard tranches. The CDX IG NA portfolio consists of 125 investment grade North American companies. The equity tranche covers losses between 0% and 3% of the principal. The mezzanine tranche covers losses between 3% and 7%. The remaining tranches cover losses from 7–10%, 10–15%, 15–30%, and 30–100%. In the case of iTraxx Europe, the tranches cover losses from 0–3%, 3–6%, 6–9%, 9–12%, 12–22%, and 22–100%.

Traders can trade a single tranche of a synthetic CDO, once it has been defined, without the structure being created. This is known as *single-tranche trading*. The synthetic CDO structure is simply used as a reference point to define cash flows between the trader who is buying protection and the trader who is selling protection.

Table 23.7 shows the quotes for iTraxx tranches at the end of January on three successive years during the credit crisis. To understand the quotes, consider the January 31, 2007, row of the table. The index level of 23 basis points indicates that (ignoring bid–offer spreads) it would cost 23 basis points per year to buy five-year protection on all 125 companies underlying the index. (For example, if $1 million of

[9] In practice, sellers of protection are usually required to post the initial tranche principal as collateral up front. When the tranche becomes responsible for a payoff on a CDS, the money is taken out of the collateral. This means that the arranger of the structure does not bear the risk that a tranche investor will default. The balance in the collateral account earns LIBOR (or another agreed interest rate).

Table 23.7 Mid-market quotes for five-year tranches of iTraxx Europe. Quotes are in basis points except for the 0–3% tranche where the quote equals the percent of the tranche principal that must be paid up front in addition to 500 basis points per year (*Source*: Creditex Group Inc.)

Date	*Tranche* 0–3%	3–6%	6–9%	9–12%	12–22%	*iTraxx index*
January 31, 2007	10.34%	41.59	11.95	5.60	2.00	23
January 31, 2008	30.98%	316.90	212.40	140.00	73.60	77
January 30, 2009	64.28%	1185.63	606.69	315.63	97.13	165

protection was bought on each company, the cost would be $0.0023 \times \$1{,}000{,}000 \times 125$, or \$287,500 per year.) A trader could buy five-year protection against losses on the underlying portfolio that are in the range 6–9% for 11.95 basis points. Suppose that the amount of protection bought is \$6 million. This is the initial tranche principal. Payoffs from the protection seller to the protection buyer depend on default losses on the iTraxx Europe portfolio. While the cumulative loss is less than 6% of the portfolio principal, there is no payoff. As soon as the cumulative loss exceeds 6% of the portfolio principal, payoffs start. If, at the end of year 3, the cumulative loss rises from 6% to 7% of the portfolio principal, the protection seller pays the protection buyer \$2 million and the tranche principal reduces to \$4 million. If, at the end of year 4, the cumulative loss increases from 7% to 9% of the portfolio principal, the protection seller pays the protection buyer an additional \$4 million and the tranche principal reduces to zero. Subsequent losses then give rise to no payments. Payments from the protection buyer to the protection seller are made quarterly in arrears and equal 0.001195% of the remaining tranche principal. Initially the payments are made at the rate of $0.001195 \times \$6{,}000{,}000 = \$7{,}170$ per year.

The equity (0–3%) tranche is quoted differently from other tranches. The market quote of 10.34% means that the protection seller receives an initial payment equal to 10.34% of the tranche principal and then receives 500 basis points per year on the remaining tranche principal.

What a difference two years makes in the credit markets! Table 23.7 shows that the credit crisis led to a huge increase in credit spreads. The iTraxx index rose from 23 basis points in January 2007 to 165 basis points in January 2009. The individual tranche quotes have also shown huge increases. One reason for the changes is that the market's assessment of default probabilities for investment-grade corporations has increased. However, it is also the case that protection sellers were in many cases experiencing liquidity problems. They became more averse to risk and increased the risk premiums they required.

The Role of Default Correlation

The role of default correlation in valuing the tranches of CDOs is important. When correlation is low, the equity tranche is almost certain to sustain losses and can easily get wiped out.[10] However, the senior tranches are relatively safe.

[10] For example, if the default rate over the five years is 5% and the correlation is zero, the probability of zero defaults out of 125 companies is only 0.2% and the probability of six or more defaults is about 60%.

As the correlation increases, the senior tranches become more vulnerable, but the expected loss on the equity tranche actually goes down. To understand this, suppose that the probability of default is 10% and that the default correlation is perfect. We are then in an all-or-nothing position. There is a 10% probability that all the companies default and a 90% probability that none of them do so. As a result, there is a 90% probability that the equity tranche will escape unscathed.

SUMMARY

Credit derivatives enable banks and other financial institutions to actively manage their credit risks. They can be used to transfer credit risk from one company to another and to diversify credit risk by swapping one type of exposure for another.

The most common credit derivative is a credit default swap. This is a contract where one company buys insurance against another company defaulting on its obligations. The payoff is usually the difference between the face value of a bond issued by the second company and its value immediately after a default. Credit default swaps can be analyzed by calculating the present value of the expected payments and the present value of the expected payoff.

A total return swap is an instrument where the total return on a portfolio of credit-sensitive assets is exchanged for LIBOR plus a spread. Total return swaps are often used as financing vehicles. A company wanting to purchase a financial asset can approach a financial institution to buy the asset on its behalf. The financial institution then enters into a total return swap with the company where it pays the return on the asset to the company and receives LIBOR plus a spread. The advantage of this type of arrangement is that the financial institution reduces its exposure to defaults by the company.

A forward credit default swap is an obligation to enter into a particular credit default swap on the maturity date. A credit default swap option is the right to enter into a particular credit default swap on the maturity. Both instruments cease to exist if the reference entity defaults before the maturity date.

In collateralized debt obligations a number of different securities are created from a portfolio of corporate bonds or commercial loans. There are rules for determining how credit losses are allocated to the securities. The result of the rules is that securities with both very high and very low credit ratings are created from the portfolio. A synthetic collateralized debt obligation creates a similar set of securities from credit default swaps.

FURTHER READING

Andersen, L., and J. Sidenius, "Extensions to the Gaussian Copula: Random Recovery and Random Factor Loadings," *Journal of Credit Risk*, 1, No. 1 (Winter 2004): 29–70.

Andersen, L., J. Sidenius, and S. Basu, "All Your Hedges in One Basket," *Risk*, November 2003.

Das, S., *Credit Derivatives: Trading & Management of Credit & Default Risk*. Singapore: Wiley, 1998.

Hull, J. C., and A. White, "Valuation of a CDO and *n*th to Default Swap without Monte Carlo Simulation," *Journal of Derivatives*, 12, No. 2 (Winter 2004): 8–23.

Hull, J. C., and A. White, "Valuing Credit Derivatives Using an Implied Copula Approach," *Journal of Dericatives*, 14, 2 (Winter 2006): 8–28.

Laurent, J.-P., and J. Gregory, "Basket Default Swaps, CDOs and Factor Copulas," *Journal of Risk*, 7, 4: 103–122.

Li, D. X., "On Default Correlation: A Copula Approach," *Journal of Fixed Income*, 9, 4 (2000): 43–54.

Schönbucher, P. J., *Credit Derivatives Pricing Models*. Wiley, 2003.

Tavakoli, J. M., *Credit Derivatives: A Guide to Instruments and Applications*. New York: Wiley, 1998.

Quiz (Answers at End of Book)

23.1. How does a binary credit default swap differ from a regular credit default swap?

23.2. A credit default swap requires a semiannual payment at the rate of 60 basis points per year. The principal is \$300 million and the credit default swap is settled in cash. A default occurs after four years and two months, and the calculation agent estimates that the price of the cheapest deliverable bond is 40% of its face value shortly after the default. List the cash flows and their timing for the seller of the credit default swap.

23.3. Explain how a credit default swap is settled.

23.4. Explain how a cash CDO and a synthetic CDO are created.

23.5. Explain what a first-to-default credit default swap is. Does its value increase or decrease as the default correlation between the companies in the basket increases? Explain why.

23.6. Explain the difference between risk-neutral and real-world default probabilities.

23.7. Explain why a total return swap can be useful as a financing tool.

Practice Questions (Answers in Solutions Manual/Study Guide)

23.8. Suppose that the risk-free zero curve is flat at 7% per annum with continuous compounding and that defaults can occur halfway through each year in a new five-year credit default swap. Suppose, further, that the recovery rate is 30% and the default probabilities each year conditional on no earlier default is 3%. Estimate the credit default swap spread. Assume payments are made annually.

23.9. What is the value of the swap in Problem 23.8 per dollar of notional principal to the protection buyer if the credit default swap spread is 150 basis points?

23.10. What is the credit default swap spread in Problem 23.8 if it is a binary CDS.

23.11. How does a five-year nth-to-default credit default swap work? Consider a basket of 100 reference entities where each reference entity has a probability of defaulting in each year of 1%. As the default correlation between the reference entities increases, what happens to the value of the swap when (a) $n = 1$ and (b) $n = 25$? Explain your answer.

23.12. How is the recovery rate of a bond usually defined? What is the formula relating the payoff on a CDS to the notional principal and recovery rate?

23.13. Show that the spread for a new plain vanilla CDS should be $1 - R$ times the spread for a similar new binary CDS, where R is the recovery rate.

23.14. Verify that if the CDS spread for the example in Tables 23.2 to 23.5 is 100 basis points then the probability of default in a year (conditional on no earlier default) must be 1.61%. How does the probability of default change when the recovery rate is 20% instead of 40%? Verify that your answer is consistent with the implied probability of default being approximately proportional to $1/(1 - R)$, where R is the recovery rate.

23.15. A company enters into a total return swap where it receives the return on a corporate bond paying a coupon of 5% and pays LIBOR. Explain the difference between this and a regular swap where 5% is exchanged for LIBOR.

23.16. Explain how forward contracts and options on credit default swaps are structured.

23.17. "The position of a buyer of a credit default swap is similar to the position of someone who is long a risk-free bond and short a corporate bond." Explain this statement.

23.18. Why is there a potential asymmetric information problem in credit default swaps?

23.19. Does valuing a CDS using real-world default probabilities rather than risk-neutral default probabilities overstate or understate its value? Explain your answer.

Further Questions

23.20. Suppose that the risk-free zero curve is flat at 6% per annum with continuous compounding and that defaults can occur at times 0.25, 0.75, 1.25, and 1.75 years in a two-year plain vanilla credit default swap with semiannual payments. Suppose, further, that the recovery rate is 20% and the unconditional probabilities of default (as seen at time zero) are 1% at times 0.25 years and 0.75 years, and 1.5% at times 1.25 years and 1.75 years. What is the credit default swap spread? What would the credit default spread be if the instrument were a binary credit default swap?

23.21. Assume that the default probability for a company in a year, conditional on no earlier defaults is λ and the recovery rate is R. The risk-free interest rate is 5% per annum. Default always occur halfway through a year. The spread for a five-year plain vanilla CDS where payments are made annually is 120 basis points and the spread for a five-year binary CDS where payments are made annually is 160 basis points. Estimate R and λ.

23.22. Explain how you would expect the returns offered on the various tranches in a synthetic CDO to change when the correlation between the bonds in the portfolio increases.

23.23. Suppose that (a) the yield on a five-year risk-free bond is 7%, (b) the yield on a five-year corporate bond issued by company X is 9.5%, and (c) a five-year credit default swap providing insurance against company X defaulting costs 150 basis points per year. What arbitrage opportunity is there in this situation? What arbitrage opportunity would there be if the credit default spread were 300 basis points instead of 150 basis points? Give two reasons why arbitrage opportunities such as those you identify are less than perfect.

23.24. The 1-, 2-, 3-, 4-, and 5-year CDS spreads are 100, 120, 135, 145, and 152 basis points, respectively. The risk-free rate is 3% for all maturities, the recovery rate is 35%, and payments are quarterly. Use DerivaGem to calculate the continuously compounded hazard rate each year. What is the probability of default in year 1? What is the probability of default in year 2?

23.25. Table 23.7 shows the five-year iTraxx index was 77 basis points on January 31, 2008. Assume the risk-free rate is 5% for all maturities, the recovery rate is 40%, and payments are quarterly. Assume also that the spread of 77 basis points applies to all maturities. Use the DerivaGem CDS worksheet to calculate a hazard rate consistent with the spread. Use this in the CDO worksheet with 10 integration points to imply base correlations for each tranche from the quotes for January 31, 2008.

Answers to Quiz Questions

CHAPTER 1

1.1 A trader who enters into a long futures position is agreeing to *buy* the underlying asset for a certain price at a certain time in the future. A trader who enters into a short futures position is agreeing to *sell* the underlying asset for a certain price at a certain time in the future.

1.2 A company is *hedging* when it has an exposure to the price of an asset and takes a position in futures or options markets to offset the exposure. In a *speculation* the company has no exposure to offset. It is betting on the future movements in the price of the asset. *Arbitrage* involves taking a position in two or more different markets to lock in a profit.

1.3 In (a) the investor is obligated to buy the asset for \$50 and does not have a choice. In (b) the investor has the option to buy the asset for \$50 but does not have to exercise the option.

1.4 (a) The investor is obligated to sell pounds for 1.4000 when they are worth 1.3900. The gain is (1.4000 – 1.3900) × 100,000 = \$1,000.

(b) The investor is obligated to sell pounds for 1.4000 when they are worth 1.4200. The loss is (1.4200 – 1.4000) × 100,000 = \$2,000.

1.5 You have sold a put option. You have agreed to buy 100 shares for \$40 per share if the party on the other side of the contract chooses to exercise the right to sell for this price. The option will be exercised only when the price of stock is below \$40. Suppose, for example, that the option is exercised when the price is \$30. You have to buy at \$40 shares that are worth \$30; you lose \$10 per share, or \$1,000 in total. If the option is exercised when the price is \$20, you lose \$20 per share, or \$2,000 in total. The worst that can happen is that the price of the stock declines to almost zero during the three-month period. This highly unlikely event would cost you \$4,000. In return for the possible future losses, you receive the price of the option from the purchaser.

1.6 One strategy is to buy 200 shares. Another is to buy 2,000 options (20 contracts). If the share price does well, the second strategy will give rise to greater gains. For example, if the share price goes up to \$40, you gain [2,000 × (\$40 – \$30)] – \$5,800 = \$14,200 from the second strategy and only 200 × (\$40 – \$29) = \$2,200 from the first strategy. However, if the share price does badly, the second strategy yields greater losses. For example, if the share price goes down to \$25, the first strategy leads to a loss of 200 × (\$29 – \$25) = \$800, whereas the second strategy leads to a loss of the entire \$5,800 investment.

1.7 The over-the-counter market is a telephone- and computer-linked network of financial institutions, fund managers, and corporate treasurers where two participants can enter into any mutually acceptable contract. An exchange-traded market is a market organized by an exchange where traders either meet physically or communicate electronically and the contracts that can be traded have been defined by the exchange. When a market maker quotes a bid and an offer, the bid is the price at which the market maker is prepared to buy and the offer is the price at which the market maker is prepared to sell.

CHAPTER 2

2.1 The *open interest* of a futures contract at a particular time is the total number of long positions outstanding. (Equivalently, it is the total number of short positions outstanding.) The *trading volume* during a certain period of time is the number of contracts traded during this period.

2.2 A *futures commission merchant* trades on behalf of a client and charges a commission. A *local* trades on his or her own behalf.

2.3 There will be a margin call when \$1,000 has been lost from the margin account. This will occur when the price of silver increases by 1,000/5,000 = \$0.20. The price of silver must therefore rise to \$27.40 per ounce for there to be a margin call. If the margin call is not met, your broker closes out your position.

2.4 The total profit is (\$90.50 − \$88.30) × 1,000 = \$2,200. Of this, (\$89.10 − \$88.30) × 1,000 = \$800 is realized on a day-by-day basis between September 2013 and December 31, 2013. A further (\$90.50 − \$89.10) × 1,000 = \$1,400 is realized on a day-by-day basis between January 1, 2014, and March 2014. A hedger would be taxed on the whole profit of \$2,200 in 2014. A speculator would be taxed on \$800 in 2013 and \$1,400 in 2014.

2.5 A *stop order* to sell at \$2 is an order to sell at the best available price once a price of \$2 or less is reached. It could be used to limit the losses from an existing long position. A *limit order* to sell at \$2 is an order to sell at a price of \$2 or more. It could be used to instruct a broker that a short position should be taken, providing it can be done at a price more favorable than \$2.

2.6 The margin account administered by the clearinghouse is marked to market daily, and the clearinghouse member is required to bring the account back up to the prescribed level daily. The margin account administered by the broker is also marked to market daily. However, the account does not have to be brought up to the initial margin level on a daily basis. It has to be brought up to the initial margin level when the balance in the account falls below the maintenance margin level. The maintenance margin is usually about 75% of the initial margin.

2.7 In futures markets prices are quoted as the number of U.S. dollars per unit of foreign currency. Spot and forward rates are quoted in this way for the British pound, euro, Australian dollar, and New Zealand dollar. For other major currencies, spot and forward rates are quoted as the number of units of foreign currency per U.S. dollar.

CHAPTER 3

3.1 A *short hedge* is appropriate when a company owns an asset and expects to sell that asset in the future. It can also be used when the company does not currently own the asset but expects to do so at some time in the future. A *long hedge* is appropriate when a company knows it will have to purchase an asset in the future. It can also be used to offset the risk from an existing short position.

3.2 *Basis risk* arises from the hedger's uncertainty as to the difference between the spot price and futures price at the expiration of the hedge.

3.3 A *perfect hedge* is one that completely eliminates the hedger's risk. A perfect hedge does not always lead to a better outcome than an imperfect hedge. It just leads to a more certain outcome. Consider a company that hedges its exposure to the price of an asset. Suppose the asset's price movements prove to be favorable to the company. A perfect hedge totally neutralizes the company's gain from these favorable price movements. An imperfect hedge, which only partially neutralizes the gains, might well give a better outcome.

3.4 A minimum variance hedge leads to no hedging when the coefficient of correlation between changes in the futures price and changes in the price of the asset being hedged is zero.

3.5 a. If the company's competitors are not hedging, the treasurer might feel that the company will experience less risk if it does not hedge (see Table 3.1).

b. The shareholders might not want the company to hedge.

c. If there is a loss on the hedge and a gain from the company's exposure to the underlying asset, the treasurer might feel that he or she will have difficulty justifying the hedging to other executives within the organization.

3.6 The optimal hedge ratio is

$$0.8 \times \frac{0.65}{0.81} = 0.642$$

This means that the size of the futures position should be 64.2% of the size of the company's exposure in a three-month hedge.

3.7 The formula for the number of contracts that should be shorted gives

$$1.2 \times \frac{20{,}000{,}000}{1080 \times 250} = 88.9$$

Rounding to the nearest whole number, 89 contracts should be shorted. To reduce the beta to 0.6, half of this position, or a short position in 44 contracts, is required.

CHAPTER 4

4.1 a. The rate with continuous compounding is

$$4 \ln\left(1 + \frac{0.14}{4}\right) = 0.1376$$

or 13.76% per annum.

b. The rate with annual compounding is

$$\left(1 + \frac{0.14}{4}\right)^4 - 1 = 0.1475$$

or 14.75% per annum.

4.2 LIBOR is the London interbank offer rate. It is the rate a bank quotes for deposits it is prepared to place with other banks. LIBID is the London interbank bid rate. It is the rate a bank quotes for deposits from other banks. LIBOR is greater than LIBID.

4.3 Suppose the bond has a face value of \$100. Its price is obtained by discounting the cash flows at 10.4%. The price is

$$\frac{4}{1.052}+\frac{4}{1.052^2}+\frac{104}{1.052^3}=96.74$$

If the 18-month zero rate is R, we must have

$$\frac{4}{1.05}+\frac{4}{1.05^2}+\frac{104}{(1+R/2)^3}=96.74$$

which gives $R = 10.42\%$.

4.4 a. With annual compounding the return is

$$\frac{1100}{1000}-1=0.1$$

or 10% per annum.

b. With semiannual compounding the return is R, where

$$1000\left(1+\frac{R}{2}\right)^2=1100$$

that is,

$$1+\frac{R}{2}=\sqrt{1.1}=1.0488$$

so that $R = 0.0976$. The percentage return is therefore 9.76% per annum.

c. With monthly compounding the return is R, where

$$1000\left(1+\frac{R}{12}\right)^{12}=1100$$

that is,

$$\left(1+\frac{R}{12}\right)=\sqrt[12]{1.1}=1.00797$$

so that $R = 0.0957$. The percentage return is therefore 9.57% per annum.

d. With continuous compounding the return is R, where

$$1000e^R=1100$$

that is,

$$e^R=1.1$$

so that $R = \ln 1.1 = 0.0953$. The percentage return is therefore 9.53% per annum.

4.5 The forward rates with continuous compounding are as follows:

Qtr 2: 8.4%
Qtr 3: 8.8%
Qtr 4: 8.8%
Qtr 5: 9.0%
Qtr 6: 9.2%

4.6 The forward rate is 9.0% with continuous compounding or 9.102% with quarterly compounding. From equation (4.9), the value of the FRA is therefore

$$[1{,}000{,}000\times 0.25\times(0.095-0.09102)]e^{-0.086\times 1.25}=893.56$$

or \$893.56.

4.7 When the term structure is upward sloping, $c > a > b$. When it is downward sloping, $b > a > c$.

CHAPTER 5

5.1 The investor's broker borrows the shares from another client's account and sells them in the usual way. To close out the position, the investor must purchase the shares. The broker then replaces them in the account of the client from whom they were borrowed. The party with the short position must remit to the broker dividends and other income paid on the shares. The broker transfers these funds to the account of the client from whom the shares were borrowed. Occasionally the broker runs out of places from which to borrow the shares. The investor is then short squeezed and has to close out the position immediately.

5.2 The forward price of an asset today is the price at which you would agree to buy or sell the asset at a future time. The value of a forward contract is zero when you first enter into it. As time passes the underlying asset price changes and the value of the contract may become positive or negative.

5.3 The forward price is

$$30e^{0.12\times 0.5} = \$31.86$$

5.4 The futures price is

$$350e^{(0.08-0.04)\times 0.3333} = \$354.7$$

5.5 Gold is an investment asset. If the futures price is too high, investors will find it profitable to increase their holdings of gold and short futures contracts. If the futures price is too low, they will find it profitable to decrease their holdings of gold and go long in the futures market. Copper is a consumption asset. If the futures price is too high, a strategy of buy copper and short futures works. However, because investors do not in general hold the asset, the strategy of sell copper and buy futures is not available to them. There is therefore an upper bound, but no lower bound, to the futures price.

5.6 *Convenience yield* measures the extent to which there are benefits obtained from ownership of the physical asset that are not obtained by owners of long futures contracts. The *cost of carry* is the interest cost plus storage cost less the income earned. The futures price, F_0, and spot price, S_0, are related by

$$F_0 = S_0e^{(c-y)T}$$

where c is the cost of carry, y is the convenience yield, and T is the time to maturity of the futures contract.

5.7 A foreign currency provides a known interest rate, but the interest is received in the foreign currency. The value in the domestic currency of the income provided by the foreign currency is therefore known as a percentage of the value of the foreign currency. This means that the income has the properties of a known yield.

CHAPTER 6

6.1 There are 33 calendar days between July 7, 2011, and August 9, 2011. There are 184 calendar days between July 7, 2011, and January 7, 2012. The interest earned per \$100 of principal is therefore $3.5 \times 33/184 = \$0.6277$. For a corporate bond we assume 32 days between July 7 and August 9, 2011, and 180 days between July 7, 2011, and January 7, 2012. The interest earned is $3.5 \times 32/180 = \$0.6222$.

6.2 There are 89 days between October 12, 2014, and January 9, 2015. There are 182 days between October 12, 2014, and April 12, 2015. The cash price of the bond is obtained by adding the accrued interest to the quoted price. The quoted price is $102\frac{7}{32}$ or 102.21875. The cash price is therefore

$$102.21875 + \frac{89}{182} \times 6 = \$105.15$$

6.3 The conversion factor for a bond is equal to the quoted price the bond would have per dollar of principal on the first day of the delivery month on the assumption that the interest rate for all maturities equals 6% per annum (with semiannual compounding). The bond maturity and the times to the coupon payment dates are rounded down to the nearest three months for the purposes of the calculation. The conversion factor defines how much an investor with a short bond futures contract receives when bonds are delivered. If the conversion factor is 1.2345, the amount the investor receives is calculated by multiplying 1.2345 by the most recent futures price and adding accrued interest.

6.4 The Eurodollar futures price has increased by 6 basis points. The investor makes a gain per contract of $25 \times 6 = \$150$, or \$300 in total.

6.5 Suppose that a Eurodollar futures quote is 95.00. This gives a futures rate of 5% for the three-month period covered by the contract. The convexity adjustment is the amount by which the futures rate has to be reduced to give an estimate of the forward rate for the period. The convexity adjustment is necessary because (a) futures contracts are settled daily while forward contracts are not and (b) futures contracts are settled at the end of the life of the futures contract while forward contracts are settled when the interest is due.

6.6 Duration provides information about the effect of a small parallel shift in the yield curve on the value of a bond portfolio. The percentage decrease in the value of the portfolio equals the duration of the portfolio multiplied by the amount by which interest rates are increased in the small parallel shift. The duration measure has the following limitation. It applies only to parallel shifts in the yield curve that are small.

6.7 The value of a contract is $108\frac{15}{32} \times 1{,}000 = \$108{,}468.75$. The number of contracts that should be shorted is

$$\frac{6{,}000{,}000}{108{,}468.75} \times \frac{8.2}{7.6} = 59.7$$

Rounding to the nearest whole number, 60 contracts should be shorted. The position should be closed out at the end of July.

CHAPTER 7

7.1 A has an apparent comparative advantage in fixed-rate markets but wants to borrow floating. B has an apparent comparative advantage in floating-rate markets but wants to borrow fixed. This provides the basis for the swap. There is a 1.4% per annum differential between the fixed rates offered to the two companies and a 0.5% per annum differential between the floating rates offered to the two companies. The total gain to all parties from

Swap for Quiz 7.1

the swap is therefore 1.4 − 0.5 = 0.9% per annum. Because the bank gets 0.1% per annum of this gain, the swap should make each of A and B 0.4% per annum better off. This means that it should lead to A borrowing at LIBOR − 0.3% and to B borrowing at 6%. The appropriate arrangement is therefore as shown in the diagram above.

7.2 In four months \$3.5 million (= 0.5 × 0.07 × \$100 million) will be received and \$2.3 million (= 0.5 × 0.046 × \$100 million) will be paid. (We ignore day count issues.) In 10 months \$3.5 million will be received, and the LIBOR rate prevailing in four months' time will be paid. The value of the fixed-rate bond underlying the swap is

$$3.5e^{-0.05\times 4/12} + 103.5e^{-0.05\times 10/12} = \$102.718 \text{ million}$$

The value of the floating-rate bond underlying the swap is

$$(100 + 2.3)e^{-0.05\times 4/12} = \$100.609 \text{ million}$$

The value of the swap to the party paying floating is \$102.718 − \$100.609 = \$2.109 million. The value of the swap to the party paying fixed is −\$2.109 million. These results can also be derived by decomposing the swap into forward contracts. Consider the party paying floating. The first forward contract involves paying \$2.3 million and receiving \$3.5 million in four months. It has a value of $1.2e^{-0.05\times 4/12}$ = \$1.180 million. To value the second forward contract, we note that the forward interest rate is 5% per annum with continuous compounding, or 5.063% per annum with semiannual compounding. The value of the forward contract is

$$100 \times (0.07 \times 0.5 - 0.05063 \times 0.5)e^{-0.05\times 10/12} = \$0.929 \text{ million}$$

The total value of the forward contracts is therefore \$1.180 + \$0.929 = \$2.109 million.

7.3 X has a comparative advantage in yen markets but wants to borrow dollars. Y has a comparative advantage in dollar markets but wants to borrow yen. This provides the basis for the swap. There is a 1.5% per annum differential between the yen rates and a 0.4% per annum differential between the dollar rates. The total gain to all parties from the swap is therefore 1.5 − 0.4 = 1.1% per annum. The bank requires 0.5% per annum, leaving 0.3% per annum for each of X and Y. The swap should lead to X borrowing dollars at 9.6 − 0.3 = 9.3% per annum and to Y borrowing yen at 6.5 − 0.3 = 6.2% per annum. The appropriate arrangement is therefore as shown in the diagram below. All foreign exchange risk is borne by the bank.

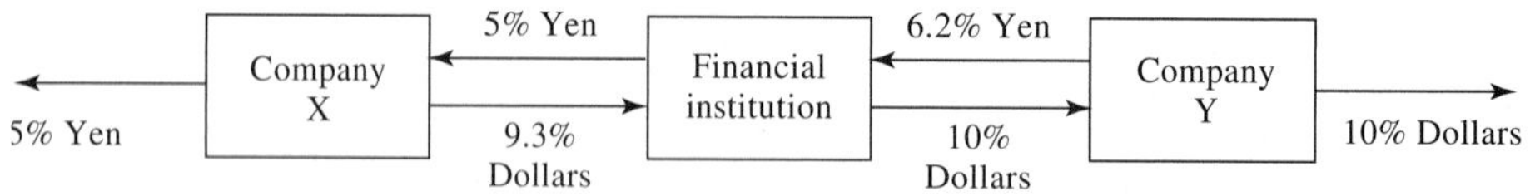

Swap for Quiz 7.3

7.4 A swap rate for a particular maturity is the average of the bid and offer fixed rates that a market maker is prepared to exchange for LIBOR in a standard plain vanilla swap with that maturity. The frequency of payments and day count conventions in the standard swap that is considered vary from country to country. In the United States, payments on a standard swap are semiannual and the day count convention for quoting LIBOR is actual/360. The day count convention for quoting the fixed rate is usually actual/365. The swap rate for a particular maturity is the LIBOR/swap par yield for that maturity.

7.5 The swap involves exchanging the sterling interest of $20 \times 0.10 = 2.0$ million for the dollar interest of $30 \times 0.06 = \$1.8$ million. The principal amounts are also exchanged at the end of the life of the swap. The value of the sterling bond underlying the swap is

$$\frac{2}{(1.07)^{1/4}} + \frac{22}{(1.07)^{5/4}} = £22.182 \text{ million}$$

The value of the dollar bond underlying the swap is

$$\frac{1.8}{(1.04)^{1/4}} + \frac{31.8}{(1.04)^{5/4}} = \$32.061 \text{ million}$$

The value of the swap to the party paying sterling is therefore

$$32.061 - (22.182 \times 1.55) = -\$2.322 \text{ million}$$

The value of the swap to the party paying dollars is +\$2.322 million. The results can also be obtained by viewing the swap as a portfolio of forward contracts. The continuously compounded interest rates in sterling and dollars are 6.766% and 3.922% per annum, respectively. The 3-month and 15-month forward exchange rates are

$$1.55e^{(0.03922-0.06766)\times 0.25} = 1.5390 \quad \text{and} \quad 1.55e^{(0.03922-0.06766)\times 1.25} = 1.4959.$$

The values of the two forward contracts corresponding to the exchange of interest for the party paying sterling are therefore

$$(1.8 - 2 \times 1.5390)e^{-0.03922\times 0.25} = -\$1.266 \text{ million}$$

$$(1.8 - 2 \times 1.4959)e^{-0.03922\times 1.25} = -\$1.135 \text{ million}$$

The value of the forward contract corresponding to the exchange of principals is

$$(30 - 20 \times 1.4959)e^{-0.03922\times 1.25} = +\$0.079 \text{ million}$$

The total value of the swap is $-\$1.266 - \$1.135 + \$0.079 = -\$2.322$ million.

7.6 Credit risk arises from the possibility of a default by the counterparty. Market risk arises from movements in market variables such as interest rates and exchange rates. A complication is that the credit risk in a swap is contingent on the values of market variables. A company's position in a swap has credit risk only when the value of the swap to the company is positive.

7.7 The rate is not truly fixed because, if the company's credit rating declines, it will not be able to roll over its floating rate borrowings at LIBOR plus 150 basis points. The effective fixed borrowing rate then increases. Suppose for example that the treasurer's spread over LIBOR increases from 150 to 200 basis points. The borrowing rate increases from 5.2% to 5.7%.

CHAPTER 8

8.1 GNMA guaranteed qualifying mortgages against default and created securities that were sold to investors.

8.2 An ABS is a set of tranches created from a portfolio of mortgages or other assets. An ABS CDO is an ABS created from particular tranches (e.g., the BBB tranches) of a number of different ABSs.

8.3 The mezzanine tranche of an ABS is a tranche that is in the middle as far as ranking in seniority goes. It ranks below the senior tranches and therefore absorbs losses before they do, but it ranks above the equity tranche, so that the equity tranche absorbs losses before it does.

8.4 The waterfall in an ABS defines how the cash flows from the underlying assets are allocated to the tranches. In a typical arrangement, cash flows are first used to pay the senior tranche its promised return. The cash flows (if any) that are left over are used to provide the mezzanine tranche with its promised return. Any cash flows that are left over after this payment are used to provide the equity tranche with its promised return.

8.5

Losses on underlying assets	*Losses to mezzanine tranche of ABS*	*Losses to equity tranche of ABS CDO*	*Losses to mezzanine tranche of ABS CDO*	*Losses to senior tranche of ABS CDO*
12%	46.7%	100%	100%	17.9%
15%	66.7%	100%	100%	48.7%

8.6 A subprime mortgage is a mortgage where the risk of default is higher than normal.

8.7 The increase in the price of houses could not be sustained.

CHAPTER 9

9.1 The investor makes a profit if the price of the stock on the expiration date is less than \$37. In these circumstances the gain from exercising the option is greater than \$3. The option will be exercised if the stock price is less than \$40 at the maturity of the option. The variation of the investor's profit with the stock price is as shown in the following diagram.

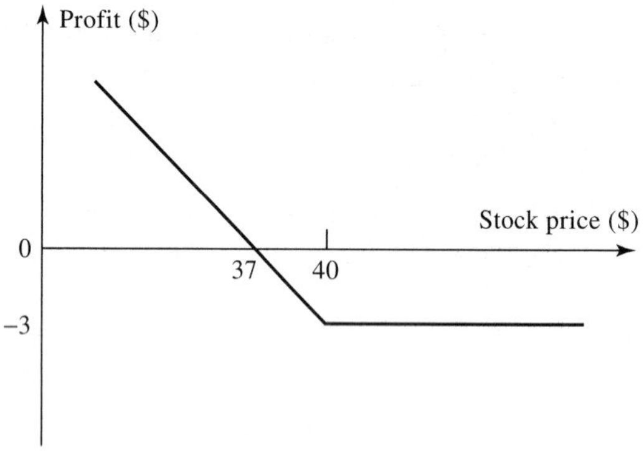

Investor's Profit in Quiz 9.1

9.2 The investor makes a profit if the price of the stock is below \$54 on the expiration date. If the stock price is below \$50, the option will not be exercised and the investor makes a profit of \$4. If the stock price is between \$50 and \$54, the option is exercised and the investor makes a profit between \$0 and \$4. The variation of the investor's profit with the stock price is as shown in the following diagram.

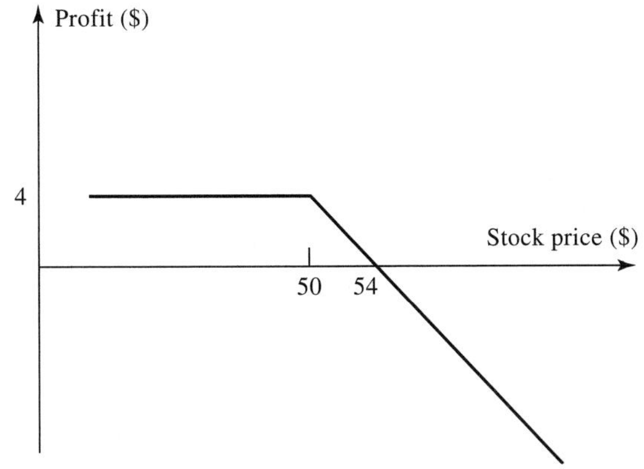

Investor's Profit in Quiz 9.2

9.3 The payoff to the investor is

$$-\max(S_T - K,\ 0) + \max(K - S_T,\ 0)$$

This is $K - S_T$ in all circumstances. The investor's position is the same as a short position in a forward contract with delivery price K.

9.4 When an investor buys an option, cash must be paid up front. There is no possibility of future liabilities and therefore no need for a margin account. When an investor sells an option, there are potential future liabilities. To protect against the risk of a default, margins are required.

9.5 On April 1, options trade with expiration months of April, May, August, and November. On May 30, options trade with expiration months of June, July, August, and November.

9.6 The strike price is reduced to \$30, and the option gives the holder the right to purchase twice as many shares.

9.7 When an employee stock option is exercised, the company issues new shares and sells them to the employee for the strike price. This increases the company's equity and therefore changes its capital structure.

CHAPTER 10

10.1 The six factors affecting stock option prices are the stock price, strike price, risk-free interest rate, volatility, time to maturity, and dividends.

10.2 The lower bound is

$$28 - 25e^{-0.08\times0.3333} = \$3.66$$

10.3 The lower bound is

$$15e^{-0.06\times0.08333} - 12 = \$2.93$$

10.4 Delaying exercise delays the payment of the strike price. This means that the option holder is able to earn interest on the strike price for a longer period of time. Delaying exercise also provides insurance against the stock price falling below the strike price by the expiration date. Assume that the option holder has an amount of cash K and that interest rates are zero. Exercising early means that the option holder's position will be worth S_T at expiration. Delaying exercise means that it will be worth $\max(K,\ S_T)$ at expiration.

10.5 An American put when held in conjunction with the underlying stock provides insurance. It guarantees that the stock can be sold for the strike price, K. If the put is exercised early, the insurance ceases. However, the option holder receives the strike price immediately and is able to earn interest on it between the time of the early exercise and the expiration date.

10.6 An American call option can be exercised at any time. If it is exercised, its holder gets the intrinsic value. It follows that an American call option must be worth at least its intrinsic value. A European call option can be worth less than its intrinsic value. Consider, for example, the situation where a stock is expected to provide a very high dividend during the life of an option. The price of the stock will decline as a result of the dividend. Because the European option can be exercised only after the dividend has been paid, its value may be less than the intrinsic value today.

10.7 In this case $c = 1$, $T = 0.25$, $S_0 = 19$, $K = 20$, and $r = 0.04$. From put–call parity,

$$p = c + Ke^{-rT} - S_0$$

or

$$p = 1 + 20e^{-0.04\times0.25} - 19 = 1.80$$

so that the European put price is \$1.80.

CHAPTER 11

11.1 A protective put consists of a long position in a put option combined with a long position in the underlying shares. It is equivalent to a long position in a call option plus a certain amount of cash. This follows from put–call parity:

$$p + S_0 = c + Ke^{-rT} + D$$

11.2 A bear spread can be created using two call options with the same maturity and different strike prices. The investor shorts the call option with the lower strike price and buys the call option with the higher strike price. A bear spread can also be created using two put options with the same maturity and different strike prices. In this case, the investor shorts the put option with the lower strike price and buys the put option with the higher strike price.

11.3 A butterfly spread involves a position in options with three different strike prices (K_1, K_2, and K_3). A butterfly spread should be purchased when the investor considers that the price of the underlying stock is likely to stay close to the central strike price, K_2.

11.4 An investor can create a butterfly spread by buying call options with strike prices of \$15 and \$20 and selling two call options with strike prices of \$17$\frac{1}{2}$. The initial investment is $(4 + \frac{1}{2}) - (2 \times 2) = \$\frac{1}{2}$. The following table shows the variation of profit with the final stock price:

Stock price, S_T	*Profit*
$S_T < 15$	$-\frac{1}{2}$
$15 < S_T < 17\frac{1}{2}$	$(S_T - 15) - \frac{1}{2}$
$17\frac{1}{2} < S_T < 20$	$(20 - S_T) - \frac{1}{2}$
$S_T > 20$	$-\frac{1}{2}$

11.5 A reverse calendar spread is created by buying a short-maturity option and selling a long-maturity option, both with the same strike price.

11.6 Both a straddle and a strangle are created by combining a long position in a call with a long position in a put. In a straddle, the two have the same strike price and expiration date. In a strangle, they have different strike prices and the same expiration date.

11.7 A strangle is created by buying both options. The pattern of profits is as follows:

Stock price, S_T	*Profit*
$S_T < 45$	$(45 - S_T) - 5$
$45 < S_T < 50$	-5
$S_T > 50$	$(S_T - 50) - 5$

CHAPTER 12

12.1 Consider a portfolio consisting of:

-1: Call option

$+\Delta$: Shares

If the stock price rises to \$42, the portfolio is worth $42\Delta - 3$. If the stock price falls to \$38, it is worth 38Δ. These are the same when

$$42\Delta - 3 = 38\Delta$$

or $\Delta = 0.75$. The value of the portfolio in one month is 28.5 for both stock prices. Its value today must be the present value of 28.5, or $28.5e^{-0.08\times0.08333} = 28.31$. This means that

$$-f + 40\Delta = 28.31$$

where f is the call price. Because $\Delta = 0.75$, the call price is $40 \times 0.75 - 28.31 = \$1.69$. As an alternative approach, we can calculate the probability, p, of an up movement in a risk-neutral world. This must satisfy:

$$42p + 38(1 - p) = 40e^{0.08\times0.08333}$$

so that

$$4p = 40e^{0.08\times0.08333} - 38$$

or $p = 0.5669$. The value of the option is then its expected payoff discounted at the risk-free rate:

$$[3 \times 0.5669 + 0 \times 0.4331]e^{-0.08\times0.08333} = 1.69$$

or \$1.69. This agrees with the previous calculation.

12.2 In the no-arbitrage approach, we set up a riskless portfolio consisting of a position in the option and a position in the stock. By setting the return on the portfolio equal to the risk-free interest rate, we are able to value the option. When we use risk-neutral valuation, we first choose probabilities for the branches of the tree so that the expected return on the stock equals the risk-free interest rate. We then value the option by calculating its expected payoff and discounting this expected payoff at the risk-free interest rate.

12.3 The delta of a stock option measures the sensitivity of the option price to the price of the stock when small changes are considered. Specifically, it is the ratio of the change in the price of the stock option to the change in the price of the underlying stock.

12.4 Consider a portfolio consisting of:

-1: Put option
$+\Delta$: Shares

If the stock price rises to \$55, this is worth 55Δ. If the stock price falls to \$45, the portfolio is worth $45\Delta - 5$. These are the same when

$$45\Delta - 5 = 55\Delta$$

or $\Delta = -0.50$. The value of the portfolio in one month is -27.5 for both stock prices. Its value today must be the present value of -27.5, or $-27.5e^{-0.1\times0.5} = -26.16$. This means that

$$-f + 50\Delta = -26.16$$

where f is the put price. Because $\Delta = -0.50$, the put price is \$1.16. As an alternative approach, we can calculate the probability, p, of an up movement in a risk-neutral world. This must satisfy

$$55p + 45(1-p) = 50e^{0.1\times0.5}$$

so that

$$10p = 50e^{0.1\times0.5} - 45$$

or $p = 0.7564$. The value of the option is then its expected payoff discounted at the risk-free rate:

$$[0 \times 0.7564 + 5 \times 0.2436]e^{-0.1\times0.5} = 1.16$$

or \$1.16. This agrees with the previous calculation.

12.5 In this case, $u = 1.10$, $d = 0.90$, $\Delta t = 0.5$, and $r = 0.08$, so that

$$p = \frac{e^{0.08\times0.5} - 0.90}{1.10 - 0.90} = 0.7041$$

The tree for stock price movements is shown in the following diagram.

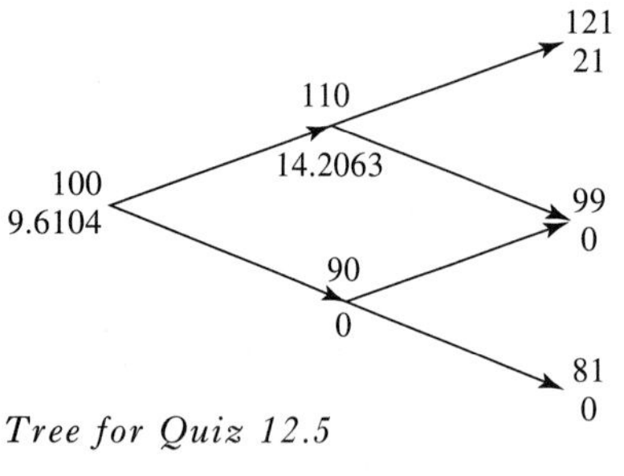

Tree for Quiz 12.5

We can work back from the end of the tree to the beginning, as indicated in the diagram, to give the value of the option as \$9.61. The option value can also be calculated directly from equation (12.10):

$$[0.7041^2 \times 21 + 2 \times 0.7041 \times 0.2959 \times 0 + 0.2959^2 \times 0]e^{-2\times0.08\times0.5} = 9.61$$

or \$9.61.

12.6 The diagram overleaf shows how we can value the put option using the same tree as in Quiz 12.5. The value of the option is \$1.92. The option value can also be calculated directly from equation (12.10):

$$e^{-2\times0.08\times0.5}[0.7041^2 \times 0 + 2 \times 0.7041 \times 0.2959 \times 1 + 0.2959^2 \times 19] = 1.92$$

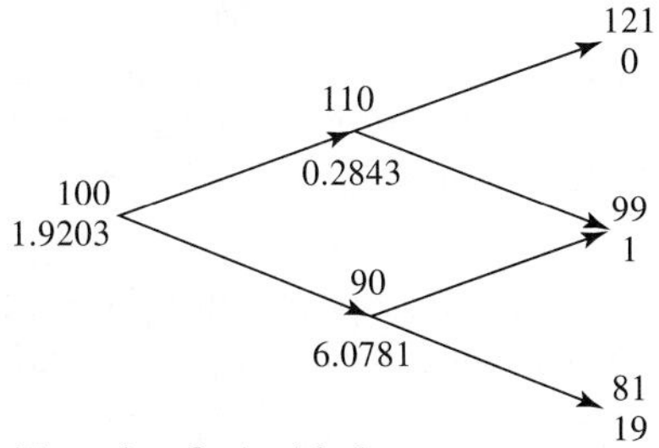

Tree for Quiz 12.6

or \$1.92. The stock price plus the put price is $100 + 1.92 = \$101.92$. The present value of the strike price plus the call price is $100e^{-0.08\times 1} + 9.61 = \$101.92$. These are the same, verifying that put–call parity holds.

12.7 $u = e^{\sigma\sqrt{\Delta t}}$ and $d = e^{-\sigma\sqrt{\Delta t}}$

CHAPTER 13

13.1 The Black–Scholes–Merton option pricing model assumes that the probability distribution of the stock price in one year (or at any other future time) is lognormal. Equivalently, it assumes that the continuously compounded rate of return on the stock is normally distributed.

13.2 The standard deviation of the percentage price change in time Δt is $\sigma\sqrt{\Delta t}$, where σ is the volatility. In this problem, $\sigma = 0.3$ and, assuming 252 trading days in one year, $\Delta t = 1/252 = 0.003968$, so that $\sigma\sqrt{\Delta t} = 0.3\sqrt{0.003968} = 0.019$ or 1.9%.

13.3 Assuming that the expected return from the stock is the risk-free rate, we calculate the expected payoff from a call option. We then discount this payoff from the end of the life of the option to the beginning at the risk-free interest rate.

13.4 In this case, $S_0 = 50$, $K = 50$, $r = 0.1$, $\sigma = 0.3$, $T = 0.25$, and

$$d_1 = \frac{\ln(50/50) + (0.1 + 0.09/2)0.25}{0.3\sqrt{0.25}} = 0.2417, \qquad d_2 = d_1 - 0.3\sqrt{0.25} = 0.0917$$

The European put price is

$$50N(-0.0917)e^{-0.1\times 0.25} - 50N(-0.2417) = 50 \times 0.4634e^{-0.1\times 0.25} - 50 \times 0.4045 = 2.38$$

or \$2.38.

13.5 In this case, we must subtract the present value of the dividend from the stock price before using Black–Scholes. Hence, the appropriate value of S_0 is

$$S_0 = 50 - 1.50e^{-0.1\times 0.1667} = 48.52$$

As before, $K = 50$, $r = 0.1$, $\sigma = 0.3$, and $T = 0.25$. In this case,

$$d_1 = \frac{\ln(48.52/50) + (0.1 + 0.09/2)0.25}{0.3\sqrt{0.25}} = 0.0414, \qquad d_2 = d_1 - 0.3\sqrt{0.25} = -0.1086$$

The European put price is

$$50N(0.1086)e^{-0.1\times 0.25} - 48.52N(-0.0414) = 50 \times 0.5432e^{-0.1\times 0.25} - 48.52 \times 0.4835 = 3.03$$

or \$3.03.

13.6 The implied volatility is the volatility that makes the Black–Scholes–Merton price of an option equal to its market price. It is calculated by trial and error. We test in a systematic way different volatilities until we find the one that gives the European put option price when it is substituted into the Black–Scholes–Merton formula.

13.7 In Black's approximation, we calculate the price of a European call option expiring at the same time as the American call option and the price of a European call option expiring just before the final ex-dividend date. We set the American call option price equal to the greater of the two.

CHAPTER 14

14.1 Prior to 2005 companies did not have to expense at-the-money options on the income statement. They merely had to report the value of the options in notes to the accounts. FAS 123 and IAS 2 required the fair value of the options to be reported as a cost on the income statement starting in 2005.

14.2 The main differences are: (a) employee stock options last much longer than the typical exchange-traded or over-the-counter options; (b) there is usually a vesting period during which they cannot be exercised; (c) the options cannot be sold by the employee; (d) if the employee leaves the company, the options usually either expire worthless or have to be exercised immediately; and (e) exercise of the options usually leads to the company issuing more shares.

14.3 It is always better for the option holder to sell a call option on a non-dividend-paying stock rather than exercise it. Employee stock options cannot be sold, so the only way an employee can monetize the option is to exercise the option and sell the stock.

14.4 This is questionable. Executives benefit from share price increases but do not bear the costs of share price decreases. Employee stock options are liable to encourage executives to take decisions that boost the value of the stock in the short term at the expense of the long-term health of the company. It may even be the case that executives are encouraged to take high risks so as to maximize the value of their options.

14.5 Professional footballers are not allowed to bet on the outcomes of games because they themselves influence the outcomes. Arguably, an executive should not be allowed to bet on the future stock price of her company because her actions influence that price. However, it could be argued that there is nothing wrong with a professional footballer betting that his team will win (but everything wrong with betting that it will lose). Similarly, there is nothing wrong with an executive betting that her company will do well.

14.6 Backdating allowed the company to issue employee stock options with a strike price equal to the price at some previous date and claim that they are at the money. At-the-money options did not lead to an expense on the income statement until 2005. The amount recorded for the value of the options in the notes to the income was less than the actual cost on the true grant date. In 2002, the SEC required companies to report stock option grants within two business days of the grant date. This eliminated the possibility of backdating for companies that complied with this rule.

14.7 If a stock option grant had to be revalued each quarter, the value of the option on the grant date would become less important. Stock price movements following the reported grant date would be incorporated in the next revaluation. The total cost of the options during their lives would be independent of the stock price on the grant date.

CHAPTER 15

15.1 When the index goes down to 700, the value of the portfolio can be expected to be $10 \times (700/800) = \$8.75$ million. (This assumes that the dividend yield on the portfolio equals the dividend yield on the index.) Buying put options on $10{,}000{,}000/800 = 12{,}500$ times the index with a strike of 700 therefore provides protection against a drop in the value of the portfolio below \$8.75 million. If each contract is on 100 times the index, a total of 125 contracts would be required.

15.2 A stock index is analogous to a stock paying a dividend yield, the dividend yield being the dividend yield on the index. A currency is analogous to a stock paying a dividend yield, the dividend yield being the foreign risk-free interest rate.

15.3 The lower bound is given by equation (15.1) as

$$300e^{-0.03\times0.5} - 290e^{-0.08\times0.5} = 16.90$$

15.4 The tree of exchange-rate movements is shown in the diagram below. In this case, $u = 1.02$ and $d = 0.98$. The probability of an up movement in a risk-neutral world is

$$p = \frac{e^{(0.06-0.08)\times0.08333} - 0.98}{1.02 - 0.98} = 0.4584$$

The tree shows that the value of an option to purchase one unit of the currency is \$0.0067.

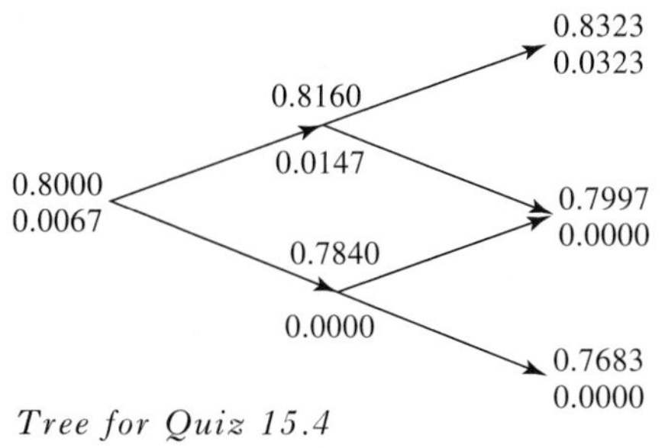

Tree for Quiz 15.4

15.5 A company that knows it is due to receive foreign currency at a certain time in the future can buy a put option with a strike price below the current exchange rate (when measured as domestic currency per unit of foreign currency) and sell a call option with a strike price above the current exchange rate. This ensures that the exchange rate obtained for the foreign currency will be between the two strike prices.

15.6 In this case, $S_0 = 250$, $K = 250$, $r = 0.10$, $\sigma = 0.18$, $T = 0.25$, $q = 0.03$, and

$$d_1 = \frac{\ln(250/250) + (0.10 - 0.03 + 0.18^2/2)0.25}{0.18\sqrt{0.25}} = 0.2394$$

$$d_2 = d_1 - 0.18\sqrt{0.25} = 0.1494$$

and the call price is

$$250N(0.2394)e^{-0.03\times0.25} - 250N(0.1494)e^{-0.10\times0.25}$$
$$= 250 \times 0.5946e^{-0.03\times0.25} - 250 \times 0.5594e^{-0.10\times0.25}$$
$$= 11.15$$

15.7 In this case, $S_0 = 0.52$, $K = 0.50$, $r = 0.04$, $r_f = 0.08$, $\sigma = 0.12$, $T = 0.6667$, and

$$d_1 = \frac{\ln(0.52/0.50) + (0.04 - 0.08 + 0.12^2/2)0.6667}{0.12\sqrt{0.6667}} = 0.1771$$

$$d_2 = d_1 - 0.12\sqrt{0.6667} = 0.0791$$

and the put price is

$$\begin{aligned} 0.50N(-0.0791)e^{-0.04\times0.6667} - 0.52N(-0.1771)e^{-0.08\times0.6667} \\ = 0.50 \times 0.4685e^{-0.04\times0.6667} - 0.52 \times 0.4297e^{-0.08\times0.6667} \\ = 0.0162 \end{aligned}$$

CHAPTER 16

16.1 A call option on yen gives the holder the right to buy yen in the spot market at an exchange rate equal to the strike price. A call option on yen futures gives the holder the right to receive the amount by which the futures price exceeds the strike price. If the yen futures option is exercised, the holder also obtains a long position in the yen futures contract.

16.2 The main reason is that a bond futures contract is a more liquid instrument than a bond. The price of a Treasury bond futures contract is known immediately from trading on CBOT. The price of a bond can be obtained only by contacting dealers.

16.3 A futures price behaves like a stock paying a dividend yield at the risk-free interest rate.

16.4 In this case, $u = 1.12$ and $d = 0.92$. The probability of an up movement in a risk-neutral world is

$$\frac{1 - 0.92}{1.12 - 0.92} = 0.4$$

From risk-neutral valuation, the value of the call is

$$e^{-0.06\times0.5}(0.4 \times 6 + 0.6 \times 0) = 2.33$$

16.5 The put–call parity formula for futures options is the same as the put–call parity formula for stock options except that the stock price is replaced by F_0e^{-rT}, where F_0 is the current futures price, r is the risk-free interest rate, and T is the life of the option.

16.6 The American futures call option is worth more than the corresponding American option on the underlying asset when the futures price is greater than the spot price prior to the maturity of the futures contract.

16.7 In this case, $F_0 = 19$, $K = 20$, $r = 0.12$, $\sigma = 0.20$, and $T = 0.4167$. The value of the European put futures option is

$$20N(-d_2)e^{-0.12\times0.4167} - 19N(-d_1)e^{-0.12\times0.4167}$$

where

$$d_1 = \frac{\ln(19/20) + (0.04/2)0.4167}{0.2\sqrt{0.4167}} = -0.3327, \qquad d_2 = d_1 - 0.2\sqrt{0.4167} = -0.4618$$

This is

$$\begin{aligned} e^{-0.12\times0.4167}[20N(0.4618) - 19N(0.3327)] = e^{-0.12\times0.4167}(20 \times 0.6778 - 19 \times 0.6303) \\ = 1.50 \end{aligned}$$

or \$1.50.

CHAPTER 17

17.1 A stop-loss trading rule can be implemented by arranging to have a covered position when the option is in the money and a naked position when it is out of the money. When using the trading rule, the writer of an out-of-the-money call would buy the underlying asset as soon as the price moved above the strike price, K, and sell the underlying asset as soon as the price moved below K. In practice, when the price of the underlying asset equals K, there is no way of knowing whether it will subsequently move above or below K. The asset will therefore be bought at $K + \epsilon$ and sold at $K - \epsilon$ for some small ϵ. The cost of hedging depends on the number of times the asset price equals K. The hedge is therefore relatively poor. It will cost nothing if the asset price never reaches K; on the other hand, it will be quite expensive if the asset price equals K many times. In a good hedge, the cost of hedging is known in advance to a reasonable level of accuracy.

17.2 A delta of 0.7 means that, when the price of the stock increases by a small amount, the price of the option increases by 70% of this amount. Similarly, when the price of the stock decreases by a small amount, the price of the option decreases by 70% of this amount. A short position in 1,000 options has a delta of −700 and can be made delta neutral with the purchase of 700 shares.

17.3 In this case, $S_0 = K$, $r = 0.1$, $\sigma = 0.25$, and $T = 0.5$. Also,

$$d_1 = \frac{\ln(S_0/K) + [(0.1 + 0.25^2)/2] \times 0.5}{0.25\sqrt{0.5}} = 0.3712$$

The delta of the option is $N(d_1)$, or 0.64.

17.4 No. A long or short position in the underlying asset has zero vega. This is because its value does not change when volatility changes.

17.5 The gamma of an option position is the rate of change of the delta of the position with respect to the asset price. For example, a gamma of 0.1 indicates that, when the asset price increases by a certain small amount, delta increases by 0.1 times this amount. When the gamma of an option writer's position is highly negative and the delta is zero, the option writer will lose money if there is a large movement (either up or down) in the asset price.

17.6 To hedge an option position, it is necessary to create the opposite option position synthetically. For example, to hedge a long position in a put, it is necessary to create a short position in a put synthetically. It follows that the procedure for creating an option position synthetically is the reverse of the procedure for hedging the option position.

17.7 Portfolio insurance by creating put options synthetically was popular in 1987. It works as follows. When a portfolio's value declines, the portfolio is rebalanced by (a) selling part of the portfolio or (b) selling some index futures. If enough portfolio managers are following this strategy, an unstable situation is created. A small decline leads to selling. This in turn causes a bigger decline and leads to more selling, and so on. It is argued that this phenomenon played a role in the October 1987 crash.

CHAPTER 18

18.1 Delta, gamma, and theta can be determined from a single binomial tree. Vega is determined by making a small change to the volatility and recomputing the option price using a new tree. Rho is calculated by making a small change to the interest rate and recomputing the option price using a new tree.

18.2 With our usual notation the answers are (a) $e^{r\Delta t}$, (b) $e^{(r-q)\Delta t}$, (c) $e^{(r-r_f)\Delta t}$, and (d) 1.

18.3 In this case, $S_0 = 60$, $K = 60$, $r = 0.1$, $\sigma = 0.45$, $T = 0.25$, and $\Delta t = 0.0833$. Also,

$$u = e^{\sigma\sqrt{\Delta t}} = e^{0.45\sqrt{0.0833}} = 1.1387, \quad d = 1/u = 0.8782, \quad a = e^{r\Delta t} = e^{0.1\times 0.0833} = 1.0084,$$

$$p = \frac{a-d}{u-d} = 0.4998, \quad 1-p = 0.5002$$

The tree is shown in the following diagram. The calculated price of the option is \$5.16.

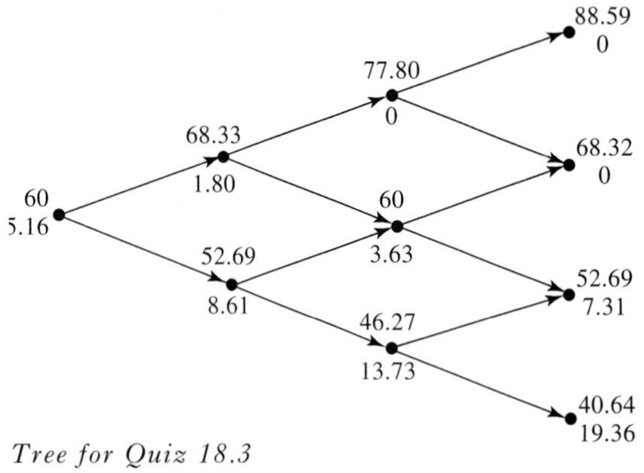

Tree for Quiz 18.3

18.4 The control variate technique is implemented by:

a. Valuing an American option using a binomial tree in the usual way (to get f_A)
b. Valuing the European option with the same parameters as the American option using the same tree (to get f_E)
c. Valuing the European option using Black–Scholes (to get f_{BS})

The price of the American option is estimated as $f_A + f_{BS} - f_E$.

18.5 In this case, $F_0 = 198$, $K = 200$, $r = 0.08$, $\sigma = 0.3$, $T = 0.75$, and $\Delta t = 0.25$. Also,

$$u = e^{0.3\sqrt{0.25}} = 1.1618, \quad d = 1/u = 0.8607, \quad a = 1$$

$$p = \frac{a-d}{u-d} = 0.4626, \quad 1-p = 0.5373$$

The tree is shown in the following diagram. The calculated price of the option is 20.3 cents.

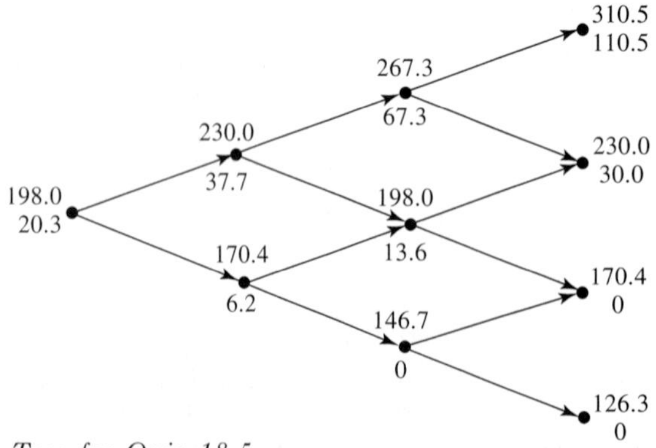

Tree for Quiz 18.5

18.6 Suppose a dividend equal to D is paid during a certain time interval. If S is the stock price at the beginning of the time interval, it will be either $Su - D$ or $Sd - D$ at the end of the time interval. At the end of the next time interval, it will be one of $(Su - D)u$, $(Su - D)d$, $(Sd - D)u$, or $(Sd - D)d$. Because $(Su - D)d$ does not equal $(Sd - D)u$, the tree does not recombine. If S is equal to the stock price less the present value of future dividends, this problem is avoided.

18.7 In Monte Carlo simulation, we sample paths through the tree, working from the beginning to the end. When a node is reached, we have no way of knowing whether early exercise is optimal.

CHAPTER 19

19.1 When both tails of the stock price distribution are less heavy than those of the lognormal distribution, Black–Scholes–Merton will tend to produce relatively low prices for options when they are either significantly out of the money or significantly in the money. This leads to an implied volatility pattern similar to that in Figure 19.7. When the right tail is heavier and the left tail is less heavy, Black–Scholes–Merton will tend to produce relatively high prices for out-of-the-money calls and in-the-money puts, and it will tend to produce relatively low prices for out-of-the-money puts and in-the-money calls. This leads to implied volatility being an increasing function of strike price.

19.2 A downward sloping volatility smile is usually observed for equities.

19.3 Jumps tend to make both tails of the stock price distribution heavier than those of the lognormal distribution. This creates a volatility smile similar to that in Figure 19.1. The volatility smile is likely to be more pronounced for the three-month option.

19.4 The put has a price that is too low relative to the call's price. The correct trading strategy is to buy the put, buy the underlying asset, and sell the call.

19.5 The heavier left tail should lead to high prices, and therefore high implied volatilities, for out-of-the-money (low-strike-price) puts. Similarly, the less heavy right tail should lead to low prices, and therefore low volatilities for out-of-the-money (high-strike-price) calls. A volatility smile where volatility is a decreasing function of strike price results.

19.6 With the notation in the appendix of Chapter 19,

$$c_{\text{bs}} + Ke^{-rT} = p_{\text{bs}} + Se^{-qT}$$
$$c_{\text{mkt}} + Ke^{-rT} = p_{\text{mkt}} + Se^{-qT}$$

It follows that

$$c_{\text{bs}} - c_{\text{mkt}} = p_{\text{bs}} - p_{\text{mkt}}$$

In this case, $c_{\text{mkt}} = 3.00$, $c_{\text{bs}} = 3.50$, and $p_{\text{bs}} = 1.00$. It follows that p_{mkt} should be 0.50.

19.7 The crashophobia argument is an attempt to explain the pronounced volatility skew in equity markets since 1987. (This was the year equity markets shocked everyone by crashing more than 20% in one day.) The argument is that traders are concerned about another crash and as a result increase the price of out-of-the-money puts. This creates the volatility skew.

CHAPTER 20

20.1 The historical simulation method involves constructing N scenarios of what might happen between today and tomorrow from N days of historical data. The first scenario assumes that the percentage change in all market variables will be the same as that between the first day (Day 0) and the second day (Day 1); the second scenario assumes that the percentage change in all market variables will be the same as that between the second day (Day 1) and the third day (Day 2); and so on. The final scenario assumes that the percentage change in all market variables will be the same as that between yesterday (Day $N-1$) and today (Day N). The portfolio is valued for each scenario and VaR is calculated from the probability distribution of portfolio value changes.

20.2 Define u_i as $(S_i - S_{i-1})/S_{i-1}$, where S_i is the value of a market variable on day i. In the EWMA model, the variance rate of the market variable (i.e., the square of its volatility) is a weighted average of the u_i^2. For some constant λ $(0 < \lambda < 1)$, the weight given to u_{i-1}^2 (which is calculated on day $i-1$) is λ times the weight given to u_i^2 (which is calculated on day i). The volatility σ_n estimated at the end of day $n-1$ is related to the volatility σ_{n-1} estimated at the end of day $n-2$ by

$$\sigma_n^2 = \lambda\sigma_{n-1}^2 + (1-\lambda)u_{n-1}^2$$

This formula shows that the EWMA model has one very attractive property. To calculate the volatility estimate for day n, it is sufficient to know the volatility estimate for day $n-1$ and u_{n-1}^2.

20.3 In this case, $\sigma_{n-1} = 0.015$ and $u_n = 0.5/30 = 0.01667$, so that equation (18.10) gives

$$\sigma_n^2 = 0.94 \times 0.015^2 + 0.06 \times 0.01667^2 = 0.0002282$$

The volatility estimate on day n is therefore $\sqrt{0.0002282}$ or 1.51%.

20.4 Measured in thousands of dollars, the variance of daily changes in the portfolio value is

$$300^2 \times 0.018^2 + 500^2 \times 0.012^2 + 2 \times 300 \times 500 \times 0.018 \times 0.012 \times 0.3 = 84.60$$

The standard deviation of daily changes in the portfolio is $\sqrt{84.60} = 9.20$. The standard deviation of changes over five days is $9.20\sqrt{5} = 20.57$. The 5-day 95% VaR for the portfolio is therefore $1.65 \times 20.57 = 33.94$, or \$33,940.

20.5 The approximate relationship between the daily change in the portfolio value, ΔP, and the daily change in the exchange rate, ΔS, is

$$\Delta P = 56\Delta S$$

The proportional daily change in the exchange rate, Δx, equals $\Delta S/1.5$. It follows that

$$\Delta P = 56 \times 1.5\Delta x$$

or

$$\Delta P = 84\Delta x$$

The standard deviation of Δx equals the daily volatility of the exchange rate, or 0.7%. The standard deviation of ΔP is therefore $84 \times 0.007 = 0.588$. It follows that the 10-day 99% VaR for the portfolio is

$$0.588 \times 2.33 \times \sqrt{10} = 4.33$$

20.6 From equation (20.5), the relationship is

$$\Delta P = 56 \times 1.5\Delta x + \tfrac{1}{2} \times 1.5^2 \times 16.2 \times \Delta x^2$$

or

$$\Delta P = 84\Delta x + 18.225\Delta x^2$$

20.7 The historical simulation method assumes that the joint probability distribution of the market variables is the distribution given by the historical data. The model building approach usually assumes that the market variables have a multivariate normal distribution. The volatilities of, and correlations between, market variables in the model building approach are usually calculated using an approach, such as the exponentially weighted moving average method, that applies more weight to recent data.

CHAPTER 21

21.1 An amount

$$\$20{,}000{,}000 \times (0.12 - 0.10) \times 0.25 = \$100{,}000$$

would be paid out three months later.

21.2 A callable bond is a bond where the issuer has the option to buy back the bond from the holder at certain times at prespecified prices. A puttable bond is a bond where the holder has the right to sell the bond back to the issuer at certain times at prespecified prices.

21.3 A swaption is an option to enter into an interest rate swap at a certain time in the future with a certain fixed rate being exchanged for floating. An interest rate swap can be regarded as the exchange of a fixed-rate bond for a floating-rate bond. Thus, a swaption is the option to exchange a fixed-rate bond for a floating-rate bond. The floating-rate bond will be worth its face value at the beginning of the life of the swap. The swaption is therefore an option on a fixed-rate bond with the strike price equal to the face value of the bond.

21.4 In this case, $F_0 = (125 - 10)e^{0.1\times 1} = 127.09$, $K = 110$, $r = 0.1$, $\sigma = 0.08$, $T = 1.0$, and

$$d_1 = \frac{\ln(127.09/110) + (0.08^2/2)}{0.08} = 1.8456$$

$$d_2 = d_1 - 0.08 = 1.7656$$

The value of the put option is

$$110e^{-0.1}N(-1.7656) - 127.09e^{-0.1\times 1}N(-1.8456) = 0.12$$

or \$0.12.

21.5 The payoff is $25 \times 87 = \$2{,}175$.

21.6 In this case, $L = 1{,}000$, $\delta_k = 0.25$, $F_k = 0.12$, $R_K = 0.13$, $\sigma_k = 0.12$, $t_k = 1.5$, $e^{-0.115\times 1.75} = 0.8177$, and

$$d_1 = \frac{\ln(0.12/0.13) + 0.12^2 \times 1.5/2}{0.12\sqrt{1.5}} = -0.4711$$

$$d_2 = -0.4711 - 0.12\sqrt{1.5} = -0.6181$$

The value of the option is

$$1000 \times 0.25 \times 0.8177[0.12N(-0.4711) - 0.13N(-0.6181)] = 0.69$$

or \$0.69.

21.7 There are two main advantages of yield curve models. First, they enable all interest rate derivative securities to be valued on a consistent basis. Second, they enable securities that cannot be handled using Black's model to be valued. An example of a security that cannot be valued using Black's model but can be valued using yield curve models is a long-dated American swap option.

CHAPTER 22

22.1 A forward start option is an option that is granted now but will start at some time in the future. The strike price is usually equal to the price of the asset at the time the option starts. A chooser option is an option where, at some time in the future, the holder chooses whether the option is a call or a put.

22.2 With the usual notation, the value is $100e^{-0.04\times0.25}N(d_2)$. In this case,

$$d_2 = \frac{\ln(50/50) + (0.04 - 0.2^2/2)0.25}{0.2\sqrt{0.25}} = 0.05$$

and

$$N(d_2) = 0.5199$$

and the value of the option is $100e^{-0.04\times0.25} \times 0.5199 = \$51.48$

22.3 Up-and-in call, up-and-out call, up-and-in put, up-and-out put, down-and-in call, down-and-out call, down-and-in put, and down-and-out put.

22.4 In an equity swap, one party promises to pay the return on an equity index applied to a notional principal and the other promises to pay a fixed or floating return on the notional principal.

22.5 When prepayments increase, the principal is received sooner. This increases the value of a PO. When prepayments increase, less interest is received. This decreases the value of an IO.

22.6 A cancelable swap gives company X the option to terminate the swap early. Suppose that the swap lasts until time T and company X terminates at time t. This is equivalent to company X entering into a new swap at time t. This new swap lasts until time T and has the opposite cash flows to the original swap. The termination option therefore gives company X the right to enter into a swap, that is, it gives company X a swap option.

22.7 The trader could enter into a diff swap where interest is paid on a U.S. dollar principal at the three-month U.S. dollar LIBOR rate and interest is received on the same U.S. dollar principal at the three-month Canadian LIBOR rate minus a 2% spread. This is better than a regular floating-for-floating swap where the Canadian dollar LIBOR is applied to a Canadian dollar principal because it avoids any exposure to the Canadian dollar/U.S. dollar exchange rate.

CHAPTER 23

23.1 Both provide insurance against a particular company defaulting during a period of time. In a credit default swap the payoff is the notional principal amount multiplied by one minus the recovery rate. In a binary swap the payoff is the notional principal.

23.2 The seller receives

$$300{,}000{,}000 \times 0.0060 \times 0.5 = \$900{,}000$$

at times 0.5, 1.0, 1.5, 2.0, 2.5, 3.0, 3.5, and 4.0 years. The seller also receives a final accrual payment of about \$300,000 (= \$300,000,000 × 0.060 × 2/12) at the time of the default (4 years and 2 months). The seller pays

$$300{,}000{,}000 \times 0.6 = \$180{,}000{,}000$$

at the time of the default.

23.3 Two possibilities are physical settlement and cash settlement. In physical settlement, the buyer of protection sells bonds to the provider of protection for their face value. Bonds with a total face value equal to the notional principal can be sold. Cash settlement involves estimating the value to the buyer of protection of being able to do this, and the seller of protection is then required to pay an amount equal to this value to the buyer of protection. Increasingly cash settlement is used and an auction process determines the required payment.

23.4 A cash CDO is created from a bond portfolio. The returns from the bond portfolio flow to a number of tranches. The tranches differ as far as the credit risk they assume. In a synthetic CDO, there is no bond portfolio. Instead, a portfolio of credit default swaps is sold and the resulting credit risks are allocated to tranches.

23.5 In a first-to-default basket CDS, there are a number of reference entities. When the first one defaults, there is a payoff (calculated in the usual way for a CDS) and basket CDS terminates. The value of a first-to-default basket CDS decreases as the correlation between the reference entities in the basket increases.

23.6 Risk-neutral default probabilities are backed out from credit default swaps or bond prices. Real-world default probabilities are calculated from historical data.

23.7 Suppose a company wants to buy some assets. If a total return swap is used, a financial institution buys the assets and enters into a swap with the company where it pays the company the return on the assets and receives from the company LIBOR plus a spread. The financial institution has less risk than it would have if it lent the company money and used the assets as collateral. This is because, in the event of a default by the company, it owns the assets.

CHAPTER 24

24.1 A day's HDD is $\max(0, 65 - A)$ and a day's CDD is $\max(0, A - 65)$, where A is the average of the highest and lowest temperature during the day at a specified weather station, measured in degrees Fahrenheit.

24.2 The average temperature each day is 75° Fahrenheit. The CDD each day is therefore 10 and the cumulative CDD for the month is $10 \times 31 = 310$. The payoff from the call option is therefore $(310 - 250) \times 5{,}000 = \$300{,}000$.

24.3 It is an agreement by one side to delivery a specified amount of gas at a roughly uniform rate during a month to a particular hub for a specified price.

24.4 Unlike most commodities electricity cannot be stored easily. If the demand for electricity exceeds the supply, as it sometimes does during the air-conditioning season, the price of electricity skyrockets.

24.5 There is no systematic risk (i.e., risk that is priced by the market) in weather derivatives and CAT bonds.

24.6 The energy producer faces quantity risks and price risks. It can use weather derivatives to hedge the quantity risks and energy derivatives to hedge against the price risks.

24.7 CAT bonds are an alternative to reinsurance for an insurance company. They are issued by the insurance company and provide a higher rate of interest than government bonds. However, the bondholders agree to forego interest, and possibly principal, to meet certain claims against the insurance company that are within a prespecified range.

Glossary of Terms

ABS *See* Asset-backed Security.

ABS CDO Instrument where tranches are created from the tranches of ABSs.

Accrual Swap An interest rate swap where interest on one side accrues only when a certain condition is met.

Accrued Interest The interest earned on a bond since the last coupon payment date.

Agency Costs Costs arising from a situation where the agent (e.g., company manager) is not motivated to act in the best interests of the principal (e.g., company shareholder).

American Option An option that can be exercised at any time during its life.

Amortizing Swap A swap where the notional principal decreases in a predetermined way as time passes.

Analytic Result Result where the answer is in the form of an equation.

Arbitrage A trading strategy that takes advantage of two or more securities being mispriced relative to each other.

Arbitrageur An individual engaging in arbitrage.

Asian Option An option with a payoff dependent on the average price of the underlying asset during a specified period.

Ask Price *See* Offer Price.

Asked Price *See* Offer Price.

Asset-backed Security Security created from a portfolio of loans, bonds, credit card receivables, or other assets.

Asset-or-nothing Call Option An option that provides a payoff equal to the asset price if the asset price is above the strike price and zero otherwise.

Asset-or-nothing Put Option An option that provides a payoff equal to the asset price if the asset price is below the strike price and zero otherwise.

Asset Swap A swap that exchanges the coupon on a bond for LIBOR plus a spread.

As-you-like-it Option *See* Chooser Option.

At-the-money Option An option in which the strike price equals the price of the underlying asset.

Average Price Call Option An option giving a payoff equal to the greater of zero and the amount by which the average price of the asset exceeds the strike price.

Average Price Put Option An option giving a payoff equal to the greater of zero and the amount by which the strike price exceeds the average price of the asset.

Average Strike Option An option that provides a payoff dependent on the difference between the final asset price and the average asset price.

Backdating Practice (often illegal) of marking a document with a date that precedes the current date.

Back Testing Testing a value-at-risk or other model using historical data.

Backwards Induction A procedure for working from the end of a tree to its beginning in order to value an option.

Barrier Option An option whose payoff depends on whether the path of the underlying asset has reached a barrier (i.e., a certain predetermined level).

Basel Committee Committee responsible for the regulation of banks internationally. Regulations are known as Basel I, Basel II, Basel II.5, and Basel III.

Basis The difference between the spot price and the futures price of a commodity.

Basis Point When used to describe an interest rate, a basis point is one hundredth of one percent (= 0.01 percent).

Basis Risk The risk to a hedger arising from uncertainty about the basis at a future time.

Basis Swap A swap where cash flows determined by one floating reference rate are exchanged for cash flows determined by another floating reference rate.

Basket Credit Default Swap Credit default swap where there are several reference entities.

Basket Option An option that provides a payoff dependent on the value of a portfolio of assets.

Bear Spread A short position in a put option with strike price X_1 combined with a long position in a put option with strike price X_2, where $X_2 > X_1$. (A bear spread can also be created with call options.)

Bermudan Option An option that can be exercised on specified dates during its life.

Beta A measure of the systematic risk of an asset.

Bid–Ask Spread *See* Bid–Offer Spread.

Bid–Offer Spread The amount by which the offer price exceeds the bid price.

Bid Price The price that a dealer is prepared to pay for an asset.

Bilateral Clearing Arrangement between two parties to handle transactions in the OTC market, often involving an ISDA master agreement.

Binary Credit Default Swap Instrument where there is a fixed dollar payoff in the event of a default by a particular company.

Binary Option Option with a discontinuous payoff, e.g. a cash-or-nothing option or an asset-or-nothing option.

Binomial Model A model where the price of an asset is monitored over successive short periods of time. In each short period, it is assumed that only two price movements are possible.

Binomial Tree A tree that represents how an asset price can evolve under the binomial model.

Black's Approximation An approximate procedure developed by Fischer Black for valuing a call option on a dividend-paying stock.

Black's Model An extension of the Black–Scholes model for valuing European options on futures contracts.

Black–Scholes–Merton Model A model for pricing European options on stocks, developed by Fischer Black, Myron Scholes, and Robert Merton.

Bond Option An option where a bond is the underlying asset.

Bond Yield Discount rate which, when applied to all the cash flows of a bond, causes the present value of the cash flows to equal the bond's market price.

Bootstrap Method A procedure for calculating the zero-coupon yield curve from market data. It involves using progressively longer maturity instruments.

Box Spread A combination of a bull spread created from calls and a bear spread created from puts.

Bull Spread A long position in a call with strike price X_1 combined with a short position in a call with strike price X_2, where $X_2 > X_1$. (A bull spread can also be created with put options.)

Butterfly Spread A position that is created by taking a long position in a call with strike price X_1, a long position in a call with strike price X_3, and a short position in two calls with strike price X_2, where $X_3 > X_2 > X_1$ and $X_2 = 0.5(X_1 + X_3)$. (A butterfly spread can also be created with put options.)

Calendar Spread A position that is created by taking a long position in a call option that matures at one time and a short position in a similar call option that matures at a different time. (A calendar spread can also be created using put options.)

Calibration Method for implying a model's parameters from the prices of actively traded options.

Callable bond A bond containing provisions that allow the issuer to buy it back at a predetermined price at certain times during its life.

Call Option An option to buy an asset at a certain price by a certain date.

Cancelable Swap A swap that can be canceled by one side on prespecified dates.

Cap *See* Interest Rate Cap.

Capital Asset Pricing Model A model relating the expected return on an asset to its beta.

Caplet One component of an interest rate cap.

Cap Rate The rate determining payoffs in an interest rate cap.

Case–Shiller Index Index of house prices in the United States.

Cash-flow Mapping A procedure for representing an instrument as a portfolio of zero-coupon bonds for the purpose of calculating value at risk.

Cash-or-nothing Call Option An option that provides a fixed predetermined payoff if the final asset price is above the strike price and zero otherwise.

Cash-or-nothing Put Option An option that provides a fixed predetermined payoff if the final asset price is below the strike price and zero otherwise.

Cash Settlement Procedure for settling a futures contract in cash rather than by delivering the underlying asset.

CAT Bond Bond where the interest and, possibly, the principal paid are reduced if a particular category of "catastrophic" insurance claims exceed a certain amount.

CCP *See* Central Clearing Party.

CDD (Cooling Degree Days) The maximum of zero and the amount by which the daily average temperature is greater than 65° Fahrenheit. The average temperature is the average of the highest and lowest temperatures (midnight to midnight).

CDO *See* Collateralized Debt Obligation.

CDS *See* Credit Default Swap.

CDS Spread Basis points that must be paid each year for protection in a CDS.

CDX NA IG Portfolio of 125 investment-grade North American companies used in credit markets.

CEBO *See* Credit Event Binary Option.

Central Clearing The use of a clearing house for over-the-counter transactions.

Central Clearing Party A clearing house for over-the-counter-products.

Cheapest-to-deliver Bond The bond that is cheapest to deliver in the CME Group bond futures contract. Also used to describe the bond that is cheapest to deliver in a credit default swap.

Chooser Option An option where the holder has the right to choose whether it is a call or a put at some point during its life.

Class of Options *See* Option Class.

Clean Price of Bond The quoted price of a bond. The cash price paid for the bond (or dirty price) is calculated by adding the accrued interest to the clean price.

Clearing House A firm that guarantees the performance of the parties in an exchange-traded derivatives transaction. Also referred to as a *clearing corporation*.

Clearing Margin A margin posted by a member of a clearing house.

Cliquet Options A series of call or put options with rules for determining strike prices. Typically, one option starts when the previous one terminates.

CMO *See* Collateralized Mortgage Obligation.

Collar *See* Interest Rate Collar.

Collateralization A system for posting collateral by one or both parties in an over-the-counter derivatives transaction.

Collateralized Debt Obligation A way of packaging credit risk. Several classes of securities are created from a portfolio of bonds and there are rules for determining how defaults are allocated to classes.

Collateralized Mortgage Obligation (CMO) A mortgage-backed security where investors are divided into classes and there are rules for determining how principal repayments are channeled to the classes.

Combination A position involving both calls and puts on the same underlying asset.

Commodity Futures Trading Commission A body that regulates trading in futures contracts in the United States.

Commodity Swap A swap where cash flows depend on the price of a commodity.

Compounding Frequency This defines how an interest rate is measured.

Compounding Swap A swap where interest compounds instead of being paid.

Compound Option An option on an option.

Conditional Value at Risk (C-VaR) *See* Expected Shortfall.

Confirmation Contract confirming verbal agreement between two parties to a trade in the over-the-counter market.

Constant Maturity Swap (CMS) A swap where a swap rate is exchanged for either a fixed rate or a floating rate on each payment date.

Consumption Asset An asset held for consumption rather than investment.

Contango A situation where the futures price is above the expected future spot price. Often also used to refer to a situation in which the futures price is above the current spot price.

Continuous Compounding A way of quoting interest rates. It is the limit as the assumed compounding interval is made smaller and smaller.

Control Variate Technique A technique that can sometimes be used for improving the accuracy of a numerical procedure.

Convenience Yield A measure of the benefits from ownership of an asset that are not obtained by the holder of a long futures contract on the asset.

Conversion Factor A factor used to determine the number of bonds that must be delivered in the Chicago Board of Trade bond futures contract.

Convertible Bond A corporate bond that can be converted into a predetermined amount of the company's equity at certain times during its life.

Convexity A measure of the curvature in the relationship between bond prices and bond yields.

Convexity Adjustment An overworked term. It can refer to the adjustment necessary to convert a futures interest rate to a forward interest rate.

Cost of Carry The storage costs plus the cost of financing an asset minus the income earned on the asset.

Counterparty The opposite side in a financial transaction.

Coupon Interest payment made on a bond.

Covariance Measure of the linear relationship between two variables (equals the correlation between the variables times the product of their standard deviations).

Covered Call A short position in a call option on an asset combined with a long position in the asset.

Crashophobia Fear of a stock market crash that some people claim causes the market to increase the price of deep-out-of-the-money put options.

Credit Default Swap An instrument that gives the holder the right to sell a bond for its face value in the event of a default by the issuer.

Credit Derivative A derivative whose payoff depends on the creditworthiness of one or more entities.

Credit Event Event such as a default or reorganization triggering a payout on a credit derivative.

Credit Event Binary Option Option that provides a fixed payoff if a reference entity suffers a credit event.

Credit Index Index that tracks the cost of buying protection for companies in a portfolio (e.g., CDX NA IG and iTraxx Europe).

Credit Rating A measure of the creditworthiness of a bond issue.

Credit Risk The risk that a loss will be experienced because of a default by the counterparty in a derivatives transaction.

Credit Spread Option Option whose payoff depends on the spread between the yields earned on two assets.

Cross Hedging Hedging an exposure to the price of one asset with a contract on another asset.

Cumulative Distribution Function The probability that a variable will be less than x as a function of x.

Currency Swap A swap where interest and principal in one currency are exchanged for interest and principal in another currency.

Day Count A convention for quoting interest rates.

Day Trade A trade that is entered into and closed out on the same day.

Default Correlation Measures the tendency of two companies to default at about the same time.

Default Intensity *See* Hazard Rate.

Default Probability Density Measures the unconditional probability of default in a future short period of time.

Deferred Swap An agreement to enter into a swap at some time in the future. Also called a *forward swap*.

Delivery Price Price agreed to (possibly some time in the past) in a forward contract.

Delta The rate of change of the price of a derivative with the price of the underlying asset.

Delta Hedging A hedging scheme that is designed to make the price of a portfolio of derivatives insensitive to small changes in the price of the underlying asset.

Delta-neutral Portfolio A portfolio with a delta of zero so that there is no sensitivity to small changes in the price of the underlying asset.

DerivaGem The software accompanying this book.

Derivative An instrument whose price depends on, or is derived from, the price of another asset.

Deterministic Variable A variable whose future value is known.

Diagonal Spread A position in two calls where both the strike prices and times to maturity are different. (A diagonal spread can also be created with put options.)

Differential Swap A swap where a floating rate in one currency is exchanged for a floating rate in another currency and both rates are applied to the same principal.

Dirty Price of Bond Cash price of bond.

Discount Bond *See* Zero-coupon Bond.

Discount Instrument An instrument, such as a Treasury bill, that provides no coupons.

Discount Rate The annualized dollar return on a Treasury bill or similar instrument expressed as a percentage of the final face value.

Diversification Reducing risk by dividing a portfolio between many different assets.

Dividend A cash payment made to the owner of a stock.

Dividend Yield The dividend as a percentage of the stock price.

Dodd–Frank Act An act introduced in the United States following the credit crisis that started in 2007. It is designed to protect consumers and investors, avoid future bailouts, and monitor the functioning of the financial system more carefully.

Dollar Duration Product of a bond's modified duration and its price.

DOOM Option Deep-out-of-the-money put option.

Down-and-in Option An option that comes into existence when the price of the underlying asset declines to a prespecified level.

Down-and-out Option An option that ceases to exist when the price of the underlying asset declines to a prespecified level.

Duration A measure of the average life of a bond. It is also an approximation to the ratio of the proportional change in the bond price to the absolute change in its yield.

Duration Matching A procedure for matching the durations of assets and liabilities in a financial institution.

DV01 The dollar value of a 1-basis-point increase in all interest rates.

Dynamic Hedging A procedure for hedging an option position by periodically changing the position held in the underlying assets. The objective is usually to maintain a delta-neutral position.

Early Exercise Exercise prior to the maturity date.

Efficient Market Hypothesis A hypothesis that asset prices reflect relevant information.

Electronic Trading System of trading where a computer is used to match buyers and sellers.

Embedded Option An option that is an inseparable part of another instrument.

Empirical Research Research based on historical market data.

Employee Stock Option A call option issued by a company on its own stock and given to an employee as part of his or her compensation.

Equity Swap A swap where the return on an equity portfolio is exchanged for either a fixed or a floating rate of interest.

Equity Tranche The tranche that absorbs losses before all other tranches.

Eurocurrency A currency that is outside the formal control of the issuing country's monetary authorities.

Eurodollar A dollar held in a bank outside the United States.

Eurodollar Futures Contract A futures contract written on a Eurodollar deposit.

Eurodollar Interest Rate The interest rate on a Eurodollar deposit.

European Option An option that can be exercised only at the end of its life.

EWMA Exponentially weighted moving average.

Exchange Option An option to exchange one asset for another.

Ex-dividend Date When a dividend is declared, an ex-dividend date is specified. Investors who own shares of the stock immediately before the ex-dividend date receive the dividend.

Executive Stock Option A stock option issued by a company on its own stock and given to its executives as part of their remuneration.

Exercise Limit Maximum number of options that can be exercised in a five-day period on an exchange.

Exercise Price The price at which the underlying asset may be bought or sold in an option contract. Also called the *strike price*.

Exotic Option A nonstandard option.

Expectations Theory The theory that forward interest rates equal expected future spot interest rates.

Expected Shortfall Expected loss during N days conditional on being in the $(100 - X)\%$ tail of the distribution of profits/losses. The variable N days is the time horizon and $X\%$ is the confidence level.

Expected Value of a Variable The average value of the variable obtained by weighting the alternative values by their probabilities.

Expiration Date The end of the life of a contract.

Exponentially Weighted Moving Average Model A model where exponential weighting is used to provide forecasts for a variable from historical data. It is sometimes applied to the variance per day in value at risk calculations.

Exponential Weighting A weighting scheme where the weight given to an observation depends on how recent it is. The weight given to an observation i time periods ago is λ times the weight given to an observation $i - 1$ time periods ago, where $\lambda < 1$.

Exposure The maximum loss from default by a counterparty.

Extendable Bond A bond whose life can be extended at the option of the holder.

Extendable Swap A swap whose life can be extended at the option of one side to the contract.

FAS Financial Accounting Standard.

FAS 123 Accounting standard in United States relating to employee stock options.

FAS 133 Accounting standard in United States relating to instruments used for hedging.

FASB Financial Accounting Standards Board.

FICO A credit score developed by Fair Isaac Corporation.

Financial Intermediary A bank or other financial institution that facilitates the flow of funds between different entities in the economy.

Fixed Rate A rate that is fixed through time.

Flat Volatility The name given to volatility used to price a cap when the same volatility is used for each caplet.

Flex Option An option traded on an exchange with terms that are different from the standard options traded by the exchange.

Floating Rate A rate that changes through time.

Floor *See* Interest Rate Floor.

Floor–Ceiling Agreement *See* Interest Rate Collar.

Floorlet One component of a floor.

Floor Rate The rate in an interest rate floor agreement.

Foreign Currency Option An option on a foreign exchange rate.

Forward Contract A contract that obligates the holder to buy or sell an asset for a predetermined delivery price at a predetermined future time.

Forward Exchange Rate The forward price of one unit of a foreign currency.

Forward Interest Rate The interest rate for a future period of time implied by the rates prevailing in the market today.

Forward Price The delivery price in a forward contract that causes the contract to be worth zero.

Forward Rate Rate of interest for a period of time in the future implied by today's zero rates.

Forward Rate Agreement (FRA) Agreement that a certain interest rate will apply to a certain principal amount for a certain time period in the future.

Forward Start Option An option designed so that it will be at the money at some time in the future.

Forward Swap *See* Deferred Swap.

Futures Commission Merchants Futures traders who are following instructions from clients.

Futures Contract A contract that obligates the holder to buy or sell an asset at a predetermined delivery price during a specified future time period. The contract is marked to market daily.

Futures Option An option on a futures contract.

Futures Price The delivery price currently applicable to a futures contract.

Futures-style Option Futures contract on the payoff from an option.

Gamma The rate of change of delta with respect to the asset price.

Gamma-neutral portfolio A portfolio with a gamma of zero.

GAP Management Procedure for matching the maturities of assets and liabilities.

Gap Option European call or put option where there are two strike prices. One determines whether the option is exercised; the other determines the payoff.

Geometric Mean The nth root of the product of n numbers.

Greeks Hedge parameters such as delta, gamma, vega, theta, and rho.

Hazard Rate Measures probability of default in a short period of time conditional on no earlier default.

HDD (Heating Degree Days) The maximum of zero and the amount by which the daily average temperature is less than 65° Fahrenheit. The average temperature is the average of the highest and lowest temperatures (midnight to midnight).

Hedge A trade designed to reduce risk.

Hedge Fund Funds that are subject to fewer restrictions and less regulation than mutual funds. They can take short positions and use derivatives, but they cannot offer their services to the general public.

Hedger An individual who enters into hedging trades.

Hedge Ratio The ratio of the size of a position in a hedging instrument to the size of the position being hedged.

Historical Simulation A simulation based on historical data.

Historical Volatility A volatility estimated from historical data.

Holiday Calendar Calendar defining which days are holidays for the purposes of determining payment dates in a swap.

IMM Dates Third Wednesday in March, June, September, and December.

Implied Distribution A distribution for a future asset price implied from option prices.

Implied Dividend Yield Dividend yield calculated from the prices of calls and puts with the same strike price and time to maturity.

Implied Volatility Volatility implied from an option price using the Black–Scholes or a similar model.

Inception Profit Profit created by selling a derivative for more than its theoretical value.

Index Amortizing Swap *See* Indexed Principal Swap.

Index Arbitrage An arbitrage involving a position in the stocks comprising a stock index and a position in a futures contract on the stock index.

Indexed Principal Swap A swap where the principal declines over time. The reduction in the principal on a payment date depends on the level of interest rates.

Index Futures A futures contract on a stock index or other index.

Index Option An option contract on a stock index or other index.

Initial Margin The cash required from a futures trader at the time of the trade.

Interest Rate Cap An option that provides a payoff when a specified interest rate is above a certain level. The interest rate is a floating rate that is reset periodically.

Interest Rate Collar A combination of an interest rate cap and an interest rate floor.

Interest Rate Derivative A derivative whose payoffs are dependent on future interest rates.

Interest Rate Floor An option that provides a payoff when an interest rate is below a certain level. The interest rate is a floating rate that is reset periodically.

Interest Rate Option An option where the payoff is dependent on the level of interest rates.

Interest Rate Swap An exchange of a fixed rate of interest on a certain notional principal for a floating rate of interest on the same notional principal.

International Swaps and Derivatives Association Trade association for over-the-counter derivatives and developer of master agreements used in over-the-counter contracts.

In-the-money Option Either (a) a call option where the asset price is greater than the strike price or (b) a put option where the asset price is less than the strike price.

Intrinsic Value For a call option, this is the greater of the excess of the asset price over the strike price and zero. For a put option, it is the greater of the excess of the strike price over the asset price and zero.

Inverted Market A market where futures prices decrease with maturity.

Investment Asset An asset held by at least some individuals for investment purposes.

IO (Interest only) A mortgage-backed security where the holder receives only interest cash flows on the underlying mortgage pool.

ISDA *See* International Swaps and Derivatives Association.

iTraxx Europe Portfolio of 125 investment-grade European companies used in credit markets.

Kurtosis A measure of the heaviness of the tails of a distribution.

LEAPS (Long-term Equity Anticipation Securities) These are relatively long-term options on individual stocks or stock indices.

LIBID (London Interbank Bid Rate) The rate bid by banks on Eurocurrency deposits (i.e., the rate at which a bank is willing to borrow from other banks).

LIBOR (London Interbank Offered Rate) The rate offered by banks on Eurocurrency deposits (i.e., the rate at which a bank is willing to lend to other banks).

LIBOR Curve LIBOR zero-coupon interest rates as a function of maturity.

LIBOR-in-arrears Swap Swap where the LIBOR rate observed on a date is paid on that date rather than one accrual period later.

LIBOR–OIS Spread Difference between LIBOR rate and OIS rate for a certain maturity.

Limit Move The maximum price move permitted by the exchange in a single trading session.

Limit Order An order that can be executed only at a specified price or one more favorable to the investor.

Liquidity Preference Theory A theory leading to the conclusion that forward interest rates are above expected future spot interest rates.

Liquidity Premium The amount that forward interest rates exceed expected future spot interest rates.

Liquidity Risk Risk that it will not be possible to sell a holding of a particular instrument at its theoretical price. Also, the risk that a company will not be able to borrow money to fund its assets.

Locals Individuals on the floor of an exchange who trade for their own account rather than for someone else.

Lognormal Distribution A variable has a lognormal distribution when the logarithm of the variable has a normal distribution.

Long Hedge A hedge involving a long futures position.

Long Position A position involving the purchase of an asset.

Lookback Option An option whose payoff is dependent on the maximum or minimum of the asset price achieved during a certain period.

Maintenance Margin When the balance in a trader's margin account falls below the maintenance margin level, the trader receives a margin call requiring the account to be topped up to the initial margin level.

Margin The cash balance (or security deposit) required from a futures or options trader.

Margin Call A request for extra margin when the balance in the margin account falls below the maintenance margin level.

Market Maker A trader who is willing to quote both bid and offer prices for an asset.

Market Model A model most commonly used by traders.

Market Segmentation Theory A theory that short interest rates are determined independently of long interest rates by the market.

Marking to Market The practice of revaluing an instrument to reflect the current values of the relevant market variables.

Maturity Date The end of the life of a contract.

Mean Reversion The tendency of a market variable (such as an interest rate) to revert back to some long-run average level.

Mezzanine Tranche Tranche which experiences losses after equity tranche but before senior tranche.

Modified Duration A modification to the standard duration measure so that it more accurately describes the relationship between proportional changes in a bond price and absolute changes in its yield. The modification takes account of the compounding frequency with which the yield is quoted.

Monte Carlo Simulation A procedure for randomly sampling changes in market variables in order to value a derivative.

Mortgage-backed Security A security that entitles the owner to a share in the cash flows realized from a pool of mortgages.

Naked Position A short position in a call option that is not combined with a long position in the underlying asset.

Netting The practice of offsetting over-the-counter contracts with positive and negative values in the event of a default or for the purpose of determining collateral requirements.

NINJA Term used to describe poor credit risk: no income, no job, no assets.

No-arbitrage Assumption The assumption that there are no arbitrage opportunities in market prices.

Nonsystematic risk Risk that can be diversified away.

Normal Backwardation A situation where the futures price is below the expected future spot price.

Normal Distribution The standard bell-shaped distribution of statistics.

Normal Market A market where futures prices increase with maturity.

Notional Principal The principal used to calculate payments in an interest rate swap. The principal is "notional" because it is neither paid nor received.

Numerical Procedure A method of valuing an option when no formula is available.

OCC (Options Clearing Corporation) *See* Clearing House.

Offer Price The price that a dealer is offering to sell an asset.

OIS *See* Overnight Indexed Swap.

Open Interest The total number of long positions outstanding in a futures contract (equals the total number of short positions).

Open Outcry System of trading where traders meet on the floor of the exchange.

Option The right to buy or sell an asset.

Option-adjusted Spread The spread over the Treasury curve that makes the theoretical price of an interest rate derivative equal to the market price.

Option Class All options of the same type (call or put) on a particular stock.

Option Series All options of a certain class with the same strike price and expiration date.

Out-of-the-money Option Either (a) a call option where the asset price is less than the strike price or (b) a put option where the asset price is greater than the strike price.

Overnight Indexed Swap Swap where a fixed rate for a period (e.g., one month) is exchanged for the geometric average of the overnight rates during the period.

Over-the-counter Market A market where traders deal by phone. The traders are usually financial institutions, corporations, and fund managers.

Package A derivative that is a portfolio of standard calls and puts, possibly combined with a position in forward contracts and the asset itself.

Parallel Shift A movement in the yield curve where each point on the curve changes by the same amount.

Parisian Option Barrier option where the asset has to be above or below the barrier for a period of time for the option to be knocked in or out.

Par Value The principal amount of a bond.

Par Yield The coupon on a bond that makes its price equal the principal.

Path-dependent Option An option whose payoff depends on the whole path followed by the underlying variable—not just its final value.

Payoff The cash realized by the holder of an option or other derivative at the end of its life.

PD Probability of default.

Plain Vanilla A term used to describe a standard deal.

PO (Principal Only) A mortgage-backed security where the holder receives only principal cash flows on the underlying mortgage pool.

Portfolio Immunization Making a portfolio relatively insensitive to interest rates.

Portfolio Insurance Entering into trades to ensure that the value of a portfolio will not fall below a certain level.

Position Limit The maximum position a trader (or group of traders acting together) is allowed to hold.

Premium The price of an option.

Prepayment function A function estimating the prepayment of principal on a portfolio of mortgages in terms of other variables.

Principal The par or face value of a debt instrument.

Principal Protected Note A product where the return earned depends on the performance of a risky asset but is guaranteed to be nonnegative, so that the investor's principal is preserved.

Program Trading A procedure where trades are automatically generated by a computer and transmitted to the trading floor of an exchange.

Protective Put A put option combined with a long position in the underlying asset.

Put–Call Parity The relationship between the price of a European call option and the price of a European put option when they have the same strike price and maturity date.

Put Option An option to sell an asset for a certain price by a certain date.

Puttable Bond A bond where the holder has the right to sell it back to the issuer at certain predetermined times for a predetermined price.

Puttable Swap A swap where one side has the right to terminate early.

Quanto A derivative where the payoff is defined by variables associated with one currency but is paid in another currency.

Rainbow Option An option whose payoff is dependent on two or more underlying variables.

Range Forward Contract The combination of a long call and short put or the combination of a short call and long put.

Real Option Option involving real (as opposed to financial) assets. Real assets include land, plant, and machinery.

Rebalancing The process of adjusting a trading position periodically. Usually the purpose is to maintain delta neutrality.

Recovery Rate Amount recovered in the event of default as a percentage of the face value.

Reference Entity Company for which default protection is obtained in a CDS.

Repo (Repurchase agreement) A procedure for borrowing money by selling securities to a counterparty and agreeing to buy them back later at a slightly higher price.

Repo Rate The rate of interest in a repo transaction.

Reset Date The date in a swap or cap or floor when the floating rate for the next period is set.

Reversion Level The level to which the value of a market variable (e.g., an interest rate) tends to revert.

Rho Rate of change of the price of a derivative with the interest rate.

Rights Issue An issue to existing shareholders of a security giving them the right to buy new shares at a certain price.

Risk-free Rate The rate of interest that can be earned without assuming any risks.

Risk-neutral Valuation The valuation of an option or other derivative assuming the world is risk neutral. Risk-neutral valuation gives the correct price for a derivative in all worlds, not just in a risk-neutral world.

Risk-neutral World A world where investors are assumed to require no extra return on average for bearing risks.

Roll Back *See* Backwards Induction.

Scalper A trader who holds positions for a very short period of time.

Scenario Analysis An analysis of the effects of possible alternative future movements in market variables on the value of a portfolio.

SEC Securities and Exchange Commission.

Securitization Procedure for distributing the risks in a portfolio of assets.

SEF *See* Swap Execution Facility.

Settlement Price The average of the prices at which a futures contract trades immediately before the bell signaling the close of trading for a day. It is used in mark-to-market calculations.

Short Hedge A hedge where a short futures position is taken.

Short Position A position involving the sale of an asset.

Short Rate The interest rate applying for a very short period of time.

Short Selling Selling in the market shares that have been borrowed from another investor.

Short-term Risk-free Rate *See* Short Rate.

Shout Option An option where the holder has the right to lock in a minimum value for the payoff at one time during its life.

Simulation *See* Monte Carlo Simulation.

Specialist An individual responsible for managing limit orders on some exchanges. The specialist does not make the information on outstanding limit orders available to other traders.

Speculator An individual who is taking a position in the market. Usually the individual is betting that the price of an asset will go up or that the price of an asset will go down.

Spot Interest Rate *See* Zero-coupon Interest Rate.

Spot Price The price for immediate delivery.

Spot Volatilities The volatilities used to price a cap when a different volatility is used for each caplet.

Spread Transaction A position in two or more options of the same type.

Stack and Roll Procedure where short-term futures contracts are rolled forward so that long-term hedges are created.

Static Hedge A hedge that does not have to be changed once it is initiated.

Step-up Swap A swap where the principal increases over time in a predetermined way.

Stochastic Variable A variable whose future value is uncertain.

Stock Dividend A dividend paid in the form of additional shares.

Stock Index An index monitoring the value of a portfolio of stocks.

Stock Index Futures Futures on a stock index.

Stock Index Option An option on a stock index.

Stock Option Option on a stock.

Stock Split The conversion of each existing share into more than one new share.

Storage Costs The costs of storing a commodity.

Straddle A long position in a call and a put with the same strike price.

Strangle A long position in a call and a put with different strike prices.

Strap A long position in two call options and one put option with the same strike price.

Stressed VaR Value at risk calculated using historical simulation from a period of stressed market conditions.

Stress Testing Testing of the impact of extreme market moves on the value of a portfolio.

Strike Price The price at which the asset may be bought or sold in an option contract. Also called the *exercise price*.

Strip A long position in one call option and two put options with the same strike price.

Strip Bonds Zero-coupon bonds created by selling the coupons on Treasury bonds separately from the principal.

Subprime Mortgage Mortgage granted to a borrower with a poor credit history or no credit history at all.

Swap An agreement to exchange cash flows in the future according to a prearranged formula.

Swap Execution Facility Place where market participants can post bid and offer quotes or accept the quotes of other market participants.

Swap Rate The fixed rate in an interest rate swap that causes the swap to have a value of zero.

Swaption An option to enter into an interest rate swap where a specified fixed rate is exchanged for floating.

Swing Option Energy option in which the rate of consumption must be between a minimum and maximum level. There is usually a limit on the number of times the option holder can change the rate at which the energy is consumed.

Synthetic CDO A CDO created by selling credit default swaps.

Synthetic Option An option created by trading the underlying asset.

Systematic Risk Risk that cannot be diversified away.

Systemic Risk Risk that default by one financial institution will lead to defaults by other financial institutions.

Tailing the Hedge A procedure for adjusting the number of futures contracts used in hedging to reflect daily settlement.

Tail Loss *See* Expected Shortfall.

Take-and-pay Option *See* Swing Option.

TED Spread Difference between three-month LIBOR and the three-month Treasury bill rate.

Terminal Value The value at maturity.

Term Structure of Interest Rates The relationship between interest rates and their maturities.

Theta The rate of change of the price of an option or other derivative with the passage of time.

Time Decay *See* Theta.

Time Value The value of an option arising from the time left to maturity (equals an option's price minus its intrinsic value).

Total Return Swap A swap where the return on an asset such as a bond is exchanged for LIBOR plus a spread. The return on the asset includes income such as coupons and the change in value of the asset.

Tranche One of several securities that have different risk attributes. Examples are the tranches of a CDO or CMO.

Transactions Costs The cost of carrying out a trade (commissions plus the difference between the price obtained and the midpoint of the bid–offer spread).

Treasury Bill A short-term, non-coupon-bearing instrument issued by the government to finance its debt.

Treasury Bond A long-term, coupon-bearing instrument issued by the government to finance its debt.

Treasury Bond Futures A futures contract on Treasury bonds.

Treasury Note *See* Treasury Bond. (Treasury notes have maturities of less than 10 years.)

Treasury Note Futures A futures contract on Treasury notes.

Tree A representation of the evolution of the value of a market variable for the purposes of valuing an option or other derivative.

Underlying Variable A variable on which the price of an option or other derivative depends.

Unsystematic Risk *See* Nonsystematic Risk.

Up-and-in Option An option that comes into existence when the price of the underlying asset increases to a prespecified level.

Up-and-out Option An option that ceases to exist when the price of the underlying asset increases to a prespecified level.

Uptick An increase in price.

Value at Risk A loss that will not be exceeded at some specified confidence level.

Variance–Covariance Matrix A matrix showing variances of, and covariances between, a number of different market variables.

Variance Rate The square of volatility.

Variance Swap Swap where the realized variance rate is exchanged for a fixed variance rate. Both are applied to a notional principal.

Variation Margin An extra margin required to bring the balance in a margin account up to the initial margin when there is a margin call.

Vega The rate of change in the price of an option or other derivative with volatility.

Vega-neutral Portfolio A portfolio with a vega of zero.

Vesting Period Period during which an employee stock option cannot be exercised.

VIX Index Index of the volatility of the S&P 500.

Volatility A measure of the uncertainty of the return realized on an asset.

Volatility Skew A term used to describe the volatility smile when it is nonsymmetrical.

Volatility Smile The variation of implied volatility with strike price.

Volatility Surface A table showing the variation of implied volatility with strike price and time to maturity.

Volatility Swap Swap where the realized volatility during a period is exchanged for a fixed volatility. Both percentage volatilities are applied to a notional principal.

Volatility Term Structure The variation of implied volatility with time to maturity.

Volcker Rule A rule in the Dodd–Frank Act restricting the speculative activities of banks, proposed by former Federal Reserve Chairman Paul Volcker.

Warrant An option issued by a company or a financial institution. Call warrants are frequently issued by companies on their own stock.

Waterfall Rules for determining how cash flows from the underlying portfolio are distributed to tranches.

Weather Derivative Derivative where the payoff depends on the weather.

Weeklys Options created on a Thursday that expire on Friday of the following week.

Wild Card Play The right to deliver on a futures contract at the closing price for a period of time after the close of trading.

Writing an Option Selling an option.

Yield A return provided by an instrument.

Yield Curve *See* Term Structure of Interest Rates.

Zero-coupon Bond A bond that provides no coupons.

Zero-coupon Interest Rate The interest rate that would be earned on a bond that provides no coupons.

Zero-coupon Yield Curve A plot of the zero-coupon interest rate against time to maturity.

Zero Curve *See* Zero-coupon Yield Curve.

Zero Rate *See* Zero-coupon Interest Rate.

DerivaGem Software

There are a number of new features of DerivaGem. The software has been simplified by eliminating the *.dll files. Source code is included with the functions, and functions are now accessible to Mac and Linux users. CDSs and CDOs can now be valued.

Getting Started

The most difficult part of using software is getting started. Here is a step-by-step guide to valuing an option using DerivaGem Version 2.01.

1. Put the disk that comes with this book into the CD/DVD drive on your computer. Open the Excel file DG201.xls
2. If you are using Office 2007, click on *Options* at the top of your screen (above the F column) and then click *Enable this content*. If you are not using Office 2007, make sure that the security for macros is set at medium or low. (You can do this by clicking *Tools*, followed by *Macros*, followed by *Security*.)
3. Click on the *Equity_FX_Index_Futures* worksheet tab at the bottom of the page.
4. Choose *Currency* as the Underlying Type and *Binomial American* as the Option Type. Click on the *Put* button. Leave *Imply Volatility* unchecked.
5. You are now all set to value an American put option on a currency. There are seven inputs: exchange rate, volatility, domestic risk-free rate, foreign risk-free rate rate, time to expiration (years), exercise price, and time steps. Input these in cells D6, D7, D8, D9, D19, D20, and D21 as 1.61, 12%, 8%, 9%, 1.0, 1.60, and 4, respectively.
6. Hit *Enter* on your keyboard and click on *Calculate*. You will see the price of the option in cell D25 as 0.07099 and the Greek letters in cells D26 to D30. The screen you should have produced is shown on the following page.
7. Click on *Display Tree*. You will see the binomial tree used to calculate the option. This is Figure 20.6 in Chapter 20.

Next Steps

You should now have no difficulty valuing other types of option on other underlyings with this worksheet. To imply a volatility, check the *Imply Volatility* box and input the option price in cell D25. Hit *Enter* and click on *Calculate*. The implied volatility is displayed in cell D7.

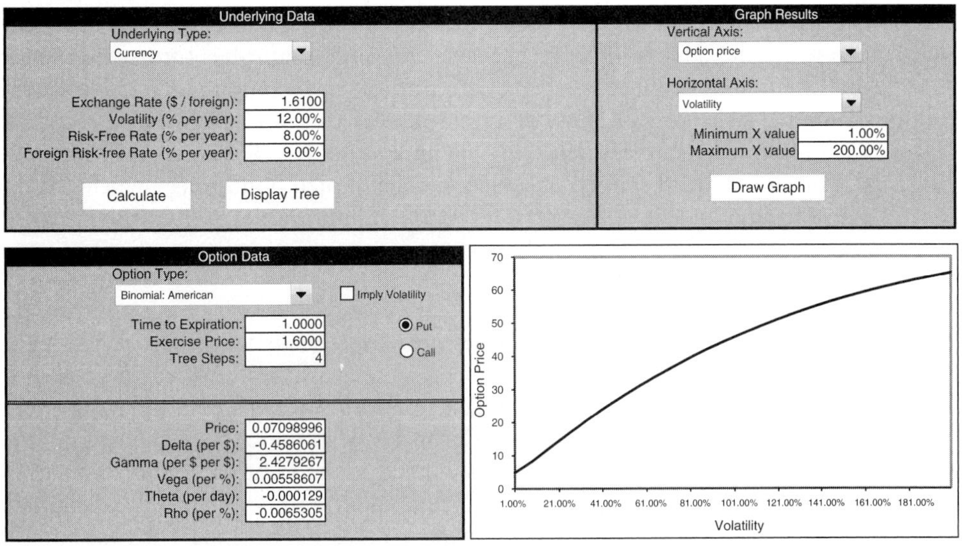

Many different charts can be displayed. To display a chart, you must first choose the variable you require on the vertical axis, the variable you require on the horizontal axis, and the range of values to be considered on the horizontal axis. Following that, you should hit *Enter* on your keyboard and click on *Draw Graph*.

Other points to note about this worksheet are:

1. For European and American equity options, up to 10 dividends on the underlying stock can be input in a table that pops up. Enter the time of each dividend (measured in years from today) in the first column and the amount of the dividend in the second column. Dividends must be entered in chronological order.
2. Up to 500 time steps can be used for the valuation of American options, but only a maximum of 10 time steps can be displayed.
3. Greek letters for all options other than standard calls and puts are calculated by perturbing the inputs, not by using analytic formulas.
4. For an Asian option the *Current Average* is the average price since inception. For a new deal (with zero time to inception), the current average is irrelevant.
5. In the case of a lookback option, *Minimum to Date* is used when a call is valued and *Maximum to Date* is used when a put is valued. For a new deal, these should be set equal to the current price of the underlying asset.
6. Interest rates are continuously compounded.

Bond Options

The general operation of the *Bond_Options* worksheet is similar to that of the *Equity_FX_Index_Futures* worksheet. The alternative models are Black's model, the normal model of the short rate, and the lognormal model of the short rate. Black's model is explained in Section 21.3 and can be applied only to European options. The other two models, which are not covered in this book, can be applied to European or American options. The coupon is the rate paid per year and the frequency of payments can be selected as Quarterly, Semi-Annual or Annual. The zero-coupon yield curve is entered in the table labeled Term Structure. Enter maturities (measured in years) in the first column and the corresponding continuously compounded rates in the second column. The maturities must be in chronological order. DerivaGem assumes a piecewise linear zero curve similar to that in Figure 4.1. The strike price can be quoted (clean) or cash (dirty) (see Section 21.4). The quoted bond price, which is calculated by the software, and the strike price, which is input, are per $100 of principal.

Caps and Swaptions

The general operation of the *Caps_and Swap_Options* worksheet is similar to that of the *Equity_FX_Index_Futures* worksheet. The worksheet is used to value interest rate caps/floors and swap options. Black's model for caps and floors is explained in Section 21.5 and Black's model for European swap options is explained in Section 21.6. The term structure of interest rates is entered in the same way as for bond options. The frequency of payments can be selected as Monthly, Quarterly, Semi-Annual, or Annual. The software calculates payment dates by working backward from the end of the life of the instrument. The initial accrual period for a cap/floor may be a nonstandard length between 0.5 and 1.5 times a normal accrual period.

CDSs

The CDS worksheet is used to calculate hazard rates from CDS spreads and vice versa. Users must input a term structure of interest rates (continuously compounded) and either a term structure of CDS spreads or a term structure of hazard rates. The initial hazard rate applies from time zero to the time specified; the second hazard rate applies from the time corresponding to the first hazard rate to the time corresponding to the second hazard rate; and so on. The hazard rates are continuously compounded, so that a hazard rate $h(t)$ at time t means that the probability of default between times t and $t + \Delta t$, conditional on no earlier default, is $h(t)\,\Delta t$. The calculations are carried out assuming that default can occur only at points midway between payment dates. This corresponds to the calculations for the example in Section 23.2 (the hazard rate in that example is 2% with annual compounding or 2.02% with continuous compounding).

CDOs

The CDO worksheet calculates quotes for the tranches of CDOs from tranche correlations input by the user. The attachment points and detachment points for tranches are input by the user. The quotes can be in basis points or involve an upfront payment. In the latter case, the spread in basis points is fixed and the upfront payment, as a percent of the tranche principal, is either input or implied. (For example, the fixed spread for the equity tranche of iTraxx Europe or CDX NA IG is 500 basis points.) The number of integration points defines the accuracy of calculations and can be left as 10 for most purposes (the maximum is 30). The software displays the expected loss as a percent of the tranche principal (ExpLoss) and the present value of expected payments (PVPmts) at the rate of 10,000 basis points per year. The spread and upfront payment are

$$\text{ExpLoss} * 10{,}000/\text{PVPmts} \quad \text{and} \quad \text{ExpLoss} - (\text{Spread} * \text{PVPmts}/10{,}000)$$

respectively. The worksheet can be used to imply either tranche (compound) correlations or base correlations from quotes input by the user. For base correlations to be calculated, it is necessary for the first attachment point to be 0% and the detachment point for one tranche to be the attachment point for the next tranche.

How Greek Letters Are Defined

In the *Equity_FX_Index_Futures* worksheet, the Greek letters are defined as follows:

Delta: Change in option price per dollar increase in underlying asset

Gamma: Change in delta per dollar increase in underlying asset

Vega: Change in option price per 1% increase in volatility (e.g., volatility increases from 20% to 21%)

Rho: Change in option price per 1% increase in interest rate (e.g., interest increases from 5% to 6%)

Theta: Change in option price per calendar day passing.

In the *Bond_Options* and *Caps_and_Swap_Options* worksheets, the Greek letters are defined as follows:

DV01: Change in option price per 1-basis-point upward parallel shift in the zero curve

Gamma01: Change in DV01 per 1-basis-point upward parallel shift in the zero curve, multiplied by 100

Vega: Change in option price when volatility parameter increases by 1% (e.g., volatility increases from 20% to 21%).

The Applications Builder

Once you are familiar with the Options calculator (DG201.xls), you may want to start using the Application Builder. This consists of most of the functions underlying the Options Calculator with source code. It enables you to compile tables of option values, create your own charts, or develop applications. Excel users should load DG201 functions.xls and Open Office users should load Open Office DG201 functions.ods. Below are some sample applications that have been developed. They are in DG201 applications.xls and Open Office DG201 applications.ods.

A. Binomial Convergence. This investigates the convergence of the binomial model in Chapters 12 and 20.

B. Greek Letters. This provides charts showing the Greek letters in Chapter 18.

C. Delta Hedge. This investigates the performance of delta hedging as in Tables 18.2 and 18.3.

D. Delta and Gamma Hedge. This investigates the performance of delta plus gamma hedging for a position in a binary option.

E. Value and Risk. This calculates Value at Risk for a portfolio using three different approaches.

F. Barrier Replication. This carries out calculations for static options replication (see Section 25.16).

G. Trinomial Convergence. This investigates the convergence of a trinomial tree model.

Note that E, F, and G are not included in the Open Office version of the software.

Major Exchanges Trading Futures and Options

Australian Securities Exchange (ASX)	www.asx.com.au
BM&FBOVESPA (BMF)	www.bmfbovespa.com.br
Bombay Stock Exchange (BSE)	www.bseindia.com
Boston Options Exchange (BOX)	www.bostonoptions.com
Bursa Malaysia (BM)	www.bursamalaysia.com
Chicago Board Options Exchange (CBOE)	www.cboe.com
China Financial Futures Exchange (CFFEX)	www.cffex.com.cn
CME Group	www.cmegroup.com
Dalian Commodity Exchange (DCE)	www.dce.com.cn
Eurex	www.eurexchange.com
Hong Kong Futures Exchange (HKFE)	www.hkex.com.hk
IntercontinentalExchange (ICE)	www.theice.com
International Securities Exchange (ISE)	www.iseoptions.com
Kansas City Board of Trade (KCBT)	www.kcbt.com
Korea Exchange (KRX)	www.krx.co.kr
London Metal Exchange (LME)	www.lme.co.uk
MEFF Renta Fija and Variable, Spain	www.meff.es
Mexican Derivatives Exchange (MEXDER)	www.mexder.com
Minneapolis Grain Exchange (MGE)	www.mgex.com
Montreal Exchange (ME)	www.m-x.ca
NASDAQ OMX	www.nasdaqomx.com
National Stock Exchange of India (NSE)	www.nse-india.com
NYSE Euronext	www.nyse.com
Osaka Securities Exchange (OSE)	www.ose.or.jp
Shanghai Futures Exchange (SHFE)	www.shfe.com.cn
Singapore Exchange (SGX)	www.sgx.com
Tokyo Grain Exchange (TGE)	www.tge.or.jp
Tokyo Financial Exchange (TFX)	www.tfx.co.jp
Zhengzhou Commodity Exchange (ZCE)	www.zce.cn

There has been a great deal of consolidation of derivatives exchanges, nationally and internationally, in the last few years. The Chicago Board of Trade and the Chicago Mercantile Exchnage have merged to form the CME Group, which also includes the New York Mercantile Exchange (NYMEX). Euronext and the NYSE have merged to form NYSE Euronext, which now owns the American Stock Exchange (AMEX), the Pacific Exchange (PXS), the London International Financial Futures Exchange (LIFFE), and two French exchanges. The Australian Stock Exchange and the Sydney Futures Exchange (SFE) have merged to form the Australian Securities Exchange (ASX). The IntercontinentalExchange (ICE) has acquired the New York Board of Trade (NYBOT), the International Petroleum Exchange (IPE), and the Winnipeg Commodity Exchange (WCE). Eurex, which is jointly operated by Deutsche Borse AG and SIX Swiss Exchange, has acquired the International Securities Exchange (ISE). No doubt the consolidation has been largely driven by economies of scale that lead to lower trading costs.

Table for $N(x)$ When $x \leqslant 0$

This table shows values of $N(x)$ for $x \leqslant 0$. The table should be used with interpolation. For example,

$$N(-0.1234) = N(-0.12) - 0.34[N(-0.12) - N(-0.13)]$$
$$= 0.4522 - 0.34 \times (0.4522 - 0.4483)$$
$$= 0.4509$$

x	.00	.01	.02	.03	.04	.05	.06	.07	.08	.09
−0.0	0.5000	0.4960	0.4920	0.4880	0.4840	0.4801	0.4761	0.4721	0.4681	0.4641
−0.1	0.4602	0.4562	0.4522	0.4483	0.4443	0.4404	0.4364	0.4325	0.4286	0.4247
−0.2	0.4207	0.4168	0.4129	0.4090	0.4052	0.4013	0.3974	0.3936	0.3897	0.3859
−0.3	0.3821	0.3783	0.3745	0.3707	0.3669	0.3632	0.3594	0.3557	0.3520	0.3483
−0.4	0.3446	0.3409	0.3372	0.3336	0.3300	0.3264	0.3228	0.3192	0.3156	0.3121
−0.5	0.3085	0.3050	0.3015	0.2981	0.2946	0.2912	0.2877	0.2843	0.2810	0.2776
−0.6	0.2743	0.2709	0.2676	0.2643	0.2611	0.2578	0.2546	0.2514	0.2483	0.2451
−0.7	0.2420	0.2389	0.2358	0.2327	0.2296	0.2266	0.2236	0.2206	0.2177	0.2148
−0.8	0.2119	0.2090	0.2061	0.2033	0.2005	0.1977	0.1949	0.1922	0.1894	0.1867
−0.9	0.1841	0.1814	0.1788	0.1762	0.1736	0.1711	0.1685	0.1660	0.1635	0.1611
−1.0	0.1587	0.1562	0.1539	0.1515	0.1492	0.1469	0.1446	0.1423	0.1401	0.1379
−1.1	0.1357	0.1335	0.1314	0.1292	0.1271	0.1251	0.1230	0.1210	0.1190	0.1170
−1.2	0.1151	0.1131	0.1112	0.1093	0.1075	0.1056	0.1038	0.1020	0.1003	0.0985
−1.3	0.0968	0.0951	0.0934	0.0918	0.0901	0.0885	0.0869	0.0853	0.0838	0.0823
−1.4	0.0808	0.0793	0.0778	0.0764	0.0749	0.0735	0.0721	0.0708	0.0694	0.0681
−1.5	0.0668	0.0655	0.0643	0.0630	0.0618	0.0606	0.0594	0.0582	0.0571	0.0559
−1.6	0.0548	0.0537	0.0526	0.0516	0.0505	0.0495	0.0485	0.0475	0.0465	0.0455
−1.7	0.0446	0.0436	0.0427	0.0418	0.0409	0.0401	0.0392	0.0384	0.0375	0.0367
−1.8	0.0359	0.0351	0.0344	0.0336	0.0329	0.0322	0.0314	0.0307	0.0301	0.0294
−1.9	0.0287	0.0281	0.0274	0.0268	0.0262	0.0256	0.0250	0.0244	0.0239	0.0233
−2.0	0.0228	0.0222	0.0217	0.0212	0.0207	0.0202	0.0197	0.0192	0.0188	0.0183
−2.1	0.0179	0.0174	0.0170	0.0166	0.0162	0.0158	0.0154	0.0150	0.0146	0.0143
−2.2	0.0139	0.0136	0.0132	0.0129	0.0125	0.0122	0.0119	0.0116	0.0113	0.0110
−2.3	0.0107	0.0104	0.0102	0.0099	0.0096	0.0094	0.0091	0.0089	0.0087	0.0084
−2.4	0.0082	0.0080	0.0078	0.0075	0.0073	0.0071	0.0069	0.0068	0.0066	0.0064
−2.5	0.0062	0.0060	0.0059	0.0057	0.0055	0.0054	0.0052	0.0051	0.0049	0.0048
−2.6	0.0047	0.0045	0.0044	0.0043	0.0041	0.0040	0.0039	0.0038	0.0037	0.0036
−2.7	0.0035	0.0034	0.0033	0.0032	0.0031	0.0030	0.0029	0.0028	0.0027	0.0026
−2.8	0.0026	0.0025	0.0024	0.0023	0.0023	0.0022	0.0021	0.0021	0.0020	0.0019
−2.9	0.0019	0.0018	0.0018	0.0017	0.0016	0.0016	0.0015	0.0015	0.0014	0.0014
−3.0	0.0014	0.0013	0.0013	0.0012	0.0012	0.0011	0.0011	0.0011	0.0010	0.0010
−3.1	0.0010	0.0009	0.0009	0.0009	0.0008	0.0008	0.0008	0.0008	0.0007	0.0007
−3.2	0.0007	0.0007	0.0006	0.0006	0.0006	0.0006	0.0006	0.0005	0.0005	0.0005
−3.3	0.0005	0.0005	0.0005	0.0004	0.0004	0.0004	0.0004	0.0004	0.0004	0.0003
−3.4	0.0003	0.0003	0.0003	0.0003	0.0003	0.0003	0.0003	0.0003	0.0003	0.0002
−3.5	0.0002	0.0002	0.0002	0.0002	0.0002	0.0002	0.0002	0.0002	0.0002	0.0002
−3.6	0.0002	0.0002	0.0001	0.0001	0.0001	0.0001	0.0001	0.0001	0.0001	0.0001
−3.7	0.0001	0.0001	0.0001	0.0001	0.0001	0.0001	0.0001	0.0001	0.0001	0.0001
−3.8	0.0001	0.0001	0.0001	0.0001	0.0001	0.0001	0.0001	0.0001	0.0001	0.0001
−3.9	0.0000	0.0000	0.0000	0.0000	0.0000	0.0000	0.0000	0.0000	0.0000	0.0000
−4.0	0.0000	0.0000	0.0000	0.0000	0.0000	0.0000	0.0000	0.0000	0.0000	0.0000

Table for $N(x)$ When $x \geqslant 0$

This table shows values of $N(x)$ for $x \geqslant 0$. The table should be used with interpolation. For example,

$$\begin{aligned} N(0.6278) &= N(0.62) + 0.78[N(0.63) - N(0.62)] \\ &= 0.7324 + 0.78 \times (0.7357 - 0.7324) \\ &= 0.7350 \end{aligned}$$

x	.00	.01	.02	.03	.04	.05	.06	.07	.08	.09
0.0	0.5000	0.5040	0.5080	0.5120	0.5160	0.5199	0.5239	0.5279	0.5319	0.5359
0.1	0.5398	0.5438	0.5478	0.5517	0.5557	0.5596	0.5636	0.5675	0.5714	0.5753
0.2	0.5793	0.5832	0.5871	0.5910	0.5948	0.5987	0.6026	0.6064	0.6103	0.6141
0.3	0.6179	0.6217	0.6255	0.6293	0.6331	0.6368	0.6406	0.6443	0.6480	0.6517
0.4	0.6554	0.6591	0.6628	0.6664	0.6700	0.6736	0.6772	0.6808	0.6844	0.6879
0.5	0.6915	0.6950	0.6985	0.7019	0.7054	0.7088	0.7123	0.7157	0.7190	0.7224
0.6	0.7257	0.7291	0.7324	0.7357	0.7389	0.7422	0.7454	0.7486	0.7517	0.7549
0.7	0.7580	0.7611	0.7642	0.7673	0.7704	0.7734	0.7764	0.7794	0.7823	0.7852
0.8	0.7881	0.7910	0.7939	0.7967	0.7995	0.8023	0.8051	0.8078	0.8106	0.8133
0.9	0.8159	0.8186	0.8212	0.8238	0.8264	0.8289	0.8315	0.8340	0.8365	0.8389
1.0	0.8413	0.8438	0.8461	0.8485	0.8508	0.8531	0.8554	0.8577	0.8599	0.8621
1.1	0.8643	0.8665	0.8686	0.8708	0.8729	0.8749	0.8770	0.8790	0.8810	0.8830
1.2	0.8849	0.8869	0.8888	0.8907	0.8925	0.8944	0.8962	0.8980	0.8997	0.9015
1.3	0.9032	0.9049	0.9066	0.9082	0.9099	0.9115	0.9131	0.9147	0.9162	0.9177
1.4	0.9192	0.9207	0.9222	0.9236	0.9251	0.9265	0.9279	0.9292	0.9306	0.9319
1.5	0.9332	0.9345	0.9357	0.9370	0.9382	0.9394	0.9406	0.9418	0.9429	0.9441
1.6	0.9452	0.9463	0.9474	0.9484	0.9495	0.9505	0.9515	0.9525	0.9535	0.9545
1.7	0.9554	0.9564	0.9573	0.9582	0.9591	0.9599	0.9608	0.9616	0.9625	0.9633
1.8	0.9641	0.9649	0.9656	0.9664	0.9671	0.9678	0.9686	0.9693	0.9699	0.9706
1.9	0.9713	0.9719	0.9726	0.9732	0.9738	0.9744	0.9750	0.9756	0.9761	0.9767
2.0	0.9772	0.9778	0.9783	0.9788	0.9793	0.9798	0.9803	0.9808	0.9812	0.9817
2.1	0.9821	0.9826	0.9830	0.9834	0.9838	0.9842	0.9846	0.9850	0.9854	0.9857
2.2	0.9861	0.9864	0.9868	0.9871	0.9875	0.9878	0.9881	0.9884	0.9887	0.9890
2.3	0.9893	0.9896	0.9898	0.9901	0.9904	0.9906	0.9909	0.9911	0.9913	0.9916
2.4	0.9918	0.9920	0.9922	0.9925	0.9927	0.9929	0.9931	0.9932	0.9934	0.9936
2.5	0.9938	0.9940	0.9941	0.9943	0.9945	0.9946	0.9948	0.9949	0.9951	0.9952
2.6	0.9953	0.9955	0.9956	0.9957	0.9959	0.9960	0.9961	0.9962	0.9963	0.9964
2.7	0.9965	0.9966	0.9967	0.9968	0.9969	0.9970	0.9971	0.9972	0.9973	0.9974
2.8	0.9974	0.9975	0.9976	0.9977	0.9977	0.9978	0.9979	0.9979	0.9980	0.9981
2.9	0.9981	0.9982	0.9982	0.9983	0.9984	0.9984	0.9985	0.9985	0.9986	0.9986
3.0	0.9986	0.9987	0.9987	0.9988	0.9988	0.9989	0.9989	0.9989	0.9990	0.9990
3.1	0.9990	0.9991	0.9991	0.9991	0.9992	0.9992	0.9992	0.9992	0.9993	0.9993
3.2	0.9993	0.9993	0.9994	0.9994	0.9994	0.9994	0.9994	0.9995	0.9995	0.9995
3.3	0.9995	0.9995	0.9995	0.9996	0.9996	0.9996	0.9996	0.9996	0.9996	0.9997
3.4	0.9997	0.9997	0.9997	0.9997	0.9997	0.9997	0.9997	0.9997	0.9997	0.9998
3.5	0.9998	0.9998	0.9998	0.9998	0.9998	0.9998	0.9998	0.9998	0.9998	0.9998
3.6	0.9998	0.9998	0.9999	0.9999	0.9999	0.9999	0.9999	0.9999	0.9999	0.9999
3.7	0.9999	0.9999	0.9999	0.9999	0.9999	0.9999	0.9999	0.9999	0.9999	0.9999
3.8	0.9999	0.9999	0.9999	0.9999	0.9999	0.9999	0.9999	0.9999	0.9999	0.9999
3.9	1.0000	1.0000	1.0000	1.0000	1.0000	1.0000	1.0000	1.0000	1.0000	1.0000
4.0	1.0000	1.0000	1.0000	1.0000	1.0000	1.0000	1.0000	1.0000	1.0000	1.0000

ndex